HUDSON TAYLOR

&

CHINA'S OPEN CENTURY

Book Five: Refiner's Fire

By the same author:

Hudson Taylor and China's Open Century
Book 1: Barbarians at the Gates
Book 2: Over the Treaty Wall
Book 3: If I Had a Thousand Lives
Book 4: Survivors' Pact

HUDSON TAYLOR

&

CHINA'S OPEN CENTURY

BOOK FIVE
Refiner's Fire

A J Broomhall

HODDER AND STOUGHTON
and
THE OVERSEAS MISSIONARY FELLOWSHIP

Back cover photograph

Together again in London, December 1871, (see pp 326–7). Hudson Taylor with Charles Edward (2) and Li Lanfeng, Emily with Herbert (10), Jennie with Fredk, Howard (8) and little Marie (4).

British Library Cataloguing in Publication Data

Broomhall, A. J.
 Hudson Taylor & China's open century. –
 (Hodder Christian paperbacks)
 Bk. 5: Refiner's fire
 1. Missionaries – China – Biography
 2. Taylor, Hudson
 I. Title
 266′.023′0924   BV3427.T3

ISBN 0 340 368667

Foreword to the Series

China appears to be re-opening its doors to the Western world. The future of Christianity in that vast country is known only to God. It is, however, important that we in the West should be alert to the present situation, and be enabled to see it in the perspective of the long history of missionary enterprise there. It is one of the merits of these six remarkable volumes that they provide us with just such a perspective.

These books are much more than just the story of the life and work of Hudson Taylor told in great detail. If they were that alone, they would be a worthwhile enterprise, for, as the *Preface* reminds us, he has been called by no less a Church historian than Professor K S Latourette 'one of the greatest missionaries of all time'. He was a man of total devotion to Christ and to the missionary cause, a man of ecumenical spirit, a man of originality in initiating new attitudes to mission, a doctor, a translator, an evangelist, an heroic figure of the Church.

The historian – whether his interests be primarily military, missionary, or social – will find much to interest him here. The heinous opium traffic which led to two wars with China is described. The relationship of 'the man in the field' to the society which sent him is set before us in all its complexity and (often) painfulness. And the story of Biblical translation and dissemination will be full of interest to those experts who work under the banner of the United Bible Societies and to that great fellowship of men and women who support them across the length and breadth of the world.

Dr Broomhall is to be congratulated on writing a major work which, while being of interest *primarily* to students of mission, deserves a far wider readership. We owe our thanks to Messrs Hodder and Stoughton for their boldness in printing so large a series of volumes in days when all publishers have financial problems. I believe that author and publisher will be rewarded, for we have here a fascinating galaxy of men and women who faced the challenge of the evangelisation of China with daring and devotion, and none more so than the central figure of that galaxy, Hudson Taylor himself. The secret of his perseverance, of his achievement, and of his significance in missionary history is to be found in some words which he wrote to his favourite sister, Amelia:

'If I had a thousand pounds, China should have it. If I had a thousand lives, China should have them. No! not *China*, but *Christ*. Can we do too much for Him?'

Sissinghurst, Kent   Donald Coggan

PREFACE

(See also the General Preface in Book One)

In the detached view of historians, the second Opium War, of 1859–60, was 'followed by about forty years of relatively uneventful relations between the Middle Kingdom and the West'. The word 'relatively' holds the key to such a statement, for the 1870s continued to see crises leading sometimes to the brink of war between China and not only Western nations but Japan as well. As dean of the Imperial Tongwen Academy of Peking, W A P Martin remarked that in twenty-five years only twenty-five riots against foreigners took place. Peace had come at last! Peace and progress, but only after a systematic attempt to crush Christian missions out of existence by mob violence. He spoke too soon. Thirty years after his elevation to this place of honour Martin himself was to be in danger of his life in the siege of the Peking legations. But that was in the future.

Friction was seldom absent in the period covered by this book (1868–75). Orchestrated agitation against foreigners and foreign policies placed the pioneers of penetration into the interior of China in extreme danger time and again. Proclamations for their protection varied in sincerity and effectiveness, and the inability of mandarins to control the scholar-gentry was often demonstrated.

If commerce was to develop and the gospel to be taken deep into China, merchant and missionary must test the unpredictable reactions of the Chinese people. Collaboration in this was unthinkable in the climate of the times. 'Trade' meant the opium traffic as much as it meant tea and silk. Hudson Taylor saw his task as involving the necessity of testing Chinese attitudes, but only as a natural consequence of his prime purpose. The enlightened attitude of Ma Xinyi, Muslim governor of Zhejiang province, had given Taylor the impression that moving up-country would be more straightforward than proved to be the case. Vehement opposition came as a surprise to everyone, consul, merchant and missionary alike. But the quiet heroism of the pioneers opened the way to better international relations and incidentally to an open door to trade.

Unconcerned about either, the missionary pioneers were intent only on spreading the gospel throughout the empire. Inadvertently they clarified the diplomatic issues, provided the pretext for armed intervention, bore the blame – and in the process vindicated their own integrity. This did not save them from being labelled the tools of the imperialists, prospecting for iron and coal!

Late twentieth-century debate is focused by political views in China on 'the Chinese experience' and 'the missionary experience', in the current jargon. But in the 1870s both were embryonic. In this book we are only just over the threshold of China's humiliation by the West. The later nineteenth- and twentieth-century experience is wholly different. When John King Fairbank used these terms in reference to a span of nearly two centuries (1800–1975) he emphasised our ignorance of the period of history considered in this series about Hudson Taylor.[1]

By offering in this volume historical facts about the individuals concerned, the kind of people they were and their activities, a better contribution to the truth about China and missions may be made than by mere assessment and opinion. 'The Barbarian Question' and 'the Missionary Question' are mid-nineteenth-century terms and are therefore preferred in this context.

Refiner's Fire continues and depends for understanding upon the other books of this series, *Barbarians at the Gates, Over the Treaty Wall, If I Had a Thousand Lives* and *Survivors' Pact*. They trace the origins of the Christian Church in China and use available sources to show the real Hudson Taylor in the perspective of contemporary events and personalities. In *Survivors' Pact* the projected China Inland Mission took shape with thirty members. Typhoons at sea and dissension in its ranks failed to destroy it in the experimental phase, and resistance by some mandarins only hardened the resolve of Hudson Taylor and his young men and women. Once again we pick up the threads as if there had been no break in the narrative. But the time has come to stand farther back from descriptive detail, to see the broader sweep of events. A year of trial and error, of training and testing of his team led Hudson Taylor to deploy those he could and to make plans for penetrating deeper into China. Fortunately the future was a closed book. To Chinese and other scholars researching the origins of the extensive Church of today, however, details of the earliest church planting will be important.

Adversity has its value however it is viewed. By testing, proving and purifying it brings out the best – the faith, fortitude and endurance of those undergoing it. In this volume Hudson Taylor and the novice members of his fledgling Mission meet with adversity far exceeding any they had yet experienced – in a spirit of acquiescence in the Refiner's work. If the theme of the series were not Hudson Taylor's humanity but his heart and soul, the problem of what to include would have been greater. Enough is retained to show the kind of man he was.

AJB

Note. Parentheses within quotations are used as follows: round brackets ( ) indicate original source material, including abbreviations and substitute Romanis-ation of Chinese words; square brackets [ ] indicate my own added comment or parentheses other than from original sources.

ACKNOWLEDGMENTS

Special thanks are due this time to my long-suffering advisers, who waded through much more preliminary typescript than usual. The abundance of source material, handled in the same way as in previous books, resulted in a draft which had to be drastically reduced for publication. The mercifully merciless advice of the panel showed clearly where the axe should fall. Some of the deleted material finds a place in the appendices, and the unabridged typescript will remain with the archives for reference.

The understanding comments of reviewers are appreciated, showing as they do a grasp of my declared intentions. In Book Six, which brings us to more recent times, I shall try, briefly, to redress the deliberate economy of assessment and discussion in the earlier volumes. Meanwhile I gratefully acknowledge the encouragement received from the late Bishop Stephen Neill, historian of Christian mission, and other correspondents, and the use of other societies' source books.

AJB

KEY TO ABBREVIATIONS

ABMU = American Baptist Missionary Union
Bible Societies = American Bible Society, B&FBS, National Bible Society of Scotland
BMS = Baptist Missionary Society
Bridge Street = Wugyiaodeo premises in Ningbo
CES = Chinese Evangelization Society
CIM = China Inland Mission
CMS = Church Missionary Society
HTCOC = *Hudson Taylor & China's Open Century*
JHT = James Hudson Taylor
LMS = London Missionary Society
MRCS = Member of the Royal College of Surgeons
New Lane = Xin Kai Long, Hangzhou
OMFA = Overseas Missionary Fellowship Archives
P & O = Peninsular and Oriental Steam Navigation Company
P & P = Principles and Practice of the CIM
RTS = Religious Tract Society
SPCK = Society for Promoting Christian Knowledge
The Mission = China Inland Mission
WMMS = Wesleyan Methodist Missionary Society
YMCA = Young Men's Christian Association

GLOSSARY OF CHINESE TERMS

Aimei	= 'beloved sister'
baojia	= government by graded responsibility, each to the next
bianzi	= hair queue ('pigtail')
daotai	= Intendant of Circuit over 2 or 3 prefectures
dibao	= local constable, police sergeant
fengshui	= 'wind and water', harmony of nature governing decisions
fu	= happiness; a prefecture
futai	= provincial governor
fu, zhou	= prefectures and cities
hong, hang	= merchant house, warehouse
Hua Yuan	= Academy of Arts
laoban	= 'old plank', foreman, boss
Nianfei	= rebels in north China
Panthay	= Muslim rebels in Yunnan
pugai	= Chinese duvet, bed quilt
sanban	= 'three planks'; skiff with oars or scull
Taiping	= rebellion led by Hong Xiuquan
Tong Wen Guan	= College of Arts & Languages
yamen	= official residence of any mandarin
xian	= county town, district magistrate
zhifu	= prefect
Zongli Yamen	= Chinese Foreign Office

BOOK FIVE: REFINER'S FIRE

CONTENTS

PART 1   RIOT   1868

PART 3   DESOLATION   1870-71

PART 4   CRUCIBLE OF FAITH   1871-75

MAPS AND DIAGRAMS

ILLUSTRATIONS

PART 1

RIOT

1868

THE BACKGROUND

Millrace of violence   *1867–70*

The eventful years 1867–70 were years of unrest and upheaval worldwide, not only in China. Towards the end of 1867 the French had entered Rome (October 30) and Garibaldi had been captured. A British expedition had embarked on the invasion of Ethiopia, leading to the suicide of King Theodore in 1868. The French had been driven out of Mexico and 'Emperor' Maximilian shot, and France herself was to suffer ultimate humiliation in the Franco-Prussian war of 1870. Defeat, with the surrender of Napoleon III and his army, led to the republic being proclaimed, Paris being besieged and a communist insurrection taking place in the capital. Paris surrendered in January 1871. Rome and the Papal States, without French protection, were annexed to the new kingdom of Italy, and Germany was proclaimed a united empire. The Age of Bismarck had begun, and William I of Prussia was proclaimed Emperor of Germany – at Versailles! The Man of Iron at last began to work for peace, his best hope of preserving supremacy.

In China the 'quiet years' were to be disrupted by a succession of violent incidents. Provocations against merchants and missionaries multiplied, and the consuls welcomed pretexts to justify an assertion of power, to protect their treaty rights. The era of high-handed action by consuls with gunboats at their beck and call was to reach its peak in a series of excesses before being quelled by Sir Rutherford Alcock, the man who had begun it all. In 1848 he had 'declared war on the Chinese empire' after the Qingpu outrage. (Book 1, pp 301–3) As minister at Peking in 1868 he had a better understanding of the successive affronts to Chinese pride against which her intellectuals were protesting.

As Hudson Taylor prepared to move 'farther on and farther in' foreigners were travelling more freely throughout China. T T Cooper, agent for the Chamber of Commerce at Calcutta, had

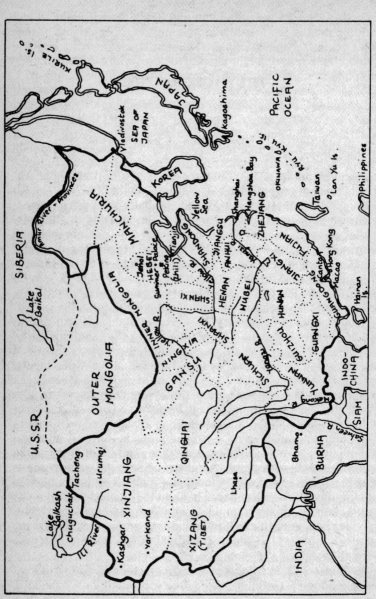

THE PROVINCES AND MAIN FEATURES OF GREATER CHINA

conceived the idea in 1862 of entering China from Burma but had had to abandon his plans during the Muslim rebellion in Yunnan. After several years in Shanghai, hearing discussion of a possible Bhamo-Dali trade route, he decided to attempt an overland journey from Shanghai to Calcutta by Captain Blakiston's route (Book 3, p 261). In January 1868 he left Hankou in Chinese clothes and travelled up the Yangzi gorges to Chongqing and on to Chengdu and Yaan. The *North China Herald* of April 11 published his description of Sichuan province and his declared intention of travelling via Batang to Nepal, a route which must take him through Lhasa. At the Tibetan border he, too, was turned back at several points south of Kangding (Tatsienlu) and conceded defeat.[1]

One of Alexander Wylie's promising young Bible Society colporteurs, named Johnson, left Shanghai, also in January 1868, and was last seen at Zhenjiang (Chinkiang) on the Yangzi, heading for Henan province. His route was almost certainly across the Yangzi to Guazhou, up the Grand Canal through Marco Polo's city of Yangzhou to Qingjiangpu (Tsingkiangpu) (map, p 38) as far as the Weishan Lake on the Shandong border. There he seems to have crossed the neck of Jiangsu province at Xuzhou into the similar neck of Anhui which shares the Shandong border for a mere twenty-five miles, for 'near the borders' he perished at the hands of 'banditti, consisting principally if not entirely of disbanded militia'. Another report of the murder of a Protestant missionary in Henan province was assumed to refer to the same person as no one else was missing.[2]

In March 1868 Hudson Taylor's young friend R F Laughton (Book 3, p 289) sent a Chinese employee to rent premises for use as a preaching point in a market-town two miles from Yantai in Shandong. Although told specifically to state its purpose, the agent lied to the owners, saying it was for use as a shop. When Laughton came and furnished it as a chapel, the owners protested, offering to refund the down payment. Not knowing the facts, he insisted on staying, whereupon they removed the roof and walled up the door. The consul, Challoner Alabaster, settled the matter by requiring the public dismissal of the employee and the restoration of the house to Laughton, warning Laughton 'in future to acquire any buildings he may need for mission purposes through the consulate'. As a petty incident of little consequence, it had its lessons for missionaries to note.[3]

Jonathan Lees of the LMS and John Innocent of the Methodist

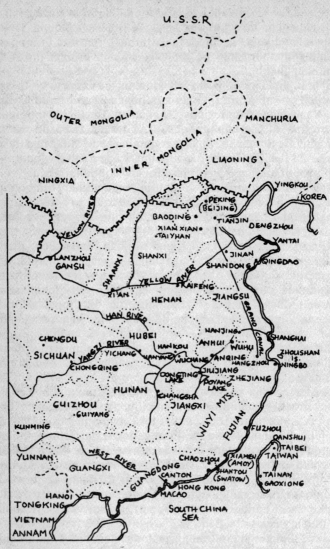

CHINA'S MAIN CITIES AND WATERWAYS

New Connexion travelled overland from Tianjin to Jinan (Tsinan) in Shandong in May 1868 to meet W B Hodge, a colleague of Innocent's. The journey took them through territory littered with corpses and destruction by the Nianfei and counter-insurgency action.[4]

On May 25, 1868, Robert Hart wrote from Peking to his customs commissioner at Tianjin, G Hughes, that he had been told at the Zongli Yamen on the previous day of Nianfei rebels having entered Zhili south of Tianjin, between the Grand Canal and the sea. Although not more than 10,000 in number, they posed a threat to the city. In April a foreign correspondent had written of corpses of men, women and children floating down the Hai He (river) at Tianjin. The court appealed to Zeng Guofan and Li Hongzhang to put an end to the Nianfei scourge, and this time Li succeeded with the aid of Mongol horsemen. A 'peaceful' region, apparently safe to travel in, could become a death trap at any time. At Xian Xian, near the Grand Canal in Zhili, Père Leboucq had nearly been killed by the Nianfei in February. In May he nearly died at the hands of the imperial troops, and in August from typhoid fever. A proclamation enjoining the populace to protect his mission and orphanage had little effect. On May 18, 1868 (the day Hudson Taylor left Hangzhou and travelled north), both buildings were pillaged by a mob.[5]

Roman Catholic missions in Guangdong had entered during 1867 upon a troubled period of three years. In October 1867 one priest was imprisoned. In August 1868 another was injured in an uprising. In December 1868 another riot led to the destruction of a chapel, the death of seven converts and the wounding of a hundred others and of their priest the Abbé Delavay. Sichuan province saw disturbances of a different nature. Friction between the Catholic community and other people led to clan fights in which the Abbé Mabileau was killed in 1865 and, as Hosea Ballou Morse recorded, 'in the years following . . . through the action of Christian converts' 105 houses were burned, hundreds of people were wounded (700 according to one of three enquiries) and 173 died. Violent retaliation followed in 1869.

As we come to the scenes of major violence in Taiwan and at Yangzhou and Zhenjiang, engulfing nine of the *Lammermuir* party (Book 4, p 155) and the four Taylor children, it should be remembered that these were not isolated incidents.

Pot and kettle *Nineteenth century*

The Roman Catholic missionaries' principles and methods of working bore few resemblances to those of the Protestants. Ultimately concerned with the eternal salvation of the Chinese through the atoning death of Christ, they worked first to secure their attachment to the Church and afterwards to instruct them. Membership of the Roman Catholic Church was what mattered: to enlist, train and care for its members in the hope that spiritual conversion would result. The means employed were secondary in importance. Treaty privileges and the French protectorate could be used for the salvation of souls, by protection from persecution, assistance with the magistrates or with litigation, just as much as through schools, orphanages and opium refuges. Sometimes whole villages or clans were enrolled in this way, and the travellers, notably von Richthofen, Younghusband and W H Medhurst Jr, remarked on some clean, orderly and industrious Catholic communities they visited, in marked contrast with non-Christian villages.[6]

Mgr Faurie, Vicar-Apostolic of Guizhou, freely used his influence to have antagonists punished, and wrote tongue in cheek if not naïvely, 'Every one of the individuals who has been punished for reviling our religion has embraced with ardour the true faith on leaving prison'. Of one in particular whom he had imprisoned and then released he said, 'The same evening he presented himself in chapel to adore the true God.' Alexander Hosie wrote of 'the handsome palace of the French Bishop' in Yunnanfu (Kunming). Pomp, ceremony and prestige could be thought of as glorifying God. But the average foreign priest lived very simply in semi-Chinese style without ever returning to his homeland. Some 'impressed travellers with the radiant strength and beauty of their lives'.

Protestant missionaries believed, however, that Catholicism was failing to give the essentials of the Christian gospel to the Chinese, and therefore disregarded its representatives. Rome to the average Protestant in the nineteenth century was anti-Christ, and Catholicism a corruption of the truth. To the Catholics, Protestant missionaries were dangerous heretics leading the people 'from Confucius to confusion'. Chinese cities were 'opened to the gospel' irrespective of a Roman Catholic presence. But anti-foreign and anti-Christian agitation drew little or no distinction between them.[7]

Burlingame, Hart and Martin   *1867–70*

The glories of Chinese culture and a wealth of values in the Chinese character appealed to some Western men of insight, while the general run of foreigners were insensitive to them. Lord Elgin, party with the French to the sacking of the Summer Palace in spite of his father's appreciation of the Grecian marbles, claimed of his co-operation with the Peking court after 1860, 'I have been China's friend in all this'.[8] His brother, Sir Frederick Bruce, first resident British envoy in Peking, shared the sentiment. The four Allies, America, Britain, France and Russia, were in fact at one in wanting to restore China to stability. Others gave helpful advice to court and government, but none to the extent of Anson Burlingame, the American minister since 1861.

At 32 Robert Hart was firmly within the counsels of the rulers. H N Lay had become Inspector-General of Customs from January 21, 1861, and with the support of the foreign envoys had resisted the Chinese officials who looked upon the customs revenue as 'their legitimate source of emolument'. But after 1863 Lay had become enmeshed in the fiasco known to history as the Lay–Osborne fleet (Book 4, pp 29–30), while Hart as acting Inspector-General made his mark in the customs service 'and from the outset gained the good opinion of all foreign envoys, Chinese officials and foreign merchants alike'. Quickly Hart was in control of all coastal and Yangzi river revenues.

This evangelical Christian, widely acknowledged to be above reproach, was China's true friend and a mandarin for fifty years. Hosea Ballou Morse's intention when he addressed himself to writing about the dynasty was to base his volumes on the life of Sir Robert Hart as a connecting thread.[9] But Hart was too modest to approve and to give him access to his seventy-four-volume diary and letters. Instead Morse had to be content to write his nine-volume history, *The International Relations of the Chinese Empire*. Alicia Bewicke Little, in a satirical passage in her biography of Li Hongzhang, attributed Hart's success and 'the apparent satisfaction of all concerned' to his 'infinite subtlety of mind and adaptability', although his integrity deserved first mention.

W A P Martin also became the personal friend of many leading Chinese officials. As a newly arrived missionary to Ningbo in 1850 he not only moved into the Chinese city but suggested that the whole American Presbyterian mission at Ningbo should transfer from the foreign settlement alongside the consulates and forge closer links with the Chinese people – as the CMS and Miss Aldersey (Book 2, Index) were already doing, while living in foreign style. He published his *Evidences of Christianity* in Chinese (*Tian Dao Su Yuan*) in 1854, a book which went through thirty or forty editions and attacked the opium traffic because no one but missionaries would do so.[10]

His involvement with the United States' envoys began when he offered to serve the Hon W B Reed as interpreter in 1858, and with Samuel Wells Williams he helped to negotiate the American treaty. Again in May 1859 he accompanied the Hon John E Ward to Tianjin, and so became known to more high Chinese officials.[11] At the time of the Peking Convention Martin was in the United States, but returned in 1862 and after some months in Shanghai began to preach the gospel in Peking, working with William Burns in the small chapel they opened. At the time, Maria Taylor's brother-in-law, John Burdon, was chaplain to the British embassy and told Martin that his *Evidences of Christianity* had reached the imperial household. (Would that Robert Morrison could have lived to see this day.) Robert Hart, already a good friend from Ningbo days, was another of Martin's close associates.

Friendly Chinese officials responded to his appreciation of their nation, but when it became known that he was translating Wheaton's *Elements of International Law* with the intention of helping China in her international relations, his future course became predictable.[12] The Grand Secretary Wen Xiang, faced with French intrusions into Annam (Vietnam), welcomed Martin's translation and his reputation was established. When Prussians captured Danish ships in Chinese waters, the Zongli Yamen (the Foreign Office) found that when they used some sentences from Martin's book, without revealing their source, 'the Prussian minister acknowledged his mistake without saying a word'. Not only that, with understanding came Chinese approval of at least some aspects of Western thinking.

Because funds for all American missions were curtailed by the Civil War, Martin was supplementing his income by teaching in the Tong Wen Guan, a school for interpreters. When, in 1867, with Robert Hart's strong backing he was offered a 'chair' or lecturership in international law and political economy, he leapt at it as yet another entrée for the gospel in influential Chinese circles. On full pay he hurried home to the States, studied his subjects for a year at

Yale (where two of his sons were undergraduates), the better to fit himself for the post, and was back in Peking the next summer, 1869. Talented young men from all parts of the empire became his students. One day they might have influence at court or even teach the emperor. His hope was fulfilled when two graduates of the Tong Wen Guan after diplomatic service abroad returned to join the staff and were called to teach the Guang Xu emperor.[13]

Martin was installed on November 26, 1869, as dean of the Tong Wen Guan in the presence of officials of the Zongli Yamen, and over the years his students went on to hold high office both in China and overseas. While most missionaries following the Biblical precedent took the gospel to the man in the street, and Hudson Taylor led his young men and women deeper into the interior of an intractably resistant China, Robert Hart and William Martin worked close to the seat of power. Like the apostle Paul who had friends among the high-ranking provincial officials of Ephesus (Acts 19: 31), they were far from silent about their Christian message. Whether at the grass roots or the pinnacle of empire, either or more probably each approach held a key to the Chinese Church of the future. Previously banned from teaching the gospel in the Tong Wen Guan, Martin was now allowed to do so discreetly. In 1869 he wrote to his mission board, resigning his membership but assuring them that he was no less a missionary than before. Always outspoken and boasting no false modesty, Martin pointed out the strategic value of his position: 'One of the highest Mandarins, an Imperial Censor, said in the presence of several others that he had declared when I was not present that "If all missionaries were like Dr Martin he would himself be a Christian".'[14]

Mrs Little introduced Burlingame into her biography of Li Hongzhang largely for 'a touch of comedy'. As a minister in Peking Burlingame was a success, obtaining by courtesy what others failed to win by bluster. In the spring of 1866 Robert Hart obtained six months' leave in Europe and proposed to Prince Kong that a Chinese delegation should accompany him to study the character of Western people. A Manchu *ex-daotai* promoted to the third rank and serving in the customs under Hart was appointed and by Western standards was well received in European capitals. But at 63 his prejudices made him unadaptable. Disgusted by the discomforts of travel and the lack of oriental decorum he encountered, he gave trouble from the start and returned without a good word for his hosts.

Not surprisingly, in November 1867, 'the diplomatic world in Peking was startled by the announcement that Mr Anson Burlingame had been commissioned by the Chinese emperor as his Ambassador-Extraordinary accredited to all the courts of the world . . .' Burlingame forthwith had conferred on him the red globe of the first civil rank, with one Manchu and one Chinese grandee of second rank as his subordinate envoys-extraordinary, together with an entourage of two foreign and thirty Chinese secretaries.

The mission left Shanghai for the States on February 25, 1868. At a banquet given in San Francisco by the governor of California, Anson Burlingame revealed what was in store. Carried away by his enthusiasm and gift of oratory, he appealed to the memory of Ricci, Verbiest, Morrison, Milne, Bridgman and others who had lived and died hoping that the day would soon arrive when this great people (of China) would 'extend its arms towards the shining banners of Western civilization'. On June 28, 1868 – when China in fact was seething with unrest – at a banquet given by the governor of New York, 'he asserted that China was ready to invite the missionaries to "plant the shining cross on every hill and in every valley," and to engage Western engineers to open mines and build railways'! In America great enthusiasm was aroused, 'but his language came as a shock of cold water to those he had left behind in China'. Peking civilities had completely misled him. Riot and murder had begun and the consuls were contemplating force to quell the mood. Incredibly, on July 28, 1868, a 'new' treaty between China and the United States was signed in Washington, reiterating the American Treaty of Tientsin (now Tianjin) with the one exception that the States undertook not to interfere in the development of China. But no power to negotiate a treaty had been granted to Burlingame!

He moved on triumphantly to Britain in September 1868, to a cool reception by Lord Stanley of the Foreign Office. At Peking the imperial regents were still refusing to grant audiences to foreign envoys; and in the provinces British subjects were being brutally assaulted and denied justice. In Paris Burlingame was granted an audience of the Emperor Napoleon III, now nearing his downfall, and proceeded to Stockholm in October and The Hague in November. Returning to London, on November 20 Anson Burlingame was received by Queen Victoria on the expressed assurance that it was only the emperor's minority which prevented him from receiving her minister Sir Rutherford Alcock. Two weeks later Disraeli resigned, Gladstone became Prime Minister, Lord Clarendon succeeded Lord Stanley and on December 26 received Burlingame for discussions.[15]

Hawks Pott summarised Lord Clarendon's policy as: unfriendly pressure, inconsistent with the independence of China, should not be applied; Britain's representatives should deal with the central government, not with unenlightened local mandarins; China would be expected to observe the treaties she entered into; and Britain reserved the right to use force to protect life and property.[16] At face value that looked reasonable. But Peking was not remotely comparable with a Western counterpart. The significance of this reversal of policy in China becomes apparent as the Hudson Taylor history proceeds.

After the new year Burlingame met Bismarck in Berlin. W A P Martin recorded, 'His last communication was a telegram, via Siberia, addressed to me for the Tsungli (Zongli) Yamen, reporting a favourable reception at Berlin, adding, "Concluded negotiations with Prussia; strong declaration by Bismarck in favour of China. Now to Russia!"'

The Tsar received him at St Petersburg on February 4, 1869, but the intense cold proved too much. On the 11th he died of pneumonia. H B Morse assessed his brief flight of fantasy by saying that Burlingame's contribution to East–West relations was, 'productive finally of good to China and to the world in general; but that in the minds of the rulers of China, its success caused such a revulsion of feeling, and created such confidence in their own judgment . . . as to retard the advance of the empire . . . for some years after.' The Empress Dowager, 'vigorous but reactionary', saw to it that Chinese customs and institutions remained as much as possible what they had been under the Qian Long (1736–96) and Kang Xi (1662–1722) emperors, and that the wheels of 'progress' dragged heavily.

So ended with some success the attempt of a sincere friend of China to open the closed minds of Western nations to all the good in the remarkable Chinese. Values the West neither understood nor appreciated would one day be acknowledged. Those like Burlingame who savoured their richness could be pardoned if they became starry-eyed. There was another side of the coin, with which Hudson Taylor and the 'Lammermuir party' had become familiar (Book 4).

CHAPTER ONE

A MOOD OF PROTEST
1868

Rebuff at Jinhua   *January–February 1868*

The success of the Huzhou riot in driving James Williamson, John McCarthy, Hudson Taylor and their battered Chinese companions away from that city in November 1867 left Williamson without a challenging objective (Book 4, pp 393–9). The Cordons and Henry Reid, newly arrived in China, had been in Hangzhou for ten days and were beginning to feel at home in their Chinese clothes and the Chinese way of living. Rather than keep them among fellow-foreigners, Hudson Taylor preferred to send them straight into a Chinese environment. Now that Williamson was free to attempt a new city, the Cordons could be with him and Reid could join his fellow-Scotsman Duncan in Nanjing.

After the Qiantang river survey south-eastward from Hangzhou (Book 4, p 322) McCarthy had lived for a month at the prefectural city of Yanzhou, and Duncan at Lanxi, the commercial centre fifty miles farther upstream (map p 38). The Jinhua river, which joined the upper reaches of the Qiantang at Lanxi, was the waterway of an extensive trading area, and Jinhua, 'a beautiful city on very high ground', was its political heart, 130 miles south of Hangzhou, the provincial capital. On January 4, while plans for Williamson were being considered, Miles Knowlton and Carl Kreyer, the Taylors' good American Baptist friends, called at New Lane with a proposition. Knowlton had travelled in the Jinhua area from his base at Ningbo, and Chinese evangelists had settled in several of the city's country areas. But he was too busy to give them the help they needed. He had come, he said, to urge Hudson Taylor to place missionaries in Jinhua. He had never known trouble on his visits there and believed they would be well received. 'This request coming just when it did, seemed to us like the Macedonian cry', Maria told the Bergers.

The next day was spent praying about it with the Hangzhou Christians, and on January 6 Hudson Taylor and the heroes of the

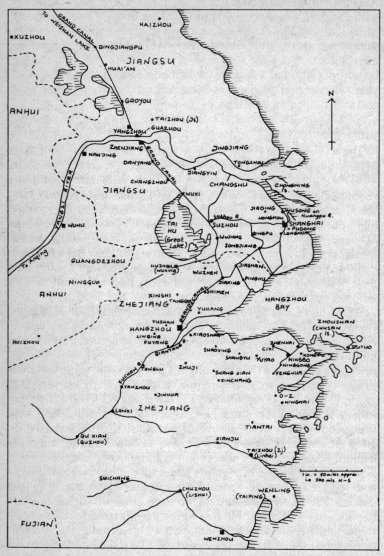

THE ZHEJIANG FRONT AND YANGZI ADVANCE

Xiaoshan and Huzhou outrages, Mr Tsiu and Liu Jinchen, set off with James Williamson and Henry Cordon up the Qiantang river.[1] Miles Knowlton had retained a room in a Jinhua home for use on his occasional visits, and the travellers were welcomed when they arrived on the 9th. The very next day they found 'a suitable house, beautifully situated' for themselves, and negotiated its rental for a year. The document was signed that night, the down payment paid, and in the morning they took possession.

Nothing could have been easier. Hudson Taylor left the same day with Cordon to return to Hangzhou, leaving James Williamson and his two Chinese companions to carry out necessary repairs. He bagged thirty birds for the larder on the way home, and arrived on the 15th with presents for Maria's birthday the next day. With no reason to delay, Henry Cordon, his wife and Chinese attendants set off at once to ascend the Qiantang river again and make their home at Jinhua. On arrival at Lanxi, however, they found one of Williamson's companions waiting for them with a message. Things had gone badly wrong at Jinhua on the 22nd. They were to go no further. James Williamson himself appeared the following morning with the now familiar story of violence and eviction. Together they all retreated downstream again.

George Duncan, alone in Nanjing, had already proved himself a successful pioneer. Living simply, with no foreign belongings or luxuries to alienate or tempt the Chinese he had settled among, and maturing steadily, his fluency in Nanjing Mandarin made him competent to give Reid, his fellow-Banffshire highlander, a good start in China. So John McCarthy was to escort Reid to Nanjing while Maria and Hudson Taylor stayed with Anne Stevenson at Shaoxing until another confinement was over. Maria would then return to her family at Hangzhou and work on her Biblical Concordance in Chinese, while Hudson Taylor at last made a tour of the southern Zhejiang cities to help the 'Ningbo five', as the earlier members of the Mission were called.

John McCarthy and Reid set off up the Grand Canal and at Suzhou stayed overnight with Charles Schmidt, the converted officer of Colonel Gordon's Ever-Victorious Army who had returned as a missionary, in September 1867, to the scene of his campaigns. Then on towards the Yangzi river, passing through the devastated countryside strewn with human bones where 'acre upon acre' lying in ruins impressed Reid with the scale of destruction by the Taiping rebellion. Late on Saturday, January 18, they reached

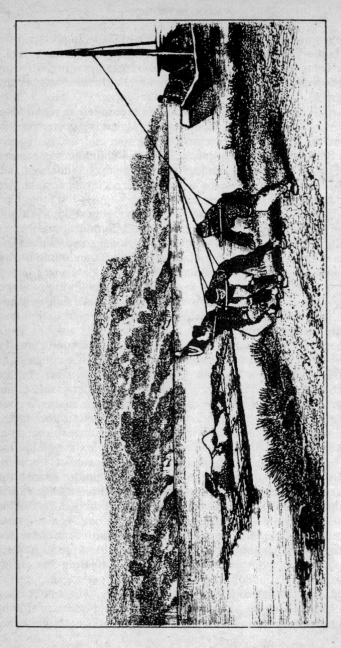

SLOWLY UPSTREAM, TOWED BY 'TRACKERS'

Nanjing and Duncan's cramped quarters – still half a poor carpenter's house. McCarthy stayed long enough to help Duncan to rent a house of his own, large enough for two families, with a roomy reception hall for use as a chapel, and by February 2 was back in Hangzhou.

The people of Nanjing, some half million in all, were friendly. But before long Duncan discovered that his new home was too near the magistrate's *yamen* for that dignitary's approval, and had to give it up. Back in the carpenter's shop, Duncan and Reid made the most of their slender foothold. At least there were two pioneers extending the Mission's deployment up the Yangzi valley and established in an ancient capital of the empire.

Hudson Taylor and Maria had left for Shaoxing on the 17th and, glad of a reason for living in a Chinese home, 'rented nice rooms in a quiet house' for themselves while waiting for the Stevenson baby to be born. They were working on a *Report of the Hangzhou Branch of the China Inland Mission* and the third edition of *China: Its Spiritual Need and Claims*, with a new ten-page appendix on the pros and cons of living like the Chinese in Chinese clothes. As always, Maria wrote to Hudson's dictation as he paced the room.

Then on Chinese New Year's Day when the city was filled with noise and merrymaking, Anne Stevenson went into labour and the two of them took turns to be with her. The weather was cold and the charcoal burner must have been in use to heat the room, for in a classic instance of poisoning by odourless carbon monoxide fumes they came close to fatal asphyxiation. Instead of the customary free ventilation of Chinese rooms, the Stevensons had put up a ceiling and papered over the cracks in their walls. By the time the baby was born, at 3.25 a m, Maria had a splitting headache but managed to wash and dress her before feeling faint and having to leave the room. Hudson Taylor, attending to Anne Stevenson, himself became so faint that he had to stop. Maria returned and took over with her head throbbing so hard that, as she wrote, 'I thought I heard the rice pounders at work'. Nearly fainting again she staggered out and Hudson put her to bed, to wake in the morning with her head aching violently and 'feeling so ill'. If the labour had been prolonged and the fumes had been undetected (accumulating from the ceiling downwards) all four could have died.[2]

Recovering, they completed the revision of *China*, and Hudson Taylor left to tour the southern cities. Early in the morning after he had gone, Maria was woken by John Stevenson hammering at her

bedroom door. James Williamson had arrived, forced out of Jinhua. She listened to his story and sent him posthaste to catch up with Hudson Taylor before he left Ningbo. On the same day, the *North China Herald* reported that the British consul had been insulted in the streets of the treaty port of Jiujiang (Kiukiang) on the Yangzi.[3] Security in China was a finely balanced thing.

Williamson's report had familiar overtones. Everything had gone favourably at Jinhua until January 14 when the landlord, a subordinate of the magistrate, had come saying he was in trouble, accused of helping the barbarians. Soon he was summoned to the *yamen* and threatened with punishment. The mandarin let him go but then sent for him again, together with the two middlemen, the agents who had arranged the deal, and an elderly Christian member of the Ningbo Baptist congregation. The house the foreigner had rented was too close to the *yamen*! They must turn him out, to find another farther away.

James Williamson had agreed to move, but the mandarin was not satisfied. He recalled one of the middlemen and ordered that he be flogged with 'four thousand blows'. (Williamson misunderstood and should have said 400.) After 'three thousand' had been administered, the man was thrown into prison. No one had dared to come near Williamson or do anything for him. His companions were in grave danger again. Tsiu had been flogged with 400 strokes and 100 more to his face at Xiaoshan, and Liu had narrowly escaped being drowned at Huzhou after a beating by the mob. Williamson went to see the middleman in prison, locked 'in a den with a number of criminals . . . like so many wild beasts in a large cage', the backs of his legs 'fearfully bruised and swollen', and realised how serious the situation was.

The next morning the landlord and the other middleman were summoned again to the *yamen*, and the wife and mother of the first man were threatening suicide and blaming Williamson for bringing this trouble on them. 'In order to save the people from further ill-usage', he reported, 'we left the house and proceeded to meet the party coming up, and returned with them to Hangzhou.' There he had reported events to the provincial governor's deputy before hurrying on to tell the Taylors.

With so many young couples of several missions within travelling distance, the Taylors' movements were often governed by confinements rather than by Mission business. Since Dr John Parker had left Ningbo and returned to Scotland in October 1867, no one else

THE OLD WALLED CITY AND FOREIGN SETTLEMENT
AT NINGBO
(*By courtesy of the CMS*)

with the medical knowledge and experience was available. Maria returned to Hangzhou for the birth of their Presbyterian friends', the Inslees', baby, and Hudson Taylor cut short his travels for the confinement of another American Presbyterian, Sarah Dodds, at the end of February. This was to be the pattern year after year.

The only record of his dealings with the consulate at Ningbo on the Jinhua matter is a reference to his taking it up with the magistrate and his superiors. But there was much coming and going. On February 10 James Williamson was back at Hangzhou with a batch of letters from Ningbo, and on the 12th was off again with a new colporteur, bearing a document from Governor Ma's deputy to the Jinhua magistrate. Liu Jinchen arrived next from Ningbo and followed Williamson to Jinhua. Then the colporteur returned with the news that the document had been delivered to the magistrate but no action had been taken. Williamson was still in Jinhua, unmolested and waiting to see results. By March 10 the picture was clear. Nothing had happened and nothing would happen. Once again the barbarian had been thwarted. The mandarins were seeing how far they could go. This time even the governor's deputy appeared to be playing safe, by putting no pressure on the Jinhua magistrate.

The American Baptists tried again and failed to secure a foothold in Jinhua, but seven years later, in 1875, when the CIM tried once more they succeeded in renting the very same house as before and were still at work there twenty years later.[4]

Southern tour   *February 1868*

When he reached Ningbo on January 29 and made his way to Bridge Street, Hudson Taylor was back at his first bachelor quarters and his first home with Maria after their marriage. Here Martha Meadows had died tragically and alone, and James Meadows had built up the congregation and proved himself as a missionary. Now with his new wife, Elizabeth Rose, it was still his home. George and Annie Crombie and their child had been staying with them only a week before. Hudson Taylor had been there only a few hours when Williamson arrived after dark. Yet another attempt to occupy a new city had been defeated.

Two nights later they were woken by a knocking at the outer gates. To their astonishment, George and Annie Crombie were standing outside with a coffin. Convulsions had quickly led to their son's death at Fenghua. Their first child had died at birth. The heartbroken parents were taken in and yet another burial at the foreign cemetery followed the next day. James and Elizabeth Meadows had lost their first not many weeks before, and Hudson Taylor had been through this grief three times already – at this same house, in London and at Hangzhou.

James Meadows, the Crombies and he then travelled together to Fenghua. Life had to go on. After consultations with the Christians, the first church in the city was organised with Wang Guoyao and Fan Qiseng as deacons and George Crombie as the pastor (Book 4, p 307). With only sixteen members it was a token of things to come, but if ten members tithing their income could support one church worker, sixteen were not to be underestimated. On the 10th he set off over the hills for Jackson's city of Taizhou, passing through Ninghai, a city Crombie was soon to occupy as well as Fenghua. Instead of taking the direct route, Hudson Taylor made a fifteen-mile detour to see Tiantai. The slender youth of Shanghai days had

'CHINESE STYLE'

become a stocky man capable of sustained physical exertion for long periods. He told Mr Berger, 'All along the way one comes to town or village every two or three miles – many of them towns of considerable size, where multitudes are born and live, and die, never leaving their native place. The thought forces itself upon one with painful intensity; and as you pass through town after town seeing others in the distance . . . it becomes more and more oppressive. When and how are these poor souls to be reached with the Gospel message?'

At Taizhou Hudson Taylor spent a few days with Jackson, writing – 'days which I have much enjoyed. He has made progress in the language recently, and lives in thorough Chinese style.' That the people all looked upon him as their friend was testimonial enough. This weak, vacillating man seemed at last to be maturing. Hudson Taylor longed to stay with him, to show him how to make more use of his opportunities and to Romanise the Taizhou dialect. But because of his promise to the Dodds he could neither stay nor go on to encourage George Stott at Wenzhou. Had he gone, he would have been with him at another time of stress.

A day at a time   February 1868

Somewhere on his journey home from the southern district Hudson Taylor wrote to his mother, on February 22, 'This hot weather opens up afresh (though they have never closed) the wounds of six months ago; and the question will sometimes arise as to how my darling little ones and dear Maria, will weather the summer. . . . I *try* to live a day at a time (but) do not always succeed (to get through everything). . . . Pray for more faith, more love, more wisdom for me (in) my multitudinous and often embarrassing duties.'

Two more couples were due at Shanghai very soon, the J E Cardwells and C H Judds. 'Where are they to be stationed?' One setback after another created its own new problems.

> Of destitute plans there is no lack [of advice], but of *open* doors – doors open for the untrained in the language and the ways of the Chinese, there are few. But the Lord will provide. In four or five directions I am called for at the same time – where should I go first? . . . As to plans and arrangements, I am obliged to *make* some, but as often as not I am unable to *keep* them . . . all my powers feel overtaxed, and I know that my head must have a few hours' rest. . . .

> A large part of my work at home consists in the settlement
> of questions which have been too embarrassing or too grave to
> be decided in my absence . . . The more hurried my stay in
> (Hangzhou), the more intense the pressure while it lasts.

Until the team gained more experience and grasp of the language
this state of affairs would continue, but as the men progressed they
must be found work and responsibilities of their own.

On February 24 the printer's proofs of the Hangzhou *Report*
arrived from William Gamble, and Maria had just handed them to
Emily Blatchley when she heard Jennie call out, 'Mr Taylor has
come!' 'I rushed downstairs and found him in the (office)!' Maria
was to write. Each time he came home from a journey her letters
echoed the Song of Solomon and her pleasure on hearing his voice
again. His journey had done him good. But when they were
together, a month's accumulation of news and problems had to be
shared.

McCarthy had come home with good news of Duncan and Reid at
Nanjing, and had gone back to Huzhou to search (without success)
for any sign of proclamations in their favour. He arrived home the
next day. Jinhua was also as unpromising as before. She was worried
about the dissident Lewis Nicol and the McLean sisters. The rift
between them and the rest of the Mission was growing. But that
could wait for a better time to discuss it. C R Alford, the new
Bishop of Victoria, Hong Kong, was in Hangzhou, staying at the
CMS with Henry Gretton. Hangzhou itself was the most encouraging place. Wang Lae-djün, the church and the school were
flourishing. Mr Yu, the teacher, and the school cook had had a fight,
had both drawn blood, and had made peace again. Henry Cordon, a
butcher by trade, had supervised the killing and dividing up of the
cow.

As for Jennie, more than ever in demand, she was being invited
into more homes than she had time for. Always riding the crests
herself, she raised the tone of the household and set a standard for
the less buoyant. On January 14 she had assured her father of her
safety and good health, before saying (in words which tell us more
about herself), 'I hope Mr Landels [minister of Regent's Park
Chapel] will not beg for (the CIM) . . . We shall be supplied, for
God cannot fail us. He feeds the ravens because He is their Creator,
how much more will He feed us who are His servants, His children? Our funds are low, and we daily look to God but without one

fear or anxious thought that He will withhold any good thing from us.'

Earlier she had written, '(The Chinese) have the very element of longevity in their unimpulsive characters. Oh that they might be won for Christ as a nation . . . Sanctified by His love what a fine people they would make! Sensible, plodding, stable, how well they stand compared with other nations.' And of the approaching Chinese New Year, 'I want the whole city to ring with the name of Jesus . . . We want them to feel that Christians may have more joy at such seasons than they have ever known as heathens. We do not wish to make foreigners of them.'

So Wang Lae-djün, the pastor, and the church members planned their Christian celebrations. With 165 seated, many more neighbours crowded the doorways. The church was in good heart. Its members were continually bringing others to the chapel. Jennie's school could take no more pupils. Every day she was having to disappoint parents who begged her to accept their children. Gone were the days when almost everything that happened at Hangzhou rested on Hudson Taylor's shoulders.

For five days after he reached home there was relative peace. Then on February 29 Mrs Dodd went into labour and the Meadows and Crombies and a friend all arrived – to stay on and off for a month – and everything began to happen all at once.

Yangzi strategy   *March 1868*

Since the New Year, and before, the Taylors and the team with them in Hangzhou had recognised the multiplying signs that their days together were numbered. The Hangzhou church was strong but should not be overshadowed by so large a body of foreign missionaries coming and going. The southern region of Zhejiang had a nucleus of missionaries and Christians from whom the work of evangelism and church-planting was expanding. Anglicans, Presbyterians and Baptists were all making their mark from Ningbo. The Huzhou area was closed to missionaries for the present, but the deep interior of China called. The foothold gained at Nanjing itself should be used in a new advance. The time had come to leave only two or three at Hangzhou and to move 'onward and inward'. Charles Schmidt in Suzhou had asked for members of the CIM to join him there. With Jinhua barred against them, the Cordons and McLean sisters were free to go north. The farther they were from

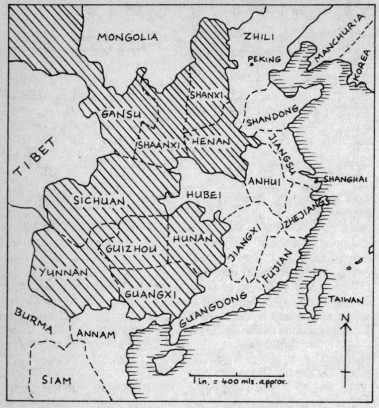

'NINE UNOCCUPIED PROVINCES'

Lewis Nicol, the less influenced they would be by his rebellious spirit. The great Yangzi waterway gave access to a chain of un-evangelised provinces, and the Grand Canal led northward to several more. The McCarthys and Jennie Faulding, most closely linked with the Hangzhou Christians, would stay while the rest launched out to tackle new cities.

This was how they were thinking and talking together. Back in October Hudson Taylor had written of the need to advance, adding, '(Before long) some may be permitted to break ground in unoccu-pied provinces.'[5] Duncan had begun the process, but it was time for others to move up to support him. If necessary Nanjing could serve as a Yangzi base, but Suzhou, Zhenjiang (Chinkiang) or one of the cities on the Grand Canal between them must also be considered. Yangzhou on the canal north of the Yangzi could be a first step towards Henan and, being close to the Yangzi and Zhenjiang, could be his headquarters. Not all his colleagues could see the wisdom of pressing inland. Even William Berger was anxious and pleaded the importance of consolidating what had been begun. But most of the team shared Hudson Taylor's broad vision of expansion.

When Jinhua and Huzhou were proving difficult to hold, John McCarthy had written, '"Let not your heart be troubled" – the voice of Him who opens and *no man can shut*. Is it a further indication that this province should not be our battlefield?' – even though Charles Schmidt had invited him, McCarthy, to move to Suzhou, a very tempting offer. And a fortnight later, quoting the prophet Habakkuk; 'Though the olive tree should fail, the harvests yield no grain and the flocks be cut off, *yet* will I rejoice *in the Lord*';

> And such faith and such faith alone, will carry us through if our mission is to do a work for God in this land; none will need it . . . more than yourself, in the midst of change of feeling and sentiments, in those to whom you would naturally look for nothing but support and assistance . . . And if our way does appear cloudy and uncertain, and the days of joy seem to be very few and far between, yet if He is with us in the fire . . . in His presence is fulness of joy. . . . *If* I have ever learned the ABC of this myself, you can thank God for having been the instrument of instruction.

This was the spirit that would win through. McCarthy agreed to oversee the Ningbo church to free James Meadows for pioneering on the Yangzi. James Williamson was game for anything. Maria was of one mind with her husband and would go anywhere with him. Where they went Emily Blatchley and 'good and kind' and competent Louise Desgraz would go with enthusiasm. And the Rudlands, fully absorbed with the presses and a growing team of Chinese printers, were willing to move with them at any time.

'More easily said than done' March 1868

The plan was one thing. To carry it out was altogether another. During March the Hangzhou premises were crowded to capacity and overflowing with visitors. Added to the Meadows family, the Crombies from Ningbo and Mary Bausum on a holiday visit, came their old friends Dr and Mrs Lord, and Susan Barnes for good measure. All this while Mary Bowyer was dangerously ill again with 'inflammation of the heart'.

James Meadows left on March 2 for Shanghai, to arrange for the arrival of the Cardwells and Judds and Mary Rudland's sister, Annie Bohannan – and then to visit Suzhou to rent premises and consult with Charles Schmidt (whom Meadows had led to Christ) about members of the CIM coming to work there. On the way back to Hangzhou he would look in at Huzhou too and encourage the converted barber. But on the same day William Gamble wrote to say the ship had made an exceptionally fast voyage of 110 days and the Judds and Cardwells were already with him. So Maria, accompanied by Ensing, the Chinese girl she had adopted, and the ever-willing McCarthy, set off for Shanghai, to introduce the new arrivals to living in Chinese style and to the difficulties of travelling with minimal privacy by canal boat. McCarthy would have the men in another houseboat.

Bishop Alford arrived for confirmations at the Anglican church on March 4, and took the opportunity to see the missionaries and arrangements at New Lane, about which he had heard criticisms. A 'crazy woman' involved Jennie in caring for her until she was shipped home to Huzhou. And the peace at No 1 was further disturbed by undercurrents of more discontent in the Nicol camp. The imminent arrival of the new missionaries meanwhile added to the unrest, and neuralgia made it difficult for Hudson Taylor to work. As Maria told his mother, 'Getting away from Hangzhou is better than medicine to him.' While there he could seldom relax.

Until the visitors had gone and the Cardwells and Judds were provided for, there could be no hope of packing up and moving northward. So the decision was taken that the Cordons and the McLean sisters would accept the Schmidts' invitation and begin work in Suzhou with his help – with one familiar complication. Mrs Cordon would need obstetric help in mid-May. Hudson Taylor's plans must revolve round that event. Taking Jane and Margaret McLean to a new environment was a fresh bid to wean them from the complaining spirit they had acquired from Lewis Nicol. Yet Margaret could say of Hudson and Maria, 'We love you so much that sooner than be a cause of anxiety to you we feel we would rather leave the mission'. Perhaps the companionship of Charles Schmidt and his Chinese wife would change their minds about being Chinese to the Chinese. Schmidt himself wore Chinese clothes and lived as a Chinese.[6]

With the Cardwells and Judds had sailed the elder son of Colonel Fishe of Dublin, another young man wanting to be under no one's control, but soon to discover how helpless he was on his own. Edward Fishe stayed in Shanghai at first, but when Hudson Taylor tried to help him, he too became dependent. Half in and half out of the CIM circle, he owed neither allegiance to the Mission nor loyalty to its leader.

Maria, Ensing and John McCarthy reached Shanghai to find William Gamble going out of his way to make the newcomers welcome. 'An invaluable friend of our mission,' Maria called him. 'All in favour of' missionaries wearing Chinese clothes and following Chinese customs, he 'kindly claimed as a privilege that it (the Cardwells' and Judds' change from foreign dress) should be in his house' rather than after they had boarded the canal boats. What other Shanghai residents might say of him mattered little. Charles Judd also came in for Maria's praise. His spirit was excellent, 'entering into the principle of making *cheerfully* any sacrifice that might conduce to the good' of the Chinese. He and Elizabeth his wife had never met the Taylors and saw relatively little of them during the first few weeks in China. But he could never forget what he did see of Maria's calm courage and good sense. 'She had no mercy on any fastidiousness about food or other matters.'

When they reached Hangzhou on March 17 and entered No 1 New Lane, the plain utilitarian nature of everything struck them. No money was being wasted. 'They had boards on trestles for tables . . . bare tables, no cloths, and it was Chinese food. There were no knives or forks . . . bare wooden chairs (just deckchairs for luxury) – nothing else . . . Plain Chinese bed-frames (with coconut-fibre ropes in place of springs) and upright posts for mosquito curtains . . . I did not see much of (Mr Taylor), he was so much away, so very busy . . . with mission matters and with patients.' Jennie's comment on their utilitarian standards had been, 'Please don't talk of my "hardships" – it is not even a trial to me to have "to rough it". I only told you about our contrivances . . . to amuse you.'

It was typical of the Taylors that the arrival of reinforcements should be an occasion for celebration. A day on the lake and exploring the hills on the far side gave time to get to know each other. A hidden cave they discovered was to Jennie a good hiding-place for Chinese Christians in time of persecution. But why only

Chinese? Hangzhou felt safe, and when they returned in pouring rain after dark, shut out of the city, the fact that the gate was opened to them as foreigners encouraged confidence. 'I suppose it is only to high mandarins to whom it would be opened', she commented.

The very next day they dispersed. The Crombies carried the Cardwells off to join Josiah Jackson at Taizhou, and James Williamson followed with their baggage, while Susan Barnes took Elizabeth Meadows home to Shaoxing. Maria trembled for the Cardwells, because both were so unadaptable, 'unbending'. It was a matter of the will, harder for some than for others. And Hudson Taylor took Charles Judd to the top of the Hill of the City God to see the temples and look out across the vast city and the lake, each the same size and shape lying side by side (Book 4, p 242). What he saw of the Judds he liked. Within a few days of arriving, both Charles and Elizabeth were throwing themselves into work and progressing well with the language, he going daily to the tea-shops with a Chinese Christian to gossip the gospel. This was the right kind of man for the interior, to pioneer the cities of the Yangzi valley for a start. But for the present he must stay behind and learn the ropes with John McCarthy's help.

James Meadows and Henry Cordon were to leave for Suzhou on March 30. Maria with Emily, Annie Bohannan and the children, Mrs Cordon and the McLean sisters would follow on April 3. Hudson Taylor would pack up his office and clinic, leaving some stock for John McCarthy's dispensary, and have the baggage ready to be shipped north when sent for. He would then join the others in Suzhou. After Mrs Cordon's confinement he would return to help Jackson at Taizhou and at last visit Stott at Wenzhou before resuming the Yangzi valley advance. So he hoped; but nothing was plain sailing.

A letter came from William Gamble, too strong a friend for destructive criticism, meaning only to help but adding to the pressure on Hudson Taylor. Knowing only a fraction of what Taylor accomplished or the reasons for all Gamble had heard, he expressed himself frankly. Naming each missionary, he advised on how they should be deployed in widespread expansion.[7]

Ill-informed, critical and contradictory though the letter was, it came as clear confirmation to Hudson Taylor and Maria of their planned deployment. Gamble would be pleased to know that within a few days only the McCarthys, Judds and Rudlands (for the present) would be left at Hangzhou, with Jennie Faulding and the slowly recovering Mary Bowyer, for whom Hudson Taylor was still anxious. One letter like that could be welcomed.

Another in a very different, bitter spirit about church government came from John Stevenson of all men, and shook Hudson Taylor to the core. His 'neuralgic headaches' had become so bad that Maria was handling all she could of his day-to-day work. Jennie knew they were caused 'solely by (nervous) prostration brought on by anxiety and overwork.' Mental distress frequently resulted in disabling physical symptoms. Knowing that Stevenson's letter would distress him, Maria waited a few days before handing it to Hudson. He replied warmly, from his heart. It was all a misunderstanding, as he would show. He had never written as Stevenson said he had. Whatever could he have misconstrued, to be so offended? 'Have I ever, dear Brother, been other than a sympathizer, a friend, a helper to you . . . as you have been to me . . . ? We always have walked in mutual confidence, as well as in love . . . The Lord use you, beloved Brother, ten-thousandfold. . . .' The rift was healed. But the next day he was 'very poorly', Maria noted. On the eve of the great migration to the greater unknown his emotional stamina did not look equal to the strain.

'The stamp of men we need'   *March 1868*

On March 12, Hudson Taylor wrote with some feeling about 'the painful experience we still have', to William Berger, who was faced with problem candidates, among them Tom Barnardo and Robert White of Dublin. Before long White was to brush aside all the Bergers' advice, marry, sail at once at his own charges and once in China to attach himself to Hudson Taylor and create his own adder's brood of predicaments.

> None should come out who do not grasp certain principles *so fully* that it shall not require 'Mr Taylor' to insist on this or that detail. The first and foremost of these principles is that of *becoming* all things to all men. . . . *Why* is it, that in every part of every province in China, Roman Catholic missionaries are both able and willing to live, while away from the ports scarcely one Protestant missionary is to be found? . . . *Our mission will prove a failure*, so far as any extensive evangelization of the interior is concerned, unless this principle is *con amore* taken up by its members as a body. Give me a score of men such as Williamson and Duncan and McCarthy and with God's blessing in less than four years' time there will not be a province

'FOREIGN DIGNITY'
(Frock coat and crinolines)

without its missionary. But let me have a few more persons who
oppose this principle at every turn, and if we are not broken up
altogether it will be of God's own special interposition. . . . We, *as a
mission differ* from *all* the other missions. As soon as some persons
arrive here they find a sufficient answer to every question in, 'the
American missionaries do this, or the Church missionaries do that;
why can't we?' . . . The missionaries of almost all the societies have
better houses, finer furniture, more European fare, etc than we have
or are likely to have. . . . But . . . there is not *one* of them settled in
the interior among the people. Unless persons are prepared to stand
alone – separate from these Societies and those who imitate them –
they should never join our mission at all. . . . Let them know, too,
beforehand, that if they are hearty, loyal members of this mission,
they may expect the sneers and even opposition of *good, godly* men.

[Two weeks later he was more precise.] I only desire the help of
such persons as are fully prepared to work *in the interior, in the native
costume*, and *living, as far as possible, in the native style*. And that I do
not *contemplate* assisting, in future, any who may cease to labour in
this way. China is open to all; but my time and strength are too short,
and the work too great to allow of my attempting to work with any
who do not agree with me in the main on my plans of action. . . .
Indeed, might not even those engaged be sent out single for two or
three years, so as to master the language and pioneer for a time

before marrying? Their intended wives also might be expected to make some little progress in the language before marrying, and thus would have a fair chance of future usefulness. . . . Might we not legitimately say . . . 'If these conditions seem too hard, these sacrifices too great to make for perishing China, *do not join our mission*. These are *small* things to some of the crosses you may expect . . . to bear . . . China is not to be won for Christ by quiet ease-loving men and women.' . . . The stamp of men and women we need is such as will put Jesus, China, souls, *first* and *foremost* in everything and at every time – even life itself must be secondary; nay more, those more precious than life. Of *such* men, of *such* women do not fear to send us too many. They are more precious than rubies.[8]

It was not wishful thinking. In time they were to come by the score.

Defiance in Taiwan   1867–July 1868

During 1867 the British firm of Dodd and Company leased premises at the market town they called 'Banka' on the Danshui river in the north of Taiwan. By the treaties of 1858 'Danshui' was a treaty port, but only at the village of Hebei at the mouth was there a deep-water anchorage. Lighters had to convey freight between Hebei and 'Banka', fourteen miles upstream towards Taibei (now the capital of Taiwan). To a man the people of 'Banka' denied possession to the foreigner and for the present there was nothing he could do.

Major trouble returned to Taiwan early in 1868. The island had been part of the Chinese empire since 1683 when the Dutch were forced out. As early as that they had provided a Gospel in Romanised Chinese, but by 1865 all signs of a Church in Taiwan had evaporated. Dr James Laidlaw Maxwell, a Presbyterian physician, had begun working at Tainan in 1865, a few years after the Roman Catholic Church, and four men were baptised the following year. (One who became a preacher was still active in 1905.) But when Maxwell attempted to rent a house, all negotiations broke down, 'an interference notoriously ascribed to the authorities'. In a memorial to Sir Rutherford Alcock, Dr Maxwell described what then occurred. A house was obtained through the Commissioner of Customs. After a few weeks 'the missionaries were stoned while walking peacefully about, the landlord of the house occupied by the Mission was threatened with violence, accusations of the most

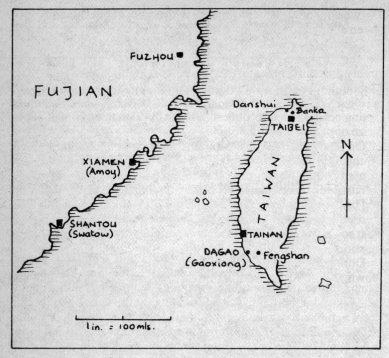

TAIWAN: SCENES OF VIOLENCE

wicked and disgusting character were freely circulated against us, and placards were posted up describing us as Resurrectionists, murderers of the most awful type, and as having then many dead bodies secreted in the house.'

He appealed to the Chinese authorities, as also did Mr Swinhoe, then British consul in Taiwan, to issue a proclamation contradicting the false rumours and warning the people against acts of violence. Promises were made but not kept. Increasingly hostile placards were posted up without interference by the authorities. 'A violent assault was one day made upon the chapel, and the district Mandarin who, after long delay, appeared upon the scene, utterly refused to protect us against the mob, unless on a promise that we should leave the place in three days. We had no recourse but to comply, and so we had to leave Taiwanfoo [i.e. Tainan] a place in which, by treaty enactment, we should unquestionably have been allowed to settle. . . .'

Consular protests had no effect in securing their return to Tainan, so they transferred to Dagao (Takao), now Gaoxiong, another treaty port thirty miles farther south, and premises were purchased. 'About a fortnight after the opening of the chapel, an assault was made up it,' led by people connected with the *yamen*. Again the acting consul failed to obtain redress and the mandarins failed to seize or punish the guilty parties.

On April 11, 1868, a mission catechist was seized in the street at 'Pithau, a District City of Hang-san' (probably Fengshan) and beaten and robbed, but he escaped and rushed into the *yamen*. The magistrate ordered him to prison. Immediately the mob, incited and led by the *yamen* underlings made for the chapel armed with knives and other weapons and began to plunder and carry off everything that could be removed, including medical and other property of the missionaries.

During the next two days they continued, unmolested, to tear down the building itself, carrying away wood, bricks, tiles and everything that could be used elsewhere. The rioters then proceeded to the house of one of the worshippers, plundered it, beat the man's wife, and drove her and her daughter-in-law into the street. One of the Christian workers was chased for three miles and escaped; the other was caught in his father's house, robbed and beaten. Other worshippers fled to Dagao for protection. Hosea Ballou Morse says that on April 24, 1868, both the Catholic and English Presbyterian churches were destroyed by mobs at Fengshan.

When news of the 'Pithau' or 'Pitow' riot spread, another catechist was accused of poisoning people, seized by local roughs, murdered with stones and knives, and his heart torn out and eaten by his murderers. By 'sympathetic magic' his courage would become theirs, they believed.[9] *The Chinese Recorder* voiced the indignation felt among foreigners. 'We have no complaint against the people for persecution at their hands, but against the authorities and their subordinates in the *yamen*.' A flood of events was developing, which was to engulf Hudson Taylor and the CIM.

On July 31 Acting-Consul John Gibson sent a dispatch to Sir Rutherford Alcock, the British minister in Peking. The day before, the rebuilt Protestant mission chapel at Pitow had for a second time been destroyed by servants of the mandarin. Clearly strong action was needed to change the *daotai*'s ways but the 'extreme pressure by the Acting British Consul' was to take a bizarre form. In the process it passed out of his control to that of a naval lieutenant with an exaggerated sense of occasion.

Responsibility lay farther up the chain of command. Sir Rutherford had called upon the Chinese government in Peking to 'compel the local authorities to do justice' in Taiwan. At the same time, as at Danshui later in the year, he thought it 'very desirable that a British gunboat should be on the station to support the consular authority'. Unfortunately, consul and lieutenant overstepped the mark[10] and eventually Alcock had to require Consul Swinhoe, to 'state specifically why he considered it necessary to proceed to this act of war'. For by then the Foreign Office and the Admiralty in London were demanding explanations.

On May 2, 1868, the Foreign Minister, Lord Stanley, referred to Sir Rutherford Alcock a letter from the LMS in London suggesting that a proposed revision of the treaty with China should have an added clause, specifically conceding to British missionaries the right to reside and purchase land anywhere in the interior as well as at commercial ports. Sir Rutherford replied, 'It does not seem to me that any new clause of a Treaty is required. . . . Article VI of the French Treaty is perfectly clear on that point, and what is acquired as a right for French missionaries, is equally acquired by the most favoured nation clause, for the British, as I have recently had occasion to remind the Foreign Board' – the Zongli Yamen. For the diplomats it was crystal clear. For others, mandarins and British subjects unacquainted with the French text, the absence of this clause in the British treaty accounted for breaches of justice. Hence the LMS's request. But Article 12 of the Peking Convention had said enough (Book 4, p 27).

As Hudson Taylor prepared to extend operations to inland China, the minister and his consuls were in no doubt that it was their duty to assist British subjects to obtain premises. They had made it plain to the mandarins of Zhejiang who had issued proclamations to that effect, and Hudson Taylor was equally aware of it – as a result of personal involvement over the years and, recently, of the Xiaoshan, Huzhou and Jinhua outrages and threatened violence at Hangzhou and Wenzhou. The trouble was that while the government of China had had to accept the grim fact of superior foreign force, the Confucian literati still rejected concessions made under duress; and mandarins out of touch with reality, as in Taiwan, shared their views and were ready to act against the barbarian as opportunity offered. Another typhoon was blowing up. The first gusts had been felt but its nature still could not be foreseen.

Converging currents 1868

Violent outbursts here and there betrayed the underlying indignation of the scholar-gentry against the foreign presence. The indignation of the consular representatives of the Western powers against violations of the treaties was no less. Undercurrents of intrigue by the most xenophobic mandarins, including some at the highest levels, flowed silently – while the outspoken foreign press in the treaty ports and Hong Kong called for stronger action to teach the only lesson they seemed to understand. Tension was growing though little other evidence was apparent.

Most sinister was the ground swell of vicious rumour widely spread, with characteristics betraying a common source. According to Du Halde in 1736, a Chinese book dated 1624 expressed the reaction of dissidents to the favour being shown by the Ming Court to the Roman Catholic Church (Book 1, pp 65–6; Book 4, p 271). It charged that the outer barbarians were kidnapping children and using their eyes, livers, hearts and other organs to make medicines. The practices of extreme unction, followed almost immediately by the individual's death, and of closing the eyes of the dead may have had a bearing on this accusation and, on the part of some, this belief. The same charges had been revived as recently as 1862 in another book, *Death-blow to Corrupt Doctrine*. And F R Grundy, the *Times* correspondent in China, had drawn attention in 1866 to a clever proclamation being circulated extensively in Hunan and presumably in other trouble spots. Blending fact with fiction about the Catholics it was calculated to inflame the emotions of its readers. Clause VII read,

> When a (Chinese) member of their religion (Roman Catholic) is on his death-bed, several of his co-religionists come and exclude his relatives while they offer prayers for his salvation. The fact is, while the breath is still in his body they scoop out his eyes and cut out his heart, which they use in their country in the manufacture of false silver.[11]

The superstitions of the general public made them susceptible to tales of this sort. After all, why should foreign men be so solicitous for young children? Other accusations of promiscuous behaviour at Christian meetings of both sexes, and of immorality by celibate priests fuelled indignation. The man in the street could be controlled by the mandarins; the danger lay in the inveterate antagonism of the scholar-gentry to everything foreign. 'Should the literati stir up the passions of the people by playing upon their superstitious fears, few officials had the moral courage as well as the ability to keep the peace for long, for their tenure of office was largely dependent upon the goodwill of the scholarly class.' Official connivance was to be expected. Official instigation would not be surprising; nor a blind eye to the facts, right up to the Zongli Yamen and the Peking court.

With hindsight we see that the advance of missionaries into the interior was coinciding with China's new mood of protest and with the consuls' impatience. So far the first indications differed little from the attitudes usually encountered. On February 6, 1868, the *North China Herald* reported that William Muirhead of the LMS had 'announced his intention of returning to China to carry out a long cherished scheme of establishing missions in the interior of the country. It has been repeatedly pointed out in our columns, that the interior of China is the place for missionaries to locate themselves, rather than linger in the treaty ports or their immediate vicinity.' Without the support of the press, Hudson Taylor intended to do what was advocated. But the reaction of the press to the protests of the literati when they took action was the measure of the editors' surprise. At Zhenjiang and Yangzhou the depth of Chinese feeling was soon to be demonstrated, and at Tianjin the lengths to which some protesters were prepared to go.

The Suzhou interval   *April–May 1868*

Until Charles Schmidt and his Chinese wife went to live in Suzhou in September 1867, the only missionaries to visit the city had preached and passed on. William Muirhead and Griffith John had been among the first. Muirhead in Chinese dress had been dragged along the street by his securely fastened *bianzi* and 'a heavy blow on his head made him think his time was short'.[12] During 1867 an American Episcopal missionary, J W Lambuth and a Chinese colleague, known since his residence in America as C K Marshall, rented a room near the Ink Pagoda in which they preached during regular visits from Shanghai. Then on his way to Nanjing in September 1867, just before the Schmidts arrived, George Duncan had commended Suzhou, once beautiful but now dilapidated, to Hudson Taylor's attention. With Charles Schmidt's encouragement James Meadows had rented premises in March, and he and Henry Cordon were going to repair them for the Cordons and McLean twins to occupy as the next new station of the CIM.

With high civil rank as a reward by the Chinese government for his part in the defeat of the Taipings, and with many acquaintances among the military mandarins of Suzhou, Schmidt was secure from interference although he gave 'public sermons' in his chapel. His deep understanding of Chinese affairs, his fluency and tact, and his ability as a preacher made this ex-soldier a model missionary. Through William Gamble he had formed links with the American Presbyterian Mission (North) who continued there after he left. But for another foreign family to attempt to put down roots in Suzhou was as much an experiment as at Jinhua.

In Hangzhou on March 30, 1868, Meadows and Cordon were ready to set out. All were aware that this was the start of a new advance towards the unoccupied provinces and, following their usual practice, the household at New Lane spent the day in fasting and prayer before the two men went down to their boat. Maria was to follow four days later with Mrs Cordon and the McLean sisters, but by then Hudson Taylor was 'prostrate' with an unnamed illness. The momentousness of this step was enough to account for his symptoms. So Maria stayed to see him through it. Whooping cough was spreading among the Hangzhou missions, and in any case he was needed to doctor the family of D D Green, the American Presbyterian, and Jane McLean, already down with it. On April 10 (the day before the attack at 'Pitow' in Taiwan) he sent Maria off to Suzhou with her four children, Annie Bohannan their nurse, Emily Blatchley and Margaret McLean. The boatmen took advantage of them as women, and the journey which he made in two days a fortnight later, had already taken them eight days when they reached Wujiang, fifteen miles short of Suzhou. By then Charles Schmidt, waiting for them in Suzhou, had become 'very anxious', fearing that they had run into serious trouble on the way. He came down the Grand Canal, met them at Wujiang and escorted their two boats back in the dark to moor in front of his own house at six in the morning. It had been 'one of the worst nights' Maria had ever spent on a Chinese boat, she said without explanation, and Margaret McLean added, 'Mr Schmidt thought (we should) get there as early as possible, so as to avoid being much observed.'

Like No 1 New Lane, the house Meadows had rented had once been a respectable home, but 'was only a shed when we first saw it,' Cordon said. With twelve rooms round the courtyard and three upstairs, it included a guest hall large enough to become a chapel seating over a hundred people. Rough repairs had made it habitable. After lying low all day at the Schmidts', Maria, Margaret McLean, Mrs Cordon and one of the children went after dark in sedan chairs and 'kept very quiet' to avoid creating excitement in the neighbourhood. They were there when Hudson Taylor arrived with Jane McLean on the 25th to find that Maria's friendliness and adaptability had paved the way and, as at Hangzhou, by May 4 he had persuaded the previous Chinese tenants to move out cheerfully.

On the way to Suzhou, Maria had had a search made through the big city of Jiaxing, fifty miles east of Huzhou, for the governor's proclamations favourable to foreigners wishing to live anywhere in the province, without finding any. Schmidt, however, had had copies made for Hudson Taylor of two such proclamations in Suzhou. The provincial boundary area between Hangzhou and Suzhou was apparently still unsafe, but at least the *daotai* at Suzhou seemed favourably disposed. With half a million inhabitants, Suzhou offered scope enough for several teams of missionaries. Hudson Taylor could have been justified in making the city a major objective, but Suzhou was the natural outpost of the missions at Shanghai. Beyond it lay hundreds more such cities with no foreseeable prospect of receiving the gospel unless from his little mission with its Ningbo and Hangzhou Christians. Two foreign and two Chinese missionaries to each unevangelised province was still his almost unattainable goal. The total of missionaries in China had grown to 'about two hundred and fifty'[13] but the CIM's thirty-four members still included seven beginners and several more who had made little progress since arriving. Among them were the Nicols, now obsessively rebellious, and at least three following their lead. Progress depended on many things, not least the readiness of the team.

Within ten days of Hudson Taylor's arrival at Suzhou, Emily was writing to Jennie, 'We are sending Wu Sin-sang and Hyiao-foh to Changchow to open a school . . . no preaching to be attempted. Evening and morning prayers with the boys but with the doors shut.' This plan was not even to be talked about in Hangzhou. But within a few days the men returned, unable to secure a footing. After setbacks in other cities as well, the tactics had to be changed to what had succeeded so well in Hangzhou – not even tea-shop evangelism until the missionaries' presence was accepted. As a proving ground, Suzhou had produced this deliberate policy for their advance to the Yangzi as soon as the Cordons' baby was born.

By then, the Taylor children all had whooping cough which kept the parents and Emily in attendance at the Schmidts' day and night. Taking turns they went to the Cordons' house to get some sleep. But the administration of the Mission had to continue. Distributing funds and advising each member, reporting to the Bergers and consulting with them, and answering questions from other missions and the consuls never ceased.

A letter critical of the *Report of the Hangchow Branch of the CIM* had been published by the *North China Daily News*. Writing to Jennie, Hudson Taylor said, 'I shall not think of answering *publickly* [*sic*] . . . but may do so privately. "The Lord reigneth." If it only has the effect of knitting us more closely together we shall have cause for gratitude to God.' As the clouds thickened, this phrase, 'The Lord reigns' was taken up by the team as a victory-sign. Come what may, God was in control and all would be well. 'Gossip must ever work mischief,' Maria wrote to Mrs Berger, 'and I fear there has been a great deal of this.' So secrecy about their movements was directed against false comment as well as against organised Chinese resistance. Someone, reputed to be Chaplain Butcher of Shanghai, had already replied in the *Daily News* to the critic, and Maria went on, 'Thus God can raise up advocates for us, when even the need of such advocates is unknown to us. I think (Hudson) is right in refusing to enter the lists against a Christian brother . . . in a worldly newspaper. . . . He has written privately to Mr Green.' Like Nehemiah, she added, he could say 'I am doing a great work, so that I cannot come down' to such levels. His *Report* was reviewed in the *North China Herald* also, 'but tho' it finds plenty of fault with "the cant", etc,' it would do no real harm. It was after all no more than a factual statement of events, receipts and expenses.

Far worse than gibes in the press was the obsessive correspondence by Lewis Nicol with William Berger and others. Nearly two years after the voyage of the *Lammermuir* he was building on the same old complaints about stockings and 'dirty Chinese cast-offs' (Book 4, p 284). Mr Berger replied to Nicol, 'It seems to me, that . . . if you cannot confide [have confidence] in us [Hudson Taylor and Berger] . . . it will be your duty to retire from the Mission.' But on May 9 Emily was writing to Jennie at Hudson Taylor's request to answer more allegations made to the Judds. Nicol had been saying that 'Large stores of English clothing and material for making such, brought out for the use of the mission in China, are stored away . . . (rather to) rot than sell them to anyone out here who would make use of them.' Hudson Taylor had 'changed his mind' after reaching Shanghai, and made them all wear Chinese clothes. It was all nonsense, Emily reminded Jennie. No such foreign clothes or materials ever existed. She herself had been in charge of preparations and Jennie had helped. The facts of the matter 'are open to the light' and ought to be made known. Moving to more pleasant topics she went on, 'We are thinking of sending someone (perhaps Lanfeng) . . . to (Yangzhou) north of the river,' to prospect. Again, this was for the Hangzhou team to pray about, but not for wider circulation. 'Mr Taylor says he hopes I have nearly "shut up" . . . so goodbye dearie – it seems a long time since I saw you.'

On May 5, William Berger wrote to Hudson Taylor, 'It is still with me a grave question whether a brother who avows he has no confidence in you (or me) should continue connected with the Mission.' His advice would have taken about two months to reach Hudson Taylor, who confided to Jennie, 'I do not see how we can keep them in the Mission after a letter, worse than ever he has written before, recently sent to Mr Berger.' The pain of dismissing a colleague, and the prospect of unpleasant repercussions, gnawed at his heart and mind while he still hoped that Nicol would reform.

Harder to face was the effect of subversion on other members of the team, for the Cordons and Barchet were the latest partisans. Stephan Barchet had been attached to the E C Lords since his arrival in China, although a member of the CIM since its inception. The influence of Edward Lord, a Baptist by strong conviction, and Stephan's engagement to Mary Bausum, Lord's step-daughter, had changed Stephan's own views. Writing to Thomas Marshall, his Congregational minister in London, he enclosed a copy of a letter he had intended to send to Hudson Taylor but had withheld. In it he expressed 'the desire to be considered a *friend*, not a member of the Mission (because) elements of the Mission tend to anarchy. . . . If it be thought proper that a Methodist should be pastor of a Presbyterian church or a Presbyterian of a Baptist church I differ in opinion, for if a church is Baptist let it be Baptist. . . .' Meadows, a Methodist, had baptised the Presbyterian Crombie's converts, and Nicol had called in an American Presbyterian to sprinkle the Xiaoshan converts rather than have Hudson Taylor immerse them. Unlike previously, the perpetuation of Western denominations among the Chinese now mattered more to Stephan than their acceptance of each other's secondary differences for the sake of unity in the Chinese church. His colleagues in the CIM, like him, had welcomed the unsectarian principle of the Mission and set no store by each other's denominational differences, although Hudson Taylor intended them to be observed in practice. Regretting Barchet's change of stance, Marshall passed his letter on to William Berger.

That was not all. Stephan continued, 'Further may be mentioned the despotic government of the Mission. So long as a man is fallible, it must be seen how dangerous it is to give the entire control of a mission into the hands of a single individual.' He had nothing against Hudson Taylor's character, he emphasised, and was not saying that he acted despotically, but objected to the principle he himself had previously accepted. Finally, and perhaps the crux of the matter, 'I would prefer not to be associated with men who are . . . under the influence of petty jealousies, and are seldom at peace.' E C Lord had resigned from his own mission (the ABMU) and become independent some years before, and Nicol and his sympathisers had been to Ningbo often enough to have sickened Stephan. He resigned in June. When the Bryanston Hall congregation ceased to support him, William Berger offered to do so instead. Before long Stephan married Mary Bausum, went to the States and became a doctor of medicine. They returned to China and forty years later were still good friends of the CIM.

News must have reached Suzhou of William Burns's death from dysentery at Yingkou (Niuchuang) on April 4, 1868. Only 53, by the standards of missionary survivors he might have had twenty more years of service ahead of him. Undoubtedly Hudson Taylor felt his loss deeply. Years later he wrote, 'His holy and reverential life and constant communings with God made fellowship with him satisfying to the deep cravings of my heart.' Burns's unsparing devotion to the Chinese and to the spreading of the gospel had also made him a man after Hudson Taylor's own heart. Seven months after reaching Yingkou he died in a cramped little room like the one he had shared with Hudson Taylor in Swatow, with little more than two chairs, two bookcases, a stove and the bench he used as a bed at night. As death approached he appealed to the Presbyterian Church to take up the torch he would carry no longer. Hugh Waddell and Joseph Hunter MD of the Presbyterian Church of Ireland responded and arrived at Yingkou in May 1869. Burns's work was continued for decades to

come. In 1869 Donald Matheson was to tell Lord Clarendon that
Burns's name was 'honoured wherever foreigners are known in
China'.[14] To soldier on without the support of Burns's prayers and
wisdom was painful to Hudson Taylor. Another ally had been
removed.

At last, on May 12, Mrs Cordon gave birth to a stillborn child. No
explanation of this frequent occurrence among missionaries is
given.[15] Life in Suzhou went on as usual until the 16th, when a boat
was hired to take all but the Cordons and McLean sisters as far as 'to
Nankin'. In spite of Duncan's difficulties in finding and keeping
good premises, his was the only foothold so far beyond Suzhou.
'Pray that if we attempt to take a house in (Yangzhou) we may
succeed,' Emily told Jennie in a letter packed as always with
business matters. The options were wide open as good, reliable Li
Lanfeng, the printer, went ahead. Meadows and McCarthy had
gone to help Jackson at Taizhou, so Hudson Taylor's return to south
Zhejiang was postponed again. On Monday night, May 18, he,
Maria, Emily Blatchley and the children, still all coughing day and
night, set off for the Yangzi valley – as China's mood of protest
deepened.

The boat-people[16]   *May–June 1868*

Little had changed, as far as foreigners could tell, in the attitude
of China towards them. There had always been sporadic outbursts
of feeling, localised and unrelated. Even this was too much for the
consuls and diplomats to tolerate. It must stop. Nationals under
their protection must be safe wherever they might be and whatever
they might do within the law, while holding passports countersigned
by China. In fact they were safe – in the normal course of events. So
when Hudson Taylor hired houseboats for his family, including
Emily, Annie Bohannan the children's nurse and their Chinese
companions, he was acting on the 'treaty of amity'. Nothing would
ever be achieved by thinking 'there is a lion in the way' (Proverbs
26: 13). On this occasion he provided roomier accommodation than
usual, for while he hoped to find a foothold in one of the great
Yangzi cities without delay, it might be weeks before they could
move into a house of their own. He was right. Leaving Suzhou
quietly after dark on May 18, they were still living in the boats six
weeks later.

In theory they were heading for Nanjing, expecting that by the time they arrived George Duncan would have found such premises as the mandarins would allow him to retain. But on the way through the cities on the Grand Canal, Wuxi, Changzhou and Danyang, they would assess the prospects, knowing of a Roman Catholic presence in the area. Nothing came of this reconnaissance, and on the 23rd they reached the 'silt-choked, fever-ridden' river port of Zhenjiang. Ruined in the Taiping war and suffocated by army camps, it was slow in recovering. But Zhenjiang impressed Hudson Taylor with its importance. With a population of 150,000, many of them the families of the Manchu garrison, the river and canal traffic it handled was 'very great', 'a place of concourse for natives of most

A MANCHU LADY

of the provinces of China' and equally strategic for merchant and missionary.[17] The LMS chapel was in a suburb manned by a Chinese evangelist. The city itself had none.

Foreign residents of all kinds seldom exceeded thirty in number, although the city stood strategically where the Grand Canal met the great Yangzi. British, American and French consuls, or at least consular offices staffed by a merchant chargé d'affaires or trainee assistant had been established there. Zhenjiang 'completed the chain of stations between (Hangzhou) and Nankin' and could be a useful business centre for the Mission and a central location for the printing press. From it as the hub, the spokes of the Mission's advance could radiate across the Yangzi and up the Canal to the north, and westward up the Yangzi itself, with quick routes east and southward to Shanghai, Suzhou and Hangzhou. From Shanghai, steamer services to Ningbo, Taizhou and Wenzhou brought the distant outposts close in terms of time.

But Zhenjiang held a factor unknown to Hudson Taylor at the time. In May 1867 a magistrate of the Chinese city of Shanghai, 'well known for his antagonism to foreigners', had unjustifiably seized and flogged a municipal policeman from the international settlement. The foreign municipal council had protested to the magistrate's superior and, degraded in rank, he had been provocatively transferred to Zhenjiang where the small foreign community also enjoyed treaty rights. There he was waiting, for his opportunity to retaliate.

Living on the houseboat, Hudson Taylor began house-hunting, and the second '*Lammermuir* day', May 26, the anniversary of sailing from London, was given up to prayer by the homeless leader of the Mission and his family. Every other member was established in a 'station' with regular work, with Meadows and Williamson standing ready to join Hudson Taylor in spearheading the penetration of the unevangelised provinces. Two days later he found a suitable house in the city only three minutes' walk from the city gate which opened into the 'concession' occupied by foreigners. He was coming to terms with the landlord when the consul's Chinese secretary told him of a Shanghai missionary who was planning to come to Zhenjiang. Immediately he halted his negotiations in order to consult Consul Lay about going on to Yangzhou, but Lay was absent in Shanghai until the 30th.

Apparently Li Lanfeng, who had gone ahead to Yangzhou, had reported favourably, and Duncan had been unable to rent premises in Nanjing, for Hudson Taylor sent the larger (family) houseboat across the Yangzi, three miles wide at that point, to wait there for him, and joined them after arranging with the consul for new travel passes and a certificate of residence for use at Zhenjiang. After spending Sunday at Guazhou, at the mouth of the Grand Canal on the Yangzi north shore, verifying that good access to Yangzhou existed, twelve or fifteen miles overland and by canal, they set off again on Monday June 1 and soon arrived at the city.

The significance of this otherwise bald statement has to be realised. Hudson Taylor and Maria with their four children, his secretary and the children's nurse – helped only by four Hangzhou Christians, employees, not teachers, Tianxi the destitute boy he had adopted eleven years before, and Ensing, Maria's protégée engaged to marry Lanfeng – had left treaty ports behind and were attempting to occupy a major city barely touched by passing missionaries in recent centuries. Even the Catholic Church had only an orphanage in the care of a Chinese administrator. If the tolerance of the Muslim governor of Hangzhou, Ma Xinyi, were to be extended by Zeng Guofan, viceroy of the two Jiangs, [Jiangxi and Jiangsu], and Governor Ding Richang of Jiangsu and their prefects, the success at Hangzhou could be repeated here in perfect peace. If not, it was as bold a step as any yet taken since the days of Robert Morrison. Apart from trial and error there was no way of knowing.

This section of the Grand Canal had been completed in AD 605, when the city of Yangzhou was called Jiangdu, the River Capital of the Sui dynasty. Linking the Yangzi with the cities of Yangzhou and Qingjiangpu it was 'the highroad from the south to Pekin and most of the northern provinces'. Curving round the south and east sides of the city, beautifully spanned by numerous arched bridges, it framed an octagonal pagoda and graceful temples and gardens inside the city. Three Nestorian churches had once existed there (Book 1, pp 51, 53) and for three of his seventeen years (1275–92) in the service of Kublai Khan, Marco Polo had been governor of Yangzhou (*circa* 1280). Scholars and painters had gravitated to it over the centuries, and one of the Qian Long emperor's libraries had been kept in the city until destroyed by the Taipings. The population of 360,000 souls necessitated the division of Yangzhou into two administrative counties (*xian*) under a prefect, the *zhifu*. Such a centre of culture, commerce and government, 'famous for its wealth and the beauty of its women', held a place of honour and pride in the esteem of its people, but most of all its literati. At the same time it was 'notorious . . . for its wickedness'.

Hudson Taylor was aware of this and from the first adopted an exceptionally cautious approach to the city. For the first week he and his family lay low in their boat, not venturing out where they might be seen. While their Chinese companions went house-hunting, they employed their time in writing the thirty-page *Brief Account of the Progress of the China Inland Mission (May 1866 to May 1868)* in the form of a letter to supporters, ending with '*Lammermuir* day', May 26, at Zhenjiang. Their minds were already at ease.

> The opening up of permanent, stationary work in the interior of China is no easy task. . . . An unsuccessful attempt to gain an entrance into a locality – even in these provinces where foreigners are best known – renders any subsequent efforts far more difficult. Hence the importance of patiently waiting till we have gained the needful experience, before attempting to enter the more remote and untried provinces. [Thanking his friends and readers for their support already given, he continued] For the future, we look with confidence to Him who has hitherto helped us. Our expenditure this year, has been about £4,100, while the income has been about £3,300. But He who gave us the balance in hand at the commencement, which has supplied the deficiency in the income, is well able to supply all the still heavier expenses which we may anticipate during the year on which we are just entering. *He* knows accurately what our needs *will* be, and there *we* need not be anxious to forecast them.

There is no evidence that anyone had yet suspected him of soliciting funds through such occasional statements of fact, but in time they would, and he would modify his frankness without loss of income.

After several days heavy rain began to fall and the houseboat leaked at every roof-seam. Oil-cloths and umbrellas inside the 'rooms' helped to keep some things dry, but the occupants could only sit huddled in the driest parts and wait for the rain to stop. By Monday, June 8, only a move to an inn on dry land was sensible. At a commercial 'hotel' inside the city, they took five upstairs rooms for the large sum of two dollars a day without food, for as long as they chose to stay. There was no alternative. After two months spent largely on the boats, their new quarters felt 'very comfortable' but, with all the coming and going of inn life beneath them, 'rather noisy' and lacking in privacy. Hudson Taylor had never before seen so clean and respectable a place, normally occupied by merchants while conducting business deals.

Soon after they had settled in, Mr Peng, the proprietor, had second thoughts and became anxious lest letting his rooms to foreigners should get him into trouble. He had not insisted on a middleman with whom to share the responsibility. So Hudson Taylor undertook to ask the magistrate to assure Mr Peng that all was well. A trial was in progress and the magistrate in court, but his subordinates assured Hudson Taylor that he need not worry. For Mr Peng this was not enough and he went out saying he would see the magistrate himself. When he returned, 'the difference in him was most marked', although he too had failed to see the mandarin. 'Instead of talking about a middleman for himself, he offered to become middleman if we wished it, in any house we might rent.' No hint of objection to their presence, only reassurance, had been encountered. Two weeks after their arrival he reduced the rent, but six harrowing weeks of close confinement were to go by before they could all move out. At first only the Chinese could leave the premises to continue searching for a home of their own. Later Hudson Taylor himself joined in, 'gently feeling our way among the people'. 'Perhaps thirty' suitable premises were found, only to be lost before negotiations could be completed. Each time the literati intervened.

'Smallpox'   *June–July 1868*

What Hudson Taylor euphemistically called 'a tedious battle with difficulties' acquired a new dimension on June 15 when Tianxi, always at close quarters with the family, fell ill with fever and a rash alarmingly like the early phase of smallpox. The children had not fully recovered from whooping cough, and the baby had not yet been vaccinated. Early the next morning Hudson Taylor took Maria and little Maria to Zhenjiang to catch the river steamer to Shanghai.

George Duncan had written proposing marriage to Catherine Brown, a 23-year-old friend in Scotland. She could reach Shanghai in July or even June, so Maria would wait in Shanghai for her even if it meant a few weeks. At eleven the same night she wrote to say that William Gamble had insisted on her staying at his place instead of on a boat as she proposed because of possibly spreading infection; Edward Fishe now wanted to join Hudson Taylor and the CIM;

Elizabeth Meadows and Eliza Nicol had both had stillborn premature babies in Ningbo; and Alexander Wylie and Griffith John had penetrated to Chengdu in Sichuan. Wylie had been stoned and in danger of his life.

After he had seen Maria on to the steamer, Hudson Taylor took his house-hunting in Zhenjiang a stage further. The way was clear for him to complete a deal for the house he had found. Then he returned to Yangzhou. Who should arrive there soon after him but George Duncan, down from Nanjing. He had walked the fifteen miles from Guazhou. All mail for Hudson Taylor had been forwarded to Duncan – but he had received nothing, not even money sent by Gamble. Where was it all? Cheques from William Berger and George Müller would be in it, and available cash was running low. To Hudson Taylor's delight, Duncan was willing to postpone his marriage for some months, until Catherine had acclimatised and learned some Chinese, so he returned to Nanjing on the 30th.

Hudson Taylor was writing almost daily to Maria with a stream of administrative instructions, but on the 27th nothing had yet reached her. On the 23rd he had been working until nearly three a m. Negotiations for house after house were breaking down after coming 'almost to the point of agreement'. Another confinement, Mrs Cardwell's this time, seemed to demand either his or Maria's presence in Taizhou at the end of July. How could they cope? A secure base in both Zhenjiang and Yangzhou seemed essential. He posted his letter of June 24 at 'the hulk', moored at the river bank as a landing stage, only to begin another. 'I expect to pay the deposit (on the Zhenjiang house) in an hour or two and to get the document signed' – at last, a foothold with possession in two weeks' time. The Rudlands should prepare to bring the printing-press and move in. Louise Desgraz was to come with them. Mary Rudland would then be near the Taylors for the last few weeks of her pregnancy.

Consul Lay was about to take the steamer up to Jiujiang (Kiukiang), but just in time Hudson Taylor discovered that although he had procured a dispatch from the *daotai* to the Yangzhou prefect it had been lying at the consulate for a fortnight or more. For lack of it, progress in renting premises at Yangzhou had been held up. As the *China Mail* of Hong Kong was to point out, 'Both natives and foreigners are obliged, when they *buy* property, to have the sale duly registered by the authorities, but there is no such rule laid down for renting a place. In fact it was never heard of until the missionaries began to move into the interior; and then it was invented as a powerful weapon to impede their progress.'[18] Of the Zhenjiang house, the consul-general at Shanghai, W H Medhurst Jr., was also to report to Sir Rutherford Alcock in Peking that Hudson Taylor had rented it, 'taking care to conduct the transaction in a plain and straightforward manner, and to record the lease, after execution and signature, with Mr Assistant Allen.' There the acceptance of a hundred dollars by the owner sealed the contract, but at Yangzhou they still had far to go.

On the 29th a whole package of closely written letters, full of detailed instructions about remittances to the team and other business, reached Maria. 'My brain seemed almost to *reel* after reading them. May the Lord help me. . . .' she wrote. For baby Maria was ill with measles and on July 1 'very ill'. Two days later she heard from Hudson Taylor again. Tianxi's 'smallpox' had turned out to be measles and all three of the children at Yangzhou had gone down with it. Samuel, just 4 years old, was desperately ill with its most dangerous complication, broncho-pneumonia. Then back to business. The Yangzhou prefect had promised him a proclamation about getting a house and another about a chapel when he was ready for it. He was said to have ordered fifty copies to be written, but none had been placarded yet.

On the night of July 1 Hudson Taylor began with business matters, so that she could take them in before he told her about Samuel. Then, 'Miss Blatchley and I sat up last night with him: we were very anxious. . . . He breathes very frequently and shallowly.' That was the softening blow. In fact his respiration rate had been one hundred per minute. At four a m they thought the immediate danger was over. On the night of the 3rd Hudson Taylor was 'hoping to get some sleep tonight'. The first, fifth and ninth moons of the Chinese calendar were inauspicious for property deals, 'hence part of our difficulty'. They might have to buy a house, because 'rents are terrible'. At two a m when he ended he still had more letters to write, to catch the five a m mail. With one went a cheque to Charles Schmidt. By Sunday, July 5, he knew about baby Maria and was 'dreading' to receive further news. In a tender, affectionate letter to Maria, longing to be with her, to weep or rejoice together, he wrote, 'Is it not Love who has separated us? . . . Perhaps we should both have been overwhelmed had we seen them both in so precarious a state. And so He did not let you know of Samuel's danger on Wednesday, nor me of darling little Maria's. . . . In Miss B's case it will be only a less trial to her than to us, if the treasure is taken from us.'

For five weeks they had lived quietly in Yangzhou and now only lacked the city prefect's promised proclamation to complete a contract for the premises Mr Peng was helping them to rent. At last the way was clear. Hudson Taylor sent to Jennie at Hangzhou for James Williamson to bring two boatloads of furniture and essentials for setting up house and 'all the things in my study (except photographic apparatus, shotguns and ammunition). . . . You will wonder at my sending for so many things at once; the reason is that the water (in the canals) will soon be so low that . . . we may have to wait months before they can come' – an important fact to be borne in mind. All mail was to be addressed to the care of J M Canny, the French consul at Zhenjiang. But news of baby Maria left 'little human hope of her recovery. . . . I know not whether she is alive or not now. I need not tell you how poorly it has made me.' Indeed, the way he became physically ill under emotional stress was an affliction he was not ashamed to admit to Jennie. She knew him too well.

CHAPTER TWO

THE RIOT SEASON
1868

'Red in the morning'   *July 1868*

So much ill-informed comment on the happenings at Yangzhou originated immediately after the events and followed from false reports and misinterpretations, even in the House of Lords, that the truth has become distorted. Caution needs to be observed by students of the period. Even the historian Hosea Ballou Morse, normally so reliable, wrote, 'In 1867 (*sic*) the Rev. James Hudson Taylor founded the China Inland Mission for the purpose of forcing the previously unsettled question of the right of residence inland, and of "planting the shining cross on every hill and in every valley of China"', either consciously quoting Anson Burlingame's New York rhetoric (p 34) or forgetting the origin of it. [1] If *this* had been Hudson Taylor's motive, he was not only brave or foolhardy but silent as to any such motive. On the contrary he acted on the declared right of residence, with the support of treaty, proclamations and 'most favoured nation clause'. He did unostentatiously what the French had done for years with flags flying above their property to proclaim their established residence and enforced rights.

In this attempt to present a more complete and factual account of the Yangzhou riot than has been recorded elsewhere, it is right to emphasise that the information exists in three categories. First-hand contemporary accounts and comments, in letters, reports and an affidavit, are most reliable. For this reason we make generous use of them. Of secondary value are first-hand reminiscences, subject to deceptive memory, and even first-hand reports by consuls and others dependent on collected evidence. Lastly, newspaper reports, pure hearsay and unbridled rhetoric such as the Duke of Somerset's, spread false statements which have clouded the issues.

The first hint of trouble had come at Suzhou. With little of the language and with a sense of insecurity, Henry Cordon, instead of cultivating friendship with his Chinese neighbours and acquaintances, kept his front door shut and behaved secretively. Soon suspicions were aroused and his landlord asked him to leave. Charles Schmidt poured oil on the troubled waters, and after Wang Lae-djün came up from Hangzhou to help, peace was restored.

But in Zhenjiang an ominous twist in events began on July 8. Posters appeared in the city alleging that young women and children were being kidnapped by being offered drugged food and stupefied by drugged tobacco smoke. Their eyes, livers, and genital organs were then being made into drugs. Thomas Francis Wade, the hero of the battle of Muddy Flat and subsequently Sir Rutherford Alcock's successor as British minister at Peking, told Consul Lay that the Zhenjiang magistrate who had been dismissed from Shanghai (p 70) was the instigator of these allegations.[2] Hudson Taylor would not have known of them on Thursday, July 9, as he wrote to Maria from Guazhou before crossing the Yangzi to Zhenjiang. The promised proclamation paving his way to possession of the Zhenjiang house had been delayed, but the Yangzhou proclamation would remove the last difficulties there. 'We may come to terms about a house at (Yangzhou) today or tomorrow. But we have so often been disappointed that we must not be too sure of anything, save of God's help and presence which He will never withhold.' The three weeks since Maria had gone to Shanghai felt like three months. And 'What shall we render to the Lord for sparing our darling children when in such danger?'

Three days later when he must have known of the inflammatory posters, he added, 'For our Master's sake, may He make us willing to do or suffer *all* His will. In this spirit we may be spared from some of the trials which might otherwise be needed; and when we do pass through the fire, He will be with us.' They were being prepared by slow degrees for upheavals ahead. He wrote to Jennie, discreetly affectionate as always, about the domestic arrangements in Hangzhou, wages, accounts, responsibilities, what to do with No 1 New Lane when most of them moved into No 2; and added about his house-hunting, 'As soon as all seems fixed . . . we are left in the lurch again.' He posted these letters 'at the Hulk' at Zhenjiang and received one from Maria. 'I hope to get a (proclamation) and then all will be well.' But this time instead of applying to the *xian* magistrate he turned to the Zhenjiang city prefect who had supplied a proclamation for the LMS chapel. 'If he will give me one, well; if not, I must go to the Consul', whose duty it was to see that the terms of the treaties were observed.

To conduct a simple matter of business was like drawing blood from a stone. In any case the sitting tenants, two brothers and two women, by inference the mother and the elder brother's wife, would not move out until 'this luckless (inauspicious) month is out'. If the Rudlands and Louise Desgraz arrived after that they could take possession. Still nothing happened. When the consul applied to the highest prefect, the *daotai*, he was promised the proclamation in a few days' time 'if all were straightforward'. 'But the (*xian*) [the ex-Shanghai magistrate] was determined that all should *not* be straightforward.'[3]

At Hangzhou it was swelteringly hot, 92 °F in Jennie's room in June and 97 °F with perspiration rolling down her face, as she wrote in July. Where could they go to escape the heat? Work that was usually a pleasure 'becomes a continual effort and one's spiritual life is in great danger of waning. . . . Oh dear! This is such weather, everything spoils! Steel rusts, moth and worms eat and mildew covers almost everything.' The Chinese felt it too. Tempers were on edge. The riot season had come. Jennie had been packing up some of Emily's and Maria's things to send with Louise. Three weeks had passed since the prefect had approved the deal. Only delay, no hostility, had been apparent so far. Hudson Taylor was living on his boat at Zhenjiang. 'My precious sister,' he wrote to Jennie; Cordon's Chinese colleague in Suzhou had been offending people by preaching that 'Confucius had gone to Hell, and that sort of thing. . . .' He was being returned to Hangzhou and 'I think he ought not to be allowed to preach at present.' Any indiscretion was dangerous. Such ineptitude was inflammatory.

Meanwhile the Yangzhou proclamation was published and Hudson Taylor returned there to complete negotiations for the lease on July 17 'with the permission and aid of the Prefect' and with Innkeeper Peng's help. To attract as little attention as possible he moved some of the family into the new premises on the 20th and the rest a few days later. 'For the first fortnight the curiosity of the people gave us some trouble, but caused no serious anxiety' was Hudson Taylor's calm recollection. Maria was more forthright in a letter to Miss Stacey. 'Excepting the annoyance of inquisitive intruders who *would* make their way in without invitation, we continued there without disturbance', and Hudson Taylor said, 'While we had many friendly callers, both from among the officials and townspeople to whom we were able to speak privately, we had no public services.'[4]

Maria was still in Shanghai, waiting with John McCarthy for Catherine Brown's arrival, and preparing Chinese clothes for her. So busy with Mission business that she was losing sleep, and unwell because pregnant again, Maria confessed her ill-health to her husband on July 23. 'But *soldiers* must not complain of hardships and I don't mean to complain, only it seems so natural to tell you of such things. . . . *Weariness* is easier to bear than *anxiety*.' For she was anxious. She mentioned complaints from several of the team. And 'I hardly dare trust myself to speak of Mr Nicol's letter (to William Berger), for the downright falsehood (of it).' If he would not resign and had to be dismissed, what an 'uproar' it might cause! Even James Meadows was restless and needed to get away from Ningbo. Such heat and humidity so easily brought out the worst in people, as she well knew of herself. Perhaps it would help matters if she, at obvious cost to herself and her own family, were to go down to Ningbo for Mrs Cardwell's confinement. What did Hudson think? But the setback at Zhenjiang was also worrying and too reminiscent of Huzhou and Jinhua, especially as the Rudlands and Louise Desgraz had been ready to leave Hangzhou on the 23rd with their staff of printers and their own two boatloads of printing-presses and baggage for settling at Zhenjiang. Williamson or Judd were to bring two more loads of household effects for Yangzhou – all before the water levels sank too low in the canals.

On the same day and again on the 29th Mrs Berger was writing to Maria one of the strong, positive letters she habitually wrote to members of the Mission in China. 'There was something about (Annie Bohannan's) spirit which invariably told for good on mine'; 'whenever I think of (good, kind) Miss Desgraz, it is with thankfulness to God for giving you such an one'; 'William often wishes there were a hundred more Miss Fauldings associated with you.' In June she had written, for them to receive in August, 'These words are comforting me concerning you at *this* time – "Underneath are the everlasting arms" . . . they will protect you when attacked, and will preserve you from all real danger. Oh *how* safe you are!' Now on July 23 she said, 'Truly your safety is in God *alone*. . . . May He . . . graciously keep you from feeling afraid!'[5] When she was writing, the prospects were good at Yangzhou and hopeful again for Zhenjiang with consular help. Accompanying a cheque for £40 for Hudson Taylor from George Müller came a letter quoting Psalm 62, 'Trust in him at all times, ye people, pour out your heart before him. God is a refuge for us.' Why so much about safety and protection?

Responses to news of violence at Huzhou and Jinhua perhaps, with awareness of potential dangers never far away, but doubly relevant by the time these letters arrived.

Dysentery, light at first, struck Hudson Taylor on the day he moved into the new house, July 20, but he had to supervise repairs to the premises and at the end of the week to go down to Zhenjiang again. The consul had taken up his problem with the antagonistic magistrate's superiors. There on Sunday the 26th his illness took a turn for the worse. He scribbled a note in pencil to Maria in Shanghai, saying he hoped a proclamation would put things right in Zhenjiang the very next day. 'But I must return [to Yangzhou]. I am so ill. Would you write to Meadows and ask if he can come and help me? Go to Ningpo, darling, if you think well. If our hearts are to be . . . a sacrifice, the will of the Lord be done. Soon we shall never part again.'

Knowing all too well the terrible toll of lives by 'dysentery' in China, Maria left John McCarthy in Shanghai to meet Catherine Brown's ship, well overdue, and sent a message to the Cardwells that she herself could not come for the confinement. Because it was the Lord's Day, which on principle she would not voluntarily secularise by travelling, she rejected the possibility of travelling to Zhenjiang by steamer, and after midnight hired a footboat to take her, the baby and an amah by canal instead, although it would take two days and nights. When the rowers tired she even took turns at the oars. Passing through Suzhou she called at the Schmidt's and carried a note from him to Hudson Taylor saying, 'I am sorry you are so ill, and we (are praying) for the Lord to spare your life . . . I think you are wanted in the field more than ever now.' He enclosed Hudson Taylor's midnight cheque with the request please to sign and return it!

Maria reached Yangzhou on the 29th to find him better, and word came soon afterwards of a Ningbo doctor having delivered Mrs Cardwell of her child by forceps. So Maria could not have helped much if she had gone. Moreover James Meadows, his most experienced colleague, was probably on his way to Yangzhou already, with Williamson, to undertake the next advance up the Yangzi.

On the 28th Anson Burlingame's treaty between the United States and China had extended reciprocity to Chinese in the States. Its Article 4 read: 'It is further agreed that citizens of the United States in China of every religious persuasion, and Chinese subjects in the United States, shall enjoy entire liberty of conscience, and shall be exempt from all disability or persecution on account of their religious faith or worship in either country.'[6] Even by the 'most favoured nation' concession by Peking this added nothing to the lot of any foreigners in China. Two days later the Presbyterian chapel at 'Pitow', Taiwan, was wrecked for the second time.

If Maria and Hudson Taylor and Mrs Berger wrote as if they had premonitions of trouble, so did Jennie and Emily. 'What may be in the future,' Jennie's home letter ran, 'we cannot tell; trials there are sure to be, perhaps dangers and sorrows and hardships which as yet we have not dreamed of, but God *is* with us and He will keep our hearts in perfect peace.' Immunity from physical harm was not promised to God's envoys. On July 19 Emily underlined, bracketed and annotated 2 Samuel 24: 24 in her Bible, 'Neither will I offer burnt offerings unto the Lord my God of that which doth cost me nothing.' News had come of another brother's death, leaving two younger sisters and her father of a once large family. It was neither unexpected nor enough to merit such a heart cry. She knew the danger she herself was in.

Premonitions or not, with August they entered a crescendo of sound and fury.

'The laugh of the tea-houses'[7]   August 1868

Jennie and the Judds in Hangzhou had a taste of trouble early on Sunday, August 2, when they heard 'a great deal of noise and confusion downstairs' and found the courtyard and main rooms 'full of rough, bad-looking men . . . between forty and fifty (of them).' A troop of beggar-banditti, flotsam of the rebellion who lived off the populace by intimidation, had invaded the premises. 'They enter respectable houses (. . . the doors are seldom closed here) and ask for money; should they be refused . . . they do not scruple to pillage the house.' Charles Judd went down to them, calmly said he would talk with them outside and 'firmly but gently led them towards the door'. They followed. Out in the street he explained who he was and preached the gospel to them while they 'listened quietly for a few moments and then went away'! When Jennie's mother heard of the potential danger her precious daughter had been in, characteristically her disapproval of Hudson Taylor's leaving Jennie behind was intensified. Had he not promised to protect her? Her attitude changed when news came of the riots he himself went through. Then she was glad Jennie was not in Yangzhou.

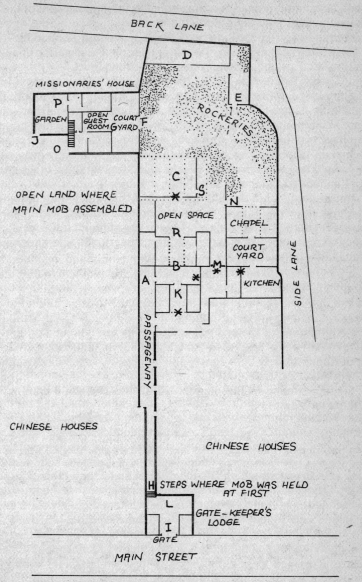

SCENE OF THE YANGZHOU RIOT

[As events follow one upon another, the deceptiveness of hind-sight needs to be resisted.]

On the same day, August 2, the Rudlands and Louise Desgraz arrived at Zhenjiang with the printing-press and their Chinese companions, expecting to occupy the premises promised for July 8. Instead they found the doors firmly closed against them. The magistrate's proclamation was still being withheld. No record has been found of their consulting Consul Lay or his assistant Clement F R Allen, although it is likely that they did so. But knowing that Hudson Taylor had moved into his own place in Yangzhou, and seeing no objections, they crossed the Yangzi and later that day arrived at his door with their two boatloads of equipment and personal possessions.

In the absence of any overt hostility in Yangzhou before August 8, apart from the evident objections to leasing property to for-eigners, Hudson Taylor did nothing to send them away. He had room in Yangzhou to house them until the Zhenjiang house was vacated and they could return there. With consul and *daotai* both helping, that could not be many days away. To ask them to manage on their houseboats or to find lodging at an inn or a temple on Silver Island, a quiet retreat in the Yangzi below Zhenjiang, might have been reasonable if Mary Rudland had been in better health and if the cost of housing the printers and servants had not been prohibi-tive. As it was, the *xian* magistrate at Zhenjiang had seen his opportunity to defy both consul and *daotai*, and made dispersal to Zhenjiang impossible.

Sensing trouble in the magistrate's tactics Hudson Taylor was later to write,

> the (Zhenjiang) landlord's family became frightened, and to avoid sharing the punishment they were led to suppose awaited the elder son (whose name alone, according to Chinese custom, appeared on the deeds of rental), they went to the magistrate and told him that the house had been let to me without their consent or knowledge. Therefore the magistrate sent for the elder son, and upbraiding him for letting his house to a foreigner, told him that one person could not be allowed to override the other three owners of the property, and that he must return the deposit-money to me. This he did not attempt to do; but the way in which the missionary and his Consul had been worsted by the cunning of (the magistrate) became the laugh of the tea-house and restaurant. [When the fact of the foreigner and even his consul being flouted at Zhenjiang became known at Yangzhou,] it

suggested the idea that it would not be difficult to eject us from that city; and while the mass of the people were quite friendly, the literary classes were looking on our arrival with great jealousy, and commencing those efforts which resulted in the attacks on us.

All too soon the details of the Yangzhou property were to become part of Foreign Office dispatches and international history as the scene of high drama. The premises were rambling. A gatehouse on the main street served several neighbouring houses, reached by a shared entrance lane about a hundred yards in length and running due south. At the far end (A) two gates opened from the lane into a complex of courtyards, gardens, rockeries and passageways between scattered buildings, each with only a few rooms, well suited to such a mixed party. Inside the gates lay the courtyards of the Chinese quarters and outer reception hall (B). Beyond them and some open ground a walled pavilion (C) gave on to large rockeries behind which kitchen buildings (D) and a well-house (E) were concealed, backing on to quiet lanes to the south and west. On the east side a latticed wall of ornamental bricks flanked an octagonal gateway (F) into the courtyard of a two-storeyed house. Entered only through the house lay another little garden at the back, surrounded by high walls between it and a vacant plot of ground. The centre of the house itself was no more than another guest hall open to the courtyard, and a stairwell, with two living rooms on each side in which the baggage was stacked. At the top of a rough staircase a trap-door could be lowered, isolating the bedrooms from the ground level of the house. Partitions divided this upper floor into seven rooms, each roughly ten or twelve feet square. Outside the Taylors' bedroom window and his office, a narrow sloping tiled roof formed a porch twelve or fifteen feet above the front courtyard (G).

For a month after he took possession on July 20, Hudson Taylor had kept several carpenters busy repairing the dilapidations and adapting the place for its intended long-term use. But when the Zhenjiang magistrate's neat ploy to thwart the rental of a house in his city became known, active hostility began at Yangzhou, and the inquisitive intruders became more truculent.

The agitators[8]   *August 1–18, 1868*

During the first week of August 'one of the agents or middle-men' who had helped Hudson Taylor to lease the property, informed him that 'there had been a meeting of some of the literary and military (graduates) at which it was determined to stir up the people by "agitating reports" and thus to eject us from Yangchow. From that time we were frequently annoyed, and sometimes endangered, by the throwing of stones at and into our windows' from the vacant ground outside. Before long, 'small anonymous handbills' were posted up in the city, 'containing absurd charges against us, and threatening us, the landlord and the house-agents'. By 'kindness' and patiently talking with the people 'we succeeded in avoiding any outbreak'.

Seeing that the handbills were not inflammatory enough, the instigators then placarded the walls in the city with posters 'nearly a yard long, calling us "Brigands of the Religion of Jesus", stating that we scooped out the eyes of the dying, opened foundling hospitals to eat the children, cut open pregnant women (for the purpose of making medicine of the infants), etc. This roused the people so much, that though we were able to prevent a riot by taking our stand at the door of the premises (A in plan), and arguing all day with them as they assembled, I felt it incumbent on me to write to the Prefect', like the apostle Paul in Acts 22 and 23 asking him to intervene. 'I wrote, enclosing a copy of the anonymous placard, on Friday, August 14, as follows',

J H Taylor, Director of the China Inland Mission to His Excellency the Prefect Sun:

Some time ago I had the honour to receive a copy of a proclamation for which I beg to thank you. . . . I rented a house in the Kiung-Hua-Kuan Street under Your Excellency's jurisdiction, which house is now being repaired. Rude persons and soldiers continually disobeyed your proclamation and day to day came to the house wandering about amusing themselves and acting most indecorously. Some of them insisted on going upstairs and regardless that there were females there entered the rooms and went hither and thither with the greatest boldness and impudence. . . .

At the present time there are persons spreading unfounded *yaoyen* (incitements) containing many scandals. Moreover these are written in large characters on yellow paper [feigning imperial authority] and placarded about in every direction . . . I now enclose a copy of these *yaoyen*, the only object of my petition being to beg Your Excellency to adopt some method of suppressing them so as to frustrate their insidious purpose. . . . For matters are in such a state that if they are not stringently prohibited, most assuredly we shall suffer great injury. Therefore I beg beforehand to apprise Your Excellency and again venture to trouble you.

May I request the favour of a reply? With many compliments etc.[9]

'The Prefect promised an answer which we received on the following day.' It was 'an evasive reply' and even facetious, but ended with, 'I will command the (*xian* magistrate) to put out proclamations in accordance with the (*daotai*'s) despatch prohibiting these things.'[10]

'The same day some of the better disposed people forewarned us [in an anonymous letter] that a riot might be expected on the morrow and advised our immediately adopting every precaution to avoid collision with the people. We at once built up as many of the entrances to the house as possible (plan *) and placing two large chairs across the passage which leads from the street to the house (plan, H) two of us seated ourselves on them and so closed the way. A crowd of from one hundred to two hundred persons was assembled; and from time to time we addressed them, with the effect of preventing any actual breach of the peace. Moreover we had a few days before engaged two of the (*dibao*'s, i.e. constable's) assistants as doorkeepers (I), who were of some help in soothing the people.'

In the evening George Duncan called in on his way from Nanjing to Shanghai to meet his bride. He had to force his way through the crowd at the gates, to find Hudson Taylor 'just up from a sickbed' facing the mob and by the force of personality and 'that remarkable tact which God has given him' holding them at bay. 'Being a fluent speaker of Mandarin, and at the same time a man of great courage and self-possession,' Duncan's arrival was most opportune, Emily observed. 'You can imagine how grateful Mr Taylor felt when he consented to waive his intended journey and stand by us in our peril.'

With the danger increasing, Hudson Taylor proposed to send the women and children to Silver Island. 'With one consent we (women) begged him not to do so,' Maria was to recall. 'For us to have gone away at that juncture would probably have been to increase to those that remained any danger that there might be.' But there was little the women could do to help, so Emily took advantage of a lull to write with characteristic verve to Mrs Berger.

Mr Taylor was boasting of God's care for us to (Mr Peng) of the hotel, who helped us to get this house. The poor man came to us late on Saturday night in great fright. He told us that our present landlord was going to remove his family away from the premises at dawn on account of the expected riot on the morrow. For himself he said he could only depend upon Mr Taylor. Mr Taylor told him *he* depended upon God; and told him to see whether God would not protect us – that we were on His business, and He would not have us in danger, and added 'Wait and see, and if God does not preserve us, never trust me again or believe my words.' What an irresistible power is in God's truth! for that heathen man . . . went away quite relieved and comforted.

Hudson Taylor's own account continued (in an affidavit required by the consul-general, W H Medhurst Jr, and later amplified for the *Occasional Paper*),[11]

When Sunday (16th) came, we found the need of all (our) preparations. From morning till night we had to keep our post at the entrance. It was clear that the attempts to enrage the mob emanated from the respectably dressed persons who from time to time came among them; but our knowledge of what they were saying enabled us at once to answer their remarks. Two or three times there were decided attempts to break into the house; and the windows were frequently assailed with stones and brickbats; but by persuasion, and by avoiding any appearance of fear or attempt at retaliation, we constrained the majority of the mob to admit, however unwillingly, that right was on our side. During this day . . . a new placard was freely posted about, more vile and irritating than the previous ones (unfit for publication). It concluded with a notification that on the 1st of the 7th moon, the local examination day (the graduates meet for graduation in Yang-chau on the 1st and 15th of the month), the graduates and the people would assemble on the exercise ground, and thence come to our house and burn it down; when all, natives and foreigners, would be destroyed indiscriminately.

No mention is made in any contemporary record of any thought of notifying the consulate, let alone of asking for help or protection. 'The great power of our God' was sufficient reality. Whether he intervened with Biblical surprises or allowed his people to be 'stoned, sawn in two or put to the sword', as in Hebrews 11, could be left to him. Physical immunity mattered less than the fulfilment of God's purposes in allowing these circumstances.

On Monday [Hudson Taylor went on] the crowding was much less but we still had to keep guard at the door. We availed ourselves, however, of the comparative lull to circulate a number of handbills, showing the foolishness of the slanders, and explaining that we could not at once throw the door open, and let the people in to view the premises for themselves, on account of the danger there might be of the falling of scaffolding and of unfinished walls, etc; that in two or three weeks' time, when the repairs were finished, we would ask them to come again. This seemed to have a beneficial effect, and though there was great crowding all Tuesday (1st of 7th moon, the day on which we were to have been destroyed), and though several attempts were actually made by literary men to stir up the mob, especially by a (graduate) of the name of Koh, no further damage was done than the injuring of some of the window-shutters and the roof by the missiles hurled at the house from the back.

THE HAIR STYLE EMILY USED, AND A CHILD'S

Emily, then 23, was in good form that day, and indeed all through 'this hurricane of trials'.

> Today (Tuesday) was placarded as the day for attacking our house and setting it on fire . . . Having done all that *we* can do to fortify ourselves, we know that whatever happens will be by God's permission, for we have put ourselves into His hands. He will not leave us. While I write He is sending thunder and the threatening of rain, which will do more for us, Mr Taylor was saying, than an army of soldiers. . . . Any attempt to set the place on fire now would be very vain indeed, for the rain is coming down in torrents.

So the day for burning and killing proved to be a damp squib, 'though some of the people were very much excited'. Ten days had passed since word of organised hostility had been received, including four 'almost in a state of siege' which they came to call 'the first disturbance'. 'It *has* been a hard battle [Emily confessed] to get ourselves established in this city. And now from hour to hour we are crying to God to enable us to hold what through Him we have gained.' The still anonymous agitators had failed to arouse the public to the extremes they urged, but turned to planning more drastic action.

A lull before the storm   *August 19–22, 1868*

Five days had passed since Hudson Taylor's appeal to Prefect Sun. The four days of uproar had in fact been since he promised to intervene. The only *yamen* underlings and soldiers at the scene had been swelling the mobs. On Wednesday, August 19, when one of the literati became conspicuous in the crowd, goading them to violence, though without success, Hudson Taylor addressed the prefect again.

> Matters being most urgent I beg you to excuse the absence of complimentary expressions.
> A few days ago I received your reply referring to the light and frivolous disposition of the (Yangzhou) people and their fondness for making trouble and stating that I was to wait until the (*xian* magistrate) should issue prohibitory proclamations. . . .
> Up to the present I have not seen any steps to repress (these agitators). Therefore the people are the more daring and fearless, daily crowding about the door. . . .
> It is not because I am alarmed that I come again to cry 'danger'.

What I feel anxious about is this: Should loss of life ensue, what then will be the consequences? May I beg your serious attention to this question? I came here to propagate religion in accordance with the will of the Emperor as given in the treaty of commerce and amity. Ought I then to be subjected to such insult? I request you to refer to the articles of the treaty which state that British subjects are permitted to buy ground and build chapels in the interior and furthermore are allowed in every place at their own convenience to travel without detention, molestation or hindrance and that in case of need they may with confidence look for protection and aid at any time, etc. It is on this ground that I venture to trouble you again. Yesterday a resident of the city (a graduate) . . . of the family name of Koh . . . came to the gate making a disturbance and . . . with loud shouts threatened . . . to collect a mob and come and beat and destroy us – using most extravagant language; to this the constable Lin Pian can bear witness. I would therefore respectfully pray Your Excellency to send officers to arrest him and to put a stop to his violence. . . .[12]

'To this note the following reply was sent by the Prefect in the afternoon' – apparently friendly but frivolously inadequate as before, 'Persons who get up this kind of report and placard generally do it in the dark and without either name or surname it is not easy for me in a short time to lay hold of them. . . . As to the man known to the (constable) who dared to make disturbance at your door I will instantly send for and examine him and issue warning proclamations.'

Thursday, August 20 – the day the naval commander issued his ultimatum to the *daotai* at Anping, Taiwan – was another relatively quiet day in Yangzhou. But, as Hudson Taylor stated, in his affidavit on August 31, 'Subsequent to the receipt of this I was informed that the Prefect, finding the man Koh was a graduate, did not send for him, but . . . matters continued to look better until August 22nd.'

Catherine Brown had at last reached Shanghai on the 20th, after five and a half months at sea, and fortunately no one brought her on to Yangzhou. But by force of circumstances, unplanned and unwelcome if only for lack of space, there were four missionary men, five women and four children in the house. Chinese colleagues, printers and servants, not the objects of attack on this occasion, numbered nineteen. Taking the prefect's letter at face value, the family became hopeful that 'the disturbance would gradually pass away', and when Hudson Taylor wrote to Jennie on Friday, he plunged straight into business matters, saying surprisingly, 'I have now the hope that ere long the press may be at work again. Our matters at Zhenjiang are looking up and we are hoping after all to get possession of the house. The (*xian* magistrate) has been made to reverse his judgment in the matter. Here we have been in great danger from an excited mob. . . . For some days . . . three or four of us had to sit all day and guard the doors. Now thank God it has passed away, and the excitement is gradually subsiding.'

George Duncan even went down to Zhenjiang to see if he could get into the disputed house, returning the next day, Saturday, August 22. While he was away peace prevailed – until two unrelated incidents played into the hands of the plotting literati.

The Saturday night riot (1)   *August 22–23, 1868*

After the riots a French priest, presumably Père Sechinger of Zhenjiang, named by Prefect Sun, wrote a brief account of his own part in events, saying,

> At Yang-tcheou we had a small orphanage, which in its recent foundation and precarious existence had been the subject of many negotiations, and vexatious difficulties. Towards the end of August 1868 a large mob stirred up by influential literati collected round the orphanage to destroy it. 'What do you want?' cried an old woman, a heathen, quite unknown to the missionaries. 'We wish to pull down the foreigners' house.' 'There are no foreigners here', said she, 'they are in another part of the town', and she showed the mob the Protestant mission house. The crowd went there at once. . . .
>
> Next day (the mandarin) went solemnly with a full retinue to our cemetery, where he disinterred twelve corpses to make sure they were not mutilated. . . . The great man could verify the fact that we disturbed neither the hearts nor the eyes of the dead – yet he issued a notice forbidding people to bring infants to the (church) in future.[13]

In 1872 Hudson Taylor issued a *Summary of the Operations of the China Inland Mission* in which he referred to the Yangzhou riot as being 'occasioned principally by the unwise conduct of (Chinese) in charge of the Roman Catholic orphanage in that city'.[14]

On the same morning, Saturday 22nd, Captain Sands, the American chargé d'affaires at Zhenjiang, and a Mr Drew visited Yangzhou for a few hours in foreign clothes to see the temples and pagodas. They found the city quiet. But as Hudson Taylor stated in his affidavit,

> Their visit would appear to have suggested another excuse for a riot. In the exercise grounds and tea-houses, and along the streets, a rumour was industriously circulated that more foreigners had come, and that twenty-four children were missing. I first became aware of danger about four p m, when one of the servants came running into the house, and asked me to come out at once, as both the inner and outer gates [A and B in plan] had been burst open, and a crowd was already on the premises. Losing no time, I went and found it was indeed so, but succeeded in getting them out, and in stationing two of our number at the end of the entrance lane [at H], as before; while the gates were repaired by the carpenters then working on the premises.
>
> [Maria supplied more detail.] Finding they had done some damage, he adopted a curious but very effectual method with them. Taking his stand at the place where they had entered, he told them now they were in they might stop in, and tell him who had done the mischief. Of course this made them all most anxious to get out; and as well as they could they slank away, until before long there was not one left. But as evening drew on a real mob began to collect outside our premises. . . . The mere fact of its being evening instead of day-time, gave affairs a very serious aspect, besides which, the evil intentions of the mob soon made themselves apparent in other ways.[15]

When George Duncan arrived home in the evening he 'found a great crowd of people gathered around the door, (saying) that the foreigners had eaten twenty-four children. As it grew dark the crowd increased until thousands of men surrounded the house trying to break into it and were throwing pieces of bricks and crying at the top of their voices, "Foreign devils!"' 'The (Chinese) say 20,000, but this is probably a number magnified by their fears,' Hudson Taylor told the Bergers. His affidavit continued,

> A little later the people began to pelt those sitting at the door – a thing not attempted before; and . . . became more uproarious. (The mob . . . were reported to us to have been armed with knives and spears as well as clubs.) We sent messengers at intervals to the Prefect; but they neither returned themselves, nor did any help come. The attack became general; some of the shutters of the upstairs rooms of the house were dashed in from behind, part of the garden wall was being pulled down [at J], and it was evident that

without help we could not long keep the people out. Mr Duncan and I, therefore, determined to endeavour to make our way through the mob to the Prefect, as there was now no hope of Chinese messengers reaching him. [Before they could go they had to barricade a window 'the shutter of which had given way and fallen down from the incessant hurling of stones at it' – a measure of the force of the bombardment.] Commending ourselves to the care of our Father, and asking the needed grace, if a violent death were awaiting us (we had previously, in the house, commended those we were leaving behind to God's care), we essayed to set out. We saw at once that it was impossible to pass through the mob in front of the house, who now also occupied the rooms [K] at the entrance and the end of the passage [L]; but by passing through a neighbour's house . . . we succeeded in eluding the rioters immediately about the door. We had not proceeded far, however, when we were recognized, and the cry was raised, 'The foreign devils are fleeing.'

Happily I knew a by-way leading through some fields, by taking which we eluded most of those following us, while our rapid pace soon distanced those who still pursued us, and the thick darkness favoured us much. Moreover, the path we had taken misled many of the people, who thought we were fleeing to the East Gate to escape from the city; and, consequently, many persons ran off by a short cut, expecting to meet us there. All this was providential, as it gave us a few minutes at a time when every moment was precious. But when we turned into the main street, we were assaulted with stones, and a mob gathered behind us, increasing at every step. Our rapid strides still kept a clear space between us and them, but we were nearly exhausted, and our legs so hurt with the stones and bricks thrown at us, that we were almost failing, when we reached the door of the *yamen*. But for the protection afforded us by the darkness, we should have scarcely reached it alive.

The gate-keepers were just closing the doors as we approached, alarmed by the yells of the people behind us; but the momentary delay gave time for the crowd to come up and close upon us; the as yet unbarred gates gave way to the pressure, and we were precipitated into the entrance hall. [Duncan said 'The door burst open, letting us fall flat on our faces'] I am convinced that had the gates been barred, they would not have been opened for us, and we should have been torn in pieces by the enraged mob. Once in the *yamen*, we rushed into the judgment-hall, and cried . . . 'Save life! Save life!', a cry which a Chinese mandarin is bound to attend to at any hour of the day or night.

We were taken to the room of the (secretary) and kept waiting for about three-quarters of an hour before we had an audience with the Prefect, all the time hearing the yells of the mob a mile or more off, destroying, for aught we knew, not only the property, but possibly the lives, of those so dear to us. And at last, when we did get an audience, it was almost more than we could bear with composure to be asked as to what we really did with the babies? Whether it was true we had bought them, and how many? What was really the cause of all this rioting? etc, etc.

At last I told His Excellency that the real cause of all this trouble was his own neglect in not taking measures when the matter was small and manageable; that I must now request him first to take steps to repress the riot, and save any of our friends who might still be alive, and afterwards make such inquiries as he might wish, or I would not answer for the result. 'Ah,' said he, 'very true, very true! First quiet the people, and then inquire. Sit still, and I will go to see what can be done.'

He went out, telling us to remain, as the only chance of his effecting anything depended on our keeping out of sight; for by this time the number of rioters amounted to eight or ten thousand. . . . We were kept in the torture of suspense for two hours, when the Prefect returned with the (governor of the military forces of the city – some three thousand men) and told us that all was quiet now; that the military governor himself, the captain of the soldiers who guard the gates, and two (*xian* magistrates) had been to the scene of the disturbance; that they had seized several of those who were plundering the premises, and would have them punished. He then sent for (sedan) chairs for us, and we returned under escort.

On the way back we were told that *all* the foreigners we had left in the house were killed. We had to cry to God to support us, though we hoped this might prove exaggerated or untrue. [Duncan added, 'As we got nearer the house we smelled a very strange smell . . .', (and Maria: 'his heart sickened as . . . he distinguished a smell . . . which suggested the thought to his mind that we were being burned,') but 'which we found afterwards were some fur garments burning.']

When we reached the house, the scene was such as baffles all description. Here, a pile of half-burned reeds showed where one of the attempts to set the house on fire had been made; there, debris of a broken-down wall was to be seen; and strewn about everywhere were the remains of boxes and furniture; scattered papers and letters, broken work-boxes, writing desks, dressing-cases, and surgical instrument-cases; smouldering remains of valuable books, etc, etc; but no trace of inhabitants within.

They searched and called but could not discover what had become of family and friends.

The Saturday night riot (2)[16]   *August 22–23, 1868*

The affidavit only summarised events at the beleaguered house after Duncan and Hudson Taylor had left to go to the *yamen*, but Emily wrote more fully after it was all over.

The next four or five terrible hours it is difficult to describe. We were separated now; and to personal danger was added the tenfold more painful suspense as to the fate of those away from us. Mr Taylor and Mr Duncan were out in the streets, exposed to the fury of the mob.

[JHT writing] Reid and Rudland (with the servants) kept the doors and entrances as long as possible, determined only to retire from point to point as actually compelled, and hoping to retard the progress of the rioters until help arrived. While they were keeping the people out at the front door [B], a wall that had been built to close up a side door [M] was pulled down, and they had to retire to a nearer point [N]. Now all the teachers' and servants' things were at the mercy of the mob. . . . Meanwhile the walls (of the house itself) were broken through [at O and P]. Mr Rudland (and Mr Reid) therefore went to try and keep the people at bay there.

[Emily] We, ladies and children, were alone in the upper storey of the house. It was unsafe to remain in any of the back rooms, on account of the stones and bricks which were being showered in at the windows; so we brought the children into Mrs Taylor's room [above the guest room] and gathered there ourselves to plead with God to protect and save us, and especially to take care of our brothers, who were in the fore-front of the danger. Sometimes a fresh out-burst among the rioters made our hearts chill for a moment, but we preserved our calmness and sustained our courage by . . . prayer.

Presently Mr Rudland came up so exhausted that he could hardly stand, and with his clothes all stained with mud. There is a trap-door at the top of the stairs, and we might at least have delayed the rioters for a time . . . by letting this down and drawing some heavy boxes upon it. But in doing so we might, perhaps, have been shutting up from Mr Reid the only means of escape from the mob. It was an anxious time; any little mistake might sacrifice all our lives in a moment. . . . We were expecting every moment to see the rioters come up the stairs, when Mr Reid called out from the courtyard below, in a hollow, hoarse voice, as if utterly exhausted, 'Mrs Taylor! Come down if you can. They're setting the house on fire, and I can't help you.'

[Maria] This however could only be done by the window of my room . . . We threw mattresses and pillows down in front [at G] as a precaution in case we should fall in the descent, and gathered together some sheets and blankets. [Emily] Mr Rudland got out upon the projecting roof under the window, and let down Mrs Rudland, Ensing (our head printer's young wife married only a few weeks before) to Reid below. [Maria] Six-year-old Freddie (Howard Taylor) was to go next, but as they were passing him through the window he said, 'Let Bertie go first; he's so frightened!' So Herbert was let down and then Howard.

[Emily] Mr Reid hurried them away, and concealed them in the well-house [E] (beneath a little summer house) and then returned for others. But in the meantime, a tall, strong man, naked to the waist, came into the (upstairs) room; and we could see others carrying off boxes from the adjoining rooms. Mrs Taylor went up to the man as he entered, and asked him 'You see we are all women and children . . . are you not ashamed to molest us?' . . .

She kept him parleying for a few minutes; but he soon began to lay hands upon us, and search our persons for money, etc. Mrs Taylor had advised me to get a few dollars, in case we should need to escape by boat from the city, and I had tied a small bag with seven or eight dollars in it upon the side-fastening of my dress. The man snatched this from me, and asked for more, threatening to cut my head off if I did not comply. . . . He next tore off Miss Desgraz's pocket, and took away her hair-ornament; and then being soon satisfied that nothing was concealed about the thin summer clothing we wore, he turned to the boxes and drawers. Mrs Taylor was speaking to him, with her hand raised when he caught sight of her wedding-ring shining in the candle light, and tore it from her finger. . . . (Annie Bohannan) escaped with baby (Maria) by going downstairs after a man who was carrying off a box, behind which she screened (her) from the stones and brickbats. She rushed through the fire at the bottom of the stairs, and so got to the front, and took refuge in the well-house.

Mr Reid was again calling to us to hasten, and the smoke was by this time becoming oppressive, while the noise of falling walls and the almost fiendish yelling of the mob warned us that no time must be lost. (Louise Desgraz) was just safely down [by sheet-rope] when the men below cast a heap of burning materials immediately under the window, and cut off escape from us who remained – Mrs Taylor, Mr Rudland, and myself. But just then our attention was directed, not to the means of escape, but to the immediate safety of Mr Rudland. The man who searched us had now turned to him as he stood upon the roof . . . caught him by the (hair) and dragged him down upon the tiles, . . . discovered his watch, and struggled to get possession of it. But Mr Rudland . . . threw it out into the darkness . . . thinking it just possible that the man might leave us to seek it. This so enraged his assailant that he attempted to thrust Mr Rudland off the roof. But

Mrs Taylor and I together caught hold of him and dragged him into the room.

The man (then) snatched an immense brick from the wall which had been partly broken down in the scuffle, and lifted his arm to dash it at Mr Rudland's head. [Rudland] Mrs Taylor put up her hand and stopped the blow; whereupon the man turned to strike her with the brick; but she said to him, 'Would you strike a defenceless woman?' The man, hearing her speak his own language and with such beautiful calmness, was amazed and dropped the brick.

[Emily] Climbing over the wall, (he) made his way across the tiles . . . crying to his fellows below, 'Come up, come up!' We were anxious now to make our own escape, (but) [Maria] 'the man had demolished our sheet contrivance.' [Emily] To go down by the staircase was out of the question; at the bottom was a large fire, by the light of which several men were breaking open and ransacking boxes. Not knowing what to do, we returned to the front room, and found that the fire (in the yard) below had been dragged away by Mr Reid . . . after being many times obliged to hide . . . from his assailants. He said there was not a moment to lose; we must jump down and he would catch us.

[Maria] The only way was to jump from the tiles, though at the risk . . . of breaking our limbs. . . . [Emily] Mrs Taylor went to the edge of the roof, and jumped from it – a height of from twelve to fifteen feet. I saw her fall upon her side, partially caught by Mr Reid; and saw that Mr Reid was ready to receive me. [Maria] But just then he received such a violent blow from a brick on the side of his face, as rendered him . . . blind and almost insensible. [Emily] Consequently, I fell upon the stones on my back. For the instant I felt that I was either dying or stunned; but to lie there was certain death. [Maria] My right leg had somehow been twisted under me in the fall, and it was with difficulty that I regained my feet – I saw Miss Blatchley fall with all her weight on her back by my side . . . It seemed to me as if such a fall *must* break her back. She was momentarily stunned, but the Chinese style of wearing her hair protected the back of her head.

[Emily] Somehow I got upon my feet and then fell again; I got up and fell three or four times before I was able to keep up. Then I saw that Mr Rudland, who had dropped himself from the roof uninjured, was assisting Mrs Taylor. (He) had been attacked by a man with a club, but had escaped with a slight bruise – (and a hernia). [As Emily led Reid away] almost stunned by the blow he had received, and nearly fainting with pain . . . the shower of bricks which were flying about us made us exert to the utmost what little strength we had remaining.

[Maria] I found I had received some hurt from which the blood was

'MR REID WAS READY TO RECEIVE ME'

flowing freely, but the principal pain was from the severe twist of my leg.[17] The night was very dark, and the glare of the fire we were leaving made the darkness seem still more dense. With what haste we could we stumbled over the broken rocks towards the entrance, but finding one of the doors by which we must pass closed and barred, we were brought to a standstill. We waited here [N] while Mr Rudland went to fetch those who were in the well-house, and when we were all together . . . made our way as quietly as possible round by an opening where the rioters had knocked down the wall [M], and so got into one of our neighbours' houses by a doorway [Q].

[Emily] We were conducted first to one room, then to another . . . as the danger of discovery seemed to increase; and were finally taken to the innermost apartments of (another) house. We sat there in the darkness – such a long, long time it seemed – hoping and fearing as to what had become of Mr Taylor and Mr Duncan. Mr Reid lay groaning with pain; the poor tired children wanted to sleep, and we dared not let them, as we might have to flee again at any moment. Mrs Taylor was almost fainting from loss of blood; and I now found out that my arm was bleeding from a bad cut, and was so painful I could not move it; while many of us were stiff and sore with bruises. [She had in fact sustained a compound fracture of her left elbow.]

[Maria] We were told that our house – from which we had just escaped – was all on fire, and I fully believed it. Whether we ourselves would live till the morning, or what would become of us we knew not. I felt there was a possibility that Mrs Rudland would be prematurely confined, and that I might have a miscarriage, that very night. But God was our stay, and He forsook us not. This confidence He gave me – that He would surely work good for China out of our deep distress. . . . One of (the children) said to me, 'Mamma, where shall we sleep tonight, as they have burned up our bed?' . . . I little thought that they would sleep . . . in their own bed in their own nursery.

From one of our teachers we learned that the Prefect had come with his soldiers, and was driving away the rioters; and that the (*xian* magistrate) himself, having discovered where we were, was guarding the house in which we were concealed. But still no word of Mr Taylor. At last, after the sounds of yelling and fighting had subsided, (we heard his) voice. He paused to speak a few words with the (magistrate) and then came in to us; he was not even wounded seriously, only somewhat lamed by a severe blow from a stone which had struck him in the hollow of the knee, on his way to the *yamen*.

We were now once more all together, and all living; and our first thought was to lift our hearts to God in thanksgiving. . . . Moreover, we found that our house had not been burned down . . . for the neighbours had interfered and helped to put the fires out. . . . Mr

Taylor having called in the (magistrate) to see Mr Reid's condition, . . . the wounded were removed as soon as possible, and we once more entered the house. It was half past twelve at midnight.

Later Maria found her own Bible, in tatters but 'not a leaf missing' – and an untouched bonnet box full of her child Grace's treasures. Exactly a year ago they had watched the life of 8-year-old Grace ebbing away and under cover of darkness had made their secret journey with her body across the lake from Pengshan to Hangzhou. This find was consolation enough. She was rich. More amazing was Emily's discovery. 'The rioters sacked every room but mine in which were all our most important papers and the bulk of our money ($300) . . . The door was standing open; they could not have entered, not a thing was touched.'

Sunday's riot[18]   August 23, 1868

Knowing that William Berger would receive a flood of enquiries as soon as the news broke in Britain, Hudson Taylor seized his first opportunity to write. His experience of distortions by the Shanghai papers prepared him for the inevitable. As usual they would be repeated in the London press. So a step-by-step statement of the facts would be the best answer. It could not be supplied soon enough. He took up the story where Maria and Emily had stopped, but could not anticipate the form the misstatements would take, or the magnitude of their repercussions.

A guard of soldiers and some men from the Mandarin's kept watch till dawn; then they left us. . . . The people soon began to re-collect; and again commenced four or five long and anxious hours. We were all nearly worn out, Mr Reid was absolutely helpless . . . and others of us stiff and sore from our bruises. . . . But the people were crowding in front and behind, and something must be done. . . . Unable to write, I . . . sent a Chinese servant over to (Zhenjiang) to inform Mr Allen, of Her Majesty's Consulate, *viva voce*, of our position. And later in the day, when the (magistrate) told me that it was unsafe to attempt to remove the wounded from the city, I sent another messenger over with a pencilled note. . . .

The rioters of last night had made a clean sweep of doors, walls, and partitions at the (key points). . . . Matters . . . looked even worse than the night before. . . . The premises in front [R] as well as behind were filled with the crowd, leaving no way of escape. A stand was made for a short time at the door [N] which we were still able to close and, leaving my brethren to guard it, I returned to the house. . . . I succeeded in getting the intruders out, and with the help of the carpenters, hastily nailed together some doors and boards, and temporarily closed up the breaches [O, P]. . . . (But) there was only a six-inch wall in front of the (pavilion) [C], and this (was) easily forced [at S], and the whole front of the building was at their mercy. Once more commending all to our covenant-keeping God, . . . I (walked through the mob unmolested and) went to the Prefect's for aid. Not a stone was thrown at me on the way. Another long and anxious delay here awaited me. The Prefect had not risen, had not bathed, had not breakfasted. After a time I was told that (he) had sent for the (magistrate) and that he would . . . accompany me to the house.

To those I had left behind the time had been one of peculiarly painful suspense. . . . Now, there was no darkness to favour an escape, and the front of the house was surrounded as well as the back. When the wall of the (pavilion) had been broken through [at S], Messrs Duncan and Rudland took their seats at the octagonal entrance [F] immediately in front of the house, the front garden and rockery being covered by a crowd which every moment increased. (When) they began to demolish what remained of a fancy wall [each side of F], Mr Rudland took his stand [at G], and assisted Mr Duncan in keeping them out of the house. A few stones were thrown in at the open front of the upstairs rooms, but . . . just as anxiety was at its (height) God sent help and the (magistrate) arrived. His soldiers began to disperse the people, and the grounds were gradually cleared; and . . . his retainers had the undivided privilege of looting to themselves.

(The magistrate said) that it was not safe for any of the members of our party to leave the city now. He requested me at once to write a letter to the (prefect); to be careful to call the proceedings a disturbance, not a riot, or the people would be more incensed than ever; and to ask him to punish those who had been arrested, and to quiet the people by proclamations. 'Thus,' said he, 'we may restore peace before night, and you will not be under the necessity of leaving the city.' . . .

I stated the case as mildly as truth would admit . . . (and) sent the letter to the Prefect; but it was opened on the way by the (magistrate) and returned to me as unsuitable. I went to him, and pointed out that the truth must be told. He replied, 'If you persist in sending that letter to the Prefect, I will go back and have nothing more to do with the matter. You may protect yourself as best you can. But I forewarn you that the lives of all your party will probably be sacrificed.'[19]

I saw very well that he wished to get such a letter from me as might be used . . . as evidence . . . that there had been no serious disturbance; but I felt that . . . there was no time to be lost, and that he might really be . . . unable to keep down the mob through another night. At his direction, therefore, and almost at his dictation, another letter was written, omitting mention of the fire and robbery. . . .

This letter he took away, but told us . . . that the only safe plan would be for him to . . . remove us, for the present, to (Zhenjiang). . . . In the afternoon he engaged four boats, and procured sedan-chairs, and coolies for the undestroyed luggage, and sent us to the South Gate.

Forty-eight hours of continuous danger and tension had ended, but not until they were through Guazhou and crossing the Yangzi could they consider themselves safe. Professedly in response to his appeal Prefect Sun and the magistrate issued this proclamation the same day, Sunday, August 23:

A Prohibitory Proclamation

The Prefect and Magistrate of (Yangzhou) have received the following communication from the English missionary Mr Taylor.

'The people have been disseminating false reports that the missionaries keep children in their house and secretly boil and eat them but the people know nothing of the matter and there is really nothing of the sort done. Last night there was a countless crowd of people (round the house) creating a disturbance and I beg that they may be punished and a proclamation be issued to quiet the populace.'

The Prefect and Magistrate therefore declare that the disorderly proceedings of the populace in the missionaries' house were exceedingly rude and ill-mannered and they accordingly issue this prohibitory proclamation for the information of the people forbidding them hereafter to create any disturbance at Mr Taylor's house. If anything of the sort occurs the offenders will be severely punished. Disobey not! The proclamation to be posted in every street.

Every Chinese reading this proclamation would see in its flippancy a snub to the foreigner. It neither denied the rumours, only quoting his comment on them, nor criticised the riots as more than 'rude' disturbances. While calling a halt, . . . it implied a licence to renew the attacks if he should return. Such an attitude to so serious a breach of the peace could not but rebound upon the mandarins.

But written on the same day was another incriminating document which fell into the hands of W H Medhurst, consul-general. A letter, purporting to be from one of the literati in Yangzhou to a friend in Shanghai, named several ex-mandarins closely connected with the viceroy, Zeng Guofan, as being implicated in the plot.

From Chiang Huang at (Yangzhou) to a friend at Shanghai

On 22nd August we had a great commotion. . . . The cause of this was that when these missionaries first came a rumour got about that the (Roman Catholics) required men's brains for food. The people of the place were filled with fear and suspicion and when on 21st, a foreigner was seen to go out of the South Gate alone with a basket . . . ten or more children's corpses were dug up and were found to have been deprived, some of the heart, some of the eyes and some of the brains. This greatly increased the excitement. . . .

Yen, formerly Viceroy of the Two Kuang (Canton), gave it as his opinion that foreigners were very much afraid of the people and that these had only to collect together and beat the foreigners to get rid of them. (ex-)Governor Li, Wu Taoutae [i.e. *Daotai*] and Pien Taoutae also (used) the same language. Now Yen was a fellow-student of the present Viceroy [Zeng Guofan] (literally of the same year), Li was a pupil of the Viceroy's and Wu an intimate friend of his father's and they are all of one mind. My idea is then that foreigners will be able again to come to Yangzhou and set up a church. They will be killed as they come. . . . Even if foreigners do write to Nanking the Viceroy will take no notice of their letters as Yen and Li will write him their joint views before they do.

This letter had reached Medhurst without its envelope but otherwise looked genuine.

After the 'typhoon'   *August 24–31, 1868*

On Monday morning, August 24, after a night on the boat under guard by the unfriendly magistrate's men, they set off with an escort of troops down the Grand Canal. Maria's thoughts were far away, on that sad journey across the Hangzhou lake with Grace's body. This time a larger party of them were themselves escaping 'from the jaws of death' she wrote, but still uncertain what they might yet meet.

'We have not had time yet to change our blood-stained clothes,' Emily added to her unfinished letter of the 18th. 'Very earnestly do I desire and plead that (God) will yet take us back to that city for His glory's sake.'[20]

They had not travelled very far before they met the British, American and French vice-consuls, Allen, Sands and Canny. Hudson Taylor's note had reached Allen and they were on their way to investigate. 'After showing us the utmost kindness,' Hudson Taylor said, 'they continued their journey to Yang-chou.' There 'Mr

Assistant Allen', after calling on the prefect, went to 'the scene of the disturbance' and 'saw for himself the debris left by the rioters' . . . returning to Zhenjiang the same day. Still on the boat Hudson Taylor was writing to William Berger, 'Thanks be to God, no life has been lost . . . if the loss of our property does not give rise to feelings of joy, it at least appears a very small matter indeed. . . . All of us are more or less bruised. Mr Reid has nearly lost his eye and several teeth.' And Maria, to Mary Berger, 'We have had, so to speak, another "typhoon" – not of so long a duration as the literal one we experienced nearly two years ago – but at least equally dangerous to our lives, and in some aspects more terrible while it lasted.' A few days later she had to add, 'We have been surrounded by a very *hurricane* of trials of various kinds: sorrows, anxieties, perplexities, evil tidings, sufferings and slanders,' for by then much more had happened.

Hudson Taylor's tribute to the Zhenjiang foreign community, published in the *Occasional Paper* ran, 'On our arrival in (Zhenjiang), we were received by the foreign residents with the utmost sympathy, and all seemed to vie with each other in their kindness and hospitality. Though most of us were perfect strangers to them, they opened their houses to us and did everything in their power to assist us.' Duncan was taken in at the Customs House, and the Rudlands and Reid by Captain Sands who gave up all his own accommodation at the US consulate to them. All the Taylor family, including Emily, Louise Desgraz and Annie Bohannan were welcomed at J M Canny's French consulate.[21]

Their reception by the antagonistic magistrate and people of Zhenjiang on the contrary was alarming. In Emily's words,

> Knowing as we did that our (Yangzhou) difficulties were closely connected with, and probably the fruit of those in (Zhenjiang), we were glad to learn, on our arrival here, Monday, August 24, that, in compliance with Mr Allen's demand, a proclamation had just been put out by the (magistrate) about our affairs, which we were led to suppose would be in our favour. But when a copy of it was procured it was found to be a tissue of falsehood and injustice, calculated only to prejudice the people against us and virtually to exclude us from the city.

The prospect of moving into the premises they had rented on June 24 receded again, and they began another, now urgent, search for vacant accommodation, necessarily in the suburb among the other foreigners. By the time it was found, the need had greatly increased.

When only hopeful news of Zhenjiang and Yangzhou had reached Hangzhou, Charles Judd and Josiah Jackson had set out with Hudson Taylor's surgical equipment and medicines. Judd recalled years later:

> When we reached (Suzhou), we heard that . . . the (Yangzhou) house was burned down and some of them burned to death . . . but we at once hastened on . . . and found them all at (Zhenjiang). . . . Mr and Mrs Taylor occupied one room with a lot of the debris – all the remains of the riot huddled together . . . on the ground floor. Others occupied rooms upstairs, not so exposed to damp. . . . Whenever others were in the same house, if anyone had to occupy a bad room it was always (the Taylors). Whatever difficulty or inconvenience he might ever ask anyone to go into, no one could ever say that Mr T was unwilling to do the same himself. When I saw them there, Mrs Hudson Taylor was sitting down in the middle of the room amidst all this confusion as composedly as possible, going on with the composition of a Ningpo Dictionary. She had a wonderful power of concentration. Mr Hudson Taylor lay sick on a bed in the same room. . . . She struck me as remarkable for her Christian faith and courage. She had a delicate, sweet face – a fragile body but a sweet expressive face of indomitable perseverance and courage.

Ever since leaving Yangzhou, Hudson Taylor had been suffering from his frequent bouts of enteritis, 'a kind of cholera' in intensity. Hearing of it 'the consul' sent him 'some chlorodyne which gave him great relief', his own medicines from Hangzhou being still crated. But the greater tribulations were beginning.

And then the press   August 1868

On receiving Hudson Taylor's hurried note on Sunday, only twenty-four hours before they all arrived from Yangzhou, Clement Allen had immediately sent word to his consul-general, W H Medhurst Jr, in Shanghai. But an unnamed correspondent in Zhenjiang gleaned what he could and sent his own account to the secular *Shanghai Recorder*. In it he said, 'They were driven to such extremities that they were forced to throw the children from the upper windows and the ladies were obliged to follow at the risk of their lives. One of them is within a month of her confinement. The outrage was caused by the literary class.'[22]

On the 27th Medhurst sent a dispatch to Sir Rutherford Alcock in Peking.

> I regret to have to report the commission of a most serious outrage upon the persons and property of certain British Missionaries resident at Yang-chou-foo. . . . Reports . . . confirmed by a hurried note from Mr Assistant Allen, state that a mob headed by the literati attacked and set on fire the premises in which the missionary families resided; that the onslaught was sudden and severe; that the children and ladies had to be thrown out of the windows to save their lives; one gentleman had his eye knocked out; and that the whole of the party have been more or less injured . . . I propose to proceed to (Zhenjiang) at once, and I have requested the Viceroy at Nanking to depute an official of sufficient standing to meet me there for the purpose of proceeding with myself to (Yangzhou), and holding a formal investigation.[23]

Distortion of the facts had started. The *North China Herald* followed on August 28 with an editorial in characteristic vein, combining truth and hearsay with advice to the minister and consuls. Under the title *Attack on Missionaries at Yangchow* it described it as,

> a very serious attack . . . which claims prompt and decided action by the Consular authorities. The literary class are said by the Chinese to have been at the bottom of the whole affair. Six of their Head-men called a sort of guild meeting at the Confucian temple about a fortnight ago, and it was there decided that the foreigners should be expelled from the city. These Head-men are well known and their apprehension may be effected without difficulty. . . . Some of the ladies and children were badly wounded and the Revd. Mr Reid lost one of his eyes. Our correspondent tells us that the ladies, who were on the upper floor with the children, were obliged to throw these out of the window, and then jump after them themselves. One lady was within a month of her confinement, and serious fears are entertained for her life. . . . We need to point out that, unless prompt and decisive punishment is inflicted for this outrage, there will be no safety for the life of any missionary in this country. The Chinese are gradually coming to believe that Consular action in the provinces is weak and inoperative.

Then followed a long paragraph putting pressure on the British authorities and making comparison with the French who would allow 'little peace for the (Chinese) authorities – local or central – till it had been thoroughly avenged. The ringleaders should first be made an example of; but, if enquiry bear out our information, the Prefect and subordinate Magistrates should also be degraded.'

Consul Medhurst needed no goading by the Shanghai press. He already knew from Consul Swinhoe of the Taiwan riots and of an ultimatum by the naval commander, Lord Charles Scott, to the *daotai* at Tainan. He was in close touch with his assistant, Allen, over a contretemps between British merchants and the mandarins at the customs barrier below Zhenjiang, and over the Zhenjiang magistrate's defiance of his own *daotai* and the vice-consul. The Chinese reaction to the replacement of Consul Lay by a Third Assistant had not escaped him. In fact, J M Canny, the French consul, told Hudson Taylor 'that the matter would be sure to be taken up by the British Government, as secret orders had been received only a few days before by the Consul at Shanghai, to take the first reasonable opportunity of making an armed demonstration up the Yang-tse-kiang [ie Yangzi river], to overawe the Chinese authorities, and to put a stop to the frequent violations of the Treaty, which threatened the arising of some *casus belli*.'[24]

Medhurst himself arrived at Zhenjiang on August 30 and lost no time in verifying from Hudson Taylor and all his party their statements in the affidavit Allen had asked them to prepare; and 'as to our losses as far as ascertained, and taking up this grievance together with the larger losses of some of the (Zhenjiang) merchants from various violations of treaties.' On the 31st he sent another dispatch to Sir Rutherford.

> . . . I arrived here accordingly last night and this morning I interrogated the missionaries most carefully. . . . The following significant inferences may, I think, be drawn from the accounts so given:
> 1. That the attack was entirely unprovoked;
> 2. That it was instigated by the literati and gentry generally;
> 3. That the outrage was distinctly premeditated and occupied time in being put into execution;
> 4. That the local authorities took no pains whatever to prevent or put down the excitement, notwithstanding that they were warned of the possible émeute [popular rising] and repeatedly and courteously appealed to for protection;
> 5. That when the rage of the mob had been permitted to take its course, and after protection had been tardily accorded, they actually threatened the victims to leave them to their fate unless

they recorded it as their opinion that the attack partook of the nature of a simple disturbance, punishable as far as the actors in it were concerned with cangue [the portable neck pillory; *see* Book 2, p 369] and

6. That since the affair took place the authorities have done nothing towards expressing their disapprobation of the conduct of the ringleaders.

He was proceeding to Yangzhou, he continued, 'to procure the condign punishment of all persons known to have been concerned, to require reasonable compensation to the sufferers' and to demand proclamations strong enough to ensure their future safety. Should he fail to obtain satisfaction from the prefect of Yangzhou, he would 'carry the whole case to His Excellency Tseng Kwo-fan [ie Zeng Guofan] himself.'

> I have communicated (this plan) together with a copy of the affidavit to Her Majesty's senior naval officer who I have no doubt will see the necessity of supporting my action by his presence and co-operation. I trust I shall have your Excellency's approval of my conduct thus far. . . . The document which . . . purports to be a letter written by a man of Yangchow to a friend in Shanghai and apparently was never intended for the eye of a foreigner . . . curiously corroborates the statement made by Mr Taylor that the literati were instigators of the attack and influenced the local authorities against the foreigners.[25]

Hudson Taylor's long affidavit, signed by himself, Duncan, Rudland and Reid, and already quoted at length, ended with this paragraph,

> During the whole time that the Mission had been stationed at Yangchow, namely since the 1st June 1868, every member of it has to the best of his and her ability, avoided giving the slightest possible cause of offence to any of the people and has borne with studied patience and endurance any casual insults which may have been offered from time to time. Even our missionary efforts have not commenced in any public shape but had been entirely confined to personal conversation with visitors to the house. We had no arms or weapons of any kind in our possession from first to last.

A victim of the Chinese protest against foreign intrusion into their country, Hudson Taylor was about to become a convenient pawn in British power politics. On August 31, the refugees moved to two adjoining houses rented at great cost and 'only a stone's throw from the British Consulate' – a fact full of unsuspected meaning. Reid, as his face and eye were recovering, took Judd off to Nanjing. For Hudson Taylor there was no respite from administrative duties, and in a business letter of August 31 to Jennie Faulding, remitting money for Hangzhou, he remarked, 'A war steamer is expected tomorrow, but I hope that all may be peacefully arranged.' She had personally assumed the financial and administrative responsibility for the school she was running, not knowing that an uncle had bequeathed to her a legacy she would be able to use.

So ended August 1868. Only twenty-four hours later the shouts of rioting mobs reached them again, this time in the Zhenjiang foreign settlement.

The Zhenjiang riot   *September 1–3, 1868*

If the flouting of Vice-Consul Allen and Hudson Taylor at Zhenjiang had been the spark to ignite anti-foreign action in Yangzhou, such resounding success there was all the resentful Zhenjiang magistrate needed to go one better. Starting with his proclamation – 'a tissue of falsehood and injustice, calculated only to prejudice the people' – he had gone so far as to say provocatively, 'you are at liberty to follow your own inclinations'. This oblique but obvious hint was quickly taken up by his supporters. Through them he dared to challenge the authority of the *daotai* and to arouse the Manchu garrison against consuls, merchants and missionaries alike. In Yangzhou the literati were celebrating, as the *North China Herald* reported. 'The mob at Yangchow have been complimented on their recent triumph; congratulatory messages and placards have been freely circulated through the city, and rewards have been promised to the popular leaders. . . . If (foreigners) present themselves at the gates they are not to be allowed to enter, and should they by any chance get inside the city walls they are to be instantly set upon and killed. . . . (At Zhenjiang) the people have threatened to attack the foreign settlement.'[26] Already this report was more than a week out of date.

On September 1, Consul-General W H Medhurst called on *Daotai* Ying, the Intendant of Circuit over three prefectures of which Yangzhou was one. All along, this friendly mandarin had done his best to get possession of the house in Zhenjiang city for Hudson Taylor. Now he directed the district magistrate 'to rejudge the case and give a verdict in accordance with the facts', that the owner and his family had already approved the contract before the magistrate intervened. He could not but comply. 'But the people . . . having accepted as facts the falsehoods of the (magistrate's) proclamation, determined to resist this new step of the (*daotai*).'

Convinced that 'the power of foreigners had already waned', members of the Manchu garrison and community, including a military mandarin, joined the riotous Chinese in attacking the premises now legally the CIM's. 'Seizing the landlord of the house, they . . . beat him for letting his house to a foreigner. Then they tied his hands behind his back, and passing the rope from his wrists over a beam in the roof hoisted him up and again beat him while suspended, and at last carried him off' to the magistrate's *yamen* where he was imprisoned.

> The next morning (Sept 2nd) [Emily Blatchley wrote], the (*daotai*) returned Mr Medhurst's call, and wished to see Mr Taylor, whom he apologetically declared himself ashamed to meet, seeing that our matters ought to have been settled more than a month ago. He said that not only had foreigners, as such, a right to rent houses in the city, but that, wearing as we did the Chinese costume, we were as one of themselves, and there was the less excuse for opposition. [Having interviewed Hudson Taylor and inspected the house and rental agreement, he declared that Hudson Taylor was the rightful lessee and ordered the magistrate to see that he was given possession of it.][27]
>
> He finally promised that Mr Taylor should have the house within three days. But at nine o'clock the same night a riotous mob, seven- or eight-tenths of whom were Tartars (over whom the *daotai* has no jurisdiction), attacked the *daotai's yamen*, burst open the front doors, and did much damage, keeping up the disturbance till four a m. His furniture was smashed and he himself accused of traitorous collusion with foreigners.
>
> The whole city by then was in a state of excitement and [Medhurst reported to Sir Rutherford Alcock] 'rumours are that this Consulate is to be the next point of attack this evening. The *daotai* has sent a message begging me not to . . . be put out, and promising that he will endeavour to fulfil his promises. . . . The anticipated arrival of Her Majesty's ship *Rinaldo* this evening or tomorrow morning will tend materially to promote this desirable result.'
>
> [Emily's account continued] The rioters threatened to come the next night to the foreign settlement and burn down the British Consulate, and so avenge the dishonour done to them in 1840. The

Tartar-General, however, was alarmed at the probable consequences of such an event, and stationed double guards at the city
gates to prevent his men leaving the city for any such purpose.

When Sir Henry Pottinger had arrived at Zhenjiang with his
expeditionary force on July 21, 1840, the Manchu Tartar-General
had put up a courageous resistance until, seeing that he was
defeated, he immolated himself. Many other Manchus followed
suit, until Charles Gutzlaff landed and strenuously intervened to
halt the mass suicide (*see* Book 1, p 263). This was the injury which
the city was determined to avenge in 1868. September 3 was
therefore another day of tension in the foreign community.

Medhurst – man of action[28]   *September 1868*

Consul Medhurst had lost no time in taking up the matter of the
Yangzhou riot with Prefect Sun and with Viceroy Zeng Guofan at
Nanjing, as his dispatches published in the Parliamentary Blue
Books testify. But his hyperbole in Chinese idiom and the literal
translation of it into English was to lead to a misapprehension of fact
which brought Hudson Taylor under undeserved criticism.

Consul Medhurst to Sun, Prefect of Yang-chow-foo

The British missionaries Taylor and others . . . have laid before
me a formal complaint in regard to their violent ejectment from your
city, and they have earnestly entreated me, as Consul for this district,
to redress the many and grievous wrongs which they have sustained,
and to secure for them peaceable possession of their late home.

In fact, neither Hudson Taylor nor any colleague at any time asked
for such intervention, as was to be made certain after the damage
had been done.

Under fifteen headings, Medhurst set out his formal protest. 1.
The CIM premises in Yangzhou had been procured with prefect
Sun's knowledge, consent and authorisation and with the approval
of HBM Consul at Zhenjiang, duly recorded. 2. From the moment
the missionaries entered Yangzhou they had been 'entirely innocent
of any offence (and had) borne with exemplary endurance, insults
and assaults'. . . . 3. The malicious rumours spread to set mobs
against them were not supported by the slightest evidence. 4. The
principal authors of the placards and slander were the gentry 'Yen

Fuan-shu [*sic*], Pien Pao-shu, Li Pao-fu and Wen-hsi'. 5. The magistrates evaded Hudson Taylor's courteous requests for intervention, and 6. detained him for two hours during which the house and possessions could have been saved. 7. By fire, plunder and violence, considerable injury had been sustained. 8. The guard had been withdrawn allowing the mob to return to their devastation, and 9. Mr Taylor had been threatened with being left to the mercy of the mob if he did not represent the riot as a simple brawl.[29] 10. Instead of protecting the victims in the *yamen* the authorities had expelled them and issued a false proclamation. So much for the facts.

Consul Medhurst proceeded to demand justice. He was laying these matters before the viceroy and the British Minister Plenipotentiary 'for adjudication and punishment, according to the laws pertaining to such official derelictions of duty'. 11. It was for the rioters to be punished by the Yangzhou authorities, but 'Should any of the culprits be members of the belted gentry, whom it is beyond the power of the Chih-fu [ie yourself the Prefect] to issue a warrant against, I must require him to report their names to His Excellency the Viceroy for degradation and punishment.' 12. Compensation to the tune of two thousand taels must be paid to him, the consul, for distribution to the victims of the riot, Chinese and foreign; 13. their house must be restored to its original condition; 14. a proclamation must state that all culprits were to be punished, and that British subjects were at liberty to rent premises and reside at Yangzhou; this proclamation was to be engraved on a stone tablet and erected at the place from which the victims were ejected; and 15. they were to be invited by letter or deputy to return there, while any and everyone imprisoned for alleged connection with the missionaries were to be released. These facts and demands, he concluded, he was placing before the prefect 'to avoid any further and disagreeable complications'.[30]

The reply received on September 6 in the name of Prefect Sun came from a deputy – none other than the magistrate who had threatened Hudson Taylor with being abandoned to the mob. The prefect himself had gone to confer with Viceroy Zeng Guofan in Nanjing. It said,

> On the 22nd August some female children were secretly buried in the Orphanage established by the French missionary, Sechinger (Chiu-chien-san), and many corpses were dug up also. . . . The people went to Mr Taylor's house, and raised a disturbance, which I, with

the magistrates and military authorities, effectually put down. No injuries were caused to, nor property stolen from, the missionaries, as may be seen from Mr Taylor's own letter.

The magistrate then quoted a dispatch from Viceroy Zeng, continued with his own equally inept comments, and concluded, 'The affair is settled; there is therefore no necessity for your troubling the Senior Naval Officer to accompany you with an escort as you propose.'[31] Meanwhile Medhurst had written to the viceroy on September 3, and Zeng Guofan's reply to Medhurst's protests also tried to evade the issue.

In Shanghai the editor of the *North China Herald* affected a languid Victorian attitude to events although well aware of their seriousness.

> We hardly remember a week in which so little of social interest has been stirring. There is nothing before the Courts, and the Consulate is only saved from oblivion by the opportunity of bestirring itself about the attack on missionaries at (Yangzhou). HMS *Rinaldo* has left for (Zhenjiang), where, we presume, she will form a sort of moral support to Mr Medhurst (and) take him on to Nanking. . . . The (prefect of Yangzhou) has seized the men who let the house to Mr Taylor and tortured them in order to make them confess that the missionaries did really destroy the children.[32]

Meanwhile in Zhenjiang the Tartar-General had succeeded in keeping his troops under control and the people took their cue from him rather than from the inflammatory magistrate.

> On the night of the 4th inst. HMS *Rinaldo* arrived, and on the 5th Mr Medhurst made a demonstration in the city. With a guard of (thirty) marines and blue-jackets he paid a visit to the Tartar-General and demanded the punishment of the military mandarin who had beaten our landlord, and also that a proclamation should be issued forbidding the Tartars from interfering with British subjects who may purchase or rent houses in the city. . . . This proceeding somewhat quieted the agitation here.

Still the magistrate failed to hand over the rented premises, and scored another victory over the *daotai* by appealing to the viceroy, in whom he had a powerful ally.

CHAPTER THREE

GUNBOAT DIPLOMACY
1868

Medhurst makes his point[1]   *September 1868*

From the arrival of HMS *Rinaldo* at Zhenjiang, consular representations to the mandarins took a new tone. Even the disgraced Shanghai magistrate at Zhenjiang played his hand more carefully. But Zeng Guofan shared the view that the power of consuls had waned. In a studied snub he sent as his deputy to investigate the Yangzhou riot a mandarin 'of very inadequate rank', no higher than *zhixian*, a district magistrate with an opaque white cap-button, inferior to the city prefect (*zhifu*), let alone to the literati responsible for instigating the uprising. Zeng Guofan instructed him to tell the Yangzhou populace that all the trouble had been due to the French Catholics and that no fault was attached to the British missionaries. But this worthy failed to arrive at the agreed rendezvous, and Consul Medhurst proceeded to Yangzhou without him.

Events of such consequence as the crop of outrages – by foreigners as well as Chinese – taking place in 1867–70, had no lack of reporters. The closest eye-witness accounts of the Yangzhou, Zhenjiang and Nanjing affairs are those of Medhurst, Hudson Taylor and those who were with them. A composite account from these sources is therefore the fullest and most dependable. Emily Blatchley, as Hudson Taylor's secretary, was in the right position to put it into words.

Consul Medhurst had been set on going up to Yangzhou with or without an armed escort, to bring Prefect Sun to Nanjing to explain in person to the viceroy why he had not responded when Hudson Taylor first reported threats of violence. *Rinaldo* strengthened Medhurst's hand.

> (Mr Medhurst) went on Tuesday the 8th, in a small steamer, with an escort of seventy marines (and blue-jackets) under the command of Captain Bush of the *Rinaldo*, and accompanied by Mr Allen and the

THE PREFECT'S PROCESSION

French Consul, J M Canny, Esquire. A French frigate which had happened to come down from (Hankou) a few days before, . . . stayed off (Guazhou) to guard the mouth of the Grand Canal until the return of the expedition. Mr Taylor was unable to go, being laid up at the time with a severe inflammatory attack; but Mr Duncan (accompanied by Mr Jackson) went up with them in our own hired boat.

The guard, Commander Bush (not 'Captain') explained to the Admiralty, was 'composed of nearly the whole of the ship's company, to prevent the possibility of (the consul-general) being insulted by the mob'.

The prefect had been forewarned and was waiting with his retinue at a minor gate of the city when the consul and naval party arrived. His intention to conduct them inconspicuously by back streets to his *yamen* had not reckoned on Medhurst's knowledge of China from childhood, or the presence of Allen and Canny, already familiar with the city. They proceeded to a main gate and marched through busy thoroughfares as conspicuously as possible. Everything seemed perfectly quiet, and without the least sign of hostility apparent they went direct to the prefect's *yamen*, took possession of it, stationed guards at the doors, and demanded an interview with the prefect.

The *North China Herald* reported that '(Consul Medhurst) was received with the utmost respect.' When Prefect Sun arrived back at his *yamen* to find marine guards at his doors and the consul in determined mood, he surprised his visitors by showing 'abject terror', Medhurst told Sir Rutherford Alcock; and a correspondent of the *North China Herald* wrote,

> It was curious to see the (prefect) during the interview. . . . He was ghastly with fear, and trembled so that he could hardly hold Mr Medhurst's despatch in his hand. . . . [And Emily, reporting Duncan's observations,] He was in a terrible state of trepidation, and endeavoured to make out that the whole affair of the night of the 22nd was nothing more than a little excitement and unruliness on the part of the people. But the Consul, after hearing what he had to say, proceeded to take up point by point in such an unanswerable way, that the Prefect was completely silenced. Mr Medhurst then set before him an ultimatum . . . [embodying the demands which the *xian* magistrate as his 'scornful and discourteous' deputy had rejected (pp 112–3)].

Some of these the Prefect acceded to; with regard to the others he said he had not the power to act without consulting the Viceroy [and some of the gentry named by Medhurst could not be arrested as they were of higher rank than himself]. It became a question, then, whether to wait where they were until an answer could be received from the Viceroy, or to take the Prefect himself up to Nan-kin. The latter course was decided upon, the Prefect stipulating that he should be allowed to go in his own boat, and not as a prisoner.

Before leaving, Mr Medhurst and his retinue, accompanied by the Prefect, the two (city magistrates) and the . . . commander of the garrison, went to make a personal examination of our desolated premises. Though cleared of *débris*, swept and repaired as the place was by the cunning mandarins, still the mended portions of the walls, the absence of partitions, the wall-plaster pricked into an almost regular unevenness by the missiles of bricks and stones which had been hurled, a pile of broken furniture yet remaining, some pieces of partially burned timber, and other traces of fire, – these told their own story quite unmistakably.

Allen and Canny had seen it all before repairs had been made, and Medhurst could see for himself the wrenched hinges, the 'piles of broken furniture' and foreign travellers' trunks. Duncan pointed out where walls had been broken down and newly bricked up again and plastered over. To Medhurst's disgust, the reaction of the mandarins to the detection of their deceit was not to show shame but to sulk. But what impressed him more deeply was the fact that the direct distance between the *yamen* and the house was only half a mile. The sound of rioting by thousands of people must have been heard long before Hudson Taylor arrived to claim protection. With any will to keep the peace, help could have reached them within minutes instead of hours.

In marching from the *yamen* to the mission and afterwards in returning to the boats, Medhurst's party was 'surrounded and followed . . . by a vast concourse of Chinese . . . even when the attendants of the Prefect thrashed the front ranks of the gazers with canes . . . to make them give way'. Yet 'not a single word of disrespect was heard . . . the inhabitants have always been rather friendly . . . and the strong feeling of antagonism . . . now said to exist can only have been conjured up by the officials and literati.'

Consuls and naval escort passed the night outside the city and in the morning were joined by Prefect Sun in a large mandarin boat for the journey down the Grand Canal to the Yangzi. 'The expedition then returned to (Zhenjiang), the Prefect (in his own boat) being escorted by two of the *Rinaldo*'s cutters. He asked to be allowed to stay the night at (Guazhou) . . . and gave his written promise to be there in the morning, and ready for proceeding to Nan-kin. Notwithstanding, he made off in the night, leaving his boat there.'

The viceroy's deputy, Zhang Zhixian, was waiting at Zhenjiang for Consul Medhurst, who took him to see Hudson Taylor and his Yangzhou party. Zhang questioned them minutely and examined what evidence of injury was still to be seen after sixteen days. Sir Rutherford in turn told Prince Kong, on February 4, 1869, of 'medical evidence of unimpeachable character having satisfied me that the injuries received by Mr Rudland, Mrs Taylor and Miss Blatchley are all of so serious a character as to entail some permanent disability.'[2] Zeng Guofan was later to inform Medhurst that his deputy Zhang had reported no evidence of injuries or bruises. So no charges had been substantiated. As for the pregnant women, neither had given birth, so the allegation that they had jumped could only be based on hearsay.

The inspection completed, Medhurst persuaded the deputy to travel back to Nanjing with him in *Rinaldo*. In the morning Zhang did set out from shore but, pleading alarm at the roughness of the water, returned to safety. With Medhurst on board, *Rinaldo* crossed the Yangzi to Guazhou to pick up Prefect Sun, only to find that 'he too proved false'. Medhurst then steamed up the Yangzi towards Nanjing. The *Times* correspondent who was with him recorded the next episode. Halfway there they overtook a river boat on which a wildly gesticulating Prefect Sun indicated that he wished to be taken in tow. Blind and deaf to his pleas, they left him behind.[3] The instigators of the Yangzhou riot being none other than Zeng's personal friends, Sun had thought he held the trump card in this game of old style diplomacy. He had calculated on reaching Zeng Guofan before Medhurst, to agree on how to thwart him.

Humiliation at Nanjing[4]   *September 11–30, 1868*

On Friday morning, September 11, Medhurst proceeded to the viceroy's *yamen* with due ceremony. 'He received me with more than customary state, and seemed inclined to be friendly; but I found it exceedingly difficult to rouse his peculiarly impassive and sluggish nature to . . . the serious importance of my object.' The reason was not far to seek. He had received a minimum of information from the Yangzhou officials and was stalling the consultation until he heard more. 'There seemed to be fair promise of his acting equitably [Medhurst thought], but nothing was immediately decided.'

When Prefect Sun's arrival was announced, Medhurst insisted on being present at an interview with him, but Zeng Guofan would not allow it and Medhurst at length withdrew. In the evening the friendly *Daotai* Ying of Zhenjiang, also in Nanjing over his own troubles, visited *Rinaldo* with a message from the viceroy and stayed two hours. Zeng was offering a thousand taels in compensation for the Yangzhou losses and injuries. Medhurst rejected the offer as unrealistic and renewed the demands he had submitted to Prefect Sun.

At this juncture Commander Bush, who had been unwell for several days, became dangerously ill with dysentery. Fearing for his life he asked Medhurst to transfer his party to houseboats, and was hurried in his own ship to Shanghai. 'The Consul was, therefore, left with only a small boat [perhaps a launch in which he had come up from Shanghai]. In the eyes of the Chinese who attach such importance to ceremonial trappings and outward insignia, he immediately became a person of no moment . . . quite unprotected and helpless.' The effect was electric. The viceroy 'changed his tone' and refused to consider Medhurst's demands. He had just received news of his translation to the viceroyalty of Zhili, he said, the highest in

A HIGH MANDARIN'S INFORMAL SEDAN CHAIR

the empire, with its concomitant title of Guardian of the Throne. So he was busy. The implication was clear, Medhurst remarked to Alcock in submitting 'the whole case to your Excellency's superior judgment and authority'.

> I can call to mind, out of my experience of British relations with China, scarcely one instance in which the outrage complained of has been more unprovoked on the part of the sufferers, and in which the evidence of neglect and culpability on the part of the local authorities has been more marked and incontrovertible.

To Zeng Guofan he replied that matters were far from resolved.

Making light of the situation, on the 14th Zeng Guofan rebuked Medhurst's 'breach of faith' in scorning his (inadequate) deputy, Zhang, and instead of himself issuing an edict, said he would order Prefect Sun to issue a proclamation, to invite Hudson Taylor to return, and to release all Chinese 'innocently' under arrest. The ambivalence of his wording was characteristic of the proceedings.

Although at such a disadvantage Medhurst was not to be browbeaten. Lacking the physical force which the mandarins appeared to understand better than reason, he gave defiant words their full weight. On September 18 he acknowledged the viceroy's 'decision', strongly questioned his statements, demanded to inspect any proclamation on the matter before it was issued, rejected the offer of a thousand taels as a charitable gift, and informed Zeng that all relevant papers, including his derisory communication of the 14th, were being forwarded to the British minister in Peking and would no doubt reach the Zongli Yamen. As not only Viceroy of the Two Jiangs but Imperial Commissioner for Foreign Affairs in the Yangzi region, from Sichuan to Shanghai, Zeng knew that this was fast becoming not a local fracas but an international incident. Yet he put his friends, the gentry of Yangzhou, before diplomacy. Medhurst challenged his defence of them. Zeng's statement that they 'could not possibly from their position and experience have been guilty of inciting the people against the missionaries' was not founded on fact, as investigation would show.

Sir Rutherford Alcock, on receiving Medhurst's first notification, dated August 27, and his report of August 31 with Hudson Taylor's affidavit, informed Lord Stanley at the Foreign Office, adding, 'The Roman Catholic missions in the interior are not exempt from the same sudden outbreaks of popular hostility; and I believe one of the chief occupations of the French Legation here, consists in pressing claims for redress, and making reclamations on their behalf.' In ponderously due time (dispatches taking weeks to reach London), Lord Stanley replied on November 20. Of Medhurst's reports he wrote, 'He appears to have acted with great prudence and firmness in the matter; and you will convey to him my approval of his proceedings.'

Consul Medhurst reported to Alcock again after passing through Zhenjiang on his way back to Shanghai. Some face-saving compromise could not be avoided. Ying would lose his office of *daotai* if he said too many home-truths about the Zhenjiang magistrate. Hudson Taylor was willing to accept a different house in the city as long as it suited his purposes. By this compromise the Chinese authorities would be spared the appearance of defeat over the first house and its suffering owners would escape further involvement. The viceroy's treatment of the delinquent magistrate had been severe, Medhurst wrote, but even the exemplary *daotai* had suffered his displeasure. Towards the guilty Yangzhou gentry who 'were in a position to bring (their weight and wealth) to bear in order to screen themselves from blame', Zeng was being lenient. 'It is my belief,' Medhurst said, 'that until the entire Chinese population, official, literary and otherwise, is distinctly informed by Imperial proclamation that British subjects are to be acknowledged and treated in a friendly spirit, and that the compact with the British nation was an Imperial act, it is hopeless to expect that our merchants and missionaries will be regarded as otherwise than objects of contempt and suspicion by the people at large.'

The strident press of Hong Kong and Shanghai as ever saw things in a less sober light. In an ill-informed editorial under the title 'Peace or War?' the *China Mail* of September 19 asked,

> What is to be the upshot of present events in China? . . . Of what use is such consular action as that recorded in the Shanghai papers last to hand? After an insult and outrage far exceeding any in the recent history of our relations with China, Her Majesty's Consul obtains from the Prefect a declaration that the would-be murderers and assassins are naughty boys, and returns having 'successfully accomplished the object of his mission'. Away with such puerile nonsense. If indeed another war supervenes, it will have been the work of 'Her Majesty's peacemongers'.

As early as September 5 the *North China Herald* was demanding action against the mandarins of Yangzhou. Overlooking the immunity of the literati to corporal punishment, the editorial claimed, 'to spare them . . . might lead to loss of life elsewhere, and eventually perhaps bring about a war . . . The mildest penalty for those men should be a public bambooing and a cangue round their necks at the city gates for three weeks.' On the 11th the *Herald* became unashamedly jingoistic and, surprisingly, took Hudson Taylor's side. 'A file of marines and a gunboat . . . would teach (them) that their literati cannot instigate murderous attacks on foreigners and then laugh in their sleeves at us.'

A week later the editor was strongly urging, in multiple columns about the Yangzhou and Zhenjiang riots, that *Rinaldo* or another warship should return lest fresh riots occur. 'We now stand as beaten hounds in the eyes of (the viceroy's) subordinates . . . Our minister is surely not going to pocket the snub we have received.' Zeng, China's senior viceroy, should be taken to Peking and charged with dereliction of duty!

On the 25th, when Consul Medhurst was back at Shanghai, Yangzhou was again the major topic for a two-column editorial. Sir Rutherford was surely over-influenced by 'the supine policy dictated from the Foreign Office' – a policy, be it noted, soon to be rejected by the next British government as belligerent. An article of the treaty had been broken! We should insist on satisfaction! Zeng Guofan's volte-face on the departure of *Rinaldo* from Nanjing was 'clear proof of the necessity for coercion. . . . So long as force is shown, compliance is insured.'

Both the *Times* correspondent and the *Herald* reported that when the Zhenjiang *daotai*, on the orders of the viceroy, issued a proclamation (declaring the right of foreigners to reside in the interior of China and that officials must aid them in obtaining houses), a counter-proclamation signed 'the People of Zhenjiang' was promptly issued. It declared that if any foreigners dared to rent premises the house would be burned down and the foreigners and the landlord thrown into the flames. Not only so, any official helping the foreigner would suffer the same fate in the flames of his *yamen*.

Hudson Taylor, who usually drew down censure upon his head, in these circumstances still won the sympathy of the press. The sworn evidence of his party had impressed even their critics. The *Herald* heaped heavy blame for the serious deterioration of diplomatic relations on Commander Bush. Even if 'dangerously ill', why had he not left his ship under his second in command at Nanjing, himself travelling to Shanghai by commercial steamer? 'Steamers containing ample accommodation for invalids were passing every day within hail. . . . The sick officer might with perfect safety have been placed on board one of these vast movable hotels and conveyed to Shanghai.' But almost in the same breath, *mirabile dictu*, the CIM was applauded for adopting Chinese clothes as 'an imitation of those great Romish pioneers of Christianity, Ricci, Verbiest, Semedo and Valignano'.

When the Admiralty and Foreign Office enquired into the manner of Commander Bush's departure from Nanjing – without question the turning-point in negotiations from imminent success to intolerable humiliation – he was fully vindicated. His condition had been too severe to admit of his being transferred to another ship. But it was the personal deposition of this honoured old officer which not only convinced his superiors but effectively influenced the policy of Lord Clarendon after he succeeded Lord Stanley at the Foreign Office. For Commander Bush had been astounded to learn of the effect of his departure.

> It never entered my head that the presence simply of a small man-of-war could have the slightest effect in influencing the action of the Viceroy of Nanking, one of the most important functionaries in the Chinese empire. . . . Under no circumstances whatever would I have allowed the ship under my command to be used as a threat to compel a compliance to the Consul's request, however just, without an official communication from the Minister at Peking or from my own Superior Officer.

Disraeli resigned on December 2 and Gladstone formed his government with Lord Clarendon as Foreign Minister, who, coming at once under the influence of Anson Burlingame, in what has been called the 'Clarendon conversion', became convinced of China's good intentions and reversed the instructions being followed by Alcock and his consuls. He instructed them and the Admiralty that Her Majesty's Government desired to deal directly with the central government of China, with Prince Kong and the Zongli Yamen, rather than with viceroys and local authorities as before. Much that had satisfied Lord Stanley now had to be explained, only to be censured. Scapegoats were needed, and in 1888 Hudson Taylor summed up the story of his unprotesting acceptance in 1869 of this role, by writing, 'An attempt was made to throw all the blame on the unfortunate missionaries. This was no small trial to us, but in the meantime we were restored to (Yangzhou), and the Lord comforted us.' There was more to it than that.

'We intend to go forward'   *September 1868*

With more than thirty colleagues looking to him for leadership and the distribution of funds, Hudson Taylor could not allow events to disrupt his duties any more than was unavoidable. The preservation of his Mission accounts and records permitted him to take up control after the riots where it had been interrupted. Business friends in Shanghai were sharing the banking, postal and purchasing chores with William Gamble, but more and more he felt the need to have a member of the Mission there to handle the increasing volume of work. With donations in Britain fewer and fewer, William Berger was sending only just as much as usual. At a time of unusual expenses in China, making it go round was difficult. Yet as refugees in the French consulate and then in the two small buildings Hudson Taylor rented in the Zhenjiang suburb, he and Emily kept the office work going.

Meeting the requirements of Medhurst and the mandarins was not least among his difficulties. His colitis, sometimes severe, was sapping his energy. Correspondence with a wide circle of people still ignorant of recent events or prompted by the papers to ask for more news, was more than he could cope with. Well-meaning friends in England were urging William Berger to press for more articles from Hudson Taylor's pen, lest interest in China flag still further. The riot and all that followed supplied that deficiency for months to come. But others influenced by criticisms of the CIM joined in the disaffection.

Maria was constantly in touch with Mrs Berger, her unfailingly faithful confidante. When she wrote on September 7, 'We have been surrounded by a very *hurricane* of trials', she could add little more. She and the children were having to lie low in cramped conditions, for fear of fomenting unrest. John McCarthy wrote from Hangzhou of problems between the different denominations in the team. 'The whole five discontented ones' – the Nicols, Susan Barnes and the McLean sisters – were 'in committee at Suzhou', without so much as 'by your leave'. And Lewis Nicol's resentments were leading him into more unfounded allegations. Cardwell was ill and unhappy at Taizhou, zealous in his work but pining to move away. Hudson Taylor agreed to his coming to Nanjing to learn Mandarin.

George Stott was in fresh trouble at Wenzhou since moving his school into more suitable premises.

> The charge . . . against me at present [he wrote], is that I am getting up a rebellion; that I invite all the leaders in the plot every night after dark to my house, and instruct them in the art of foreign warfare from foreign books, and harangue them to excite their courage; and that I am in secret correspondence with some foreign magistrates in Ningpo, having the same object in view.
>
> These handbills have so alarmed the mandarins, that the city gates are now shut immediately after sunset. Then a guard of soldiers is posted at each end of the street leading to my house; and a watchman walks all the distance and reports at both ends, beating all the time he walks a brass gong, which is heard all over the city. For three nights I have been hardly able to sleep for the sound of it.

In his insecurity Stott thought the closing of the city gates, the guard of soldiers and the watchman were part of the threat against him. No letter from Hudson Taylor on the subject has been kept, but he would certainly have pointed out that, on the contrary, they had assuredly been ordered by the mandarin to protect him.

To Hudson Taylor and his team, the deliverance from Yangzhou was clear confirmation of God's hand upon their venture. Three weeks after the Yangzhou riot and ten days after the Zhenjiang mob wrecked even the *daotai's yamen*, Hudson Taylor voiced to William Berger the conclusions he had reached. They were not to be foiled by difficulties.

> We are all now getting over our wounds and bruises. . . . It is no child's play, and our funds are very low. . . . But the Lord reigneth. By His grace we intend *to go forward* and He will not leave us in the lurch.
>
> 'He'd never have taught us to trust in His name,
>
> And thus far have brought us to put us to shame.' . . . We may before the winter possibly be able to attempt some new province. Many of our number are stirred up to press into the interior; and our recent disasters, if such I may call them, only make us the more determined to go on, leaning on the almighty power of our Captain. . . . I shall have to put away one of the *Lammermuir* party – Nicol – from the Mission. He has done us much harm; and unless restrained by the Lord, if the most unscrupulous lying can do us any harm, he will still cause us much injury.

Three steps were needed. First, to consolidate the work so far begun. He had made provision for it to be carried on in each city so far occupied, and was dealing with its problems. Second, to clear the decks of encumbrances and dangers. For over two years he had dealt patiently with Lewis Nicol and those who sided with him. Suggestions that Nicol should resign if he could not co-operate peacefully had led to nothing. The time had come to grasp the nettle. And lastly, to reconnoitre farther afield and place teams where possible. From Wuhan, Griffith John and Alexander Wylie were exploring Sichuan and northward into Shaanxi as far as Hanzhong. Hudson Taylor had his eyes on Henan province, northward up the Grand Canal; on Anhui province farther up the Yangzi, on both sides; and on Jiangxi province to the south. James Meadows and James Williamson were poised to begin this advance, and Hudson Taylor himself longed to play a part in it.

With fifty or sixty members, the church at Ningbo could manage its own affairs with the help of John McCarthy from Hangzhou, and of George Crombie from Fenghua. In Hangzhou itself, after three years a congregation of twice that size had Wang Lae-djün as its good pastor, strongly supported by his wife and Jennie Faulding. Jennie often said when writing home that she would choose to be nowhere else and with no other colleagues than the McCarthys. Last of the *Lammermuir* party – the rest had all scattered – she welcomed the freedom to work with fewer distractions. 'I could not imagine for myself a happier lot.' Running her school, constantly invited to visit Chinese homes all over the city, she felt fulfilled, without a care or fear for the future. One day was much like another. Long might it continue so.

John Stevenson was at last seeing a church of true believers taking shape at Shaoxing. South of Ningbo the little church at Fenghua and its outlying daughter churches were expanding. Three men came from Taiping to Taizhou, a two-day walk of forty miles, expressly to hear the gospel. They had with them Luke's Gospel and the Acts, presented to them by a missionary years before, and said there were twenty more men at Taiping who would gladly come as they had. The bush fire was spreading slowly but surely.

Goodbye to Nicol   *September 1868*

On September 13, the day Hudson Taylor wrote, 'We intend to go forward', he also wrote to Nicol. He could hope no longer for a change of heart. The letter is a window on both men.[5] William

Berger had sent him, he said, a copy of Nicol's 'disgraceful' letter of
February 13. Naming missionaries who had testified to the fact that
the 'falsehoods and misrepresentations' in the letter had been
repeated in conversation with members of his own and other
missions 'in the habitual breach and perversion of the truth', the
only course left was to 'terminate your connection with the China
Inland Mission'. In doing so he was 'acting after conference with
and with the concurrence of all the brethren of the *Lammermuir*
party and as many of the other brethren of the Mission as I have had
opportunity of meeting, since I received the copy of your letter . . . I
do not dismiss you because of your denominational views . . . nor
yet for your preference for the English costume; nor indeed on any
other ground in whole or in part than that of habitual and deliberate
falsehood.' William Berger had sent Nicol a gift of twenty pounds
for his current needs, and 'through the kindness of a friend I shall be
able to procure a passage to England for you and Mrs Nicol'.
Another forty dollars could be made available to him if he needed
an outfit for the voyage within the next two or three months.

Believing it to be necessary to have this letter delivered by hand,
Hudson Taylor sent it to John McCarthy, apparently asking him to
vet it before taking it to Xiaoshan. On September 20 McCarthy
replied, 'We hardly knew how much we valued your love, till it was
nearly lost to us [in the riot]. May we be bound closer and closer
together – for the Lord's sake . . . for the sake of this needy
land. . . . Thank God, dear brother, and take courage, for if ever
you were helped in writing a letter, I believe you were in the one I
have just handed to Nicol. What pain it cost you to write that letter I
can guess.' To Berger he wrote at length, applauding Hudson
Taylor's qualities and defending him against all accusations. His
only crime was that of trying to do ten men's work instead of one.

At the time Nicol made no reference to the contents, but William
Berger commented, 'Your letter to Nicol . . . was everything that
the case required, and how sad was his reply to it.' To the Taylor's
grief, by October 5 they had received letters of resignation from
Susan Barnes and the McLean sisters. They had hoped that the
dismissal would dissolve the alliance and save these three for the
Mission, but it was not to be. Maria told Mrs Berger that after 'many
prayers that the Lord would remove . . . those who were not really
of us', this must be accepted as the answer. 'Perhaps after all these
storms the Lord will give us a calm, but all these sorrows and
anxieties tell sorely on my beloved Husband's health. If he *can* get

away for a little quiet and change he will DV do so, and if possible I shall accompany him.' Jennie was expecting them to visit Hangzhou. Instead 'the advance' claimed priority.

Among Maria's papers is a sad soliloquy. Sooner or later the reckoning had had to be made. 'If (the Lord) has suffered some to come who have caused us untold sorrow, may we not regard this as part of the storms that are to make our young Mission strike its roots into . . . the rock?' Jennie remarked in her home letter, 'I think it is better so. [And as for dismissing Nicol] Everyone . . . felt that he *ought* to do it. Poor Mr Taylor! Very few people know how unselfish and devoted he is, nor how much he has to endure (from) those who treat him so ungratefully. . . . God knows, and He will bring the truth to light sooner or later.'

Little information has come to light about the five lost from the Mission. Nicol chose to stay at Xiaoshan, but before long was helping briefly at the hospital in Ningbo. After that nothing more seems to be known. 'Some of them' applied to the LMS, but were not taken into membership. Susan Barnes and Margaret McLean worked at the Union Chapel of the LMS in Shanghai until August 1869, but there the trail runs cold. Jane, too, worked in Shanghai and by 1874 she and Hudson Taylor were on as friendly terms as ever (*see* p 397f).[6]

Action to advance   *September–November 1868*

September and October were full of diplomatic activity and no foreigner doubted that strong-arm persuasion would be used as soon as possible to resolve the mounting differences between China and the European nations. That Anson Burlingame in Europe was urging peaceful negotiations with a well-intentioned Chinese government stood in marked contrast with the mood on both sides in China, especially in Taiwan and the Yangzi region.

After *Rinaldo* and then Consul Medhurst withdrew from Nanjing it was no time for those who had been thrown out of Yangzhou to attempt to penetrate beyond the city to the north of Jiangsu, on the way to eastern Henan. Yet this was what Hudson Taylor and James Williamson were planning to do. In a little boat on the Grand Canal they could remain out of sight until well clear of Yangzhou, and even a man in poor health could travel in comparative comfort. For a start they would reconnoitre Qingjiangpu, a hundred or more miles beyond Yangzhou. James Williamson hoped eventually to pioneer in Jiangxi province, but initially he and James Meadows were to secure a footing at Anqing on the Yangzi in Anhui province. Anqing, about two hundred miles above Zhenjiang, would be a forward base for the next advance to Jiujiang, the best starting-point into Jiangxi. As the weeks passed they were watching for their opportunity.

Catherine Brown had at last reached China. The prescribed month in a consular centre before British subjects could marry in China would end for George Duncan and her on September 25. On the 17th he and James Meadows left Zhenjiang by steamer for Shanghai to arrange for the wedding and for Meadows to bring his family from Ningbo. The next day Maria set off with Catherine in the Mission's canal boat, to give her a leisurely introduction to this kind of travel. During the same period Hudson Taylor was also away, making preparations for the bride, and for Mary Bowyer to keep her company. Arriving back at Zhenjiang on the same day, for Mary Rudland's confinement, Maria and he found it was all over. The riot baby was in perfect health.

All through October the papers were full of rumblings about the riots in Taiwan, inflammatory anti-foreign placards were being posted in Shanghai, and foreigners were being stoned on the streets of Wuhan. HMS *Dove* was ordered back to Zhenjiang as a precaution, and the jingoism in the Shanghai papers approached hysteria. But on Monday, October 26, Hudson Taylor and Williamson started up the Grand Canal. On November 3 he began a letter to the Bergers. 'I am now returning from a journey of exploration as far up as (Qingjiangpu) . . . a large and important town . . . some three miles below where (the Grand Canal) formerly crossed the Yellow River. . . . With a view to our ultimately commencing work in K'ai-fung-fu, the capital of Honan, or failing that, in some other city in the province, it seems desirable to have a half-way station.' Qingjiangpu was the farthest point any missionary of any society had so far penetrated from the south (Book 3, p 182).

On the same day, Consul Medhurst left Shanghai to return to Nanjing and Zeng Guofan – this time on the flagship HMS *Rodney*, with a squadron of supporting warships. The editor of the *North China Herald* preened himself with the comment, 'We hope, for the sake of the Chinese themselves, that they will yield to what is asked, and not await the seventy-eight guns of the *Rodney*!' Safely home on November 6, Taylor and Williamson were in time to observe the activity and to be caught up in it dramatically.

Berger takes the strain   *1868*

The editorial letters of William Berger in the *Occasional Paper* from the time of the *Lammermuir* party's sailing have been said to form a worthy monument to the memory of this good man. His and his wife Mary's frequent personal letters to the Taylors and each member of the Mission provide material enough for a book in its own right. Without the part they played, the missionaries could hardly have survived as a team. And without their encouragement and advice Hudson Taylor would have found it even harder to keep going. William Berger had given a great deal of thought to problems of church government and wrote long letters on the subject. While still ignorant of developments in China, he said of their differing denominational views, 'We cannot enforce our own views . . . indeed we can scarcely say a standard is established in the Word, except for essential doctrines.'

He also thought constantly about how their aim to evangelise the inland provinces could be realised. 'If you will not smile at my planning in our dining-room, I will tell you my musings concerning your future – namely: I fancy you will some day move your headquarters to some desirable city or town very near the (Yangzi), perhaps within easy reach of Hankow; thus you would, I suppose, have easy access to a consul, facility for going to Shanghai and up the river, so as to reach many provinces.' By the time his letter arrived to supply strong confirmation of the step, the dining-room strategist was vindicated – the deployment to the Yangzi had begun. In another letter he mused prophetically on taking violence and robbery in the right spirit, only to laugh at himself – 'as dear Duncan said, "It is very easy to go to the interior of China in Mr Berger's drawing-room."'

Well-to-do, though not very wealthy, the Bergers devoted their home and most of their time to the Mission's welfare. Capable of contributing very largely to its expenses, they firmly believed that such generosity on their part was neither necessary nor in the will of God. The China Inland Mission and its work in China were the responsibility of a wide circle of Christian friends in most denominations, who were not to be deprived of the blessing of giving in the service of God. In the financial year 1867–68, £3,300 had come from the wide circle of donors. Remembering an inflationary factor exceeding twenty we may appreciate this scale of giving. So, when for a variety of reasons the donations the Bergers received for transmission to China fell uncomfortably low, they restrained themselves from the temptation to make up the difference. Instead, they helped when they could in subsidiary ways, as in their offer to pay for the Nicols' passage home.

Their contribution was far more valuable than mere cash. They themselves were wholly immersed in their role of administrators in Britain. After a few years, when the pressure of work became too great, William Berger sacrificed his favourite pastime. He sold the agricultural part of his estate at Saint Hill, East Grinstead, mostly to his own farm manager. Jennie's parents bought and built on another part but lived there less than two years, from 1869 to 1870. At one time he retired from the management of his factory, but took it up again to allow the added income to give him greater liberty in his Christian activities.

Neither William nor Mary Berger felt competent to write about China or to address meetings as Hudson Taylor had done and would do if he were at home in Britain again. In any case they had no time nor strength for more than they were doing. Their prayers and strong moral support meant more to the Taylors than any material help. Mary Berger's fine, legible handwriting filled page upon page, overwritten at right angles in a different colour, of information, comment and love, as genuine as it was effusive, and as prophetic in the truest sense. 'May the knowledge of (God's) great love to us quicken us to endure everything . . . that He permits in the course of our service to Him . . . even though misunderstood, misjudged and unrepresented.' In the letter which would have arrived just before the Yangzhou riot in which she said, 'Underneath are the everlasting arms', she went on, 'They will protect you when attacked, and will preserve you from all real danger. You may . . . quietly stay yourself on Him.'

Jennie had had to stay at Hangzhou, but in Emily they had 'such a treasure'. When news of the murder of Dr Maxwell's Chinese colleague in Taiwan reached Britain, Mary Berger wrote on July 29, ignorant, of course, of events at Yangzhou, 'Truly your safety is in God *alone*. . . . May He . . . graciously keep you from feeling afraid.' And again on September 23, 'We are . . . intensely interested in your movement northward (to Yangzhou). . . . I think the caution you are all using is most commendable.'

William Berger's candid letters were those of a man of affairs in which his affection and confidence constantly came through.

Your life . . . is so valuable that every means for its prolongation must be adopted. So I shall . . . deliver my message. . . . You are going beyond your physical powers, and to such an extent that unless you relax I fear the worst. If (you work to excess) during the night as well as the day . . . you will assuredly fail and have to give in. Our Father has given us the spirit of a sound mind and holds us accountable for its use. . . .

[In July] You must not allow the strong language employed by some who have received such limited education unduly to affect you; they are not aware how they wound. . . . Be of good cheer! Walk holily and humbly with thy God and He cannot fail thee. . . . No weapon that is formed against thee shall prosper.

[And a few weeks later] Never apologize for your letters, dear Brother, they are always lucid and to the point. I wish I had the same facility of expressing myself. . . . I shall gladly defray the cost of this third edition (5,000) [of *China: Its Spiritual Need and Claims*] thus saving trouble as to keeping accurate account of copies we lend or give away or put on sale.

As the allegations started by Nicol and relayed by those he spoke to spread to Britain, losing nothing in being relayed, William Berger kept Hudson Taylor informed. Unshaken in his faith in him, he waited patiently for the explanation. 'I deeply deplore afflicting you so much, but I see not how to keep (it) back from you. . . . If I am wrong kindly say so and I will strive to be more reticent.' The fortnightly mail, taking fifty days in each direction at the fastest, was at best a poor means of communication. Carbon copies, with the stylus, were not yet in general use. Copying each letter consumed too much time. Sometimes a contrite Berger explained that he thought he had mentioned things which Hudson Taylor needed to know, when in fact he had not. And often members of the team made passing references to things the Taylors had omitted. 'The difficulty of acting at such a distance from you and without the power of conferring is very great.' Even the Foreign Office and Minister in Peking had the same problem.

With the transfer to England of the campaign against Hudson Taylor and the Mission, the strain became as much as the Bergers – in fickle health – could bear. William Berger had not only to present the factual situation in interviews with leading Christians, but to answer troubled questions from correspondents, arising from reports they heard. The confidence of some could not be shaken. Others withdrew support and sympathy. Copies of the plan of No 1

New Lane spoke for the truth more eloquently than anything. Even before she knew that accusations were being sent to friends in England, Emily had sent a room-plan to Mrs Grattan Guinness, who had shown it to others.[7] Well into 1868, when worse attacks of a different nature imposed new stresses, the aspersions on Hudson Taylor's integrity and policies continued.

After news of the riots arrived, the Bergers' sympathy shone from their letters. 'That this outrage will serve for the Gospel I quite hope and think, and shall expect to hear of your being back again in the same house.' That they might be afraid to return to Yangzhou did not enter his head. The motherly Mary Berger said to Maria with penetrating insight,

> Had we not been realizing that the work in which you are engaged is *God's* work, the painful, harrowing tidings which reached us three days since, would have been overwhelming. Our hearts are stirred to their very depths, yet the love and sympathy they can offer are so utterly below your deep need that we turn to Him who *alone* can be to you *all* you require. *He* saw it all! He permitted, but He protected too! So far, but no further! . . . Perhaps He would show . . . that the Christians have confidence in the living God whom they are seeking to make known [– exactly what the Chinese said]. Perhaps He would teach unconverted Europeans in China that there is a reality in the faith of the missionary. . . . It may be, that by this dreadful outrage He may call the attention of His own dear children all over the world, to China: its spiritual need and claims; and such a desire for their souls' salvation may be aroused as never was known before! [Again, exactly what happened.] . . . We may well leave it all in His hands. . . . How could *you* jump from that height? Yet you were injured.

The newspapers were saying that the children had been thrown from the upper windows. How was it, Mary Berger asked, that in the first letters from Hudson Taylor, Maria, Emily, Duncan and Reid, no mention was made of them? (Lowering them from the upper windows had been the least of the difficulties that night.) And then a tremor of apprehension lest what she was writing should reach Maria when it was hard to relive those experiences. Far from it. Maria read it on December 14 in the very house they had escaped from. 'You are a marvel to me, beloved friend,' Mary Berger wrote. But in the intervening months what had happened? What of the unborn babe? As far as the Bergers knew, Hudson Taylor had appealed to the consul for help and they could not understand why or know how to defend him. Still they remained unshaken.

They had their own difficulties. Mr Aveline, his secretary, and as devoted as William Berger to the Mission, began to go blind and had to stop work. Criticism of the Mission, stemming both from Nicol and from false accounts of the riot, seemed almost to stop the flow of donations. Then one donor who had said his latest gift would be his last, learned the truth and sent £500 (£10,000 today?), while George Müller asked for the names of five or six more 'thoroughly trustworthy' missionaries to whom to send gifts. George Müller, in channelling to the CIM money entrusted to him for distribution, sent it direct to the individuals. Berger did not know how much was going to China, and Hudson Taylor could not know how to share most equitably the funds at his disposal. When Mr Berger took this up with George Müller he agreed to send his contributions through them.

Editing the *Occasional Paper*, seeing it into print and distributing it issue after issue in his 'spare time' took many hours. Usually content with stating the balance in hand, he sometimes enlarged on how timely donations had arrived in a 'refreshing and encouraging' manner. Occasionally he even referred to future expenses – in a way he soon abandoned, confessing to Hudson Taylor that he wished he could have consulted him first. In August 1868, after the marked inflow of funds, he said in his editorial,

> The number of labourers already in the field connected with this mission . . . is now considerable. The amount required to supply their needs and that of the home department will probably not be less than £100 per week, £5,200 for the current year. . . . The questions naturally arise – shall I continue sending out missionaries if in all respects suitable? Will the needed funds be supplied? And, shall I be overpowering dear Mr Taylor? Then China's *four hundred millions* . . . rise up before me, and seem to cry with a loud voice – 'Come over and help us!' . . . I would now ask you my dear friends, to share this responsibility and service with me by giving yourselves to prayer, and seeking in every way in your power to make known the deep need of this poor people, so that labourers may be thrust out into this vast field, connected with our Mission and with others. . . .
>
> By God's help, I hope never to go into debt, and only to enlarge the work *as* He may put it into the hearts of His people to sympathize and send in the needful supplies from time to time. Towards the end of last month, the balance in my hands was reduced to about £97. I

greatly desired to send £300 to Mr Taylor on Mission account, fearing
he might be in need; whereupon we made our prayer to God, were
kept calm, and were able to believe that He would help us in due
time. On August 1st, over £220 was sent in; and on the 13th, over
£500, and in all from the 1st to the 24th, [the three weeks of the
Yangzhou 'disturbance' and riots] over £950, as though our heavenly
Father would say to us, 'If thou canst believe, all things are possible
to him that believeth.' . . . I mention these facts that you may joy
with us, even as you so lovingly share our burdens.

A qualified medical man has not yet been raised up to assist Mr
Taylor; we therefore continue to pray and wait.

He had noticed an impatience among supporters, with no understanding of the difficulties, to hear of advance into the unevangelised provinces. In spite of publishing many pages of letters about
dangerous opposition, he had to remind them that nearly all the
team were still novices facing resistance at almost every turn.

The hardest part – assessing candidates   1866–68

The selection and training of candidates weighed most heavily
upon the Bergers in their inexperience. Hearing of how one and
another whom they had thought well suited to be missionaries, in
new and difficult circumstances had revealed bad flaws of personality, while the best was drawn out of others, they felt incapable of
sound judgment and continually turned to Hudson Taylor for
advice.

It is intensely difficult even when men and women have been here
long under our eye and roof really to know how they will turn
out. . . . I feel it right now to refer to the disaffection . . . to set all
upon their guard. . . . We loved (one in particular) but with us he
was excitable, and we thought not likely to prove a wise leader or
captain over others. [So it was cheering to receive a good account of
him.] Still . . . be very slow in taking any into your full confidence,
rather let them make their own way. . . . I am declining almost all
(candidates) but those of whom we have very much reason to think
them desirable persons. . . . It seems to me . . . we should not accept
such raw recruits as we have done.

The responsibility of candidate selection was 'so great that unless
I was sure God had brought me into the work I should certainly feel
led to retire from it – even as you state of yourself in China'. A
month later he said, 'I am sure none of the Societies could become

so intimately acquainted with their missionaries. On the other hand we may lack perception of character. Our hope is in God.' All too many without education were asking to be sent to China, and had to be disappointed. The rough men of the *Lammermuir* party had yielded too high a proportion of failure to justify sending more of the same type without careful training.

William Berger drafted a letter to all applicants, setting out unequivocally the 'exceptional character' of the CIM, and asking for 'thorough openness' between the candidates and himself. 'The operations being unsectarian . . . are you prepared (to go) avoiding the enforcement of such views as Christians may be allowed to differ upon?' This was an extension of the principle the *Lammermuir* party had agreed to. It required agreement not to press their denominational differences as some Baptist and Presbyterian members already in China had been doing. Hudson Taylor did not question Berger's wording.

Several very suitable women were in touch with the Bergers, but until they heard from Hudson Taylor that single girls could be placed with suitable married couples they could only be asked to wait. Meanwhile Mr Berger was acting on the advice that all unmarried men should be challenged to defer marriage until they had found their feet and learned as much as possible of the language in two or three years. Some responded well.

In contrast, one of the Dublin men of Mrs Gainfort's circle (Book 4, pp 121–2), Robert White, was as intent on marrying her daughter Frances as on going to China. 'He seems spellbound.' The girl had a diseased hip, probably tuberculous. And her mother proposed to go with them! 'Impulsive to a degree' and 'a dangerous person' to have in China, Mrs Gainfort created 'a painful scene' when told she should not go. Together they drove the Bergers to distraction. 'We are quite ill with anxiety,' Mr Berger wrote, unable to change the Gainforts' minds. He managed to obtain a signed document from them that they held neither him nor the Mission responsible for any of them, and on arrival in China would all three adopt Chinese dress! Then suddenly Robert married Frances and sailed, without her mother. With the three Dublin students, Tom Barnardo, Charles Fishe and Thomas Harvey, and Jennie's mother and sister Nellie and others, the Bergers saw the Whites off at the East India dock, but warned Hudson Taylor in detail not to admit them to the Mission when they arrived. All too soon his advice proved well founded.

Barnardo, Fishe and Harvey were candidates of whom Mr Berger was more hopeful. Handsome Charles Fishe lived at Saint Hill with them. The others visited them frequently. Thomas P Harvey, a master-butcher who had turned his attention to medicine in spite of a deficient education, was paying his own way as a student at the London Hospital. He looked 'strong and well', but his father and brother had died of 'consumption'. 'I should say it is in his system. Would this be sufficient reason for refusing him?' William Berger asked Hudson Taylor. With Maria, Emily and Duncan known to have the disease, and with tuberculosis so widespread and little understood, it would be a difficult question to answer. Harvey was overbearing but 'improving' in personality, and might sail with Charles Fishe in 1869 without completing his medical course 'if eventually approved' for the CIM.

Unlike Edward Fishe, who had gone out to China at his own charges without approaching William Berger, Charles Fishe wished to join Hudson Taylor. Serving as the Bergers' secretary for a year, he was their ideal candidate. Without him, Berger feared, his own health would have failed under the pressures on him. Charles was like a son. '(Quiet, and content not to take) a forward place . . . his sterling worth is not seen on the surface, but once known, you will find you have a treasure. There is that in his daily life which produces an influence even when he is silent. . . . (He) has been (unknown to himself) my silent comforter. His holy walk, and prayers, and public addresses have . . . helped me beyond explanation. . . . He is not easily led, he thinks for himself; yet there is such a spirit of subjection and humility as you find in great minds.'

This paragon was in fact all that the Bergers thought of him, with the one reservation that he was still young and immature. But there was more they had not noticed. Colonel Fishe, his father, wisely withheld permission for him to go abroad until a year older. Yet William Berger wrote in August 1868, 'Except C. Fishe I have no one ready to go.' And in September, 'We hope God is fitting him to bear much responsibility and (to) prove a right hand to you. He is calm and of such general good judgement.' His mother had no doubts about Charles but with reason feared for Edward, should he be 'left alone to act for himself'. Accepting a year's delay was not difficult for Charles. He and Nellie Faulding were attracted to each other.

Another unexpected problem also faced the Bergers. Although a CMS clergyman, Frederick Gough had come to feel more at home with the CIM, of which his wife (as Mary Jones) had in a sense been a founding member at Ningbo. From the time of the *Lammermuir*'s sailing in 1866, friends of the Mission had met each Saturday to pray in their homes for China. But, wrote William Berger, 'A sphere has been offered Mr G which I think would perhaps suit him, viz. training (Chinese) youth for becoming evangelists, etcetera. . . . (But) can he also continue his connection with the CIM? He loves to realize the union of true believers and to co-operate with them. . . . It is a critical time.' To belong to a trans-denominational society would have suited him well, but as a result of their consultations, the Goughs returned to Ningbo in the CMS.

Tom Barnardo[8]   *1868*

In spite of the need of experienced doctors being made widely known, none had offered his services to the CIM. Thomas Harvey and Tom Barnardo could not qualify for several more years. The medical student named Evans who had responded to Hudson Taylor's appeals in Dublin seems not to have kept in touch. Barnardo had arrived in London in April 1866, only a few weeks before the sailing of the *Lammermuir*. Though not quite 21, had he been more mature he might have gone to China with the rest. But his father was opposed to his doing so, and Hudson Taylor, seeing 'his youthful assertiveness and somewhat overbearing manner' advised him to take up medicine, allowing him time to mature. So when the Coborn Street houses were given up and Barnardo moved into lodgings nearer to the London Hospital, his intention was to take the entrance examinations without delay.

An evangelist at heart, he could not but be stirred by East London's milling crowds of people. By his own claim, the cholera epidemic of 1866–67 – in which, according to *The Times*, 3,909 died in this area alone – opened his eyes to their hopeless degradation. Soon he was preaching in the streets and on Mile End waste and like William Booth at roughly the same time and place, was being abused and pelted for his pains. The Bergers had doubts about Tom Barnardo's future in the CIM. 'I fear he will not work harmonious-ly, except he can be allowed to have his own way and go where he likes; and yet he seems desirous to have your counsel, and to follow it as far as he feels led.' Frederick and Mary Gough thought he would never be able to work under anyone.

Then, in December 1867, Barnardo fell seriously ill, but recovered so that William Berger could write, 'Tom Barnardo came to us on Christmas Eve and appears to have China before him as ever. He is still suffering much and has had I think a narrow escape. . . .' Ten days later Tom himself was well enough to write to Hudson Taylor. His exuberant, effusive letter, lavishly larded with quotations from Scripture, like Hudson Taylor's own in his days at Hull, said in essence that he hoped to sail for China in the autumn. Again and again he had weighed up his motives, his 'fixity of purpose' and 'in short my whole heart'. 'The leadings of God Chinaward have not slumbered in my breast'; 'the taper that God through you first lit in my soul has now really become a fire'. On and on he went in this vein, only turning briefly to report progress in his medical studies. In view of his preoccupation every evening and at weekends with the sea of destitution around him in London's East End, his achievements as a medical student were considerable. But he wanted to cut short his medical course, to bypass the examinations and go to China. He was looking for a successor to take over his work among the children, his Bible classes and the congregation of about ninety members he had brought into being. Yet Barnardo could not reconcile his views on authority and leadership with the policies of the CIM. Unimpeded (or impelled?) by his physical size, 5 feet 3 inches in height, he never would lose his inner urge to lead, command and be second to none. Alert and competent himself, he could afford to be as resolute and 'obstinately persevering' as his thoughtfulness and intelligence directed. Yet he longed at this time to go to China, as he longed to do all he could for the children of London's slums.

In June William Berger thought Thomas Harvey was wanting 'to be connected' with the CIM. Harvey was sharing in Barnardo's street preaching and had his scalp laid open 'by a missile', painfully enough to deserve mention. As for Barnardo, by the end of July Berger was writing, 'We are somewhat anxious about him. . . .' He had passed the preliminary examination of the Royal College of Surgeons, and there was talk of his going on to take the final examinations of the Royal College and the MD in 1870. But he was neglecting his studies in favour of his wider interests.

Ultimately Tom Barnardo became more and more deeply committed to the East End and never went to China. His close friendship with the Bergers continued, however, and also his correspondence and co-operation with Hudson Taylor.

PART 2

ATTACK

1868–70

CHAPTER FOUR

THE LIMELIGHT
1868

'An anvil, not a hammer'[1]   *May–June 1868*

The Yangzhou riot was as nothing to Hudson Taylor and the Bergers in comparison with the violence of verbal attacks they suffered throughout 1868 and 1869 from fellow-Christians and the secular world. William Jowett's Instructions to John Tucker of Madras in 1833 (quoting the advice of Ignatius to Polycarp of Smyrna, 'Stand steady as an anvil when it is struck,' and Tucker's own comment, 'Be an anvil not a hammer,')[2] had become relevant to their situation. The criticisms directed against the CIM in 1867 (*see* Book 4) were still circulating in 1868, reinforced by Bishop C R Alford's airing of them after his arrival in China – objections to the adoption of Chinese dress, to the inclusion of young women as missionaries, and to Hudson Taylor's position as the only experienced leader of so many novices. In terms of Mission policy alone the climate of opinion was against them in Britain as well as China, owing to a difference of outlook.

In *The History of the Church Missionary Society* Eugene Stock explained the policy of Henry Venn and the CMS on women as missionaries.

> In 1859 the Rev. W. Pennefather, then at Barnet, wrote to the Society offering to train ladies [for service at home and abroad] at an institution he proposed opening. The Committee . . . undertook to pay the expenses of any candidate they might send to it. But they still shrank from saying much in print about even the few women the society was employing. . . . In October of (1863) . . . they passed the following resolution: 'that as there are already two Societies in whose principles this Committee have full confidence, whose professed object it is to send out ladies for schools and zenanas in India; this Committee are not prepared to take up that branch of missionary operations, except under very special circumstances. . . .'[3]

Several offers from ladies to serve with the CMS were therefore declined, the Committee pointing out that wives, sisters and daughters of missionaries were working among Indian women, but that the policy of the CMS was not to expand this side of its work. Other major missions shared this outlook. So Hudson Taylor had embarked on an unconventional practice.

When George Smith, first Bishop of Victoria, Hong Kong, retired in 1864, C R Alford, the vicar of Holy Trinity, Islington, an active member of the CMS Committee, was appointed to the see of Victoria. But W A Russell returned to Ningbo as Secretary for China, 'almost a quasi-bishop' with 'powers of superintendence', and less than five years later (December 15, 1872) he became the first missionary bishop for 'North China', including Ningbo.[4]

That Hudson Taylor should be affected by these events was coincidental. C R Alford reached Hong Kong in October 1867 and, with characteristic energy, within a year had visited every Anglican chaplain and missionary on the coast of China, the Yangzi river and at some treaty ports in Japan. At the beginning of March he was in Ningbo and Hangzhou to ordain the new arrivals (in 1867), H Gretton and J Bates, and to conduct confirmations. On or about March 4 he 'visited Mr Taylor and Party' and on the 11th wrote at length to his cousin Robert Baxter, who had given them a royal send-off from London in 1866 (Book 4, p 157). The form of Alford's letter implied that he had been requested to investigate the reports in circulation about the CIM. After little more than four months in his diocese and only weeks in treaty ports on the mainland so new to him, he could claim no personal knowledge or ability to judge by observation, so he noted the remarks of some missionaries whom he met and reported these. The form and content of his letter followed those of George Moule in 1867.

Doing his best to be fair, but faced with judging a situation from hearsay and a brief social call upon Hudson Taylor and his Hangzhou household, Alford commented on their zeal, potential and energy, but added, 'There is a very strong feeling in (the minds of Anglicans and Nonconformists) against the Mission!' He then repeated the familiar allegations of 'the autocracy of Mr Taylor' – 'hard dealing and there is no appeal!'; of scandalous housing arrangements; of novices engaging in pioneer work, 'prejudicial to the success of missions in general'; and of adoption of Chinese dress – 'considered absurd! and calculated to lower the missionaries in the presence of the Chinese.'

'I think there is some truth in these unfriendly criticisms,' he went on to say. 'Perhaps they are sometimes *unduly* pressed and magnified. But if the Taylor mission is to last and prosper, 1. Someone or more should be associated with him to bear the responsibility of the movement. 2. Even *Chinese* not to say English notions of propriety in reference to the familiar association of young men and women must be respected. 3. One member and that a very young member of the missionary body [Hudson Taylor], should respect the judgement and feelings of the body corporate. 4. Manifest peculiarities, perhaps *absurdities* should be avoided.'

This well-meaning report reached Robert Baxter in late April or May, when his friend Captain Fishbourne of the Far Eastern fleet (*see* Book 2, p 128; Personalia) became 'greatly incensed against' Hudson Taylor and at first declined to meet William Berger to hear the allegations answered.

At last they dined together and discussed the complaints, as outlined by William Berger to Hudson Taylor:

'1. The dwelling of the brethren and sisters under the same roof and with partitions of only half-inch board between the bedrooms.' – 'I replied that the (*Occasional Paper*) would show that the house No 1 has or had two wings and two staircases, the single men being in one wing and the females in the other, and that since obtaining house No 2 the single men had been removed thither.'

In a London drawing-room it all sounded unpardonably primitive. Had William Muirhead been present, as intended, he would have described the construction of not only Chinese houses but Asian homes throughout the tropical and subtropical regions, and the conditions in which foreigners tolerated reduced privacy for the sake of free ventilation from room to room – and still do in the late twentieth century.

'2. Your intimacy with and kissing the sisters.' – 'I explained the long intimacy between your family and yourself with Mr and Mrs Faulding and also spoke of how Miss Blatchley needed your protection, that these two were more like part of your own family and therefore the kiss upon retiring to rest was easily accounted for; that only under peculiar circumstances had you kissed some of the others and lastly that you and Mrs T had of your own accord thought it wise to desist from the practice, so far back as Jan. or Feb. 1867. . . . I said, "I have a copy of a letter, signed (I believe) by all the single sisters (save one, who was engaged to be married at the time), testifying to the purity of your life and manners and in every respect satisfactory."'

Mr and Mrs Faulding had invited the Bergers for the night, supporting them through this inquisition. Knowing the facts from Jennie as well as the Bergers, they were untroubled. To them the relationship between the Taylors, Jennie and Emily was wholly above board.

'3. (Your position as) "Pastor, medical man, Paymaster and something of Confessor."' This echo of Nicol was easily explained. Robert Baxter seemed satisfied, but to the Bergers' grief Captain Fishbourne continued to discuss the subject with his acquaintances. Hearing of the accusations, Dowager Lady Radstock asked for particulars and with Miss Waldegrave wrote to encourage the Bergers. 'The baptism of trial for the Mission in England seems fast drawing on, but we need not fear, so long as we are sincerely desiring to follow holiness and to please the Lord', wrote William Berger, closer to the truth than he realised.

'A soft answer'   *June 1868*

A few days after their consultation, Robert Baxter sent Mr Berger a copy of Bishop Alford's letter, and William Berger replied with a restrained memorandum, naming neither Lewis Nicol nor those he had misinformed. Nor did he mention those of other societies who supported Hudson Taylor in his policies and practice and had dissociated themselves from the allegations. More than a year had passed and here they were again confronted by the same objections from the same source. The bishop was only the latest one to take them up.

The complaint of autocratic direction by Hudson Taylor was not borne out by his correspondence, which showed instead a firmness tempered with friendliness and tolerance. 'Distinct and separate accommodation' had been Hudson Taylor's first concern in renting No 1 New Lane and in hiring boats. Chinese Christians had helped them to find and adapt the premises and, far from it being a scandal, no Chinese, Christian or otherwise, and no other missionaries in possession of the facts had taken exception to the arrangements. After long experience Hudson Taylor knew exactly how Chinese women travelled, and always provided for the comforts and privacy of his colleagues by separate covered quarters and usually a separate boat for the women. Any and all missionaries who left the treaty ports and the foreign coastal and Yangzi river steamers had no choice but to use '*native* boats'. This was only one of the skills (and delights) acquired by purposeful travellers. Every one of the early missionary pioneers had worked by 'itineration' – Burdon, Aitchison, Wylie, Edkins, Muirhead, Griffith John, Hudson Taylor and others. Missionaries who confined their lives and work to the treaty ports and lived in European style while waiting for China to open up would wait a long time. Pressure on Hudson Taylor to disperse his team was as strong as this criticism of his doing so. But the successful occupation of eight cities by these means, in spite of opposition, was already the answer – as the preaching of the gospel with the occupation of every province and hundreds of cities would in a few decades place it beyond challenge. In at least three of those eight cities (Taizhou, Wenzhou and Nanjing) 'no missionary or native assistant had ever been stationed'.

Bishop Alford had accepted the opinion of one school of thought about adapting to Chinese dress and ways. All Mr Berger said in comment was, 'A matter of opinion! Time will show who is wise as to this. The (late) Revd. W. C. Burns and others and the Roman Catholic Missionaries have worn the dress for many years and not seen ground for abandoning its use. Let every man be fully persuaded in his own mind.' He could have sent many pages on the subject. As for saying the CIM women looked like 'the disrespectable class', prostitutes and vagrants, this was echoing certain elements of the secular press. Both Hudson Taylor and Maria had answered it by detailing the way prostitutes customarily dressed – very different from the dress of Jennie and her friends.

The expression 'a very young member of the missionary body' did Hudson Taylor scant justice, for he was 36 and had already been a missionary for fourteen years, longer than any other in Ningbo or Hangzhou with the exception of Dr and Mrs D B McCartee (1844, 1852) and E C Lord (1847), and of W A Russell (1848) and F F Gough (1849), both in Britain on prolonged leave of absence. In the whole of China only twenty-eight others, including wives, of a total of 261 missionaries, had been longer in China – most of them by less than five years. By these standards Hudson Taylor was a veteran. He certainly longed and prayed for a colleague with the vision and ability to share the burden of leadership with him.

Without apology William Berger had ranged himself firmly alongside his embattled friend – and found himself stoutly backed by loyal supporters.[5]

News of the riot   *July–December 1868*

When he was in Ireland in July, William Berger spent an evening with his and Hudson Taylor's friends, including Henry Bewley, the Dublin printer of the *Occasional Paper*, himself an evangelist. The reports about Hangzhou had reached them and many others whom Berger named. He read Bishop Alford's report to them and explained it. 'They were quite satisfied and considered the affair just Satan raging and striving to overthrow (the Mission).' He also met John Houghton of Liverpool, who showed his confidence by sending two hundred pounds from his father and twenty from himself, generous sums at the time. The Grattan Guinnesses also rose to the occasion and declared they would give several weeks, if not months, to working for the CIM before moving to Paris for evangelism on the Continent.

William Pennefather had spoken up for the CIM at the popular Mildmay Conference. 'His confidence in you was unshaken. Dear Lord Radstock has not a moment's question as to your integrity, and he spoke out so . . . frankly. So did Lady Beauchamp and Sir Thomas . . . The Goughs expect to be in China by the end of January. . . . I do not think we ought to be discouraged, perhaps some few friends may not feel quite so warmly as they once did to the Mission, though I know of none. If there are such we can only expect this, on the other hand we have fresh friends.'

When news of the riots became known in Britain, a flood of sympathy and enquiries inundated the Bergers, who wrote, 'Our difficulties are as a feather in the scale compared with yours. . . . All minds are upon Yang-chau. The public papers, *Times*, *Telegraph* and others, have about a column and a half each upon the subject. . . .

'I received a letter from Mr Tarn of the (Religious) Tract Society [Maria's cousin] very strongly reflecting upon your having taken your wife and children and other females to Yang-chau.'

The next letter read, 'The excitement, indeed I may almost call it a storm, seems now bursting over us. The *Times* is very severe and incorrect in some things. Whether to reply to the false statements I scarcely know. I should not like to get into a paper war with its correspondent. Perhaps the Lord will put it into the hearts of some of His people to do so and it would come better from them than me.' He wrote all the same.

Criticism of Hudson Taylor over the Yangzhou riot led William

Scott of Dundee to write to George Müller for his opinion. But he sent the letter to William Berger to read and forward. In the light of new information from Maria and his own letter to *The Times*, Berger returned it to him, asking him to reconsider what he had said. When he wrote again to George Müller and received a reassuring reply, Scott sent a donation of fifty pounds in place of the twenty he had intended.

It was an incessant struggle. As criticism mounted on the Yang-zhou affair, even the Bergers could not disguise their fears that Hudson Taylor had brought it on himself.

> Many think your party was too large for commencing in a city and the property too much to have had there so early and that it might have been a temptation to the Chinese. Perhaps another time it might be well not to state the amount of property involved as it gives the idea that you urge redress and restitution. For myself I confess I felt it a difficult subject to form a judgment upon. Though I have to think it the most excellent way to take the spoiling of our goods joyfully if we can when we are really engaged in the Lord's service, and to flee from one city to another if the people will not allow us to remain in their midst. I do trust the Chinese will not identify the Lord's servants with the British guns or if they do, it may only be from our authorities not allowing any British subjects to be maltreated . . . [As for complaints about taking women and children there] I have stated that I conceive you must have thought it safe or you would not have taken your wife and children and two or three sisters with you. Yang-chau being so near (Zhenjiang) a free port you probably did not think any riots would arise.

So intense had the flood of correspondence become, that Mary Berger confessed in December, 'I seldom sleep more than half the night.' Pages of sympathy and admiration of the Taylors continued to flow from her pen, though she still thought they had appealed to the consul to intervene.

The first news of the riots had reached them all through the newspapers with their inaccuracies. Letters from China only came later. Mrs Faulding told Jennie,

> On Monday (October 19) your father had been dining in the city, when quite accidentally his eye was struck by the word China in the *Daily News* which was lying close to him, you may imagine what he felt on seeing Mr Taylor and Mr Reid's names in connection with the accounts of the dreadful outrages at Yang-chow. . . .

[November 5] Mr Berger felt obliged to send extracts from the letters to the . . . *Daily News* and *Revival* . . . (and) Mrs Berger wrote . . . to all who had relatives at Yang-chow.

[December 4] The Mission is going through the fires, not only from the persecution of enemies . . . (but from) the misrepresentations of those who should have been its truest friends. . . . Some of our English Papers are as usual blaming the missionaries, foreboding that a war will be the consequence. When I saw the leading article in the *Times* of yesterday, I sent it to Mr Landels requesting he would answer it which he has very kindly done and brought it on himself. . . . I, myself have written to the Editor of the *Daily Telegraph*. . . . The details in the (*Occasional Paper* No 15) are of thrilling interest, so many people are asking for them. . . .

[December 18] I trust war will not be the result. . . . Of course the Mission would be blamed and its enemies would rejoice.

Consul Medhurst's request for a naval squadron had received Sir Rutherford Alcock's approval and armed diplomacy in China was entering upon a new phase.

Who asked for gunboats?   *September–December 1868*

What appeared as isolated incidents involving merchants and missionaries in Taiwan, Huzhou, Zhenjiang and Yangzhou, assumed much greater significance for the men at the diplomatic helm in Peking. When *The Times* of December 1 echoed the Hong Kong and Shanghai newspaper headlines, 'Peace or War?' and wrote of real danger in this direction, it was not mere jingoism. Zeng Guofan, appointed Guardian of the Throne, though still at Nanjing, had humiliated Her Britannic Majesty's consul-general and had shown that a threat of force was necessary to negotiation if he was to talk seriously about the blatant injustices complained of. Furthermore, Prince Kong had failed to 'compel the local authorities to do justice' in Taiwan. A series of provocations had persuaded Lord Stanley (at the Foreign Office in London until December 9) and the minister plenipotentiary in Peking, to look for the right moment to make that show of force. China's response would decide which it was to be, peace or war. French Consul Canny's remark about 'secret orders' (p 108) explained the activity in Taiwan and on the Yangzi in September, October and November. British prestige was to be restored.

In Taiwan the whole Gaoxiong (ie Dagao) outrage against Catholics and Protestants involving Dr J L Maxwell and the death of a catechist had to be investigated. Finally, a proclamation must enjoin respect for Christianity and the rights of British citizens under the treaties of amity! The *daotai* did nothing.[6]

Acting-Consul Gibson's request for a gunboat was granted and the steam-sloop *Icarus*, Commander Lord Charles Scott, proceeded to Tainan. Thereupon consul and gunboat commander 'grasped the opportunity to demand a settlement of all outstanding grievances' in Taiwan. On August 21 the commander conveyed to the *daotai* at Tainan an ultimatum for the righting of outstanding wrongs. The *daotai* himself held the monopoly of the camphor trade and was unwilling for the British to trade in camphor. A Mr Pickering of Ellis and Company had been fired on by a company of soldiers and his cargo seized. His Chinese agent's son had been imprisoned. A certain Tinhai had stabbed a Mr Hardy. The murderer of the Presbyterian catechist must be brought to trial.

Then on September 22 Acting-Consul Gibson reported three ambuscades, by sixty or seventy men armed with spears and knives, upon himself and the 'Senior Naval Officer', 'with the object of killing' them. Sir Rutherford Alcock urged Consul Swinhoe to travel at once to the scene. A landing party under a young lieutenant overreacted, seizing the forts at Anping (the port of Tainan), killing twenty-one and wounding as many defending soldiers. On the strength of this act of war the consul and naval commander also went too far, obtaining 40,000 dollars in cash to guarantee satisfaction of their demands, 5,000 dollars as indemnity for the coal and ammunition expended, and 5,000 more, purely as prize money. Their superiors were alarmed. 'My Lords view with extreme disapproval these pecuniary demands', the Admiralty reported to the Foreign Office. Lord Stanley agreed and repudiated them, and also other exactions to indemnify the Catholic and Protestant missions.

Admiral Sir Harry Keppel blamed the consul and complained to Sir Rutherford and the Admiralty of these 'reprehensible actions' and in 1869 'of the frequency with which consuls requisitioned for gunboats, "inconsistent with strict international law towards the Chinese"'. But where armed diplomacy ended and unlawful coercion began was not apparent, for by then the greater coercion of the great Zeng Guofan, Viceroy of the Two Jiangs at Nanjing, had taken place.[7]

The terms imposed at Tainan were repudiated, but 'in the end all who could be punished were punished, and all who could be compensated were compensated'. It took Lord Clarendon – after the change of government in Britain – to denounce all these 'rash and inexcusable warlike acts'. But as late as December, British and other foreign residents were still being molested by people under the authority of the same *daotai*. Modification of the severe initial demands appeared to have been interpreted as another climb-down, another humiliation.

In contrast, in the north of Taiwan, at Danshui and 'Banka', the 'silent pressure' of the presence of a gunboat ensured the return of the merchants. On September 30, 1868, the highest regional mandarin in Taiwan assured Dodd and Company (p 57) that there would be no impediment to their return to 'Banka', from where they had been evicted. Two representatives of the firm moved in. A mob of 500 thereupon 'brutally ill-treated them' and seized the premises. The British consul refused to act without the support of gunboats, and 'under their silent pressure, but without the overt exercise of force, he obtained complete satisfaction of his demands'. His superiors approved his action, Lord Clarendon commenting, 'He has succeeded in obtaining redress without employing force'.[8] But the house in 'Banka' had to be given up, and for thirty years no foreigner was allowed to live actually in the town. Instead the merchants 'fired and packed' Formosa tea a mile downstream – and a larger, more prosperous town grew up around them. Again on December 6, two Taiwan merchants named Bird and Kerr were mobbed and severely injured. Even so, 'obtaining redress without employing force' won Lord Clarendon's approval.

On the mainland Medhurst's dealings with Zeng Guofan were accompanied by more trouble on the Yangzi. In October some missionaries were 'constantly being stoned' in the streets of Wuchang, so on the 29th Consul G W Caine sent a dispatch to the senior naval officer on the Yangzi, Captain Heneage, urgently requesting a gunboat. He sensed that the new mood had been 'brought about I have no doubt by the Yangchow affair'. But Hankou and Wuchang were hundreds of miles farther up the great river. With a 3- or 4-knot current to overcome, HMS *Dove* had previously taken a month to get there and another gunboat had had to be towed by a more powerful river steamer. After all the dust of these riots and counteraction had settled, Sir Rutherford Alcock sent a dispatch to Consul Caine, putting his request into perspective but exposing a diplomatic volte-face on his own part. With the disturbances of a very serious nature at Taiwan requiring the immediate presence of more than one ship-of-war, and the necessity of so distributing the force available for all exigencies from Singapore to Hakodate, it was 'quite obvious' that the navy could not respond to minor provocations. And then, illogically, 'If the missionaries cannot carry on their labours peaceably and without an appeal to force for their protection, it seems very doubtful how far HM Government will hold themselves justified in resorting to measures of a warlike character for their protection away from the ports.' But in Taiwan, Yangzhou and Wuchang it had been, not missionaries but, 'consuls (who) requisitioned for gunboats'.

This change of stance in January 1869, to putting blame on the missionaries, was new to the situation and part of the political manoeuvring occasioned by Lord Clarendon's return to the Foreign Office in place of Lord Stanley. To the end of 1868 Sir Rutherford had himself been carrying out Lord Stanley's policy, but a sequence of excesses by his subordinates, extending into the new year proved too embarrassing for him.

A matter of face[9]   *October–November 1868*

Consul Medhurst's report on his rebuff at Nanjing (p 122) reached Sir Rutherford Alcock at Peking late in September (three months before Lord Clarendon took office). Alcock acted at once. As minister plenipotentiary he was free to take decisions within his brief from Whitehall and must answer for them. He agreed that armed persuasion was needed on the Yangzi and asked 'that grand old man Admiral Sir Harry Keppel' to mount a squadron for the purpose. On October 12 he reported to Lord Stanley that Viceroy Zeng Guofan had 'turned a deaf ear to all remonstrances' from the moment of HMS *Rinaldo*'s departure and he, Alcock, was therefore asking the commander-in-chief to send a force to Zhenjiang to resort if necessary to determined pressure. The Yangzi authorities, he explained, 'have long shown a great disposition to treat with neglect all complaints, and either to invite or tacitly connive at popular violence and hostility towards foreigners, to the regret, I believe, of the Central Government and, to all appearances, without regard to their instructions'.

Sir Rutherford proposed to blockade the mouths of the vital Grand Canal where it crossed the Yangzi, and even to seize a high official. 'But whatever be the means, recent occurrences in Formosa, at Yangchow and at (Zhenjiang), have plainly shown the necessity for decisive action. . . . The popular outbreak at (Zhen-jiang) [against the *daotai* and consulates] is nothing but an extension of the violent attacks on inoffensive missionaries at Yang-chow. . . .' In view of the turn of the political tide as the year ended, his phrase 'inoffensive missionaries' is to be noted. He applauded Medhurst for his firmness and the moderation of his demands, and secured the agreement of Prince Kong and the Zongli Yamen to a full inquiry at Yangzhou. Peking even welcomed action to curb this powerful viceroy who thought little of being out of tune with the Court.[10]

On October 13 the East gate of Shanghai city was placarded with anonymous posters of the familiar type, about children being kidnapped for gruesome purposes. Immediate action by the French consul-general induced the Shanghai *daotai* to have the offensive placards torn down and to substitute a counter-proclamation strongly condemning them. Then the *North China Herald* carried news of the appointment of a new viceroy, to succeed Zeng Guofan as soon as he had settled the Yangzhou and Zhenjiang affairs. The fact that he was Ma Xinyi, the friendly Muslim governor of Zhe-jiang, boded well for peace on the Yangzi, however much he would be missed at Hangzhou.[11]

The regulation that foreigners must report negotiations for the rental or purchase of premises was peculiar to Zeng Guofan's jurisdiction, the *Herald* maintained, imposed by him to impede the progress of missionaries. The paper also published a three-column protest by an enlightened anonymous 'Spectator' against pressing the Chinese authorities too hard. The fault lay not with Zeng Guofan, he suggested, but strictly with his friends at Yangzhou. Enemies must not be made through insensitive blunders. The wording of an engraved stone tablet about the riots would hold the key to future tranquillity. 'We ought to take care that the guilty only are punished, and do anything rather than awaken the anger of the well-meaning populace, a result that would certainly occur if we compelled them to erect a tablet to their own disgrace.' The tablet should not even refer to the riot. 'Face' mattered supremely. How true this was, would soon be demonstrated.

W H Medhurst left Shanghai on November 3 for Zhenjiang. On the sixth a full squadron of three steam-sloops, *Rinaldo*, *Icarus* and *Argus*, and two gunboats, *Dove* and *Slaney*, escorting HMS *Rodney*, 'steam line of battle', flagship of Sir Harry Keppel, arrived there on the way to Nanjing with 700 men-at-arms aboard. The issue was no longer the right of missionaries to reside unmolested in inland cities. As the *Times* correspondent put it, 'The case has now grown beyond a mere question of reparation for injuries sustained. Our political prestige has been injured and must be recovered'.[12] The *North China Herald* went further. 'We hope for the sake of the Chinese themselves, that they will yield to what is asked, and not awake the seventy-eight guns of the *Rodney*.' '(Zeng Guofan) may find the British lion unmuzzled, if he waits at Nanking till the *Rodney* gets up.' For this kind of arrogance Britain and the Chinese Church are still paying the price in the late twentieth century.

During October the viceroy had not only cashiered the offending prefect and magistrate of Yangzhou but had degraded by three degrees the Salt Commissioner, a mandarin of higher rank. He himself expected to evade another confrontation with Consul Medhurst by leaving Nanjing to take up his new post as viceroy of Zhili. However, both a memorial from the Zongli Yamen to the emperor on the subject of foreign missions and religious freedom, and the emperor's response (published by the *North China Herald*), although ill-informed, were moderate and conciliatory in tone. Both called upon Zeng Guofan to complete the settlement of matters under his jurisdiction before leaving Nanjing to take up his new viceroyalty.

Zeng Guofan had therefore delayed his departure. But great preparations were being made. 'It is expected that (he) will be escorted at least as far as Yangchow . . . by such a following of Mandarins as never before accompanied a viceroy. He had always been popular with his subordinates.' Zeng's crowning glory, however, was to be a 'handsome new steamship' of his own in which to travel, the *Tien-chi*, with a foreign captain. The *daotais* of Shanghai and Zhenjiang and the prefect of Suzhou were being taken up to Nanjing in her, to help in the negotiations.

Leaving HMS *Dove* at Zhenjiang to survey the Grand Canal, the naval squadron proceeded to Nanjing on November 9 and Consul Medhurst marched with an escort and appropriate ceremony to the viceroy's palace. There he presented Zeng with an ultimatum simply reiterating the original demands rejected in September.

Consul Medhurst was not a man to be trifled with. An officer and men boarded the *Tien-chi*, anchored near by, with a message from Captain Heneage of *Rodney* informing the ship's captain that it was now 'attached' to the squadron. He was not to weigh anchor without orders, on pain of having a prize crew placed in charge. He at once went to inform the viceroy and returned saying that 'the effect of this seizure was electrical'. When Zeng Guofan was told at six p m what had happened, his face had 'changed colour violently'. This blow at his personal prestige was intolerable. 'There was a general explosion of rage.' But he was helpless. He yielded unconditionally to all Medhurst's terms.

Together Zeng and the viceroy-designate, Ma Xinyi, confirmed the capitulation in a 'conjoint letter' and issued a proclamation that foreigners were not to be opposed; and on the 12th Ma was entertained on *Rodney*. Leaving one warship to hold the *Tien-chi*, the squadron returned to Zhenjiang the same day, and with his immediate reinstatement at Yangzhou decided upon, Hudson Taylor was invited to dine on *Rodney* on the 14th. The *Times* correspondent's comment voiced the general belief that the court at Peking would be secretly glad that Zeng Guofan had been humiliated. For in Alicia Bewicke Little's view 'Everyone at that time was full of the idea that (Zeng) and Li [Li Hongzhang] together could become masters of Central China.'[13] Too powerful and too influential, he had largely taken to doing as he wished. His antagonism to foreigners was only a case in point, at variance with the current policy of the Zongli Yamen.

Although Yangzhou was the main issue, W H Medhurst had also finally settled the two Zhenjiang disputes. The authority of the friendly Ying *daotai* had been established against the opposition of the Manchus and the defiant magistrate, and the parties to exactions and outrages, including torture, against British merchants and their Chinese employees at the customs barrier were brought to book.

The reinstatement   *November 1868*

Hudson Taylor had been told to hold himself in readiness to attend a consular court on November 15. This may have been a briefing on the return to Yangzhou, but it appears that a formal hearing of evidence before a high-ranking grain commissioner and the *daotai* of Shanghai took place in Yangzhou city itself on the 17th. While the squadron was at Nanjing, the commander of *Dove* had made soundings of the Grand Canal for sixty miles north from Guazhou, to see how far gunboats could safely go. On the 16th both gunboats, *Dove* and *Slaney* escorted Consul Medhurst to Yangzhou with between three and four hundred marines and sailors and some fieldpieces, and anchored off the East Gate. Duncan, Rudland, Reid and W G Stronach, an interpreter in the consular service, travelled independently in the Mission boat. Stronach's father had been the closest friend of Maria's father before his tragic death in 1843 (Book 1, p 280). Sentries took command of the gate and the marines were conducted 'to the Temple of Ten Thousand Genii'. A Catholic priest (Sechinger?) described the occasion.

> Mr Medhurst . . . and Mr Taylor are taken solemnly through the streets to a large pagoda to accommodate 400 men. Literati with buttons precede the retinue of mandarins. The two ringleaders had been arrested; the others, by joining the procession, gave the necessary satisfaction to foreigners. Two heralds at the head announced to the people in the streets, 'People – take care not to hurt the foreigners; or to call them "foreign devils"; but give them the titles of great men.' Mr Taylor is taken back to his house, perfectly repaired at the expense of the mandarins.

But the Yangzhou officials had once again taken the troops through minor streets, so Medhurst and the naval commander mounted a full parade the following day. Marching across the whole breadth of the city by the main streets from the East Gate to the parade ground outside the West Gate, they staged two grand exercises, firing their field guns to impress the populace.

In the presence of the Chinese commissioners the case against the prefect, magistrates and literati was then investigated, as a preliminary to ensuring that all Medhurst's demands were met in full. When Rudland was faced with the murderous plunderer who had twice tried to kill him on the night of the riot, he could not be mistaken. The ringleader Koh was harder to identify, until as Interpreter Stronach informed Medhurst, 'He broke out into a long and incoherent appeal for mercy which had at least the effect of enabling the missionaries to announce, if possible, more confidently the identity of the man, as his voice and manner irresistibly recalled the impressions of the night of terror.' The leading member of the literati, ex-viceroy Yen of Canton was declared absent, so Medhurst held 6,000 taels against his arrest, and demanded as a formality that the new prefect and magistrate be dismissed if he were not apprehended within two months.

Medhurst had had twenty-seven years of experience in consular service, some of it as a youth while his famous missionary father was still living. He knew that the real culprits behind the riot would be difficult if not impossible to bring to justice. A proclamation by the viceroys denouncing the previous prefect and magistrates and the leaders of the riot, also announced the impending return of Hudson Taylor and his party.

> Be it known to all that British subjects have liberty to go into the interior without let or hindrance as clearly stated in the Treaty ratified by the Emperor. . . . Hereafter should anyone insult, hinder or annoy (British subjects) they shall be immediately seized and severely punished. No mercy shall be shown them. Tremble at this![14]

When he had done all he could, Medhurst reported to Alcock on November 20 and 26 that it was not found possible to bring evidence to bear upon the gentry for their complicity in the attacks. It was more than any man's life was worth to testify against them. Alcock protested at this but nothing more could be done.[15]

Justice for the Chinese victims of the riot was as much part of Medhurst's demands as for the foreigners. When on the consul's insistence during his September visit to Yangzhou the Taylors' landlord had been released from prison, a pack of 'yamen runners' had been set on him to persecute and ruin him. Mr Peng the innkeeper had also been 'utterly ruined'. Seven or eight yamen runners had dogged his footsteps day and night. 'They lived upon him, smoked opium at his expense, took possession of his house and property. . . . Six weeks ago he was a prosperous and independent man; at present he is an utter beggar . . . simply because he was friendly towards foreigners.'

The inquiry over, the financial losses by the Chinese and missionaries all agreed and reparations settled, Hudson Taylor was formally reinstated at his house on November 18. Consul Medhurst announced that the whole Mission party, including the women, were invited to return, and summarised the indemnities paid to them as 1,128.40 taels for losses by them and their servants, including further repair to the premises, 500 taels in compensation for their injuries, and 197.75 taels to the landlord and carpenter, in all 1,826.15 taels. He had earlier advised Hudson Taylor not to take the women back there until later. With renewed confidence he now asked him to do so at once, knowing full well that Maria's confinement was due at any time. They all returned on November 23, and on the 29th her baby, Charles Edward, was born. On December 1 she wrote to Mary Berger,

Last Sunday, in the very room from which . . . after seeing Mr
Rudland twice nearly murdered – I had with Miss Blatchley . . . to
take what might have been to my [unborn] infant, not only to myself,
a *death-leap* – . . . God had given me the desire of my heart . . . that
if safety to myself and my infant permitted, I would rather it were
born in this city, in this house, in this room, than in any other
place – your own beautiful spare room . . . not excepted.

They gave the baby the Chinese name of Tianbao, 'protected by
Heaven', as a testimony to the miracle of his survival. But ever since
the riot she herself had been frail and ill. She believed that with her
'chest so weak lately', the sentence of death was upon her. Sir
Rutherford Alcock, himself a surgeon, wrote to Consul Medhurst:
'Now that the medical certificate is before me, I see that three of the
party, Mrs Taylor, Miss Blatchley and Mr Rudland (p 119) have
suffered permanent and serious injury. Money, unfortunately, can
afford no adequate compensation for injuries which cause permanent and disabling effects.' At the time it was thought that Henry
Reid's eye had recovered, but in fact he had suffered the most
serious lasting injury, eventually losing the sight of that and probably of both eyes.[16] 'I do not think 500 taels at all adequate,' Sir
Rutherford continued, 'and have to instruct you to make a demand
of 2,000 taels, to be equally divided among the three already
named.' Sir Rutherford also addressed Prince Kong in unam-
biguous terms, defending the peaceful and good behaviour of the
missionaries (including Dr J L Maxwell of Tainan), and declined to
admonish them to cause no offence, as the Prince had suggested.

An engraved stone tablet was erected at the street entrance to the
CIM premises, making no mention of the riot. Forward-looking, it
referred only to the right of foreigners to live there in peace and to
propagate their religion, a generously face-saving show of wisdom
on the consul's part which the people of Yangzhou did not fail to
note. When all was over, Hudson Taylor wrote to him saying
'We feel the more grateful for these measures, because they will
facilitate, as we believe, not only our own work in Yangchow,
(Zhenjiang) and Nanking, but Christian missions generally
throughout the interior of China.' In his *Summary of Operations of
the China Inland Mission* (1872) he had more to say.

It is, perhaps, also due to the members of the Mission to state, that of
the indemnity claimed on our behalf by the British Government,
more than half was for Chinese whose property had suffered in the

disturbance; and that all that was for the missionaries themselves was handed over by them to form a fund for the furtherance of God's work in Yangchau.

In June 1888, Hudson Taylor recalled the events at Yangzhou and Zhenjiang with these observations on the lessons to be learned 'from this and similar experiences'.

> One was to be longer known in a city through itinerant visits before renting houses and attempting to settle in them. Another was not to take much luggage to a newly-opened station. . . . A third was, not to commence work with too strong a staff, and not to attempt to open contiguous stations simultaneously. . . . The lessons learnt there have . . . enabled us since peacefully to open many cities in remote parts of China.
>
> 'There is no command to open mission stations, in the Word of God, and there is no precedent to be found there. The commands to evangelize, to go into all the world to preach the Gospel to every creature, and the examples recorded in the New Testament of the methods of the early workers, might have led us from the first to give itineration a greater prominence than we did. It must be admitted that stations become necessary to some extent; the itinerant work of the Church cannot be carried on without them. It is, however, a grave mistake to make location our first aim, instead of keeping it in a strictly subordinate position as auxiliary; in proof of which, one notorious fact may be adduced – namely, that the best spiritual work in connection with all missions is to be found in out-stations at a distance, rather than at the station where the missionary resides.[17]

Alexander Michie in his memoir of Sir Rutherford Alcock, *The Englishman in China*, was to write in 1900, 'For the last thirty years Yangchow has been the most peaceable missionary field in the whole empire.' In 1868, however, another major riot, the success of itinerant evangelism and the fundamental value of these foci of the Chinese church a little remote from the foreign missionary, had first to be experienced. With 1870, a new era of the expansion of the CIM was entered upon. Casting the seed, and the net, widespread, with a minimal intrusion of foreignness upon the Chinese, became the aim and practice – while consolidation of the resulting churches in settled situations followed as a matter of course.

Viceroy Zeng Guofan's steamship (p 155) was released on November 26. He promptly handed his seal of office to Ma Xinyi and left Nanjing. An unnamed source quoted at length in *Li Hung-chang*:

His Life and Times[18] described Zeng Guofan's departure. 'On the 15th December the all but Imperial Tseng Kwo-fan left the city which he had so long ruled more like a king than a viceroy. . . . All along the road . . . altars, with candles and incense burning, had been erected; and . . . the people again and again bowed down and worshipped him as if he had been a god.'

By December 2 Consul Medhurst and his staff had returned to Shanghai and, not yet having received his minister's demand for higher compensation for the injured, on the 8th he declared the Yangzhou affair ended. A Christian himself, he had treated the missionaries throughout with sympathy and concern. To thank him Hudson Taylor asked William Berger to send as soon as possible the best calf-bound edition of the Bible he could obtain.

Anqing and Anhui next   *December 1868*

The end of the era of opposition to foreigners by literati under the patronage of the old school of viceroys was approaching, but still far from over. Li Hongzhang remained viceroy of Hubei and Hunan, but he was young and well acquainted with foreign ways and power. Under Ma Xinyi as viceroy of Jiangsu, Jiangxi and Anhui, the prospect for peace between the nations was better than it had ever been. The prospect for peaceful penetration by the CIM had therefore suddenly blossomed. With homes assured at last at Zhenjiang for the Rudlands and the printing-presses, and at Yangzhou for the Taylors' administrative centre, nothing stood in the way of the advance they had begun in April. The Judds were to come to Yangzhou to understudy the Taylors in planting a local church and to support Maria whenever Hudson Taylor's duties took him away. And other young missionaries were to join them from time to time, beginning with Edward Fishe.[19]

Three weeks after the birth of Charles Edward, weeks spent in distributing the reparations to his landlord and other Chinese, and restoring the premises to their former state, Hudson Taylor left Yangzhou again, on November 16. He had hoped to visit every station of the Mission from Nanjing to Wenzhou, but instead was at Nanjing over Christmas, to launch the pioneers of Anhui on their way and then to travel alone until March. Meadows and Williamson were to reconnoitre Anqing on the north shore of the Yangzi. They left Nanjing on December 26, eventually to gain an uncertain footing in the city after months of hard work against determined opposition. Briefly returning to Yangzhou, Hudson Taylor was away again on December 28 to meet Alexander Wylie in Shanghai and learn all he could from him about Sichuan, South Shaanxi and Hubei before he sailed for Britain.

Maria had Louise Desgraz and the Judds with her, but life in Yangzhou was far from plain sailing. In asking the Judds to come to Yangzhou Hudson Taylor had said, 'I do not hide it from you, that it will be exceedingly dangerous, the people threaten to kill the first Europeans that go in, and they have banded themselves together to do it, but God will protect you.' Judd recalled:

> For some weeks after we arrived, the shutters of our house were stoned night after night – battered and shattered with stones. We were stoned or mobbed nearly every time we went out on the street. My wife was once delivered marvellously from a mob by two Chinese soldiers coming up just in time and they brought her home. Later on I escaped from a mob of probably 2000 or 3000 people who were stoning me, by going on my pony across a narrow plank over a brook.[20]

All was otherwise well in Yangzhou. The fact that they had been able to open both a boys' and a girls' school indicated confidence among their neighbours. Better still, three Chinese were asking for baptism and several were interested, including Mr Peng the inn-keeper. Because Judd needed more exercise but could not afford a pony, Hudson Taylor himself had 'bought a good one' and asked Judd to keep it exercised for him when he himself was away on his travels. Not until long afterwards did Judd discover that Hudson Taylor had never intended to use it himself.

In this one year of difficulty Jinhua had been lost, Wenzhou, Suzhou, Zhenjiang and Yangzhou had been occupied. Ninghai and other outstations had been opened in Zhejiang. Qingjiangpu had been reconnoitred and, boldest step of all, Anqing was being attempted. To the friends who believed in him Hudson Taylor was indomitable, but to Sir Rutherford Alcock and many critics he was only incorrigible – as the coming year was to show.

CHAPTER FIVE

'THE DEVIL'S GROWL'
1869

The gunboats go too far[1]   *January 1869*

Commander Bush's successful vindication of his action in September 1868 expressed, if it did not initiate, a change of mind in the Foreign Office in London. His indignation that the ship under his command should be used to coerce a viceroy of the Chinese empire, on the word of a consul and not of his own admiral or the minister-plenipotentiary, illuminated the whole scene of gunboat diplomacy. While Lord Stanley's policy in China was not belligerent, he approved of Sir Rutherford Alcock's preference for prompt, decisive action on the right occasions. But even he, on December 1, the day before Disraeli's government fell, pacifically advocated that all cases be dealt with by the minister and decisions by the Peking government be carried in the *Peking Gazette* for Chinese officials to see. Mellowed from his headstrong early days, Alcock remained formidable. His consuls followed his lead, successfully in W H Medhurst's case, leading eventually to his own knighthood and elevation to minister, but disastrously where misjudgment by inexperienced men led to excess.

The tardiness of communications made consultation between even consuls and minister difficult at any time. Because of *fengshui* (Book 4, Appendix 8) the telegraph was not being installed in China. With cables taking at least two weeks between Peking and London, because of the need to send a message by courier to Kiakhta in Russian Manchuria for dispatch by trans-Siberian cable, Sir Rutherford could only seek approval if no great urgency existed. Written reports still took two months by the fast 'overland' route. News of the Anping ultimatum on August 21 and the Yangzhou riots on the 22nd and 23rd reached London in October. Comment came back in December. Sir Rutherford's dispatch to Lord Stanley of September 11 reached him on November 30. His request to the Admiral in October for a show of naval strength on the Yangzi would not have been on the Foreign Minister's desk until December. The change of government in Britain on December 9 and Lord Clarendon's 'conversion' through Anson Burlingame's diplomacy, could have no direct effect in China until two months after Lord Clarendon declared his policy on December 28. Events in China during January and February 1869 were still governed by the consuls' understanding of policy as it had been in 1868.

When Lord Clarendon commented to Alcock on January 14, 1869, 'I consider Mr Medhurst to have acted very rightly,' for limiting his coercion to a show of force without its use, he also rebuked Sir Rutherford for sending a naval squadron to Nanjing and risking war without consulting Her Majesty's Government. Sir Rutherford barely knew by then of a change of Foreign Secretary, let alone of a new policy. The action in October for which he was being rebuked had been in keeping with Lord Stanley's directives. Consultation with Anson Burlingame, Lord Clarendon said, had shown how the whole matter could have been handled through the central government at Peking in a friendly manner. 'Provincial governors are too often in the habit of disregarding the rights of foreigners,' he had protested to Burlingame. But Burlingame had confirmed the wisdom of Lord Stanley's dispatch of December 1 – as if the effectiveness of the fiat of Peking could be counted on where men like Zeng Guofan chose to differ. It could not. They were a law to themselves. Distance and delays were too great for proper consultation.

On January 28 another dispatch from Lord Clarendon signalled the end of the era of high-handed action by consuls, gunboats and even Her Majesty's minister-plenipotentiary. In future all such matters *must* be referred by consuls to the ministers in Peking for reference to the Zongli Yamen, and if necessary to London. But even before this order could reach the consuls, two more outrages had been perpetrated in the name of British prestige.

The first was relatively mild. A certain Revd Wolfe, a missionary at Fuzhou, bought land on Sharp Peak Island on which to build a holiday cottage or 'sanitarium'. When a local Chinese gentleman stirred up the people to prevent him from doing so, he asked the consul to help. The consul called upon the commander of HMS *Janus* to intervene, and on January 20 an armed force overawed the villagers by destroying the instigator's house – whereupon terms were signed to permit Wolfe to proceed with erecting his own 'place of coolness'.[2]

The second incident was more serious. By the treaty of 1858 and the Peking Convention two other cities became open ports – the city of Chaozhou, near Chao'an (where William Burns had been arrested), and its deep-water port of Shantou (Swatow) 'with a reputation for piracy and turbulence'. In January 1869 the American consul was stoned at a large village or market-town called 'Aotingpow' in the Admiralty reports, 'notorious for its hostility to foreigners'. A few days later, on the 20th, boats from the gunboat HMS *Cockchafer* exercising on the river were stoned from the same place. Men landing to demand an explanation were fired on and ten were wounded.

Consul Challoner Alabaster saw his opportunity to settle at the same time some trade disputes. While Admiral Sir Harry Keppel consulted the viceroy of Canton, the naval commander at Hong Kong lost no time in sailing with four warships to Shantou, landed men on January 29 to attack 'Aotingpow', set fire to the villages the force passed through, and 'by sunset a great part of the town' of from seven to ten thousand inhabitants 'was destroyed', at the price of six men slightly wounded.

The navy protested at being used so freely and when Lord Clarendon's firm statement of policy reached Peking at the end of February the practice of 'isolated acts of coercion . . . on the initiative of the consul' originated by Sir Rutherford himself twenty-three years ago, had to end. The 'vicious circle of irritation and repression' was broken. In response to Sir Rutherford's claim that 'relations with China had never been more satisfactory', Lord Clarendon made the surprising pre-judgment and admission, 'The injudicious proceedings of missionaries in China, the violence engendered by them on the part of the Chinese authorities and people, and the excessive and unauthorised acts of retaliation to which British consular and, at their requisition, the naval authorities had resorted, were indeed sufficient to cause Her Majesty's Government to look forward with apprehension to the intelligence which each succeeding mail might bring.'[3]

This state of mind – blaming missionaries but not merchants or others – was to influence public opinion in Britain and add to the Bergers' and Taylors' discomfort. As for the Clarendon policy, Hosea Ballou Morse concluded, 'It is noteworthy, that for some years to come, there were almost no acts of violence committed against English mission stations, while those against the Roman

Catholic missionaries, under the protection of France, increased in number and gravity.'[4]

If relative peace was restored, it was only relative. Not until the latter half of the 1870s did atrocities cease for a while and foreigners of any nation feel safe. 'Almost no acts of violence against English stations' was cold comfort to young men and women scattered hundreds of miles apart, intent only on peacefully sharing their own knowledge of the gospel with the Chinese around them.

A growl – in the press   *January–March 1869*

For the present the action was over; Yangzhou was quiet and Hudson Taylor was away on his five-month tour of the Zhejiang cities. But the recriminations had begun – in Spurgeon's phrase, the devil's growl. Hearsay news of the riot had reached London in October through the China papers and the *Times* correspondent's articles in November and December. His news of the Yangzhou settlement followed in the January 21 issue. Criticism of Hudson Taylor had begun on the assumption that he had appealed for consular intervention, quickly exaggerated to asking for gunboats (a canard as alive today as then). W H Medhurst's first dispatch had mistakenly supported the myth of an appeal. But as late as mid-January the Bergers were writing of mails having gone astray and vital information being denied them. He dared not draw upon himself the attention of the press until he had facts to go on, but at Mrs Faulding's request William Landels, minister of the fashionable Regent's Park Chapel, had written on December 4 to the Editor of *The Times*.

> So far from 'finding the people as well as the authorities dead against them . . . first in one city, then in another', in which they have tried to 'force their way', (the China Inland Mission) have succeeded in opening mission stations in various cities of the interior. . . . [Miss Faulding] who went out from my church (and) is now in (Hangzhou), is known in every part of the city and has never had a rude word addressed to her. The people invite her to their houses, and press their hospitality on her to an extent which proves often embarrassing.
>
> Mr Taylor is the last man to seek to involve his country in hostilities with the Chinese on any ground whatsoever. It was not his wish that a 'gunboat' should appear on the scene.[5]

That was true, so far as it went, but Joseph Tarn's objections to Hudson Taylor's taking women and children to Yangzhou were shared by others and the reasons were still not known. Nor why so many had congregated there. In the *Occasional Paper* William Berger bemoaned the missing mail, but fell into the trap of believing newspaper reports of 'the appeal made by Mr Taylor to HBM's Consul'.

'The diplomatic action which has resulted, the peremptory demand for redress and compensation, and the demonstration of force, must not be attributed solely to Mr Taylor's request for protection.' Meanwhile in China, neither Hudson Taylor nor Maria mentioned the subject in their letters, having no inkling that the facts had been misrepresented. By December 18 many were fearing war as a consequence of Sir Rutherford Alcock sending a naval squadron to Nanjing. What was Hudson Taylor's 'foolhardiness' leading the nation into? Another 'typhoon' was 'bursting over' the Mission.

When Lord Clarendon at last received (in January) the dispatch detailing the strong action taken by Medhurst and the squadron in November, he censured his minister in Peking. In future 'the active interference of H.M. naval forces should only be had recourse to in cases of sudden emergency or of immediate danger to lives and property'. Then followed the withdrawal of powers from Alcock; when once any matter had been referred from the scene of action to him in Peking, it must be referred to the Foreign Office for a decision whether to use force in support of diplomatic pressure![6] But how could the minister in Peking convey in a dispatch all the intricacies of dealing with an international incident involving people like Ci Xi (the Empress Dowager), Prince Kong and Zeng Guofan? How could he bring home to British statesmen accustomed to European diplomacy the contrasting character of dealings with the Peking court? A new era had begun. The minister's hands were badly tied. But the era of overbearing action by consuls had to end, and Lord Clarendon had ended it by one clear order.

Strong expressions of opinion on the whole question of consular support for missionaries, both for and against, naturally proliferated as news of Taiwan, Yangzhou, Fuzhou, Hankou and elsewhere hit the headlines. But the authorities had done a great and lasting disservice to missions and to the Church in China by using the Yangzhou episode to serve their own predetermined ends.

As late as February 11, William Berger was writing to Hudson

Taylor of Mrs John Eliot Howard 'thinking you did call in British men-of-war'. 'Will you kindly send me word whether you sent for the gunboat. . . ?' At the same time, Jennie was writing to her parents,

> I wonder whether this will be the last time Mr T's movements will excite world-wide notice? Perhaps not, for I have often heard him say that it is his impression that in seeking to spread the truth he will lose his life by violent means. He longs to go forward now more than ever and is hoping that the end of this year may find him in (Sichuan).
>
> Mr Medhurst having learned all particulars of the steps taken in Yangchau, said to Mr T, 'Well, I think you have done all that any man could do. There is nothing in your actions here that I would have had otherwise, except it be that I think the ladies should have been moved at an earlier period.' When Mr T explained that he had nowhere to send them to and that . . . it was at (the ladies') request that the thought of removing them was abandoned, then Mr Medhurst said, 'Under those circumstances you were quite justified in the course you have taken.'

A growl – in the Lords[7]   *March 1869*

Hudson Taylor and the China Inland Mission had been in the unwelcome limelight of debate, of criticism and of abuse for two years over the Hangzhou allegations, and for six months over the Yangzhou riot. All that had gone before now paled into shadow under the glare of an attack by the Duke of Somerset in the House of Lords on March 9, 1869. In an astonishing and 'most lamentable display of ignorance on the part of some of the members of that noble body' he led the 'anti-missionary sentiment' in a speech beginning by naming the China Inland Mission correctly and asking, 'what right have we to send missionaries to the interior of China?'

To the amazement of many he then described Hong Xiuquan, the fanatic Taiping rebel leader and his hordes, linking missionaries with them, and continuing, 'It is most unjust that the English naval power should be used to support them.' When he protested that 'every missionary almost requires a gunboat' the noble lords laughed, but he pressed on, 'The fact is, we are propagating Christianity with gunboats, for the authorities of inland towns know perfectly well that if they get into trouble with the missionary a gunboat will soon come up. They turn the French missionary out of the town, and they knock the English one on the head; so that there is perfect religious equality. We ought, I contend, to recall these inland missionaries.' His unfactual rhetoric became even more vulnerable, however, when he declared surprisingly that nobody was more responsible for this mischief than the London Missionary Society!

When the Foreign Secretary rose to reply, he tried to be fair. 'I cannot help admiring the spirit which animates missionaries, and (their) fearless zeal,' he said, yet Sir Rutherford Alcock had referred to the riots (in Taiwan and Yangzhou) as proof that 'not only the authorities and influential persons but the whole population of China (were) averse to the spread of the missionary establishment'. As for the LMS, they had asked on February 5 how far they could go in taking up the great opportunities in China without embarrassing her Majesty's Government. The Foreign Secretary had replied advising them to consult the minister in Peking in specific instances, as he was not prepared to apply the provisions of the treaties to hypothetical situations. Finally, he too laid himself open to a devastating riposte by advising that 'the missionaries will do well to follow in the wake of trade when the people have learned to see in it material advantage to themselves, rather than to seek to lead the way.'

The Duke of Somerset was grateful and drew the noose more tightly round his own neck. 'My noble friend (the Earl of Clarendon) is quite right in saying that Christianity can only go in the wake of civilization and progress.' But present in the House was Dr Magee, Bishop of Peterborough, who had yet to make his maiden speech. He seized this opportunity.[8]

On the spur of the moment Bishop Magee rose to deliver a defence 'which at one bound established his fame as one of the most brilliant debaters of the day'. The advice of both duke and earl was unlikely to be accepted, he began. To leave that part of the world unconverted or to give up the attempt because British commercial interests might be prejudiced was unlikely. The youngest and least zealous missionary would reply, 'There is something more sacred even than that sacred opium trade for which Great Britain once thought it worth while to wage war!' That something was obedience to the command of God to seek the conversion of his fellow-man at whatever risk to himself or others. It was hardly generous for one in the safe security of their lordships' House to taunt a man who took his own life in his hand, with imperilling the interests of English trade. Should he by becoming a missionary lose the rights he would retain as a trader? British subjects were equally entitled to protection if they sold Bibles or cotton. But had missionaries always been prevented from becoming 'troublesome', neither the noble duke nor he would have been Christians today. Would the noble earl like to mention what kind of trade the missionary should follow? 'Should he wait till the beneficent influence of fire-water or opium had made the people amenable to the Gospel and then preach to men whom the trader had demoralized or intoxicated with his liquor or his vices?'

Little remained to be said. Certainly trader and missionary should be treated alike, Earl Grey agreed, but Britain had abused her superior force, protecting even the abominable coolie trade. She should withhold protection from missionaries, traders and smugglers who penetrated beyond consular protection and incurred hostility. Lord Shaftesbury's comment was no kinder. Those who had raised this fuss were a small independent body of men, 'in no way connected with the great missionary societies' [naming CMS, LMS, Wesleyans and Baptists], acting under no central authority. The great missionary societies should 'be exonerated from the charge which had been *justly* brought against that small independent body.'

Reaction to the Lords[9]   *March 1869*

The Times of March 10 carried a full report of the debate, losing nothing in the telling. 'Parliament is not fond of missionaries,' it said, 'nor is the press, nor is general society. The missionaries are certainly the most independent, perhaps the most wrong-headed of men.' Even so, not until a month later did William Berger feel sufficiently in possession of the facts to write to the editor. By then the need to do so had increased immeasurably.

Some societies naturally needed to justify themselves in the face of accusation. They did so, not realising that dissociating themselves from allegations could further incriminate the CIM. Others consciously pointed the contrast. Both in China and at home some had been cautious to a fault, not to take avoidable risks or to conflict with government policy. On March 31 Donald Matheson spoke for the English Presbyterian Mission. After thirty years as a merchant and partner in Jardine, Matheson, and later 'in missionary operations', he protested to Lord Clarendon against his censure of missionaries, especially in Taiwan. Dr Maxwell had quickly discovered that it was the mandarins who 'entertained an inveterate hatred of all foreigners,' but 'as a mission we deprecate the idea of seeking the support of an armed force in carrying on our work, and our missionaries are prepared to meet dangers and opposition in the conflict of Christianity with heathenism'.

Joseph Ridgeway, the outspoken editor of the *Church Missionary Intelligencer*, observed of Lord Stanley's hope that missionaries would 'conduct themselves with circumspection' – 'By all the great Societies with whose principles and modes of action we are acquainted this has been done. There has been no startling invasion of the interior; no sudden irruption of a strong body of Europeans into the midst of a heathen city, with which they have had no previous acquaintance.' Ridgeway's purpose was defensive. While only newspaper reports and parliamentary blue books were available, without the underlying facts, his dissociation of the major societies from Hudson Taylor's 'startling invasion of the interior' and 'sudden irruption by a strong body of Europeans' was to be expected. As late as 1899, when Eugene Stock's *History* of the CMS was published, Hudson Taylor was still being blamed. But with better understanding, Stock recorded of 1869,

> There was no lack of sympathy for the missionaries who suffered, or of approval of the action of the British Consul at Shanghai in going up the river at once in a gunboat, examining into the affair, and demanding reparation from the authorities at Nanking. The attack on the Mission, however, was rather the occasion than the cause of his action. . . . The English Government had been on the look-out for a convenient opportunity of making a demonstration. It was in the interest, therefore, more of the merchants than of the missionaries that a fleet of seven ships-of-war presently appeared. But of course it suited the anti-missionary public at home to indulge in the usual tirade about 'the Gospel and the Gunboat'; and this was done with the omission of no element of offensiveness by the Duke of Somerset in the House of Lords.

What was true of Britain was also true of the press in China, before and after news of the Lords' debate arrived.

In the *Chinese Recorder* a letter under the pseudonym 'Arthur Challoner', patently the British consul Challoner Alabaster, came to the defence of missionaries in general, ridiculed in the *Saturday Review*, with Hudson Taylor bearing the brunt of 'the uncalled-for attacks which seem to be the fashion . . . This attack – light, yet bitter – the last and happiest production . . . of the *reviler* – will be a matter of surprise to no one.' Directed against the losses sustained by 'the Taylor Mission' it had read,

> Would Mr Taylor have done his duty to those who sent him out, had he refused to state (the value of the property destroyed) when called on by the authorities? A concertina and a sedan chair seem extra-ordinary to the writer at home, but to people out here who know the necessity of chairs, and to missionaries who know the utility of some musical instrument . . . it would be an evidence that Mr Taylor's Mission approached apostolic simplicity in its appoint-ments, that one chair only, and a humble musical instrument only, were the extent of its possessions. . . .
>
> Never was such little justice (done) as against Mr Taylor and his companions. Poor, unfriended, unbacked by a powerful society at home, they had no opportunity, even had they had the inclination, for excess. . . . For years and years the mission-haters have abused the Protestant missionaries for not going into the interior; and now they do so, the cry is at once that they must be confined to the ports.[10]

Reports of the debate in the House of Lords were the next to reach China and drew the wrath of the *Chinese Recorder*'s editor. 'Hostility to foreigners as such, on the part of certain literati . . . was plainly the *animus* of the whole affair.' Suppose that the Duke should be the victim of violence after shipwreck on Taiwan, that one of his eyes [like Reid's] should be injured and that the consular authorities should exact prompt reparation – would that be propa-gating the British system of nobility by gunboat? No more was Mr Taylor propagating Christianity with gunboats! He and his party were assaulted because they were foreigners, to drive them out. As for the duke and earl saying that Christianity should follow 'in the wake of civilization and progress', they should have recognised that 'If England has any civilization and progress to bring to China, they are the result of Christianity. . . . Christianity is not accustomed to travel in the wake of anything.' His Grace was 'anxious to know what chance we have of reducing these missions, or, at least, of not allowing them to go still further up the country'. 'None, may it please your Grace – not the slightest imaginable chance!' As for sending British missionaries out of China, 'a country where they have as much (legal) right to be as the Duke has to his place in the House of Lords', he shows a disregard for constitutional law.

Lord Clarendon fared no better. In Africa, India, Burma, China, the best response to the missionary's message has been 'away from the marts of trade'. How could he think that 'material advantage to themselves' would be a good basis of Christianity? And was *The Times*, in accusing missionaries of being impudent, uneducated and ignorant of Chinese thought and culture, perhaps ignorant of Wells Williams' masterly *Middle Kingdom* and James Legge's incomparable *Chinese Classics*? – and of the fact that 'no class (of foreigner) makes more rapid advancement, after arrival here, in these regards' than missionaries? Finally, 'All this talk is wide of the case in hand. No want of "learning", no lack of "knowledge of mankind", no rushing in to "controversy" had anything to do with the Yangchow outrage.'

Such vindication by others spared Hudson Taylor the necessity to set the record straight and eased the suffering which so many slanders inevitably caused. But the circulation of the *Chinese Recorder* was small. It reached few outside China. The damage done by the newspapers and wild rhetoric in Parliament extended throughout the British empire and into the palaces of China's rulers. Li Hongzhang had taken up his post at Wuchang as viceroy of Hubei, Hunan and Anhui when Griffith John wrote of him,

> Our Viceroy is a very intelligent man, and anti-foreign to the backbone. He knows just as well as I do all that has been said in the House of Lords, and all that has appeared in *The Times* on missionary enterprise. He sees that we are despised and distrusted, and he knows that we are at his mercy. It is certain, too, that the Chinese Government will grant us no privileges willingly. The policy of the Government is, was, and ever will be to oppose the hated foreigner, whether missionary or merchant, in his every attempt to obtain a foothold in the interior.
>
> (As for attacks in the press), the work and the agents have been misrepresented, calumniated, and ridiculed in no measured terms by many of your leading newspapers, and by some of the peers of the realm. Here in China, too, they have been handled rather roughly. . . . Men who have never put a foot within the door of a missionary's house, chapel, or schoolroom think they have a right to speak authoritatively of him and his labours.

The damage had gone further than Griffith John anticipated. Before long the LMS in London issued instructions that all their missionaries should confine themselves to the treaty ports. Griffith John had been extending his work through the Wuhan complex of three cities, Hankou, Wuchang and Hanyang, and into the provinces. His epic journey through Sichuan and Shaanxi had ended only recently, in September 1868 – a journey from which he confessed that he hardly expected to come back alive. He looked forward to establishing a church at Chengdu in Sichuan, where Alexander Wylie had been stoned. At this point the storm in Britain stirred up by the Duke of Somerset and the papers had caused the LMS, and the Wesleyan Methodist Missionary Society also, to shackle their great pioneers in China. Not until twenty years later was the first LMS missionary stationed at Chongqing in Sichuan.

Griffith John protested vigorously against being told to withdraw even from Wuchang. His foothold had been resisted for four months by the literati and only the help of the consul had secured him his treaty right to reside there. To retreat would be to close down everywhere. The LMS premises had been built by contributions from the European community who would have to be consulted. He won his point, over Wuchang only. Wardlaw Thompson, John's biographer, commented on this episode, 'When the spirit of the pioneer is dead, the Christian Society which has to record the fact begins to write its own epitaph.'[11]

Speak or be silent?   *March–September 1869*

Hudson Taylor's silence during this long period as the scapegoat speaks more loudly than the little he wrote. But a letter to his mother, to whom he could always unburden his heart, showed how deeply he was feeling the criticism. Reading it superficially and out of context, some might miss the point and see Hudson Taylor's resolve being undermined, with 'self-pitying isolation' creeping into his correspondence, as has been said. In the same context, Latourette, on the other hand, rightly continued after summarising some of the adversities Hudson Taylor was up against, 'Yet Taylor was undismayed and prayed and planned for the expansion of the Mission.'[12] Isolation he certainly never experienced while enjoying strong friendships with those around him. From Ninghai on his southern tour he confided to his mother on March 13,

> Often have I asked you to remember me in prayer; and when I have done so there has been *need* of it. That need has never been greater than at the present time. Envied by some, despised by many, hated,

perhaps, by others; often blamed for things I never heard of, or had anything to do with; an innovator on what have become established rules of missionary practice; an opponent of a strong system of heathen error and superstition; working without precedent in many respects, and with few experienced helpers; often sick in body, as well as perplexed in mind, and embarrassed by circumstances; had not the Lord been specially gracious to me; had not my mind been sustained by the conviction that the work was the *Lord's*, and that *He* was with me in – what it is no empty figure to call – the thick of the conflict, I must have fainted and broken down. But *the battle is the Lord's*. And He *will* conquer. *We* may fail, do fail continually, but *He* never fails. . . . My own position becomes more and more responsible, and the need of special grace to fill it greater, but I have continually to mourn that I follow at such a distance, and learn so slowly to imitate my precious Master. I cannot tell you how I am buffetted sometimes by temptation; I never knew how bad a heart I had. Yet I do know that I love God, and love His work, and desire to serve Him only, and in all things. . . . Never were there more thick clouds about us than at this moment; but never was there more encouragement than at the present time. Nay, might I not say that the very *dis*-couragements are themselves *en*-couragements?[13]

He had passed through Ninghai thirteen months ago and prayed that the gospel might soon be preached there. For months now the city and surrounding villages had shown a willingness to listen, and five men were asking the evangelist Feng Nenggui for baptism.

These are very great results, accomplished by *God* in a new station and in a very short time (but) I incline to think we are on the eve of no slight persecution in China. The *power* of the Gospel has been little felt heretofore. The *foreign* element *has been* the great stumbling block.

Sir Rutherford Alcock's attitude to missionaries in his communiqués to the Foreign Office had become known through Lord Clarendon's speeches, to the indignation of the whole Protestant missionary body. On the following day in writing to Maria, Hudson Taylor said he thought the (British) government might even compel them to stop wearing Chinese clothes 'or otherwise interfere with our freedom of action'. On June 9 he went further in telling an unnamed colleague to 'wrestle in prayer' and work hard while she could, 'It seems very likely that we shall be recalled from all our stations in the interior in a short time, or that the Chinese will be told that we shall no longer be sustained in our residence there. . . . Our position is not, however, more dark than that of the Jews in the time of Esther, nor is God less mighty and gracious.'

In Britain the pressure on the Bergers increased immensely after the Lords' debate on March 9. In his March 20 editorial of the *Occasional Paper* No 17 William Berger said many were urging him to write to the press. And to Hudson Taylor, '*The Saturday Review* is very bitter, indeed so much so that I think no one will be turned aside in consequence. Dr Landels kindly offers again to reply to it if I will supply the facts.' William Berger preferred to let it pass, but James van Sommer, Mary Berger's brother, believed it essential 'to correct the erroneous statements . . . propagated in public', so with his help Berger was drafting a letter to *The Times* while he still waited for Hudson Taylor's lost letters to arrive.

When pressure to present the facts overcame his unwillingness, he simply gave the gist of reports from the victims of the riot, stressing that they only notified Vice-Consul Allen late in the events. 'We could have written far more strongly,' he said, 'but we thought it best to act cautiously and as Christians not recriminatingly.' But after he had posted his letter, days passed and it was not published, until during an evening with a friend named Brodie, who has 'a share in *The Times*', they discussed Yangzhou and Brodie offered to unearth and 'secure the insertion' of William Berger's letter. A month later the picture had changed considerably. 'One of the Editors of *The Times* (he who offered to have it inserted) was very pleased with it and sent me a guinea for the Mission.' Correspondence all the more dominated the Bergers' lives, with many commendations of the letter. 'We really have done comparatively little else. Today James (van Sommer) and I have been writing Lords Clarendon and Shaftesbury, the Duke of Somerset and Bishops (of) Peterboro' (Magee) and St David's' enclosing copies of the letter to *The Times*, and to three of them *China: Its Spiritual Need and Claims* and the *Occasional Paper*. R C Morgan also reproduced the letter in *Revival*.

Some of Hudson Taylor's missing letters at last turned up on May 1, leaving two earlier ones still to be accounted for. Meanwhile Maria had answered the vital questions and it looked as if the subject of Yangzhou had 'had its day'. People were wanting normal news again.

What Maria had written on February 11 was,

In the riot we asked the protection of the Chinese Mandarin: my dear Husband did not see it right to neglect this means of possibly saving our lives. After our lives were safe, and we were in shelter, we asked no restitution, we desired no revenge. . . . All that my dear Husband did in the way of giving details etc was at the Consul's request. Perhaps one secret of our matter being taken up so warmly was that it was looked upon as a climax to a series of provocations which the English had received from the Chinese. And the representatives of our government were I believe not sorry to have an opportunity of good ground for settling off a number of 'old accounts'. *We* felt that it was *our God* who had so disposed events that our matter should have happened at such a crisis. And is there not a great difference between resisting evil ourselves and defending ourselves by offensive means such as the use of fire-arms etc (which some missionaries out here think it right to do) – and availing ourselves of the protection which our Government surely *pledges* itself to afford us when it renders it compulsory on us to take out Passports every year? . . . We did not in this instance even ask our Consul to right our wrongs. . . .

As to the harsh judgings of the world, or the more painful misunderstandings of Christian brethren, I *generally* feel that the best plan is to go on with our work and leave God to vindicate our cause. . . . It would be undesirable to print the fact that Mr Medhurst – and through him Sir Rutherford Alcock – took up the matter without application. The new Ministry at home censures those out here for the policy which the late Ministry enjoined upon them. . . . The fact that my dear Husband had his wife and children with him stamped him in the eyes of respectable people as a respectable man – not one likely to swindle them or be off without sign or trace. . . . As to the *number* of persons that were in the house at the time, that was occasioned by circumstances beyond our control.

[And on May 2] I don't think it ever occurred to us that Christian friends at home might be stumbled by our rulers espousing our cause, and requiring for us both restoration and restitution. We fully believed that God could and would far more than make up to us our losses – perhaps not in kind, but . . . in His own way of supplying our need.[14]

Warm letters and generous gifts from George Müller, Philip Gosse, the Howards, Lord Congleton and others did more to encourage the battered Bergers and Taylors. An anonymous contributor to the *Chinese Recorder* by his cogent observations also showed that they had more firm friends in China, taking the offensive against the critics.

Should it not be rendered illegal, for noble Lords, Dukes, or Earls to attempt to speak or legislate upon subjects about which they are profoundly ignorant, without first at least *reading* the *Parliamentary Blue Books* printed for their special information? Even a cursory glance at the sworn statement of facts, which forms a part of the *Parliamentary Blue Book* on the Yangchow riot, would have nipped many of the most plausible speeches against missionaries in the bud.[15]

Not every friend used anonymity to command attention. One in particular rose to the CIM's defence.

Miles Knowlton sums up   *May 1869*

Strong intervention to do justice to the maligned missionaries came from the American Miles J Knowlton, DD, the Taylors' faithful friend since the days of their painful courtship in Ningbo. He as much as anyone in the treaty ports knew what it was to 'itinerate' deep into the countryside. Known as 'Christlike', his obituary in the *Chinese Recorder* five years later, when he succumbed, as yet another victim, to virulent dysentery, said of him, 'There are no people, we are persuaded . . . who possess the power of gauging character in a more accurate manner than the Chinese . . . He was often designated by them "the Western Confucius", the highest compliment they could possibly pay him. . . . They gave him credit for very high moral placidity.'[16]

In a ten-column paper dated May 22, 1869, he examined the reports on the Yangzhou riot, the debate in the House of Lords, editorials and letters to the press and official documents reproduced in the *Parliamentary Blue Books* and *Morning Star*, emphasising that no one had asked him to do so. It was owed to all missionaries that the facts should be established and that blame should rest only where it belonged. No more than a summary of his arguments can be given here. In China, at least, they satisfied serious questioners and removed the growing necessity for Hudson Taylor to speak out in defence of the truth.

'Ignorance of the facts' was Knowlton's starting-point. 'All the speakers in the debate, and all the editors whose papers I have noticed, appear to take it for granted that the riot arose from the "imprudence" of the missionaries.'. . . How strange, he said, that 'these zealous decriers of missions to the Chinese, have nothing to say, no fault to find with the infamous opium trade'.

1. They had complained of the imprudence of going to Yangzhou 'so far inland' beyond consular jurisdiction, whereas Yangzhou was 'in sight from the (Zhenjiang) British Consulate' and only an hour and a half by pony from the river. What use was a consulate if its writ did not extend so short a distance?

2. The Yangzhou missionaries had passports, the requirement by agreement between governments to permit unlimited travel within the Chinese empire. A passport holder was under the protection of his own government and that of the nation which ratified it. Yet Lord Clarendon had spoken of 'places where no consular authority is at hand'. Merchants and men of science as well as missionaries were constantly travelling far from the consular ports. Was the passport system to be dispensed with?

3. Before going to Yangzhou the missionaries had consulted consular officials 'of different nationalities [American and French] as to the propriety and practicability of residing there'; and they had all agreed that they had the right, and that it was undoubtedly feasible for them to do so.

4. They had obtained an official dispatch from no less than the *daotai* to the Yangzhou mandarin, stating the missionaries' purpose 'and directing them to afford them protection and aid' in exerting their right to rent premises. 'That the Chinese government and the provincial officers do admit this right, is proved by the fact that foreigners do actually possess houses and reside in every province in the empire' – the Roman Catholics.

5. A proclamation by the Yangzhou magistrate in obeying the *daotai*'s order had allayed any fears the people might have had, and greatly helped in the rental of premises in a quiet part of the city.

6. Hudson Taylor had been blamed for going to Yangzhou 'in so large a party'. But only he and 'his family' had been there, quietly living in boats and then in an inn for a month, during which they found both people and authorities friendly and co-operative. Only when the Rudlands had been prevented from staying at Zhenjiang had they joined the Taylors in Yangzhou, for lack of anywhere else to go. Others were merely visitors passing through, 'one or two having arrived on the very day of the riot'. '*The Saturday Review* makes itself merry over the "indemnity for losses extorted from the Chinese."' Far from overcharging, Hudson Taylor's inventory of property stolen and destroyed had fallen short by several hundred dollars. '*The Saturday Review* misrepresents them as *demanding*

indemnity; but they did not, and the compensation and penalties demanded by Consul Medhurst were most moderate and just.'

7. 'The preaching of Christianity, and especially by declaiming against ancestral worship' had been generally assumed but 'had nothing whatever to do with exciting the disturbance.' No preaching at all had yet taken place. 'Indeed, if "a small body of independent men, acting under no central authority," act with so much discretion as facts proved they did, what paragons of . . . prudence must be the missionaries . . . of "the great Missionary Societies"!

'How then was the riot caused? . . . By the instigation of the gentry (who) held a secret meeting . . . and deliberately formed their plan for ejecting the foreigners,' emboldened by the withdrawal of the British consul from Zhenjiang and by the Zhenjiang magistrate's success in thwarting Hudson Taylor's attempts to rent premises there. An American Baptist missionary (Horace Jenkins) had only just received rough treatment at Jinhua. 'The contract for a house had been signed but the gentry compelled the owner to sell it instead to them and proceeded to dismantle and move every stick and brick of it' – in spite of the Burlingame treaty of reciprocity![17]

Miles Knowlton then recounted the provocations by handbills and posters and the events of the Yangzhou riot, of Hudson Taylor's repeated petitions to the prefect of Yangzhou, whose failure to act clearly implicated him in conniving with the literati who had raised the mob.

> Where in the whole history of that affair is there any act, any course of procedure of the missionaries, to which the blame can be attached? . . . No, no, noble Dukes, Earls and Lords . . . it was *not* the propagation of Christianity but the persistent reiterated report that the foreigners 'boiled and ate babies'!
>
> Even Sir Rutherford Alcock has 'referred to the riots . . . as a proof that . . . the whole population of China are adverse to the spread of missionary establishments, (hence) that it would be very inconsistent with wisdom or prudence' (to negotiate an article in a new treaty) 'empowering missionaries to purchase land and reside in the interior.' . . . The root of the opposition . . . is not found in any repugnance to Christianity, but in *hatred to all foreigners, as such*.

Miles Knowlton had enquired carefully among Chinese and learned that fear lay behind the opposition, fear of unprincipled foreigners coming after the missionaries, 'with sufficient capital to take the trade out of the hands of our native merchants'. 'Merchants have . . . often been driven from places in the interior . . . a merchant and his servants had been beaten and robbed by an official and his lictors, at a place not far from Yangchow, previous to the Yangchow riot. . . . At Taiwan . . . gunboats were called in more to vindicate the treaty rights of the merchants, than those of missionaries. The same was substantially the case at Yangchow.' At Shantou and Xiamen (Swatow and Amoy) the serious disturbances had nothing to do with missionaries. Dr Maxwell's protest in the *Chinese Recorder* for April 1869 made the truth about the Taiwan riots abundantly plain. China and the Chinese were exceedingly tolerant of Christianity. Neither they nor the missionaries were culpable. The 'unjust and unrighteous mandarins' and the literati out of office were entirely to blame.

Knowlton finally summarised Consul Medhurst's August 31, 1868, dispatch to Sir Rutherford, reprinted from the Parliamentary blue book in the *Morning Star* of February 18, 1869. He applauded his settlement of the whole affair, before offering his own views on how diplomatic relations with the China of the mandarins were best conducted, locally as they had been and not by central governments. In a word, missionaries and Hudson Taylor in particular had been made the butt of unjustified blame, the scapegoat for the sins of others.

By September Hudson Taylor was able to write, 'Mr Knowlton's paper on the Yangchau riot has done good here in many quarters and has helped to draw back to their former sympathy some who were a little shaken by some of the false reports which had been industriously circulated. Strange work for some of the Lord's people to be engaged in!'[18]

A few late firecrackers had yet to break the silence, but the Yangzhou issue had run its course for the present and both Hudson Taylor and the Bergers could breathe again. *The Times* was among the last to relent. Someone using the nom de plume 'Veritas', in a letter from Shanghai, dated August 17, described Protestant missionaries as '(enjoying) perfect immunity from all personal danger (with) the inevitable gunboat under the window'. 'The readers of *The Times* will of course understand,' the *Chinese Recorder*'s editor commented, 'that gunboats in China always anchor directly under missionary windows, and are kept here exclusively for the protection of missionaries, who, having "perfect immunity from all personal danger" must always be in need of them.'[19] Taunt and riposte could both have been just for the laugh, but bitterness lay behind the jibe – just another way of baiting the Hudson Taylor bear.

In 1872 when the dust had settled to some extent and Hudson Taylor published a slim report of the years since 1865, he allowed himself this statement,

> We cannot but remark upon the unfair view which was taken of this matter at the time in the public papers at home. We do not remember to have seen it once noticed, that the armed interposition which was made, unsolicited by us, had mainly for its object, and actually resulted in, the settlement of commercial difficulties, the obtaining of pecuniary compensation for mercantile losses, and the restoration of waning British *prestige*.[20]

The bear's head was still sore – but from new baiting.

'The Missionary Question' again   1869

Building the next chronological tier upon those already laid we have reached the critical period recognised by Hudson Taylor in his references to the threat of being forced back from the 'interior' to the ghetto settlements of the treaty ports. While Anson Burlingame spoke in glowing terms of China's imagined welcome to messengers of the 'shining cross' (p 34), the Court and Grand Council of the Chinese government were pressing for greater restrictions, and the British government was inclining in the same direction. In April 1869 *The Scotsman* in an article from China on *The late Disturbances in China* had usefully pictured the ruling body in accurate if uncomplimentary terms.

> The Government of Pekin consists of a boy of thirteen years of age, the Emperor (Tong Zhi), of whom little is known, except that he is not intelligent, and that he has a violent temper; his mother, the Empress Dowager, who is believed to be a shrewd woman; a eunuch, who is the favourite of the Empress Dowager, and has secretly great power; Prince Kong, who is a subtle quick-witted man, fond of dissipation, and has a strong head for liquor. All these are Tartars, and, although they govern through a mixed body of Tartar and Chinese Ministers, they are the heads of the Government.[21]

In his memorial to the throne on the 'barbarian question', the viceroy of Hunan and Hubei, Li Hongzhang, had advocated far-

H E WEN XIANG

aching 'restrictions to missionary liberty (through) regulations for
e control of Missions', even to the extent of 'placing missionaries
der Chinese jurisdiction', with all that those ominous words
plied. And it was in 1869 that Wen Xiang, Grand Secretary of the
uncil (Book 4, pp 220, 380), in addressing Sir Rutherford as
itish Minister said (according to Hawks Pott), 'Do away with your
traterritorial clause [allowing Western justice on Chinese soil]
d merchant and missionary may settle anywhere and everywhere;
tain it, and we must do our best to confine you and our troubles to
e treaty ports.'[22]

The riots and outrages already experienced at the instigation of the literati left little room for the hope that the annulment of extra-territorial privileges would result in a change of attitude. The objection of the literati was not so much to concessions wrested from China by force as to foreigners and things foreign. With or without protection by treaty, foreigners threatened the ancient institutions, the merchants by their newfangled machinery, railways, telegraph and tainted merchandise, the missionary by offensive architecture and doctrines which challenged the ancient beliefs and practices. Sir Rutherford therefore resisted the Zongli Yamen's proposals, while advocating to the Foreign Office in London an equivalent shackling of British subjects' movements. Certainly he was in no doubt that (to understate the case) the submission of foreigners to Chinese law would deprive them of the kind of justice they could expect from their own governments.

When news of the debate in the House of Lords (on the Yangzhou riots) and its repercussions in the press had reached Peking, the missionaries there responded with characteristic energy. Astonished by what they read, John Burdon and William Collins of the CMS, and John Dudgeon MD and Joseph Edkins of the LMS boldly asked Sir Rutherford if they might read his dispatches to Lord Clarendon – which had not been published in the Parliamentary blue books, in order to answer them. They knew their man. Sir Rutherford had nothing he was ashamed of. He furnished them with 'copious extracts', and on July 14 they addressed to him a long and closely reasoned letter, expressing their intention that it should be seen also by the Secretary of State for Foreign Affairs.

The 'Missionary Memorandum' as it came to be called (Appendix 8) challenged Alcock's claim that missionaries should be confined to the treaty ports before they did more damage to Britain's commercial interests in China. It protested that any hostility by the Chinese was to foreigners, not to missionaries as such. As for commerce being Britain's main object in China – as their figures showed, opium was the main commodity! 'Honourable commerce has nothing to fear from Protestant missionaries.' Then Sir Rutherford complained of the revolutionary tendencies of Christianity. True, from the beginning it had been turning the world upside down, but was in no way *seditious* or comparable with 'the settlement in Peking of a British Minister, at the point of a bayonet'! Sir Rutherford's thesis could not bear examination.

Alcock replied briefly, promising to forward their letter to Lord Clarendon with comments. A week later John Burdon (Maria's brother-in-law) sent a copy of the joint letter to the *Chinese Recorder* for publication, with his own introduction.

In this he drew attention to the salient points at issue. Writing strongly in support of Hudson Taylor, he went further to resist the move to restrict missionaries to the treaty ports. Lord Clarendon appeared to lean too hard upon Sir Rutherford's 'great experience in China', and had been misled by what he understood him to be saying. 'According to Lord Clarendon, Sir Rutherford "doubted whether any prospect of success . . . would compensate the dangers (the missionaries) incurred in disregarding not only the laws but the advice of their own government." Thus the British Minister was made to accuse the Protestant missionaries of "disregarding the laws of China!"' And not only Lord Clarendon; the *Pall Mall Gazette* had made 'a ludicrous mistake' by misinterpreting a vague reference by Lord Clarendon in the House to 'a most offensive placard against the Roman Catholic religion (posted on) the walls of Shanghae'. According to the *Gazette*, the Protestants had contrived the offending placard! So what would they not do to revile the religions of China? Foreign Minister and fallible press needed to know the facts.

> When it comes to be understood by Lord Clarendon, as it will be by and by, that the Chinese government is half, if not wholly, in sympathy with those local mandarins and native gentry in their opposition to foreigners, and that the authority of the central government over their subordinates and the literati is at best a very questionable thing, it will then be seen that in certain extreme cases, such as that of Yangchow, Sir Rutherford Alcock's *action* is of more avail toward bringing the problem of foreign intercourse with China to a peaceful solution than all his *theorisings* about restricting missionaries to the treaty ports. J. S. Burdon, Peking, July 23rd, 1869.[23]

In his comments to the LMS directors on the same issue of shackling the missionary, Griffith John was no less explicit (Appendix 9)[24] – but even after his powerful pleading, the London-based ruling body of the LMS declined to retract their own strong restraints upon their missionaries in China. In loyalty they were reluctantly obeyed, while the CIM surged forwards – until the climate of opinion changed and the irrepressible spirit of the pioneer evangelist was given rein to extend its frontiers. Meanwhile, true to his word, Alcock sent the 'Missionary Memorandum' to London where it was published in the *Parliamentary Papers* of 1870.[25]

After protracted negotiations, Sir Rutherford concluded an Anglo-Chinese Convention with the Zongli Yamen on October 23, 1869. Alcock's signature should have been final; Prince Kong and four other ministers signed for China, and the emperor's seal was affixed to the treaty. When commercial, not missionary, criticism led the British government to refuse to ratify it, the emperor was deeply insulted and his ministers humiliated beyond redress. As they saw it, British perfidy had yet again been unmasked. That Sir Rutherford had lost face mattered little.

Not only the British were involved, the French were a law unto themselves. But American missionaries and their successive ministers at Peking were by no means silent. In May 1869 the American missionaries of Ningbo petitioned the Hon J Ross Browne to secure protection for them in the rental of land and buildings. In June Miles Knowlton wrote personally, and in July conveyed to the *Chinese Recorder*[26] the substance of the US minister's reply. To Ross Browne he said,

> The British Government (influenced by the representations, or rather misrepresentations, of Sir Rutherford Alcock) appears disposed to withdraw all protection from residents in the interior, taking in fact a retrograde step. This measure if carried out, will be sure to make those officials and literati who are opposed to foreigners all the more bold and contumacious. . . . Should that policy result in the driving of the numerous Protestant missionary establishments from the interior . . . the result would be to put back the friendly relations of the Chinese with foreigners more than twenty years.
>
> [The minister replied]. Your memorial and letters are now on the way to Washington, with my most cordial endorsement. . . . From my first despatches . . . I took up their cause with all my energy. At first I thought it would be better for them not to press too hard against native prejudices, or incur risks by pushing too vigorously into the interior; but I soon gave that up as untenable, and entirely inconsistent with the object in view. . . . Opposition must be expected and must be overcome. It will never be overcome by standing still or retreating.

The 'Missionary Question' would never cease to be harped upon. In 1871 the Chinese government raised it with renewed vigour. Over a century later it is again under inquiry, this time prompted by the viewpoint of the People's Republic of China. Just as Robert Morrison by sheer force of circumstance became inseparable from his fellow-countrymen of diametrically opposite motives and practice, so each generation of missionary continued to be inextricably implicated in the use of force and the traffic in opium. As the historian George Woodcock put it, 'Always, until the end of the British presence in China, the missionary was beset by a conflict of loyalties. He owed one duty to his religion and the people he was trying to convert; another duty to his country. And there were times when, even against his will, his very presence became an excuse for his country's power to be tightened over the land in which he worked.' Today he is having to answer for it.[27]

CHAPTER SIX

'A FLEA IN A BLANKET'
1869

Alford's mission[1]   *January–May 1869*

The Bishop of Victoria's prolonged 'visitation' of his scattered diocese had opened his eyes. Complimenting the missions he had visited, he stressed the inadequacy of all that was being done to give the gospel to this huge empire, and 'boldly faced the question of founding a new (Anglican) society' to remedy the situation. But his proposition of a new Church Mission for China had a frigid reception in London.

The uproar over the Yangzhou riot, the notorious debate in the Lords, and its repercussions in the press, had needled the big societies into defending their own reputations. 'No startling invasion of the interior; no sudden irruption of a strong body of Europeans' had expressed their defensive attitude. Even if innocent of either a startling invasion or sudden irruption, Hudson Taylor and the CIM were believed to be guilty of both epithets. So they were embarrassing comrades-in-arms. Alford's proposal was condemned (to use Stock's words), 'on the ground that it would be an imitation of the China Inland Mission!' 'The conception is grand', its opponents declared; 'the execution impracticable, and, if attempted, disastrous' – like the charge of the Light Brigade. To send 'numerous missionaries' to China, would only mean 'a lowering of the standard, and a mistrust of Native evangelists who would do the work better.' But where were the Chinese evangelists? Sixty-two years after Morrison arrived in China, few converts and fewer trained evangelists even existed. In August 1869 Protestant missionaries in China numbered in all 151 men, 129 women, with 365 Chinese Church workers of all kinds, and fewer than six thousand communicant members in a nation of hundreds of millions. However unwelcome, foreign missionaries in growing numbers would have to share the spadework for a long while to come if the job was to be done and enough Chinese Christians won to permeate the empire. So Bishop Alford's scheme was never carried out. 'The pioneer work in the interior was to be done by the humble and despised agency which Alford was supposed to be imitating.'

But Eugene Stock was writing thirty years later. At the time Hudson Taylor seemed to stand alone. All but crushed by the difficulty of putting his vision into effect and by disappointment over some of his team.

'Always on the move'   *January–May 1869*

While all the aftermath of the Yangzhou riot was in motion, it had been 'business as usual' for the Mission and the Taylors – except that for them the usual was the constant cropping up of the unusual. Much was happening and many letters remain to illuminate this difficult year. Its very complexity may best be seen by following Hudson Taylor through it, travelling with him as he led his team, constantly at their beck and call. Within the complexity the pattern is apparent.

Yangzhou was home, at least as the place where the Taylors' personal possessions and mission records were kept. From there frequent journeys were made, across the Yangzi to Zhenjiang on business; upriver to Nanjing and beyond, or down to Shanghai as need demanded; and south by the Grand Canal or coastal steamer to the work centres of the southern region.

In the Yangzi area he now had Meadows and Williamson two hundred miles to the south-west at Anqing, living on a boat after their arrival there on January 8, and then at an inn. Fifty miles away George and Catherine Duncan and Mary Bowyer were at Nanjing with Elizabeth Meadows and her two children. The rudiments of a congregation and little schools for boys under George, and girls under Mary Bowyer, fully occupied them and their Chinese colleague Li Tianfu.

William and Mary Rudland and their printing staff in the Chinese city of Zhenjiang were making what use they could of the presses, pending the move into their own house in the Chinese city on January 15, and providing a staging-post and business centre for members of the team. Missionaries passing through, renewing passports at the consulate or wanting Hudson Taylor's medical help, stayed with the Rudlands.

Charles and Elizabeth Judd and Louise Desgraz, with Mr Yu's help after he joined them from Hangzhou, supplied the continuity

A *'FENGSHUI'* GEOMANCER AND A NUN

at Yangzhou, inconspicuously giving the gospel to enquiring Chinese no longer afraid to visit them. Edward Fishe, Emily Blatchley, Maria, Annie Bohannan and the children came and went as circumstances directed.

The Cordons and Henry Reid were at Suzhou. Absent for six weeks at a time to preach in the villages, Reid himself had apparently recovered from his riot injuries, except emotionally. Apprehension of violence sapped the enjoyment of his work. Robert and Frances (Gainfort) White lived with the Cordons, although not members of the CIM. In the Yangzi region alone, Hudson Taylor therefore had eighteen missionaries and their children and half a dozen Chinese Christian workers under his care.

The southern field was correspondingly depleted by the move northwards and the resignation of Stephan Barchet, Susan Barnes, the McLean sisters and the Nicols. The John McCarthys, Jennie Faulding, Wang Lae-djün and his wife were building up the Hangzhou congregation, with McCarthy also overseeing the Ningbo church. Midway between the two cities, John and Anne Stevenson were slogging on at Shaoxing with a handful of newly-baptised Christians at last to encourage them.

Thirty miles south of Ningbo, George and Anne Crombie with Fan Qiseng and Wang Guoyao served the growing local church and its outposts, now including Ninghai, halfway to Taizhou, a hundred miles southwards. Josiah Jackson and the Cardwells, not one of them either contented or effective, hung on at Taizhou, still seeing greener grass over the fence in other places, and leaving their post from time to time on one pretext or another.

A hundred miles still farther south, George Stott tenaciously ran his little school for boys and preached to any Chinese who visited the chapel. But Stott seemed slow to learn wisdom, and often faced difficulties of his own making. One night death-wails startled him at two a m. A child had died of 'croup' in a near-by house. The father called in the *fengshui* expert (Book 4, Appendix 8) to discover why it had happened.

> After casting about for some time, (he) pronounced it to be the furnace in my kitchen which had caused the sudden death. A deputation soon waited upon me to request me to pull down the unfortunate thing, as it had an unlucky number of holes in it; but I maintained the innocence of the fire-place, and would not consent to its removal. Then another expert said it was my horse; he was put in a place which was not primarily intended for a horse, and so had upset the equilibrium of the elements. . . . The poor afflicted father thought I was bent on the destruction of his family, for another child was sick by this time. . . . Then he went to the city temple; the gods there said he must move away; so he did next morning.[2]

Superstitions made it difficult for Stott, but an unbending attitude could not help. He was lonely and had written to Glasgow to ask Grace Ciggie to marry him.

The medical care of missionaries, and others, made increasing demands on Hudson Taylor's time. There was a doctor in the international settlement at Ningbo, but his fees excluded most members of the CIM from consulting him. Hudson Taylor was willing to attend them whenever possible, and planned his visits to fit in with confinements, but the abnormal life they lived made calculation of when he would be needed difficult for them. All were young, and pregnancies were frequent. Often severe illness and emergencies tore him away from whatever he was doing. Because of his coming and going, members of other missions, merchants and consular officials, far from Ningbo, Shanghai and Hankou and other doctors, also looked to him for medical attention.

Long business and pastoral letters flowed from his pen, often headed 'on a boat near' wherever he might be. Canal travel was smooth and relatively fast. He was fully at home sitting on his bed-roll in a footboat or lying full length working. Once he arrived at his destinations, he joined in the local activities. Always in demand for doctoring, preaching and discussing problems he, and more often Maria, had to play matchmaker for local church members. Arranged marriages were customary in China and, with Christians so few, they depended on help in finding wives and husbands for each other. When visiting E C Lord's or other girls' schools in Ningbo, Hudson Taylor would enquire on their behalf or negotiate for a particular one.

Maria sometimes travelled with him and sometimes joined him at his patient's home to nurse the mother and infant after Hudson's work was done. Emily went with her if she took the children to stay with the McCarthys for a change of company. Emily's secretarial work continued wherever they were. If Hudson Taylor was up-country he would send the letters he wrote via Maria and Emily to be given serial numbers and copied for filing before being posted.

George and Annie Crombie had already lost two babies. Hudson Taylor's gratitude for their sacrificial spirit when Richard Truelove had forfeited his passage on the *Corea* (Book 3, p 421), made him doubly willing to go early to Fenghua and wait for the birth of their third. At the end of January he went first to Hangzhou on the way to Fenghua. Not until June 25 was he to reach home again. Maria, Emily and the family arrived at Hangzhou on February 2 for their first reunion with their many friends since the previous year, and Hudson Taylor invited Wang Lae-djün and all fifty or more church members to a Chinese New Year feast. But no sooner had they reached New Lane than the baby Charles Edward fell ill with

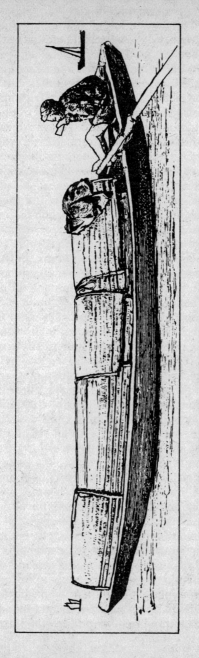

FOOTBOATS ARE ROWED BY LEG-POWER

bronchitis. After a week he was better and they went on to Ningbo, within call of Fenghua.

Early in January Stephan Barchet and Mary Bausum, now eighteen, had been married. A week later her mother, Mrs Lord, fell ill with pneumonia and died on the 15th. As Mrs Bausum she had been the staunch friend of Maria and Hudson Taylor through the opposition to their engagement and marriage, and ever since. Her death was the removal of yet another prop in their vulnerable lives, and the loss of one of the hardest working missionaries of any society in China. For Hudson and Maria to move with their family into their first home above the Bridge Street chapel, and from there to visit the Goughs and E C Lord and Mary, aroused deep emotions. They had only just left their own daughter Grace's grave and wrestled with Charles Edward's sudden serious bronchitis.

On February 28 all were at Fenghua, and Annie's confinement appears to have been safely over. For on March 13 Hudson Taylor was with Feng Nenggui and Ninghai on the way to Jackson and the Cardwells at Taizhou. He sensed the approach of 'no slight persecution in China' and advised George Crombie, who was with him, not to delay in baptising the five believers he found there. Rumours were flying. To have burned their boats would help them if persecution broke out. News of Sir Rutherford Alcock's attitude and the change of policy by Lord Clarendon and the British government had reached them. 'We need to pray especially that the Gov. may not compel us to put off (Chinese) dress or otherwise interfere with our freedom of action,' he wrote to Maria on Sunday, 14th, after three church services during the day. The Duke of Somerset's attack in the House of Lords and the onslaught in the London newspapers had been during the week just past. It would be May before he knew of them.

He went to Taizhou for a painful few days of listening to Jackson's and the Cardwell's complaints about each other and other missionaries, their work and limitations. Mrs Cardwell could scarcely conceal her dislike of the Chinese. J E Cardwell's ill-health made Hudson Taylor anxious, but it might be simply that he had set his heart on pioneering far up the Yangzi river and nothing less would restore him. Hudson Taylor advised as best he could and kept it to himself for the present.

The quickest postal route to Taizhou or Wenzhou was by Ningbo and coastal steamer, so Maria sent a note to Hudson, saying that the *Chinese Recorder*'s editorial correcting '*The Times* strictures on us' had cheered her. But Annie Crombie had fever and each of their own children was ill. On the 25th her news was worse. Little Samuel was 'much worse, passing blood every hour or so', with much pain. He was to suffer incessantly from it, but so patiently that they marvelled – until he died eleven months later. She was giving him chlorodyne, but was it the right treatment? A Chinese baby in the lower part of the Crombies' house had smallpox and 'Tianbao' (Charles Edward) had come out in a rash. After reading Hudson's medical books she hoped it was a false alarm.

By then Hudson Taylor and Jackson were with Stott at Wenzhou, a large and important city, like Ningbo and Shaoxing in size. From a high hill on the overland journey they had seen the city ten miles away and counted thirty-five towns, villages and hamlets in the fertile plain around it. Taizhou in contrast had given up much of its agricultural land to growing opium poppies. Wenzhou was the farthest point on his journey and so far the least productive. Stott and his servant-companion were the only Christians, and this was the first visit by any other foreigner since they had arrived there. But after a few days with them Hudson Taylor and Jackson had to return.

The Wenzhou dialect was so different from either the Ningbo, which Hudson Taylor used in the south, or the Taizhou colloquial familiar to Jackson, that Wenzhou people could hardly understand them. The value of putting each dialect into roman script had been proved beyond doubt, and Hudson Taylor was working with Jackson to express the Taizhou dialect phonetically in roman letters. Nenggui, a completely uneducated farmer, was reading, writing and teaching his congregation at Ninghai, using the roman-ised New Testament and other books. Now (in the 1980s) that there are tens of thousands of Christians in each area, these humble beginnings take on new meaning.

Maria in Fenghua was schooling herself not to expect Hudson for another ten days or two weeks, when he arrived unannounced on April 5. The three weeks they had been parted 'seemed almost like so many months', she told Mary Berger. Samuel was better, but the Crombies' new baby was now ill with bronchitis. From Wenzhou Hudson Taylor had suggested that she invite Jennie for a short holiday to visit their honeymoon beauty spots with them. Travelling with Alosao, the first Hangzhou Christian woman, in the care of John McCarthy in another boat, she reached Fenghua on Tuesday, April 13.

The Crombie baby was 'out of danger'. But early on Wednesday morning it had 'a convulsion of the throat' and died. They all set off for Ningbo and on Thursday Hudson Taylor conducted the funeral in 'the little cemetery where the remains of the Crombies' first two lay', with Maria's first, and Martha Meadows, Dr Parker, Mrs Bausum and so many of their friends. George and Annie left the next day for their outpost at 'O-z', to be surrounded and consoled by converted Chinese friends. 'You would have shed tears of joy at the sight,' they wrote.

Hardly an hour after they left Ningbo a messenger arrived with an urgent letter from Cardwell to say that for the last few days they had been besieged by students attending the civil and military examinations and were 'in constant fear of trouble' and almost worn out. John McCarthy and Mr Tsiu, victim of the Xiaoshan flogging, and together involved in the Huzhou outrage, immediately offered to go with Hudson Taylor. The danger would continue for the month of examinations, and Mrs Cardwell and her child, 'great curiosities', would have to be sent to the Crombies. But when Hudson Taylor arrived 'the crisis had passed'. As soon as it became known that a message had been sent to Ningbo 'the abusive mobs (had) ceased to make trouble' and 'a great number of quiet hearers' took their place.

Hudson Taylor had decided to walk the hundred miles back to Ningbo, but that night 'evil-disposed persons' threatened them again, and he was afraid that 'if we leave and trouble should arise (Jackson and Cardwell), wearied out, might be impatient' and make matters worse. On the 26th he could only say to Maria, 'I *hope* the worst is over', but he did not know when he could come home. 'I do long to be with you, darling, but God has called me away and we must be content. . . . Now, my love, my precious one, my own fond darling, rest in Jesus' love, lie in *His* arms, lean on His bosom.' The letter included a page of detailed business, about handling cheques, and trying to buy plate-glass mirrors at Shanghai and Ningbo for the Yangzhou magistrate, and ended, 'Give my love to Miss Blatchley, Tell her if she loves me to take care of herself. . . . My heart yearns for you. Fondest love. J H T.' In the end he stayed the whole month, not leaving for Ningbo until about May 12.

Jennie's holiday had begun, continued and ended strangely. Without having got farther than Ningbo, she left on April 21 to return to Hangzhou, sleeping head to foot with Alosao in a foot-boat. She scarcely knew what to tell her parents in her letters home.

'I have got so accustomed to Chinese life and ways now, that it is difficult to know what to write about.'

For Maria it was hard to wait for possible news of a riot at Taizhou, to keep her five children happy in the Bridge Street garret and to carry on the Mission correspondence in Hudson Taylor's absence. On May 2 she told Mary Berger of a cheering letter from the Judds in Yangzhou. Among several new Christians was Mr Peng, the landlord of the inn they had occupied before the riot. 'I think he was much struck by my dear Husband's uprightness towards him in the matter of his indemnification . . . handing over such a large sum without deducting or at least requesting a portion, larger or smaller, as "thanks".' And on the 7th to Hudson, 'I have been writing all day and nearly all last night. Having got off the mail. . . . I turn with such different feelings to rest myself in writing to *you*. I need not weigh my words lest I give offence or cause misunderstanding.'

In long letters to the Bergers, Miss Stacey and others in Britain she was trying to set straight the tangled maze of misstatements about the Yangzhou affair. Meeting the Goughs, the Knowltons and other old friends of bygone days in Ningbo, she had ample opportunity to give them also the facts about the riot. Miles Knowlton's vigorous letter to the *Chinese Recorder* in defence of them was written on May 22. But Maria also had more news of criticisms in the Shanghai papers to share with Hudson.

Back from Taizhou he made a flying visit all the way to Yangzhou and a week later was with Maria in Ningbo again. Writing to his mother about the 'five not very little voices' of his children around him, he commented, 'I have been astonished at the wilful false-hoods circulated by the newspapers and political men, to suit their own ends. . . . Well, the Lord *reigns*. We must keep our eyes fixed on *Him*.' A passing reference to the baptism on May 17 of their boatman is all that points to long conversations and daily expla-nation of Scripture to him as they travelled long distances together. So week succeeded week, and as this chronicle proceeds, enlarging on the major events, the background of similar comings and goings, griefs and delights, needs to be kept in mind.

After all they had been through without a holiday in the past year, and with no urgent demands upon them for the present, they decided to take Emily and the children to the beautiful island of Putuo in the Zhoushan (Chusan) group. Peaceful and beautiful with a profusion of rhododendrons, Putuo with its beautiful, long sandy beach and tranquil temples was popular as a resort of Ningbo and Shanghai residents. For once he would drop work completely and they would enjoy the children together.

'Incurable idiot'[3]   *June 1869*

For a·full fortnight they seem to have made the most of this holiday. Not a line to anyone hints that any work disturbed their peace. By deduction from references before and afterwards they appear to have enjoyed Putuo from about May 20 until June 5. Then that bliss was over. By June 8, Maria, Emily and the children were with Jennie at Hangzhou and in the lakeside hills. But Hudson Taylor in Ningbo had taken up the threads of work, brought himself up to date on world news and was writing to tell a colleague to 'wrestle mightily' in prayer that they might not all be forced out of their hard-won stations in the interior. The Abbé Gilles was flogged to death at Zunyi in Guizhou on June 14. To Maria, Hudson wrote on the 15th, 'My ague is over', and again on the 19th, but from Shanghai.

To his astonishment he found on reaching Shanghai that he was under attack yet again, the butt of merciless slander. Instead of completing the business he had come to do, and going straight on to rejoin Maria at Suzhou, he stayed to find out what was happening. In the *Shanghai Evening Courier* of June 14 he read,

> A report has reached us from Ningpo that the Reverend Mr Taylor of the Inland Mission, recently went on a preaching tour to Pootoo; an island, as is well known, exclusively devoted to the worship of Buddha. The priests who are the sole inhabitants of the island, protested against such an invasion of their privileges, and laid the matter before the (*daotai*). Instructed by the latter, Mr Bowra, commissioner of customs at Ningpo, appealed to the British Consul, who has summarily ordered Mr Taylor to retire from the island.

The *North China Daily News* repeated the paragraph, and an editorial in the following evening's *Courier* enlarged on it.

Mr Taylor's Visit to Pootoo
Mr Taylor's religion is peripatetic. Today at Hangchow, tomorrow at Soochow, the next day making philters of babies' eyes at Yang-chau, and finally alarming the peaceful seclusion of shaven and placid

BUDDHIST PRIESTS ON TRANQUIL PUTUO

priests at Pootoo, this restless apostle is as difficult to lay hold of as a flea in a blanket. . . . It was unnecessary to invoke the aid of the Consul to banish him from the little island where he was last heard of, for his own unquiet disposition would have carried him off speedily enough. . . .

We are not altogether surprised that Mr Taylor found himself at this particular time at Pootoo. Christians of his stamp whose every step is dictated by an immediate inspiration of the Holy Spirit, are generally guided to the most pleasant places attainable without too great an appearance of inconsistency (and at the pleasantest season to do so).

On the morning of Hudson Taylor's arrival at Shanghai, a wag in another periodical, the *Shanghai Recorder*, in an equally ill-informed article went one better.

> Giving Mr Taylor full credit for his clerico-surgical character, we imagine that he has forsaken his vocation. In various parts of Great Britain there are to be found institutions (in many of which) the possession of a surgeon who could also officiate as chaplain would be an inestimable advantage. Among the institutions of this kind which present themselves to our memory one stands out with exceptional clearness – the Hospital for Incurable Idiots. We wish Mr Taylor could obtain admission in some capacity to this excellent asylum. Were he an inmate, much trouble that now occurs would be prevented . . .

Meanwhile Hudson Taylor called on the editor of the *Courier* to give him the facts, and wrote to Maria, waiting at Suzhou for him.

> A series of articles in the papers here (has stated) that I went to P'u-t'u for purposes of propagandism and had made a disturbance thereby. . . . You may suppose the anti-missionary papers did not let this pass without comment. 'The pestilent folly (of Mr Taylor) at Pootoo . . . it is not to be borne that an individual who has already by his stupidity produced serious political complications, should be permitted to roam about the country preparing ill-feeling and ill-treatment for every foreigner who may be unfortunate enough to follow his route.'

The editor of the *Evening Courier* tried to extricate himself by a curious bit of duplicity. Complaining of the paragraphs in the *Shanghai Recorder* and *North China Daily News* having led to 'an unusually severe article on Mr Taylor and his Mission in the *Evening Courier* of the 15th', he drew attention to another article in the *Shanghai Recorder* 'so rude as to be almost brutal'. He then proceeded to repeat the facts Hudson Taylor had given him, and to say,

> Going there in search of health, they confined themselves strictly to that pursuit. There was no preaching; no discussion; no distribution of religious books; there was not even a religious conversation with a priest. . . . There was no tumult, no representation to the (*daotai*), no mediatory message through Mr Bowra [of the customs] to the Consul, and no order from the latter for Mr Taylor to leave. . . . No

persons, perhaps, were more astonished on perusing your article than Mr Bowra and the Consul at Ningpo. . . .
Yours truly,
    'Scrutator'

On his own copy of the *Courier* Hudson Taylor made the note, 'Scrutator is the Editor himself. JHT'! The next morning the *North China Daily News* simply published an 'official denial' by W H Fittack, HM consul at Ningbo,

> I deem it right to state that no complaint whatever has been made to H.M.'s Consul at this port, of the nature referred to; that Mr Taylor has not been inhibited as stated; and that the British Consul has not summarily ordered Mr Taylor to retire from the island, on the appeal of Mr Bowra, the Commissioner of Customs, or the appeal of any one else.
>
> As the assertions referred to have no foundation in truth, and as they are of a mischievous character, I consider it my duty to give them my official contradiction and shall feel obliged by your publishing the same.

By then the European mail steamer had sailed and Hudson Taylor had to tell Maria, 'I regret that the statements have gone home a mail before the retractions can do. Nevertheless "the Lord reigneth".' While the troublemaker in Ningbo chuckled over his success, and 'Veritas' sent home to *The Times* his 'gunboat under the window' letter (p 181), Hudson Taylor's uncomfortably sensitive nature smarted under the taunts. Petty in themselves, they added to the strain on the camel's back.

Waiting in Suzhou for him to join her, Maria knew how despised he felt and wrote '*I* want you'. But the mischief was not easily laid. The missionary *Chinese Recorder* for July cited the falsehood and only retracted it in August with a denial that Hudson Taylor 'had endeavoured to establish a branch of his mission on the island, and had been required by the British Consul to desist.' Miles Knowlton's reply to the attacks in the House of Lords and *The Times* was published in the same issue of the *Chinese Recorder*, a whole year after the misreported events at Yangzhou.[4]

Anqing at last[5]   *January–July 1869*

Hardly had the reinstatement at Yangzhou been effected in November 1868 than James Meadows and James Williamson were preparing to advance 200 miles up the Yangzi to Anqing. Boarding a river junk with Chinese companions on December 26, they arrived on January 8, 1869, and lay low, moored among the many other boats along the bank. Li Hongzhang, a native of Anhui province, (returning from his final, successful campaign against the Nianfei rebels in the north and on his way to take up office at Wuchang as viceroy of Hubei and Hunan) was staying at Anqing with a huge retinue until after the Chinese New Year in February. Every available house in the city was occupied. So, leaving their Chinese colleagues to prospect for accommodation, Meadows and Williamson went on to Jiujiang (Kiukiang) 100 miles farther upstream, to arrange for mail to be forwarded and to confer with W H Lay, the acting consul at this trading post. There they made the acquaintance of an American Methodist Episcopal missionary, V C Hart and of M G Hollingworth, a merchant, the only Protestants in Jiangxi. Both were to become good friends of the CIM. (Josiah Cox, the English Methodist, had already been withdrawn.)

Li Hongzhang was in no hurry to move on and made the most of the celebrations at Anqing until ten days after the New Year (on February 10). As soon as he and his followers had gone, Meadows and Williamson called on the prefect and district magistrate who received them courteously and promised to help them find accommodation. But the sub-prefect to whom they were referred 'seemed anything but pleased, and remarked that our passports said nothing about renting houses. We replied that the treaty did, and showed him a treaty proclamation. . . . A day or two after, we sent our servants to engage a room for us at the inn. . . . The innkeeper was quite willing, and said it was no matter whether we were foreigners or (Chinese), so long as we paid for our accommodation.' But when they themselves arrived, having sent their baggage ahead, the troubled innkeeper said there was no room for them – 'some persons had been trying to frighten him. We were now in an awkward position. If we took back our luggage to the boat, it would soon be reported all over the place two "foreign devils" wanted to get into an inn in the city but had been put out. . . . We then sent a message to the district magistrate, who immediately sent for the innkeeper and told him to provide a room for us, which he then gladly did, and the same evening even offered to rent us the whole house.'

Two days later the garrison commander sent for their servant. 'Suspecting they might be planning some mischief,' Meadows went with him, to the mandarin's alarm. Asked why he had set men to watch them as if they were thieves or robbers, he claimed with profuse apologies that the provincial governor, a Manchu named Ying Han, had reprimanded him for allowing them to enter the city. Yet only a few days later the prefect and sub-prefect received them very politely. The governor, they explained, had consulted the viceroy, Ma Xinyi, at Nanjing, and a reply had come that,

> we had a right to preach our doctrine; but there was one thing they did not understand exactly about our passports. When any of the French priests came there, they always brought a letter having the seal of the viceroy, and if we would write our Consul and get such a letter, it would simplify matters. . . . Mr Meadows then went to (Jiujiang), and stated the matter to Mr Lay . . . who told him it was evidently a subterfuge on their part to get rid of us, that our passports and the twelfth article of the treaty were sufficient [Book 4, p 27].

A week after Meadows' return from Jiujiang a proclamation by prefect, sub-prefect and magistrate was displayed outside the inn door saying 'that the religious teachers . . . were there to preach their religion and had passports certifying their respectability and that it was perfectly optional for anyone to connect themselves with the religion but not compulsory. They issued the proclamation to inform the soldiers and people so that they will peaceably pursue their own business, keep the laws, and respect the treaty.'

So far so good, but it said nothing about renting premises. While the mandarins were known to be obstructive, however superficially polite, the townsfolk dared not be friendly. 'It is very trying, wearying work having to deal with unscrupulous officials who, while outwardly professing to be very friendly, may secretly be doing all they can against us,' Williamson wrote,

> Whereas in other places, if we go into a teashop we soon have numbers of persons about us, asking questions, etc, here they will not take the least notice of us. We often give away a few tracts in a teashop, but seldom get into conversation. . . . Meanwhile, I am staying at the inn, and busy making inquiry about houses. The forenoon is generally spent studying Mandarin with a Nankin teacher, while in the afternoon I mostly go out and pass a little time in a teashop; the reserve and evident suspicion of the people prevent my doing much in this way. . . . We must be very careful to guard against doing anything which might cause disturbance, and thus frustrate our efforts.

At last on April 21, while Meadows was visiting his wife and new baby, born at Nanjing, Williamson succeeded in renting a house with three upstairs rooms, breezier and freer from mosquitoes than the ground floor. Well situated on a small hill in the heart of the city near the governor's *yamen*, it showed promise of being healthier and safer than anything they had expected to find. Since December 26 their only home had been their little boat. On Meadows' return they reported their deed of rental to the authorities and the landlord agreed to improvements. At once 'some of the literati, with the neighbours, threatened to burn down the premises'.

Hudson Taylor received the news with the remark, 'I hope no trouble will arise there.' So far every inch of the way was being contested. The natural route to the far western province of Guizhou was up the Yangzi to Wuchang or beyond, and then overland; and further up the Yangzi to Sichuan. But all remained peaceful at Anqing. Mrs Meadows (Elizabeth Rose of the *Lammermuir*) and the children joined them and, undeterred by threats, the Meadows family and Williamson moved into their rented premises on July 9, 1869, the historic date of their 'occupation' of the city and province, the first of 'the eleven'. 'But for the (Yangzhou) affairs, (Anqing) would not have been so easily opened,' Hudson Taylor suggested. He spoke too soon. It was only a matter of time before 'Yangzhou' was repeated at Anqing, without consular intervention.

Undercurrents of danger   *June–October 1869*

Alarm elsewhere had not ended. News of the plundering of the Catholic mission at Zunyi in Guizhou on June 14 and the flogging of the Abbé Gilles so severely that he died from the effects on August 13, must have reached Viceroy Li Hongzhang, Anhui governor Ying Han and Viceroy Ma Xinyi within two weeks or so. Also in 1869 the French chargé d'affaires, Comte de Rochechourt, while visiting Shanxi province to assess the commercial possibilities and to scotch rumours that all foreigners were soon to be expelled from China, narrowly escaped assassination in Taiyuan, the provincial capital.[6] This too would have been known before the summer had passed.

In August another James Williamson, of the LMS (*see* Book 4 p 218 – the younger brother of Alexander Williamson), and William Bramwell Hodge of the Methodist New Connexion, left Tianjin in a boat to visit outstations. Soon after midnight of the

25th, while moored in a canal which daily carried merchants with large sums of money and unguarded goods, they were attacked and plundered. When Hodge was woken by the boatmen's shouts and jumped ashore, he saw no sign of Williamson. A gang of armed men attacked him with the flat of their swords, 'unaccountably not using the edges' until he was 'severely bruised from head to foot'. Making his way to the local magistrate's *yamen*, he met the mandarin already coming 'with a company of soldiers' – a highly suspicious fact. They 'set off in pursuit of the robbers' and began to search for James Williamson. His body was found three days later, in the canal twelve miles away.[7] The *North China Daily News* later carried the observation, 'Who ever heard of a mandarin and his followers being up and on the watch between twelve and one o'clock in the morning? Those who have lived long in China know how unlikely, if not impossible, it is for a band of robbers to commit such a deed and remain undetected, if the authority had the will to do it.' Circumstantial evidence was strong that the mandarin was implicated.

September saw the emergence of a dangerous new factor. In Hunan, 'always conservative and anti-foreign', a placard was published which found its way throughout the empire and lay at the root of a deepening animosity. Summarising the history of Christianity in China, it declared that 'pernicious doctrines were daily gaining ground'. Jesus was born during the Han dynasty. Was the world without a divine ruler before that? 'This young serpent must be crushed before it attains its full monster growth!'

In October when a missionary of the American Board attempted to take possession of premises he had leased at 'I-cho' [probably Yi Xian] only seventy miles south-west of Peking, the doors were locked against him. The magistrate had the middleman heavily fined and flogged on his legs and face until the flesh of one thigh was sloughed to a depth of an inch, allegedly for helping a foreigner to obtain premises so near (seven miles) to the imperial tombs. The people of the city had been friendly and willing to have missionaries live among them. When the Zongli Yamen supported the magistrate, the US Minister at Peking chose to take no action. C A Stanley (possibly the missionary referred to) concluded that success or failure in any locality depended upon the liberality or prejudices of the local mandarins and literati. In some instances the risk to the Chinese implicated was greater than that to the foreigner.[8]

Too much for one?   *July–December 1869*

For the last six months of the year Hudson Taylor was like a cork on a choppy sea. Willing to a fault to go to the aid of anyone in need, he still adapted his other work to those claims. After five months on the move, he and Maria were home again in Yangzhou on June 25, but already planning to return to the trouble spots of Taizhou and Wenzhou as soon as they could. Emily and the older three children were with the McCarthys at Hangzhou. 'It is a real trial, and not a small one, to her to be away from us,' Maria told Mrs Berger, 'and we shall much miss her loving attentions and invaluable help.' Since leaving Britain Emily had developed 'a maturity of Christian character' which marked her as one of the Mission's most valuable members.

In contrast with what they had found in the south, there was a good spirit among the missionaries and the handful of Christian Chinese at Yangzhou. The Judds' zeal and Louise Desgraz' stability made them a good team. Looking back only a year to when they were still homeless, cramped together in leaking boats while trying to gain a toehold, they took heart from the contrast. For here they were in their own house with hardly a trace of riot or arson or personal injury, but, instead, their landlord, their loyal carpenter, Mr Peng the innkeeper, their boatman and others who had been no more than pagan bystanders, were 'one in Christ' with them.

For two months they came and went between Yangzhou and Zhenjiang, torn between duty and the illness of one and another. Meadows and Williamson had at last gained possession of the rented premises of their own in Anqing. On July 20 George Duncan succeeded in occupying a house in Qingjiangpu, a hundred miles up the Grand Canal. While Alcock was forging his shackles they were pressing 'onward and inward'.

But Hudson Taylor could join none of them. The Judds were unwell and had to go on holiday while the Taylors did their work. Then urgent news arrived from Emily and McCarthy at Hangzhou. Howard and little Maria were ill with symptoms alarmingly like those from which Grace had died two years ago. What should they do? Take them to Ningbo and by steamer to Shanghai, Hudson Taylor replied. But while letters travelled up and down the Grand Canal between them, how ill were the children? The emergency drove the Taylors to the realisation that this life of homelessness, of travelling and bivouacking, exposed to disease, and staying with other missionaries for short periods was no life for their family. 'It is a serious question with me whether I may not have to send the elder children home before long,' Hudson Taylor confided to his mother. By the time they reached Shanghai the threat of meningitis had passed. John McCarthy put Emily on the river steamer to Zhenjiang and returned home to Hangzhou.

On August 7 they were all together again. But on the 22nd Hudson Taylor was wondering if he himself was developing pneumonia, and if Samuel's incessant 'dysentery' was tuberculous enteritis. Hardly had he himself picked up than Maria was 'very ill'. Her pulmonary tuberculosis had shown fewer symptoms recently, but a tormenting suspicion that she and Samuel shared the same lethal disease was growing on him.

September had to be given to another visit to Hangzhou and Ningbo. To travel farther to see Stott again was out of the question. Even in the 'state room' of their streamlined footboat, 'little more than a canoe', as Maria described it to Mrs Berger, they continued their unceasing correspondence. 'Carefully packed up together with sundry small boxes and baskets – in a space (less than six feet by four) considerably smaller than your dining room table,' she, Hudson and Samuel lived, ate, worked and played for days at a time. 'Comfort is as much a matter of the mind as the body, if not more so,' she concluded. While they were away the Anqing magistrate had sent for Meadows and Williamson and warned them to lie low during the literary examinations, the first hint of the trouble to come.

October brought new anxieties, painful letters to be written to unhappy colleagues, and separation from Maria again when Hudson Taylor returned to Zhenjiang while she stayed in Hangzhou and Ningbo to help in Jennie's preparations for a girls' school, in addition to the one for boys. Month after month the funds of the Mission were at a low ebb. Loss of confidence attributable to the press attacks had followed the accusations of irresponsible behaviour. 'The Mission funds are lower than they ever were before,' he told the team. Some took for granted all he did for them and even complained of neglect, not seeing, or forgetting, that he did as much for each. Occasionally he reminded them of this to make them think. Hudson Taylor wrote (always by hand in his duplicate 'manifold') to James Meadows, his most senior and experienced colleague after six years in China, who had just written thoughtlessly.

(Zhenjiang), October 31, 1869

As to correspondence, I do my best to keep up to it, but there is a limit to one's time and strength. . . . What can I do beyond trust to your consideration and forbearance? My personal incompetence for the many and onerous responsibilities devolving upon me, is far from being unfelt by me. So far from this, I have very seriously considered the question of attempting to retire from them. And if I am led to work on, it is from the belief that I have neither sought nor pleased myself in the position I now find myself in, and that He who placed me in it, can and will work through me all He intends to be done through me in it. And this thought gives me indescribable peace and comfort, under a burden that would otherwise be intolerable. . . . I have no Mission soap, but I am expecting some of my own in a month or so from England. I might perhaps be able to let you have some of that if you like. Would you wish one quarter or one half (hundredweight)? . . . P.S. It just occurs to me to add that some of the members of the Mission may be unaware of the amount of labour involved in helping them. It is *real* pleasure to do so; but it is none the less onerous. For instance, I have to write to Mr Müller to thank him for your cheque, to Mr Lord asking him kindly to sell it, as he gets a better price than the Shanghai banks will give. Then to enter it in his account, and in my cash account. Then to send the amount to Mr Hart [the American Episcopal V C Hart at Jiujiang] with a note requesting him kindly to forward it. Of course I must also advise you of it. . . . Just now I have seven different portions of Old and New Testament (whole books), and long tracts sent me in several dialects with requests to revise them. This, if possible, is the work of weeks if not months. Yet I am praying for guidance as to whether I may not have to leave *tonight* for one of our most distant stations on account of a case of sickness.

Tempted as Hudson Taylor might often have been to abandon the role of leader and return to pioneering with a few loyal friends, the very thought was sterile. No one could replace him and few had the determination to persist without him. So far not one in the team, not even McCarthy or Stevenson, was ready to share his load as an assistant or deputy. He must soldier on. So to Mary Bowyer at Nanjing he next wrote,

This morning I was called up early and ere long Mrs Rudland presented us with a fine little girl. . . . I enclose the stamps you wrote for. Some tincture of benzoine shall be sent to Mr Duncan. We increasingly feel the power of the truths we were speaking of together; they are joy and strength every day. There is good work going on at Yangchau. Five were baptized last month. . . . I enclose the santonine I spoke to Mr Duncan about for Mrs Duncan. . . . The best thing you can do for Mrs D if she suffers in her back is to try ten drop doses of Sweet Spirits of Nitre with three drops of Laudanum three or four times a day.

PS I must see what I can do about quinine.

And, urgently to John McCarthy, because of another confinement to attend, 'I should have left for Hangchau this evening, but my boatman's (partner) has refused to go. We cannot hire another here, and I should be too late for Mrs Dodd if I wait for Thursday's steamer, or travel by a slow boat. The Lord will doubtless order all for the best.' To George Crombie at Fenghua, 'If you like to send the copy of *Ecclesiastes* here I will try to finish revising it and have it printed.' And to Cardwell at Taizhou, 'I see no objection to your proposal as to (Jiujiang), if attempted solely as a basis for action as soon as possible in the interior.'

Even so, within an hour or two of Mary Rudland's delivery Hudson Taylor was on his way to Hangzhou, leaving Maria to look after her, and travelling fast by footboat. By November 5 he was there and none too soon. He found the McCarthy children and Charles Kreyer very ill – so ill was Kreyer that after recovery he left Hangzhou and his mission. Sarah Dodd's child arrived safely, but serious news arrived from Zhenjiang and Hudson Taylor could not delay more than three days. Jennie wrote home,

A Romish priest reported that the house we had at (Anqing) (inhabited by Meadows and Williamson) had been pulled to the ground. . . . He had come down (to Zhenjiang) to put matters into the hands of the French Consul. . . . Then we heard that the Shanghai papers reported the disturbance and added that the missionaries had this time paid with their lives the penalty of their position, or words to that effect. This is all we know. . . . I trust that we shall find that much has been made out of little. . . . Still the Lord reigneth, He has allowed whatever has taken place. . . . It may be that as a Mission we are to be baptized with His baptism and so made more fruitful. His will be done.

The news was two weeks old already. As he travelled Hudson Taylor reported events to the Bergers. Saying nothing of the alleged loss of life at Anqing, he spoke of being most anxious lest his friends had been injured and needed his help. But as he neared Zhenjiang where the full facts would be known, he unburdened his heart to his old friend George Pearse.

> Some seem to think the whole party were killed. . . . I know not and can only throw the burden on the Lord. . . . And now, it may be, He is about to take us through more trying and painful experiences than we have previously experienced. What shall we say? 'Father, glorify Thy name', says the spirit, though the flesh is weak and trembles. *He* is our strength, and what we cannot do or bear, *He* can both do and bear in us.

After that, the Anqing affair would have filled his time and thoughts had not new troubles of many kinds descended upon him. December was fraught with tension. Maria and he decided that their four eldest children – Herbert, Howard, Maria and Samuel – must go home to Britain. It held Samuel's only hope of recovery, if indeed he lived through the journey. At great personal grief, Emily undertook to escort and mother them. Maria herself became more and more frail. Serious lapses in morale and conduct among their missionaries tore almost as painfully at their heart-strings; and, ominously, the Bergers' health was failing. The pressures of the Yangzhou riot aftermath had told severely on them. Mary Berger could eat nothing without severe pain. Then William wrote of growing convictions on a subject already theological dynamite in the world of the 'evangelical revival' which provided most of the Mission's support. Andrew Jukes was propagating the revolutionary idea of the 'non-eternity of punishment'. Not only was it the negation of Hudson Taylor's beliefs, so strongly expressed in *China: Its Spiritual Need and Claims*, but it was resisted as unbiblical and therefore heretical by evangelical Christians as a whole. William Berger knew and declared to Hudson Taylor that if his openness to Jukes' arguments became known, the CIM would be doomed. So he had better resign. Hudson Taylor should come home – for other reasons also.

How could he go? He could not be spared from China. How then could the year end on the note of another advance, into yet another province? But it did. This time it was Jiangxi – by the disappointing J E Cardwell, in a dramatic change of character.

Silver lining   1869

To look back very briefly – when he launched the Mission in 1865 Hudson Taylor had no illusions about the difficulties ahead. But knowing what to expect did not make it less hard to bear. Opposition from the Chinese was acceptable. Scorn from cynical foreigners could be tolerated. Opposition from fellow missionaries was a greater test of resilience. But a sense of personal failure and sinfulness when he was sincerely trying to serve and please God he found to be supremely distressing. In his cri de coeur to his mother from Ninghai on March 13, 1869 (p 174) it was not his health or persecutions or perplexities but his failure to be as Christlike as he longed to be that distressed him. His brother missionaries and Maria knew his failings well enough. 'Oftentimes I am tempted to think that one so full of sin cannot be a child of God at all.'

Readers unfamiliar with the Pietism of this period (not in the sense of exaggerated or feigned piety but of the historical movement) may be interested to follow the process of thought which had such far-reaching results. Not surprisingly, he had confessed to 'irritability of temper' as his besetting sin, his 'daily hourly failure'. It was hard to suffer fools gladly. And long separations from Maria subjected him to added tension. During 1869 *The Revival* magazine in Britain carried a series of articles by R Pearsall Smith, whose influential addresses at Oxford largely gave rise to the Keswick Movement which still draws thousands together annually in several countries around the world. As John McCarthy recalled, his expositions 'had led many of us to think of a much higher (plane) of life and service than we had before thought possible'. Copies of *The Revival*, reaching every CIM station, were creating a desire in many of the Mission to attain to this spiritual goal which for convenience at this point was being called 'holiness' or 'the victorious life'. Before long other terms superseded these to express the answer discovered. In the CIM 'the exchanged life' and 'union with Christ' or just 'union' came to sum up their thinking.[9] William Collingwood, Louise Desgraz' former employer, wrote to her on the subject and in Yangzhou she and the Judds were 'seeking holiness'. In Zhenjiang the Rudlands, at Suzhou the Cordons and in Hangzhou the McCarthys and Jennie Faulding all responded with the same longing as Hudson Taylor himself. Only Maria was unmoved, wondering (as McCarthy put it) 'what we were all groping after . . . (an) experience she had long been living in the enjoyment of. . . . I have rarely met as Christlike a Christian as Mrs Taylor.' In Judd's words '(It) gave her that beautiful calmness and confidence in God (in which) up to that time she so surpassed her husband.'

The subject has been well documented by the Howard Taylors

and in Hudson Taylor's subsequent writings and addresses. Here it is enough to show how his own life came to be revolutionised – in timely preparation for the hardest experiences yet to come his way. J J Coulthard, who in time married Hudson Taylor's daughter Maria, recalled in 1905 that Hudson Taylor used to say that when he could bear his distress no longer and was crying to the Lord for help, the words of Scripture, 'He that cometh to me shall never (at any time) hunger, and he that believeth in me shall never thirst' came to him with such power that he knew his search would soon end. 'Cometh' in the sense of 'keeps coming' was the secret. He need never be thirsty again.

Towards the end of August, after his illness at Yangzhou with what he thought to be pneumonia and Maria's subsequent attack of enteritis, he advised Duncan to bring Catherine, his wife, and Mary Bowyer to Zhenjiang because of the Yangzi flooding at Nanjing. They needed boats to move about the city. There at Zhenjiang in the first week of September Hudson Taylor found a letter from John McCarthy waiting for him. They had been in Shanghai together, both dissatisfied with themselves, both on the same search, discussing their spiritual hunger yet unable to help each other. But by August 20 McCarthy was back in Hangzhou surprised by the joy of discovery and quick to share his find with his friend.

> At the time that you were speaking to me, (Holiness) was the subject of all others, which occupied my thoughts. . . . I have thought of others whom I have met – (Grattan) Guinness for instance . . . who seemed able to guide the minds of those with whom they came in contact – *influencing* instead of *being influenced*, really accomplishing that which the Saviour said we should – not only themselves *full*, but full to overflowing, and overflowing for the good of others. Do you know dear Brother I now think this striving effort, longing, hoping for better days yet to come – is not the true way to happiness, Holiness or Usefulness. . . . I have been struck with a passage from a book of yours here – 'Christ is All' – it said, 'The Saviour *welcomed*, is all Holiness begun. The Saviour cherished is all Holiness advancing. *The Saviour never absent*, is Holiness complete. . . . A channel is now formed, by which Christ's fulness plenteously flows down. The barren branch becomes a portion of the fruitful stem. . . . The limbs receive close union with the head, *and one life* reigns throughout the (whole). . . . To *let* my living Saviour work in me *His will* – my sanctification – is what I would live for . . . Abiding, not striving, nor struggling. . . .'
>
> I seem as if the first glimmer of the dawn of a glorious day has risen

upon me. I hail it with trembling – yet with trust. I seem to have got to the edge only – but of a sea which is boundless. To have sipped only of that which can fully satisfy. Christ *literally 'all'* seems now to be the power, the *only* power for service.[10]

The next day he had posted the book, and another letter in which he wrote about believing 'with a true heart in full assurance of faith' that we can boldly *'enter into the holiest'* with hearts cleansed from an evil conscience – because of all that Jesus has done for us and now is to us.

How then to have our faith increased? Only by thinking of all that Jesus *is* – all he is *for us*. . . . Not a striving to have faith or to increase our faith. But a looking at the faithful One, seems all we need, a resting in the loved One.

This truth had dawned upon Jennie too, now happier than ever. In Zhenjiang as Hudson Taylor read, the light broke for him also and the next day he wrote to Louise Desgraz at Yangzhou that he had shared McCarthy's letter with all the others. Louise had found the answer before him. 'I have seldom seen so remarkable a change in anyone as has taken place in Miss D. . . . Now she is calm and happy.'

To me it has been the happiest day I have spent for a long time [he said]. The part specially helpful to me is 'How then to have our faith increased, only by thinking of all that Jesus is *for us*. His life, His death, His work.'. . . Here I feel is the secret. Not asking how I am to get sap out of the vine *into* myself, but remembering that Jesus *is* the vine – the root, stem, branches, twigs, leaves, flowers, fruit – all indeed.[11]

On September 4 Emily Blatchley had written in her journal, 'He too has now received the *rest* of soul that Jesus gave to me some little time ago.' Instead of *'trying* to abide' in Jesus the Vine and asking to be kept so abiding, as if Jesus were the *root* and we as the branches having to 'get hold and *keep* hold', he wrote, 'the truth is that He is the whole vine and we are in Him.' So relax! Enjoy the flowing sap!

He seems to have paid a quick visit to Yangzhou, his home, for Charles Judd recalled years later,

Late one evening, I went into his house to welcome him back and at once saw that his heart was full of joy. He walked up and down the room saying 'Oh Mr Judd, God has made me a new man! God has made me a new man! I see that I *am* a branch in Christ, really united to Him; I have not to *make* myself a branch, He says that I am one ('Ye are the branches') and I have simply to believe in Him.' If I have a thousand dollars in the Bank and ask the clerk at the counter to give me five hundred, putting out my hand to receive them, he cannot refuse them to my hand and say 'They are Mr Taylor's; for my hand is part of myself: what is mine is my hand's also, and my hand can take it. I am part of Christ, and what is His I can take.' His faith had now taken hold of the fact of his union – living and actual union – with Christ.[12]

He was due to go down to Ningbo again and took Maria with him by canal. It gave them a day at Hangzhou with McCarthy and Jennie, and a chance to share his discoveries with Wang Lae-djün and Mr Tsiu. At Ningbo he called as many missionaries together as he could meet and shared with them and with Frederick Gough 'our oneness with the risen, exalted Saviour . . . the mighty power of absolute and indissoluble union with Him. . . . O the years I have struggled to abide in Him . . . to get virtue out of Him . . . practically forgetful of the fulness of Him in whom we are.'

The difficulties of life did not lessen, but he could write to encourage the disconsolate William Berger on October 8 by pointing out that five of the missionaries he, Hudson Taylor, had chosen had been a disappointment, but only two or three of those sent by Berger. Yet he did not despair, for now he was trusting that 'the fruit of the vine comes from *abiding*, not *striving*'. God in His wisdom would give him the ability he needed and use him.

Familiar with *The Revival* articles, the Bergers took exception to the overstressing of the passive, receptive aspect of 'holiness'. They replied emphasising the need for active resistance to evil and of effort to obey God, just as Bishop J C Ryle in his books was to balance the Keswick Movement's emphases a few years later.

Far from denying the rightness of his friend's cautions, Hudson Taylor and several of his team were finding in their newly-discovered truths the answer to their present need. Sharing the apostle Paul's paradoxical experience he could say, 'In all our troubles my joy knew no bounds.' (2 Cor. 7.4) 'Now He makes me happy all day long, makes my work light, gives me joy in blessing others . . . I have no fear now of our work being too heavy for Him in Britain or China,' he told the Bergers. Yet funds were lower than ever before, inflammatory placards were being posted again, and in Anqing the riot was only days away. He was ready now for whatever the future might hold. Little could he imagine what that would be.

The Anqing riot[13]   *August–November 1869*

In Anqing the regional literary examinations were about to begin. The magistrate sent for Meadows and Williamson, asked them to suspend public preaching and indirectly urged that they should leave the city, 'hinting at . . . the lawless character of the candidates'.

> We informed him that we had not yet commenced public preaching, and . . . intended to take every precaution . . . to avoid coming into collision with these students. [But even so in August] 'it was rumoured abroad, that by some mysterious influences . . . we had brought over to our views 135 persons the first night, and almost as many the second; and that 240 children had been stowed away, eaten, or otherwise disposed of'. . . . The trouble, time and expense . . . put it out of the question to leave the city with Mrs Meadows and children and the greater part of our goods for three months; . . . and we were the more encouraged to stay in the city during the prefectural examinations seeing we were not so much as insulted during the time of the district examinations.

On November 2, however, an inflammatory placard in large letters was posted on the walls of the Literary Examination Hall, calling on the students and others, to pull the mission house down on the 5th because it was occupied by 'Religious Brigands'.

Meadows and Williamson therefore called on the *daotai*, whose refusal to see them was taken by 'a large number both of literary and military candidates' in the large court of the *yamen* as an excuse for attacking them. 'Williamson's chair was . . . nearly knocked over, with horrid shoutings of, "Kill the Foreign Devils, Beat the Foreign Devils!"' Rushing back into the *daotai's* judgment hall and calling, according to custom, for protection, they were besieged by a mob shouting for their death.

Meanwhile Elizabeth Meadows and the children had been assaulted by another mob at home. The doors she had barricaded with furniture and boxes were battered down, and 'with my Louise in my arms, Sammy screaming at my side, and (the amah) crying, my own heart aching, the blood running through my veins with an icy coldness, I watched' scores of people plunder the premises.

> Each one for himself tore open drawers, boxes, and cupboards, carrying off everything in them . . . – now an armful of crockery, now one of clothes, another of books, now and then stopping to break out the windows. Boxes and cupboards as they were emptied were thrown out. . . .
>
> I got downstairs somehow, receiving some severe blows by the violent manner in which the men carried the things out. I did not know where to go, but went first to the teachers' room hoping there to be protected. . . . There was a gentleman in the room whom I had not seen before, and he was helping us, taking all he could from the thieves and stowing them in this room. He made way for me to get into the room and kept the mob out as long as he could, getting his face bruised for his pains.

The mob then plundered this place also, and her person, taking the few dollars she had secreted, and her wedding ring, and even making 'violent efforts to get my Louise' from her.

At last the magistrate arrived. A faithful Christian servant then took her hand and led her through the mob to join her husband in the *yamen*. After dark they were given some bedding and money for food and, otherwise completely destitute, were put on board two little river boats, to go wherever they could.

On the same day the Roman Catholic mission at Anqing and 'Kienteh' were similarly pillaged. According to the *Shanghai Recorder*, 'It is known that the mob made two visits to the China Inland Mission, and . . . destroyed the Roman Catholic Mission in the interval.'[14] While the Meadows family and Williamson painfully made their way to Jiujiang, an English Catholic priest managed to board a steamer and reached Zhenjiang on the 5th, bringing the first news of the riots. No more was heard until Charles Judd was told that 'a foreigner had been killed' at Anqing 'endeavouring to keep the mob from entering the house'.

The night was wintry and bleak. A strong wind blowing upstream met the river current head on and whipped the surface of the Yangzi into angry waves. Nothing could be done but to sit huddled together and endure. Still dishevelled from the riot, they had not even a comb between them, no soap nor towel. 'I took off my chemise to make a napkin for Louise,' Elizabeth wrote. And in this state they reached Jiujiang on November 9 only to find that the friendly

American Episcopal V C Hart was away until the next day. Preparing to spend another wretched night in the boats, their delight may be imagined when M G Hollingworth, the merchant, hearing of their arrival came looking for them. He had his own house full of guests, so he 'did all in his power to make us comfortable' in an empty house, sending 'table, chairs, bedding, coal; and two ladies to inquire into our circumstances . . . (one sent me two changes of underclothing and the other a complete suit of outer clothing). He sent us (food) direct from his own table, and came early the next morning to fetch us to breakfast.'

To Williamson, Jiujiang had 'a nice foreign settlement' with thirty foreign residents, 'a small, neatly built church, and a resident chaplain'. When the Harts returned they brought the refugees into their own home, H N Lay, the consul, took a statement from them and Hollingworth procured free passages on a steamer to Zhenjiang. On the night of the 11th he and Hart saw them on board. 'The Captain treated us with great kindness' and on reaching the Zhenjiang 'hulk' at midnight on the 12th handed them over to the foreign customs official who made up beds in the customs house for Elizabeth and the children. To reach the Rudlands in the morning was like arriving home, but Elizabeth wrote, 'I felt like Naomi when she said, "Call me not Naomi, call me Marah . . . I went out full and the Lord hath brought me again empty".' Not one relic of their most prized possessions, personal mementoes of home and parents, remained to them.

There Hudson Taylor and Maria joined them.

After Anqing   *November 1869–February 1870*

Knowing from experience what it was like to go through a riot, and to be separated from each other during it, the Taylors' sympathy and encouragement carried weight. As time was to show, this for the present was the best contribution they could make. Hudson Taylor could see beyond the physical and emotional trauma to wider issues. Sir Rutherford Alcock, the minister, happened to be in Shanghai, and hearing from Consul Lay went himself to Anqing to confront the guilty governor and *daotai*. As Hudson Taylor told William Berger,

From the first I could not but see that the opponents of missions, and especially those opposed to us, might make a trying use of (the

Anqing riot). . . . Sir R Alcock has inquired into the matter and the Mandarins, I am told, promised him to repair the house and make good the losses, but would give no guarantee of exemption from future molestation. . . . ('They may return but at their own peril.') Messrs. (Meadows and Williamson) are now directed to proceed to Shanghai to give evidence as to their losses. I really do not see that they can refuse to do so, or to receive the compensation, if any be really offered to them. For to refuse this would be to affect the safety of others, and embarrass our officers. Friends at home really cannot understand these things here, and they must give us credit as seeking to please God, and do, as far as we know it, what is right and best. Often our property and not rarely our lives are in jeopardy. We can, in some measure, even rejoice that it is so. But those who neither know, nor can understand, our position must not expect the reasons of all our steps to be apparent to them. . . .

If you have another typhoon about the (Anqing) riot do not be cast down, dear Brother, the Lord will strengthen you and us by His own might to bear much more than this. The day may come when we have to look alone to and lean alone on the One sufficient stay. I hope it is so now indeed. When Rome and Jew combined to oppose, God carried His cause through, and He will *now* carry it through.[15]

That day did come, when even the ambassadors were in fear for their lives.

In March 1870 Hudson Taylor was in the dark as to what the minister was doing. Alcock did not confide in him as Consul Medhurst did. Li Hongzhang, newly enthroned as viceroy at Wuchang, had 'issued an edict which was popularly interpreted as a condemnation of Christians'.[16] The pillaging of the Catholic premises at Anqing being attributed to Li's action, the French chargé d'affaires proceeded at once to Wuchang with an escort of two gunboats to enforce justice. And the visit of one vessel to Anqing ensured satisfaction being obtained there. Hudson Taylor commented,

The state of affairs since the riot, up to the time that the French expedition arrived, I have been unable as yet to ascertain; but it seems that the visit of Sir Rutherford Alcock was followed by rumours of the French armed expedition, and the people were very much frightened. Many of them made preparations for leaving the city, but the majority said that there was nothing to fear from the foreigners, who were not like the rebels, for not only would they not touch private property but would also pay a good price for what they wanted. . . .

> There can be no doubt that the French demonstration has been the means of facilitating our return to this city, as well as of bringing down punishment on the rioters. . . . What is the true disposition of the people towards us, as yet we cannot ascertain. . . .[17]

The direct intervention of Sir Rutherford and the French was not as significant as the attitude and actions of the new viceroy at Nanjing, Ma Xinyi, supported at last by the provincial governor of Anhui, Ying Han. As a Manchu, Ying Han had been true to type at the time of the riot, leaving the prefects to aid and abet the expulsion of the foreigners. So it can be assumed that his role in events after the riot was dictated by the viceroy, Ma Xinyi.

At a time when the great Muslim 'Panthay' rebellion in Yunnan (1855–73), the equally threatening Muslim rebellion in Gansu (1862–76) and the conquest of Kashgar and Urumqi by Yakub Beg (1864–77) had become the Peking court's chief preoccupations, Ma Xinyi might well have taken a less contentious line. Instead he went even further than when the missions had been attacked in Hangzhou. He issued a proclamation in no uncertain terms, commanding mandarins and people to respect the Anqing missionaries and not molest them in any way (Appendix 10). Yet the leniency of the punishments, the association of the culpable prefects with the viceroy instead of demotion in rank, and the frank distinction between missionaries and secular foreigners (to whom no reference was made), confirmed the reputation for wisdom of this enlightened viceroy. None of the people, officials or victims of the riot could object.

Leaving Elizabeth and the children at Zhenjiang for the present, James Meadows and Williamson went back to Anqing on February 23, 1870, to be 'well received by officials and people'. 'The landlord seemed rather disappointed . . . having hoped to pocket the two years' rent which had been paid in advance, and to let it out to other tenants as well. We proceeded to the (*daotai*), who received us with due courtesy and took up some time excusing himself for not having seen us on the day of the riot. . . . He was ready to do all in his power to assist us . . .' – and as an extreme mark of courtesy, accompanied them to the outer door of his palatial *yamen*. The occupants of their own house began moving out the next day – and in possession again Meadows dug up the earthen floor of one room and found one hundred and three silver dollars still where he had buried them. He left Elizabeth to decide whether to return, for she had suffered most, and she bravely agreed; but neither of them could shake off the pall of terror their home continually represented to them.

James Williamson's ambition extended far beyond the provincial capital. 'I have long been anxious to live entirely in a boat and travel from place to place, endeavouring to obtain a footing wherever an opportunity might occur. Here such a boat can be hired very cheaply.' The experience of two disturbances, at Jinhua and Anqing, had failed to stifle his urge to pioneer.

Three years later when Hudson Taylor assessed the progress of the Mission during the first few years of its existence, all he wrote of the episode was, 'After months of persevering effort, (Meadows and Williamson) were ejected for a time by the literati, but were able to return, and the work has since proceeded without interruption.'[18] By 1872 far more harrowing events elsewhere had placed Anqing in a different perspective and Hudson Taylor could be excused his brevity. But the province of Anhui had been 'opened' and 'occupied', and soon would have its growing church. Not for twelve more years was any other mission to join the CIM in Anhui. As 1869 ended J E Cardwell arrived at Jiujiang in Jiangxi (a story in its own right) and Hudson Taylor could claim, for what understanding it conveyed, that the extent of the Mission's territory had increased to 200,000 square miles, about the size of France. The whole of Britain boasts less than 95,000. His own travelling as supervisor increased accordingly.

Looking back and far ahead   *1855–1935*

For fourteen years, since 1855, Sir Rutherford Alcock had had to deal from time to time with trouble arising from this incorrigible visionary's penetration into new territories. Only the fulfilment of duty as consul-general and then minister in Peking governed Sir Rutherford's policy and his impartial attitude to Hudson Taylor. Never friendly, as Consul Medhurst and others were, he remained scrupulously fair and impersonal in reporting his objections to missionary 'provocation' of the literati. In contrast Medhurst was warm in his thanks for Hudson Taylor's gift of 'the best Bible available'. By then Medhurst had received Lord Stanley's congratulations and his successor Lord Clarendon's faint praise intended to be read as reproach.[19] So his letter continued,

That action (at Yangzhou) has certainly not met with the approval at home which I had anticipated for it. But I nevertheless believe that it has had its good effect in a marked degree, and I trust that the policy which has since arisen out of it although based upon somewhat different principles, may in the end secure for all missionaries throughout the country, what it was my simple desire to obtain for you, namely, freedom to pursue their avocation without molestation or restraint, so long as they keep within the bounds of reason and discretion.

In November 1869 when the Anqing affair was still an open wound, Medhurst tackled Alcock about the need to settle the still unresolved matter of compensation to the Yangzhou victims, from the indemnities demanded by him from the Chinese government, and sent Hudson Taylor 500 taels as indemnity for personal injuries sustained by the party.

Knowing that Medhurst was under fire from Whitehall for his strong action at Yangzhou and Nanjing, Hudson Taylor did what he could to support him. On January 18 he wrote to James Meadows, 'Mr Medhurst evidently considers the indemnity as *claimed* by you. . . . It is important not to word anything you may write so that it may get into print that the claim was made contrary to your wish. We are placed in a very difficult position, are we not? May God give us wisdom and grace.'[20]

Because critics were accusing the Mission of profiting from the receipt of indemnities, Hudson Taylor was encouraging all who received compensation of any kind at Yangzhou and Anqing to contribute what they received to funds 'for the permanent benefit of the city . . . in trying to remove this slur.' They all did. He and Maria then personally refunded the losses so that they would not suffer more than they had already.

On January 28 Hudson Taylor followed his usual policy of providing factual publicity to counteract falsehoods. Writing from Yangzhou to the editor of the North China Herald, he said,

. . . In conducting the negotiations Mr Medhurst so combined courtesy with firmness, as to secure the necessary redress, without unduly violating the prejudices or irritating the feelings of the people. The demands which he made were so just, and at the same time so moderate, as to commend themselves to the people's own sense of right. . . . The good discipline, too, of our troops, has often been commented on by the Chinese; . . . the confidence of the people, and the cordiality of the literati . . . have been unmistakably indicated during the year. There is, perhaps, no more delicate criterion of the former than the willingness or reluctance of parents to send their children to our schools . . . we have had to refuse children from want of accommodation.

It will be remembered that Mr Medhurst secured for us a stone tablet bearing a proclamation from the Prefect stating that we were here at the consent and approbation of both local and foreign authorities. By this admirable diplomacy, he not only conclusively set at rest all questions of our right to be here, but also, with a delicate appreciation of the feeling of the (Chinese), placed us in the position of invited guests, when otherwise our mere presence might have galled them as an evidence of their defeat. . . . Numbers of the literati daily visited us during the examinations (as many have done before and since) and appeared fully prepared to reciprocate courtesies shown to them . . .[21]

Twenty years later, when Hudson Taylor assessed the lessons learned from the Yangzhou riot and 'similar experiences', the sting had gone from the criticisms of 1868–69 and the reasons for the apparent mistakes of previous days were understood. Apart from others lost by death, disease and retirement, by then the CIM had 285 members in China and supported 117 full-time Chinese colleagues, besides many more voluntary workers. To avoid distortion and wrong interpretation of the facts, and secondary issues such as national prestige overriding the Mission's best interests, the CIM shunned publicity whenever possible. Molestation was to be endured up to the point at which it ought to be reported to the Chinese and foreign authorities and their help requested, but never demanded as of right. Vindication by the Lord was always more satisfying than that obtained by the intervention of officials. 'Take joyfully the spoiling of your goods' and the thought 'Better be had than hard' gave more lasting satisfaction than indemnities wrested from the offenders. Compensation, though never demanded, could be accepted and used for their benefit. As the first printed form of the Mission's *Principles and Practice* expressed it in 1884,

While availing themselves of any *privileges* offered by the British or Chinese Governments, (missionaries) must make no *claim* for their help or protection. Appeals to our Consuls . . . are to be avoided. Should trouble or persecution arise inland, a *friendly representation* may be made to the local Chinese officials, failing redress from whom, those suffering must be satisfied to leave their case in God's hands. *Under no circumstances must any Missionary on his own responsibility make any appeal to the British authorities.* As a last resort, the injunction of the Master can be followed, 'If they persecute you in this city, flee ye into another'. . . .

Where prolonged stay in a city is likely to cause trouble . . . and where residence cannot be peaceably and safely effected, (it is better to) defer the attempt.[22]

If so long afterwards such counsel needed to be given, certainly at Yangzhou in 1869 the threat was far from over. But no one could foresee that, of all places in China, relations between people, officials and missionaries were to become better in Yangzhou than perhaps in any other city. Yangzhou became the location of the women missionaries' training school. And Anqing, the capital of Anhui, Li Hongzhang's home province, became (according to his biographer, Alicia Bewicke Little), 'best known to English people as the training centre (for men) of the China Inland Mission'.[23]

PART 3

DESOLATION

1870–71

CHAPTER SEVEN

'THE DARK CLOUD'
1870

'Don't doctor, work!'   *1870*

Dissatisfaction with himself had been partly due to Hudson Taylor's gnawing dissatisfaction with several of his team. Most were turning out well, but some were exasperating. In Meadows, Stevenson, Williamson, Rudland, Duncan, McCarthy and Judd he now had reliable and increasingly valuable men, most of them well matched in their own way by their wives; he also had four dependable single girls, Jennie Faulding, Emily Blatchley, Louise Desgraz and Mary Bowyer. But whatever upheavals came his way, Hudson Taylor was the administrator responsible for keeping in touch with each missionary, good or mediocre, to advise them in their work, to supply them constantly with funds and to maintain their morale in anxious and discouraging times.

No fully qualified doctor had yet come to help him. The smattering of medical knowledge which Edward Fishe, Robert White and Thomas Harvey boasted was not enough to relieve Hudson Taylor of medical responsibility for all his growing team and several in other missions. Soon, while threats to the foreign communities increased, to make up for their lack of the language these inexperienced newcomers tried their hand at doctoring Chinese. Hudson Taylor had to urge greater caution. Quite apart from untoward results of treatment, the wild rumours about foreigners drugging people and stealing their organs could put them in great danger. An experienced surgeon, warmly commended by George Müller, was preparing to leave his practice on the south coast of England and bring his wife and six children to China, when unaccountably he suddenly dropped out of the picture. So while the claims of widely deployed 'workers' constantly called for visits from Hudson Taylor, an almost unbroken sequence of illnesses and obstetric cases had to take priority.

Had it been possible to see more of his team, to talk with them and hold them to even their personal principles, his problems might have been fewer. But without his pastoral oversight, some were temperamentally vulnerable to vitiating influences. John Mara, the Free Methodist whom Hudson Taylor had helped to send to Ningbo, had to be invalided home with delirium tremens. But his own colleague, the once admirable George Crombie, was following the same trend, frock-coated and liking to be called 'Reverend' while drinking and smoking to excess. To William Berger, in the course of a long business letter on the distribution of funds, Hudson Taylor said, 'Those who . . . spend in Port, Claret, Brandy, Cigars, more than is good for them might be increasingly dissatisfied'.

Cardwell, while at Taizhou with Jackson, was 'a cipher', of no value. 'I am afraid that Cardwell has mistaken his calling altogether and that his dislike of the Chinese and everything Chinese, his bad judgement and temper will prevent his ever being of use as a missionary. Still I *may* be wrong, and China sadly needs missionaries. . . . Crombie is a missionary, though of very low stamp.'

Cardwell's health had steadily deteriorated until Hudson Taylor almost despaired. Then, instead of letting Hudson Taylor manage his wife's confinement, Cardwell ran up a bill at the Ningbo hospital which he could not meet. At last he had revealed that his heart was set on pioneering in virgin Jiangxi, not Zhejiang. When Hudson Taylor agreed to his making Jiujiang his base for extensive evangelism in Jiangxi province, he had travelled up the Yangzi by steamer for a fare he could not afford, and by his quick temper so offended the shipping company that they ceased to grant discounts to missionaries. But no sooner had he received a welcome from V C Hart in Jiujiang, than Cardwell's health and morale recovered dramatically. He quickly made a reputation for courageous pioneering over great distances, soon had a number of converts as the nucleus of a church, and proved Hudson Taylor wrong.

Before Cardwell and his wife left Taizhou, 'Jackson's city', another chapter of incidents involved the restless Josiah Jackson. 'As to Jackson,' Hudson Taylor confided to Willian Berger, 'he has some very nice points about him, and has done some work. He speaks *well* the Ningpo and Taichau dialects and has a considerable knowledge of the Wenchau dialect. He gets on well with the Chinese – perhaps *too* well sometimes, sacrificing principle. . . . But he is shallow. He smokes and jests and laughs with them until he loses all power to influence them seriously.' Jackson had proposed by letter to a girl in England whom he had never met and Hudson Taylor warned the Bergers, for her own sake on no account to let the lady come to China until she knew what she would be in for. Berger replied, 'Alas! what will be the end of poor Mr Jackson? I do not think I could have taken from him what you have . . . would strongly advise a *loving* but *firm* policy from the first, with those who are under your guidance.' Clearly Berger thought that Hudson Taylor was, if anything, too tolerant.

In another letter to Jackson, Hudson Taylor had said, 'You speak of my letter scolding you for leaving Taichau. . . . You know, I think, that I am not a scold.' Perhaps he was not being firm enough. Whether it was the same lady or another, in 1873 a Miss Fanny Wilson, equally a stranger, did go to China, persuaded by Hudson Taylor not to say 'Yes' to Jackson until she had seen enough to form a sound opinion of him. She married and for ten years did wonders for him.

Poor Henry Reid was another problem. In spite of damage to his eye, his worst injury in the Yangzhou riot had not been physical but psychological. Still intent on doing his best, he toured the villages round Suzhou for weeks at a time, and later Qingjiangpu, trembling with apprehension that the violence might be repeated. When the Cardwells left Taizhou, the Rudlands took their place. William Rudland's limited education was not up to running the printing-press at Zhenjiang and Reid was a suitable substitute. So Rudland found his niche and was still at Taizhou forty years later, building a thriving community of Christians. But Reid added to Hudson Taylor's worries by having a tiff with his Chinese colleague.

When the 22-year-old Edward Fishe had told his parents about the 'Annie' he had met in the Taylor's home in Yangzhou and wanted to marry, he had not said that she was older than he and the uneducated, widowed nursemaid to the Taylor children. Colonel Fishe learned of it through the Bergers and remonstrated with his son, saying he must at least delay long enough to weigh carefully the difficulties he would face from their intellectual and social differences. But he did not forbid the marriage. Edward married her at once, so Hudson Taylor may have planned deliberately to put the excellent Mary (Bell) Rudland in Taizhou with her sister Annie (Bohannan) Fishe, to make a missionary of her. Edward also needed to be held to the essentials, for he too found amateur doctoring an attractive 'bypath meadow'. 'I do not think it at all . . . feasible for you to attempt the cure of opium-smokers,' Hudson

Taylor wrote. 'Even had you the requisite knowledge of medicine it would not pay you for the time. . . . Consider six or eight hours a day *sacred to the Lord* and His work, and let nothing hinder your giving this time (to language study and practice) till you can preach fluently and intelligibly.' Every hindrance to making Jesus known to the Chinese must be decisively rejected. 'Satisfaction is not to be found in any position or circumstances – it must spring from within or can never be found at all. It is very easy to fancy that we should be happy and useful in any position or circumstances save those we are in.'

Edward's brother Charles was a totally different type of man. Younger, and still youthful when the Bergers (who looked on him as a son) felt they could keep him in Britain no longer, he sailed with Thomas P Harvey in the *Lammermuir* in July 1869, to arrive at Shanghai on November 9 and go straight to the Taylors and Judds at Yangzhou. On the Bergers' insistence they were to be protected from unsettling influences in Shanghai. To become a missionary he had sacrificed his chosen career in civil engineering and the social standing of his Dublin home circle – and for the present his secret love of 'Nellie' Faulding, Jennie's younger sister. Quiet, discreet, sound in judgment and with Hudson Taylor's magnetic way with children, it was not long before he was asked to become Hudson Taylor's personal secretary, when Emily Blatchley returned to Britain. Of all the team, Charles had more potential as a leader than any other, taciturn Stevenson and amicable McCarthy included.

Thomas Harvey had studied medicine at the London Hospital with Tom Barnardo long enough to have attended more than fifty midwifery cases and to begin surgical operations on cadavers, but was not yet fully qualified as a doctor. He also had 'a tendency to consumption' and an arrogant, overbearing manner when he was not, in contrast, quite charming. The Bergers had warned that he was excitable, 'ardent but easily damped, and as quickly cheered again'. Before long he also had to be told to stop doctoring and get on with the language. But Harvey was a law unto himself and frequently an anxiety to Hudson Taylor, who advised William Berger that in future candidates should complete their medical training or do none at all.

Robert White and his bride, Frances Gainfort, though not members of the CIM lived at Mission premises as if they were, while pleasing themselves. He too played the doctor and had to be warned of the risks. Many Chinese were afraid of this tall, dark stranger in foreign clothes. But by December 1869 White was in Shanghai looking for secular employment. In February 1870 Hudson Taylor wrote, 'Some persons seem really clever in doing the right thing in the worst possible way, or at the most unfortunate time. Really dull, or rude persons will seldom be out of hot water in China; and though earnest and clever and pious will not effect much. In nothing do we fail more, as a Mission, than in lack of tact and politeness.' And again, 'With a very wrong head, (White) has a true heart.' 'I think that as a general rule the man, and certainly the woman who does not take an interest in children, and *who is unable to make children take an interest* in himself or herself . . . is a somewhat uncertain boon to a work like ours.' Williamson, the Judds and Jennie were all fond of children, and children and adults liked them. The successful missionaries and potential failures came from varying social backgrounds. It was not the policy of enlisting artisans that was at fault. The medical students were little better. Encouraging the uncultured to be missionaries would have been in doubt if several had not been shaping well. Spiritual maturity or immaturity explained the difference.

Emily and the children   *January–June 1870*

Ever since March 1869 5-year-old Samuel had been suffering from tuberculous enteritis, unable to eat or drink without adding to his abdominal pain. Maria and Hudson Taylor kept him with them, even on their travels, leaving the other children with Emily and their nurse and coming back to them whenever possible. But Herbert, Howard, Maria and the 1-year-old Charles Edward were too often ill and upset by the unsettledness of life. The meningitis scare of August and the onset of 'ague' were followed by purulent conjunctivitis affecting each of them in November. By December all the family were ailing. Maria was writing of it being little Maria's 'day for an attack' of malaria, and of Hudson that 'such a little thing knocks him up, and renders him quite unfit for work: as you know, he keeps on long after most people would give up'. In January it was Emily whose 'chest is worse than it has been for a long time', but Maria thought herself better than before.

Only with pangs of grief had they decided to ask Emily to take all except Charles Edward home to England. The prospect of parting with the children was 'the dark cloud which lies before us. Sometimes it seems for a time to take all one's strength and heart away.'

To so affectionate a father the tunnel of grief looked endless. Samuel was so ill that he might not survive the journey, but it was his only hope. The long voyage round the Cape would be fatal and via America too expensive, so a French steamer taking two months via Suez was decided on. Hudson Taylor thought he might go with them as far as Suez. An absence of three months could be tolerated and a sea voyage always did him good. But no, he could not leave Maria and the team for so long. He might take Emily and the four children as far as Hong Kong. In the end he could not even do this although, as he later told Jennie, Emily's health was fragile. She would have died but for the change of climate. To trans-ship at Hong Kong would tax her severely, but the missionaries there would help her.

So they began preparing Western clothing for the growing children, and all Emily would need for them on the voyage, including school-books. Herbert was nearly nine, and learning Greek. He must keep working at it. Samuel was worse as their departure time was approaching, in March to avoid winter gales in the China seas and extreme heat in the Indian Ocean and Red Sea. After the new year Hudson Taylor went to Shanghai to arrange for the voyage, to see Consul Medhurst about the Yangzhou property and the reinstatement of the Meadows family and Williamson at Anqing, and to get back to Yangzhou for Emily's twenty-fifth birthday on January 24. But as he told George Müller and E C Lord on the 23rd, the day before he arrived home, 'our little invalid became suddenly and rapidly worse' and 'never rallied fully'. Samuel died on February 4, when he was nearly 6, and was buried the next day at Zhenjiang. A few hours after his death, a packet of cheques totalling £250 (a large sum at the time) arrived from George Müller for distribution to the team. The grieving parents welcomed it as a token of God's love in the midst of ordeals.

A month later when they were all in Shanghai waiting for the ship, Maria managed a letter to Mary Berger, '(Samuel) was the most patient child I had ever seen.' Uncomplaining in spite of constant pain from the ulceration of his intestines, he had endeared himself exceptionally to them.

On February 6 George Müller's wife died, and on May 20 the wife of James Wright, his fellow-director of the Bristol orphanage. Sleepless with grief Müller recorded his thoughts in a leaflet entitled *Satisfied with God*. It reached Hudson Taylor in time to console him when his own supreme test came.

Emily felt the approaching separation from the Taylors as intensely as the death of Samuel. 'The thing I dread', tuberculosis which had carried off several of her own family, was already far advanced in her own lungs. But in her own words, she had reached a contented state of wholehearted 'Acquiescence, not submission' to the will of God. Submission only was too grudging. 'I delight to do Thy will, O my God' had become her attitude. Yet the Taylor's help in bearing her illness was hard to forgo. 'Receive her as a daughter,' Maria wrote to Hudson's mother, 'for our sake to begin with, but soon you will continue to do so for her own sake. . . . And . . . call her Emily and not Miss Blatchley. . . . In leaving *us* she is leaving *home* for she has been to us as a daughter and a sister, both in one.'

In mid-February they left Yangzhou and Zhenjiang, travelling by canal boat to Shanghai to be there when Grace Ciggie arrived at last. Time and again, low water levels led to long delays when they ran aground, 'stuck fast for days together at shallow places'. Jennie came from Hangzhou with Mrs Wang Lae-djün to say goodbye to Emily at Suzhou – and without knowing it until long afterwards this was the factor which revolutionised a young man's life. A new believer at Suzhou named Ren was so impressed by her prayerful spirit and accounts of the spiritual life and influence of the New Lane church in Hangzhou, that he 'longed to be in that atmosphere'. After being baptised in November, he went to Hangzhou as a teacher in Jennie's school and, in the course of years, married Wang Lae-djün's daughter. When Lae-djün retired, Ren succeeded him as pastor of the whole Hangzhou circuit of churches – 'one of the most gifted and devoted Chinese pastors in China'.

By March 5 the Taylors, Cordons and Emily were in Shanghai, living on their houseboats. Like so many foreigners in her situation, Mrs Cordon could not say precisely when her baby would be born, and for weeks to come travelled with the Taylors wherever they went. In a note to Stephan Barchet, Hudson Taylor wrote hopefully of 'running over to England' in a year or two, to consult with the Bergers and make permanent arrangements for the children. Grace Ciggie arrived and went on to Ningbo. But Hudson was preoccupied with administrative duties.

On the evening of March 22 Maria and he saw Emily and the children aboard the French steamer and he went ashore again. After midnight he began a business letter to the Bergers with, 'At 5.30 a m they steam away for Hong Kong and we leave for Su-chau, DV . . . Miss Blatchley will be better than twenty letters; being more intimately acquainted with Mission matters than any other members.'

As soon as they had gone, the Taylors and Mrs Cordon, still 'daily expecting her confinement', started back to Suzhou. 'The moment I can leave her, I must hasten on to Yangchau as Mrs Judd (has dysentery). I feel very uneasy about her – one of our most useful female missionaries.'

On April 9 he was writing from an overcrowded houseboat in Zhenjiang. Elizabeth Judd had been brought there, 'near the point of death', needing to be nursed day and night. 'I found the Judds here, and Mr Meadows and family and Duncan, so we are pretty thick on the ground. Mrs Judd I was quite shocked to see. Her face drawn to one side, her strength gone. . . . She is *very* ill.' In asking Mary Bowyer to come and help, he added, 'There is *very* little hope of her recovery.' What neither he nor Maria said in their letters, Charles Judd recorded. Although very unfit for travelling at all, Maria had left the boat as soon as she heard of Elizabeth's condi-tion, 'took a (springless) wheel-barrow and came about thirty miles across country,' the fastest route. 'She arrived at (Zhenjiang) late in the day, very much worn,' but insisted that Charles Judd should get some sleep while she herself sat up with Elizabeth all night long. Mary Bowyer came at once from Nanjing, but even then Maria shared night duty.

The reinstatement of the Meadows family at Anqing 'with the exception of little Sammy whom *we* have borrowed for a couple of months' (Hudson Taylor said), relieved the overcrowding, and on April 14 Elizabeth Judd was beginning to recover. But Hudson Taylor, still living on the houseboat, had to go up to Yangzhou on business and was away when Maria, sleeping after night duty, was called just in time to receive 'Miss Cordon' into the world.

As soon as Elizabeth Judd was well enough, Hudson Taylor sent her with her husband Charles and Mary Bowyer to Putuo for five weeks of sunbathing, keeping her baby in Maria's care. 'Sometimes the longings for (our) dear absent ones (Grace and Samuel as well as the other children at sea) are indescribable,' he confessed to his mother. Yet his administrative work had to be carried on regardless of all else. The marriage of orphans and others committed to the care of missionaries was one of their responsibilities. To E C Lord he wrote, 'You were wishing to get a good husband for Pao-tsie. If we are not too late, we should be glad to propose on behalf of Ah-liang, our head-printer under Mr Rudland . . . superintendent

TRAVEL BY WHEELBARROW, EVEN FOR LONG
DISTANCES

over the other workers. Have you any other girls . . . whom you are prepared to betrothe?'

By April the Bergers had disclosed painstaking plans for meeting Emily and the children. Friends at Cannes and Dijon, a German pastor and a man at the harbour in Marseilles were 'on the lookout night and day . . . for the French Mail packet'. The Grattan Guinnesses in Paris would keep them for a brief rest. Then the Bergers would meet them at Dover and bring them home to Saint Hill. Both were there when the travellers landed on the 24th. Until they caught sight of Herbert's Chinese shoes, they could recognise none of them. In Paris Herbert had had what was feared to be 'hydrocephalus'. Mrs Faulding told Jennie, 'I was quite shocked to see dear Emily she is *so* altered – no one who has not known her intimately would recognise her, even dear Mr and Mrs Berger did not know her as she stood on the steamer.'

Mrs Berger had more to add for Maria, 'Beloved Miss B gives me *most* concern. . . . (On June 2) a ring at the bell announced the arrival of a gentleman in his gig. . . . It was her father, who could keep away no longer; . . . the meeting was most affecting – but I left the room immediately. . . . She is now walking about with her father in the grounds and round the lake. . . . And now farewell, my precious friend. The Lord throw around you His everlasting arms!' – prophetic words again. Maria would never read them, for with June in China they entered upon two months more tense and terrible than they had yet known.

By the end of June when Emily and the children moved to live with Hudson Taylor's sister, Amelia, in Bayswater, they were 'all much improved in health'. '(Even) Miss B,' Mary Berger wrote, 'seems to be rallying.' She needed to, for much of her time at Saint Hill had had to be spent briefing the Bergers about China, and working with him on accounts and on the *Occasional Paper*. Business matters she had been commissioned to attend to in London would need all her feeble strength for three more weeks.

The Stott and Ciggie story   *March–August 1870*

After nearly two years constantly in Wenzhou without another western colleague, and never speaking anything but Chinese, George Stott had written to Grace Ciggie. Would she be his wife? For three years she had persevered as the friend of 'fallen women' in the Glasgow Salt Market, maturing and regaining her physical strength. But China was her goal and the Bergers had kept in touch with her. She consulted them about Stott whom she barely knew. They had been together in the Taylor household in Mile End for only three weeks before he went to China. Then she waited while they consulted Hudson Taylor.

At last his reply was received in London and Grace Ciggie came down from Glasgow ready to sail. Try as he might, William Berger had been unable to find a missionary escort for her. All others were travelling by steamer, while careful use of funds still meant the cheaper route by clipper ship for members of the CIM. Grace was game for anything. So a ship was found, the *Kaisow*, with a genial captain and his wife for company. The Bergers fitted up a cabin and the Fauldings saw her off on December 4, 1869, alone among strangers. She was imperturbable.

When the captain said the voyage could take one hundred days at best from the Channel to Shanghai, or two weeks longer even with good winds, she declared that the hundredth day would be her twenty-fifth birthday. Would he please get her there on March 12? In the South China Sea she was still hoping for 'a real storm' and was not disappointed. They reached Wusong on the ninety-ninth day and the captain took her up the Huangpu river to Shanghai by steam-launch on her birthday. He and his wife remained her lifelong friends. She was the last member of the Mission ever to go to or from China by sailing-ship.

George Stott arrived at Shanghai. Four and a half years had passed since they had last seen each other at the London docks when Stott and the Stevensons sailed. He carried her off to Ningbo, and put her in the care of the ever-obliging Lords for the month's residence required by consular regulations before their marriage on April 26, 1870. Wenzhou was only one hundred and fifty miles away – three or four days by sea-going junk. But pirates still infested the lonely waters among the many islands down the coast. George wanted to leave at once and take his bride to the humble Chinese home he had prepared for her, but no junk owner would sail without a full convoy and war junk escort. For three weeks they searched before being able to start. And even then, when they reached the Zhoushan Islands their escort would go no farther without more war junks for protection. For nine frustrating days they kicked their heels, while a tearful Grace endured her rude initiation into rough travelling conditions in the cramped and crowded junk.

At last after fifteen days they reached 'home' – a bedroom,

living-room and study above George's noisy school – only to be
besieged day after day by insatiable crowds wanting to see the first
foreign woman to visit Wenzhou. Hardly had the excitement died
down than the whole of China was electrified by the news that, in
June, a massacre of foreigners had taken place at Tianjin in the
north.

For three months it was unsafe for George Stott to leave the
house, let alone for his wife to show her face. When he had to
venture out he was cursed and stoned.

A climate of unrest   1869–70

Ever since the proclamation of the September 1869 anti-foreign,
anti-Christian 'Hunan manifesto', a growing disquiet had been
apparent to everyone in touch with the people. The alarms in
Wenzhou were only the local expression of a nationwide excitement, an orchestrated surge of antagonism leading directly to the
most serious international incident in China between 1860 and 1900.

Unrest was not confined to China. Jealous of Christian progress
in Chieng Mai, Thailand, the northern king beheaded two church
members and threatened the rest and their missionaries. Dr Daniel
McGilvary wrote on September 29, 1869, 'If you never hear from us
again, know that we are in heaven, and do not . . . regret the loss of
our lives. We are all peaceful and happy.' For four months nothing
more was heard of them. But they survived and the king himself fell
ill while on a visit to Bangkok and returned home to die.

In Japan William Gamble reported in January 1870 his personal
observation of the mass abduction, by Japanese government troops,
of hundreds of Roman Catholic Christians from the valley of
Urakami near Nagasaki.[1] Refusing to recant, more than seven
hundred were sent by ship into exile and, according to his information, three thousand had already been taken from their homes.

But in China the superstitions and gullibility of the masses were
being exploited by the lurid tales about foreigners. The ancient
practice of ancestor worship and *fengshui* (Book 4, Appendix 8) lent
itself to exploitation. In the words of the *Cambridge Modern
History*, 'It was impossible to describe the alarm and consternation
of the Chinese when at first they believed that native magicians were
bewitching them; nor their indignation and anger when they were
told that these insidious foes were the agents of foreigners.'

The excitement of the people had been encouraged in the sum-

mer of 1869 by the news that Zeng Guofan 'was making preparations for the expulsion of foreigners from China; – his removal
from Nankin to (Zhili) was considered from the first to be connected
with such a plan. Thus one thing after another has increased,
deepened and extended the anti-foreign feeling.' 'No sooner was his
approach announced than we heard rumours of the intended destruction or expulsion of foreigners. Every month or two these were
revived. . . . Even in (Tianjin), where foreigners had for so many
years engaged in business and missionary operations, so great was
this fear that it was with much difficulty that buildings could be
rented in new localities.'

That feeling had been strongly exacerbated by the activities of the
so-called French Protectorate. Through the concessions made in the
treaties of 1844, 1858 and 1860, all Roman Catholic missionaries
and their converts had come under the protection of France. The
issue of French passports to priests of other nationalities, the
enforcement in the inland provinces of treaty concessions, and the
exemption of Catholic Church members from taking part in non-
Christian observances and celebrations put the missionaries in a
strong position. In 1870 an edition of the Imperial Code, the *Da
Qing Lü Li*, was issued with its old articles interdicting Christianity
deleted and anti-Christian decrees abrogated. But the return to the
Church of properties long since confiscated and put to other uses,
could not but create deep resentment, as did foreign interference in
the natural processes of the Chinese courts of law.

Growing tension everywhere became focused alarmingly on
Tianjin when a date was openly cited in other cities for a destructive
attack on the French consulate and missions in Tianjin. On June 14
people were saying in 'Shan-ts'ing', one hundred and fifty miles or
more from Tianjin, that attacks would begin on the 21st. In Tianjin
itself foreigners first heard these reports a day or two later. 'Some
servants in foreign employ . . . removed their bedding etcetera, . . .
gave the reasons for doing so, and told when the attack would take
place.'

Far away in Dengzhou (now Penglai) in the neighbouring province of Shandong, while John Nevius was visiting Hangzhou, ugly
rumours of danger to the American Presbyterian missionaries led to
their being evacuated to Yantai by British gunboat.[2] The rumours
included an intended massacre at Tianjin, long before it took place.
Everywhere missionaries recognised the extent of the threat and
were asking, as C A Stanley of the American Board in Tianjin put it,

'Will missionaries be allowed to stay (in China)?' Their own consuls and ministers might order them out, even if the Chinese did not.

Count-down at Tianjin[3]   *May–June 1870*

There had been foreign residents at Tianjin since 1858, when the British, French and Americans, represented by Lord Elgin, Baron Gros and the Hon W B Reed, had captured the Dagu forts and established themselves in the former imperial palace of Huanghailou and adjoining temples for the negotiation of the 'Treaty of Tientsin'. These sacred precincts at the junction of the Grand Canal, the Bei He (North River) and the Hai He (the river to the Gulf) had been occupied by the French in 1861 after the capture of Peking. Facing the Chinese walled city, they stood close to the *yamen* of Chonghou, the imperial commissioner for foreign affairs. There the French had built their consulate and the provoca-

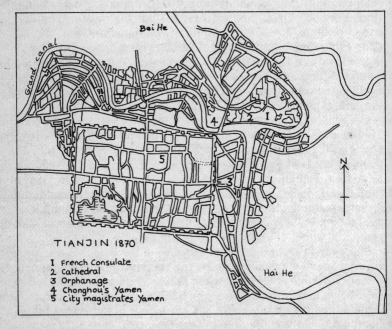

TIANJIN 1870

1 French Consulate
2 Cathedral
3 Orphanage
4 Chonghou's Yamen
5 City magistrates Yamen

TIANJIN 1870

tive Notre Dame des Victoires, a cathedral due to be destroyed twice and defiantly rebuilt a third time.

In the suburb between the North Gate of the old city and the Hai He, the 'Sœurs de Charité', known also as Sisters of Mercy and Sisters of Saint Vincent de Paul, had an orphanage staffed in 1870 by five French, one Irish, two Belgian, and two Italian nuns. An international 'settlement' housed the merchant community and Protestant missions, the LMS, American Board and Methodist New Connexion, whose chapels were dotted about the city and suburbs.

Chonghou's influence and prestige, derived directly from the Zongli Yamen, were directed towards foreign relations, but he 'had no place in the provincial administration'. In other words, 'he could bring in the imperial authority, but could not move a policeman.' Among foreigners he was highly respected for 'his benevolence, his pleasing manners, and his perfect courtesy' – in Admiral Keppel's words, 'the most finished Chinese gentleman he had ever met, with the exception of the Viceroy of Canton'.

A summary of many subsequent accounts of developments in 1870 epitomised the common understanding of events.

> There can be no doubt that the indiscretion of the poor sisters brought upon them and their Mission this terrible blow. They were accustomed to purchase children, with a view to baptizing them and thus saving their souls. Many that were sold to them were sickly; and also an epidemic broke out; and the result was that small coffins were continually coming out of the establishment for burial. This seemed to the ignorant populace to confirm the belief that the eyes and hearts of children were used in the manufacture of drugs; and one woman who had been employed as cook declared that she had herself witnessed the whole operation and had fled in horror.

Although it was reported that the nuns bought the babies, this was stoutly denied in subsequent inquiries. But they did receive abandoned babies and those that would otherwise be discarded.

A Baron Hübner carefully investigated the facts and the historian H B Morse relied on Hübner and first-hand witnesses when he wrote,

> As at Yangchow the final incitement to riot had been the rumour that 'twenty-four children were missing' and therefore presumably kid-napped; so at (Tianjin) the first sign of trouble was manifest in rumours current towards the middle of May, that 'certain

children had disappeared, kidnapped by persons in the pay of the
missionaries . . .'

The practice of kidnapping children and selling them for immoral
purposes was known to be common throughout China; and this
practice was popularly associated with the horrible mystery hanging
over the fate of the children who disappeared into the orphanage. . . . Matters were made worse by an epidemic, which visited the
orphanage early in June, and caused the death of between thirty and
forty children whose bodies were disinterred by crowds of hundreds
of Chinese who raided the cemetery daily. This stirred the people to a
fiercer rage, and the search for kidnappers became active. On June 6
and later dates, four men were arrested, tried and executed without
much formality; and on the 18th another, being arrested and sent for
trial, confessed, under torture of course, that he had relations with
the cathedral verger (Chinese), to whom he sold his stolen children.

By June 16 even devotees were staying away from both Catholic
and Protestant missions, and evading the missionaries when they
went out. 'Application was made to the authorities on several
occasions . . . by both the English and French Consuls – for
proclamations to quell the excitement, but *no notice* was taken of
them – they were not answered.' The prefect issued a proclamation
against the kidnappers, tacitly endorsing the testimony of the
convicted men by its silence about the orphanage and accusing
'other parties' (understood to mean the Catholics) of employing the
kidnappers. At once an honorific 'Ten Thousand Name Umbrella'
was presented to him by 'a grateful people'. The mandarin hier-
archy of Tianjin 'solemnly affirmed the guilt of the Sisters and
demanded an inquest', while Commissioner Chonghou pleaded
that the matter was outside his jurisdiction.

A mob dominated the inquest and the allegations were declared
factual. The local magistrate then demanded an investigation into
conditions at the Catholic mission and orphanage. Chonghou
arranged for it to be made, and M Fontanier, the consul, thought
the whole affair as good as settled. On the morning of June 21 the
daotai, prefect and local magistrate went in state to the cathedral,
followed by a large crowd, and confronted the verger with the
19-year-old witness who had claimed to sell children to him. His
tales were there and then proved to be false. The accusations had
been pure invention, to provide a pretext for rabble-rousing.
Chonghou claimed he was actually drafting a proclamation in
exoneration of the Catholics when the sound of uproar reached him
from the direction of the cathedral.

Massacre[4]   *June 21, 1870*

Soon after midday fire-gongs were sounded and a mob immediately collected. Witnesses confirmed that instead of carrying fire-buckets, the volunteer firemen poured on to the streets armed with weapons, headed for the French consulate, and attacked it. Consul Fontanier at once donned official uniform and made for Chonghou's *yamen* to demand protection.

Commissioner Chonghou's report to his superiors, the Zongli Yamen, was later confirmed by C Hannen, the Tianjin Commissioner of Customs, to his own superior officer, Robert Hart. Chonghou had already sent a military mandarin to the scene of the uproar when he was told that M Fontanier had arrived, demanding to see him. Going to his reception hall, Chonghou was met by a display of fury. The consul, with two pistols in his belt and accompanied by M Simon, his consular secretary, wearing a sword, rushed towards him, smashing cups and other objects on a table. Then, 'keeping up an incessant torrent of abuse' he drew a pistol and fired it. 'He was seized,' Chonghou reported, and 'to avoid a personal collision I withdrew'. On returning, Chonghou 'told him that the crowd outside had a very threatening aspect . . . but, reckless of his life, he rushed out of the *yamen*.' Chonghou sent men to escort the consul, and the district magistrate meeting him on the way tried to prevent him from going further, but he fired at the magistrate, hitting one of his attendants. At this the mob surrounded and killed him, stripped him of his clothes, mutilated his corpse and threw it into the canal.

In the short time he was away the consulate had been looted and burned down and everyone in it murdered. At this point a brigadier in the Chinese army named Chen Guorui, a protégé of Zeng Guofan, arrived with a body of men who joined in the destruction and firing of the Catholic cathedral and mission residence. Enquiry later confirmed that a bugle had been sounded at Chen Guorui's quarters at about the same time as the fire-gongs. (More was to be heard of Chen Guorui. He had commanded the garrison which had joined in the riot at Yangzhou, and two years later was to repeat his rabble-rousing there, with Hudson Taylor again as his prime target.)

The mob then made for the orphanage about a mile away, demolishing the 'English chapel' on their route. The orphanage was plundered and burned, the ten nuns were stripped naked before the mob, barbarously stabbed, hacked to death and thrown into the flames. 'Every French man and woman who could be laid hands on was killed, with every accompaniment of outrage and mutilation . . . and between thirty and forty Chinese employed in the mission and orphanage.' Only the charred remains of the Sisters were found afterwards, but the horribly mutilated bodies of most of the other victims were recovered from the river. Among them were the consul and secretary, two priests, four other French men and women, including a merchant and his wife living a mile from the main scene, two Russian men and the wife of one of them. These three Russians were killed amid shouts of 'Kill the French first and then the other foreigners.' But three other Russians were allowed to escape on pleading that they were 'not French but Russian'. A British doctor named Fraser was attacked, but being on horseback at the time, like W H Medhurst twenty-five years before (Book 2, p 151) escaped at speed. Two Swiss subjects were protected by the mandarins and sent under escort to the British consulate. As the victims' bodies were found they too were delivered to Lay's consulate.

In reporting this to the British chargé d'affaires in Peking (no longer Sir Rutherford Alcock but Thomas Francis Wade, the hero of the Shanghai Battle of Muddy Flat and later, with Harry Parkes, an interpreter to Lord Elgin in the 1860 campaign), Consul Lay declared on July 24 and 25 his conviction that the assault was directed against the French only. Other members of the community strongly challenged this opinion. Certain of reprisals, rich Chinese merchants began leaving Tianjin. Lay warned that 'the Chinese are very determined now, and I am quite certain will take up the gauntlet and fight' if the French attempted reprisals. So the French chargé d'affaires had to beware. If only a small force were to be sent, the Chinese troops would react against the whole foreign community.

On June 21 as the consulate, cathedral and orphanage were burning, Lay's assistant dispatched a courier with a message to the British naval commander at Hong Kong and another to Consul W H Medhurst at Shanghai. Medhurst received his on June 22, six days later, and the commodore at Hong Kong on July 4. Sent on immediately, the news was telegraphed on July 23 from Point de Galle on the southern tip of Ceylon, still the most easterly extent of the cable, and reached London on the 25th. This was the first intimation received in any of the chancelleries of Europe, a week after the outbreak of war between France and the North German

THE GUTTED CATHEDRAL AT TIANJIN

Confederation. The first report from Wade in Peking, dispatched on July 6 and telegraphed from Kiahkta on the Manchurian border with Russian Amur, reached London on the same day, July 25, more than a month after the massacre. Undoubtedly France would in normal circumstances have taken drastic action, but Napoleon III was in no position to undertake war thousands of miles from home.

The CIM at risk   May–July 1870

February and March had been busy and fraught with the illness and death of 5-year-old Samuel and the departure of Emily and the older children to England. April came in with Elizabeth Judd at death's door. But May was like no other month. 'We had previously known something of trial in one station or another; but now in all, simultaneously, or nearly so, a wide-spread excitement shook the very foundations of native society.'[5] A crescendo of excitement took everyone by surprise.

In writing to George Müller on February 17, Hudson Taylor had said, 'Mr Wade, our new chargé d'affaires at Pekin, is strongly opposed to Christian missions and may cause us much trouble.' In the event Wade did make life difficult but without much effect, and to his own discredit. The first sign of his becoming a thorn in the flesh of Hudson Taylor and other progressive missionaries was his prohibition of the purchase of the Yangzhou and Anqing premises. But the year had begun with few hints of other tensions. On March 19 conditions had still been calm enough for three merchants, including the Meadows' friend M G Hollingworth, to set out from Jiujiang on a 550-mile journey southwards, crossing the Wuyi mountain range (map, p 28) to reach Fuzhou without incident on April 16.[6] Yet to William Berger on May 30 Hudson Taylor said, with strong premonitions,

> I increasingly feel that the time is short, very short, and we must not be thinking of pleasing ourselves, but of fulfilling the work our loving Master has given us to do . . . the work is quiet but the congregations are good. . . . The weather is now becoming warm and . . . might occasion some anxious thoughts – Shall we suffer much from sickness, or lose any of our number before the season is over?
>
> [And on June 13] At Yangchau we have had (rumours) again, owing to a most unwise attempt of the Roman Catholic missionaries to remove some children from Yangchau to Shanghai. At (Anqing) also rumours have been rife, and Mr Meadows is in trouble about his house; his rascally landlord having taken steps to try and eject him.

Louise Desgraz had been given a third Chinese baby (left on her doorstep) to bring up in the care of Chinese women, and Mary Bowyer had another, being mothered by Catherine Duncan. The one Jennie Faulding had accepted and wisely left in the care of the Chinese, had died while she was away from home. The rumours being circulated about the Catholics had suddenly made this fostering of children an increasingly risky practice.

It appears that there has really been some kidnapping going on, which has been industriously fathered upon the foreigners, notwithstanding proclamations put out by the mandarins, threatening to punish anyone who should circulate such lies; and the people have shown their belief in the lies by making large white crosses in every street, that the trampling underfoot of the Romanist sign might work evil for the foreigners.[7]

Then on June 14, C T Gardner, the acting-consul in Zhenjiang, sent this dispatch to Hudson Taylor.

I have to inform you that the country round about Nanking, (Zhenjiang) and Yangchow is at present in a very excited and riotous state on account of rumours. . . . Popular excitement has run so high that the authorities have already been constrained to execute several individuals. . . .
Under these circumstances I have to warn you to be exceedingly cautious . . . not leaving your house after nightfall and (when this is found impracticable) carrying a lantern with your name in Chinese upon it. The authorities at Nanking have had to yield so far to popular prejudice as also to notify that (Chinese) women and children are not to be allowed to go out of doors.
I need hardly remind you that when the passions of the people are roused the authorities have not always the power even where they have the will to protect you from outrage.
I have to request you to forward – with as little delay as possible – a copy of this letter to the various members of your mission.[8]

Soon afterwards, Consul Medhurst sent another dispatch, in even stronger terms, primarily for Duncan and Harvey in Nanjing.

No. 20   Shanghai, 15th June 1870
Gentlemen,
. . . at the coming examination season you are likely to be in peril of your lives and property . . .
I have addressed the Local Authorities a communication request-

ing them to afford you all the protection in their power, but you will do well nevertheless to be cautious how far you exasperate or intensify the ill-feeling against you by too persistently maintaining your position within the city whilst the excitement prevails. . . . Chinese mobs have already in similar instances shown themselves capable (of acts of violence) in their blind fury against foreigners. And you must be well aware by this time that . . . Her Majesty's Consul cannot undertake to extend protection by forcible measures to persons resident in the interior. . . .[9]

The unsettled state of affairs was not Hudson Taylor's only anxiety during June. Maria's confinement was approaching, and she was as frail as she had ever been. In a note to Louise Desgraz from Zhenjiang on June 14 he explained, 'I am sorry to be away so long . . . and sorry that you should be left alone. But Mrs Taylor cannot be left now safely even for a day; the effect of the last two journeys on her was such, that I dare not risk another.' Their friendship was deep, and now in his note about Maria he went on,

I have got the very passage for you, and God has so blessed it to my own soul. It is in John 7, vv.37–39. 'If any man thirst, let him come unto *Me* and drink.' Who does not thirst? . . . No matter how intricate my path, how difficult my service. No matter how great my need, how obstinate my disease. No matter how sad my bereavement, how far my loved ones may be away. No matter how helpless I am; how deep are my soul-yearnings – Jesus can meet all (my need), and more than meet (it).

To James Meadows he wrote on the same day, one of many letters to his missionaries which reflect upon his leadership. 'Matters were in a frightful state in (Nanjing) when I last heard. But two hundred proclamations had been put out by the (viceroy) and it was hoped matters would blow over. (Rumours) are also serious, to say the least, at Yangzhou.' Two days later he told John Stevenson at Shaoxing, 'The people are agitated to a degree . . . but in any case, "The name of the Lord is a strong tower: the righteous flee into it and are safe."' And on June 20 to Duncan and Harvey at Nanjing, from whom he had heard nothing since the 11th.

Please let me have a line, if ever so brief, either from you or Harvey every other day till the excitement somewhat subsides. . . . I scarcely know how or what to advise you. I had thought it might be well for you and Mr Harvey to go out of the city with books etc into the surrounding villages and towns. . . . In the event of any stir it would be ascertained that you were absent, and your house *might* not be molested; or if you were, you would escape all personal violence. But I learn that the excitement is even greater in the country than in the city, so that this course is probably not desirable, and might lead to still further misconceptions. [It might be misconstrued as an expedit-ion to collect babies or kidnap people.]

If the danger of riots seems to increase; the effort, bona fide or otherwise, of the Mandarins to suppress them seem unavailing, . . . consider whether you should not retire for a time . . . . To leave *unnecessarily* would be very undesirable, lest the people in authority should think it a good plan to get rid of us, to keep up chronic excitement against foreigners. On the other hand, to stay and to be injured or killed, at a time when you are powerless to help the native Christians, and can expect little fruit from immediate efforts to spread the Gospel, would be unfortunate, especially as even if *you* escaped unhurt, there would be a good deal of talk and writing about your obstinacy in remaining after so many warnings.[10]

On the same day he enclosed cuttings from Shanghai newspapers and copies of 'Consular Notifications' with a letter to William Berger, this time about unfounded criticisms being levelled at the CIM.

Just a hasty line. We are in great perplexity. . . . Around (Nan-jing) (we are informed by one of the Romanists), rumours have sprung from the missionaries having sent out native agents to baptize beggars and children. . . . I should leave at once for (Nanjing) were it not for the state of my dear wife, who might need my help at any time – indeed I am not sure that in spite of that I must not run up there to see how matters are; the Lord guide! You can scarcely conceive how destitute of news we are, tho' the place is only (35 miles) from here. Hence our embarrassment. The cellars under the RC building at Nankin are at all times a great mystery to the (Chinese). And to their minds a prima facie evidence of something suspicious and wrong.[11]

Almost certainly they were wine cellars, adding incidentally to the coolness of the house.

On June 21 (the day of the massacre at Tianjin, though news of it would not arrive until the 29th), Hudson Taylor acknowledged receipt of Medhurst's dispatch saying,

The latest tidings I received from our Nankin missionaries were favourable. The popular excitement . . . appeared on Friday, the

17th inst, to be about over. Throughout its duration our Missionaries received no insult, even in the streets, nor were they treated otherwise than usual. . . . Some months ago we had arranged for the absence of (Mrs Duncan and Miss Bowyer) from Nankin during the exams, and had maturely deliberated on precautionary measures. (The viceroy's deputy) approved of them, and intimated to Mr Duncan that the Mandarins are fully prepared to protect them while quietly remaining in their houses (the chapel being closed during the exams).[12]

But as so often, it was to Jennie Faulding that Hudson Taylor turned that day,

Dear Sister, We need your prayers; things look very dark. One difficulty follows another very fast – but *God* reigns, not *chance*. At Nankin the excitements have been frightful . . . Our people have met with no insult . . . but had the (RC church) been sacked, they would scarcely have escaped scot free.

As tensions, difficulties and setbacks increased, this phrase, 'God reigns!' was used more and more as a victory slogan by one after another in the team.

Writing again to encourage Duncan at Nanjing, he reminded him that Ezra and Nehemiah rebuilt the walls of Jerusalem 'in troubled times like these'. 'There has been a strange and erroneous article in the *Shanghai Evening Courier* about (Nanjing). . . . It will be a *very great* thing, and a most *important precedent* if you can manage to remain in the city through the [literary] exams – a precedent that will bear more or less on work in every city of the three provinces subject to the (viceroy)' – Ma Xinyi, viceroy of Jiangsu, Jiangxi and Anhui. Another long letter on the 25th gave more careful advice, ending with 'I may come up after Mrs T's confinement and relieve you perhaps.'

Anxious to keep the Bergers informed, but still unaware of the massacre at Tianjin, he sent them a long letter on June 27.

The accounts in the papers have I believe been very incorrect and exaggerated. . . . It may be of importance to you to know the *Dove* has never left (Zhenjiang), and that *no* French gunboat has been to (Nanjing) about these matters, and that we have neither desired or needed any help of this kind, or of any other kind. I would advise extreme caution in publishing anything about these matters, as we do not know what use the Authorities may make of them.

The most trying thing that occurred was the sudden illness and death of a child in our (Yangzhou) school in the absence of its mother. Mr C Fishe guided by a very worthy and capable (Chinese) helper, acted with commendable discretion. The child was sent to two or more native doctors, the disease was at once pronounced incurable by them. The prescription of one of them was secured as an evidence, as well as for use. The medicine was administered and though the case terminated fatally there was abundant evidence that all was done for the child which could have been done for it. Finally they got the constable to bury it, he having previously in the presence of numerous witnesses examined the body to see the eyes etc were there and that there was no scratch on the body in front or behind, and that the fingers and toes and other parts were perfect. The next thing was to get some evidence of the funeral having been conducted by the (constable). Had he been asked to write one, doubtless he would have refused. He was therefore asked by a native teacher for a bill for the expenses that the latter might be able to show to me in evidence that he (the teacher) had had bona fide to pay away these sums. The bill was at once made out, and is an evidence, should one ever be needed, that the funeral was attended to by him. It has given rise however to no trouble so far; and is not likely to do so.[13]

Maria also wrote to Mrs Berger (with the thermometer 'at times over 90°'),

We have far more to fear from the cool false statements of some of our own countrymen, who probably care nothing about us. . . . (For instance) one of the Shanghai newspapers – stated a short time ago that Mr Taylor had ordered his missionaries away from Nanking, thus leaving the RC missionaries to bear the brunt alone. Now in Nanking what excitement there has been against foreigners has been almost entirely against the RCs; Mr Duncan has been there the whole of the time, and Mr Harvey only absent a few days. . . .

The 'Interpreter in Charge' here wrote a few days ago to the Commander of the Gunboat stationed at (Zhenjiang) requesting him to send a boat up to (Yangzhou) in order if necessary 'to cover the retreat of the missionaries'. The judgement of the Commander differed from that of the 'Interpreter in Charge' and he wrote a reply accordingly. Now 'the missionaries' had no idea of beating a retreat; and certainly had circumstances compelled them to leave Yangchau they would – after the absurd nonsense that has been current in England about 'Missionaries and Gunboats' – have preferred doing so in some other way than under the 'cover' of a man-of-war boat, *but* – and here is the danger to us – this correspondence being official, goes home to (the Foreign Office), and I suppose it would be almost impossible to convince those in authority there that we had known nothing whatever of the proposed step until afterwards, that such an idea had never entered our heads, and that when we did hear of it we hardly knew whether to be more *annoyed* or *amused* at it.

But God is our *refuge* and *strength* and surely we may as confidently trust Him about (rumours) in England or amongst the foreigners in China as about (rumours) in Inland Cities in China.[14]

After news of the Tianjin massacre arrived, Hudson Taylor sent Reid as his messenger to Duncan in Nanjing.

I thought you should know first how serious was the attack on the French, second that as far as we know the English had been un-molested. . . . Now everyone knows that the Nankin students are under a stronger rein and are more easily governed than those of any other place in China . . . (so if) you can safely hold on, I would say by all means do so, or give me the opportunity of exchanging with you for a time, which I will cheerfully do. [Several times he made this offer in replying to nervous missionaries wondering if they should pull out. Relief 'for a time' could do them good.]

You will note that all I have said is based on the assumption that there is no special risk to life in staying; nor of provoking a riot by your presence. Should things so change as to lead you to see that there was seriously increased danger in remaining, it might be worth your thought as to whether you should come down here and person-ally confer with me. . . .

By all means hire a boat by the month and *do it at once*. If matters look in the least threatening, have a trustworthy servant in the boat when you are not in it; that the boat people may not desert you. Do not be too anxious about your things in the case of real danger. Do not leave the house till compelled, if any sudden attack should be made on you when you are in it – for the poorest wall is a great shelter from all but fire and some shelter from that. If the house should be attacked in your absence, I would then make either for the boat or a *yamen*.[15]

On the 27th he had written, 'I advise you to engage a Hupeh boat by the month. Hupeh men are in general bold and faithful to their employers.' Such a leader deserved the gratitude he received from his colleagues.

After the massacre[16]   *July 1870*

As the mob came to the end of their gruesome work at the orphanage in Tianjin, shouts were heard of 'determination to attack' the foreign settlement and merchants' warehouses. If Consul Lay had not acted so swiftly to bring all the foreigners together under the resolute protection of the defence volunteers, and if a heavy thunderstorm had not sent the rioters running for shelter and quenched their fires, the slaughter could have been far worse. It stopped at sixty to seventy Chinese Catholics killed, more, including many Protestants, wounded, and twenty-two foreigners dead, only one unmutilated.

The remaining missionaries retreated to a merchant steamer on the river, but Consul Lay saw danger in any hint of fear, and (Wade reported to Lord Clarendon) 'fully alive to the dangers surrounding him . . . opposed every proposition made him to quit his post, and it is in chief part to his firmness that I attribute the security of the foreign residents. . . .' Chonghou was persuaded to calm the people, but his offer of Chinese troops to guard the settlement 'was declined with thanks'. Lay's certainty that an inadequate use of force by the French 'would be the signal for the rising of the whole of the troops in the city' led him to urge Wade to prevail upon the French chargé d'affaires in Peking to ensure that it did not happen. So an extremely tense peace returned to Tianjin during the succeeding days.

As soon as word of the massacre reached Peking, the foreign envoys realised that 'the interests of all foreign nations and the lives of all foreigners were at stake'. A collective note was addressed to the Zongli Yamen, pointing out that 'foreigners are not everywhere sufficiently protected by local authorities in China'. Justice should be seen to be done or the outrages would be repeated elsewhere. The very next day, June 25, an imperial decree exonerated Chonghou and condemned the prefect and other magistrates with the words, 'their delinquencies admit of no palliation', but no arrests were made until two weeks had passed.

The spectre of war rose visibly before the Court and Council. On the 28th Chonghou was commanded to investigate with the viceroy and then to proceed to France to explain and apologise. Zeng Guofan, the viceroy of Zhili, whose word alone could have done all that was needed, took his time, not arriving from his palace at Baoding until eighteen days after the massacre, a fortnight after receiving his orders. The orphanage was declared innocent of all charges against it, and the people misled by inflammatory placards from elsewhere in the empire – an attempt to protect the magistrates. Not until August 7 was the order issued to put the prefect and *xian* magistrate on trial. Brigadier Chen Guorui, 'a military officer of evil reputation' but the protégé of Zeng Guofan, present and leading the attacking mob on June 21, was passed over as of no importance.

On July 5 Wade wrote to Consul Medhurst in Shanghai saying that Peking was entirely peaceful, as if the crisis was limited to Tianjin, but this was far from the case. 'Either as a result of the outbreak in (Tianjin), or . . . as part of the universal and premeditated anti-foreign agitation', H B Morse wrote, the whole of China seethed with unrest throughout the rest of the year.

The trouble at Nanjing had begun at about the same time as at Tianjin, with multiplying reports of children missing and the presentation of 'evidence' implicating the Catholic mission in the kidnapping. In spite of strong action by the viceroy, Ma Xinyi, including decapitations, the agitation increased and an attack on the mission became imminent. On the orders of the viceroy, the prefects, magistrates and 'a number of the gentry and literati' of Nanjing visited the priests and sisters. Their report that no foundation existed for the accusations, was for the moment enough to restore confidence. Ma Xinyi reported to the Zongli Yamen that he had advised both French and English missionaries 'to move out of the way while the provincial examinations were going on', which in Duncan's case meant lying low in his unpretentious home.

The British naval commander reported to Wade on July 2, 'Both Nankin and Yangchow are in an unsettled state', and on July 16 Wade's dispatch to Lord Clarendon reported alarm at Yantai (Chefoo) – 'fear that some attempt was about to be made upon the foreign settlement'. Letters had come from Cantonese in Tianjin before the massacre, to Cantonese at Yantai, inciting them to violence. With no ship or force of men available, the British consul assembled the foreign residents, mounted a guard of volunteers with less than a dozen rifles and a few revolvers, and sent for the *daotai*, who came shortly before midnight. The timing of his visit could have been significant.

After the return of George Moule to Hangzhou in February 1870, Henry Gretton of the CMS opened a 'station' at Shaoxing near the Stevensons. (The word 'station' was used for a complex of premises and activities, 'mission' meaning a unit of missionaries however few.) Following the Tianjin massacre a mob burst into his house, excited by talk of impending mass extermination of foreigners. He turned quietly from directing some carpenters in their work and by his friendliness calmed them so effectively that they withdrew 'half-ashamed, half-reassured'. Stevenson himself was left in peace.

In Hangzhou some ten thousand candidates were attending the literary examinations, and anxiety for the missionaries was great; but no trouble erupted. In fact Jennie's home letter of July 12 showed more concern for her parents than for herself.

> I have just this evening seen the account of the massacre of French Romanists at Tientsin. . . . I am feeling for you, for I know that you will be anxious about us. There is no sign of dislike to us among the people of (Hangzhou). . . . Unless it is God's will no one can harm us, if we are in the circumstances in which He places us . . . all must be well even tho' trouble should come. 'Fear not them that kill the body . . . the hairs of your head are all numbered.' [She filled a whole page with such quotations from Scripture, to make her point.]

Vigilance committees were formed in Ningbo, as on such occasions in the past, but here too the city rode out the tensions without disturbances. Past history gave the lie to accusations against the missionaries. But the danger was real. Eugene Stock wrote, 'In [Zhejiang province] missionaries and converts alike were openly threatened with extermination; but they quietly clung to their posts and looked to the Lord's Almighty Arm for protection.'

Vile placards accused the Stotts in Wenzhou of atrocious crimes. 'Had not some seen barrels in which we salted down babies? . . . Crowds of excited people came daily and wandered all over the place, examining closely every corner to find traces of children's bodies. . . . When the excitement became general, I had to call on the Mandarin and request a proclamation, which he gave. . . .'

Stott planned to send his bride away but she protested, she might never get back again, so she must stay and trust the Lord. 'We got so used to threatening placards and having the day of our death posted up,' she wrote, 'which passed by as quietly as other days, that we began to feel less anxious.' Yet all though this time one and another Chinese came asking for Gospels to read – the first signs of a sincere response to faithful perseverance.

At Shanghai it was a different story. News of the massacre arrived on June 27. Five foreigners returning to the settlement along the Pudong shore of the Huangpu river were 'roughly handled' and one, a Mr Grant, was later found bleeding and senseless in a creek, with his hands and feet bound. On the 30th W H Medhurst Jr sent a dispatch to the Earl of Clarendon relaying the particulars and reporting that ships and men had been sent to help at Tianjin – only ten old soldiers employed as policemen, a reflection on the knife edge of danger at Shanghai also. To Wade at Peking he wrote that the Chinese at Shanghai were very disturbed . . . He himself protested to the *daotai* about inflammatory placards posted in the city. 'The animosity is principally directed against the French, but foreigners generally are looked upon as objects of hatred . . . Last night,' he went on, 'an alarm was given that the French settlement was about to be attacked, and their volunteers turned out at once, but nothing happened.' Admiral Sir Harry Keppel reported to the Admiralty '(the) threatened extermination of all foreigners'. On July 28, the *North China Herald* said, 'The night passed off quietly; and the display of force had a good effect . . . when it showed that we were thoroughly prepared to meet any attack.'

Before the alarms and excursions finally died down, mission chapels, Catholic and Protestant, had been destroyed at Yantai and Dengzhou, Nanjing, Zhenjiang, two cities in Jiangxi, and at Shanghai and Canton. Through June, July, August and beyond, when Hudson Taylor's personal circumstances were the most harrowing he had ever known, this was 'the climate of unrest' in which he remained the leader of so many threatened young men and women. What had happened at Yangzhou in 1868 and, worse still, at Tianjin now, could happen in any of his fourteen stations at any time. On July 4 he wrote to William Berger,

> As matters now are in China it is some comfort to have the dear ones (Emily Blatchley and the children) out of the way. . . . A little Chinese girl given some time ago to Miss Bowyer, was suddenly taken ill and died about half an hour after I was called to see her. . . . We had her immediately carried (as a live child might be) out of the city to Mr White's, which is in an isolated position, and then got the constable to . . . bury her. Thus public notice was avoided and no one was the wiser. Indeed the whole question of the care of infants, in stations in the interior, is evidently a grave one, . . . any such young children and infants should be nursed in (Chinese) families and not in our premises.

Grim circumstances and the pall of danger on a nationwide scale could not rid him of day-to-day administrative problems. In 1887 he told a small conference of missionaries,

> I received letters almost daily from one and another, saying: 'It seems no use our staying here; there is not a soul in this vast city that

will listen to us. . . . Would it not be better to go somewhere else?'
(They) did not know that other cities were just as bad.

I was led to advise that some of the Sisters should be sent to the
ports (so that the brethren might feel relieved of anxiety on their
behalf), but in every case they should hold the fort themselves. I said,
'You are now placed in a position to help the Chinese as you have
never been before. They see that your being a foreigner is now no
protection, but increases your danger. Let them see that you are
rejoicing in God . . . that you do not need any other protection, and
that you are not going to run away. . . . The native Christians, who
see that you do not go away, although you might; that you put your
trust in God, and are prepared either to suffer or be delivered as He
sees best, will learn that there is something in the Gospel worth
risking life for.' What was the result? In almost every place where
there were native Christians they grew (in spiritual maturity) as never
before.

Life could hardly have been more difficult or the prospects more
uncertain, yet greater tests of his fortitude and faith lay only days
ahead.

CHAPTER EIGHT

'THE HARDEST YEAR'
1870

Maria and Noel[1]   *July 1870*

In the closing days of June, Maria asked Emily Blatchley in her weekly letters from Zhenjiang to tell Hudson Taylor's parents not to be alarmed, whatever the newspapers were saying, 'but pray that *wisdom* may be given us'. One slip over a Chinese child could be the pretext to make the Yangzhou riot insignificant. Then news of the massacre arrived. Already Catherine Duncan and Mary Bowyer had been withdrawn from Nanjing, and Louise Desgraz from Yangzhou, so the Zhenjiang house was full when the Rudlands arrived unexpectedly from Hangzhou. During the 'intense excitement' a message had been sent to stop them. They had not received it. The Taylors gave up their room, Maria joining Louise, Hudson Taylor and Henry Reid sleeping in the communal living-room (a passageway to everyone in the house). Work had to continue as though all were well. On July 1 Hudson Taylor wrote to make peace between Edward Fishe and Josiah Jackson in Taizhou.

> We do not know whether we shall be able to hold our own ground at any of our (Yangzi) stations. . . . (Jackson) has felt annoyed by some of your letters: you have been tried by some of his. He may have been mistaken in some of his steps; you may have erred in some of your judgements. . . . (He) has had an invitation from Mr Stott . . . and you will have *exclusive charge* and control over the work (at Taichau) . . . not of course excluding my own general superintendence. . . . You are not sent to preach death and sin and judgment, but life and holiness and salvation – not to be a witness against the people, but to be a witness for God – to preach the good news – Christ Himself. . . . You have to win the people's esteem and confidence and love.

And the next day, to E C Lord, 'The excitement seems to be on the wane, but any spark may relight it.' Ten days later he was to add, 'That spark may be supplied by the (Tianjin) news.'

Day after day the temperature in the shade was in the nineties and they were in the Chinese city, within the high walls, close and airless. Maria's breathing was 'fast and shallow'. Then,

> After we parted on the night of July fifth my dear wife took a bath . . . (and) threw herself down on the bed to rest. [The bedroom was divided by a curtain between her bed and Louise's.] So, with the window open, (she) fell asleep. . . . It became very cold and windy . . . and a sharp attack of English cholera came on (with great abdominal pain) and yet she would not wake me nor wake Miss D. . . . When I came in to see her in the morning I was shocked to see the change. . . .
>   By noon of the 7th all the unfavourable symptoms were subsiding. . . . Williamson was just leaving us for (Anqing) with Sammy Meadows. . . . (I) told her I thought I would see him to his boat and on my way back buy a little brandy for her.

He satisfied himself that it was all right to leave her, but having bought the brandy, he left Williamson and Sammy to go on and himself returned home.

> When I got back the baby was already born. . . . I did not like the feel of (Maria's) pulse. As it got dusk she had a little doze, from which she awoke expressing herself refreshed. At this moment Mrs Rudland brought in a candle, I saw the colour leave (Maria's) lips and she turned deadly pale. . . . I believe that if I had been out of the room, or if we had had no brandy in the house, she would never have recovered.

A severe post-partum haemorrhage was taking place and 'but for instant measures she would not have lasted many minutes'. He was up all night with Maria and the baby, but had to go on with his work the next day. His letter to Henry Cordon at Suzhou on the 8th said, 'It has been reported here that all the Foreign Residents of Suchow have been murdered – but we take little notice of this.' Maria, he said, was very ill. 'I am very anxious about her.'

During the next week she 'seemed to get weaker instead of stronger but . . . felt sure she would soon be well'. She called the baby 'Noel', simply because she liked the name. To her it meant 'Peace', and for a week 'he seemed to do famously'.

By the 11th the Chinese were saying, 'It is too hot for business.' Hudson Taylor agreed but had to continue working. Thomas Harvey wrote that day from Nanjing, 'All is quiet here [on the 11th] though the people are still bent on burning down the Roman Catholic establishment.' On the 14th Hudson Taylor had to answer another complaining letter from Edward Fishe and tell him that if he did not wish to bear the responsibility for Taizhou he must either leave, or accept and work under William Rudland's leadership. In confidence he also asked John McCarthy to keep a pastoral eye on all the south Zhejiang missionaries, as he himself could not visit them. This would train McCarthy for leadership. The 15th saw him assuring the US consul at Zhenjiang that he himself saw no immediate danger from the Chinese.

> I ascertained that *even at its height* the hostility was against the French, who were shamefully blind; and that there was *little* or *no* danger to persons of other nationality, unless mistaken for Frenchmen. . . . My numerous correspondents, native and foreign, keep me well posted up in matters. This is the more needful, as some of our missionaries inland might need timely notice of any event of moment, or their lives might be needlessly sacrificed. . . . Nothing would sooner induce (the Chinese) to take hostile action, than an impression, however erroneous, that we are afraid of them.

Only the next day, however, Hudson Taylor wrote to Charles Judd at Putuo where his wife was still recuperating. 'No one knows what may be the next news, however. Yesterday I was officially notified that in case of danger we were to take refuge on the gunboat, and that if desired the ladies in the City could move there, the Captain kindly placing his cabin at their service. This will show you the feeling here. I do not think there will be trouble . . . (but you had better stay at Putuo for another month).' To Charles Fishe at Yangzhou he wrote on the 16th, 'Continue to use all care to avoid trouble. Some seem to look on it as only *deferred*, not over.' And to Duncan and Harvey, 'Do not relax your vigilance in the least. *Alert*, but not anxious.' This was the day of crisis at Yantai (p 254).

Writing on July 18 to keep the Bergers informed, he reported that outwardly all was peace and quiet.

> The foreign residents here are in some uneasiness as to their safety. I do not think there is much reason to fear. There are probably several gangs of thieves about, and they may try to avail themselves of the unsettled state of affairs. But we shall have more notice before anything very serious is to be apprehended from the people generally. . . . You will think me very remiss about my accounts. . . . This

is a time of special pressure, and I've not got Miss Blatchley's help. Were she here it would be better both for my dear wife and baby too. Others may be as kind, but few possess her ability. . . . When shall the Gospel reach the vast neglected districts of this poor Empire?

Even in such circumstances, Maria and he had been planning the house they would like to buy or build in Zhenjiang for a school and work among women, like Jennie's in Hangzhou. Yet the baby had severe 'thrush', an infection of the mouth, with diarrhoea. And the unmistakable signs of terminal tuberculous enteritis convinced Hudson Taylor that in the long run there was no hope for Maria. It was only a matter of time. But he could not believe the end would be soon. Everything failed to arrest Noel's disease and he died on Wednesday evening, July 20, just thirteen days after his birth.

Charles Fishe had come over from Yangzhou to be with them. Of Hudson Taylor he wrote on the 24th, '*He* felt it much; *she* said she did not think it right to allow herself to dwell too much upon it, in her weak state.' But that evening, though her own condition became worse, she chose two hymns to be sung at Noel's funeral. A letter came for Maria from Mrs Berger. Hudson Taylor replied, 'Could (you) have known that it would arrive and be read beside the coffin . . . (you) could not have written more suitably.' By the same mail came the news that Emily and the children had reached England safely.

[July 26] She (Maria) revelled in the enjoyment they would have, and was prepared for the trial of the closing of the little coffin, which had to be done then. . . . I little thought when I read to her your concluding words, 'And now farewell, my precious Friend. The Lord throw around you His everlasting arms', that they were a final farewell, that she would so soon fare so well, that the Lord was about so truly to throw His arms about her and carry her to His own bosom. 'Even so, Father for so it seemed good in Thy sight.'

The prevailing tensions could not be forgotten, however poignant personal experiences might be. The French consul, J M Canny, had asked him for an account of the massacre plot at Ningbo in 1857 (Book 3, p 43–51). He wrote it on July 21. A letter and more generous donations had come from George Müller, by then a warm friend. He read it to Maria 'her infant babe lying in its little coffin near her side, and we together thanked God'. The cheques he forwarded at once, some before and some directly after she herself died.

On Friday the 22nd, 'in the cool of the evening', Noel was buried beside his brother Samuel in the little walled cemetery about a mile from the river bank. Hudson Taylor took the burial service himself, and afterwards said to the grave-digger, 'I trust I may not have to trouble you again soon.' Then, turning to Charles Fishe he said, 'I think she is needed for the Lord's work; that is a comfort to me and leads me to hope for her.'

They returned via Robert White's house in the cooler suburb, arranged to move Maria there, and reached home again about eight o'clock. 'Maria seemed much as when I left her' and sitting beside her he explained his plan for her. 'Could I have my bath there as often as I like?' she asked. He was very tired and soon fell asleep.

> She asked Miss Desgraz to cover me over, lest I should take cold. I awoke about 9.30 and asked if there was anything I could get her. She said 'No, you must go and get some tea, Mrs Rudland has some waiting for you.' I went into the next room . . . and we were chatting together . . . when Miss Desgraz who was sitting at the door between the two rooms, heard my name faintly called. I rushed in, and found Maria up and very faint, unable to speak or to get into bed. I lifted her in, withdrew the pillows and bolster and put them under her hips and legs, used stimulants, and heat to the extremities. . . . I feared she would die . . . and asked the Rudlands (and others) to pray God to keep my heart quiet and guide my judgement and He did so. When she felt better the reaction became alarming, violent palpitation came on and it was but too evident the lungs were unequal to the work required of them. . . . By 12.30 a m I persuaded the Rudlands and Reid to go to bed. . . .
>
> When she began to come round she said her head was hot. . . . [He offered to thin out her hair for her but found her head so 'congested' that he cut off all her hair.] When I had (finished) she put her hand up and said 'That's what you call thinning out, is it? (and smiling) Well I shall have all the comfort, and you all the responsibility as to looks.' . . . And she threw her loving arms – so thin – around me, and kissed me in her own loving way for it. We were now able to apply cold to the head to her great comfort and relief. Soon after she dozed, and I left her with Miss Desgraz.

He sent a lock of hair home to his parents and to each of the children, writing on the envelope containing it 'One half: I dare not risk all by one ship. *Take great care of it*. J.H.T.' It is very fine; a light brown, almost blonde.

With Reid and the Rudlands he went to pray in another room, and noticed that neither he nor they could pray unreservedly for Maria's recovery. At midnight and two a m he gave her food and medicine, and sat with her till three. Louise would not go and lie down so he asked her to wake him at four. She did, and while he was in the next room Maria woke. The light of dawn upon Saturday, July 23, showed him unmistakably that she was dying. All the household and the young men, Charles Fishe, Harvey and White from the other house gathered round her.

> As soon as I felt sufficiently composed, I said to her, 'My darling, are you conscious that you are dying?' She replied with evident surprise, 'Dying! Do you think so? What makes you think so?' I said 'I can see it, darling. . . . Your strength is giving way.' . . . She continued conscious till about 7.30 . . . after which she slept till Jesus took her home, to be 'for ever with the Lord', at 9.20. She suffered no pain. Only felt weary.
>
> [Writing to her cousin William Tarn he added,] The Chinese servants and teachers who all respected and loved her, came into her room. She had a message for each, and an earnest exhortation for those who were unsaved to come to Jesus and meet her in heaven. She gave me her dying kisses for her little ones in England, and messages for them. Then language failed her and her last act of consciousness was to put one arm around my neck and one on my head, to look up to heaven with a look of unutterable love and trust. Her lips moved but no sound was uttered. . . . Then she fell asleep. . . . Her sleep became lighter and lighter, and it was not easy to say when it ceased and her ransomed spirit entered into the joy of her Lord.

An undated copy of a note in Hudson Taylor's hand to the American Presbyterians in Hangzhou reads, 'Would Mr Dodd gently break these tidings to Miss Faulding and Mr and Mrs McCarthy? Excuse the request and brevity. Mrs Taylor died of consumption of the bowels; baby also of diarrhoea. They are truly blessed! And I too. My heart *wells up* with joy and gratitude for their unutterable bliss, tho' nigh breaking. "Our Jesus hath done all things well." Yours in Jesus, J Hudson Taylor.'

Sixteen years later Hudson Taylor mentioned something he had kept to himself,

> When I said, 'My darling, do you know you are dying?' . . . She said 'I am so sorry, dear,' and paused, as if half correcting herself for venturing to feel sorry. I said 'You are not sorry to go to be with Jesus, dear?' I shall never forget the look she gave me, and as looking right into my eyes, she said, 'Oh, no, it is not that; you know, darling, there has not been a cloud between my soul and my Saviour for ten years past; I cannot be sorry to go to Him. But I am sorry to leave you alone at this time. . . .' I knew what she said was perfectly true.

She had made a habit of confessing and receiving forgiveness for any conscious sin. William Rudland also recorded Maria's words – and the fact that Hudson Taylor himself went out to buy a Chinese coffin. In such heat it was imperative to lose no time. When Maria's body was laid in it Hudson Taylor took a last look and in Job's words said 'The Lord gave and the Lord has taken away; blessed be the name of the Lord.' Then he 'hurried to his room'. But where could he go? Their own bedroom they had given to the Rudlands. William Rudland closed the coffin.

'My happy one'[2]   *July–August 1870*

That same day Hudson Taylor began his letter to the Bergers. 'As I have just re-read (yours) I could not but weep to think that soon I shall have lost the precious letters of Mrs Berger to my dearest earthly treasure. . . . Am I too selfish? Forgive me.'

But his grief was quickly submerged in a rapture which did not surprise his friends. By Monday, July 25, he was able to continue a normal business letter, calmly beginning, 'I hasten to fulfil my promise to my happy one that I would thank dear Mrs Berger for her kind letter and for all the love' shown to Emily and the children on their arrival. Towards the end he added, 'dear Miss Blatchley will be able to explain to you better than I can (that we) have little cause to boast as a Mission . . .'. The tribulations of leadership could not but penetrate his mourning. On Wednesday he wrote again, this time about the repercussions from the massacre and apparently 'deliberate machinations' by unfriendly foreigners. More difficulties, right on his doorstep, had coincided with Noel's birth and the deaths first of Noel and then Maria. The request by the well-meaning interpreter-in-charge to the commander of the gunboat 'to cover the retreat of the missionaries' from Yangzhou was a case in point. Misrepresentations in Britain seemed to be 'equally unfounded and perhaps more maliciously circulated' than the equivalent tales in China.

The funeral was on Thursday, July 28, when the great heat yielded a little towards evening. Following Chinese custom, Charles Fishe and Thomas Harvey in white gowns, the dress of mourning, walked ahead of the coffin born by eight Chinese. Behind came Hudson Taylor and all the missionaries, also in white, then the British and American consuls, the foreign officers of the Imperial Maritime Customs, 'and most of the English and American residents here', the merchants. 'They wished to erect a tombstone for her' but, though grateful, Hudson Taylor asked that he might provide it himself. At the graveside he read the burial service and a brief paper about Maria's family, conversion and life in Ningbo, in the Yangzhou riot and since.

Emily Blatchley (hearing from her friends in China) wrote, 'For many days her husband seemed to stand on the threshold (of heaven) with hardly a glance to turn on the desolated earth. . . . He himself conducted the funeral with a calm, sustained mind. . . . To him death was *swallowed up* in victory. He realised her joy, her rest. His joy *in her joy* was unbounded almost.' He himself went down with dysentery the following day, with the onset of fever, and was seriously ill for two months. 'I had to bury a sailor . . . from the gunboat,' he told his parents, 'and could hardly get through that service.'

He completed his letter to the Bergers on Monday, August 1, probably to catch the mailboat, and at once began another.

> My heart is *overwhelmed* with gratitude and praise. My eyes overflow with tears of joy mingled with sorrow. When I think of my loss my heart, nigh to breaking, bursts forth in thankful praise to Him who has spared her from such sorrow and has made her so unspeakably happy. My tears are more tears of joy than of sorrow. But most of all I joy in God through our Lord Jesus Christ – in His works, His ways, His providence – in Himself. He is giving me to 'prove (know by trial) what is that good and acceptable and perfect will of God'. And I do rejoice in that will. It is acceptable to me, it is perfect. It is love in action. [He filled a page with Scripture and a hymn, the thoughts that buoyed him up, and continued] Forgive me for rambling on in this way, dear Brother. I feel like a person recovering from a long prostrating illness – yet I am not really weak, I was able to take the service at the Consulate and three Chinese services yesterday.

He was sleepless, 'partly from the great heat and partly from the deep joy in the happiness of my beloved one' – but also from his dysentery and fever. He still could not send his statements of account. In fact he was keeping little cash in hand while the country was so disturbed. 'The merchants here and at (Jiujiang) object to cashing dollar bills. . . . I have already £sd accounts, dollar accounts, Chinese cash accounts, and now I must keep a tael account.' Nanjing was quiet, he went on, but George and Catherine Duncan had been separated for two months, so Hudson Taylor proposed to take over in Nanjing for a week or two. Not until October when the literary examinations ended would it be safe for Catherine to return there. His illness foiled the plan.

He wrote to George Müller and to his own boys on the same day, August 1, saying, '(Noel) had soft, sweet little eyes, and long silky eyelashes, and a dear little mouth just like Grace's used to be.' He told them about 'Maria's last thought of and messages for them,' and then 'it may be that God will take away your dear Papa too before very long. But God will *always* be a Father to you.' News of their mother's death would seem to have been enough for them in one letter. So why did he add that mournful note? The dangers were hourly, and going to Nanjing would increase them. After re-reading Mrs Berger's last letters to Maria on October 16, he wrote of perhaps sending Charles Edward home to join the others, 'which would be better for him, especially were I taken home either by sickness or violence'. Depression may explain the timing of it, though happiness for Maria was the dominant note in the first weeks after her death. The Tianjin massacre and nationwide excitement evoked a different, defiant reaction. He firmly believed that the apprehensions of the consuls and talk of mass extermination of foreigners were unrealistic. A few weeks later it was a different matter. At the time, his dysentery – the great killer – was the more likely reason for his remarks. So many expatriates died of it and more of his close friends were soon to be its victims. Only two months previously he had written, 'Shall we suffer much from sickness, or lose any of our number before the season is over?' He could not complain. Indeed, he could say to the Bergers, 'with the disposition the Lord has made of our precious ones I am content, fully content, and grateful for it. But that does not prevent my feeling at times sad, oh, so sad!' How much had happened since May! The euphoria could not last interminably.

In Emily's words, 'Then the blank left *here* turned upon him all its terrible vacancy; he began to realize more what her joy was to cost *him*. . . .'

'*To be the friend of God demanded even if it repaid, everything he had.*'[3]

How many heads?[4]   *August–October 1870*

Nothing stood still in Tianjin or the other treaty ports. Alarm and indignation over the massacre prompted the usual outcry for retribution from the press and public. Though they worded it differently, even the missionary body called for justice to be seen to be done – or the days of a foreign presence in China were numbered. Jonathan Lees of the LMS and William Hall of the Methodist New Connexion made a strong representation to Consul W H Lay (July 21). And C A Stanley of the American Board (July, November, 1870) closely investigated the circumstances leading to and during the riot. They made their protests public, and the leading newspapers published their correspondence.

They ranged themselves alongside not only the Roman Catholics but the French in general in saying that they wanted 'not to be separated from our suffering French brethren in any settlement', and sent their condolences to the survivors.[5] Of the mandarins they wrote, 'The excuses which unhappily served them so well in regard to the outrages at Formosa, Yangchow and elsewhere, fail them now' – for their involvement with the fire guild, the troops led by Chen Guorui and the rioters had been reliably witnessed. 'We are not crying for war and vengeance,' the missionaries wrote to Lay, 'but we do claim justice.' So they refused Chonghou's premature offer of reparations. But the United States envoy took their claim that 'the path of safety and honour . . . is to stand by our fellow-sufferers in the hour of trial' to mean no less than that 'a war between France and China must first take place before it is proper to adjust any claims.'[6]

'No money indemnity can satisfy the demand for justice,' the *North China Herald* editorial trumpeted. 'The lives of all the authorities concerned ought to be forfeited. . . . If (Chonghou) is allowed to escape, disaster may be expected for every European in this country.'

The universal demand for the punishment of the guilty mandarins was handled adroitly by Prince Kong and the Zongli Yamen.[7] The

viceroy, Zeng Guofan, apparently escaped blame as his seat at
Baoding was a hundred miles from Tianjin – only a stone's throw to
a schemer, however. Chonghou was sent as an envoy to Europe.
The prefect and *xian* magistrate suffered exile for incompetence.
But eighteen rioters were decapitated (in October) for murder and
thirty more banished for a few years. To behead mandarins, as
demanded by the Comte de Rochechouart, the French chargé
d'affaires, would humiliate the emperor and people, Robert Hart
explained to his Customs Commissioner in Tianjin. So common
law-breakers must bear the brunt – and Prince Kong had offered
fifteen heads, later increased to twenty![8] The foreign representatives rejected this as being 'in no way satisfactory'.

The Comte had been joined at Tianjin in July by his admiral, and
threatened to withdraw his legation and call in the navy to maintain
the honour of France – until on August 4 the news of France and
Prussia being at war stole the wind from his sails. From then on the
Chinese pleased themselves. Instead, five French men-of-war,
three British and one American at Tianjin, with six more at Yantai,
co-operated 'for the protection of all foreign interests' while tension
in Shanghai continued.

Assassination[9] *August 1870*

Suddenly a new shock wave swept through the nation. At Nanjing
the Muslim viceroy, Ma Xinyi, had repeatedly shown his determination to abide by the treaties, however unjust, and to defend the
Christians at Hangzhou and, since his promotion, at Anqing,
Jiujiang, Zhenjiang, Yangzhou and Nanjing. He had vigorously
suppressed all attempts to repeat the Tianjin outrage on the Roman
Catholics under his protection. By Hudson Taylor's direction,
Duncan and Harvey had lain low while Nanjing was full of examination candidates and their companions, 'fifty thousand strangers', a
powder-keg of political violence, rather than to withdraw from the
city and risk being unable to return.

On August 22 Ma Xinyi was stabbed in his own *yamen*. Lingering
for a day, he succumbed as the news swept through the provinces.
The restraining influence in central China had been removed. The
North China Herald of August 25 reported great excitement in the
city. But Duncan wrote, 'Who would have thought that the viceroy
who had so many soldiers continually guarding him from danger,
should have been laid low by the assassin's hand, whilst we, who

seemed so much exposed (should live on in safety)?' He was probably nearer the truth than he knew.

Deep resentment over the removal of Zeng Guofan and his replacement by Ma Xinyi had been felt by the troops from Hunan, Zeng's home province – and resentment was even more widespread over Ma's repression of the Anqing riot (involving the French Catholics and the CIM) and the recent plot against the Catholics in Nanjing. The fact that Zeng Guofan was reappointed to Nanjing in Ma's place is significant; it may be inferred that Zeng's transfer to the inferior viceroyalty of Nanjing was considered to be a disgrace. Both Charlotte Haldane and Alicia Bewicke Little painted a pathetic word-picture of his vainly pleading old age and blindness. 'So the ageing and ailing old warhorse had no choice.' He only lasted two years, and when he died in harness the Empress Dowager called him, in a commemorative decree, 'the very backbone of the Throne'.[10] His anti-foreign sentiments were her own.

'Universal alarm was (again) felt in foreign circles in China.' The defence volunteers rearmed and patrolled the settlements. As the weeks passed, foreigners increasingly felt unsafe. Even before the assassination, an army of forty thousand was reported to be marching eastwards from Shanxi into Zhili, in anticipation of strong French retaliation for the massacre. The Tianjin municipal council (or merchants) considered that the legations should withdraw from the capital before hard winter conditions made it impossible for rescuing troops to reach them. Wade disagreed. While he urged the merchants and missionaries in Tianjin to assess their losses at the time of the massacre, they replied indignantly that they could not even safely appear in the streets to inspect their premises.

Meanwhile Hudson Taylor expressed surprise (on August 29) over the excitability of Vice-Consul Gardner.

> I saw in (his) letters another evidence of that state of panic in which many foreign communities have been ever since the Tientsin murders. Mr Duncan could scarcely do less, in courtesy, than come down (from Nanjing) and explain [to Gardner?] that all was quiet in Nanking. . . . Mr Harvey was unwell and had his things packed for coming down, before the arrival of Gardner's letter; so his movement was entirely independent of it. . . . Mr Duncan has left (again) for Nanking. In Yangchau there has been no excitement whatever about it – nor here.[11]

His own information was that the assassination had been a private revenge, an explanation not widely shared.

When Chonghou reached Europe he 'found France prostrate at the feet of Germany; (and) the Emperor gone into captivity'. The powerless government in defeat had no time for Chinese affairs and told Chonghou they wanted no bloodletting, only protection for Frenchmen in China. But although Peking had already assumed it, the court took nothing for granted. On September 9 Robert Hart wrote to his commissioner in Tianjin, 'There is great military activity in this province, and the Chinese are preparing – they say so – to meet France in the field. . . . Winter prospects are not agreeable. We'll be safe enough in our houses, but it may not be so pleasant in the streets.'[12]

Knowledge of this made anti-foreign elements throughout the empire the more eager to act. On August 29 J L Nevius, again in Dengzhou, reported to the US vice-consul that serious threats to foreigners' lives had been made, should action at Tianjin go against the Chinese. It was being openly stated that foreigners would be murdered on September 16. So they were evacuated by ship. And in October the foreign residents of Canton notified their consul that threats to their security were daily increasing.

Sixes and sevens   *September–October 1870*

From the beginning of this crisis Wade was 'the only one in step'. Full of praise for W H Lay's heroism, efficiency and tenacity in an extremely ugly situation, Wade disagreed with Lay's diagnosis of the underlying causes. He repeated to Medhurst in Shanghai his conviction that 'the popular belief that children were received into the orphanage of the Sisters of Mercy for unholy purposes' lay behind the attack, and not a general anti-foreign movement. Why? 'There has not been in or about this city (Peking) the slightest display of hostile feeling towards religious or other foreigners'[13] – as if ignorant of the distinction between the moving spirits, the literati (including mandarins) and the peace-loving but gullible and superstitious populace with an eye for plunder, on whom they played with provocative rumour and placard. According to H B Morse, 'the gentry were manifestly filled with the belief' that the orphanage Sisters had bought infants for immoral purposes. Of some inferior literati this may well have been true, but the true intellectuals were more intelligent and clever. As for Wade, as

HBM chargé d'affaires he had the ear of Lord Clarendon and, after Clarendon's death in 1870, of Lord Granville.

By September, however, while admitting the insecurity of ministers and others alike at Peking and Tianjin, he gallantly declared himself opposed to withdrawal before the winter. The danger persisted. In December there was still much talk of war, with many dispatches passing to and fro. The *North China Herald* columnists shrugged their shoulders. 'If March finds the foreigners in Peking alive and well, all that can be said is that the luck of the storm passing over enabled the umbrella-less man to get in with a dry skin.'[14] At some point in this climate of danger, the Scottish Presbyterian James Gilmour dressed as a rugged northerner and escaped to the wilds of Mongolia as a missionary far from all diplomats and plots.

On October 18 the Chinese death sentences were carried out like a charade, 'to satisfy the vengeful wrath of foreigners'.[15] Instead of emaciated, tortured prisoners going to the block, the men wore silk, superior coffins were ready for them, each family received 500 taels and a bonus of 100 more from Chonghou on the way to Paris. Their heads were not exposed on the city wall in the usual way, but an aura of martyr-patriot was created for them. For the massacre an indemnity of 250,000 taels was paid, of which 130,000 went to the Roman Catholic Church. The vicar apostolic or bishop refused an indemnity for the murdered victims, but accepted the allocated sum to augment that for reconstruction of buildings destroyed. This included re-erection of the cathedral on its previous, greatly resented site, in Morse's words as 'part of the triple symbol of Roman dominance and French prowess in arms – the church of Notre Dame des Victoires on the site of the imperial temple of Hwanghailow at Tientsin; the cathedral at Canton on the site of what, up to 1857, had been the viceroy's *yamen*; and the (Beitang) cathedral at Peking, erected on land the gift of an emperor [Kang Xi in 1693], and dominating with its towers the grounds of the imperial palace'.[16]

Samuel Wells Williams, missionary and US diplomat, author of *The Middle Kingdom*, sympathised with Prince Kong and his colleagues in the Zongli Yamen, saying, 'The whole history of the riot – its causes, growth, culmination, results and repression – combine as many of the serious obstacles in the way of harmonizing Chinese and European civilizations as anything which ever occurred.' In other words, 'the Missionary Question' was as deeply involved as 'the China Question'. Alexander Michie, the Shanghai newspaper editor with no love for missionaries, wrote in his life of Sir Rutherford Alcock, alluding to what would have happened but for France's war in Europe, 'the Chinese government narrowly escaped a signal retribution for its continued guerrilla warfare against foreigners as represented by the missionary vanguard.'[17]

A national embarrassment   *September–October 1870*

Wade was not content to trust his own judgment on the Tianjin affair only. Dispatches between London and Peking discussed the part played by Protestant missions and Hudson Taylor in particular. Wade's message to Lord Granville on September 17 contained these words,

> I disapprove, and so far as in me lay should oppose, the establishment of Protestant missions at a distance from the Treaty ports. But when a foreign community has formed itself, its hasty withdrawal is greatly to be deplored. [It crossed en route the dispatch from Earl Granville of September 15, saying] . . . It is from knowing that missionary zeal might lead to consequences not only fatal to those devoted persons who apply themselves to spread Christianity in China, but calculated to put in jeopardy the lives and interests of the whole foreign community, that Her Majesty's Government have felt it their duty to discountenance missionary operations which seemed likely to give rise to difficulties with the Chinese Government and people; and Her Majesty's Government trust most sincerely that British missionaries will take warning . . . and conduct their operations with the utmost prudence, and with a steady purpose to abstain from exciting suspicion or animosity among the Chinese.[18]

If they thought any of this exchange would alter the intentions or actions of the particular person in mind, they did not know their man. The dispatches were barely on the way when one from Consul Medhurst in Shanghai added fuel to Wade's thoughts. Hudson Taylor's dysentery had dragged on for weeks. The Rudlands had left Zhenjiang to take up the task in Taizhou which they then continued for forty years. Duncan came down from Nanjing to report, and returned. Hudson Taylor found himself 'alone' in the Zhenjiang city house among the single men, ill, 'as weak as a child', and feeling utterly bereft. Painfully conscious of three graves at the foot of the hill outside the city walls, another at Hangzhou, three more of his children far off in Britain, and Charles Edward, not yet two, in the care of the Judds at Yangzhou, the meaning of Maria's death came home to him poignantly (Appendix 4). In two of her last letters she had said, 'T'ien-pao (Charles Edward) likes to cuddle and cosset . . . nestling in his Papa's arms . . . playing with his moustache with both his hands, or laying his little head on his shoulder.' All that was over. A week after Ma Xinyi's assassination he brought Elizabeth Judd and 'Charlie', both ill again with dysentery, to the relative safety of Zhenjiang and, with Catherine Duncan to mother his child, took the river steamer to Shanghai, called on Medhurst, and went on by coaster to Ningbo. There Charles Edward hovered 'between life and death' but recovered enough to complete the journey to the holiday island of Putuo, his best hope of a cure.

Closely in touch with his colleagues at their locations, Hudson Taylor had information valuable to his friend Medhurst – that all was at present quiet as far as his missionaries were concerned, in Anqing, Jiujiang, Nanjing, Zhenjiang, Yangzhou and Qing-jiangpu. All were keeping discreetly within their premises. But anti-French feeling was still strong and liable to erupt into violence in which the rioters might not distinguish between French and British. When he had gone, Medhurst informed Wade, and Wade took the opportunity again to deprecate the residence of British missionaries outside the treaty ports – the treaties with their clear provision for doing so seemingly forgotten, like Bishop Magee's powerful maiden speech in Parliament, about missionaries' rights being in no sense inferior to merchants' rights. The Parliamentary blue books contain it all.[19] Medhurst immediately conveyed Wade's message to all members of the CIM through Hudson Taylor, quoting the minister's directive to his consuls, 'Although you are hereby distinctly instructed to refrain from assisting in the acquisition of land or premises away from your Port, it is in my opinion extremely inexpedient that any position now occupied by a British Mission inland shall be, in this period of alarm, precipitately abandoned.'

When this eventually reached Hudson Taylor, he replied (tongue in cheek?), 'It is to me personally a matter of gratification to find that the views expressed by HM Chargé d'Affaires accord with those I have urged on the members of the Mission, and on which we acted during the last summer.' Nothing was new. His letters to his advance guards, urging the inconspicuous removal of women from dangerous situations, but not the men, and avoidance of all publicity had in fact all been written three or four months ago, in June and July. Unaccountably, a full year later Wade and the Foreign Office had not taken it in and were still harping on this theme.

Oh for MEN!   *August–October 1870*

If the first seven months of 1870 had been made difficult by successive crises, Hudson Taylor found the remaining five harder in other ways. Each political crisis had been a vicious turn of the blade in the wounds of death and separation from those most dear to him. That he could fix the eyes of his faith on Maria's joy 'with Christ, which is far better', did not mean that the stresses became fewer or less painful. 'Eye hath not seen; ear hath not heard; neither hath it entered into the heart of man what God hath prepared for them that love Him,' confirmed the certainty of 'no grief, no pain' in which he rejoiced for her. But as his colleagues returned to their work and the Rudlands moved south to replace Jackson at Taizhou, his own desolation could not but come home to him. Suddenly he was single again, thrown together with the men, instead of sharing with Maria as home-makers to whom the young men and women naturally turned. His dysentery robbed him of sleep and strength. Left alone with his thoughts, he felt bereft yet comforted. Writing from White's bungalow outside the city of Zhenjiang with a panoramic view of the Yangzi, he opened his heart to the Bergers. 'My house was full – now it is still and lonely. . . . "I go to prepare a place for you." Is not one part of the preparation the peopling it with those we love?'

News of war in Europe had just reached him. Soon it would be Paris under siege and Napoleon III captured, with a dramatic fall in the receipts of missionary societies as donors' thoughts were full of events on the Continent. The onus of guiding his Mission weighed on Hudson Taylor's shoulders all the more since Maria could no longer share it. Jackson had gone into foreign clothes again. Another Chinese baby in Jennie Faulding's care in Hangzhou had died, still potentially a dangerous thing to happen. Shortly afterwards some parents removed their children from her school, although the teacher was a Chinese. She herself was like her phlegmatic father, but news from China was throwing her mother into a frenzy of anxiety. In February she had written, 'When (the Taylors return) I should not at all like you to be left in China. . . . We gave our consent to your going quite with the understanding that we placed you under their care. . . . It would not be keeping to their promise to leave you there.' But in August it was, 'When China gets the news of the terrible defeats France has sustained . . . they will feel emboldened to go on with their attacks on Europeans (in China).' On Jennie's birthday, October 7, her mother wrote,

> Almost all our friends are anxious about you. . . . Your lives are not safe in China . . . and surely life is too valuable to be thus risked. Do let me *beg* of you to return to us . . . and then those intensely horrible cruelties – it makes me tremble to think of them – it cannot be right of you to remain if war should have broken out. . . . Today's paper . . . contains a telegram from Hongkong . . . 'Rumours are current of further assassinations . . . . Troops are massing between (Tianjin) and Pekin, ostensibly to protect foreigners, tho' their real object is considered doubtful.' If you could but know how the thought of your danger is ever uppermost in our minds you would not delay your return a day longer than absolutely necessary. . . . (The) coffins (of Grace Taylor and the Rudland baby) being on your premises has troubled (us).

In July Jennie had written sympathising with her parents and saying, 'There is no sign of dislike to us . . . in Hangzhou.' To her relief they replied that they were less worried, and Jennie commented, 'There is really no profit in "self-consuming care".' After hearing of Maria's death her thoughts were for Hudson Taylor. 'They were so much to one another but I believe he will be sustained in spirit. I only fear that his physical strength may fail.' And when Hudson Taylor was making one of his rare visits to Hangzhou, she extended her letter to reassure her parents,

> God will overrule all. . . . He will bring me home to you at the right time. . . . Troublous times might come again, what then? Well, dear Mamma, am I not safe in *God*'s keeping? Is it not best for me to be in the path of duty? He who notices the sparrows fall will not forget to care for me. . . . And if He should appoint it then surely to suffer for Him would not be the worst thing that could happen to me. Would it not rather be an honour?
>
> [And later] Mr Taylor is going to send down our own boat when he gets to (Zhenjiang) to fetch the two little coffins that they may be placed in the (Zhenjiang) cemetery.[20]

Such strength of purpose that he could count upon, in her and several others, supported Hudson Taylor when sadly many of his team were quailing in the face of threats. George and Grace Stott, the Duncans, Stevensons and McCarthys, the Rudlands, Judds and Charles Fishe were unshakable. But after the Tianjin matter had been settled, Cardwell, Harvey and even James Meadows returned like Jackson to foreign dress for self-protection. To Hudson Taylor's mind it was a sad departure from trust in God.

In the cooler climate of Putuo Island where he hoped to save Charles Edward's life, in spite of losing sleep from the child's constant need of care, he took up the correspondence he had been unable to do while ill at Zhenjiang. But it was as much as he could manage. 'My head is so tired with night (duty) and exhaustion that I scarcely know what I am doing,' he told the Bergers. 'Mail day comes and finds me sick or behindhand. It needs *your* love to bear with such inefficiency. You will pray for me that I may not *faint* under the chastening of the Lord.' Then on with endless business until, again, 'I am feeling sick and faint and must lie down.' They were far away but, after Maria, his closest confidants. He had been accused again of sabbath breaking, of deviant views on the subject, and had to set out his beliefs in detail for the Bergers to defend him. 'I do not think any member of our Mission save Mr Judd (and possibly Miss Desgraz) would tolerate buying and selling on Sunday.' Another old chestnut had also reappeared, that he had published criticisms of other missions. Again there was no truth in it, but some ghosts were hard to lay.

Jackson had been talking wildly, about someone offering to pay his return fare to England to find a wife. Worse still, Hudson Taylor wrote to Jackson from Putuo, 'It is far from improbable that subscribers to the Mission who do *not* look on faith in God as a "farce", or looking to Him for guidance as "nonsense", or profession of it as "cant" – to quote words and sentiments attributed to you – may be inclined to object to your continuing a member of the Mission of which these views are the distinctive features.' Even in such a situation when the big stick of authority might well have been used, a quality of firmness without heavy-handed autocracy is apparent in his letters. Referring to the case of Jackson, Hudson Taylor commented to the Bergers, 'I love to think of Jesus as one who upbraids not, and He is our pattern.'

Henry Reid, too nervous to be left in an advance position like Qingjiangpu, had taken over the presses from Rudland. But when Duncan fell ill, he bravely took his place at Nanjing with Thomas Harvey. In October Hudson Taylor had to ask Reid, 'Have you heard anything of dear Harvey? He cannot surely have been so terrified as to have left China for good, and have said nothing about it to any of us. Ah! for quiet faith in God. I feel greatly troubled about him. I thought he had more love to some of us than to leave us in such suspense.' It transpired that Harvey, without so much as 'by your leave' had gone to Japan and back for a change of scene! At Nanjing Harvey was doing some doctoring, another dangerous practice at this time. 'Medicine is a very sharp knife,' Hudson Taylor wrote, 'and should be well-handled or not at all.' At another time he told Reid,

> I was very glad to hear from you, as I always am, though I do not quite understand some parts of one of your letters. Might I suggest to you always to date your letters; to write them on sheets of paper of uniform size and colour; to number the pages – or at least the sheets; to add up and carry forward accounts, numbering consecutive pages, so that one may not have to lay them aside in hopeless despair of ever unravelling the confusion, two or three times before mastering them. . . . And this while I am longing all the time to know how you are in body and soul. . . .

Then he hoped he had not written too strongly. Reid seemed 'to have no mind . . . . The Chinese say (his discourses) are chaff with little grain in them.'

He missed the efficient secretarial help of Emily Blatchley and asked Charles Fishe to join him as personal assistant – and by the way, he wrote to his mother, would she arrange for Emily to have her lungs examined? If seriously ill she must have the help of another governess, to understudy her and get to know and love the children. Only youthful Charles Fishe already appeared to have the makings of a director of the Mission, but he could not yet be appointed over men so much his senior in age and experience. Stevenson, the lone wolf, and McCarthy, so mild, were unsuitable. 'McCarthy would work a province better than many would a Fu (prefecture), but to get persons willing to help (in administration) is the difficulty.' As for poor Judd – his not always gracious ways of stating his views 'may cause sorrow to himself and others. No one will be able to work or even to live with him.'

The greatest disappointment came, however, from an unexpected quarter. His reliable friends Williamson and Meadows had had enough of living under strain, exacerbated by illness, and asked to be withdrawn from Anqing. 'Everyone stands aloof, and we feel that . . . neither rulers or people are to be trusted,' they said. They had already sent Elizabeth Meadows to the relative safety of Jiujiang, though even there some foreigners were attacked. A minor mandarin called on them and warned that their house was not safe. It could have been a ruse to make them leave, but their language teacher heard a report that foreigners in the north had been defeated and 'the people in the city were . . . trying to pluck up courage to attack the two solitary foreigners in (Anqing).' Ma Xinyi's assassination compounded their fears, and to Hudson Taylor's grief they withdrew to Shanghai, briefly demoralised. He wrote of going himself to replace them, while they rented a house in Shanghai and then gave it up after paying the rent. It looked as if Meadows needed a long leave in England. 'I wish we had a few consistent *men* among us!' Hudson Taylor groaned to Berger. 'You can form no idea of the absurd and unreasoning panic that prevails among some of our communities. And those who leave their work and have nothing else to do are naturally the most easily infected.' Oh for the right kind of men! But in so small a mission he must soldier on, still virtually alone in bearing responsibility as leader.

While at Putuo, he wrote to thank Jennie for her letters of sympathy after Maria's death and Charles Edward's dangerous illness. Beginning formally with 'My dear Sister', he told her about little Charlie's ulcerated mouth and inconsolable misery, saying 'I am almost worn out.' But he had always been able to confide in Jennie, so his letter moved gradually, by way of saying that Emily would have died by then if she had stayed in China, to an unburdening of his own heart about Maria and himself.

> The more I feel how utterly I am bereaved, and how helpless and useless I am rendered, the more I joy in her joy, and in the fact of her being beyond the reach of such sorrow. But I cannot help sometimes feeling, oh! so weary. . . . My poor heart would have been over-whelmed and broken, had I not been taught more of His fulness and indwelling. . . . I am not far from her whom I have loved so long and so well; and she is not far from me. Soon we shall be together. . . . Goodnight. [And then as if calling to mind that Jennie was single.] Jesus *is* your portion. . . . Yours affly. in Him,
>
> J Hudson Taylor.

'*How to meet difficulties*'   *September–November 1870*

Undated notes for a paper on *How to meet Difficulties* lie among his documents of this period.[21] The nature of them suggests that he wrote it while at Putuo. Its keynotes read, 'What are difficulties? Circumstances in which our needs are, or appear to be, great in proportion to our resources.' Should difficulties be squarely met or avoided? To determine the will of God is the key to the answer – and he expressed his conviction that God's will may be known, and suggested how to find it. The difficulty may be a temptation, or a God-given obstruction to one on the wrong path. But it may be something to be confronted and overcome or to be met with suffering, to our benefit. So 'Fear them not; look them in the face; determine to overcome them in the strength of the Lord.'

Both the Crombies were ill and needed to return to Britain, and the Fenghua church asked for James Williamson to come as their pastor. As another Presbyterian he was well fitted to do so. But when James Meadows wanted to return to Ningbo he had to be told that the Bridge Street church had been successfully indigenous for too long already to be set back by the re-appointment of a foreigner. Hudson Taylor replied,

> It would throw matters back considerably now for any foreigner to be resident in Ningpo. The Church are beginning . . . to grasp the idea that they should not always be dependent on foreign teaching. And much of McCarthy's labour in this direction might be thrown away.

Crombie had been arguing his Presbyterian beliefs too forcibly for harmony within a trans-denominational society. He might do better to return in a Presbyterian mission, William Berger was warned, unless he became satisfied with the principles of the CIM before returning. Part of the trouble was that all three Crombie children had died and Anne was pregnant again. Unknown to George and Anne, Williamson, Meadows, Hudson Taylor and the Bergers were combining to pay their steamer fare, hoping that the latest baby would live if born at home.

Hudson Taylor was seeing them off at Shanghai in mid-October and spent the night on board ship with them before they sailed early next morning. During the night 'a miscarriage took place and she was in such a dangerous way that it was with difficulty that I was able to leave her to get the change of clothing etc I had on shore – the (sailing) was kindly delayed for me for half an hour or more by the Captain, who agreed and even wished me to go, as Mrs C could not be moved. . . . She gave me great anxiety.' Ever since George and Anne had risen so nobly to the occasion and taken Richard

Truelove's place on the *Corea* at a few hours' notice (Book 3, pp 418–24), Hudson Taylor had been looking for an opportunity to show his gratitude. As soon as Anne recovered enough to continue the journey, Hudson Taylor made the most of an 'enforced holiday', stayed in Hong Kong (very likely with James Legge of the LMS, always hospitable to CIM travellers), visited Canton and caught the French mail ship back to Shanghai. An LMS chapel had been burned down in Fushan (Fatshan) 'a place further from Canton than Yangchau is from Chinkiang'. And Christians were suffering in several places in Guangdong province while the long crisis in China lasted. 'The Clarendon policy has done an injury that, I fear, will not soon be recovered from,' he surmised. The complete change of scene had done him good, his love of the sea taking his mind from his grief. When he learned that the next ship to follow him from Hong Kong had been caught in a typhoon and lost without trace, he was impressed that his life was in God's hands.

After Charles Edward's dangerous dysentery at Ningbo and severe 'thrush' at Putuo, Mary Gough (Mary Jones of thirteen years' friendship) had offered to keep him as one of her family. So, trans-shipping at Shanghai, Hudson Taylor went down to Ningbo, planning to visit each station between there and Zhenjiang on his way home to Yangzhou – now only home in that his possessions and precious memories were there. On arrival at Ningbo he found Charlie desperately ill again, this time with croup.[22] He had been black in the face and at midnight Dr John Parker had with difficulty saved his life. To go on with the journey demanded determination. 'My heart aches at the prospect of leaving him again,' he groaned – the last living link in China with Maria.

In gratitude to Mary Gough he went to great trouble to arrange for his parents, the Fauldings and others to do what they could for her son Tom Jones, now a young man of 18 taking up medicine. Reunion with the faithful Wang Lae-djün and his wife, and with the McCarthys and Jennie Faulding for nearly two weeks was the tonic he needed. But on arrival at Hangzhou he was called to see one of George Moule's church members who had already 'been left three or four days with her infant partially born'. It was too late to save her life. Two days later he attended Mrs McCarthy in a hazardous confinement which could also have been fatal if he had not been there.

A letter arrived from his mother. The doctor had examined Emily's lungs and gave her 'no hope'. Her tuberculosis was far advanced. 'My heart felt almost overwhelmed' for a few minutes, he wrote in reply. Was Emily to be taken too? Maria's dying wish had been that the children 'should all be kept as a little family together; and under (Emily's) care'. So now, 'O death, where is thy sting? O grave, where is thy victory?' had new meaning for him.

> *Formerly* I had thought those *taken* were to feel this. *Now* I know those *left* may also triumph over death. . . . Often I find myself wondering if it is possible for her who is taken to have more joy in His presence, than He has given to me. If He has taken her to heaven He has also brought heaven to me here – for *He is* heaven. . . . In His presence is fulness of joy . . . 'It is *I*, be not afraid.' '*I* took them.' And my heart He fills with such deep true unutterable gladness.

Even more disquieting was a note detectable in the Bergers' letters, of failing health and even failing resolve. Their invariably kindly, humble letters carried a hint of waning confidence in their own ability to do what was required of them, not only in the selection of candidates. Shock after shock from the international news and then of Maria's death, following all the trauma of the Yangzhou riot aftermath and the defence of Hudson Taylor and the Mission, were more than they could stand. Mary Berger was still suffering pain whenever she took food. William Berger was wilting. On September 23 he wrote, 'I feel my inability . . . my nerves have become so shaken by events.' Letters of sympathy for Hudson Taylor and his team were pouring in and had to be replied to. Mrs Faulding's alarm and concern for Jennie were taxing too. So William Berger confessed, 'I bear burdens too heavy for me.' 'I get weaker year by year.' And as the year ended, 'I am very weakly in body but the Lord knows my need.' How could the Mission continue without the Bergers? There was no one in Britain so far known to Hudson Taylor with the same commitment and liberty to take on the work involved.

All the same, long, affectionate and efficient letters continued to come, dealing with administrative matters, but always so carefully expressed – with pages of accounts, especially if any apparent discrepancy should need clarification. Philip Gosse (the naturalist) had sent his greetings and sympathy, but advised, 'Mr Taylor has more and more disappeared from our view. . . . Now, seeing that . . . he is manifestly the only mastermind in (the Mission) the recession from communication with the supporters . . . is much to be deprecated. The cream of former Papers was his *coup d'oeil* over the Mission, his estimate of work done and his anticipations of progress.' 'Did Mr Gosse know,' Mr Berger commented, 'what you are asked to bear and pass through, he would not be surprised at your silence.' Still, he was right, a few lines from time to time were essential. Stern business was well balanced by encouragement. 'I see in you what God can do, keeping you in peace and even joy when his billows are going over your soul. (He) has been preparing your soul, dear brother, for stripping it of its chief earthly joy. It has been most marked. . . . The furnace has been heated by an all-wise hand, and shall only purify the gold.'

Another struck down   December 1870

Leaving Hangzhou, Hudson Taylor went next to Suzhou, to be greeted by Henry Cordon with the news that George Duncan was seriously ill at Zhenjiang, incessantly coughing blood. Something about Hudson Taylor impressed Cordon more than this emergency. 'He came to us full of the Spirit. Although he had so lately experienced such deep sorrow, he only spoke of the wisdom and goodness of the Lord.' Hudson Taylor set off at once for Zhenjiang. Starting with the same disadvantages as his companions in the team, and yielding like some of them to the pitfalls of culture-shock, criticising and rebelling until he found his feet, Duncan had faced the difficulties and overcome. In pioneering Nanjing he had been wise and not fearless but brave.

Catherine Brown had taken a risk in coming to China to marry a man she scarcely knew, but had all the qualities to make her the right wife for him if they were not 'as unsuited to one another as they well can be'. Unfortunately, as the victim of Victorian mores, like so many of her kind, 'of what marriage involved, she appears to have been in absolute ignorance', while from the first George was rough and demanding. At Nanjing they had quarrelled incessantly and she had been on the point of leaving him, when Hudson Taylor and Maria had gone to the rescue, explaining and advising them over several days. As a result the love and respect of each couple for the other became profound, though the Duncans still found it hard to adapt to each other.

When extreme danger forced Catherine and her companion Mary Bowyer to leave Nanjing for a while, and when Maria was ill and died, Catherine repaid her debt of gratitude in every way she could, mothering Charles Edward and seeing to Hudson Taylor's comfort.

For her sake and George's he hurried to help them. There was little
he could do. Tuberculosis, the inveterate enemy of so many, with no
known cure, had struck the strong Highlander down. He lived,
working hard, for only two more years.

The saddest week and hardest year   *December 1870*

Perhaps it was too soon, but Yangzhou as 'home' to the Taylors,
though they had so seldom lived there, held all Maria's possessions,
and Hudson Taylor had to spend a few days disposing of them. Two
days before Christmas he wrote, 'Last week was perhaps the saddest
I have passed since my dear wife's removal. I was going over many
of her things – our betrothal presents, her wedding dress, and many
things . . . connected with the birth and death of some of the dear
children and with my darling wife herself.' A flood of memories had
been inescapable.

He had asked Emily Blatchley to compile material for a memoir
of Maria for the children, and then to write it herself. She began but
as her health failed had to put it aside. Little survives, but scattered
reminiscences and tributes in letters of sympathy confirm the impression of a highly competent, caring and self-effacing wife,
mother and missionary colleague. James Williamson recalled her
constant attention to the single men's clothes, keeping them laun-
dered and mended. Charles and Elizabeth Judd knew her only from
the six weeks they were together in Hangzhou, and then in Zhenjiang after the riots, when Hudson Taylor was down with dysentery.
In spite of her injuries Maria had risen to the occasion and struck
Judd as being 'the backbone of the Mission at that time'. A false
inference has been drawn from his remark – that without Maria,
Hudson Taylor would have been weak – but throughout the collected correspondence (her own, the Bergers and Hudson Taylor's)
the clear impression is given of a consistently unobtrusive but
positive personality supporting her husband loyally, and obediently,
in his strong leadership, never asserting her own opinions when they
occasionally differed from his. It was true, however, that while
dysentery disabled him, Maria's quiet strength had inspired her
colleagues.

The shattering experience of her death in a year of crisis upon
crisis, emphasised the nature of Hudson Taylor's own personality as
perhaps nothing else would have done. In Grattan Guinness he had
an understanding friend to whom he could open his heart.

The difficulties and dangers . . . and the sickness and sorrows of the past year, I think I may say they have equalled if not exceeded, those of the previous sixteen years of my missionary labour in the aggregate. But be this as it may, the Lord had previously taught me *practically*, as I never knew it before, our *present*, *real* oneness with Christ. And with the exception of the last two months, it has been the happiest and most joyous year of my life.

To William Berger he announced that he was sending the Meadows family home before the summer, and gently held Berger to Mission principles undergoing strain.

As to appeal, I would suggest we make that to God alone so far as *funds* are concerned. If the Lord sends still less, and some were to leave us in consequence we might be rather stronger than weaker for the loss. [Then he answered a suggestion that he himself should visit England, to relieve the Bergers and encourage the Mission's supporters.] I need not say how my poor desolate heart often longs to see you all, and how I should like to make some arrangement about family matters, to say nothing of seeing face to face the friends of the Mission. But I think you will see with me that in the present state of matters (in China) *I* should not be out of the way. . . . Mrs Faulding has written to Jennie in great trouble urging her to return. There is really no need for it *now*, so far as immediate danger goes. And she could not leave her work at present without grave injury to it – and to others. . . . But I *must* close. It is 2 a m and I rose at 6 a m and must not attempt more.

Jennie herself answered her mother's pleas by writing on December 7,

The panic of the summer has quite passed away. . . . Fresh missionaries are being sent out by the different societies, but I have not heard of any leaving on the score of 'prudence', not even the most timid. . . . *Now* is our opportunity, the people are willing to hear, our opportunity might be short, ought we not then to make the most of it? I have health and am able to work. I will not court danger, but you mustn't want me to come home before God makes it clear to me that I ought. . . . I *hope* you will give me your permission to stay. . . . I think you will.

To Cardwell at Jiujiang, timidly seeking protection in foreign clothes, the symbol of Western power, Hudson Taylor had written after returning to Zhenjiang, to instil some courage, 'As a rule the sooner we, as an inland Mission, can get away from the ports the better. . . . Living in the interior of China, and especially in the unoccupied provinces is not, and is not likely to be, an easy task. . . . Let us take courage and press forward.'

Looking back over 1870, Hudson Taylor himself said, 'Wave after wave of trial rolled over us; but at the end of the year some of us were constrained to confess, that we had learned more of the loving-kindness of the Lord than in any previous year of our lives. Perhaps, also, more was done during this year than ever before to teach the (Chinese) Christians not to lean upon the arm of foreign protection and support, but upon God alone, on whom, as they had seen, the missionaries themselves had to lean in the hour of trial and danger.'

'The year,' he was content to add, 'was not wholly without some visible sign of progress.' During the less tense periods Stevenson had extended the Shaoxing church to Xinchang beyond Sheng Xian (map, p 38) where he had begun work in 1869; Wang Lae-djün had opened a country chapel at his own expense; the Hangzhou evangelists had returned to Lanxi on the Qiantang river, and to other cities; McCarthy had made an evangelistic journey north-east from Hangzhou, Harvey northwards into Anhui from Nanjing, and Rudland and Edward Fishe in two directions from Taizhou. The freehold of the Nanjing house had been successfully purchased, and land outside Zhenjiang on which to build. The invisible signs of progress were not long in making themselves apparent when churches came into being in those cities in which beleaguered young men and women had thought they were achieving nothing.

PART 4

CRUCIBLE OF FAITH

1871–75

CHAPTER NINE

'TUNNELLING THROUGH ROCK'
1871–72

Holding on   *January–June 1871*

If the year just ended, 1870, was the hardest in Hudson Taylor's experience so far, the first half of 1871 was in some ways 'harder still'. The new year began well. Someone went so far as to tell Emily Blatchley in a letter that Hudson Taylor was 'never looking better'. He was disciplining himself to go to bed between nine and ten o'clock and to begin the day at six-thirty. After the customary day of fasting and prayer on December 30, things began 'to look up', with conversions and baptism in most of the Mission's cities, and fewer problems with the team. Whenever he was at Zhenjiang he acted as chaplain to the community and preached at the consulate as well as in the Chinese chapel. In March he organised the congregation as a church, Chinese and missionaries sharing the leadership. But six or seven hours of meetings in a day were too taxing for his strength and the improvement in his health was short-lived. Charles Fishe, as his assistant, was picking up the administrative duties of accounting and routine correspondence, and being called the Secretary in China of the Mission. So Hudson Taylor began to think of making a quick visit of a few months to Britain and back, as the Bergers were urging him to do. To consult with them, renew links with the Mission's supporters, and make arrangements for Emily and his 'three strong, rompy' children, were crying needs.

He had noticed on his visits to his scattered team that they – Chinese and foreign evangelists and their congregations – followed each other's progress with interest. So he launched a little house journal, the *Monthly Gleaner*, printed on the presses at Zhenjiang, and Fishe took responsibility for producing this. When Hudson Taylor fell ill again and had to cancel a planned visit to Ningbo and the southern area, he very carefully delegated his pastoral duties to John McCarthy. McCarthy was already advising the church leaders of the Hangzhou, Xiaoshan and Ningbo (Bridge Street) congregations. If he were also to visit his missionary colleagues, the Stotts, the Rudlands, Edward Fishe, Williamson and Jackson he could encourage them and help in any way he saw fit. He could be in practice a real though 'not a nominal bishop or overseer'.

> You are really their head as you become their helper and servant. I wish you to feel responsible before the Lord for seeking to help . . . really help them, really pray much for them, and, as far as possible, with them; feel and *evince* a deep interest in all their out-stations and work generally. And above all, don't let them dream you are taking a higher place than their own – leave God to show that in due time.[1]

As a pattern for superintendence as it developed in the years ahead, this basic statement stands as relevant today as then.

After all they had been through, James and Elizabeth Meadows were preparing to return to Britain on leave. They left Zhenjiang for Shanghai on April 7, but were delayed by the premature birth of Elizabeth's baby and continuing ill-health, so that they decided to wait and travel with Hudson Taylor. They were still waiting in July. By the time they arrived home James would have been away for nine years of rebellion, war, riot, threats and recurring dysentery. Knowing of Hudson Taylor's concern for his little Charles Edward, still in the care of Mary Gough though she was ill with liver abscess, Elizabeth Meadows offered to take him home with them. By then Hudson Taylor's illness and the pain of being parted so far from little Charlie, his last link with Maria, made him unable to think the question through. If he himself could get away he would be able to have Charlie with him. Outwardly he was composed and cheerful, but John Stevenson had seen evidence of weeping.

By mid-January when he was struggling again with constant pain in his side and chest, he told Jennie and his mother, 'everything is a burden'. But 'matters look encouraging at most of our stations, and the prospects of peace increase. I have midwifery engagements up to the end of June' – including the British and American consuls' wives – but after that he would try to come home. His pain was like the pain that had driven him home in 1860, and as then he feared the worst. It continued for months, but this time without jaundice. Actual gallstone colic was to come later. He preached at the consulate on January 22, and then went down with 'bronchitis' for ten days, nursed by Louise Desgraz. Even so he had to keep up with his correspondence and complete his share of work on the *Monthly Gleaner*.

On the whole China was calm again, but at Anqing and Yangzhou the mutterings of anti-foreign feeling kept being heard. 'We hold our own with great difficulty.' When Thomas Harvey began doctoring again at Nanjing, after saying he would not do so, Hudson Taylor wrote patiently, reasoning at length with him that he was playing with fire. The danger and potential damage could extend far beyond Nanjing to affect the whole work of the Mission, and others too, by limiting them to the treaty ports.

> As you know the Nankin people still believe (that) foreigners . . . bewitch people with medicines. And you can scarcely be ignorant that since the return of (Zeng Guofan) . . . any medical efforts are open to *accidental*, not to say *intentional* misconstruction. Such a case might easily arise as would result in the destruction of all missionary property, Roman Catholic and Protestant, lives might be lost, war ensue. And I cannot but think that no small responsibility would rest on the shoulders of the unintentional but still highly reprehensible author of so much trouble. . . .
>
> You have made most commendable progress in the written character. I do not know any member of the Mission who has made such good progress in the same time as you have done; and not many, if any, can write the characters so neatly as you can . . . but your ear is as evidently needing help. . . . Your own servants often misunderstand you; and many (Chinese) have told me that not more than half you say is intelligible to a stranger. . . . Concentrate your efforts on the language and on direct missionary work till you are truly efficient. . . . I beseech you not to attempt *any cutting* operations in Nankin. Trifling ones about the eyes, or the removal of tumours, may cost many lives. I would advise you to sell your medicines; they would be worse than useless to you, they would be a temptation. And if it be known that such a supply of medicines has gone to Nankin, who could prevent the report that further bewitching was on the way? The Viceroy himself could not do it.

It was after all only seven months since the Tianjin massacre. Instead Hudson Taylor suggested that Harvey should visit the coast of Jiangsu to find, if possible, a seaside holiday place like Putuo. At the end of March he did go by river and across-country from Qingjiangpu, north-eastwards as far north as Haizhou near the Shandong border, an adventurous journey with a Chinese companion. But he found only mile upon mile of tidal swamps.

Henry Reid had written proposing marriage to a complete stranger. 'Don't let her out!' was the only advice Hudson Taylor could give William Berger. But Reid was doing well at supervising the erection of new school buildings at Zhenjiang, planned with Maria before her death and now a memorial to her. Designed as a home and school for Louise's and Mary Bowyer's work among women and children, it stood outside the city where the air was fresh and the surroundings peaceful. So Hudson Taylor rented rooms near by for himself.

For a short while in March he was better and gave lessons in Greek to the Zhenjiang household, to their delight. But by the end of the month he was in bed again and so ill that he thought this time death was not far off. He told his father, 'The joy of life has fled', and wrote about committing his children legally to Emily Blatchley if he should die. Perhaps he half wished he could.[2] Far away in England Emily, too, was tearful and lonely, finding the care of his children as much as her failing strength could stand. When his mother and others in China suggested that he should marry her, he replied,

> Poor Freddie [Howard Taylor] . . . needs a person of pretty strong nerves and firm deportment to manage him. And Miss Blatchley suffering as she does must often be very unequal to this. I can fully endorse all you have said of her value to me and to the children, and might add much more. The Mission would never have been what it is, but for her ability, diligence, and faithfulness. On at least two occasions, I am convinced, my dear wife owed her life to her kind and vigilant nursing. . . . Miss Blatchley's present condition is largely the result of her unceasing care of dear little Samuel during the winter of '69–'70. In cold rooms, she was up night after night – sometimes frequently, to save my dear wife whom she loved with a devotion no-one else has ever shown. So that if I did not love and value her, I should be ungrateful indeed. But that is quite a different thing from entering into the relationship you so delicately allude to. This has been advised, I do not say urged, by some here, who know her loss to the (Mission), love her and think it would add to my happiness and efficiency. But I have always replied that if there were no other reasons against it, the state of her health was too uncertain to admit the question. . . . I am, however, rather looking forward to reunion with my own Maria, than to any earthly union. . . I can very well foresee that if I do return home my position will be both delicate and trying.

His letters to the children were warmly affectionate, reminding them of his love and friendship while they were with him, and exhorting them to be considerate and good. For Freddie he had this to say, 'There is one thing (God) never does . . . He never *undoes* what we have done, no matter whether it be *right* or *wrong*. And its consequence goes on, and on, and on . . .' – but letting Jesus rule in our hearts is the secret of overcoming the bias to do wrong.

Emily was comfortably established in Bayswater with a sister-in-law of W G Lewis of Westbourne Grove, close to Amelia and Benjamin. But the expense was more than Hudson Taylor could justify, and supporters of the Mission might misconstrue his children's being housed in stylish new West End quarters. A seaside town on the south coast would be better for them all. But he was too far away to intervene – or to help Benjamin, whose business partnership had had to call in the receivers and come to an end. A deliverance from the wrong kind of company, Hudson Taylor thought. But it meant that Amelia, with eight children of her own, could not help Emily. He himself was needed at home.

Still his illness continued. In editing the April issue of the *Monthly Gleaner*, Charles Fishe wrote 'Mr Taylor has been very unwell for the last three months, almost wholly unable to engage in any work.' By mid-May he was writing of having an irregular fever and of months on and off a couch, unable to be up all day. Yet all through these months he continued to carry the day-to-day administration of the Mission, constantly training Charles Fishe to keep it going when he himself would at last be free to leave.

Progress   *May–June 1871*

The Mission's work continued to look up. The New Lane church at Hangzhou had fifteen candidates for baptism, about to swell the church membership to sixty-seven. Wang Lae-djün, declining any salary from Mission sources, and trusting God to meet his needs, had opened four country outposts with regular services, and was supervising seven full-time evangelists and colporteurs. He had been up the Qiantang river to Lanxi preaching the gospel in an area where new churches were to result as this evangelism progressed – and on beyond Lanxi to Qu Xian. John McCarthy's continuous training classes were preparing more to join them either locally or far afield as missionaries to other cities. Jennie's friend, the future pastor Ren was among them. Her schools were doing well, finan-

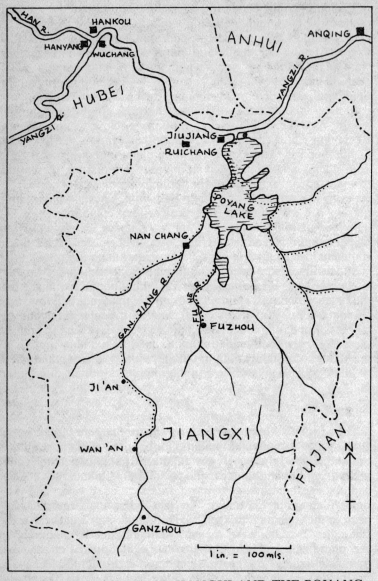

CARDWELL'S DREAM: JIANGXI AND THE POYANG
LAKE

ENDLESS WATERWAYS IN THE POYANG LAKE REGION

cially independent of the Mission, and several older pupils had so far memorised the whole New Testament with the exception of two Gospels. Apart from managing and teaching in the school, with Mrs Wang she was still visiting house after house in the city as she had done since her arrival there in 1866. To stay and carry on, as if massacres and uproar elsewhere in China had no relevance in Hangzhou, was in her view the best way to maintain calm, and she was probably not mistaken.

Acting on Hudson Taylor's advice, John McCarthy walked all the way to Taizhou and back, 'preaching along the way' and discovering a personal ability which was to become part of the history of China. At Ningbo, Fenghua, Taizhou and Wenzhou his coming cheered the churches and missionaries, who wrote appreciatively to Hudson Taylor. At Wenzhou and Taizhou such crowds were thronging the premises (a hundred or more day after day to hear the gospel preached) that larger chapels were urgently needed. The response of the people to the foreigners' quiet endurance of threats and stoning was their just reward.

J E Cardwell at Jiujiang had acquired a boat and begun evangelistic journeys along the 'endless' rivers and shores of the Poyang Lake. At long last he was realising his ambition and was beginning his major penetration of the province of Jiangxi. After an initial five-day journey he ventured deep into the province for a month. Sailing to the southern extremity of the lake, and up the Gan Jiang, a large river, to the provincial capital of Nanchang, he went on up the Fu He a hundred miles beyond to a subsidiary city called Fuzhou, in the same latitude as Wenzhou on the coast.

When stones were thrown from an excited crowd he asked bystanders, 'Is this the way to treat a visiting stranger?' and taking his side they stopped the offenders. Another day a man put his hand beside Cardwell's and said, 'They are the same.' 'Then why do you call me "foreign devil"?' he asked. If their bodies were the same and one was a foreign devil, the man answered, then the Chinese must be native devils – and they all laughed. 'You're right,' they said. From then on Cardwell made a point wherever he was of discussing the absurdity of the epithet, 'foreign devil', and heard people change their expressions. At Nanchang literary examinations were in progress and the mandarins sent a gunboat to see him safely on his way, welcoming him back after the unruly students had dispersed.

News of such expeditions, reminiscent of Hudson Taylor's own early adventures before obligations to others tied him down, gave him hope of eventually achieving his ambitions for spreading the gospel throughout China. Only at Anqing and Yangzhou was opposition being maintained and progress slow. Continuing attempts to buy the premises they had rented, expressly to turn them out, kept Hudson Taylor, Meadows at Anqing, and Judd at Yangzhou at their wits' end. To be evicted would make a return well nigh impossible. Yet in both places a church was steadily taking shape as members increased in number and maturity.

Writing to his mother on June 21 Hudson Taylor said, 'Nearly all my things are packed, and I had hoped to be away from (Zhenjiang) by this time. But two cases of confinement which I have engaged to attend have not yet come off, so I am detained – and yet may be for some time. . . . I have seemed to realize those thin loving arms almost around me again, as they were when she gave me her parting blessing.' Feeling drained and exhausted, he was doing all he could to get unco-operative members of his team to pull together. When Reid wrote of going into 'the English costume', Hudson Taylor replied on the 24th,

> No change in your views or action in this matter will in the slightest degree affect my Christian love and esteem for you. . . . (This question of dress is) one of the topics I propose for conference with Christian friends at home, in its bearing on our work, and on my movements. . . . [It was a serious matter. If he could not get his colleagues to follow his lead, perhaps he should not continue as leader – or should limit the Mission to those who would?] I wish to

develop my own conscientious convictions òn this subject; at the same time I do not wish to constrain any to act contrary to their own feelings and wishes. . . . It must be borne in mind that not merely the feelings and interests of those who would discard the principles and practice of the Mission have to be considered; those who adhere to them, and friends who support them, are not to be forgotten.

Abandoning Chinese clothes, he continued, could embarrass his colleagues who did not, could start another spate of newspaper criticism at the time when more publicity would be most unwelcome. 'We are just now in particularly delicate circumstances politically.' It was impossible to foresee the outcome of any action to disturb the status quo. He did not add that young Reid was probably too out of touch with affairs to realise that a second plot to attack the Mission in Yangzhou, and the concerted attempt in Peking to force all missionaries back to the treaty ports were currently hot issues.

Then came the news, that after a long, long wait for Tom Barnardo to qualify as a doctor and reach China he would not after all be coming. It could not but deepen Hudson Taylor's despondency. Protests from Britain that Hudson Taylor should not be so tied by babies – waiting for confinements – were all very well. No one else could relieve him of the duty and he was unwilling simply to deny his help to consuls' wives, let alone his own missionaries. So while the Meadows family waited to travel on the same ship as he, he had again to defer his own departure until the pending confinements were over.

The second Yangzhou plot[3]   *April–June 1871*

For months Hudson Taylor had been trying to negotiate the purchase or lease in perpetuity of the Yangzhou premises, using the indemnities received and contributed by each missionary victim. The terms of reinstatement after the riot in 1868 had provided for permanent tenure of the property and had been carved in the stone tablet set up at the gate. But at every turn he had encountered difficulties, until deliberate obstruction could be the only explanation. On January 29 he noted that negotiations in Yangzhou were no further forward than a year ago. Only if all went well could he expect 'to return to England for a short time in August or September'. By April 9 he was more hopeful of success, but doubtful, as others were too, of his own survival. A week later the root cause of his 'fruitless negotiations' suddenly came to light, and rapid developments revealed the seriousness of the situation. A second plot to expel the foreigner from Yangzhou had the backing of two instigators of the Tianjin massacre.

After the murder of Viceroy Ma Xinyi and the investigations into the Tianjin outrage, the aged Zeng Guofan returned to Nanjing as viceroy of the Two Jiang, the provinces of Jiangxi and Jiangsu, with Anhui – and therefore of Yangzhou and Anqing. From having a protector in Ma Xinyi, Hudson Taylor and the CIM had returned to the state of affairs in 1868 and 1869 when their enemies had been supported by Zeng Guofan. But this time Zeng had returned with the unsavoury reputation of sheltering the literati responsible for the Tianjin massacre, if not of instigating it, while Brigadier Chen Guorui had again been given command of two army camps at Yangzhou, the scene of his earlier crime.

For safety's sake and because of another approaching confinement, Elizabeth Judd had moved to Zhenjiang to be near Hudson Taylor, but Charles Judd, Louise Desgraz, her Chinese language teacher, his mother, wife and children, and a Chinese Scripture-reader or 'Bible woman' and about fifteen girl and boy boarders in the Mission remained on the Yangzhou premises.

The actual owner of the property was a retired military mandarin, a Grandee called General Li, who lived in Henan. At various times he had been a Taiping rebel general, a Nianfei rebel leader and an imperial army commander, 'as best suited his purpose for the time being and brought in the largest income'. 'A man of undoubted bravery, he (was) also a man of violent passions and great determination' who kept 'a few private gunboats and some soldiers of his own'.

Hudson Taylor had always negotiated with the owner's uncle, his official representative, a dignitary with the style of Great Father, 'Da Lao Ye' (Book 2, Appendix 3), who from the first had been 'most anxious that (Taylor) should retain possession of the premises'.

> Summoned (it is said) by Zeng Guofan, (General) Li suddenly appeared in Nankin. There he had an interview with (Zeng Guofan) immediately after which (on April 17) he wrote a most violent letter from Nankin to his uncle at Yang-chow, accusing him of ruining his reputation by letting his property to foreigners, insisting that by fair means or foul, he must turn them out of the premises on or before (May 4) and insisting, also, that if they were not out of the premises

by that time, he, the uncle, *should go to the premises, close the first gate and commit suicide within*, upon which, said he, '*I will at once come and avenge your death*.' He warned the uncle not to attempt to escape, 'for if you do,' he continued, 'I will seize on your wife and children and kill them.'

The uncle and his friends were appalled for, knowing Li's character and reputation and the veneration in which Chinese normally hold their elder relatives, they knew this was no empty threat. The sudden change of tone implied strong influences upon General Li and an intention to do as he said. The uncle went at once to Judd (on April 19) and told him he 'must immediately get ready to quit' the premises. But to his distress Judd replied that the agreement had been made, the deposit had been paid and the balance of payment was ready for the contract to be signed. 'We could not think of giving it up.'

To appeal to the Yangzhou prefect would be futile, for he was greatly inferior in rank to General Li, and Chen Guorui commanded the troops which the prefect would normally call upon to quell a riot. Chen, since his arrival at Yangzhou, had 'been endeavouring to regain his popularity among the most dangerous class of Chinese, by large distributions of money amongst them. And simultaneously with this, there has been a marked development of anti-foreign feeling amongst the people . . . Before, and up to the time of his interview with (Zeng Guofan) Li and Chen were sworn enemies; suddenly they became fast friends, to all appearance, to the great astonishment of the (people) of Yangchau.' It was the talk of the town that another attempt to drive out or kill the foreigners had brought them together. Judd crossed the Yangzi to consult Hudson Taylor, and they decided that the schools should be disbanded, Louise should come to Zhenjiang, and Judd should hold on at Yangzhou for as long as possible. From then on, he was largely alone as the fateful date, May 4 drew nearer.

'(On April 25) Li himself came to Yang-chow from Nankin, and in conjunction with (Chen Guorui) ripened his plans, and they and their soldiery became almost irrepressibly excited.' Charles Judd and the Christians in Yangzhou were then in considerable danger, with nowhere to flee to in the event of an attack. Urgent messages began to pass between all the parties involved, Vice-Consul Gardner himself consulting urgently with the *daotai* of Zhenjiang. May 4 came and went, and the next day one of the Christians pleaded with Judd to appeal to the magistrates for protection. 'I thought of . . . Ezra when he was ashamed to ask the king for a body of soldiers,' Judd replied, 'So we only waited on our God with fasting.' By then Hudson Taylor suspected that Zeng Guofan and the provincial governor were implicated. Only three days remained before the fateful 9th, when murder and destruction were expected. Already Yangzhou was 'full of rowdies' openly boasting of their intentions, and Chen Guorui of his past doings.

Things were getting out of hand. The provincial authorities were alarmed. Expulsion from the city was one thing, but another massacre could call down retribution on their own heads and precipitate a war. Zhang Futai, Governor of Jiangsu, appointed the *daotai* of Zhenjiang to handle the crisis, and the *daotai* immediately notified General Li and the prefect of Yangzhou that they would be held responsible for any disturbance. To Judd's amazement General Li 'became friendly on the governor's orders'. But the façade was transparent and short-lived. Urgently seeking a solution, the *daotai* persuaded a friend named Zhao to buy the Yangzhou premises for whatever General Li would accept and, at Consul Gardner's instance, to lease them to the Mission, initially for five years. There was no time to lose.

General Li still had the whip hand. He arrogantly demanded 4,500 taels – an exorbitant sum – or he would carry out his threat. Early on May 6 his terms were sent to the *daotai*, the consul and Hudson Taylor in Zhenjiang by mounted courier. They must accept the terms or the attack would be made. The messenger could have arrived back on the same day but was hindered. The old uncle and his middleman came to Judd in great distress and would not leave. On the second day the messenger still had not come, and when night fell they were still at the Mission, sick with apprehension. 'They said . . . the next twenty-four hours might find our house the scene of bloody slaughter.' Judd and the Chinese Christians discussed 'how best to dispose of the (Chinese) women and children', but there was nowhere for them to go. When word came at noon on the 8th that the *daotai* (through his friend Zhao) had agreed to pay the full amount, they were told that the attack would undoubtedly have been made on the 9th.

General Li had won, bought off by a ransom price. But had he? The *daotai* had also won, wresting ownership of the Yangzhou property from Li and paving the way for Hudson Taylor to buy the freehold in due course. At 1.30 a m on May 11 Hudson Taylor was writing to his mother while documents for the consul and the *daotai* were being made out in Chinese. 'We have had a very narrow escape from another Yang-chau riot, stirred up by (Chen Guorui) – the Tientsin murderer and our landlord. The labour and anxiety are almost more than I can bear.' Later the same day Hudson Taylor attended the American consul's wife, in her confinement.

In the *Occasional Paper* of April and of June 1873, Hudson Taylor gave the sequel of this bizarre episode. Just as, after the Yangzhou riot of 1868, the prefect and his family came to a tragic end and the leading agitators were impoverished, so in 1870,

> Many who are friendly to us warned Li and Chen that they would lose their *luck* (a terrible thought to pagan Chinese) if they molested us. . . . Within a month of the settlement of these matters, they had a quarrel between themselves . . . Both finally reached Nankin, underwent trial by the Viceroy, and have received sentence, confirmed from Pekin, which deprives Li of all rank and title for ever, and reduces Chen to the rank of a major. The latter is further sent to Honan to help in quelling the rebellion there. [Earlier it had been stated that] Li had been *beheaded*, and Chen degraded and *banished* from Yang-chau. . . . The people were awed thereby. But if the sentences *were* actually pronounced, they were in some way evaded in great measure, as is often the case with the rich in China; for Li is reported to be now *living* in retirement, in his own native place; and Chen has returned again to Yang-chau, and is leading a private life there, though without his former rank, wealth, or influence.

Most likely Zeng had said what was required of him, and saw to it that his friends came to no greater harm. Knowing the story would soon be learned and reported (erroneously) in the Shanghai papers, Hudson Taylor composed as factual an account of events as was possible and arranged for it to be released anonymously in the *Shanghai Evening Courier*. The whole incident had taken place while he was packing up, preparing to sail for Britain as soon as his last obstetric case was over. There was no knowing what would happen next.

Tilting at a windmill?[4]   *June 1871*

True to the precedents he had set, Wade was working for the withdrawal of Hudson Taylor and his mission from the 'interior' to the treaty ports. By the autumn the Foreign Office would be putting more pressure on them through William Berger, but in

June the beginnings were simple enough. Writing to George
Müller on May 15, Hudson Taylor said enigmatically, 'the Chinese
and our own Foreign powers seem growingly inimical to the
gospel'. And to William Berger on May 19 he hinted at trouble
ahead.

> I learn that Mr Wade has made a representation to the Chinese
> Foreign Office about our Yangchau affairs. Of its nature I have been
> unable to learn. He must, I should think, have heard of (Chen
> Guorui's) boastings of what he was about to do against us and have
> written in consequence. It may be well for you to know that nothing
> done has been owing to any report from us, directly or indirectly; Mr
> Gardner does not know himself what or why (Wade) has so written.
> The Senior Naval Officer also is said to have been ordered to go to
> Nankin and make representations to the Viceroy (Zeng Guofan). I
> do not know their nature either, nor why the Admiral has so directed
> him.

After the way the Yangzhou riots of 1868 had been inflated into
international incidents, Hudson Taylor could be forgiven if he was
apprehensive. On June 8 the new consul-general in Shanghai, J
Markham, wrote to C T Gardner, his vice-consul in Zhenjiang,

> I have just received a note from Mr Wade and he strongly advocates
> that Mr Taylor should leave Yangchow, not hurriedly, but in the
> course of a few months – quietly. . . . I might run up to Yangchow
> myself. . . . Don't let it out that Mr Wade wishes Taylor to remove,
> but acquaint that gentleman privately, with his wishes, and say that
> although everything is quite quiet and settled now, there is no
> guarantee that the trouble will not be remembered on some future
> day. . . . PS Mr Wade bids me caution you 'not to tell any Chinese
> that we shall support or shall not support the Dynasty in case of
> Revolution.' J.M.

Gardner passed Markham's letter on to Hudson Taylor, who (in
spite of fever) replied on June 15,

> It is perhaps the best thing for me to write you a private note on the
> subject, which . . . if you think it desirable you can send to Mr
> Markham, through whom I should be glad to convey my thanks to Mr
> Wade for his suggestion.
> We are most anxious to promote our work with all possible
> caution; and while, I trust, not unprepared to meet personal danger
> when inevitable, we seek to avoid everything likely to involve

ourselves, and are still more anxious not to involve others, in needless difficulties. We have endeavoured, and not without a fair measure of success, to conduct our operations in the interior, in a conciliatory spirit. The recent difficulty at Yangchow was not, I believe, either caused by, or aided and abetted by, the people there, nor by the local officers or the literati, but was entirely confined to Li and Chen, with their partisans and associates. I incline to think that now, our position there is more firmly established in the minds of the people than ever it was. . . . The satisfactory conclusion of the recent difficulties has convinced many that we are favoured by Heaven, and that therefore those who attempt to assail us, are likely to be both unsuccessful and unfortunate. This impression, which existed before, cannot but have been deepened by the recent capture of (Chen Guorui) and the disgraceful outrage perpetrated on his and Li's wives. I therefore think, that there is now very little danger of troubles arising *spontaneously* at that city in connection with our work.

Our entire removal from Yangchow would, I fear, give rise to grave difficulties in a number of other stations, and might even seriously affect (Zhenjiang). . . . It is undeniable that (Zeng Guofan) could, if he wished it, make trouble (at Yangzhou). Of such trouble we should have ample notice. . . . The projected attack on May 9 was known to us by the middle of April.

In two paragraphs he detailed his 'mode of working' in the interior. Much coming and going by the missionaries, often on account of illness, but also in the course of their work, had accustomed the Chinese to their movements. 'Temporary absence being therefore the rule rather than the exception, is deprived of the significance it might otherwise have had.' People would no longer think the foreigners were afraid and running away. The schools at Yangzhou and Nanjing had been closed, and the women in charge transferred to the newly-built school at Zhenjiang.

Were (these) facts made known to Mr Wade, he would feel satisfied that we have done all that present circumstances render requisite. . . . Mr Wade is fully alive to the fact that the danger of leaving is sometimes greater than that of remaining – so far as National Interests are concerned.

Christopher Gardner replied the same day,

Thanks for your letter, in the spirit of which I cordially agree. With Asiatics a bold and determined front to danger is the most prudent course. Sir Harry Parkes and Mr Locke owed their life to their not being afraid (Book 3, p 218). And I believe in the recent trouble at Yangchow, had Mr Judd showed any signs of fear, that the riot would have taken place. . . . I venture to believe Mr Wade will be perfectly satisfied and will approve the measures of prudence you have taken. . . .

> Believe me, yours with the greatest respect,
> Chr. T. Gardner

Consul Markham duly visited Zhenjiang and Yangzhou, but Hudson Taylor was unable in the stormy weather to meet him. Instead he wrote on June 22,

> I believe you saw the only boarders in the Boys' School (at Yangzhou). Double the number might easily have been admitted, but prudential motives [to avoid suspicion] and want of accommodation, have required the refusal of many applications, some of which were made since the settlement of the recent difficulty with Li and (Chen Guorui). . . . A written indenture drawn up and signed by the parents or guardians of each child is required before admitting him into the school, both for our own protection in the event of any false charge, and in order that he may not be removed before his education is sufficiently advanced to be of some real service. I need scarcely say that this willingness of the people to entrust to our care . . . their own children, on whom they expect to rely in old age, is one of the strongest proofs that we have really gained a position among them, and a considerable measure of their confidence and respect.
>
> It is impossible to view Yangchow as an isolated place. Any removal from it would not only affect other stations of our own Mission . . . I submit for your consideration whether it would not also seriously affect foreign relations in this Port, and possibly at (Jiujiang). It would likewise affect the work of other Missions elsewhere. . . . (At Huzhou) local officers referred to Yangchow as a precedent. A few months ago, a Yangchow man now (magistrate in Shaoxing) took a similar course. And it is not six months since the Prefect in (Taizhou) referred to Yangchow as a precedent authorizing the protection and favour of Protestant Missions.

Gardner capped the correspondence four days later with a surprising note,

> Mr Wade had more reason than we knew of for the advice he gave you – facts have come to my knowledge today that render it very advisable gradually to give up your schools at Yangchow, gradually

of course. And so to have matters that no lady should reside there. Wade mentioned two or three months. You have that time to make arrangements for disbanding the schools. As for Judd, he is a brave man – my advice is he should stay at Yangchow – he will always get warning enough. The danger will not be to Foreigners alone, but there is a rebellion on foot, and there are reasons to dread that Yangchow will be one of the spots where it will break out. . . . I will try and see you today.

Hudson Taylor could not but act on such insistence. During July Charles Judd closed the Yangzhou school and joined his wife at Zhenjiang. Charles Fishe quietly took his place at Yangzhou. Five boys of their own or their parents' volition followed Judd to Zhenjiang and entered the new school there. But letters continued to refer to the likelihood of both Charles and Elizabeth Judd returning to Yangzhou, once the baby was born. Whether Wade was tilting at a windmill of his own imagining or of Prince Kong's contriving, Hudson Taylor could not know. No more was heard of the alleged rebellion, and such diplomatic pressure on Hudson Taylor had if anything the reverse effect, making him more secretive in pursuing his aims. Instead, what came to light was a strong initiative by the Zongli Yamen to curb all missionary activity. Wade used it to restrict Hudson Taylor and the CIM, by directing the attention of the Foreign Minister, Lord Granville, to him.

The 'Zongli Memorandum'   April–June 1871

Habitual use of certain terms has endowed historical events and highlights with labels never designed for them. A document emanating from the Zongli Yamen and circulated at first among high-ranking mandarins became known to foreigners and in early 1871 was being referred to as the 'Chinese Circular'. Some continued to use this term to apply to a document issued by the Zongli Yamen to ministers of the foreign powers. Others distinguished between the two and referred to the latter as the 'Zongli Memorandum'. Each was in fact a new twist in the old 'missionary question', too general a term to apply to the specific proposals of 1871.

An editorial note in the *Chinese Recorder* of May 1871 entitled 'A Remarkable Plan for settling the Missionary Question' reported that . . . 'The Mandarins of the (Zongli) Yamen at Pekin have been devising a plan to settle for ever the missionary question. They have actually proposed to send all missionary ladies home; to confine each Mission to forty-five converts; to register all baptisms; to compel missionaries, whenever they have business at the Yamens, to appear *as natives* in the presence of native officials; together with one or two other points. . . .' These propositions were simply submitted to the foreign ministers for their consideration.

The Memorandum itself was 'dignified and courteous', but radical in its proposals. In addition to the clauses mentioned in the *Recorder*, only the children of Christians were to be admitted to orphanages, women were to be debarred from churches, and members of missionary sisterhoods were not to enter China. . . . 'Excessive and unusual penalties were not to be demanded by foreigners for the murder of missionaries and Chinese Christians.' Passports issued to French missionaries were to limit them to a specific province and prefecture. Officials would regularly inspect mission premises; and local officials were to be consulted and to inspect land before its purchase by foreigners, to ensure against violation of *fengshui* (Book 4, Appendix 8).

Transparently directed at Roman Catholic missions, these proposals threatened Protestant missions also. Even if sincerely intended by the Zongli Yamen to correct abuses, they were open to interpretation at the whim of local mandarins and the public. Although the Memorandum and 'Chinese Circular' were only consultative documents, they were released in the provinces and had immediate repercussions at the grass-roots. James Williamson reported from Fenghua in June, 'Rumours have been circulated that a dispatch has been sent out by the Ningbo *daotai* to the district magistrate here, ordering him to inquire about the number of people who had joined the foreign religion, with a view to their apprehension and punishment. The first part seems to have some bearing on the circular of Prince Kong. Such rumours, even if unfounded, are at all times a great hindrance to our work.'

Each of the eight articles of the Memorandum affected the prospects of the CIM. No Protestant orphanages had been opened, but the first article would affect schools and the compassionate adoption of foundlings. Women's work, such as the CIM was doing on a growing scale through its single and married women, would be prohibited. The third article would deny missionaries the protection of extra-territoriality and subject them to the capriciousness of local magistrates. And the seventh, binding them to observe the same ceremonies as observed by or 'exacted from the literatès', would include kneeling before mandarins, prostrating themselves and knocking their heads on the ground (*see* Book 4, p281). As Sir Ernest Satow, a later minister-plenipotentiary, put it, 'The Protestant Powers replied that the abuses complained of did not concern them; while the French Government rejected the whole of the proposals as inadmissible'.[5]

June 3, 1871, saw a great leap forward in communications between West and East, the inauguration of the telegraphic cable link between San Francisco (and therefore London) and Shanghai, and from Singapore (itself an extension from Ceylon) to Hong Kong. But on June 8 T F Wade sent a long dispatch to London by slow means. Recorded as reaching London as late as August 15, it included translations of the Memorandum and eight propositions appended to it. According to the *Standard* for December 15, 1871, it drew from a supplement to the *London Gazette* relating to 'the Missionary Question in China' containing verbatim copies of letters between Earl Granville, Foreign Minister, and T F Wade, British Minister in Peking.[6] Wade wrote,

> . . . the people at large do not distinguish between Romanist and Protestant, nor between foreigner and foreigner . . . The Chinese government would have the missionaries all brought under the same control. . . . At present they constitute in China an *imperium in imperio*; and it is to be apprehended that . . . of this will come an uprising of the people beyond the power of government to control. The responsibility of foreign governments will be great if they do not join China in devising precautionary measures. [Summarising each article, Wade continued circuitously with his own heavily loaded deductions.]
>
> To secure the missionary against the hostility of the lettered class, one of two courses must be pursued – either the missionary must be supported, out and out, by the sword of the protecting powers [an option already excluded by London], or he must be placed by the protecting powers under restrictions which, whilst leaving him always as much latitude of action as, if simply intent on Christianizing China, he is justified in desiring, will yet enable the Chinese government to declare . . . that he the missionary, is not authorized by the power protecting him to put forward the pretensions objected to. . . . [The missionary must be shackled by his own government and submitted to the will of the mandarins.]
>
> Romanism, in the mouths of non-Christian Chinese is as popularly termed the religion of the French as the religion of the Lord of heaven. A dread of Romish ascendancy, as I have more than once reported . . . or that the Romish community will throw itself for

support upon the French . . . is, in my belief, the suggesting cause of (both Zongli Memorandum and Chinese Circular).

Earl Granville apparently did not see Wade's dispatch until after he had sent a lengthy one of his own, dated August 21. In it he protested that the assertions of the Zongli Memorandum were against 'missionaries' in general without recognition of the fact that not one of the abuses alleged in the Memorandum 'is in any way connected with any British missionary establishment'. There was no wish to secure for missionaries 'any privileges or immunities beyond those granted by treaty to other British subjects'. The treaty of June 1858 had stipulated that 'the Christian religion, as professed by Protestant or Roman Catholics . . . shall alike be entitled to the protection of the Chinese authorities. . . . Her Majesty's Government, therefore, . . . could not be indifferent to the persecution of Christians for professing the Christian faith.' To prevent women from attending divine worship would be in violation of the treaty, and 'Her Majesty's Government would not countenance any regulation which would cast a slur upon a sister whose blameless life and noble acts of devotion . . . are known throughout the world.'

Missionaries do not forfeit their rights under the treaty, so Her Majesty's Government 'cannot allow the claim that (they) must conform to the laws and customs of China to pass unchallenged'. 'It is impossible to prevent enterprising persons penetrating through a country. Sooner or later they will find their way (even to Sichuan); and the true interest of China is to facilitate rather than to restrict the flow of foreign enterprise.' If British missionaries behaved improperly they should 'be handed over to the nearest Consul for punishment', like other British subjects, as provided in the treaties. Until it could be proved that the minister and consuls were unable to control British subjects in China, Her Majesty's Government must decline to supplement the existing treaties.

When Wade's dispatch arrived, asking for missionaries to be restrained, it therefore received the brief (even curt) reply on August 31 that it had already been answered. But this was not known to Hudson Taylor or others threatened by 'disturbing rumours' based on the Circular, by the Memorandum and by Wade's directives to his consuls – until it was all published in the Parliamentary blue books and the press after he reached England. Meanwhile Wade continued to write, focusing his attention on Hudson Taylor by name. 'The Foreign Office believe him,' Hudson Taylor told Meadows.[7]

The suspense made little difference. If the time was short, all the more strenuous efforts must be made 'while it is day'. More and more Chinese evangelists were joining in the work. 'This year witnessed more extensive and important itineration and colportage than any preceding one. . . . Such journeys would have been even more numerous, had not sickness to a very serious extent prevented them.'

Winds of change[8]   1871–72

The wider world of which the Hudson Taylor saga was a part, must again receive a glance to keep perspective. With the end of the Franco-Prussian war, ushering in the era of consolidation by Bismarck of his conquests, Europe entered upon what was a long period of peace. No major war erupted until 1914, long enough for an accumulation of wealth and power to tempt with new thoughts of domination. In Asia the Russian annexation of Kuldja and Ili from Chinese Turkestan, the continuing annexation by France of Indo-China and the rapid expansion of Japanese strength and ambitions, further reduced the stability of East Asia.

By a Sino-Japanese treaty at Tianjin on September 13, 1871, the Qing dynasty recognised the emergence of Japan from being a tribute-bearing vassal state into national identity, however inferior. But only three months later the seeds of the Sino-Japanese conflict were sown. Since 1372 the Ryukyu Islands had been tributary to China, and since 1451 to Japan also. From the time of the Ming emperor Yong Lo (1403–25) the princes of Ryukyu had received their investiture from China, but after 1609 from the emperor of Japan as well. In December 1871 some Ryukyuan sailors, ship-wrecked on the east coast of Taiwan, were killed and eaten by independent aboriginal tribesmen. Japan demanded redress. The percipient Li Hongzhang advised admission of responsibility, but the unstatesmanlike imperial ministers at Peking (in July 1873) told Japan that they claimed no control over the savage tribes in eastern Taiwan. A Japanese force of 6,000 thereupon mustered at Xiamen (Amoy), and landed on the east coast of Taiwan – outside Chinese jurisdiction. At that point Peking changed its mind and sent 10,000 troops to Taiwan. China and Japan were heading for a war neither nation wanted nor was ready to undertake. Settlement was effected through skilful diplomacy by T F Wade, of which more was to be heard.

Manchu-Chinese obscurantism was slowly yielding to outside

influences, but all too slowly. In August 1871 an imperial decree
even sanctioned an educational mission to the USA. Robert Hart in
his favoured position as inspector-general of the Imperial Maritime
Customs was exerting all the influence he could for the good of
China, but wisely played his hand as carefully as circumstances
demanded. His powerful Chinese opposite number in Canton,
successor to the 'Hoppo' of Robert Morrison's day, had the approval of Peking for historic reasons. 'If the Board of Revenue had to
choose between *him* and *me*, it would throw me over,' Hart wrote to
his commissioner, E C Bowra, in February 1871, 'for honest collec-
tion and truthful report means *impecuniosity* for the *Board* . . .'
Graft and corruption appealed even more strongly to those officials
than the integrity of Hart, although it was Hart who was strengthen-
ing China's government with unprecedented speed.

China must break out of her encrusted ways if she was to survive
in a changing world. 'Try to get (the local officials) out of their
shells, and put new ideas into their noddles when you get the
chance,' was Hart's advice to his Tianjin commissioner. To some
extent they were succeeding. 'Steam is taking hold of the official
mind,' he could tell Bowra in December 1871, 'and in a few years, if
not disgusted by too much pressure, the horse will drink heartily of
the water to which he has been led.' (A railway – little more than a
tram-line between Shanghai and Wusong – projected in March
1872, was completed in 1876, only to be torn up again when handed
over to Chinese control.)

Li Hongzhang was more enlightened than most contemporary
mandarins. Closest to Peking in his new position as viceroy of Zhili
(after Zeng Guofan's return to Nanjing), he also had most to do
with foreigners. He became 'the one man to whom the distracted
Manchu Government inevitably had recourse, each time that the
crass ignorance of the Princes of the ruling Imperial House had
brought the country to the verge of ruin'. Standing physically head
and shoulders above his average countryman, he also 'excelled
them in mental calibre'.

His relations with foreigners were varied. When he had ascended
the Yangzi river to Wuchang in 1869 as viceroy of Hubei and
Hunan, he had pandered to popular feeling by leaving his steamer
to complete the journey in a junk – under tow by a steamer and
escorted by three others.

When Admiral Sir Harry Keppel wanted to borrow a small
steamship to investigate the upper Yangzi, Li had refused him his

request. When the then British consul of Hankou insisted as Her Britannic Majesty's representative on being admitted by the main entrance to his *yamen* and not at a side entrance as high Chinese officials were, he complained that the consul visited him too often, giving him a reputation for being mixed up with hated foreigners.

At the time of the Tianjin massacre a British consul wrote, 'I take it for granted that (Li) will not tolerate any outrage on foreigners within his jurisdiction', and this was indeed his reputation. But it was not forgotten that the proclamation by him while he was at Wuchang was blamed for encouraging the literati of Anqing to riot against the Catholic and CIM missions. He it was who memorialised the throne to curb the admission and activities of missionaries – the initiative behind the 'Chinese Circular' and 'Zongli Memorandum'; and he had been quietly building up the navy which was to come into conflict with the Japanese. Keeping the measure of his compatriots, he was bent on reforming and modernising China no less than was Robert Hart, but at his own pace.

The great revolution of 1868 in Japan had overturned the shogunate of feudal barons, in favour of the Mikado. January 1869 saw the reception of Western envoys in public audience, and the arrival of the first English missionary, George Ensor of the CMS. (Americans of the Presbyterian and Episcopal Churches were in Nagasaki and Yokohama already.) But proclamations continued to forbid Christianity to the people. Descendants of the old Jesuit converts of Urakami were being persecuted and banished (p 238). The British minister to the Yedo court, Sir Harry Parkes – he whose name scintillates with tales of valour in China – pointed out the inexpediency of persecution concurrently with the pursuit of Western civilisation. 'Why!' Japan replied. 'Our employment of Christian teachers in schools and colleges and use of Christian books of education shows that we have nothing against *religion* of any kind. It was the *conspiracy* by the Christians, which nearly overthrew the government of a previous century, that is remembered! Public opinion demands control of seditious communities in self-defence.' At the end of 1872, however, in a change of attitude all anti-Christian proclamations were withdrawn and the surviving exiles of Urakami were brought home. The year 1872 was also to see other astonishing developments in Japan, in the army, navy, civil service, schools and colleges, the post office, newspapers, railways, telegraphs and coastal navigation. The contrast between Japan and China could hardly have been more marked.

In China several revolutions had failed or were failing – even the great Muslim revolt of the north-west. The ancient system was being re-established, Christians were again being regarded as suspect or traitorous, and missionaries as 'the outposts of western penetration'. Ironically the slow wheels of history were to bring China back to the same situation a century later. To the literati of 1872, trained in Confucian doctrine and practice which identified politics and religion as inseparables, the 'left-hand, right-hand' relationship between foreign missionaries and their governments was indubitable. Persuasion such as Parkes had used in Japan might have had its influence, but T F Wade was not Parkes. Rejecting the Zongli Memorandum in a point by point rejoinder to the minister, Wen Xiang, in June 1871, he simultaneously sought to curb the progressive missionary enterprise – until he failed to win Lord Granville's support. Paradoxically, within five years he himself was to play a major part in the removal of restrictions upon missions.

In 1872, W H Medhurst Jr, the Shanghai consul-general before Markham, was to publish a book entitled *The Foreigner in Far Cathay*. In it he set out his opinions on foreigners being 'disguised' in Chinese dress, of which he disapproved, and on missionaries, whose champion he chose to be. We cannot but surmise that he was answering Wade indirectly and supporting Hudson Taylor whom he admired. 'I have no sympathy with those who, for want of consideration or from mere prejudice, think lightly of the work and character of the missionary.' Comparisons of Catholic and Protestant were impossible, he insisted, so different were they in organisation, method and even definition of 'convert'. Each kind was doing good work. Of the Roman Catholics he said,

> Their system is to penetrate deeply into the interior the moment they arrive, to dissociate themselves entirely from the mercantile classes of foreigners, and to work disguised as natives, unobtrusively and unremittingly, at the various stations which have been occupied by them for years, in some cases for centuries. Their devotion is as remarkable as their success has been astonishing, and I am one of those who believe that they have been the means of accomplishing . . . a vast amount of good. . . . I have been often struck by the quiet and respectability which prevails amongst (the Christian families) as compared to the heathen around them.

It was unfortunate that the French government had exacted toleration of Christianity as a treaty right, which had led the Church into claiming property, privileges and judicial rights in such a way as to arouse antagonism to the point of massacre, 'a foretaste, it is to be feared, of what we may yet have to mourn in the future'. How right he was!

From intimate personal knowledge, he denied that Protestant missionaries showed partiality for the use of force or coercive measures, and insisted that they were entitled to full protection and the maintenance of their rights. But 'to erect pretentious edifices after the foreign style of architecture', with steeples and towers in Chinese cities, could only create ill will. He knew that Chinese shrank from entering foreign buildings, while they would willingly enter Chinese houses occupied by friendly foreigners.

As for the merchants, Medhurst was equally frank. The term 'merchant', so long and so constantly associated with traffic in opium, was almost the synonym in Britain, he wrote, for 'adventurer' or 'smuggler'. 'No man who has the slightest spark of philanthropy in his heart but must deprecate the existence of the trade.' On it the merchant lived in affluence, scorning the Chinese around him.

It was a courageous essay. The merchants were powerful in Britain as in China. He could have prejudiced his prospects as career diplomat. But Medhurst was as courageous morally as physically. His integrity was recognised in his knighthood and appointment as HBM Ambassador to Peking in due course. Hudson Taylor did not need to vindicate himself.

Sister missions   1871–72

With the new liberties obtained through the treaties of 1858–60, Catholic and Protestant missionaries were pressing out in ways impossible in China for centuries. Although the papacy had fallen on hard times, the Roman Church retained its missionary momentum. The limiting factor for the CMS was still what Joseph Ridgeway had called in the *Church Mission Intelligencer*, 'a babel-like determination to build up the Church at home, instead of "replenishing the earth"'. With its goal of taking the gospel to hundreds of millions of Chinese, the personnel and funds released for the purpose were still pitiably inadequate. Reinforcements were barely enough to replace casualties. Advance such as the infant CIM had made was still being achieved at a high cost in health and lives in all societies.

The story of the CMS in Hangzhou and Shaoxing was typical. In

AN ANGLICAN CHURCH IN SEMI-CHINESE STYLE
(By courtesy of the CMS)

early 1870 when George Moule returned from home and Henry Gretton 'opened a station' at Shaoxing alongside Stevenson and two American missions, he was joined by J D Valentine and his wife in November, on their return in renewed health. But Gretton had to retire ill, and the Palmers took his place in the autumn of 1871, only to withdraw to Britain themselves in shattered health in 1873. Arthur Moule returned to Ningbo in December 1871 with Dr and Mrs James Galt of the Edinburgh Medical Missionary Society, who joined George Moule in Hangzhou. Galt opened a hospital for opium addicts with the funds the CMS had offered to Hudson Taylor in 1863.[9] But W A Russell left Ningbo again in the spring of 1870 to be consecrated in Britain as 'bishop in North China'. Continuity and progress were always difficult to attain. Chaplains and missionaries north of the twenty-eighth parallel of latitude (through Wenzhou) came under Russell, and the remainder to the south under Alford. So Alford resigned in protest, and Hudson Taylor's friend and brother-in-law John Burdon, chaplain in Peking, became the third bishop of Victoria, Hong Kong.[10]

In Shandong the Baptist Missionary Society had lost missionary after missionary. 'Disaster overtook most of them' and of twelve colleagues only the young Timothy Richard survived to continue working alone. Latourette's tribute to him read, 'This lone representative, Timothy Richard, was, however, one of the greatest missionaries whom any branch of the Church, whether Roman

Catholic, Russian Orthodox or Protestant, has sent to China.' The *Chinese Recorder* voiced the sympathy of the missionary community with the BMS, saying, 'When will this afflicted Mission see better days?'[11]

Of the Presbyterian, John Livingston Nevius, W A P Martin was to write in his *A Cycle of Cathay*, 'He was the first missionary to establish himself at (Hangzhou), the capital of the province, unless Bishop Burdon may contest that honour, and one of the first to break soil in the province of (Shandong).'[12] With Helen his wife, Nevius had pioneered and lived in Hangzhou in 1859, at the same time as John Burdon. By 1869 he resolved to set up an institution there 'for the instruction of candidates for the ministry', with Samuel Dodd, but found the foreign influences in Hangzhou too strong for this to be the right venue. Then in 1870, Nevius, 'patient, kind and deferential to the opinions of others', was elected moderator of the Presbyterian Synod of China and returned to Yantai. By 1871 under his leadership, Chinese Christians were 'fast gaining influence in our ecclesiastical courts' – an early move towards 'the Nevius Plan' for a strong indigenous Church, so successfully applied in Korea twenty years later.[13] Slowly but surely, though at a price, the Protestant church in China was growing and maturing. But it still numbered no more than 7,000 communicants in all.

In 1872 Dr D B McCartee, the American Presbyterian veteran in Ningbo, accompanied a Chinese envoy to Japan and negotiated the release of hundreds of victims of the coolie traffic imprisoned on the *Maria Luz*. For this service he received a gold medal from the Chinese government. But he remained in Japan for five years (1872–77) as professor of law and natural science in Tokyo University.

William Muirhead, the first missionary to reside in Suzhou after Charles Schmidt and the Cordons (pp 62–8), had a remarkable experience that same year, 1872. Ten years previously, when visiting the headquarters of the Taiping rebels at Nanjing he had heard 'shrieks and groans' coming from a wounded boy up on the city wall. Taking him to Shanghai, he had seen that he was well cared for. In 1872, when Muirhead was trying to rent premises in Suzhou, a young rice merchant offered to help and found him a prime site for a chapel on the city's main thoroughfare. It was the boy he had rescued.[14]

Slowly but surely the gospel was inching forward, taking root where not so long before it had been stubbornly resisted.

CHAPTER TEN

A 'COUNCIL OF MANAGEMENT'
1871–72

Priority to the Bergers   *1870–71*

Time and again, the prophetic messages of William and Mary Berger to one and another of the Mission team, and particularly to Hudson and Maria Taylor, had proved uncannily timely. William Berger's New Year greeting for 1870 had proved to be such a voice from God. 'Moses prayed "Show me Thy way". The Lord replied "My presence shall go with thee and I will give thee rest". . . . Had the Lord shown Moses all the way by which He intended to lead him , . . would it not have overpowered or slain (him)? Oh! the Wisdom and Love of God! As we are able to bear it, He shows us His way. . . .'

If for Hudson Taylor the year 1870 had proved to be 'the hardest yet', and in different ways 1871 was harder still, for the Bergers the same was true. Repercussions of the Anqing riot, ill-health, making a home for Emily Blatchley and the 'rompy' children, answering criticisms of the Mission, watching the donations decline, especially when the Franco-Prussian war excited the British nation and a republic in France became the 'all-engrossing subject' – all weighed on their minds. Alexander Williamson of Shanghai and Yantai had been to see them and had unblushingly spoken of his efforts to dissuade Duncan, Reid, Judd and others from wearing Chinese clothes, until William Berger protested. Yet Alexander Williamson was a true friend of the CIM in most respects.

When the Tianjin massacre foreboded ill for the young missionaries far from human protection, they redoubled their faithful praying. And their devotion to the cause was complete. They decided to sell all but forty acres of their estate at Saint Hill, retaining only pasture land and woodland around the house. His bailiff was to farm on his own account. So, while it lasted, the sale of wagons, horses, sheep, cows, pigs and equipment added to the work. Producing the *Occasional Paper* from whatever news arrived from China strained their ingenuity, but knowing Hudson Taylor's difficulties, they restricted their requests to such remarks as, 'Friends at home, I am sure would exceedingly prize reading your lucid statements of affairs.' Berger's factory in Bow shipped thirty-two boxes of supplies, personally ordered and checked by him. And the next note said how 'stunned' they were by news of Maria's and Noel's deaths. If only they could come and be with Hudson Taylor in his desolation. 'Out of this (your) deepest sorrow and trial . . . shall surely flow some inconceivable blessing. . . . Our Father never takes away and leaves us poor.' 'Nearly every day brings fresh notices in the public papers of rumoured rising of the Chinese against all foreigners indiscriminately. . . . The thought of your daily fearing some attack may take place . . . is most painful.' The assessment of candidates increasingly seemed beyond him. 'After four years . . . I can only say I am sorely discouraged and feel very loathe to have more on trial.' Without doubt the Bergers needed to be relieved of their duties at least for a while.

But William Berger's references to Andrew Jukes, the ultra-independent and eccentric preacher and writer, held for Hudson Taylor the surest signs of an approaching end to Berger's place in the Mission. As early as January 1870 he had written, 'Pray . . . that I may be guided into Truth respecting a Doctrine I am examining,' of the 'non-eternity of punishment' of sinners not justified by faith in Christ. As the year closed he returned to the subject. 'At Hackney the dear Brethren have put away several from Communion for teaching the doctrine. Some . . . are personal friends. . . . If I receive them will the brethren receive me afterwards? . . . Need I say that I desire to be incognito as to the subject, . . . for were it to get abroad that I even favoured it, my usefulness, some say would be at an end.' More than that, the stigma among the orthodox of the period could end support of the Mission of which he was a director.

With January 1871 the fall of France was expected at any time and the Bergers' sense of strain increased. Both were in very poor health, Mary 'very weakly' and often in great abdominal pain. But they still had no one able or willing to deputise for them. Mary's brother, James van Sommer, a frequent helper, was tied by his growing family. So William Berger warned, 'The matter of your visiting England . . . as early as you conveniently may be able, grows exceedingly upon me in importance, both as regards my own future and the well-being of the Mission. . . . The bare possibility of your visiting us in the autumn or winter of this year is a light to our eyes. Truly we shall rejoice almost without bounds.' Then letters ceased, in expectation of Hudson Taylor's sailing from China during June.

Hudson Taylor wrote, 'I cannot but regret that your mind should be so occupied about (the eternity of future punishment). At one time my own was very much so. It resulted, however, in my being more satisfied with the old view. Mr Jukes' book seems to me the most inconclusive I have seen on the question. . . .' He was praying that William Berger's 'usefulness' would not be 'seriously curtailed' on account of it. And again in June with detailed references to Scripture, 'While God (wishes) that all men should be saved, and offers (salvation) to all freely, He does not decree it.' But it was far too complex a subject to debate by correspondence, and in his state of mind and health. Gardner's letter about rebellion in the wind had just given him more to think about. He spared William Berger the news.

Hudson Taylor's style in writing sometimes bore strong traces of his mother's generation, drummed into him at home. But his spirit and convictions, shining through stilted phraseology, gave a luminescence William Berger's stolidity could not achieve. Urging Hudson Taylor to write for the *Occasional Paper*, to come home to revive the drooping interest of the Mission's friends, so easily distracted while no less sincere, he voiced a principle held by Hudson Taylor himself. That God as Father would provide for his children as they obeyed and served him was undoubted. That he would normally do it through his Church was Biblical doctrine. That his Church is all too human and prone to neglect its stewardship made it necessary to inform, instruct and exhort his people. Only Hudson Taylor with his knowledge of China and vision for her evangelisation could (of available members of the CIM) convey such a message. In China the resurgence of spiritual morale among the missionaries and churches, and his own obligation to recoup his health and see to the needs of his children, confirmed that the time was ripe for him to go to the Bergers' relief.

Jennie   *1871*

The friendship between the Fauldings and Bergers, and William Faulding's help with the Mission's business matters, had led to his buying part of the Saint Hill estate. They took to staying at the Bergers' home farm while sinking a well and building a house in the current architectural vogue, of concrete. 'Is your home like the

Bergers?' Jennie asked (*see* Book 4, p 61). But before they sold their home at 340 Euston Road their circumstances changed. Financial difficulties such as many suffered through the war in France and panic on the Stock Exchange, and William Berger's talk of retiring and perhaps of espousing heterodox interpretations of Scripture, led the Fauldings to abandon their intentions, to put up their Saint Hill property for sale and to stay in London.

Anxiety at home increased Mrs Faulding's anxiety about Jennie as the news went from bad to worse and (Hudson Taylor conjectured) was inflated for political ends. As early as February 1870 she was reminding Jennie that she had talked of going to China for five years initially. In August what upset her was anti-foreign feeling at Shanghai, the French consul at Canton having to take refuge in the British settlement, and the appearance of placards at Hong Kong and other ports predicting extermination of all foreigners. By October it was the threat of war in north China, with the Chinese 'buying and manufacturing large quantities of fire-arms' and the thought of 'those intensely horrible cruelties' at Tianjin that provoked the appeal for Jennie to come home without delay. In December, however, 'the fighting all round Paris and dreadful loss of life,' and the danger of war with Russia unless 'all goes right with Austria and Turkey' distracted her mother's thoughts from China.

Jennie's own letters avoided the subject of returning home and chattered cheerfully on as usual. In the winter, 'we all look so stout with fur and wadding'. 'Mr Taylor got my likeness taken in Suchau and Emily will bring the negative home.' In March 1870 she confessed to having malaria and to taking quinine at frequent intervals – not knowing of the mortal danger of 'blackwater fever' from this practice. John Eliot Howard, the quinologist and manufacturing chemist, was supplying them all with quinine. 'I have been vaccinating (two Chinese). I got a scab from Mrs Dodd's little baby.' When news of the Tianjin massacre came, 'the Lord reigns, we will not fear' was the steady tenor of her letters. 'It is easy at home to be a professing Christian. I sometimes wonder how many would stand the tests and influences that (Chinese) Christians out here have to encounter. How many are there who are prepared to give up everything for Christ's sake?' At the back of her mind she could have wished her mother would let go of her in that spirit.

When Hudson Taylor wrote of visiting Hangzhou, Jennie told her parents, 'Mr Taylor is thinking of coming here on his way to (Zhenjiang), I hope he will.' But he had to accompany the Crombies to Hong Kong. Then it was, 'I hope he will soon be able to get back again.' In mid-November he arrived at last and stayed with the McCarthys for two weeks. His advice to Jennie about her mother's fears was reflected in her letters.

After he left, he wrote to her (on January 19, 1871), 'My loved Sister, . . . It looks as if . . . I shall need to go myself and arrange (for the children). The constant pain in my side and chest reminds me to work while it is day and keep my account balanced.' He said no more, but being with her had disturbed him deeply. With so large a capacity for loving, and with so many women in his team to care for and having now to care for him, having no wife made his relationship with them difficult. His thoughts had naturally turned to Maria. They had loved Emily and Jennie together. Alone, he could love them no less. His mother had encouraged him to think of remarrying, and he had ruled out Emily, so ill and unable to be the support he and the Mission needed. He prayed and thought about it during the next few months, but the difficulties seemed insuperable. He could only struggle on alone.

Jennie was absorbed in her work. In February 1871, in answering her mother's letters she said about one of her schoolgirls with smallpox, 'I, of course, went to her constantly, but having been vaccinated felt little fear. . . . The horrors of the Tientsin massacre did indeed make one's blood run cold, and yet – are we not ready to think *too* much of what only affected the *body* and that for a very short time?' The reputation of her schools, her teachers, housemothers and of herself ensured no lack of pupils. Several years later Wang Lae-djün was to state that of his congregation in Hangzhou no less than fifty had become Christians through Jennie's influence.

Hudson Taylor's long drawn-out illness had relapsed after a temporary improvement in March, and he remained in no doubt that he must get back to Britain as soon as the confinements still dependent on him were over. Cardwell, for so long a thorn in the flesh, wrote sympathetically from Jiujiang urging him to go. 'We can spare you for a time, but how can we part with you for ever?' Jennie's malaria dragged on too, undermining her strength. But leaving Hangzhou and her schools and many Chinese friends was almost more than she could face. On April 8 as the state of political affairs looked up, Hudson Taylor told the Fauldings that he might be free to leave by the end of July if he lived to do so.

Under these circumstances I write about your dear daughter. I am not unmindful of the trust you reposed in my precious wife and myself in committing her to our care . . . I hear that you have expressed the desire that in the event of my return, she should fulfil the proposal of returning after five years, and she should accompany me. You will be better able to judge, upon reflection whether in my altered circumstances this is desirable or not . . . (And) whether it might not be well to leave the matter of her immediate return to her own judgment. . . .

I am alone and sick – yet *not* alone. Your dear daughter has been as a Sister to me; . . . I need not say that her companionship on the voyage would be pleasant to me, and more still helpful with my motherless darling child; but I believe she deals with God, and were she my own daughter, I should hesitate before *requiring* her to come irrespective of the state of her work, and of her conviction of duty. . . . Kindly reply by return . . . (and) to her also by the same mail.

He told Jennie what he had done, and a week later she told her mother what she knew – that he was 'asking you to leave it to me as to whether I shall come too. This I think you will do. God will make my path plain step by step . . . whether I should come or not. . . . Mr Taylor's health is in a very critical state. May God spare him to us and to China. Missionaries such as he is are scarcely to be found.' Many of the missionaries' letters referred to the books they were currently reading, and in this one Jennie went on to mention hers – Law's books on the Pentateuch.

In May she had a jubilant letter from Charles Fishe, to confess that in February he had written proposing to her sister Nellie, and the answer had just arrived, with her parents' permission. Then on the 29th Hudson Taylor told William Berger that the Judds had arrived for Elizabeth's confinement in a few days' time, and that Mrs Gardner's should follow soon after that. Mrs Shepherd, wife of the American consul, was safely through hers, and two more had taken place elsewhere. 'I propose to leave as soon as I can after they can safely be left,' he said. Half his packing was already done, he told his boys in a fatherly letter. 'I have sold the harmonium, to help me complete the building of (the) school, in remembrance of dear Mama. . . . I have played on it today, for the last time, some of (her) favourite tunes.'

Instead of going ahead, the Meadows family had decided to wait for Hudson Taylor, but it was also 'manifestly unsafe for Mr Meadows to spend another summer in China'. Having them with him would remove one problem. 'I wrote to Miss Faulding suggesting that . . . any difficulty which might otherwise have been felt as to her return with me would be largely abated. . . . (But) I judge that it is not likely that she can leave, even were we delayed till July. . . .'

John McCarthy and Jennie came up to Zhenjiang to consult with Hudson Taylor, and reached a clear plan of action. McCarthy would take over all Jennie's responsibilities in addition to his supervision of the work in the southern cities, and Jennie would join the Meadows family in Shanghai and sail with them. As to travelling with Jennie, Hudson Taylor was in two minds. She had always been careful not to show her feelings about him. To suggest marriage and be disappointed would only deepen his grief. To reach London and seek her parents' permission first might be the better way. But still his last two obstetric cases showed no sign of action. He handed over all his accounts to Charles, now the official secretary in China of the Mission, and his credits – £1,200 in the bank, nearly $200 in cash, and £748 in dollars of indemnity money subscribed by the victims of the Yangzhou riot – to buy the house if possible. But on July 5, with Jennie alone in attendance, Elizabeth Meadows suffered yet another premature birth, of a dead baby. This changed the whole picture. She no longer needed to wait for Hudson Taylor. Now they could sail with Jennie and escape to sea from the great heat. The *Nestor* would leave on July 14 via Suez.

Hudson Taylor would follow as soon as he was free. 'I should much prefer the Cape route,' he wrote, 'but time is precious.' He was at his lowest ebb, 'physically and mentally worth very little,' so he would keep Charles Fishe with him when he travelled to Shanghai and on to Ningbo to collect little Charles Edward. Nine months had passed since he had left him with the Goughs. Then the Duncans arrived from Nanjing with a sick baby (born in February) for Hudson Taylor to doctor, and at last Consul Gardner's wife was safely delivered with his help. News then came that Jennie was going through a serious exacerbation of malaria and passages on the *Nestor* were very expensive. There was another ship, the *Ajax* and her parents' permission had come, to travel with or without Hudson Taylor.

At long last Frederick Hudson Judd was born on Sunday, July 23, destined to become a leading member of the next generation in the CIM. Duncan started the following day with Hudson Taylor's baggage by canal to Shanghai, for him to follow by steamer as soon as Elizabeth Judd could be left. A plaintive note came from Jennie on the 27th (so unlike her – and yet so typical), asking him to pray that she might recover on the voyage. She did not want to reach home 'too much an invalid' lest her mother make it difficult for her to return. And another from Mary Barchet (née Bausum) confirmed that Jennie was in 'very poor health'.

Hudson Taylor decided to catch the French mail on August 5 and came down to Shanghai on the 1st. The only other passenger on the Yangzi steamer turned out to be Père Sechinger, the Catholic priest so closely involved in events following the first Yangzhou riot, and since then head of his mission at Anqing. 'He seemed an earnest and devout man . . . and spoke of the converts in a way that greatly pleased me', Hudson Taylor told Emily Blatchley. To his surprise the Meadows and Jennie had not gone. He had expected to find that they had left a week ago. It was 'very pleasant' to have fellow-travellers after all. The same day he enquired about all available shipping and 'passages in the French mail', the cheapest dependable accommodation to be had. French shipping was beginning to return to normal after the end of the war in France. His heavy luggage, thirty cases of books and personal possessions (much of it probably Maria's) he sent home by sailing-ship. Then he took a coaster to Ningbo. By August 2 he was with his child at the Goughs, 'so (thin and) grown and altered that I could not have recognized him.' Li Lanfeng, the printer, Ensing's husband, had agreed to go to England with them and was waiting, ready to sail. Like Wang Lae-djün he was to live with Hudson Taylor and be given personal tuition.

Hudson Taylor was in Ningbo just long enough to see a few of his friends before catching the same steamer back to Shanghai – 'another of those partings of which my cup has been so full – and then Charlie and I and Lanfeng were on our way from much-loved Ningpo.' Then followed more partings at Shanghai, from Charles Fishe, McCarthy, Duncan and Reid who had come to see them off, and on the 5th Hudson Taylor, the Meadows family and Jennie were on their way to England, with only Lanfeng and the children in good health.

'The only one'   *August–October 1871*

Leaving China on a wave of rumour about missions being banned from 'the interior' demanded faith. On the other hand, if Hudson Taylor personified the troublesome element in missions, a notice in the papers of his departure in poor health might calm the agitation against him. So it turned out, though the wheels of diplomatic action turned slowly. He had provided for the routine distribution of funds through Charles Fishe, and for him to keep the team in touch with each other's work and welfare through the *Monthly Gleaner*. Each had a clear assignment and knew his own sphere, so apart from emergencies everything should continue steadily until he returned. Twenty-five missionaries (with eighteen children) and forty-five Chinese 'workers' in ten cities, with responsibility for the churches in three more, could do good work during the year he expected to be away.[1] Problems needing a decisive answer could be referred to him by cable. William Berger was remitting funds and George Müller still distributing sums from his Scriptural Knowledge Institution's missionary fund from time to time. Müller's independent action worried Berger, lest some missionaries should count on him and choose to become independent of Hudson Taylor and the CIM.

Weighing anchor at midday on August 5, the French ship *Volga* came almost immediately into collision with two junks and had to call a tug to help her down the crowded Huangpu river. But otherwise all went well. On going aboard, however, even Hudson Taylor had been appalled. 'The third class accommodation of the *Volga* was very bad and my heart sank when I saw it . . . (until God) inclined their hearts to put us into the second class cabins. . . . Miss F kindly took Charlie with her.' So in comfort on a quiet sea they steamed slowly to Hong Kong, and had two days with James Legge and the CMS and German missionaries before trans-shipping on August 11 to the Messageries Maritimes liner *Ava* for Saigon and Marseilles. 'Lanfeng has very good quarters, and I hope is as comfortable as he can be under present circumstances. We have family prayer together twice a day [in Chinese].' The journey from Singapore to Point de Galle, Ceylon, took two weeks and from there to Aden another nine days – where they took on 'a hundred and twenty Arab firemen for two new steamers at Marseilles,' men accustomed to great heat.

Long weeks together on board ship, with shopping and visits to friends and 'the gardens' at each port, had thrown the travellers together. James Meadows' low state of health and Elizabeth's preoccupation with her children left Hudson Taylor and Jennie with hours in each other's company. With like-minded Jennie to talk and pray with, he revelled in complete relaxation from the pressures of life in China, 'a time of great spiritual joy to me'.

He wrote a long, affectionate, descriptive letter to Emily Blatchley, but had to tell her what was happening. Any doubts about loving Jennie and wanting to marry her had evaporated. He could not reach home and meet Emily without the matter being settled. She had to be told. However painful the news might be, she was too ill ever to return to China as his wife, whereas Jennie, so highly respected by all the Mission, was ideally suited to share his life, impossible although they both knew it was for her to replace Maria.

He had to speak. 'My feelings *could* no longer be hid,' he confessed to Jennie's parents from the Red Sea. 'I do not so much . . . ask you to give up a daughter . . . as to ask you . . . to make room in your hearts . . . for me also.' It was all that a Victorian suitor would be expected to write, although Jennie was 28 and Hudson Taylor 39.

> You know the affection with which I and my late dear wife watched over her, prayed for her, and desired to do all we could (for her). . . . Nor will you deem it unnatural that when I found myself week to week more and more unable to carry on efficiently the work which the Lord has committed to me, my thoughts and prayers respecting *the only one* possessed at once of the heart for the Lord's service and of that peculiar preparation for sharing my peculiar duties, should unconsciously have been . . . intensified. . . . Each time (I) concluded that there were insuperable difficulties in the way. . . . It would be impossible for her to leave (the work in Hangzhou); I found her so fully absorbed in and so happy in it . . . that there was no probability at all of (her favouring) any proposal from me.

Rather than travel on the same ship it had seemed 'better not to be too much thrown together, lest it should involve me in further sorrow . . . (so) I do not know whether I more longed or dreaded to find' on arrival in Shanghai, that she had already sailed. When they found themselves together, therefore, he had days of mental turmoil, until 'the expression of my feelings became irrepressible and incapable of further delay'. 'To find my love and my feelings so fully reciprocated as they are,' made it possible to talk freely. Jennie's logical habits of mind so closely resembled Maria's that they talked about her, the first true love he could never forget nor put from his thoughts. Jennie knew and had faced it already. She loved Maria too. They would always be able to talk about her unreservedly. There was no need to delay their marriage.

France had declared war against Prussia in July 1870 and after a rapid sequence of defeats, Napoleon III and his army had surrendered on September 2. A republic had been proclaimed two days later, and the German army besieged Paris on September 19. A communist insurrection in Paris at the end of October had been followed by the capitulation of Paris to the Germans on January 28, 1871, and soon afterwards peace talks began with an immense indemnity being demanded by the conquerors. But in May the communists were still destroying the Tuileries, the Louvre and many other public buildings, until French government troops entered Paris and crushed the communists. While Hudson Taylor and his party were at sea, France was restored to peace. On their arrival at Marseilles on September 21 they were able to take a train to Paris, cross to Southampton and reach London in the evening of September 25.

Three obstacles at once   *October–December 1871*

Emily was at Barnsley with the Taylor children but sent her congratulations to greet Jennie and Hudson Taylor on their arrival in London. For herself she printed on a card, to keep before her, the words of Jesus, 'EVEN SO, FATHER' – 'for so it seemed good in Thy sight'. It was she, too, who wrote of those painful months for the Mission as 'tunnelling through rock', a picture of determined progress against odds, with no thought of giving up.

They separated, each to their own families, but met again in London before all going together to the Bergers at Saint Hill on October 10. By then, Jennie's parents had plunged them into deep distress by agreeing to their eventual marriage only after she had been at home for a year! Jennie's tearful pleading and Hudson Taylor's persuasion eventually drew from Mrs Faulding the protest that neither of them was physically fit for marriage – her only objection to an early wedding, she said, and nothing would move her. Again, Emily wrote sympathising with Jennie. When Hudson Taylor saw Jennie from time to time he could tell she had been weeping.

He took rooms in Bognor for a fortnight to see if the seaside suited Emily and the children, but Bognor he found depressing and he went to Mildmay 'on the outskirts of London', to consult William Pennefather's curate, Hay Aitken. With his help he rented six rooms at 64 Mildmay Road for 'forty shillings a week with light and attendance' and his mother moved in to make a temporary home for him and Emily, the four children – Herbert, Howard, Maria and

Charles Edward (aged 10, 8, 4 and 2) – and Lanfeng. 'It is better perhaps to know well the advantages and disadvantages of a neighbourhood before renting a house,' he said, with Bognor in mind. On October 19 he brought his family up from Bognor to join his mother, and went straight on to Saint Hill.

William Berger had received a notice from Lord Granville, Foreign Minister, through the Rt Hon E Hammond, urging Hudson Taylor's removal from Yangzhou and revealing serious misunderstandings of the situation there. The tenor of the dispatch suggested that another political storm might be blowing up, so they decided to take time before replying. Hudson Taylor went from Saint Hill to Tottenham, to renew his friendship with the Howards and Miss Stacey, and probably to consult with them about this threat. Then on November 3 he was at the Fauldings' home at Euston, writing business letters to Charles Fishe and others in China, and drafting a letter to William Berger for him to enclose in his reply to Lord Granville on the subject uppermost in their minds. A week later, back at Mildmay Road, he sat down to write a letter to Jennie's parents – of which the copy is in her handwriting – a gently worded ultimatum pleading for their compliance.

It was never good, he wrote, for Christians to be unable to speak freely to each other, so how much more true of his relationship with them. 'If you *will* let me love you as a son, and confide in you . . . what a happy relationship will exist . . . after our marriage.' In rejecting his view that he and Jennie would benefit rather than suffer from marrying soon, were they not treating his medical experience of more than twenty years as of no weight? 'We feel it is mistaken *kindness* on your part, but *very mistaken* and very wrong. . . . The whole responsibility rests on us. . . . Do not longer withhold your consent.'

There was too much in this contretemps that reminded him of Miss Aldersey's opposition in 1857. Only two days before Maria's death, she had said to him, 'Miss Aldersey's unkindness has caused you so much sorrow and anxiety [through influencing others against him] and me so much weakness; I have never got over it.' Now Hudson Taylor repeated this to the Fauldings and went on, 'I do not want to hear similar language again.' Next week his mother would still be in town and his sister Amelia and William Berger were expected. They could be present if the wedding were to be on Wednesday. Why not agree to it, and all share the joy together?

William Berger and he were treating the content of their reply to

the Foreign Office as more important than its date, until the 14th
when Berger wrote to say he had posted it. Burdened with his own
ill-health and anxieties he underestimated Hudson Taylor's, for he
went on to add another hammer-blow. 'In all probability it will be
desirable for me to retire altogether, or at least greatly into the
background; both on account of my being unable to bear the weight
of the Home department as heretofore; and likewise from my
religious opinions being so changed from what they were before.'
He proposed that they should consult together with George Müller
about 'the grave undertaking of reconstructing the Mission'.

Hudson Taylor was suffering 'intense nervous headaches' –
'almost worn out with the strain on body and mind' which rivalled
the tensions he had endured in China. He could not handle all these
problems at once. Getting married was the one most readily overcome. No one had questioned the propriety of his becoming engaged fifteen months after Maria's death. George Müller and his
colleague James Wright, whose wives had died in February and May
of the same year, 1870, were also about to remarry, Wright on
November 16 to Müller's daughter, Lydia, and Müller on November 30 to Miss Sangar, 'mother' of his orphan homes. Death and
early remarriage were commonplace in times of high mortality,
especially when children had to be provided for. The Fauldings
must let him marry without delay. Then he could cope better with
the Foreign Office and the Mission's future.

This time Mrs Faulding capitulated, and William Faulding who
had stood loyally by his wife while not sharing the strength of her
feelings, helped to arrange the wedding. On Tuesday, November
28, Dr William Landels performed the ceremony at Regent's Park
Chapel. In the circumstances they dispensed with a honeymoon. On
December 30, 1873, two full years later, they found themselves in
Fenghua in the absence of other missionaries, and recorded that this
was the first time they had been without companions since their
marriage. After the wedding Hudson Taylor's mother returned
home, and they joined the children at 64 Mildmay Park, while
Emily, approving but nonetheless lonely and grieving, had a brief
holiday.

In acknowledging a letter of congratulation from Elizabeth Judd
(whom he and Maria had done so much to bring back 'from the
verge of the grave' and whose delivery he had attended just before
sailing), he opened his heart in a way that showed how close their
friendship had become.

The *last* wish (Maria) expressed to me [between dawn and 7.30 on her last morning (p 263)?] was that if she were removed, I would marry again. . . . Seeing the love I have for her is not likely to undergo any change or diminution, I do not want one or two years, or five, to forget her in. You do not know *how* I love her, nor how seldom for one hour she is absent from my waking thoughts. . . . And my dear (Jennie) would not wish it otherwise. She has *her own* place in my heart, which Jesus has given her, a place all the larger because her love is not jealous.

So began his life with Jennie, as romantic as it was sacrificial, of nearly three times as many years as the twelve he had enjoyed with Maria, and as rich. With the obstacle to their marriage surmounted, he returned to work.

Lord Granville takes the point[2]   *October–November 1871*

The Foreign Office letter of October 13 to William Berger as Director in Britain of the China Inland Mission was a late response to F T Wade's dispatches of June, but a time lapse covered a further exchange of dispatches on the Zongli Memorandum already described. In spite of the disclaimer in Lord Granville's replies to Wade, this courteously worded letter to William Berger strongly hinted that, if not complied with, it could lead to stronger measures later.

Sir,
. . . It would appear that the continued residence of the Reverend Mr Taylor at Yang-chow, notwithstanding the recent attack on his Mission House, is likely to be productive of further difficulty; and that it would be advisable that he should remove from that place. . . . Lord Granville does not hesitate to appeal to you to withdraw that gentleman from Yang-chow, where by the treaty he has no right to reside, and where his residence may possibly lead to most serious complications. . . .
Mr Wade has been desired to urge Mr Taylor to leave Yang-chow, and to warn him that if he persists in residing there he will do so at his own peril, and that he must not expect any interference on the part of Her Majesty's Government to ensure his safety, or to obtain redress from the Chinese Government for any injuries he may receive.
I am, Sir, your obedient humble servant,
E. Hammond.

Even if a new political storm was blowing up, the rights and wrongs of the Yangzhou situation had to be made plain to the

Foreign Minister. He, or at least his junior minister, appeared to have overlooked, firstly, the fact that the Mission's presence in Yangzhou was the result of strong action by Sir Rutherford Alcock and W H Medhurst, consul-general, to secure Hudson Taylor's reinstatement, and secondly, that no new attack had been made against the premises since 1868, but only a plot. The actions of the Chinese government and local mandarins supported the presence of the Mission at Yangzhou and only the upheaval caused by the rebellious General Li and Chen Guorui expressed anything to the contrary. Viceroy Zeng Guofan's part in the proceedings was as always shadowy, even when correct to outward appearances. But although Yangzhou was nominally his base, months had passed since Hudson Taylor had lived there. To bring Charles Judd into the matter was unnecessary, beyond a mere mention of his name.

When Hudson Taylor was at Saint Hill on October 20 to consult with the Bergers about a reply, he said in a note to his mother, 'I may have to return to China suddenly, perhaps at once – but do not mention this to *anyone*.' They decided that he should send William Berger a statement which he in turn would forward to the Foreign Office, and await developments. Yangzhou was under threat, not from any Chinese but solely from the pro-trade, anti-missionary stance of the minister in Peking, T F Wade, without valid reason. *The Times* of October 31 joined in, attacking missionaries in general and advocating the necessity of suppressing them, while acknowledging that the British government could only influence British subjects and were powerless against the French Catholics. The new editor of the CMS *Intelligencer* then countered this with the retort that merchants whose stock-in-trade was opium could also have 'their warehouses sacked and gutted as readily as if they were nunneries'. Missionary Jonah might be thrown overboard, but it would not ensure that the ship would reach shore. Why not leave Jonah alone?

Hudson Taylor's statement of November 8 was the result of careful thought and made some strong points:

> In deference to Mr Wade's wishes, the work there has been so narrowed up as to be all but abandoned, and that we have not only gone as far in this direction as in the estimation of Mr Markham (our Consul at Shanghai) could be needed, but fully as far as he considered safe, and even justifiable. . . .

There has been *no* recent riot at Yangchau. Our former landlord there . . . did, in April or May last, threaten trouble if his demands were not complied with. Those threats, however, never had sufficient influence on the people to even disturb the price of silver – that most sensitive barometer of political feeling in China. . . .

(Mr Markham) inspected our work and expressed himself highly satisfied with what he saw, and gratified at the evident hold we had on the respect of the people. He fully concurred with me in the opinion that our remaining there was very unlikely to become a cause of difficulty or danger, while our leaving the station was almost sure to be so misunderstood as to produce the very evil sought to be avoided. . . .

One or two years ago we were apprised that if we continued to reside and work in the interior, it must be at our own risk and peril, but that if prepared for this we were quite at liberty to do so.

I may further add that the Consular representatives of the United States and France communicated to me their conviction of the danger and impolicy of any further retrograde steps with regard to Yangchau, an opinion shared in by the leading members of the mercantile community of Chinkiang.

Writing with a preoccupied mind only three days before his strong letter to the Fauldings, Hudson Taylor had omitted an important point which he recalled on the 13th and sent as a postscript.

My dear Mr Berger, That you may be the better able to reply to Earl Granville's despatch about Yangchau, allow me to state what has been done with respect to the station in question. It will doubtless afford satisfaction to His Lordship to be informed (that the *daotai* of Zhenjiang), before purchasing the Yangchau property, asked me whether I intended to keep it permanently, and on the faith that I should do so, purchased it at a price more than double its value to a native. . . . He secured himself by a written guarantee from me binding me to a heavy loss if I gave up possession of the premises under five years. I believe it would cause great annoyance as well as loss to him were I to leave the station at present.

As soon as the Foreign Office officials verified the date of Wade's despatch about Hudson Taylor, they would see that they themselves were out of step. William Berger replied to Mr Hammond on November 13,

It would appear that Earl Granville has been incorrectly informed . . . and that the wish of Mr Wade has been already complied with, as far as the circumstances of the case allowed. The present relations of the Station having been personally arranged by Mr Taylor with the (*daotai* of Zhenjiang) could only be safely interfered with by Mr Taylor himself.

Mr Taylor is now in this country, but purposes returning to China at no very distant period, and will seek by every means in his power to avoid any danger of hostile collision with the Chinese.

Even this was too much for William Berger. On the following day he told Hudson Taylor that he wished 'to retire altogether'. Then for several weeks they waited for the next move from Downing Street, and the wedding took place under this shadow. But they heard no more.

A forward look is justified at this point. Yangzhou not only came to be known as the most peaceful mission centre in China and the home of the women's language school of the China Inland Mission until shortly before the second world war, but perhaps the most colourful episode in the Mission's continuing presence in that historic city occurred in 1912. General Xu Baosan, commanding the Second Army Corps of the new Republic of China, gave an unprecedented opportunity for CIM missionaries to distribute Christian literature to his troops and deputed his younger brother, the military governor of Yangzhou, to arrange for regular preaching of the gospel to his officers and men. When the resident missionary, A R Saunders, left Yangzhou for Britain, General Xu Baosan ordered all members of his own staff and a guard of honour of 5,000 officers and men to escort him to the Grand Canal. By then, of those who had experienced the Yangzhou riot only William Rudland and the Taylor children were still living. Charles Judd also saw the reward of the faith and tenacity he had displayed during the second Yangzhou plot.

The CIM in China[3]   1871–72

After Hudson Taylor and his party of invalids left China, Charles Fishe took over from Judd in Yangzhou. Combining oversight of the churches in Yangzhou and Qingjiangpu with his secretarial duties, including the distribution of funds remitted from Britain, he edited and printed the *Monthly Gleaner*. Receipts continued low but adequate. Cardwell pursued his ambitious penetration of Jiangxi province from Jiujiang, and had the heartening experience of being sought out by a one-time army officer, a major and commander of a gunboat, who bought a New Testament, believed what he read, resigned his commission and declared his wish to be a missionary. With an intimate knowledge of the Jiangxi waterways this gentleman, Chen Zhaotong, was a godsend. Together they travelled far and wide. Later they were joined by another converted soldier, Lo Ganfu, a strength to their team, who succeeded in leading three more soldiers and two Daoist priests to Christ. Meanwhile, an ex-officer of Gordon's Ever-Victorious Army, a Colonel Rohde, came to Suzhou wanting to be associated with the CIM, and was preaching with Henry Reid through the Suzhou countryside.

In September 1871 George Duncan, with advanced tuberculosis but feeling stronger, and Thomas Harvey, who at his own expense had erected 'the first Protestant chapel which has ever been built in Nankin', made a long cross-country journey together. Meeting at Wuhu they travelled south-eastwards through Ningguo and Yanzhou [not Yangzhou] to Hangzhou. When Harvey fell dangerously ill, Duncan, himself febrile and coughing blood, took him to Shanghai where he recovered. Duncan then returned to Nanjing and from there up the Yangzi to the Yuxi river below Wuhu. Penetrating up the Yuxi, through Yuncao to Chao Xian on Lake Chao where 'scarcely a house was left standing' after the Taiping rebellion, he and a Chinese companion crossed the lake westwards and, ascending another river, came to the city of Lüzhou, only 120 miles from Anqing. Unacquainted with foreigners, some people called him, 'a Ningbo man', others 'a real foreign devil' and one bent on trouble said, 'The gentry should unite to put him out' of the city. Undeterred by mere words he preached and sold hundreds of Christian books, all he had brought. Duncan had all the makings of a great pioneer.

No record seems to exist of conversations between John Nevius and John McCarthy in Hangzhou, but McCarthy's loyal attachment to Hudson Taylor and faithful implementation of his policies are enough to account for his deep interest in promoting a truly indigenous Chinese Church. Nevius did not publish his principles until 1886–87. In November 1871 the *Monthly Gleaner* carried important notes from McCarthy as 'a member of the China *Inland* Mission', here abridged. His concept was that of the Pauline 'tent-maker', widely adopted in years to come.

> How is the Gospel to spread in China? . . . While by no means undervaluing itinerant labours . . . in *addition* there must be *lengthened* residence of the preacher among the masses. . . . Of course not

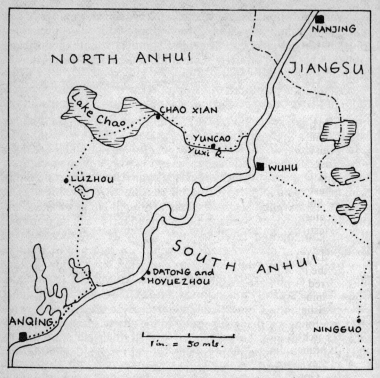

DUNCAN'S ROUTES IN ANHUI ASTRIDE THE YANGZI

foreign labour . . . there must of necessity be a large influx of the (Chinese) element. . . . That houses should be rented . . . is *not* necessary; nay more, not *desirable*. . . . The *Foreigner's* (house and) chapel are looked upon by the Christians as the Foreigner's. Thus the spirit of self-support which we hope to see grow and mature, is almost strangled at its very birth. . . . The *spirit* of the Gospel would certainly lead men to self-support, and thankful effort for Him who has done so much for them. . . . Is it not *unfair* to expect them to be bound to our arrangements for them? . . . A Chinese tradesman finds no difficulty in getting lodgings in any place he comes to. . . . Where God has blessed their labours it would not be difficult to arrange for the baptism of converts. . . . It may be asked, where are they to meet? . . . Why not in the house of one of their number? . . . If, however, the number increased (they would) get their own meeting-room or chapel . . . the point being that the room and all its surroundings would grow out of the felt need on the part of the *native* (Christian). . . . Such converts would be more likely to stand, and in their turn advance the cause of the Redeemer.

McCarthy was writing from personal observation and experience, as Hudson Taylor recognised in his *Summary of the Operations of the CIM*, in 1872.

> In both Ningbo and (Hangzhou) districts he has a large number of (Chinese colporteurs and evangelists). The work of some of these has been itinerant, but settled work is on the increase, and is by far the most effective. . . . For the harvest we must be content to wait. . . . It is God's Word that is being preached and sold. . . . A very industrious man works at his trade all the week, but always gives up his Sundays to God. Wang Lae-djün says that it is a subject of the greatest wonder to the people at his lodgings, when a man so industrious and earnest should be satisfied to 'waste' every seventh day. . . .
>
> (Lo) Ah-ts'ih (was) for a year or two engaged in evangelistic work in the interior, far away from (Hangzhou), and his whole soul was stirred with a deep sense of his countrymen's need, and of the wide opening for (the) Gospel. . . . When in (Hangzhou) he called the Christians together and [quoting McCarthy] 'explained his plan for the formation of a native missionary society; namely that each (church) member should give something each month . . . and select some man or men to be their representative, supported by them. This money, he said, should not be used for any purpose but the spread of the Gospel; *not* for the poor (or) a fund from which they could borrow money. . . . Wang Lae-djün then told them how glad he was to hear of (it). . . . The popular belief that they got so much a month for being Christians would be effectually refuted, if it were known that, instead . . . they themselves *gave out* money for the spread of the Gospel. . . . They collected more than sufficient for one man's support for a month and . . . intend to send to the other stations of our mission . . . inviting (the Christians) either to co-operate, or else to act in the same way independently'. . . .
>
> When we remember how recently the work at (Hangzhou) was commenced, and how poor the native Christians are in this world's goods, we . . . thank God and take courage.

This tale had a sequel. William Rudland's head printer, Tsiang Aliang, had one day said to Rudland, 'My little brother at home (near Fenghua) is feeding the cows and is nearly as stupid as they are. I wish you could use him here in some way.' 'Bring him back with you after the New Year', Rudland replied. The boy, Tsiang

A CHINESE EVANGELIST IN ACTION BY THE
ROADSIDE
(By courtesy of the CMS)

Liangyong, became a Christian, and in 1874 was chosen by the Hangzhou church to be their missionary. He developed into one of the most effective pastors, in charge of the Yushan church, in Jiangxi, and his son became a devoted Christian doctor. James Williamson had reported a similar initiative from the Christians in Fenghua and its outstations. They had rented a room in a large village for regular preaching.

A discussion at the Fuzhou Missionary Conference in 1870 on how to establish Chinese churches on a self-supporting basis had been followed by an appeal from Sia Sek-ong of the Methodist Episcopal Church, to his fellow-ministers,

> The trouble is with us. We are afraid to trust God in this matter. But why should we fear? . . . (God) knows where our support is to come from; can we not trust Him? . . . Will He not feed us who go forth to preach His Gospel, and to suffer for Him? Don't trouble yourselves so much about the people; don't be always looking back to see where your supplies are to come from. . . . If we were to give as much for Christ as the heathen give to the devil, we would soon be able to support our own pastors. We pay less money as Christians than the heathen do. We must give money to support the Gospel, and give liberally, or the church can never be established here. . . . Henceforth let everyone say – 'The Saviour is my Saviour, the Gospel is my Gospel, the Church is my Church, the preachers are my preachers', and let us never cease our efforts until the Church of God is firmly established in China.

Today as we see an ever-expanding Church in a hostile environment, as rid of foreign restraint as of foreign funds, the insights of a century ago remain for our encouragement.

In December 1871, soon after Hudson Taylor's marriage to Jennie Faulding, disturbingly incomplete accounts began to reach him from China of Charles Fishe being ill, of the missionaries being in financial difficulties, and of Robert White becoming involved in a fracas which could have precipitated another diplomatic storm.

What began with a small abscess in Charles's 'hip' led to complications affecting the whole Mission. Soon he had to be taken to hospital in Shanghai, came close to death and after an operation was still in hospital in March 1872. Hudson Taylor was 'in the dark' as to what was happening. News travelled slowly, and towards the end of April he heard that Charles was still dangerously ill. During his long illness no one had assumed Charles's responsibilities or acted to keep Hudson Taylor informed!

George Müller had taken to sending his donations through William Berger, instead of direct to the missionaries as before, and although regular remittances were being sent en bloc from Britain, they were not distributed in China. As early as December 27, Hudson Taylor was asking, How was it that several sums had not been transmitted to John McCarthy, who had suffered a robbery? 'His distress must have been extreme.' Blame undoubtedly lay with Charles, but his illness plunged his foreign and Chinese colleagues into yet greater deprivation, testing their faith in God to supply them by other means. Wang Lae-djün, to show his concern, went so far as to pawn some of his clothes and present the money to John McCarthy towards the expenses of the two boarding-schools in Hangzhou. Ample sums for all were inaccessible. As soon as Hudson Taylor knew what was happening he remitted money direct to each missionary, and more to E C Lord for distribution.

Robert White was a law to himself. He wore foreign clothes and paid sedan-chair carriers at the inflated rates they demanded from foreigners, but Charles Fishe wore Chinese clothes and paid the same amount as Chinese customers. Under White's influence, Charles resumed foreign dress and was promptly charged at the foreign rate. One day when White refused to meet the inflated charge on Charles's behalf, the carriers 'became insolent, whereupon he gave them a sound beating'. On another occasion he gave three men into custody, had the mandarin called, and sat with him in judgment while 'they were condemned, sentenced and flogged then and there'. White claimed independence but still attached himself to the CIM at his own convenience. So when it was reported to Consul Gardner, Hudson Taylor wrote to Fishe, 'Wade will get to know and will make capital of it, I fear.' It was plain that he must return to China as soon as possible. But with William Berger's retirement imminent and no one yet in sight to replace him, he was needed as urgently in Britain.

Goodbye to the Bergers   December 1871–March 1872

William and Mary Berger had not spared themselves in representing the Mission in Britain, or in sacrificing their home, Saint Hill, to be its headquarters. But ceaseless work had tied them to it. His gifts did not include public relations, and as the years had passed since Hudson Taylor's departure in the *Lammermuir*, the *Occasional Paper* alone became inadequate to maintain interest. The continental wars had ended, but great political issues captured attention instead – issues leading to the legalisation of the trades unions, and (in 1872) extension of the franchise to more citizens than ever before, through the secret ballot box.

Because China was seen to be getting the measure of other nations and peace in east Asia could not be counted on, a wait-and-see attitude spelt inertia among supporters of missions. False reports from China and attacks in the press had made even sympathetic Christians sensitive to criticisms against the CIM. And 'party questions agitating the Brethren' and others, especially on the current issues of 'non-eternity of punishment' and 'universal restoration', were undermining confidence. Hudson Taylor told Charles Fishe, 'Many Churches of England, Baptist, Brethren, etc are expelling all who hold non-eternity. Some work is quite broken up on account of it. Mr Berger himself greatly fears our work will suffer on his account.' Mary Berger was distressed by his views and had no sympathy for them.

The Christian public needed to have their consciences stirred again, to look away from affairs close at hand and to show concern for the wider world. 'Slipshod stewardship was still handicapping missions,' however urgent their appeals. Hudson Taylor believed as strongly as he ever had, that the Church would respond to the Holy Spirit's prompting to contribute to missions if it first responded in terms of love and commitment to God himself. His own responsibility was therefore to reawaken those Christians who had responded so strongly before to China's spiritual need and claims. Griffith John, on leave from China, was enrapturing great audiences with his oratory, claiming that the scope he had in the Hankou field was greater even than Spurgeon's in London. The Church in Britain needed to be told, and responded when it was.

The Bergers' health had broken and they were spending more weeks on the south coast than at Saint Hill, while Hudson Taylor gave his thoughts to finding successors. In the lodgings at 64 Mildmay Park, over Christmas and the New Year, he faced the immediate prospect of being alone, not only as the leader in Britain as well as China but in all the daily work of correspondence, public relations and accountancy. He had Emily Blatchley's help again, while Jennie helped her with the children, but both lacked the strength to do much, Emily with phthisis and Jennie still weak from malaria. Emily's 'Even so, Father' had progressed beyond resignation to contentment. 'My one cry is for perfect Christ-like acquiescence in the Father's will. Then . . . I shall have joy, and even undisturbable peace,' she wrote in her diary. So by March she was 'as happy as ever', en famille again with Jennie and Hudson Taylor. Without others in the home he did not have to call her 'Miss Blatchley'. She was 'Aimei', 'loved sister', all the time, reliving the past while writing her memoir of Maria.

Early in January, he rented a new house on the fringe of fields near the village green and duck-pond of Newington Green, and moved in on January 15. At the other side of the Green, a country lane led away past Henry VIII's old hunting-lodge and Inglesby House, an old residence, through fields as far as Manor House and the Seven Sisters. For twenty more years that district would change only slowly. Emily was the first to use the new address, 6 Pyrland Road, in a letter of January 3. They restarted the almost defunct Saturday prayer-meetings, and Hudson Taylor addressed a meeting of the evangelical Week of Prayer, the first of a constant succession of lectures and church meetings, sometimes nightly, from then until October. At Welbeck Street on the 18th he renewed old friendships, and at Portman Square, Tottenham, Hackney – all the familiar places – he was welcomed with all the old warmth and no loss of confidence in him. Yet he still felt deflated, needing more time to recover, unequal to the demands on his vitality, but compelled to defer his public appearances no longer. All his old friends wanted to hear him report on the great adventure. Nor could he stay away from London's theatre services, good opportunities to preach the gospel to the unconverted.

William Berger and he spent three days at Bristol with George Müller, discussing the Mission's problems. They found him sympathetic, and left him with a clearer understanding of their difficulties and determined to help them. While he applauded the faith of young missionaries who took responsibility for the expenses of their own work, he saw the danger of fragmentation and of personal domination of a local church. Working as a team, with interchangeability of personnel from city to city according to necessity, was preferable, he suggested. No note on his attitude to William Berger's view on 'non-eternity' remains, but the silent comment of all Müller's donations being withheld until after Berger's formal retirement from the Mission led Hudson Taylor to attribute cause and effect, and reinforced his own convictions on the subject.

From Bristol, Hudson Taylor went straight on to Dublin for a strenuous round of meetings and interviews, with Colonel Fishe and John McCarthy's brother William, and others. Still he had 'no strength, nor Jennie' (true in both senses), and was glad to get back to Pyrland Road and routine under his own control, however demanding. Copies of his correspondence reveal the impossibility (which he had always pointed out) of directing, let alone leading a team in China, so far away.

Frequent letters to Josiah Jackson tried to hold him to his purpose, keeping him informed of progress towards sending Fanny Wilson to whom he had proposed by letter, out to China. She married him in December 1872 and transformed him (while she lived) into a worthwhile missionary – the reward of Hudson Taylor's long patience. Henry Cordon wrote that his wife's low state necessitated their return home. In view of Cordon's own poor record, Hudson Taylor replied that if they came it must be with a view to not returning to China. So when the Cordons withdrew and Reid irresponsibly followed without consulting his leader or making provision for the property or the work established in Suzhou, Hudson Taylor handed it over to William Muirhead and the LMS. To the troublesome but ailing Thomas Harvey he wrote, 'I am sorry that you and dear Mr Duncan have not got on happily together. . . . You must part *friends*, if you cannot get on together. . . I do not doubt that you have tried him, as much as he has tried you. You cannot correct his failings, you can forgive them; your own, however, you have more serious concern with.'

Cardwell had sent a long account of his epic journey up the waterways of Jiangxi, and of his close encounter with mobs at the capital, Nanchang. Hudson Taylor's acknowledgment went on to say,

> Owing to the touchy state of public feeling here about China, it would not be safe to publish *in extenso* the account of all the treatment you were subjected to. Everything which so eventuates as to leave hostile collision possible, excites the general public to a degree. They say 'Those missionaries want to embroil us in another Abyssinian war' and much more in that style. We must have as little as possible to do with our Consuls, as they report to Pekin, and Wade who hates missions and missionaries, I fear, will make the most of what can be made to tell against them. . . . It would seem wise for the present to avoid the (provincial) capital as there are so many other cities open to you.[4]

But the most important overseas letters were to young Charles Fishe, to whom he said, 'I hope nothing will require me to leave England before early in September, and that you will not fail me in this crisis of the Mission.' With Hudson Taylor's strong support

Charles was urging Mrs Faulding to allow Nellie out to marry him, but against stronger resistance. As for the fashion-loving Nellie, she longed to get away from the influences of London, 'full of eloquence, politics, anything but Christ' which held her back. Two months had passed since news had come that Charles's health was improving rapidly. How was it that no letter had come from him? Had he relapsed? But to business – Hudson Taylor had had a gravestone made and engraved in memory of Maria and each of her deceased children, and was about to ship it to Zhenjiang. And finally, 'Mrs Faulding is coming round to Nellie's going with us.' More than a year later they were still exhorting her mother even to be willing to let her go.

Editing the fourth edition of *China: Its Spiritual Need and Claims*, his *Summary of the Operations of the China Inland Mission from its commencement to the year 1872*, and *Occasional Paper* Nos 29 and 30, absorbed hours of concentration as he prepared a table of the stations and current staff of the Mission, Chinese and foreign, with a map to show how widely they were deployed, in many cases a hundred miles from each other. When Christians knew what was going on they rose to the occasion and joined in. When feeling out of touch, their gifts and even praying seemed to dwindle. Information led to dedication – of their whole lives in many instances. That Hudson Taylor learned this lesson – brought home to him by Philip Gosse – is apparent in his change of practice over the years ahead. If William Berger had been unable to make bricks without straw, no one could. Good reporting from the field of action was imperative. When Hudson Taylor lacked reports hot from the field, he drew upon personal knowledge, and gave vivid pen-portraits of his Chinese colleagues whose example put to shame many a Western Christian.

Twice he spent five days with William Berger, going through the financial accounts from his sailing in 1866 to March 1872, and reviewing all outstanding business. Only one error in accounting emerged, an omission at the time of the Yangzhou riot; and another bizarre episode had been safely weathered, in which the French bank at Shanghai had mislaid and failed to credit the Mission with cheques to the value of £1,106, but found them five months later! On March 16 he returned to London to preach for James Vigeon ('he is doing a good work in London') and then back to Saint Hill for William Berger's formal handover of his audited accounts – which revealed a balance of £336 1s. 9d. – and of official records on the

18th. The next day each of them wrote an editorial letter for the *Occasional Paper* No 29, announcing Berger's retirement and Hudson Taylor's assumption of the directorship at home as well as in China. 'Our fellowship together has been a source of unmixed and uninterrupted joy,' Hudson Taylor said in his tribute to his friend, but 'we have, for the past two years, seen unmistakable evidence that the same kind and measure of co-operation was becoming impossible with Mr Berger's failing health and strength'. No one was yet available to take his place, but God would provide in this as in every need.

As for the future, it looked as if Hudson Taylor himself must return to China in the autumn and be back in Britain again after fifteen or sixteen months. With steamers cutting the voyage to a mere six or seven weeks at only £50 per person, by third-class passage on the Messageries Maritimes, travel to and fro had become less time consuming. Experience had shown that, in spite of the difficulties, the unoccupied provinces of China could with determination be entered, and he had every intention of continuing towards that goal. To this end he wrote to George Duncan to lease or purchase premises in Anqing, even if expensive. They must hold on and reach out from there. The loss of William and Mary Berger must not prevent progress.

Alone yet not alone   *March–October 1872*

In James Vigeon, the accountant so committed to going to China until forcibly detained at home in 1866, might have lain the answer to the Mission's need for a representative in Britain. But the silence of the records provides no clue as to why he was not. Instead, from March to September Hudson Taylor carried the full load, often 'weary and in pain', but with no alternative, 'sparing everyone but himself', taking Lanfeng with him to meetings and showing him the Crystal Palace and the historic sights of London, interviewing and advising candidates, trying to acknowledge personally every donation received, and constantly rethinking the administrative problems of the Mission. A period of probation before becoming a full member of the Mission, he thought, might encourage young men and women to make a better start. And labelling some 'associates' could help critics to recognise that the CIM held no responsibility for their actions, as in the case of those who sought Hudson Taylor's help, but went their own way. Still no answer emerged to the most outstanding need, for someone to share the burden.

News came that John Stevenson, who had been ill since October 1871 with malaria and then typhoid fever (one account said cholera), was desperately ill with confluent haemorrhagic smallpox. Vaccination still tended to be unreliable, and the need to repeat it at intervals was not fully realised. Steady, reliable, indefatigable, with strong churches already firmly established in the three cities of Shaoxing, Sheng Xian and Xinchang, to the credit of his Chinese colleagues and himself, his future was full of promise. For nine months he lay ill and out of action, with no medical help beyond what his wife and Chinese friends could give him, while the churches learned to stand on their own feet. But he recovered and, as soon as he was strong enough, visited Sheng Xian.

A scholarly gentleman named Ning, a graduate in the classics and student of Western science, 'a man of ability and considerable standing and influence' but sceptical about Christianity, after meeting Stevenson said to himself, 'Here is a foreigner, a perfect stranger to me, yet so concerned about my welfare that he will pray for me though I do not so much as pray for myself.' Mr Ning began in secret to pray for himself and soon experienced a change of heart which he could not account for. He, his wife and son became strong Christians. 'When I see what he has done, and the persecution that he is exposed to,' John Stevenson wrote, 'I cannot hesitate to say that the age of heroes is not past.'

Hudson Taylor took courage. In June he retraced his steps through the West Country, visiting Bath, Bristol, Barnstaple, Teignmouth, Torquay, Exeter, Yeovil and other towns, some more than once. When the Franco-Prussian war had ended Grattan Guinness's mission to France and Spain, he had returned to Dublin and then to Bath to write his great tome, *The Approaching End of the Age*. Hudson Taylor addressed a meeting in the Guildhall there, and conferred with Guinness whose expansive soul had developed a concern for the whole world, not only for China.

'Grattan Guinness was a man of vision and had become a man of learning. He could inspire and teach, he could move men but he had little understanding of the labour that makes the vision possible.'[5] So even if willing, he was not the administrator needed to direct the CIM in Britain.

Again Hudson Taylor conferred with George Müller, and addressed meetings in the parish church and the historic Bethesda Chapel in Bristol. He met Robert Chapman again at Barnstaple, and other leading Christians who later became the first 'referees' of the China Inland Mission, and was back at Pyrland Road in time for the Mildmay Conference of June 26–28. William Pennefather had invited him to give some of the main conference addresses, beginning with the opening address on the first morning. Sharing the platform with D L Moody (on his first visit), Lord Radstock, the Earl of Cavan, and Stevenson Arthur Blackwood, he faced an audience of hundreds of like-minded Christians, the kind he most wanted to arouse to concern for China. Rising at the end of the popular missionary hymn, 'Waft, waft ye winds His story', he captured the attention of the conference with his first words, 'My dear friends, the wind will never waft it! If the blessed story of His love is to be taken to the dark places of the earth, it must be taken by men and women like ourselves . . . who wish to obey His great missionary command.' He reported on what had happened in China since he had last addressed the conference and had distributed the first thousand copies of *China: Its Spiritual Need and Claims*. And citing electricity and steam, forces of nature always available but only recently put to use by men, he went on, 'There is a power in us who believe . . . a power that men may wield . . . God's power' upon which we may call. He told them about the dangerous experiences of the past few years in China, and of how the power of God had been displayed in answer to prayer, delivering Chinese idolaters from Satan to serve the living and true God.

Henrietta and Lucy Soltau were staying at 6 Pyrland Road during the conference. According to Henrietta, one day after lunch Hudson Taylor led the household – Jennie, Emily, Henrietta, Lucy and 'one or two gentlemen' – into the sitting-room, to stand round a map of China. 'Now,' he said, 'have you the faith to join with me in laying hold of God for eighteen new men, to go two by two to the unoccupied provinces?' They 'covenanted with him to pray daily for this, till it was accomplished.' Then 'we all joined hands while Mr Taylor prayed'. That his team in China had been reduced to twenty-five, with more leaving soon afterwards, and that the 'crisis' of William Berger's resignation and replacement had not been resolved, were as irrelevant to the task needing to be done as to the power of God in response to believing prayer. Funds were low and donations coming in painfully slowly. With the Mission in some ways at its lowest ebb since its inception, this seemed no time for expansion, yet Hudson Taylor was in no doubt that the will of God was unchanged – for advance, not retreat.

Two and a half years later they were still praying, little nearer to their goal – except that God's time had come.[6]

'A council of management' – for home affairs[7]   July–October 1872

Hudson Taylor's good friends of Bryanston Hall, Portman Square – Thomas Marshall, John Challice and William Hall – could see that he was bearing too much for one man and reminded him of Jethro's advice to Moses, 'You will only wear yourself out' – you must share the load with others. He knew it only too well and had been looking for lieutenants for five years. None had come forward. Nor did Challice and Hall offer more than their support. They were waiting to be asked. In the week after the Mildmay Conference on July 5, Hudson Taylor was spending the evening with Richard Harris Hill, the architect and civil engineer, and Agnes his wife, one of the Soltau sisters, when Hill made a proposition. If Taylor would form a council of friends he could trust, he himself would be willing to serve as its honorary secretary. 'Not seeing any hope of a colleague, (to replace Berger) he adopted my suggestion,' Hill noted.

At last there was light at the end of the tunnel. More than once Hudson Taylor had stated his objections to the often cloying effects of committee control in China, and before the *Lammermuir* sailed from London, he and William Berger had opted for the freedom of judgment and action Berger would have as an independent director while the Mission was small. Memories of the failure of the Chinese Evangelization Society with its large board of management and committee of armchair strategists were too vivid. But William Berger had been a co-founder, committed body and soul to the Mission. Many strong supporters were fit and willing to play a minor role, but until now no one had offered to do more. Perhaps Richard Hill underestimated what would be involved, or having offered to be secretary to a council was carried along in subsequent conversations with Hudson Taylor to take on more than he had intended. William Berger had managed his factory and farm as well as Mission affairs in Britain, and found them too much. Richard Hill was adding the Mission to his professional practice. His new undertaking was to suffer, for all his good intentions.

At the end of July, Henrietta Soltau, a petite young woman, 'a very nice girl, well-educated', with a strong and buoyant spirit, came to Pyrland Road to help for two or three months in any way she could – the beginning of an association which led to her being one of the Mission's most venerated veterans. Consultations between Hill and Hudson Taylor continued, and, realising that at all costs he must leave for China in October, only a few weeks away, he concluded that an advisory council to share the responsibilities *in Britain* was the right provision to make for his absence. No potential member knew enough of his principles, of the brief history of the Mission, or about China, to replace William Berger as director. So Hudson Taylor would remain as the general director while the council served the Mission. John Challice and William Hall accepted his invitation to be members, and also the Soltau brothers, George and Henry, and Joseph Weatherley, a family friend of Maria's and trustee of her marriage settlement for the education of her children.

Planning matured while the 'almost overwhelming' pressure of daily duties on Hudson Taylor showed no sign of easing. In a note to his mother on July 20 he even had this to add, 'Mrs Meadows was confined last night of twins at 7 p m prematurely. Both died ere midnight.' Again! This had happened to Elizabeth so often, and he felt for her.

Too late to be included in the *Occasional Paper* No 30, a slip was attached announcing that Richard Hill and Henry Soltau had 'agreed to act as Honorary Secretaries during our absence from England.' The Taylors went to the Radstocks the next day, speaking at two meetings, and stayed overnight for long conversations. And then to the Howards and Miss Stacey at Tottenham for the same purpose. On August 22 the Hills and George Soltau met with Hudson Taylor again, and through this month and September a list of those willing to serve as referees in different parts of the country began to grow (Appendix 7). William Pennefather and John Eliot Howard were naturally the first to be included. George Müller's acceptance was received on October 9, the day the Taylors left for China. After a long conversation with Henry Soltau on August 30, Hudson Taylor and Jennie spent another weekend with the Robert Howards at Tottenham. On September 4 John Eliot Howard attended an early morning meeting at 6 Pyrland Road to bid farewell to the Crombies and Lanfeng, escorting Fanny Wilson and a 'Miss Potter' to China. Richard Hill then went with Hudson Taylor to meet the Marquis of Cholmondeley and agree his functions as a referee. And a few days later Hudson Taylor's host at Bath, Colonel Woodfall, also agreed to serve.[8]

Hudson Taylor was preparing boxes for packing up and sailing

within a month, but still had a tour of the north to fit in. On the 11th
the Judds and Thomas Harvey arrived at Liverpool and came on to
London. Elizabeth Judd had become so ill in China that Mary
Bowyer at a day or two's notice had joined them to care for her on
board ship. Harvey had returned to complete his medical course at
his own expense. On the same day Grattan Guinness and Tom
Barnardo, two more referees, came to tea – well met, for it had
been through Barnardo's friendship and Guinness's *Voice of thy
Brother's Blood* that Judd had been directed to China. Barnardo
and Guinness, living opposite one another in Bow, were each
building up his own great achievements while serving the CIM in his
own way.

On September 15 Hudson Taylor preached for William Landels
at Regent's Park Chapel in the morning and for William Garrett
Lewis at Westbourne Grove in the evening – two more of his new
referees. Then, at last, on the 20th he began his farewell visit to
Yorkshire on the way to Dundee for a three-day conference, and
from there to Kendal. He spent two days with his old friend William
Collingwood in Liverpool, left by the 1 a m train and rejoined his
family at 7.30 a m on the last day of September 'greatly prospered'
and 'not too tired'. Only ten days remained before he would have to
catch the French Mail at Marseilles.

On Friday, October 4, Hudson Taylor, Joseph Weatherley, John
Challice, George and Henry Soltau and Richard Hill met at 51
Gordon Square, Weatherley's home, 'to inaugurate a Council for
the management of the Home affairs of the China Inland Mission'
(Appendix 7). The Council was to deputise for him in his absence
and to advise him when he was in Britain. They clearly understood
how it differed from the controlling councils and committees of
most other societies, and approved of his principles in this respect.
Hudson Taylor then requested and authorised the council, in the
event of his decease, to make 'all necessary arrangements for
carrying on the work of the Mission'. William Berger's part in the
growth of the Mission, and his activities as director in Britain were
reviewed as an indication of what the council and secretaries could
expect to shoulder, and Hudson Taylor went on to brief them on the
complexities of property, rental and purchase in China, and (as the
minute read) on the appointment of 'missionary agents' – the term
died hard in the thinking of those accustomed to it. Hudson Taylor
then handed over the small balance lying at the bank.

On Saturday they met again, as much to pray as to conduct

business, with Joseph Weatherley in the chair and Hudson Taylor, Challice, Hall, Hill and Henry Soltau present. One final meeting followed on October 8 at Gordon Square, with Grattan Guinness attending by invitation while the selection and training of candidates was discussed. George Soltau undertook to train and test candidates at his Lamb and Flag Ragged School and City Mission. Hudson Taylor delivered his cash in hand, £21, to the treasurer, and £15 to Emily Blatchley, and at last was free to do his own hurried packing and preparations for departure. Shortly afterwards Theodore Howard, Robert's son, also joined the council. To ease the parting Hudson Taylor's children were in the country at Godalming with his sister Amelia and her big family. He had said goodbye and his heart was heavy. Of all farewells, he confessed, those from his children were the most painful.

Third-class French Mail   *October–November 1872*

The Crombies had been home from China only two months when Annie wrote in January 1871 from the House Beautiful at Saint Hill to Hudson Taylor, 'I long for the day when we shall start again for China. . . . All the kind friends and many comforts of England are not worth a tenth of the privilege of being allowed to bear the burden and heat of the day in China.' But they were not well enough to return until September 1872. By then Lanfeng had been away from his wife and home for more than a year. Travelling third class with the Crombies and Fanny Wilson (through a typhoon in the China Sea) and due the same treatment as other passengers, Lanfeng had found himself exploited by the crew and made to work his passage all the way to China. When Hudson Taylor learned of this, he took it up with the shipping company to recover the fare for Lanfeng.

The Taylors and Emmeline Turner, a new recruit, were seen off at Charing Cross station on October 9 by such a crowd of well-wishers and with so little time for registering their baggage that he could not bid any a proper farewell. Worse still, his father could not get through the barrier to the platform and failed to see him. Nellie and her father missed Hudson Taylor completely, and in the confusion Mrs Faulding left her handbag in the carriage. Hearing too late that he had gone, Major C H Malan, a garrison commander at Singapore, sent a hundred pounds for his own use. 'Your visit to me at Singapore on my birthday, August 19, 1871, was one of my brightest days there.'

They had second-class tickets to Marseilles, apparently Richard

Hill's parting gift, and after the 'excessive fatigue' of finally clearing up and leaving Pyrland Road, welcomed it as God's special provision for them in the circumstances. The journey of fourteen hours to Paris and twenty-five from there to Marseilles, brought them to the steamer *Tigre* of the Messageries Maritimes. They went aboard to see their third-class cabins – Jennie and Emmeline together with a nine-berth cabin to themselves, and Hudson Taylor sharing with other men in the adjoining cabin. They left their note of introduction and cards for the captain, and spent the night ashore. He wrote 'so cheerfully', Emily told Henrietta Soltau. 'He says Jennie is hardly like herself, she is so well. . . . He told me to send his love to you (you hardly deserve it!)' But beneath this exterior Emily was lonely, ill and very sad. 'But it does not *tear* my heart now as it used to do, for I realize that ties are not made for time (but) for eternity.'

All the routine work had fallen upon her, seeing the *Occasional Paper* through the printers and then distributing them, and dealing with the mail, everything that did not have to wait for the secretaries or treasurer. Finding her so competent and reliable, they soon began to overlook her frail health until she carried more than she could bear. At the same time she had Hudson Taylor's four children to mother, and Tom Jones to keep at his books, working for medical entrance examinations.

Crossing the Mediterranean, Hudson Taylor and Jennie worked on No 31 of the *Occasional Paper*, in a long letter to friends of the Mission introducing the 'Council of Management of the home department'. One part of the council's work was 'so momentous . . . as to call for special remark', the selection and training of reinforcements. He enlarged on the need for them, on the painfully difficult life they would be called upon to lead, and on their necessary qualifications. 'The work of a true missionary is *work* indeed, often very monotonous, apparently not very successful, and carried on through great and varied but unceasing difficulties.' He then introduced the list of referees 'in various parts of the country, whose known sympathy will be helpful to strangers to the mission, and from whom such may learn its character and *bona fide* nature'. Matters which could not at once be made public would be referred to them for advice, should such dire circumstances arise again. He made a careful statement of arrangements for banking and exchange, of how he followed the market fluctuations in order to change sterling into silver taels and Mexican dollars at the most favourable times, and of how this careful stewardship also brought in substantial interest – as a by-product, not the result, of deliberate investment of current funds.

> We shall seek pecuniary aid from God by prayer, as heretofore. He will put it into the hearts of whom He sees fit to use, to act as His channels. When there is money in hand, it will be remitted to China; when there is none, none will be sent; and we shall not draw on home, so there can be no going into debt. Should our faith be tried, as it has been before, He will prove Himself faithful, as He ever has done; nay, should our faith fail, His faithfulness will not; for is it not written, 'If we believe not, He abideth faithful?' . . . Pray that (the) principle – of becoming one with the people, of willingly taking the lowest place – may be deeply inwrought in our souls, and expressed in our deportment. With regard to missionaries wearing the native costume, there will always be differences of opinion, and we do not, therefore, make its adoption a *sine qua non* of membership with the mission. But for work in the interior we value it *much*, seeing year by year more reason to value it.

Most significantly he harked back to his early experiences of years ago when he, with William Burns and others, engaged in itinerant preaching and colportage where residence was impossible. The result had been

> to convince (him) of (the) comparative inutility (of this type of work). Where interest was excited it could not be sustained; enquirers had to be left with no one to lead them on. . . . It became more and more apparent . . . that any who might be brought to Christ would need the constant care and teaching of older and more experienced Christians. [Here he stressed fundamental principles:] *How* could this be done? As we foreigners could not then reside in the interior, it seemed desirable at first, to labour (at Ningbo) until a native church was formed; to spare no pains in thoroughly instructing the converts in the Word of God; to pray that evangelistic and pastoral gifts might be developed among them; and then to encourage them to locate themselves in the interior, visiting them frequently, and aiding them in their work in every possible way.

He then told at length the story of Tsiu Kyuo-kwe and his mother ('the manhunter'), to show how effective the policy had been. This was the way the Mission's work was developing everywhere and would be continued. 'We shall seek by God's help to plant the standard of the cross in new and unoccupied regions; to get as near as possible to the people, and to be as accessible to them as possible, that our *lives* may commend the gospel.'

The work on the manuscript was finished as they approached Port Said, and it was posted home. After that it was correspondence until they were 'tired of writing'. From Aden he asked that his mother should copy and send him all the Mission's statements of account for the past seven years – which he later received and prepared for publication. The long tropical voyage on the Crombies' ship through the Indian Ocean had been too much for Miss Potter, and she had been put ashore at Singapore to recover. When the *Tigre* arrived and most third-class passengers disembarked, Miss Potter joined Emmeline Turner (only to relapse in China and be sent home to die in July 1874).

Approaching China 'in heavy seas', Hudson Taylor quailed at the thought of what lay ahead. 'I should tremble indeed, had we not God to look to.' From Aden he had written, 'Difficulties will be very thick on our arrival but God will perfect that which concerns us.' At Shanghai he would meet 'the first crush of matters' for to T F Wade the Yangzhou affair was still a live issue. If only he could avoid secular business and give himself to spiritual activities! But he could see no remedy while he was the sole leader. A visit to Gutzlaff's grave at Hong Kong must have rallied his spirit, for the memory of Gutzlaff's vision was always an inspiration.

Unknown to them, Henry Reid had passed the *Tigre* in another ship, homeward bound, and George Duncan's health had steadily deteriorated until Catherine had to bring him and their child home on a second ship. Reid's baggage and theirs was on a third vessel which went down with all their worldly possessions. On October 9, the day of the Taylors' departure from London, only nine missionary men, Louise Desgraz and five wives remained in China. Where was the China Inland Mission? The Crombies and Fanny Wilson arrived soon afterwards.

The journey over, Hudson Taylor admitted that he did not enjoy travelling as he had on clipper ships under sail. Little glamour was left. They anchored at the mouth of the Yangzi. Even with Robert Hart's buoys and lightships to mark the channel, it was too dark and thick a night to proceed, so they lay at anchor. 'I can form no conception of what our course (on landing) may be – north, south, east or west – I never felt so fully and utterly cast on the Lord. . . . My heart too aches at the remembrance of the past, and at the distance which separates me from so many loved ones.' In the morning, on November 28, the first anniversary of his and Jennie's wedding day, they reached Shanghai.

CHAPTER ELEVEN

'A LONG STRIDE'
1872–73

Taking up the reins   *November–December 1872*

Landing at Shanghai on their first wedding anniversary aroused in Hudson Taylor and Jennie a flood of memories, and a surge of qualms, immediately justified. Before anything else came a visit to the post-office to collect their mail. Whom should they meet there but Charles Fishe, looking better and stronger than they had ever known him, but shamefaced, in foreign clothes. The pressure of opinion had been too much for him. Being 'a Chinese to the Chinese' was all very well in 'the interior', and out of place among Westerners in an increasingly Westernised international settlement which treated its thousands of Chinese residents as aliens without a say in its government. But Charles was not only wearing them in Shanghai. Unconvinced, it had been easy for him to forget Hudson Taylor's principles and to take the line of least resistance, to do as others did. He was quickly set at ease. Hudson Taylor himself was in foreign clothes and so soon swept up by the need for immediate action as Charles gave him all the news, that he could not get Chinese travelling clothes made before he had to leave Shanghai. Even Jennie and the two girls, Emmeline Turner and 'Miss Potter', could not complete their shopping before they all set out for Hangzhou by canal boat forty-eight hours later.

The news from Hangzhou was bad. All Chinese who had sold land to foreigners, on which to build their foreign homes and churches, were in prison and one of them in chains, with the exception of the New Lane landlords. But no more had been heard of moves to force the CIM out of Yangzhou. The Mission's finances in China were in such a state that Hudson Taylor had to exchange all the foreign currency he had brought with him, regardless of an adverse exchange rate, for no remittances had arrived from Britain. 'Our present supplies will soon be exhausted,' he wrote to the secretaries in London, assuming that they had no funds to send. 'What a comfort it is to know that . . . our Supplier never can be so.' James

Williamson, Charles reported, was in a state of nervous exhaustion close to breakdown. Hudson Taylor sent him a message to hand over his work in Fenghua and Ninghai to Crombie and come to Hangzhou ready to be sent home to Britain. News of Reid's irresponsible defection from Suzhou was a greater shock, the first Hudson Taylor had heard of it; and the rapid acceleration of George Duncan's tuberculosis before he sailed for home almost certainly heralded his early death. As painful a reminder of Hudson Taylor's own experiences lay in the news that both the Rudland and Edward Fishe families had lost another child. In the political field reports were hopeful. China seemed to be peaceful again and, on the whole, persecution had ceased.

Preaching to village audiences and at the city of Songjiang on the way to Hangzhou took Hudson Taylor back in thought to his very first journey with Joseph Edkins in December 1854. This time his congregations were drawn by the sight of foreign women in foreign dress, 'the women examining our bonnets and dresses and peeping at our petticoats to their hearts' content,' so that they paid no attention to the speaker. Jennie was in her element, happily chatting with them as she revealed more mysteries to the curious women. Emmeline Turner at once caught the spirit of the occasion.

Hurrying on, they were in Hangzhou of happy memories by December 5. Apart from lapses by some Christians, 'on the whole I see *very* cheering and decided progress here,' Hudson Taylor could tell Richard Hill. Wang Lae-djün, 'a wise as well as a godly man,' as pastor in Hangzhou and several outstations, was still supporting and directing a team of evangelists and colporteurs deployed hundreds of miles apart, including some at Lanxi again, the scene of Duncan's and Tsiu's early pioneering, and at Qu Xian, the city they had failed to reach on the first Qiantang river reconnaissance. Better still, two had crossed the provincial border into southern Anhui and occupied Huizhou, one of the cities visited and reported on by Duncan and Harvey on their long journey through southern Anhui in 1871. One of Lae-djün's team was being victimised by extortioners, but resisting the demands for money. The Hangzhou schools were in good order, and Emmeline was game to step straight into Jennie's previous post and live among the girls. 'Miss Potter' on the other hand was in a precarious state of health. 'Inflammation of the right lung' had left her an invalid incapable of anything. Jennie was enjoying the bloom of her first pregnancy and delighting in the comfort of getting into Chinese wadded winter clothing at last, snug in the bitter cold.

Before Duncan had had to admit defeat by his illness, he had rented good premises in Anqing as a base for evangelising the province. The Chinese missionaries left in charge had sent word, however, that attempts were being made to wrest this new foothold from the Mission. John McCarthy agreed to go and see what he could do, and left Hangzhou on December 14, little knowing that this step would lead to his becoming one of the internationally famous pioneers of inland China. For the present, Anhui was the province they most wanted to see evangelised in 1873, its northern half from Anqing and its southern half from Wuhu. Jennie took McCarthy's place as servant of the church at Hangzhou, while Hudson Taylor prepared to visit the southern cities immediately after Christmas.

In Hangzhou for a short three weeks, he gave himself to the work he most loved – teaching the Christians and preaching the gospel – but also in showing that warm affection which they so prized. He put on a Christmas fellowship-meal for all the church members – and on Christmas Day received £495 in cheques allocated by George Müller from his missionary fund, enough to keep the Mission going. Hours had to be spent on drafting the main contents of *Occasional Paper* No 32, an account of all he was learning of recent development, and a biographical essay on Feng Nenggui, the basket-maker responsible for Wang Lae-djün's conversion. So useful had the Mission's *Monthly Gleaner* proved, that another monthly bulletin in Chinese had to be started, for the Chinese missionaries who already outnumbered the foreign.

On December 28 Hudson Taylor set out on his visit to the southern district, calling first at Xiaoshan, the scene of Mr. Tsiu's flogging in 1867 and still unproductive. Only two Christians were known to the evangelist who had taken over when Lewis Nicol left. Then on to Shaoxing where Charles Fishe rejoined him. Hudson Taylor had discovered that Charles's sense of disloyalty in forsaking Chinese dress was making him think of resigning from the Mission. Potentially a valuable asset, he needed to be encouraged. Important though adaptation to the Chinese was, dress was not the most important issue where Charles was concerned. His secretarial help was indispensable if Hudson Taylor was not to be bogged down by administrative detail. Would he agree to their travelling together for a few weeks, to act as his personal assistant? Gradually, Hudson

Taylor hoped, he could bring about a complete change of outlook and save Charles from giving up. It took him more than six months of close friendship to achieve this, but only a few days to know that beneath Charles's unrest lay his pining for Nellie Faulding. Broadly hinting that he need not wait to marry her if he came home, her mother was refusing to let her go to him.

John Stevenson had recovered from his succession of serious illnesses, but this tall, upright, once handsome man was now covered with deep pockmarks from the haemorrhagic smallpox that had all but claimed his life. Instead of letting it affect his mind or commitment to the growing churches in Shaoxing, Sheng Xian and Xinchang he now added responsibility for the Ningbo outstations. His and the newly converted gentleman-scholar Ning's single-mindedness were in Hudson Taylor's mind when he wrote affectionately to Emily from Shaoxing, 'My dear, more-than-dear, Sister, . . . If I could, I would write you often and long, as I think of you often and much. . . . You are *never* forgotten [underlined five times]. I am greatly cheered . . . the time is drawing near for us to attempt one or more new provinces . . . before the year is out.'

Emily was already doing most of what William and Mary Berger had done, correspondence, account-keeping, publishing and distributing the *Occasional Paper*. So this letter had to deal mostly with business matters. Richard Hill's first letter, written on Christmas Day, apologised for letting so many sea-mails go by without writing. His other letters at intervals frankly confessed that he had taken on too much. As a busy architect and civil engineer he had little time to give to Mission affairs.

To Jennie in Hangzhou Hudson Taylor also wrote frequent love-letters about business and pastoral matters, such as he used to write to Maria. Jungeng, the household servant who had failed them from time to time, had fallen again (Book 4, p 361). 'May the Lord bless and forgive Ah-djün [ie Jungeng]. Could you call on him, God is very forbearing with us – we must be like Him. Send Mr Stevenson the four volumes of Chinese classics (Mr Legge's) which I bought in Hong Kong.' James Legge's great achievement in translating the main Chinese classics into English, to create appreciation by foreigners of the Chinese people, was to win him the first professorial chair in Chinese at Oxford after he retired. Hudson Taylor planned to retrieve these books on a later visit, to provide for his own intellectual needs. Then he set off with Charles Fishe for Ningbo.

China peaceful? 1872–73

The arrest and imprisonment of landowners in Hangzhou who had sold sites to foreigners, was another example of the importance of *fengshui* in the thinking of the people, including the literati (Book 4, Appendix 8). E B Inslee of the American Presbyterian Mission (South) and his colleagues, all young and inexperienced, had been sold some property on the Hill of the City God and had proceeded to build foreign-looking houses. To the scholar-gentry these monstrosities, on the hill and at the south end of the city, significant breaches of *fengshui*, offended every sense of priority, towering as they did over the *yamens* of the high mandarins.[1]

While the imprisonment of the Chinese landowners gave some satisfaction, the safety of all foreigners had been in jeopardy in August 1872, until the intervention of the British and American consuls in Ningbo restored calm and secured the landlords' release. E C Lord was American consul at the time. Friendly consultation then led not only to the Presbyterians handing over their property to the mandarins, but to their reinstatement (in 1874) in 'far more commodious' premises at the north end of the city (again of significance in *fengshui*) and generous compensation for the inconvenience caused. An offending schoolhouse on the hill was pulled down to satisfy the geomancers, but geomancy had to compete with market values. The larger building was allowed to stand, 'perhaps the first foreign house ever owned by Chinese in the interior', H C Du Bose observed. But most interesting in this episode was the readiness of the Hangzhou mandarins to deal reasonably with the offending missionaries, victims of their own neglect or ignorance of the Chinese outlook. Great advances had been made in a decade.

The sudden death of the aged viceroy, Zeng Guofan, at Nanjing in 1872 had removed one of the greatest figures from the Chinese scene – and a dangerous antagonist of the CIM from the Yangzi valley. But greater events were taking place in the capital, Peking, greater than the attempts of the new French envoy to negotiate another treaty, or of the Portuguese to claim jurisdiction over the islands dominating the harbour of Macao.

On April 30, 1872, the boy emperor, Tong Zhi, only son of Yehonala, the Empress Dowager Ci Xi, came of age.[2] Since his accession at the age of 5 in 1861, after the Jehol plot (Book 3, p 257), he had been under the control of his mother and Yong Lu, the imperial Bannerman appointed as his imperial counsellor. 'Passionately devoted to horses and riding' and archery, under Yong

Lu's tuition, Tong Zhi was growing up to be a healthy, intelligent and even precocious boy. By the time he was 12, when by tradition the choice of his future consort and concubines began, Ci Xi had trained him to sit on the Peacock Throne and to repeat what she told him from behind a bamboo screen. But as soon as he was 13 he began to go his own way, sowing his wild oats in the brothels and opium dens outside the palace, and dismissing those who tried to restrain him.

Coming of age at 17, by Chinese reckoning from conception, he had attained the right to make the final choice of his consort and concubines from among the Tartar girls of his own age, or younger, favoured by his regents. Tragically, for he had an unscrupulous mother, he chose the daughter of Chonghou's brother, granddaughter of the Prince of Cheng condemned to death by the bowstring or 'silken cord of self-despatch' in 1861. Ci Xi's choice for him had been the daughter of Yong Lu's friend Feng Hua. 'To compose the feuds' between Manchu clans, Ci Xi accepted the decision, though Alude (A-lu-de), the young empress, would not be as tractable as Feng Hua's daughter who became the first concubine. The wedding ceremony was to be in October, and the *fengshui* experts, the geomancers and astrologers, ordained that the bride should leave her home at 11.30 p m on the 15th and cross the threshold of the imperial palace a few minutes after midnight. In that auspicious half-hour her sedan chair of imperial yellow would be borne in solemn silence through the torch-lit streets.

To the amazement of the foreign envoys in Peking, they were asked by Chonghou, recently back from France, to stay indoors and have no part in the celebrations. The ministers to a man were indignant, sensing an international slight and even danger to foreign interests, for what nation on earth does not give prominence to the respect paid by ambassadors of other nations on such occasions! The French envoy reported that 'the two ministers of the (Zongli) Yamen had been received by Mr Wade with an outburst of anger, by General Vlangaly (the Russian envoy) with a sharp lecture, by Mr Low (the American envoy) in a . . . very disagreeable (manner), while at the Spanish legation they encountered a veritable tempest'.

On October 21 the young emperor decreed that the regency of the two dowager empresses, Ci Xi and Ci An, was soon to end. On November 15 an edict was issued declaring 'His Majesty today assumes control of the government' and on February 23, 1873, a day of yellow bunting and dragon banners at every masthead, Tong Zhi actually assumed control. The very next day the foreign envoys requested an audience, and in April Li Hongzhang, to aid his delicate negotiations over the Taiwan confrontation with the Japanese ambassador, secured for him an audience which was afterwards extended to the representatives of other nations. On June 14, therefore, an imperial decree in condescending tones granted the audience which took place on Sunday, June 29, 1873 – not in the palace but in a garden pavilion in the imperial city where the envoys of tributary states were normally received. Eighty years had passed since Lord Macartney had been denied an audience in 1793 for refusing to *ketou* (kowtow) to the emperor (Book 1, p 91f), and now 'the defiant vassal state' of Japan had been given precedence over the Western nations, at a time when Japan assumed suzerainty over the Ryukyu Islands and China undertook to keep the savage tribes of Taiwan in order.

Alude from the first took a strong interest in the affairs of state, and with Tong Zhi attempted to establish their independence from his domineering mother, Ci Xi. After twelve years in power, Ci Xi was not willing at the age of 37 to be relegated to comparative obscurity. But when Alude was known to be pregnant, Ci Xi saw herself in danger of being displaced even as dowager empress, for having an heir would in time make Alude the dowager. Meanwhile Tong Zhi returned to his dissolute ways.

While Peking was preoccupied with its own affairs, the Muslim rebellion in south-west China was finally quelled with ruthless slaughter. It had been active for nearly twenty years, mainly in the province of Yunnan. Marco Polo, passing through Yunnan (Carajan), in the service of Kublai Khan, had written of encountering Saracens and Nestorians as well as idolaters.[3] Over six centuries later the natural fortress of Dali, walled by mountain ranges with readily defensible passes only on the north and south, was inhabited mainly by Muslims. Known later to the West as Panthays, their appearance was distinctly Han Chinese or Mongol, but often with strongly Arab features as in the north-west.

The first rebellion in 1818 had been followed by others in 1826–28 and 1834–40, but that of 1855 to 1873 was the greatest, with repeated massacres perpetrated by both sides, Chinese and Muslim. At one time the Muslim forces had invested Kunming the provincial capital and controlled most of the province, but with the end of the Taiping rebellion and the release of imperial troops, the Muslims were slowly forced back into the west. The final stand at Dali

A STRONG STRAIN OF ARAB IN A YUNNAN MUSLIM

depended on the defence of Shangguan and Xiaguan, the upper and lower passes, and these were lost by treachery. The traitors themselves were decapitated by the enemy they had helped and on January 19, 1873, according to reports, 30,000 of the 50,000-strong Muslim garrison were put to the sword, with hundreds if not thousands of the common people. On June 10 the fall of Tengyue, near the Burma border, signalled the end of this long rebellion, only less bloodthirsty than the Taiping rebellion itself.[4] So was the south-west 'pacified' and theoretically opened to travel. Twelve years later George Clarke of the CIM described the pathetic lot of Muslim survivors, and after thirty years John McCarthy commented on the abundance of ruins still in evidence. But with peace in 1873

Hudson Taylor's thoughts returned to his dreams of entering China through Burma.

To rescue Charlie
January 1873

High winds, snow and sleet made the journey from Shaoxing to Ningbo in a footboat slow and dangerous. Taking three days to cover ninety miles Hudson Taylor and Charles Fishe arrived to find a storm-damaged city under snow and a welcome by the Goughs, who had lost a chimney. But at Bridge Street they found the church members disheartened and lacklustre, in need of an infusion of faith and teaching through a visit by John Stevenson. They lunched with the Lords and Barchets and caught the steamer to Shanghai, where Hudson Taylor visited 'most of the missionaries' of other missions before boarding the Yangzi steamer for Zhenjiang. 'It does seem *so* long since I left you, yet I have to go further away,' he wrote to Jennie. However, at Zhenjiang on Saturday, January 11, he had to say, 'Here, it is high time I came. . . . In effect Charlie has been out of the Mission for months – or worse.'

As the Zhenjiang city house was empty and unswept they had gone to the Whites. In their comfortable suburban bungalow at the foot of the hill outside, the painful truth came home to Hudson Taylor as the weekend progressed, a revelation more distressing than failure by those members of the team of whom he had never expected much. Instead of living as a Chinese among the Chinese Christians, as intended when left in charge at Zhenjiang by the Judds, Charles had moved in with the independent Whites, an alien among aliens in foreign clothes. By nature receptive to his environment, he had soaked up the Whites' influence.

'The work here is and has been *utterly* neglected,' Hudson Taylor told Jennie after a cheerless Sunday with a disconsolate remnant of Christians. 'Mr Fishe preaching there *sometimes*, not even going into the city to (lead the services). . . . The (Christians) have been perplexed and disheartened, and the wonder is that there (are any of them left).' Their survival could be attributed to Louise Desgraz who, responsible for her school, had done what she could to hold them together. One thing was clear, whatever happened Charles must be kept away from the Whites. 'Goodbye, darling,' wrote Hudson Taylor ending his letter to Jennie, 'I must go to my cold, lonely house in the city.' He at least would choose to live among the Chinese. To McCarthy he confided, 'I have had many thoughts which I do not care to put on paper.' He was planning on taking Miss Potter with Jennie to Nanjing, and to keep Charles under his eye too. For Charles it would clearly be a rescue operation demanding patience and perseverance, but he seemed to be responding.

Moving into the city house paid off at once. The evangelist, inactive in imitation of his missionary colleagues, had 'fallen into gross sin' and had to be suspended. 'We *all* need helping,' Hudson Taylor commented. How he dealt with this situation held lessons for the Mission. Because of the low morale he must show that he cared. He invited the fourteen church members and 'inquirers' – 'to dine with me tomorrow, Sunday, after the morning service. . . . They will soon look *up*, with God's blessing, if they are looked *after*.' He had twelve good Christians to work with, the nucleus of a potentially thriving church, and enlisted one as a colporteur. The school-work was important, too. He bought land above Louise's girls' school (the memorial to Maria) to build a boys' school. That would show Zhenjiang was not forgotten.

Sending Charles to Nanjing to get the house ready, on January 22 he himself was on his way to Hangzhou to bring Jennie and Miss Potter back. Nanjing was another difficult place, resistant to the gospel, still a pioneering situation more than five years after Duncan had begun there. Hudson Taylor intended to stay with Jennie until after her baby was born, so what better than to preach the gospel and plant a church, with her and Charles to help. Nanjing was central to the northern field of the Mission. He would be within easy reach of Zhenjiang and Yangzhou by river steamer, and with the other Yangzi cities, Wuhu, Anqing and Jiujiang, too. To take down the foreign scaffolding and leave established churches in Chinese hands was his dominant thought, moving his foreign missionaries to pioneer new regions – if they were willing to do it.

'If we are well supplied with funds,' he wrote to Emily as he travelled, 'we may make a long stride, DV, this year. If not, we must hold on in faith. . . . CTF has been a *wet blanket* (in Zhenjiang) for some time, I fear – of course without intending it. . . . If our native helpers improve as they are doing, we shall soon *need* very few foreign helpers for our older work. If we have a few men of the right stamp, we shall soon see more than one unoccupied province invaded.'

In another letter to the Bergers he also wrote frankly about arrogance towards the Chinese on the part of some missionaries, and their influence on Charles. 'One of my objects in going (to

Nankin) is to be *alone* with him. I hope . . . to talk over these matters with him alone . . . for I should be so sorry for a young and devoted missionary to be spoiled, as dozens [in various missions] have been, in this way.' The Chinese Christians were developing well, he went on, and 'I hope we may be able to break ground in several new provinces within the next three years.'

He had been away from Jennie for a month when he arrived at Hangzhou on the 28th, and was off again directly after celebrating the Chinese New Year with the church – but this time with her in his big footboat and Miss Potter and her Chinese companion in another.

Attrition   *October 1872–May 1873*

Henry Reid's unannounced arrival in London after abandoning Suzhou caused more surprise than he himself received when Hudson Taylor wrote to tell him he should not think of returning to China. Both knew how damaging the Yangzhou riot had been to his emotional balance, and his injured eye was unhealed. When the Council made generous allowance for the shock and injuries he had suffered, refunding his travelling expenses, Hudson Taylor saw further than they and warned that no unauthorised expenditure should be refunded. It would open the door to irresponsibility. But after his return home to Banff, Henry Reid addressed a letter to the friends of the Mission which was published in the *Occasional Paper*. His experiences in China had so shattered his nervous system he said, as 'thoroughly to unfit me for a sphere where courage is so essential. My acquaintance with Mr Taylor has been one of unbroken fellowship, and I cannot resign . . . without testifying to his abounding kindness to us . . . to his holiness of life . . . and more than ordinary self-denial and gentleness.' He could hardly have bowed out more gracefully, but once again the lesson was not lost on Hudson Taylor or the council: zealous people, however attractive, do not necessarily make good missionaries; the assessment of applicants' personalities before they entered the Mission mattered profoundly. Two years later Hudson Taylor wrote that Reid was not only losing the sight of his injured eye but would probably lose that of the other also, by 'sympathetic ophthalmia'.

When George and Catherine Duncan and their child arrived unannounced in London with Mary Bowyer in attendance, ten days after Reid, the shock for the council was even greater, for the tall

Highlander was a physical wreck, 'very broken down'. For two weeks the Duncans stayed with the Meadows family, until the doctors sent them to Torquay among friends of the Mission, in a last desperate bid to let the mild climate and sea air do what no other known treatment could do to heal him.

Emily Blatchley felt deeply for him, knowing how hard she had found it to accept the inevitable. His phthisis was only a stage more advanced than her own. On November 25, 1872, she wrote to Henrietta Soltau (herself nursing her very sick father and sister at Barnstaple). 'He *craves* for restoration to health.' She could wish him to be submissive to God's will, and better still, to delight in it as she was learning to do.

She knew Hudson Taylor as well as he knew her, and she had known George Duncan on days of confession, prayer and worship, on the *Lammermuir*, in Hangzhou and since the Yangzhou riot. When he died on February 12, 1873, aged only 29, it was Emily who wrote for the *Occasional Paper* extolling his faithfulness, his indomitable perseverance, his faith at Nanjing in the Drum Tower days (Book 4, p 366) and his courage in staying at Yangzhou when he arrived to find the riot beginning. To 'the comfort afforded by his presence and help, and calm self-possession in the face of danger and death,' she could testify from personal experience. His success in pointing Chinese to Christ and tending an infant church at Nanjing where 'there is hardly a corner or street or teashop in the whole place where the gospel has not been proclaimed by (him)', was only secondary to his greatest gift, of being 'essentially a pioneer'. The church at Qingjiangpu was another star in his crown. After his illness had taken a serious turn, he had also added James Meadows' responsibility at Anqing to his own, and had undertaken his longest exploratory journeys in Anhui. At the end, in great pain, 'his patience in suffering (not natural to him), his submission to the will of God, and his thankfulness (showed how) his spirit was ripening'. Dying, he named some of his Chinese friends, and his last words were 'Bless the Lord, O . . . (my soul)!'

Death claimed so many in 1873. Emily's thoughts and the Taylors' were often turned to think about it. Henry Venn died on January 13; William Pennefather on April 30; and on May 11 Richard Hill wrote to say that Lucy Soltau had just died and Henry W Soltau, their father, was sinking. On March 4 Griffith John's wife died on reaching Singapore, on their way to China. Robert Howard of Tottenham had died, and on May 3 the great missionary explorer of Africa, David Livingstone, died kneeling by his camp-bed. When word came in May that Emily herself was finding it hard to keep going, the impression Hudson Taylor received was that her end must be near. He suffered pangs he could have been spared, for she was still working hard. He had written every month, however busy he was, taking her into his confidence. Had he asked too much of her? She must not economise on food or warmth, but perhaps he had written too late. To lose her would be far too costly a price to pay.

'I wish you *definitely* to get (secretarial help). . . . If you break down where will things be?' – seeing the honorary secretaries were not coping. She should ask Catherine Duncan to give a year to helping her. 'She would be happy with you . . . and she loves us and the dear children.' But had he misjudged her strength? In May he wrote 'My own dear Ae-me' [dialect for Aimei] and again, after some stern pages of business, 'I don't like to send you such wretched letters, when you send me such dear, loving, long ones'. Happily married to Jennie, her closest friend, with perhaps only months remaining to Emily for such candour, he knew he was on safe ground in writing 'May God bless you, my own *dear* Ae-me'.

Teething troubles in London   October 1872–May 1873

Apart from carrying a heavy share of routine work on behalf of the secretaries and council, Emily was finding herself to be Hudson Taylor's mouthpiece, in duty bound to speak out when she learned of their acting, through misunderstanding, in conflict with the Mission's policies. 'You *must* pray for me, dear, dear Brother. I cannot be blind to the fact that as yet the real responsibility of the work at home rests on me. Mr Challice told me the other day that the Council do depend on me.' As treasurer he had such confidence in her account-keeping that he saw no need of frequent checks on it. 'Mr Challice *now* sees (since I had a talk with him about it) that we are right in not making collections or asking for money . . . though he did not when you left. I wish *all* the Council did. I must seek an opportunity of talking with Mr Weatherley about it. He as good as asked for money yesterday, though he had just said, "We do not ask".' She signed herself 'Your loving Me-me', the Chinese for 'little sister'.

She was writing during the Mildmay Conference of packed audiences overflowing even outside the great hall, though it held three thousand.[5] She herself had been asked to join Charles Judd and Grattan Guinness in addressing a garden meeting with the Earl of Cavan as chairman. His concern for China had been reawakened, he said, by Elizabeth Judd whom Lady Cavan had invited to their home. After the meeting a Mrs Grace of High Wycombe came up to Emily and promised to give £50 annually to the CIM – and later gave Charles Judd £140 for opening a new station. Grattan Guinness and James Meadows had been touring a number of cities together, speaking about China and calling on young men to commit their lives to Christ, to serve him there. As a result, a young medical student named Arthur William Douthwaite was to attend Guinness's training institute and the London Hospital before sailing with Meadows in February 1874. Douthwaite was to become one of China's notable missionaries, decorated by the emperor.

Guinness moved shortly afterwards to Mile End, and opened the East London Institute for Home and Foreign Missions at Stepney Green, Bow Road, in the poorest part of London, to be among the narrow alleyways and undrained streets with sounds and smells resembling those of distant parts of the earth. He wanted to accustom his student missionaries to life and evangelism in the roughest and most demanding conditions. He himself wrote 'I selected East London as a training sphere because it contained the largest number of people of any dark and needy district in England' – and because Tom Barnardo was there, but also because of its association with the CIM at Coborn Street. As 'a natural result many of our early students selected China as their sphere and became connected with the China Inland Mission . . . about a hundred . . . some of them numbered among the martyrs. . . . It would be impossible to estimate the results for good . . . throughout the world' from Hudson Taylor's making his home in East London.

The Institute had made a tentative beginning when Richard Hill wrote to Hudson Taylor on February 18, 1873, a letter which must have alarmed him by its lack of understanding of what the secretaries had undertaken to do.

> By the time I have sent receipts and a letter to the almost daily batch of donors, I have done about as much as I have time for – and H Soltau being divided into three parts, viz., secular calling, 'Lamb and Flag' work and CIM has of course little time left. . . . I fear that I may have seemed to aim at what I cannot get through. [He was right. The

Bergers had carried more, without an Emily to relieve them of half
the load.]

Mr G (Guinness) has taken a house in Stepney for a temporary
training place for candidates, with a view to Spain, China and other
parts of the mission field. He tells me that he will attend to their
spiritual training and they will practise mission work in Barnardo's
district. Barnardo will reside in the house as major domo – I don't
know how far he will have private spiritual influence over them.
Some people think he is not old enough for the post, but Mr G
considers him precisely the man for it.[6]

The Institute soon moved into its permanent quarters at Harley
House, near Coborn Street, Bow, and became known as Harley
College. In the next twenty-one years, Grattan Guinness trained
and sent abroad 588 men and women, to every continent, in thirty
different societies, including some which he himself founded; and
under his son, Dr Harry Guinness, the Institute trained almost as
many more.

The first meeting of the London Council after Hudson Taylor's
departure in October 1872 had been concerned with the application
of a candidate named Frederick Groombridge, one of Charles
Haddon Spurgeon's students. 'Having had him under his eye for
two years,' Spurgeon gave him 'the highest character', and George
Soltau after seeing him in action at his Clerkenwell mission found
him 'very intelligent and spiritually advanced . . . indefatigable in
visiting, his heart being entirely taken up with missionary work'. So
he was accepted 'without any further hesitation'. A physician who
had been a missionary passed him as fit for China, and Groombridge
left with another, John Donovan, 'a true Cockney from Limehouse'
on December 31, 1872. The council were to learn that appearances
can be most deceptive, and references may suffer from an uncon-
scious bias.

Donovan had had an unfavourable 'past history', Grattan Guinness warned, but as his referees considered him a reformed character he, too, was accepted by the council as fit to go. Both signed
agreements to work under Hudson Taylor's direction and to wear
Chinese dress 'and not to discontinue to do so without first conferring with the Director of the Mission'. Almost from their arrival in
China they were to be more trouble than use, finally finding secular
employment before returning home. The assessment of candidates
would never be easy and would always be more the concern of the
Mission abroad than of those entrusted with the decision at home.

Restoring order   *February–May 1873*

It was Emily who notified Hudson Taylor of the expected sailing of Groombridge and Donovan from Marseilles on January 5, but her letter reached him on February 23 after they had arrived at Shanghai on the 13th. Fortunately she had wisely repeated the information in a later letter, of December 19, which outstripped the first and reached Hudson Taylor on the 13th. John McCarthy was to have met them but had been delayed. Instead Charles Fishe, still in foreign dress, tracked them down on February 24 when they had already spent ten days listening to Shanghai opinions of Hudson Taylor and his principles. To repair the damage Hudson Taylor took them under his own care at Nanjing, and introduced them to Chinese clothes and Chinese ways; but before long they chose to follow the majority, rejecting his advice and their own promises made in London, in favour of being foreign in appearance and behaviour. Groombridge showed signs of having advanced tuberculosis and Donovan was so uneducated that Hudson Taylor wondered whether he would ever learn the language.

'Nanjing has proved hard ground,' he wrote, 'but we must sow in hope.' By showing 'magic lantern' slides to draw a crowd he was soon preaching the gospel to two hundred who came in spite of persistent opposition by Muslims. The few Christians were encouraged and within a few weeks the hopefulness George Duncan had instilled in them was returning. Li Lanfeng arrived to be their pastor-evangelist, they were organised as a church, and Hudson Taylor was free to give his attention to other cities.

Again he confided in Emily,

> We sadly want some real men with enough faith in God to trust Him and do His work, and a good, not an irritable conscience . . . one that worries about everything. . . . Kiss the dear children for me. How I wish I could save you the trouble! [He was hoping to get Herbert and Howard into the City of London School.] A little rough discipline might . . . make them strike their roots deeper, give you more hold of their affections, make them men not girls. . . . Expensive schools beget expensive habits, cheap ones often lead to vulgar habits, so it is very difficult to know . . . what to do.

Inflation was affecting all missions, and receipts in Britain were low, but how was it, he asked Richard Hill, that Major Malan's donation of £100 had not been forwarded to China? There was no need to wait for a larger sum to accumulate before transmitting it. In mid-March he had reached the point of having 'not a cent of money in hand' – after instructing Tsiu and a colleague to rent premises in Wuhu. The Yangzi advance was as much part of the ongoing commitment of the Mission as feeding its members, and donations had been given specifically for that. To Rudland he wrote, 'I have not a dollar in hand for all the expenses of the Mission. The Lord doubtless *will* provide; it is specially for His glory to do so now, as many doubtless thought we were trusting to Mr Berger before.'

Never since the Mission began had such a situation developed. Yet the funds were there, in London. With greater political stability in China he judged the opportunities to be more promising than ever. To Emily, Hudson Taylor had confessed 'I am much crippled just now for want of Mission funds. . . . It seems to me that our good friends have forgotten that the main object of *all* the home operations is the reception and transmission of funds *to China*. I've been in China nearly four months, and not a penny has been sent.' He had been reduced to using his personal funds for Mission purposes. To her he could say, if the work was to grow, a steady supply would be essential. 'We shall require £250 a month, besides Mr Müller's remittances (which were) uncertain, both as to time and amount.' The secretaries should send fortnightly all they had available. Emily's role was a difficult one, to coach the secretaries into dealing with God, not men, when they had little in hand to transmit, but she succeeded.

Then, at last, gifts including £50 from the Bergers, as friendly as ever, and a transmission of £300 from the secretaries eased the difficulties. But why did Emily rather than Richard Hill send two cheques that did arrive, for £100 and £150, without explanation from either of them? Was each expecting the other to do it? Tactfully he tried to show Hill that the arrangements he had made were falling between two stools, that Emily was carrying too much, that funds received must flow, for they were constantly needed in China. He explained at length what they were used for, and how he did his best to provide each missionary with a remittance at regular intervals. 'I need scarcely say the missionaries themselves know nothing of these calculations. . . . They look to the Lord [and receive provision through various channels including Mr Müller's Institute], but so far as *I* can, I seek to know and supply their need, and so to supply it as to keep them in circumstances of moderate comfort' – by the standards of the CIM.

Richard Hill had misunderstood a request from William Berger, to be allowed to know 'the state of the funds' from time to time, as a request to be informed when funds were needed. Berger wrote to Hudson Taylor, 'I did not desire to be informed of the low state of the funds whenever that might arise – far from it. . . . I might not be able or willing to carry (the burden).' He had no thought of being 'responsible for any need there might be'!

The confusion was understandable, and Hudson Taylor replied, 'The only question in my mind was this, Should your enquiry come at a time when our funds were low, how far could we consistently, *at the time*, give this information?' That, too, was straightened out with the secretaries. A frank answer to a frank question would leave an enquirer with what he had asked for, without in any way being solicitation of help. His action then would be his own affair, between himself and the Lord. On May 2 William Berger wrote giving approval of the Yangzhou building fund (to which he had contributed generously) being used for other purposes while building was impossible – but he would prefer it to go to established work rather than to extension in the present circumstances.

Another complication was the fact that Jennie's legacy from her uncle in Australia was coming into her correspondence with her father and others. Joseph Weatherley, Richard Hill and Henry Soltau, as the trustees, were to invest it and remit the interest to her. Instead of welcoming it as a steady source of personal income, at a time of perplexity she wrote, 'I should like to dedicate all my interest for the furtherance of God's work in different ways and . . . to have some of the principal at command for the same purpose. God has all along cared for our personal need, and I shall feel happiest in still looking to Him for the supply of our ordinary wants.' And again to her mother, 'You must not think that because I want £1,000 of the principal of my money sent out here that I shall be reckless with it. . . . If it can be used for China wisely at any time, surely that is not waste, but the best way of putting it out to interest that I know.' The trouble was that such mature thinking looked immature to those who knew little of trusting God as she did from day to day.[7]

Not only the Zhenjiang church had been neglected. Keeping clear of Yangzhou lest he draw T F Wade's attention to himself and the Mission's presence there, Hudson Taylor learned from the Chinese that the Yangzhou Christians were also 'in a bad way'. 'They are more to be pitied than blamed, for they have not been fed or watched over as young Christians need.' Edward Fishe, the resident missionary, was not sufficiently able, and his wife, Annie (Bohannan), had been ill for six months. But the critical expiry date of the contract made after the second Yangzhou plot was approaching. Long-term renewal of the lease would make possible a new attempt to establish a strong church. In April Hudson Taylor told his mother, 'The time for the owners [the *daotai* and his friend] to give us notice if they wished us to leave Yangchau has passed. They have not done so.' It therefore looked as if the plot and Zeng Guofan's attempts to oust him had died with the old viceroy himself. The time had come to act.

Meanwhile in Nanjing hardly had funds arrived and that particular problem diminished, than Jennie went into labour, on Saturday morning, April 12. After twenty-four hours she was exhausted and at dawn on Sunday Hudson Taylor anxiously sent a message asking a Dr Macartney, attached to the Nanjing arsenal, to come and advise him. He spent most of Sunday with them. But Jennie went into convulsions and afterwards did not know her husband. At 1.30 p m a stillborn boy was born, and when Dr Macartney left they thought all was well. Not until nightfall did they know there was an unborn twin! She went into labour again on Monday afternoon, 14th, and gave birth to a stillborn girl at 11 p m. Typically resilient and matter-of-fact, Jennie recovered quickly and told her mother, 'It was a very intensely anxious time for (Hudson)'. She was looking forward to moving to Yangzhou in mid-May, making it their base while putting the church back on its feet, and to working and travelling with him again.

China's hope   1873

Returning to China with a mental picture of a team in each province and established churches actively reproducing themselves, Hudson Taylor had found his first priority to be rescue operations. Long letters about struggling colleagues and dwindling funds, flagging evangelists and dispirited church members, also carried shafts of confidence. Stripling churches, however few their numbers, he saw as not only good potential but as the source of workers to plant more churches in other towns and cities. To wait for their own local church to be strong was unnecessary. The fact of contributing to the expansion of the Church at large would strengthen the sending church. The absence of several foreign missionaries from China in this respect had its advantages.

CHINESE CHRISTIANS PREACHING TO A WAYSIDE AUDIENCE
(from a visual aid: black stands for sin; red for the blood of Christ; white for a cleansed heart; gold for eternal glory)

In asking John McCarthy in February to take up George Duncan's work in Anhui and carry it into every one of the province's eight prefectures, Hudson Taylor also had the good of Hangzhou in mind. He planned to go there himself but to be busy with administrative work while delegating much of McCarthy's work to Chinese. They would have him and Wang Lae-djün, their pastor, to consult while they found their feet. Complete devolution to the church would follow naturally. Already Wang Lae-djün would not accept a salary; 'he really looks to God for his sustenance'.

If we can remain in China for a time [he explained in a letter to Emily] the Mission may be put on an entirely new footing, I think. I am striving to make the work more and more *native* and *interior*, so as to be workable with as few foreign helpers as possible.

[And to his mother a week later] I am aiming at such organization of our forces, as will make us able to do more work with fewer foreign missionaries. I think I may *eventually* attain to one superintendent and two assistant foreign missionaries in a province, with qualified (Chinese) helpers in each important city, and colporteurs in the less important places. *I hope* I may be able ere the year closes to commence a college for the more thorough training of our native helpers. Long desired, there is more *probability* of our attaining this than heretofore.

[In June he added] Pioneers are trying in several parts of (Anhui) to establish themselves. . . . The path of patient perseverance in well-doing, of voluntary taking up of the Cross, of forbearance under annoyance, and even persecution, without attempted retaliation is a difficult one; none perfectly pursue it; those whose work involves much of it need our special prayers.

[And in July, 1873, in a statement of classic significance in the strategy of mission] The work . . . is steadily growing and spreading – especially in that most important department, *native* help. The helpers themselves need much help, much care and instruction; but they are growing more and *more efficient* as well as more numerous; and the future hope of China doubtless lies in *them*. I look on all us foreign missionaries as platform work round a rising building; the sooner it can be dispensed with the better; or rather, the sooner it can be transferred to other places, to serve the same temporary purpose, the better for the work sufficiently forward to dispense with it, and the better for the places yet to be evangelized. As for difficulties and sorrows, their name is legion. Some spring from the nature of the work, some from the nature of the workers. Here Paul and Barnabas cannot see eye to eye; there Peter so acts as to need public rebuke; while elsewhere private exhortation is required.[8]

Hope for China lay in trained Christians, and the missionary scaffolding (not necessarily foreign) being moved elsewhere. This fundamental principle has been repeated, forgotten, and revived again and again in the century since then, until today it is the keystone of missionary strategy.

As early as February Jennie was telling her parents, 'We want to draw off our strength from the places near the coast with a view to more and more work.' And Hudson Taylor told Richard Hill, 'I do so hope to see some of the destitute provinces evangelized. I long for it by day and pray for it by night. Can He care less for it?' In March he went on, 'I find our present position – trying in some respects from the absence of so many (missionaries) – most favourable for the extension of our work, and for the redivision of the outstations. This . . . with God's blessing may result in our very soon having a new and very extensive work in hand.'

The most mature Christians were from the longer-established churches in Zhejiang, but the mandarin-speaking Christians of the Yangzi valley were more recently converted and untaught. His plan was therefore to send a mature Christian, whatever his dialect, with a newer one, to teach and train him while working together.[9] It would be costly, but 'I must ask you . . . and all members of the council to help by believing prayer in the name of Jesus, and we will go forward and trust Him not to fail us.'

To George Müller he could say, 'The work is generally *very* cheering' and found great pleasure in adding, 'Miss J McLean, formerly of our Mission, is now working for the Lord here in Shanghai faithfully . . . looking to Him only for support.' Hudson Taylor had himself contributed to her expenses and would gladly be the channel of donations if George Müller or others wished to help her anonymously. By May Hudson Taylor's notes to Jennie were also about his deployment of Chinese and foreign missionaries. Administration, writing for the *Occasional Paper*, travelling or doctoring, his thoughts were seldom far from this theme.

With John McCarthy's departure to Anqing leaving his family at Zhenjiang, and Mr Tsiu at Wuhu, the development of the 'Yangzi strategy' took a stride forward. To thwart McCarthy when he seemed determined to stay in the property he rented in Anqing, the wily landowner erected another building at the entrance in such a way that access to the Mission house was through a pigsty. With few callers willing to negotiate this obstacle, and with such a landlord, the only course for McCarthy was to move. He found another house and began work. 'McCarthy is about to attempt a *great* work for God,' Hudson Taylor told Emily, 'greater than he is aware of', while to Richard Hill he said of the eight prefectures McCarthy hoped to occupy, so far 'he has had two (Chinese) pioneers for some time in two of the cities of this province (of Anhui)'.

Mr Tsiu, as one of the most mature and tested members of the team, had a recent convert named Han to train at Wuhu – none other than the proprietor of the inn at which the Meadows family and James Williamson had lived before the Anqing riot. Two others had already been at Huizhou for seven months, and two more were beginning at Guangdezhou, each pair a hundred and more miles apart from the others (maps pp 38, 334). By June two were added, at Hoyuezhou and Datong, halfway between Anqing and Wuhu, where Mr Tsiu established another bridgehead and Hudson Taylor found him 'surrounded by friendly people'. Tsiu's going from Wuhu left Mr Han and another new Anqing convert to spread the gospel at Wuhu. The seed had taken time to germinate, but when it did George Duncan had been there in Anqing to teach and then baptise them. The churches in Anqing and Wuhu today can look back to these beginnings. McCarthy's work was to visit and encourage all these men, discussing their problems and joining in their work. He himself was a hard worker who gave himself to his task and accomplished it.

Farther up the Yangzi beyond Anqing, J E Cardwell's ambitious pioneering with Lo Ganfu, the converted soldier (p 333) was meeting with both success and opposition. Based at Jiujiang since December 1869 and travelling widely in his 'mission boat' since March 1871, he had visited hundreds of cities, towns and villages and sold thousands of Old and New Testaments, Gospels and Christian books.[10] Between Ningbo and Wenzhou the CIM had nine or ten stations and outstations, but between Jiujiang and the southern city in Jiangxi province called Fuzhou, not one outpost of the gospel existed. In September he travelled far to the south of the Poyang Lake and Nanchang, the provincial capital (map, p 294), following the Gan river beyond Ji'an to Wan'an, 400 miles from Jiujiang, before turning for home again.

With Lo Ganfu and the three other soldiers and two Daoist priests who became Christians through his testimony, Cardwell had a training class of future missionaries. 'It is my heart's desire and daily prayer, that the Lord may send me four or five more such men, so as to form a class of students who shall . . . be fitted to work in the interior. . . . Our household now numbers sixteen souls,' including three orphan boys whom he was employing someone to teach. Such good letters told also of a Buddhist priest who, on professing to believe, had abandoned his robes and joined the class, but before long proved to be an opium addict out for what he could get! Of seventeen candidates for baptism, seven were soldiers. Forbidden by their mandarin on threat of beheading to attend his teaching, after the first scare they were coming surreptitiously. 'Oh, these officials!' Cardwell wrote. 'When will they cease to be the barriers of all true religious, social, moral, intellectual and political progress?' An anti-Christian riot against the American Methodist Episcopal Mission twenty-five miles away at Ruichang (Shuichang in the reports) early in 1873, was traced to the local literati, but the Cardwells met with no personal animosity.[11]

Zhejiang had been the nursery of all this growing Church, and continued to provide evangelists, colporteurs, Scripture readers and schoolteachers from its thriving congregations, although the peculiarity of its dialects handicapped the Christians at any distance from their homes. Apart from the American Baptists, and Miles Knowlton in particular, who penetrated the province to the south-east of Ningbo, most other Zhejiang missions still worked on the principle of concentrating on Ningbo, Hangzhou, Shaoxing and a few outstations.[12] Since three other missions had joined him in Shaoxing, John Stevenson was giving more time to the new churches in Sheng Xian and Xinchang in keeping with the CIM's policy to move onwards as others followed them. The Confucian scholar Ning, the 'man of uncommon ability', and his family were being persecuted for their faith and thereby drawing attention to it, so that more conversions resulted. At Taizhou, too, was one of the most progressive churches, keeping William Rudland stretched to seize his opportunities. 'No part of our work gives greater promise at the present time than the country outstations of Taichau,' Hudson Taylor wrote. 'Had we more suitable (Chinese) helpers, their number could be rapidly increased.' At one responsive village a new Christian bought a Buddhist nunnery, threw out its idols and furnished it as a chapel. The fact was widely known and talked about.

Miles Knowlton, looking back over a decade since the end of the Taiping rebellion, reported a fivefold increase in the number of Chinese preachers in the province, from fifteen or twenty to one hundred, and of Christians from four hundred to over fourteen

A TEMPLE ENTRANCE

hundred communicants. 'In view of the assertion often made, that the converts are all from the ignorant and un-influential classes, (it should be noted) that over a hundred . . . are literary men; a number of them having literary degrees, and several have obtained their degrees since having become Christians.' Knowlton himself, renowned among Chinese for his Confucian excellence of character, baptised sixteen literary men. But his days were numbered. He died of acute dysentery (and his wife and daughter barely survived) on September 10, 1874.[13]

A new phase of the Church in China had become discernible – a Church becoming strong enough to play the major role in the empire's evangelisation.

North or west?   *March–August 1873*

When Hudson Taylor told Emily Blatchley in January 1873 about his hopes of making 'a long stride' upcountry, the man he largely set his hopes upon had returned to Britain with an exhausted wife. Elizabeth Judd, a great spirit in a diminutive body, could not keep pace with her powerful and impatient husband. 'She will never recover while he is in England,' Hudson Taylor dared to say. But after a break of a few months he should be able to return, and Hudson Taylor was counting on him to take the longest stride. Again it was to Emily rather than the preoccupied secretaries that he explained his plans. With too many irons in the fire and failing to attend to detail, so that Hudson Taylor's accounts with London were becoming impossible to keep, Hill and Soltau could be spared tentative information about immature plans for the future. Emily could be trusted to pray, to comment wisely, and to share her knowledge only with discreet friends. 'Our present thought . . . (when) Judd comes, (is) to send him if possible to pioneer to the west or north in some wholly unoccupied province,' but nothing must come to the ears of the minister at Peking. Even the fact that McCarthy was buying land in Anqing with a view to building must be kept very quiet. 'It is *most important* that this be not made public, as Mr Wade would certainly cause us trouble if he knew it' – legal though all the plans were by Chinese and British law.

The two major possibilities for strategic advance were, firstly, northwards up the Grand Canal from Qingjiangpu, across the old bed of the Yellow River and into Henan province and southern Shandong. With this in mind, Hudson Taylor determined to go himself and gain some impressions of that route. Secondly, westwards, beyond Jiujiang to Wuchang and Hankou (now the metropolis of Wuhan), which could form a mission base. Always studying his map, his mind dwelt on the great heartland of Hubei with Henan and Shaanxi to its north, and Hunan to the south, leading on to the south-western provinces of Guizhou and Yunnan with their aboriginal tribes. Westward beyond Hubei, far up the Yangzi river, was Sichuan, the teeming rice-bowl province bordering Tibet. To go northwards might be limited in scope, but would be a natural

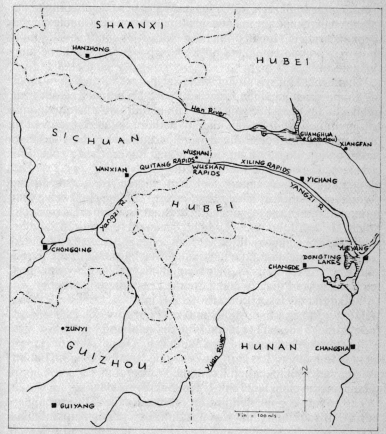

KEY TO THE WEST: THE UPPER YANGZI, HAN AND YÜAN RIVERS

extension from Yangzhou with communication by canal-boat. To go west, far up the Yangzi, would have the advantage of river steamers to the base at Wuhan and beyond to the mouth of the Wushan gorges, the gateway of Sichuan. This was the more ambitious choice, the one that said, 'Every province shall be opened to the gospel and at that, soon.'

The claims of the northern option Hudson Taylor set aside for the present. Apart from everything else, it would be more directly under the observation of Wade. To Charles Judd he wrote from Nanjing on March 13, 1873, suggesting that he leave his wife and children to recuperate at home while he returned to China for a year of pioneering in Hunan or Sichuan. Meadows could possibly do it, but with a good command of the Ningbo dialect would be more valuable in Zhejiang.

On May 21 Hudson Taylor wrote again, carefully weighing up the pros and cons on which Judd must base his decision. Even if the whole family came back together, pioneering would involve months of separation from one another. Whether they were prepared for the personal sacrifice involved in either choice, they must decide for themselves. Judd took his time and had not reached a conclusion when the London Council met on July 27.[14]

Hankou and Wuchang had had missionaries of LMS and Wesleyan Methodist Missionary Society (WMMS) for twelve years already, and of the American Protestant Episcopal Church since 1868. Griffith John of the LMS had been there since 1861 and had baptised 353 adults by 1875. Medical colleagues had joined him for part of this time, and in 1868 Alexander Wylie and Griffith John had made their dangerous journey through Sichuan to Chengdu, north to Hanzhong in Shaanxi and down the Han river to its junction with the Yangzi at Hankou ('mouth of the Han').[15] A great stride for the CIM would be in their wake until new territory was explored and settled work began far beyond Wuhan (map, pp 28, 379).

Josiah Cox had been the first Wesleyan to reach Hankou, in 1862 at Griffith John's invitation, and the saintly David Hill and W Scarborough had arrived in 1865. Scarborough's journey up the Han river to Laohekou (now Guanghua) beyond Xiangfan, was the most ambitious since Griffith John's. In a decade they had baptised a total of 104 adults. Progress was difficult and slow, and there was ample room for more missionaries even in these Wuhan cities, but Hudson Taylor's intention was primarily to use Wuhan as a springboard.

He had other thoughts as well. With Charlie Fishe unready to take up the responsibilities he had relinquished through his long illness, what the Mission in China most needed was an administrator who could set Hudson Taylor free to lead in the fieldwork, the advanced pioneering, evangelism and church planting. He therefore appealed to Henry Soltau to wind up his professional and personal commitments at home and to come without delay.

> Had I here the co-operation of *one* able, thoroughly reliable, fellow-worker, of faith in God, tact and influence with our missionaries, I should say that in three years' time our work might be doubled in extent and increased manyfold in usefulness. But here I have no one who is sufficiently superior, educationally *and* mentally *and* spiritually, to the others to take the position I propose. C T Fishe is very nice and gentlemanly, and is superior to any of the others in education, but he has no *power* in him. McCarthy is by far the most useful of our workers, but I need him in the work, which is his forte, and for the post I propose he is not adapted.
>
> Now, my dear Brother, will you not come out and go into the work with me? There is a sort of lull [in opposition and counter-claims] which is opportune for extending the work into new provinces; we have several converts from provinces which are destitute of missionaries, who may with God's blessing be of great help. . . . And other things . . . lead me to hope that ere long we may be able to take a decided step in advance towards the fulfilment of the prayer of some years – the preaching of the gospel in every province of China proper.
>
> Is it not a worthy object, can *any* sacrifice be too great to hasten its realization? Is not He whom we serve deserving of *all* our time, our strength, our powers? If you come you can bring with you others to help in this great work and can exert an influence over many at home, which few could do, as well as one (too) which your position as Hon. Sec. entitles you to. . . . China is so large, the work so great and so widespread, that without further help, our onward progress will be greatly retarded.
>
> I do not write in any hasty excitement. I know as much, perhaps, of the difficulty of obtaining what I propose, as most do. I know, too, something of the sacrifice which this step would involve to you. But in view of eternity can we weigh these things? Each of these provinces is as large as an European kingdom, can we seriously contemplate their populations of 15, 20, 25 millions each, and be willing to leave them to perish?

Two months later he returned to the subject before a reply could have reached him. 'I hope that you and your sister (Henrietta) and

Miss Faulding (Nellie) will join us this year.' Again in April he
confessed to a strong urge to exhort Soltau to consider the strong
case in Scripture for leaving his secular occupations to give his whole
time to God's service. Could he not trust the Lord to supply all his
needs? 'Our eyes must be upon *the Lord*, not upon His people. *His*
means – not *ours*, not *theirs*, but *His* means are large; and to a
faithful steward He will prove a *faithful* master.'

'I do wish Mr Soltau had faith to cast himself upon God,' Hudson
Taylor wrote to Emily. 'I wish you could find time to talk to and pray
with him about it.' But Lucy Soltau's and their father's last illnesses
preoccupied Henry while the seed-thought germinated, to take
dramatic effect a year later. Meanwhile Theodore Howard, a son
of Robert Howard, had joined the London Council, taking the
chair on January 20, 1873.[16]

On July 18, Hudson Taylor and Jennie set out from Zhenjiang,
picked up Groombridge and Donovan at Nanjing, and went on in
houseboats up the Yangzi to introduce them to travelling evangelism in China. Calling at each city where Chinese and foreign
missionaries of the CIM were based, they visited Mr Tsiu at Datong,
and the Chinese holding the fort at Anqing while McCarthy was
away. To hold a communion service in the house from which the
Meadows family had been ejected in 1869 seemed symbolic of
victory against all odds.

Leaving Jennie and Donovan there, Hudson Taylor took Groombridge on to the Cardwells at Jiujiang to put him in the care of an
English doctor.[17] His tuberculosis had advanced so alarmingly as to
threaten his survival. 'Sometimes I think (he) will not live through
the winter', Hudson Taylor wrote. Before long the poor man
resigned, and after a period in Shanghai returned home to die. Both
Groombridge and Miss Potter had been passed as fit by the same
London doctor, yet now she was not even well enough to go home
by ship. When it transpired that Groombridge had followed her to
China in order to propose marriage, only to be rejected, a tragic
series of mistakes was exposed, which cost much money and effort
before they were both back in Britain again. She died in July 1874,
and he not long afterwards.

A sidelight is thrown on Hudson Taylor's life by his mention in a
letter from Jiujiang that eighty-nine letters were waiting for him
there. He dealt with sixty-seven to catch the mail steamer and took
the rest on with him, collected Jennie and Donovan at Anqing,
returned to Zhenjiang on August 5, and set off the next day for

Yangzhou and Qingjiangpu, cheered by the progress he had observed in each place. This time he took Charles Fishe with him, visiting the dried bed of the old Yellow River and preaching to an attentive crowd at Huai'an until his voice failed.[18] Then down to Zhenjiang again only to set off on September 20 for 'the southern stations' of Zhejiang – and two months of 'extreme trial' of the most unexpected nature.

Meanwhile, in London the council were facing another unusual situation. Charles Judd having decided to return to China within a few weeks, though still uncertain about his wife and children, asked that he might take 'a *new* missionary' with him. No known candidates were ready to go, but Grattan Guinness when consulted answered, Yes, three admirable young men in his training institute had China on their hearts and could be ready in time. They were M Henry Taylor, Frederick W Baller and Arthur Wm Douthwaite, the medical student, who was prepared to defer qualifying until after gaining experience in China.

On August 12, Guinness presented each of them for interview, and three days later chaired a subcommittee of the council with Judd present, at which it was decided that Baller, Taylor, Mary Bowyer and the Judds should sail early in September via the United States, to avoid the tropics. Mrs Grace (who had promised £50 per annum at the Mildmay conference, and had since given Charles Judd £140 for 'a fresh mission station') had then increased it to £300, not knowing of the three men being available. Now she took the Judds' eldest child, Rossell, into her own home. Douthwaite was to stay a few months longer and travel with James Meadows. These three were to be among Hudson Taylor's most outstanding pioneers in 'the long stride' to both west and north, Baller as a linguist and Sinologue, Henry Taylor as the intrepid spearhead into Henan, and Douthwaite, in company with Hudson Taylor, in Jiangxi and then Shandong, winning the Order of the Double Dragon in the Sino-Japanese war twenty years later. (*See* Book 3, p 307 and Note 30)

'All seems very dark'   *September–November 1873*

While Hudson Taylor was on his Yangzi journey, things were going sadly wrong in the southern area. The timing of his movements was governed by the approaching confinement of Annie Stevenson and of Fanny (Wilson) Jackson. He also needed to have a long talk with the Rudlands. After a spell of success at Taizhou, what looked like spiritual pride had overcome them. He 'is getting very up-ish and conceited. . . . Printing his papers and letters (in the *Occasional Paper*) is not doing him any good' – until a surge of threatening behaviour by the anti-foreign, anti-Christian factions in the city had so scared Rudland that in panic he changed into foreign dress to awe them. That garb meant the power of consuls and gunboats behind him, and the threat of reprisals if they should go too far – as if trust in God was a fair-weather safeguard. His Chinese colleagues were dismayed. But worse was to come. Mary Rudland thought she saw one of the younger Chinese missionaries kissing the evangelist's wife. So Mary spoke out. Both men left, insulted, as two others had done previously, and in shame William Rudland wrote offering to resign from the Mission.

Little did Hudson Taylor realise that this was only the prelude to what he already felt was his worst experience 'since Nicol's time'. It had hardly begun. Groombridge had been Nicol all over again in his attitude to Chinese dress, and Edward Fishe was talking of leaving the CIM to join the Robert Whites as an independent missionary. If he did, it would be at the price of separation from his wife, staunchly loyal to Hudson Taylor. 'For myself I shall be far from sorry to lose him,' Hudson Taylor confided to Emily. 'I am pained that (after) long and confidential conversations with him . . . he should have (bought) land to build on, and never breathed a hint of it to me.' 'If (Rudland) leaves in a bad spirit, reaping up all the troubles . . . since and in Nicol's time, he may cause much sorrow.' And poor McCarthy; his wife wanted to give up and go home. 'Now what do all these things indicate? I think, that Satan sees the spreading of the work, dreads it, and is making a strong effort to uproot it. But he will fail. The Lord who is with us, is stronger than he.'

More bad news of Emily's condition had come in several letters. Because of it the Taylor children had been taken to their grandparents, young Tom Jones had at last left Pyrland Road – a welcome guest for his mother's sake, but an intolerable burden for Emily – and Henrietta Soltau, freed from nursing at home, had come to look after Emily. Someone must do Emily's work, so Hudson Taylor wrote asking Henry Soltau and Henrietta to give themselves to it for a year. As the news became worse and worse – Emily on a water-bed, everyone so kind, Emily 'fading', Emily's condition 'precarious', 'I fear, going home', dying – Hudson Taylor felt badly shaken. What could they do from a distance? Could his parents take over her work? 'There is *no* one able to do the work she has been doing,' he wrote. 'If this work is left undone all my work for all these years may come to nought.' Much as he loved Jennie, he loved Emily too. On the anniversary of Maria's death, July 23, he had written to her, 'I thought that writing to you would be a comfort to me. . . . What a happy, happy three years these have been to (Maria).' With an aching heart he could do nothing more than pray.

Anxieties close at hand demanded no less attention. Passing through Hangzhou, Hudson Taylor learned that students in the city were planning to pull down one of another mission's buildings. 'We need to be very careful.' But Wang Lae-djün's wife was dangerously ill, so while Jennie stayed to nurse her dear friend, Hudson pressed on to Shaoxing to cope with an emergency in Anne Stevenson's pregnancy, three weeks from 'term'. Details are not given, but a placenta praevia seems likely; potentially a matter of life and death to mother and child. While he was there, letters came from Jackson and Rudland reporting that Fanny Jackson had had a spate of fifteen fits at half-hourly intervals. Black in the face, she seemed likely to die each time. But the letter had been two weeks on the way.

If Fanny was still living, her eclampsia was likely to be fatal, but all Hudson Taylor could do was to send Charles Fishe to Taizhou with medicines, telling Jennie to come by fast canal-boat as soon as she could leave Mrs Wang. 'You need not fear being alone for one night' on the way! She reached him on October 4 (in time for her thirtieth birthday)[19] and Anne's baby was born on the 10th. For twenty-four hours Anne seemed unlikely to live, but pulled through. Waiting another day or two until it was safe to leave, the Taylors travelled by fast footboat, raft and then mountain chair, and were at Taizhou on the 15th. On a little scrap of paper (preserved by his mother) he said that Fanny Jackson had given birth to a stillborn child after her convulsions and was recovering, but swollen with oedema and 'water in the chest' as she was, it had been touch and go.

> I feel almost overwhelmed. I have scarcely time to write even a line, I have to think over so many matters, and am so filled with sorrow about dear Miss Blatchley's illness. For the Mission's sake the house at Pyrland Road *must* be kept on, at least for the present. I don't want the boys to miss getting into the City of London School. . . . I hope either Mrs Duncan or Miss H E Soltau will care for the housekeeping and dear Miss Blatchley and the children for the present. . . . Could you not edit the *O P* for us?

How in these circumstances could he himself also produce

another issue of the *Occasional Paper*? It was expected of him and he did his best. But the immediate pressure came from a letter announcing the imminent arrival of the Judds' party at Shanghai, with no time to make arrangements to receive them. He would have to go himself. In an agitated letter to Richard Hill, he wrote, 'I cannot possibly meet the party . . . as requested. . . . I question whether any circumstances can render it advisable to send a party without giving us a month's more warning. . . . Men get dissatisfied and put out *before* they begin their work' if, like Groombridge and Donovan, there is apparent neglect in arrangements for them on arrival.

Morale was low among the disillusioned Taizhou church members as well as their missionaries. If their teachers failed to live up to their teaching, what hope was there for Christians newly out of a pagan environment? 'The presence of heathenism is very deadening to the soul; and when their hope and zeal run down, we cannot wonder if the (Chinese) do so too.' So Jennie agreed to stay while Hudson made a dash for the Ningbo coaster and by fast walking interspersed with stretches in a mountain chair, arrived in time. On the way he had called in at Ninghai and found another case of sub-Christian living like that at Taizhou. George Crombie had been undermining Jackson's loyalty to their leader again, and his Chinese colleagues were asking for higher 'wages' – as if they were employed to preach the gospel! 'Oh for a baptism of the Holy Ghost . . . the only remedy for our troubles,' Hudson Taylor wrote to Jennie.

Sitting in the mountain chair somewhere between Taizhou and Ningbo, he scribbled another line to his mother. He had stopped a postal courier carrying mail addressed to him in Taizhou, and took delivery there and then. Emily had been to stay with the young Radstocks at Richmond, but was no better when she returned to Pyrland Road. 'No words can express my sorrow over what I fear will be the end of this attack,' he told his mother. 'It is selfish to sorrow so, for what will be infinite gain for (her). But "Jesus wept" . . . and can sympathize still.' He had thought Emily's tuberculosis 'so far quiescent' that she would live until he and Jennie could get home again and look after her as she had tended his dying Grace. So it was good to know that Joseph Weatherley was getting the boys into the City of London School, and Catherine Duncan was nursing Emily. But he and Jennie were so far away and 'all seems very dark'.

From Ningbo on November 21 he dashed off another line to

ONE KIND OF MOUNTAIN CHAIR – FOR SHORT
JOURNEYS

Jennie, enclosing a cable received from Catherine, dated October 21. 'Emily not expected to live many weeks. She would like you to come.' 'It greatly perplexed and distressed me. But I do not see any reason for going home which we had not before.' If from the secretaries, or if more strongly worded than 'like' it would be different. Judging by the letters received, it was already too late to see her alive, but he could make a quick journey, separate Emily's possessions from his family's, arrange for his children to be cared for *together*, sort out business problems with the secretaries, and press Mrs Faulding for Nellie's release.

But he was needed in China no less. 'There is nothing *feasible* and *right* which I would not gladly do for our precious Ae-me – the debt I *owe* her I can never repay. . . . As dear Ae-me says, we *must* trust (*the Lord*) implicitly.'

He was thinking of having a permanent Mission agent in Shanghai, with Lanfeng and his wife and the printing-press, to handle shipping, postal matters and purchases. Edward Fishe could do that better than church work. It was all put into action in December – the CIM's first business department in Shanghai, an institution which under the management of others was to become renowned through the decades for its scope and efficiency.

The coaster came in, and when Hudson Taylor next wrote he was in the Chinese city of Shanghai in a room with four bedsteads, two chairs and a little table, waiting cheerfully for word of the Judd party's arrival.

They arrived the next day, November 5, a day never to be forgotten by Fred Baller, a born raconteur, on whose fourteen-page reminiscences of their meeting this account depends. A thoroughly Chinese figure, 'the oddest figure I have ever seen', greeted them on landing and invited Baller and Henry Taylor back to his 'hotel' while the Judds and Mary Bowyer went to a friend's home. They found Hudson Taylor such a light-hearted, humorous and saintly person that they had no inkling of what he was going through. While they were with him he wrote again to Emily, 'I have seen very little of the Judds and Mary Bowyer yet, and indeed my heart is so filled with sorrow that I can see nothing. . . . I know that He will not forsake me nor leave you.' And to his mother soon afterwards, 'He can spare her and hasten our return . . . ; if not, we must bow to His blessed will. The words "God my exceeding joy" have been so constantly on my heart lately. He is making me in this heart-breaking trial, to *rejoice* in Himself, "with joy unspeakable and full of glory". The most painful part of it, perhaps, . . . to me and to dear Jennie is (Emily's) desire to see us once more, to resign her charge [the children and Mission matters] into our own hands.'

He launched Baller and Henry Taylor straight into Chinese ways, of living, eating, washing and dressing, and took them to Nanjing on November 7. To give time to talk and get to know them, he devoted himself exclusively to them over a period of ten days, introducing them to intensive preaching in the street chapel, before returning alone to Shanghai. 'He stamped us at once . . . with his own stamp.'

> The thing that impressed me [Baller wrote] was that Mr Taylor knew how to make a bargain. . . . Since then I have often been with him when he has been hiring boats, making contracts, buying land or houses. The Chinese were always loud in his praises on these occasions . . . because of the ability with which he conducted the

transaction. . . . He was never in a hurry. He would calmly and deliberately raise points, or go into those raised by the other party, . . . This lack of hurry was a great power. The average foreigner makes a beeline between the two nearest points, but the Chinese goes round the circle instead of along the diameter. And there can be no doubt that the business capacity Mr Taylor possessed saved the Mission large sums of money. . . . His abilities would easily have placed him in the front rank had he taken up any line of business.[20]

The respect was mutual. Two real 'MEN' had joined him, and more were soon to follow. He was on the verge of a new era of the Mission, and of China.

Back in Shanghai, he was again in harness. A local resident, David Cranston of the Shanghai and Putong Foundry and Engineering Company, met Hudson Taylor at Jane McLean's house, and wrote a few days later, 'You shall ever be a favourite of mine. . . . I should like to sit at your feet and hear all you have learned of the riches that are in Christ Jesus.' The heartaches of life had not silenced him, but were still heavy to bear.

The reasons for staying in China were greater than for going home to Britain, Jennie assured him from Taizhou, far enough from pressures to think dispassionately. She had been trying to exert a good influence (she said), working hard at visiting homes in the city. 'Numbers that I went to came on Sunday.' The chapel was crowded with some standing. 'Miss Happiness' (Book 4, p 238) had been thinking and had a message for Hudson when he needed it. 'It's unbelief that saps our strength and makes everything look dark; and yet He reigns and we are one with Him and He is making everything happen for the very best, and so we ought always to rejoice in Him and rest though it isn't always easy.' She was the right wife for him.

Back in Ningbo again Hudson Taylor was 'so weary' of being separated from her. As for Emily, what could he do? He made a brave attempt to write to her about the cablegram – Emily who might not be alive to read his letter, dating it November 24, 1874, by mistake. 'Dear Ae-me! . . . He has placed me here, you there. For the time being He has separated us. . . . I feel bewildered, dear, precious sister. . . . I think of how you nursed me in the (guest hall) at Yangchou. . . . Of your care of Gracie and Samuel and their sainted mamma – who seems to die again in you, to leave again my precious children bereaved, and me so, so far away. I do pray, "Lord, what wilt *Thou* have me to do?"'

But Anne Stevenson needed his help again, so he went next to

Shaoxing and on to Hangzhou for a Sunday with Wang Lae-djün and the New Lane church before travelling through Sheng Xian, explicitly to meet the scholar Ning and his family. John Stevenson was there. The deep scarring of his face by smallpox was regarded by pagan Chinese as an asset, a sign of death-defying good luck. As Hudson Taylor later recounted in the *Occasional Paper*, at a fellowship meal in the chapel he (Taylor) told the Christians how, on his first overland journey from Taizhou in 1867, he had climbed the hill of their city god 'and saw the whole city at my feet . . . and after preaching to the people (at the temple) till I could do so no longer, I went higher upon the hill, and all alone . . . entreated (the Lord) to have mercy on them and to open the door for the gospel. . . . I could have wept with joy to hear the record of what (His) grace had done for one and another.'

Wanted: workers who WORK!   *October–December 1873*

When Hudson Taylor at last reached Taizhou, impatient to be with Jennie again, she had gone. 'Imagine my dismay,' even before reaching the house to learn 'that you had left this morning' – for Ninghai escorted by Rudland. 'I have been kissing you, darling, in mind all last night, nearly, and all today.' Jennie had been as excited, imagining because she had not heard from him for several days that he was ill, alone and needing her. So she had gone to find him. He caught up with her at Ninghai, and they went on to stay overnight with Feng Nenggui, the basket-maker, at his outstation.

At long last, after Hudson Taylor had been travelling almost incessantly since the beginning of the Yangzi journey on July 17, they reached Fenghua on December 13. Looking back he called it not five months but seven weeks of travelling – reckoning from the day he left Jennie at Taizhou and overlooking their forced marches from the Stevensons to save Fanny Jackson's life, let alone from Zhenjiang to Shaoxing before that. The Fenghua mission house was empty. James Williamson had gone home to Scotland on the verge of a nervous breakdown. But in the time he had been at Fenghua the church had thrived.

This was their chance to work with the church while writing issue No 36 of the *Occasional Paper*, his first opportunity since sending No 35 off in September. In the summer he had hit upon a good source of material, asking Stott, Crombie, Stevenson and others to write year by year reports of the start and progress of their own work, while he himself wrote ten portraits of the Mission's Chinese colleagues. Each issue therefore answered the questions in the minds of friends at home in Britain who looked for evidence of their support being justified. As soon as the *Paper* was posted, they would go by sea to Wenzhou for their long-deferred visit to George and Grace Stott. So they thought. Before the time came they were off on two more hectic forced marches to save the lives of colleagues.

For the present they were alone together, for the first time since their marriage two years ago, and for Christmas. On Christmas Eve William Rudland sent them the love of the two Taizhou families, his own and the Jacksons. 'Tell (Jennie) that . . . we *are* enjoying *rest* in (the Lord). My work though hard is a *pleasure*, not *task*-work, and God does help me to do more than I could before. May God make her as great a blessing to others as He has done to us.' The change from what she had found at Taizhou on first arriving there was profound.

For months, Hudson Taylor had been mulling over the need of colleagues who could be counted on to keep up their standards and drive on at their work, whatever their circumstances. Men and women like the Stotts, McCarthy, John Stevenson and the Judds were the right kind because they were examples to Chinese Christians and to younger missionaries. In praising Emily to his mother in 1870 he had said, 'Though there are others willing to help, some lack ability, others reliability.' It was true of church work, too. In March he had reminded Henry Soltau, concerned with the assessment of candidates, that it was better to weed out the weak ones before they left home than to discover their failings in China.

> The nature of our work here needs to be remembered. It is very trying to the temper and to patience. One must be willing to sow in faith, to work maybe for years ere the fruit appears. Persons who cannot *wait* are not suited for China. It might sometimes be a test of the earnestness and patience and ability of candidates to suggest a line of self-improving study for six months or a year, with a view to their ultimate efficiency. Many would never be heard of again, but those who were, would be more likely to prove men of the right stamp. Another important thing in missionaries is *tact* and power of *adaptation*. . . . Young men accustomed to please customers in a shop will often be able to adapt themselves to their audiences here better than work-people who are of a rougher mould. And the latter . . . do not value direction and are often impertinent to (Chinese) authorities to the great detriment of the work. . . . New workers

should come out on probation . . . and are not at liberty to marry for
the first two years.

The council in London had worked this out with him in October
before he left: 'That candidates should go out on probation for two
years, as missionary students, but that no one should be sent out
who would not consent to remain for three years in the service of the
Mission.'[21] On the subject of marriage, Hudson Taylor wrote on
December 8, 1873, that 'newly married missionaries lost the first
twelve months' through preoccupation with wife and home. In fact,
finding themselves in a new environment as part of the socially
mixed missionary community did strange things to some, especially
if they had more money under their control than they had had
before. 'Two out of three men are very different in thought about
themselves twelve months after leaving England, from what they
were twelve months before,' he told John Challice. Adaptation
must start before they were uprooted from the homeland, and
certainly on the voyage out. To begin with luxury travel was bad for
them. Even third-class conditions could spoil a man or woman.

> If two or three kinds of meat, two or three of vegetables, soup, bread
> and potatoes ad lib and one pint of wine per meal are not enough; or
> if the privation of a few weeks' loss of privacy, and separation in the
> case of husbands and wives, who must sleep in separate state rooms,
> is too appalling, this is such positive luxury and comfort compared
> with what will be found here, that such persons would do well to stay
> at home. The only persons wanted here are those who will *rejoice* to
> work – *really* to labour – not to dream their lives away; to *deny*
> themselves; to *suffer* in order to *save*. Of such men and women there
> is room for any number and *God* will support *any* number – they are
> *His* jewels and *He* values and cares for them.

In October Richard Hill wrote asking what the council should do
about women wishing to join the Mission. 'There are two or three
apparently suitable ones who have offered themselves; but none of
us seems quite to know your mind about it.' This was the legacy of a
change of secretaries without sufficient overlap in office. William
Berger had known Hudson Taylor's mind on the subject, and Emily
could have told them if they would accept it from her. Back in 1867,
Hudson Taylor had asked Berger not to send any more women until
there were couples or experienced single women with whom they
could live. Since then, no couples in the southern area had been
willing or proved suitable to have them, and of the suitable experienced single missionaries, Jennie had married and Mary Bowyer

had gone home with the Judds. Hudson Taylor and Jennie had come back with Emmeline Turner, who was shaping well, and with Miss Potter. Only her breakdown in health was forcing her home as soon as fit enough to travel. Louise Desgraz' gifts were of a different nature, though 'but for her the Chinese Christians (of Zhenjiang) would have given up . . . in despair' during their year of neglect under the Fishe brothers. And Catherine Duncan had proved her worth even when handicapped by an unhappy marriage. With the Judds and Mary Bowyer back in China again and Catherine Duncan expected before very long, Hudson Taylor hoped (as always) that more women could come. 'If there are one or two *suitable* female candidates, who could harmonize with Mrs Duncan, live with her, and work under her, by all means send them if you can. The great difficulty . . . is to find them suitable homes.'

Never had he wished to restrict the part women, married or single, should play. Convinced in 1850 by the rightness of Charles Gutzlaff's principle (Book 1, p 332), and confirmed in his belief by the effectiveness of Mrs Lord, Mrs Bausum, Mary Jones, Mary Gough and Maria among Ningbo women (Book 2, pp 252, 399, 407) the record of the last few years provided absolute proof. Jennie had needed no teaching. From the day of her leaving Shanghai for 'the interior' she had loved to sit and talk with Chinese women and children (Book 4, p 232). Mary Bowyer had quickly followed suit. Not only the church in Hangzhou was a living tribute to their influence; the friendly attitude of the city towards foreigners with a right regard for the Chinese bore witness to their attitude as much as to Hudson Taylor's and McCarthy's. Catherine Duncan had imbibed the same spirit and would show others how to emulate it. Already they could say 'Emmeline Turner gives promise of making a valuable missionary. She has thrown herself heart and soul into the work.' Given people like them, the more women the better. His conviction that they would play a powerful part in the evangelisation of China had never wavered. Now it was stronger than ever.

'Our hearts sing for joy'   *December 1873*

Some miscellaneous notes left by Hudson Taylor include this statement, 'During the latter part of November, December and the first part of January, I asked the Lord to make it specially clear whether He would have us prepare to work in some of the new provinces or not, and also whether we should seek to occupy more stations in (Zhejiang). My mind was assured that we ought to do both.' Tangible conformation was being given at the same time. On December 5, 1873, Mrs Emma Grace (of Naphill, High Wycombe), wrote to Richard Hill saying she was arranging for £800 to be paid to the China Inland Mission in addition to the £300 already contributed for its advance into more provinces. Eight hundred in 1874 may be thought of as well over £16,000 today, enough to give Hudson Taylor confidence that he was not mistaken in his understanding of God's will, and his prayers were being answered. In reporting this development on the 10th, Hill added that James Meadows would be leaving early in January with A W Douthwaite, the third of Grattan Guinness's young men. From her Fenghua working 'honeymoon' Jennie wrote to her father on Christmas Day to say that she and Hudson had decided to put the whole of the principal and interest of her uncle's legacy in the care of trustees, to be used at her direction for the work of God, not only in China. None was to be for personal use, except sometimes to pay for their passages between China and Britain. Her father had exhorted her to think very carefully about how she used the money, and she assured him that over a period of months she had become certain of her duty, 'and I am sure you would be the first to say – Then, do it.'

> We have not used a farthing of Uncle's money for ourselves from the first, and decided not to do so, and my thought has been . . . that we should go on looking to God for our own support as before. . . . We have already been looking to God for support for years, and if we were to use this money for ourselves, we should have to give up taking what He sent us and live on our interest. This we do not think well for two reasons, 1st. We should lose the influence on others of our example; we are asking the members of the Mission to look to God without any definite income, and we wish for their sakes to do the same ourselves. 2nd. . . . I *could not* expect God's blessing if I let work for eternity be left undone, because I withheld the money when I had it. . . . No, it is safer to trust in God than in 'uncertain riches' . . . 'for where your treasure is there will your heart be also'.

When a copy of Mrs Grace's letter reached China with its insistence 'Remember! FRESH provinces', Hudson Taylor wrote, 'It caused our hearts to sing for joy.' And now like Paul, 'assuredly gathering that the Lord had called us to preach the gospel to the regions beyond', the word was given for Judd to make the long stride to Wuchang. But four prefectures and forty-eight *xian* (county) cities of Zhejiang province still had no known Christians or preachers of the gospel in them. Zhejiang must see advance as well.

CHAPTER TWELVE

TORN IN TWO
1874–75

'A disturbed year for China'   *1874*

The Tong Zhi emperor's attainment of his majority and the sumptuous celebrations associated with his wedding had meant a heavy drain on the empire's coffers. No official or eunuch of the court or state government was content without his share. When Prince Kong tried to limit the profiteering by high ministers preparing palaces for the empresses Ci Xi and Ci An on their retirement from the regency, he was even punished by degradation in rank for one day.

The long campaign against the Muslims of the far north-west continued to deplete the empire's wealth, led by Zuo Zongtang (Tso Tsung-t'ang), 'a blunt soldier, with a fine reputation for leadership, and free from the covetousness characteristic of the Chinese officials generally'. Even though 'he halted his army, sowed and harvested a crop of grain, and then continued his advance', the costs of an expedition far up the 'panhandle' of Gansu and across Turkestan (now Xinjiang, the New Dominion) were immense (map, p 26).

The government's blunder into confrontation with Japan (p 309) quickly led to a change of direction. A collision between Japanese and Chinese forces could embroil the western nations or greatly embarrass them in their professed friendship with both nations. Sir Harry Parkes in Yedo (Tokyo) and T F Wade in Peking did their best to resolve the situation. Robert Hart from his privileged watch-tower chuckled to observe that *fengshui* no longer stood in the way when Li Hanzhang, Li Hongzhang's brother, and Chinese forces in Fujian, opposite Taiwan, needed telegraphy in their emergency. But Wade had an inspiration. Sensing that both governments were looking for a way out, though ignorant of the fact that the Japanese negotiator had come to Peking prepared to reach 'a settlement on almost any terms', Wade devised a formula to save face on both sides. Japan was recognised as justified in avenging the death of Ryukyuan sailors at the hands of Taiwan tribesmen, and withdrew her expeditionary force on payment of an indemnity explained as compensation for the victims' families and payment for roads and buildings constructed by the Japanese.

'Unstinted praise' rewarded Wade. But in accepting this way out, China had to surrender her tributary dependency of the Ryukyu Islands at a time when Britain was annexing Burma by stages, France was taking Annam, and Japan had her eyes firmly on Korea. Hanoi had been occupied on November 20, 1873, and a Franco-Annamese treaty of alliance was signed in Saigon on March 15, 1874. Alexander Michie characteristically observed that 'the transaction really sealed the fate of China, in advertising to the world that here was a rich empire which was ready to pay, but not ready to fight'.[1]

A bone of contention existed between China and the foreign powers in the existence of a tidal bar of silt where the Huangpu river flowed into the Yangzi near Wusong. In 1874, only thirty years since Captain George Balfour, the first British consul, began turning empty mud flats into a commercial foothold on the mainland (Book 1, p 271 ff), Shanghai was handling sixty per cent of all foreign trade with China. For two years, demands that the bar be dredged had been rebuffed by Peking. As Hart told his Tianjin commissioner, 'the question of the Woosung Bar . . . may develop into a *casus* of something very like *belli*'!

Ever since the French concession at Shanghai had been extended in 1863 to include the north gate suburb of the Chinese city, in which Hudson Taylor had experienced his earliest adventures (Book 2, pp 183 ff, map), plans had been made public to move the cemetery of Ningbo residents to another site, to make way for new roads. No objections had been made, but when action was due to begin a riot erupted on Sunday, May 3, 1874. Foreign houses were fired, beginning with the French surveyor's, a score of foreigners and Chinese were injured and seven Chinese rioters were killed when the fire brigade, 200 men of the Volunteer Defence Corps and 100 American and French naval ratings helped the *daotai*'s troops to restore order. James Meadows and A W Douthwaite had arrived from Britain two days earlier and were staying with Edward Fishe at the new premises in Hongkou (Hongkew). On the way to a meeting in the home of a Mrs Jenkins in the French settlement, Douthwaite and Fishe realised that trouble was afoot and arrived to find

THE FRENCH CONCESSION AT SHANGHAI

American naval casualties having their wounds dressed in Mrs Jenkins' house.[2]

(The rioters) had attacked Miss (Jane) McLean and utterly destroyed her house and furniture [Douthwaite wrote]. She ran into the garden but was knocked down and dragged along by the hair. Mr Weir [p 415] and a friend named Cranston [p 389] came upon the scene at this juncture and ran to her assistance. Mr Cranston was knocked down and his head beaten with a stool. They left him for dead (but) a man whom he used to employ picked him up and carried him inside. He soon recovered a little and then tried to walk away. When the rioters saw that he was still alive they rushed at him again and would have killed him but for the man who had befriended him. He begged them to desist, saying that he knew him to be a good man and no Frenchman, so they left him and he was taken to hospital. Mr Weir also received some severe cuts and bruises about the head and arms. Miss McLean got away into the street but was knocked down several times and would certainly have been killed but for some of the Chinese who protected her by pushing her into a teashop and forming a circle round her. They called to the mob that she was not French but was a good woman who kept a school. When she had so far recovered herself as to be able to speak she called out in the Chinese language that she was an English woman. That satisfied them and they went away. By the time I got there her house had entirely disappeared. She bore the ill-treatment she had received in a lovely, joyous, Christlike manner and refused to put in a claim against the Chinese for damages. . . .

[Years later Douthwaite commented] My first year was filled with a succession of riots in one of which I lost most of my possessions and narrowly escaped losing my life also.

The grievances of the Chinese were recognised as just, and the French undertook to leave the cemetery undisturbed for all time and kept their promise until two years before the Boxer uprising of 1900. Samuel Wells Williams, who was American chargé d'affaires in Peking in 1874, reported to Washington that all Chinese could be expected to sympathise with those whose ancestral graves were to be violated and to condone their riotous action. Three more riots were to follow in other cities.

The sick and the dying   *January–April 1874*

The events of early 1874 present a picture of the Taylors' hectic life. The Edward Fishes' first child had died in infancy in 1873, and the unvaccinated second child died of smallpox soon after they moved to Shanghai. The toll continued. Some parents wished to send their children home as the Taylors had done, and during his working 'honeymoon' with Jennie at Fenghua, Hudson Taylor was weighing up whom to ask to escort them. He needed an efficient, balanced member of the Mission in London to take over Emily Blatchley's work and responsibility for his own children who were 'like orphans'. Louise Desgraz was ideal. He asked her to meet him in Shanghai and was about to go there on Friday, January 2, when an urgent message came from the Crombies at Ninghai, thirty miles away. Both children were very ill and one apparently dying. Sending Jennie to the Goughs at Ningbo, he 'came at once – no easy journey in the snow.' Persuading the officer on guard to open the city gate to him after dark, he was with the Crombies by midnight. One child was 'in a very precarious state' with whooping cough and the other little better.

On January 7 Hudson Taylor wrote to Jennie that he hoped to be able to leave the Crombies by Monday, 12th, and be in Ningbo on Tuesday. But his note crossed one from her. Fanny Jackson had joined her in Ningbo, she said, and in the night had had convulsions and been semiconscious for two or three hours. Dr John Parker had been sent for. Hudson Taylor came at once, reaching Ningbo on Saturday, January 10. Annie Stevenson was said to be still very ill at Shaoxing but, Hudson Taylor wrote, 'An hour before my arrival (at Ningbo) an express messenger had arrived from (Taizhou),' saying that William Rudland had smallpox, and two of the children had not been vaccinated. Louise had come on from Shanghai and agreed to escort 'poor Miss Potter' and two or three children to London, and to mother them and the Taylor children at Pyrland Road, but Jennie and he waited only for the carriers to arrive from Ninghai with his medicines and set off for Fenghua again, on the way to Taizhou.

Together they wound up the Mission business they had been working on, and she returned the thirty miles to Ningbo while he continued southwards. [Drawing on two letters,]

I went on in (the dark), the wind and rain (and snow), and reached [the Crombies at] Ninghai this afternoon, leaving again with a new sedan and fresh coolies. We have made 30 *li* [ten miles], (twenty *li* in the dark), and are waiting while rice is cooked, and then go on again. I have promised to walk 20 *li* (6–7 miles) if they will go on 20 more. . . . This will still leave us 110 *li* (33 miles) tomorrow, a long walk with a heavy burden and some high hills as steep as stairs in some places. . . . May God help poor Mrs Rudland in her trouble, and if it be His will spare her husband and children. . . . [Reaching an inn between midnight and 1 a m he and the bearers had slept and set off again at 7 a m to cover the last 40 miles by 7 p m.] Well! The Lord reigns, and my heart does rejoice in Him. Sadness cannot rob us of this unchanging source of joy and strength.

Jennie was in Shanghai by Wednesday, 14th, arranging for Miss Potter's journey, when Hudson Taylor was writing to her from Taizhou on the same day, 'Rudland, wife and three children have all had smallpox and are nearly all well again.' He himself had been using his time in Taizhou arranging a long lease for the Mission premises and preaching in the countryside.

With the Rudlands out of danger, his problem was how to shake off the contamination of his own clothing and possessions before going among other fellow-missionaries again, yet he did not seem to be aware that even his letter could carry the infection. Being about eighty miles from Wenzhou, he wanted to visit the Stotts but once again had to disappoint them. Because no Chinese in contact with smallpox considered it necessary to restrict their movements, he felt he would be justified in travelling on the open road for four days to

THE GRANITE FLAGGED 'MAIN ROAD' THROUGH A
HILLSIDE VILLAGE

Jinhua (map, p 38) and from there by river to 'Gyü-tsiu' (ie Ch'ü-chou, now Qu Xian) and Lanxi before going down the Qiantang river to visit Hangzhou and Annie Stevenson at Shaoxing again. He ended his letter by asking Jennie to find suitable wives (in the Ningbo schools) for three Christians at Taizhou.

On Sunday, January 18, he was in the temple which had been converted into a chapel, exposed to a cold wind and uncertain whether Emily would be alive to read what he was writing. He could not see how he could leave China within a few months, and wrote to her, 'The Lord says stay, and I *cannot, would not if I could*, reverse it.' Jennie told Emily, 'I dream so, so often that your wish has been granted and that we are with you.' When love and duty appeared to conflict, duty came first in the will of God.

But by January 26 Hudson Taylor was in Taizhou again for a few days and writing to Richard Hill. Louise Desgraz would not need any Mission funds for her personal support while in Britain as he would be personally responsible for her. 'You will find her somewhat reserved in manner, and at first sight might fail to duly estimate her sterling worth. For humility, fidelity, truth and conscientiousness, for perseverance in spite of difficulties and discouragements, few equal her. Our work in (Zhenjiang) owed its continued existence to her, and her alone. . . . But for her, the Christians would have given up in despair.' The Rudlands, Stevensons and McCarthys 'cannot be expected long to hold out without (home leave); and if they did, their families could not.'

He had written to Jennie that the Rudlands were all right and he must change his plans, travelling to Ningbo, Hangzhou and Shanghai to see Louise off to Europe. Two nights later all had changed again. His mountain-chair had come and he was ready to go, when Rudland in distress said that Mary and two of the children had a high fever again. The baby now had unmistakable smallpox. If by the 30th he could not leave, he would send bearers for Jennie. He could not – and by then he himself was not well, so he wrote again. 'My anxieties about (Grace Rudland) are far from diminished. . . . Come as soon as you can', and he detailed his arrangements for fresh carriers to be at each stage of the 150-mile overland journey, and Christians to meet her at some points. 'Little Gracie, now my only anxiety, will be at the height on Sat night or Sunday.'

Jennie went, and the child survived, but Hudson Taylor himself was ill, so, as soon as they could, they set off for their haven of Fenghua again, hoping to recover and spend a Sunday teaching the

Christians at the temple-chapel. Instead, on the way he was unfit to
travel or even to leave his bed in 'a very large house more like a barn
inhabited by a good many families'. The villagers 'came crowding in
to see us', Jennie wrote. In a large room, a space had been
partitioned off on three sides by bamboo matting, but there was no
privacy except after dark, because all the children kept peeping
through the cracks. 'On Monday morning I made H's (mountain-
chair) as much like a bed as possible and on we went. . . . The road
was very rough, and we crossed a high series of hills. . . . There was
so much climbing and such a sloughy road that the men . . . begged
us to stop, an hour before dark.' The rest of the letter is missing.

From February 8 to 20 Hudson Taylor had a nightly fever, and on
March 3 was in bed at the garret at Bridge Street, Ningbo, expecting
to travel all the way to Hangzhou by boat, because a bed could be
made up in it for him. Ten days later he was 'slowly recovering'. 'A
severe attack of remittent fever' was his description to George
Müller. They were heading for Shanghai, this time to meet the
Meadows family and Douthwaite, but without information as to
when they would arrive. Then, he hoped, back to Wenzhou at last,
and Taizhou again. But on March 30 he was still in bed, seemingly
unable to shake off his fever.

They reached Shanghai on April 7 to find a financial crisis on their
hands, with Mrs Stevenson's condition such as to need an early
return to Britain, but no funds for passages. 'Precious Ae-me,' he
wrote to Emily, '*you* know I should come if I could', but – with funds
so low, so many needing his help and such promise of advance to
promote into action – 'my way is not open'.

They went up to Zhenjiang to confer with Judd about the advance
he was to lead. The Mission houses in the city and suburb were
crowded with all who could be there for a day of fasting and prayer
on April 14, before the question was settled, to advance north or
west? The Whites had packed up and gone home, but Donovan,
Baller, Henry Taylor, McCarthy, the Judds and Mary Bowyer (in
charge of the school), Jennie and Hudson Taylor were present, and
'local residents', unnamed. Only the Cardwells of the Yangzi team
were absent, with a sick child, when the decision was taken – to
make the long stride to Wuhan and the far west.

Prayer had also been focused on the financial crisis. On April 10
Hudson Taylor's balance for general purposes had been 67 cents.
Yet Annie Stevenson must get away before the tropical summer
descended on them. The missionaries present, whose own basic

needs had been met by George Müller's remittances, contributed 200 dollars towards the family's fares, and Hudson Taylor 'found' the rest. He wrote on the 24th instructing Richard Hill to send £700 of Mrs Grace's big donation, to be used at once for sending the Judds to Wuhan and leasing premises there. On that day Cardwell came down on the Yangzi steamer with his dying child, too late for anything to be done but to comfort him and bury her beside the growing family of Mission graves, where Maria and her children lay. Only two months later Cardwell had to put his very sick wife and two remaining children on a ship for England. The price in disease and death seemed never-ending.

No 6 Pyrland Road   *January–July 1874*

Once Henrietta Soltau's father and sister had both died, she was free to rejoin Catherine Duncan in nursing Emily Blatchley. Faithfully they carried on the Mission's routine business on behalf of the secretaries, and the weekly prayer-meetings to which few others came, as well as mothering the Taylor children. As Emily became weaker they nursed her on a 'water-bed', a poignant reminder to Catherine Duncan of George's last days, and to Henrietta of her sorrows in Barnstaple. Mary Berger wrote on February 5 that Emily was 'so calm and patient . . . I believe she enjoys real rest in our blessed Lord.' Emily had come a long way in a few years.

Louise Desgraz sailed from Shanghai the next day, February 6, commissioned to take charge of the children and the Mission office, and when she arrived in March the *Occasional Paper* said no more than that Emily was 'patiently suffering the Lord's will'. She too had developed terminal tuberculous enteritis and was going steadily downhill. 'Mrs Duncan has promised not to leave her as long as she lives,' Jennie's mother wrote, 'but is looking *very* jaded with disturbed nights.' And Mary Berger said, 'They became so attached – I cannot say whose love was the stronger of the two.'

Having children in the house had increased their difficulties immeasurably, especially with two boys of 13 and 12 of whom Miss Stacey wrote, 'I do not remember ever being acquainted with a boy of such energy as Freddie [Howard Taylor]; it is no easy matter to keep pace with the variety and intelligence of his ceaseless questions.' Inevitably Richard Hill declared that Louise and the children would have to be in another house, which he would find for them near by. And when Joseph Weatherley entered Herbert and

Howard at the City of London School (founded 1442) it was to everyone's advantage. The wisdom of Maria's marriage settlement had come to fruition, leading to Howard acquiring high academic distinction in medicine and surgery before following Herbert (1881) and their sister Maria (1884) as a missionary to China in 1888.

One day in 1873 when Freddie had been sent with a message for Grattan Guinness, the door of Harley House was opened by his 11-year-old daughter Minnie. They stood looking at each other – and neither lost the first impression formed on that occasion. Minnie, Geraldine Guinness, also went to China in 1888, and there they became engaged.

But on April 24, 1874, Hudson Taylor was agonising in Zhenjiang over Emily's sufferings and his sure path of duty. 'My own dear Ae-me,' he wrote, 'you know how dearly I love you, and how I long to see you (and) the dear children. But I dare not doubt that the Lord is doing *the* best thing for them and for you.' By July Emily was sinking and 'Miss Potter' had died.

Scraping the barrel   *January–July 1874*

So much was happening at once, that a coherent account of this period again demands separation of its elements and more retracing of steps. For the two long years in China after marrying Jennie, Hudson Taylor was having to run the Mission on what looked like barely enough funds for survival, let alone for advance. A strong brake was being applied to his abounding enthusiasm and zeal for expansion. Had he possessed the means, who knows how over-stretched his depleted team might have become. From time to time large sums dangled before him, the promise of future freedom of action, still out of reach. At the same time tangible though small advance payments were giving substance to the dream.

Jennie's legacy from her rich uncle in Australia, Francis Hardy Faulding, was one of these, in all about ten to fifteen thousand pounds (at that time). 'My dear wife is left one of five residuary legatees. There are certain persons having annuities out of the estate. Not till after their death can the whole of what will ultimately be divisible be divided. . . . In the meantime the executors have commenced paying interest. . . . She feels the whole is the Lord's, and wishes to use it for Him, and has so used it, and not for private purposes. . . . The whole cannot be realized – half of it, perhaps, may be twenty, thirty or forty years before it can be realized.' The trust she had formed in London was to handle that part of the bequest already distributed, and interest in small sums had begun to reach her at infrequent intervals. To be able to apply them to her colleagues' needs was in her power, such as for fares to Britain or to replace loss by theft. But through Jennie's mother telling the Bergers and others about the legacy, Jennie and Hudson were receiving more advice than they knew how to accept. They had the impression that this highly personal matter had become a threat to the future support of the Mission. Lest misinformation should lead donors to withdraw their support, the Taylors asked the council to publish a statement of their intentions. Instead the council showed that no such danger yet existed, and at last Jennie and Hudson Taylor were left to do as they had intended.

A case in point had involved none other than William Berger, who since his retirement had sent gifts to the Mission from time to time, unpredictably. Since June 1873 he had ceased sending any to Hudson Taylor personally, explaining that if anyone sent him, Berger, £100 as a gift he would feel obliged to return it, seeing that he had no need of it. He was one who had expressed an opinion on how the legacy should be used. But he sent £200 to Richard Hill in May, and again in July, for the Mission, and told Hudson Taylor that he had named the CIM to receive a small legacy in his will.

The generous gifts from Mrs Grace were strictly for advance into a 'fresh province' and could not be used for other immediate purposes. But, month by month, Hudson Taylor was scraping the barrel of available cash. Where was the previously adequate supply for general purposes? In March he had confided to Emily, trusting her to hint tactfully to Richard Hill or Henry Soltau, that 'nearly eleven months have elapsed since I had any (statement of) accounts'. By the end of March when he wanted to distribute funds to all the stations, he had only £5 and $25 in hand. When he arrived in Shanghai on April 7 hoping to find £500 in cheques from Britain, they totalled £25. On the 10th his note to Jennie said, 'The balance in hand was 67 cents! The Lord reigns; here is our joy and confidence.' The Meadows party were expected daily. It was providential that they did not arrive until May 1. Remittances began to come in, as he told his mother in some detail when he could look back in July and see how events had dovetailed together.

Asking Richard Hill on April 23 whether he and the other members of council could carry on beyond the two years they had agreed to serve, if circumstances in China should delay his return, he wrote, 'I never was happier in the work, or freer from care, tho' I have no funds. . . . PS. Let me beg that no *appeal* be made for funds.' It was as though he feared what they might do, even to making public in the *Occasional Paper* his frank, confidential letters to them.

The very next day he wrote in the same vein to the treasurer, John Challice, a letter which he quoted to his mother, editing it for clarity, so that we may draw upon both.[3] No more than £20 or £25 should be spent on a new missionary's outfit; to guard against 'the *great* risk of young men being spoiled'. And then,

> I am truly sorry that you should be distressed at not having funds to send to me. May I not say 'Be (anxious) for nothing'? . . . We should use all care to economize what God does send us; but I do not think that God would have us *bear*, ourselves, any care about apparent or real lack. After proving God's faithfulness for many years, I can testify that times of want have ever been times of spiritual blessing, or have led to them.
>
> I do beg that never any appeal for funds be put forward, save to God in prayer. When our work becomes a begging work, it dies. God *is* faithful; *must* be so. The Lord is my Shepherd, I shall not want. . . . Take *no* thought (anxiety) for your life, what ye shall eat . . . but seek first (to promote) the kingdom of God, and (to fulfil) His righteousness, and *all these things shall be added unto you*. . . . It is doubting . . . not trusting, that is tempting the Lord. . . .
>
> The Lord . . : makes our hearts so *very* glad in Himself alone – not Himself plus a bank balance – that I have *never* known greater freedom from anxiety and care. The other week when I reached Shanghai I was in *great* and immediate need. The mails were both in; no remittance and . . . no balances at home. I cast the burden on the Lord. Next morning I awoke and felt a little inclined to trouble, but the Lord gave me a word, '*I* know their sorrows, and I am come down to deliver them . . . .' He said, *Certainly* I will be with *thee*' (Exodus 3:7, 8, 12). Before six a.m. I was as sure help was at hand as when near noon, I received a letter from Mr Müller . . . which contained more than £300. My need now is great and urgent, God is greater and more near. And because He *is*, and is *what He is*, all is, all will be, *all* must be well. Oh! my dear brother, the joy of *knowing* the *living God*, of . . . resting on the *living God*. . . . I am but His agent; He will look after His own honour, provide for His own servants, supply all our need according to His own riches, you helping by your prayers and work of faith and labour of love.

On May 1 a pencilled scrap of a letter to his mother said the work was going well but,

> Pray for funds. We have over 100 agents native and foreign, 170 mouths to feed daily and that number to clothe, not to count the wives and children of the native helpers. I feel no anxiety tho' for a month past I have not had a dollar in hand for the general purposes of the Mission. The Lord will provide. But in the meantime it is impossible for me to return home, or even to go to any distant station here, as I must be on the spot to distribute at once any sums which God may supply.
>
> [And on the same day to Emily] I cannot leave China in the present state of our funds. I have written to Mr Hill, Mr Challice, Mr and Mrs Guinness begging them not to *appeal* for funds. If God try our faith it is to show *His* faithfulness, and we shall lose the blessing by appeals etc. The work is very cheering. Mr Stevenson has just baptized eight persons and writes of new inquirers and candidates. Lae-djün has recently baptized firstfruits in three outstations. New doors are opening before us, and Jehovah Jireh ('The Lord will provide'). Is that not true, my precious Sister, of you and me too?
>
> Yours *so* affectionately in His deep true love,
>
> > J Hudson Taylor
>
> [*And a week later*] I have sent all Mr Berger's £170 home to you for housekeeping. [To his mother he continued] We were kept waiting on God till May 5th, when £104 2s. were received from the Secs. . . . On the 15th $222.22 reverted to the funds which had been temporarily appropriated in February to an object for which it was no longer needed. And Mr Judd on leaving Nankin for Wuchang was able to hand in $240.71, a surplus of funds given him in December and which had not been required. In these ways, by the sale of some stationery, and by profits on exchange, the most urgent needs of May were met; leaving us *all the promises of God* to meet the expenses of June, and nothing more.

By May 29 a new setback had occurred. John Challice had sent cheques made payable to 'the Bearer' and no Shanghai bank would cash them. They must be made out to the China Inland Mission.

> I asked urgent prayer of some of the brethren for £500 to meet the manifest and unavoidable outlay of that month. Perhaps never in the history of the Mission have we all been so low together. As it proved, the outlay of the month required above £100 more than the sum I had named; and therefore the Lord who meets all our need, supplied it too [detailing the sums received]. The aggregate of these sums comes

to about £100 in addition to the money sent from home; so that not only were the current expenses of the month met, but Mrs Cardwell, and her two surviving children were able to return to England . . . leaving me with a balance in hand of $3.57 on July 1st.

You will wonder how my dear fellow-workers bear (their own) trials. . . . I will give you some extracts from the letters of . . . June. 'When you said, Pray for £500 for this month's expenses, the sum seemed so insignificant when we referred it to God, that I felt ashamed that we should *have* to make it a subject for special prayer – though to you and to us, it would be everything so to speak. But God's inexhaustible riches rose up before my mind so vividly, that £500 seemed to me no more than 500 stones of the street. I have not the slightest doubt that He will give you this, and much more, as soon as *His* time comes. What I have to watch against is impatience at *waiting* His time.'

[From another] 'Many thanks for . . . the money which I received safely this afternoon. My last cash was spent yesterday morning, and I was waiting on our heavenly Father today for money to pay my teacher. Blessed be His holy name, He still answers our prayers.'

[Hudson Taylor himself said in a June 11 letter to Emily] I am so thankful for the remittances. The last few months have been the greatest trial of faith since the Mission was formed. My soul has mercifully been kept in much peace; sometimes indeed in great joy and God has helped us wonderfully. During the long time in which we had *no* Mission money the Stevensons were helped home, and by a series of providential circumstances . . . we have been helped on from day to day.[4]

On July 11, on the way to all the southern stations again, he told his mother, 'Our work is now so extensive, that it cannot be carried on without much difficulty and trial, at less cost than £100 a week. . . . We have more than 50 buildings – houses, chapels, and schools – to keep in repair, and four-fifths of them to pay rent for. . . . The travelling expenses involved in the work in China, now extended to five provinces, are not small. . . . Of course, all my own expenses for all purposes, at home and here, are outside of this.'

If ever there existed a recipe for bankruptcy and the destitution of scores of colleagues – Chinese and foreign – as well as of school-children and other dependants, this was it – unless he was not mistaken and the message of Scripture 'Jehovah Jireh: the Lord will provide' was being correctly understood and applied. Events showed that it was, and that '(God's) thoughts are not your thoughts'.

The Zhejiang momentum   *January–July 1874*

Hearing as we do in the late twentieth century of the extensive, lively Church in Zhejiang province, the history of its origins captures our attention. Returning again to January 1874 we follow another sequence of events. Hudson Taylor was at the Crombies after his working holiday with Jennie had ended in a forced march to save their alarmingly ill children. By Sunday, January 4, he had dosed them, rigged up steam-tents to ease their breathing, set them on the road to recovery and soothed the agitated parents. George must have been ashamed to receive such attention (*see* p 398), for back to his pre-furlough behaviour, he had again been setting Josiah Jackson against Hudson Taylor.

After the Sunday services Hudson Taylor turned to letter-writing. His winter travels to save the lives of Annie Stevenson and Fanny Jackson had given him an exciting insight into the teeming density of the population, the state of the churches and individual local Christians in 'the Shaoxing circuit' (of Shaoxing, Sheng Xian, Xinchang and their village outposts), as well as in the Taizhou field and in scattered, sometimes remote, places en route. His own conversations with Chinese, as he travelled or stopped at wayside inns, had revealed a spiritual hunger in places beyond the range of the existing team of evangelists. The tone of the articles in the *Occasional Papers* from his pen betrays his enthusiasm as he wrote of 'revival' in the Shaoxing churches, and progress almost everywhere. After telling Jennie about Taiping on market-day (so packed with people for two or three miles of city streets that he could hardly move through them and chose to return along the top of the city wall) he went on,

> This morning at the *van-tin* (foodshop) as we were breakfasting, the people began to ask many questions. Among them a young man showed much earnestness in enquiring of us and in listening to what we said. . . . I think we shall hear of him again. On our way back to the boat I went into the (temple of the city god) and preached to a little knot of people who gathered around me. Some seemed to hear with pleasure. As we neared the boat we met two men who were seeking us to tell us of a house which we could rent. I sent (my companions) and they took it at 1,000 cash a month (*see* Book 2, page 130), and met two women whose deep earnestness to learn the plan of salvation evidently moved and encourged them. In the boat I had like encouragement. Among a number of others an old man of

seventy-two years manifested such a real solicitude as I have never seen exceeded in China. I asked him to come in and sit down. He did so. I began as usual to ask his name. He replied, 'My name is Dzing, but the thing which troubles me is this: the world is all vanity and what is to be done about our sins?' 'Yes,' I replied, 'that is *the* question, and it is to reply to it that we missionaries have come to China.' 'Our Scholars say that there is no hereafter, that the several elements of the soul (three *weng*, six *pah*) are scattered at death – but I cannot think it is so.'

So now, on January 4, after telling his mother about the Crombies' straits and his plans for Louise Desgraz to relieve Emily, he wrote,

> I am now in the act of arranging for the eventual opening up of the whole of this province to the gospel as the Lord gives us men, open doors, and means. Pray for these three things. This province (Zhejiang) contains thirty millions of souls. It is divided into: circuits (four) we have workers in each. Prefectures (eleven) we have agents in 6. We alone in 3, with others in 3. (One of these we opened, others came later.) 1 is opened, not by us. 4 are still unopened. County towns (seventy-eight) 4 Prefectures have each 2 (*xian*) cities in their walls. So there are – 74 walled cities, 11 of them (prefectures), making 63 (county towns). We opened 10 of these. Others opened 5 of these. 48 (*xian*) county cities remain unopened. . . . In this province they average nearly 400,000 people in the whole (*xian* or county). . . . Others began to work this province in 1842; we in 1857; the CIM in 1866. It shows that there was work for us to do; that we have done some, but there is much (more to be done).[5]

Trekking along the hilly trails had helped him to mull it over. He shared his latest thoughts with Jennie.

> I will try to get Stott to work (Wenzhou) [he used the dialect, Weng-tsiu] and Jackson (Quzhou) [Cü-tsiu, now Lishui]. Then perhaps Lae-djün and Meadows when he comes might work Hangchau (Jiaxing) and (Huzhou). . . . Let us pray much for *men*, *means* and *open doors*. . . . I do believe that this year will be one of much blessing to us as a Mission.

By January 26 his thinking had progressed a stage further when he told Richard Hill to send two '*suitable*' young women with Catherine Duncan, and continued,

1874

Jan 27th Tai-chau. Asked God for 50 or 100 additional native evangelists & as many foreign superintendents as may be needed to open up the 4 fu & 48 hien still unoccupied in Cheh-kiang. Also, the men to break into the 9 unoccupied provinces. Asked in the name of Jesus. I thank Thee, Lord Jesus, for the promise whereon Thou hast given me to rest. Give me all needed strength of body, wisdom of mind, grace of soul, to do this Thy so great work. Amen!

Feb. 1. Tai-ping hien opened
   Sin-hü " "
Ap. 1 Gü-hang " "
   Hu-chau fu " "

HUDSON TAYLOR'S PRAYER FOR CHINESE
MISSIONARIES
(from a flyleaf of his Bible)

Should the Lord present suitable men for the work, you might send four more with advantage this year. . . . The work is now greatly extending, and I hope will yet do so. . . . If the Lord spare me and permit me to labour here a year or two more, I trust there will be no . . . county left in this province in which we have not preached Christ either by located or itinerant (evangelists). At present there are many such – fifty, perhaps. [At their own expense, that is – many more than the CIM was supporting financially.]

That last remark 'fifty, perhaps' seems to have been the spark that fired his thoughts through that night. For his first birthday after their marriage, Jennie had given him a new Baxter polyglot Bible, a facsimile in larger type (for his changing eyesight) of his favourite pocket edition. As always, he annotated it with the dates on which he read through each year, systematically day by day. And on a blank page at the end he wrote in pencil,

Jan. 27th, 1874, T'ai-chau. Asked God for 50 or 100 additional native evangelists and as many foreign superintendents [Gutzlaff's word for the more mature Christian missionary] as may be needed to open up the 4 *fu* [prefectures] and 48 *hien* [xian, counties] still unoccupied in Cheh-kiang [Zhejiang]. Also for the men to break into the 9 unoccupied provinces [ie the eighteen of the prayer pact made during the Mildmay Conference (p 345)]. Asked in the name of Jesus. I thank Thee, Lord Jesus, for the promise where on Thou hast given me to *rest*. ['He who keeps coming to Me shall never hunger, and he who keeps drinking of Me shall never thirst.'] Give me all needed strength of body, wisdom of mind, grace of soul, to do this Thy so great work. Amen!
   [Below this note he added later on] Feb. 1. T'ai-p'ing hien, Sin-kü,opened; Ap. 1 Yü-hang, Hu-chau-fu opened.

The pencilled note to his mother from Ningbo on March 3 when he was recovering from his 'intermittent fever' said, 'We have forty or more stations now' – not only in Zhejiang. And to Emily on March 30, again pencilled in bed because he had not yet recovered his strength, he wrote about the second anniversary meeting of the Chinese missionary society (p 335). 'Having 70,000 cash in hand (about $58) they elected one of their number as their evangelist, to be sent at their own expense to some district destitute of the gospel.'[6] The next day, March 31, he wrote in his editorial letter to friends of the Mission, 'There are more than forty stations and one hundred labourers, foreign and native, connected with our work, and about fifty children and adult students are studying the Word of God.' Baptisms were being reported from almost every occupied city and outstation, including Lanxi and Qu Xian far up the Qiantang river, and at last from Yangzhou, Qingjiangpu and even – the latest development – from a second city of the same name, Taizhou in Jiangsu, east of Yangzhou.

An evangelist had also succeeded in getting a footing at Huzhou again, where McCarthy, Yi Zewo and Liu Jinchen had been so badly mauled in November 1867 (Book 4, pp 393–6). So far he was unopposed. At Wuhu where Mr Han, the converted Anqing innkeeper was the evangelist, a native of Hunan province had become a Christian. Hunan was one of the 'fresh provinces' the long stride was to penetrate. What did it matter if they were all 'scraping the barrel' for mere cash and living more frugally than ever, if such things were happening! The lighter their purses, the more they looked up to their Father who fed the sparrows, and the more they did that, the more happened on the spiritual front.

The momentum in Zhejiang had spilled over to the Yangzi provinces, too. Had circumstances not led unmistakably to the Taylors leaving China for another period in Britain, who could tell what they would be witnessing next? On July 13 Hudson Taylor listed ten places in the southern region he proposed to visit once again before at last sailing for Europe at the end of August, and declared frankly and factually with confidence in his mother's long-proved discretion,

> I feel like one almost torn asunder by the claims at home and here. No mission aims at the definite evangelization of China – or even a single province. All are helping towards it . . . in their own way. . . . A few . . . are approximating to the work I hope to see effected, and we are influencing more largely every year older missions to step out and onwards. My plans are now so developing that were I able to remain in China, and had I a few more men of the right stamp, in two or three years we might have (DV) missions founded in every province otherwise unoccupied – nine – in each prefecture of (Anhui); and in each (county of Zhejiang); if funds were adequate. To see the bare possibility of this, and to have to defer it by coming home, is a great trial to me; on the other hand to return may be needful in order to effect it.[7]

As long ago as 1870, the *Missionary Magazine* of the American Baptist Union had published a letter by Miles Justice Knowlton DD of Ningbo about the CIM, because it was 'beginning to make some stir in the Western as well as the Eastern world'.

1. They have an excellent spirit – self-denying, with singleness of aim; devotional, with a spirit of faith, of love, of humility.

2. Their operations are carried on with great efficiency and economy.

3. They are able and willing to bring themselves into close contact with the people, by living in their houses, using their dress, and living for the most part on their food. . . .

4. They are widely scattered, but one or two families in a city.

5. They are having good success; many are doing a great amount of teaching and praying, and souls are 'added to the church'. . . .

6. They are not generally educated men, but . . . showing zeal and aptness to preach and labour for the salvation of souls. . . .

7. They are willing to 'rough it'. . . .

My principal fear, from what I saw, is that their health will suffer; but whether it will suffer more than in the case of the missionaries of other Societies, remains to be seen.

I notice that the English Baptist Society is beginning to be influenced considerably by the example of the 'China Inland Mission'. Could not all the old Societies learn some lessons from it? Could they not send some men of piety, good commonsense, energy, and perhaps of some experience, who had not been through the usual college course? . . . [8]

Hudson Taylor had still to descend to greater depths of tribulation, but he was nearer than he thought to the great breakthrough when his 'mad venture' would succeed on a far greater scale. Religious and secular observers alike would soon credit him with having been right all along, and take up his methods to an increasing extent.

The accident[9]   May–June 1874

In the final days of May, as Hudson Taylor and Charles Judd prepared to travel 500 miles farther up the Yangzi to Wuhan, the Hunanese Christian from Wuhu was baptised with three others at Zhenjiang. Soon afterwards he was joined by another Hunan man. Judd could have no better companions when he ventured into their province. The home of the scurrilous anti-Christian tracts and placards, Hunan gave promise of being as resistant as any province yet penetrated. While the Stevensons arrived in Shanghai, to sail on

June 7 – another family to go home as a matter of life and death – the westward advance was beginning.

June 1 found Hudson Taylor and Charles Judd on a little river-steamer, the ss *Hanyang*, travelling as Chinese passengers in quarters unsuitable for Jennie to be with them. 'It was one of McBain's, there were no cabins at all, just a few bunks, it was not much larger than a tug-boat.' 'I was going too,' she told Emily, 'but afterwards concluded that my being in Hankow at a (Chinese) inn might afford food for gossip'. On the same vessel was the Shanghai businessman Thomas Weir, just one month after his adventures with David Cranston in the Shanghai riot. A firm friend of Hudson Taylor (Book 4 p 75) he had used his influence to obtain fifty-per-cent discounts for members of the CIM on passages between Shanghai and Europe, and for some years secured most favourable terms with the Castle Line for Mission travellers from the United Kingdom.[10]

By Tuesday, June 2, they had chugged slowly upstream, stopped long enough at Jiujiang for a brief visit to Cardwell and the Christians there, and were due at Wuhan on Wednesday. 'I saw him on the steamer,' Weir wrote. 'He had fallen down a ladder one foot nine inches wide. He was lying on some bales of cargo between-decks where he fell . . . in great pain, could not move.'

On arrival at Wuhan, Judd, it seems, found accommodation for them in a Chinese inn, and Hudson Taylor wrote the same day, 'Wed. June 3. The steps were very steep, and when on the 2nd or 3rd from the top, my foot slipped and I came down feet first to the bottom [taking the impact on his heels]. The shock was very great, and for a time the agony was intense. After a while I was able to breathe a little and was helped to my bed. (I could not breathe properly for several hours.) . . . My spine was very painful. . . . This afternoon lying still, with my left ankle, which was sprained, elevated, I have no pain, and I can move with much less pain. . . . I feel very good for nothing today.'

The weather was very hot and the mosquitoes in the inn very many and troublesome. Josiah Cox, the Wesleyan, as soon as he knew of their arrival and what had happened, insisted that Hudson Taylor move into his home, while Judd stayed with a missionary with whom he had travelled to China, and looked for premises to rent. 'My back,' Hudson Taylor mistakenly wrote to Jennie, 'is evidently not seriously injured,' and by June 8 he thought his back was 'nearly well'; he could bear some weight on his feet.

Griffith John, Hudson Taylor's old friend of Shanghai days,

invited him to move in and stay, although not understanding, yet, why a fourth mission should be added to the LMS, WMMF and Protestant Episcopal Church in the three cities now forming the metropolis of Wuhan. 'I think that the Wesleyan missionaries will be good friends to us,' Hudson Taylor's note to Jennie ran, that same day. 'The London Miss. Socy not *quite* so warm, perhaps, but they see the need of a place here, *if* we are to go beyond' – which was his intention.

By June 9 Judd had rented a house and left by Chinese steamer to pack up at Nanjing. Young Baller and Henry Taylor were to stay on in Nanjing with Chinese colleagues, while Judd brought his wife and second son, Frederick Hudson, back with him. But on the same day, June 9, a letter from Jennie reached Hudson Taylor. Mary Bowyer had smallpox – 'We have completely isolated her.' 'I left Hankow the same night,' he wrote 'and reached (Zhenjiang) last night. . . . The populousness of the three places, Wuchang, Hanyang and Hankow, exceeds all I have hitherto seen in China – there must be at least a million souls in them. I propose forming a distinct branch of the Mission – under the superintendency of Mr Judd – for opening up work in these regions.'

At Zhenjiang John Donovan was 'brooding'. He had proposed to Mary Bowyer and been disappointed. Her reason was not long in coming to light, for when Frederick Baller knew that she had smallpox he could not wait to confess his love for her – or she for him. They had not travelled out to China on the same ship for nothing. She soon recovered from her smallpox, a light attack, and was undisfigured. 'Should she have her health,' Hudson Taylor commented to Richard Hill on June 18, 'they will probably soon be one of the most useful couples we have in the Mission. He is able, and humble; a man of piety and purpose; and his progress in the language is *very, very* good indeed.' At last the right kind of reinforcement.

In the same letter he wrote of more conversions and more baptisms. China was ripe for the gospel. The Hunan man converted at Wuhu 'seems all on fire for the conversion of his own people'. As for Hudson Taylor himself, apart from the temporary need of a crutch, the accident appeared to be a past event.

> My soul yearns, oh how intently for the evangelization of these 180 millions of the nine unoccupied provinces. Oh that I had a hundred lives to give or spend for their good. . . . Better to have pecuniary

and other outward trials and perplexities, and blessing in the work itself, souls being saved, and the name of the Lord Jesus being magnified, than any measure of external prosperity without it.

London's greater claims   *May–August 1874*

Nothing was static in the Taylors' lives. (Looking back yet again) – while they were at Zhenjiang for the conference about expanding north or west and, after it, preoccupied with monetary matters and the death of the Cardwell child, James Meadows and A W Douthwaite arrived at Shanghai. Edward Fishe welcomed them into the Mission's first business centre, near the Ningbo wharf on the Huangpu river, in 'Hongkew' – little more than a shop-front with rooms behind and above it – and two days later they were involved in the Shanghai riot.[11]

When Meadows learned of Annie Stevenson's urgent need to leave for England, he gladly accepted Hudson Taylor's request that he step into John Stevenson's shoes at Shaoxing, with oversight of the churches in that 'circuit'. At Shaoxing alone Stevenson had established a church of forty-six communicants. Expecting it to be a temporary post, Meadows was so deeply involved when news came at the end of the year of Stevensons' designation elsewhere, that he was glad to continue there – as he did with only one furlough in the next forty years, until he died.

With their passage money contributed entirely by their fellow-missionaries, John and Anne Stevenson and their five children were in Shanghai by May 29, to sail on June 7, while Hudson Taylor rested on his Yangzi tug-boat before his accident, 'reading and sleeping' and sorting his correspondence files. The financial crisis in China was extreme, but news of remittances from home and £500 of capital from Jennie's legacy being available had changed the picture. The Taylors could leave their colleagues provided for and still have enough for their own fares to Europe. John McCarthy and Donovan with Mr Han of Wuhu were on a pastoral visit up the Grand Canal to the growing church at Qingjiangpu, while Judd was contemplating his approach with the two Hunan Christians to their province, 'one of the most difficult in China'. The intense heat of the summer had begun, and Mrs Cardwell could not face the worst of it in her low state of health, so she sailed for home and her husband stayed to continue his pioneering in Jiangxi.

At last the need for Hudson Taylor to be in London exceeded the need in China. If no more pressing situation developed, as well it might in Yangzhou or Anqing, he could leave. They might be in time to be with Emily after all, though the news of her was bad. She was suffering more than ever and slowly sinking. On July 10 Hudson Taylor set off on another quick tour of the Zhejiang region, intending to do most of his travelling by canal-boat and coastal steamer, to spare his ankle and back. The Rudlands, especially Mary, were not recovering from their succession of illnesses, so he must see them – and the Stotts in their remotest station of Wenzhou, busy with successful work but often persecuted. To catch the French mail-steamer at the end of August was his goal.

On July 13 as he passed through Jiaxing by canal, he recalled his first visit there with Edkins twenty years before. Then a day or two at Hangzhou to encourage Wang Lae-djün and the church, a day or two more with Meadows, settling in at Shaoxing with Douthwaite, and Emmeline Turner at her school. On the 19th Jennie and he met at the Goughs, she having come down by coastal boat. Then with the Crombies at Ninghai on the 22nd, and by the 24th they were looking for the Rudlands at Taizhou, tracing them at last to an old temple in the hills near the mouth of the river. There the sea breezes made the heat tolerable for Mary, at the end of her endurance. Almost eight years had passed since she, as Mary Bell, and William had arrived in China on the typhoon-battered *Lammermuir*.

At once Hudson Taylor told them to be in Shanghai by August 29, ready to leave on the same ship as himself – funds permitting. Another crisis caused by no remittance from London would mean no sailings until it had been weathered. 'I have not a dollar of Mission money in hand now,' he had to admit yet again, 'but our *Father* has all the gold and silver at His disposal, and if He wish, He can easily provide all and more than we need.' Meanwhile he and Jennie had some money of their own, at God's disposal if he should want them to share it with the rest. The Taizhou church and outreach would be in the good hands of 'some of the best Chinese Christians'. He had intended taking the overland route between Taizhou and Wenzhou in order to see the new believers at these places on the way, including the old man who had gone straight to the point about his sins (pp 409–10). But time was running out and the heat was prohibitive. So he and Jennie boarded a coastal boat on July 28 and bucked their way against head winds to Wenzhou for a long weekend with George Stott and Grace (Ciggie).

Returning, they had the choice of ten days on a Chinese junk or longer by sedan chair overland to Ningbo. They chose the junk and almost regretted it. 'It was a question all the time of being either roasted or stewed according as we crawled out of or remained in our little berth. We were twelve days on the way including two . . . at anchor.'

Finally, on the way up to Zhenjiang for a last quick consultation and farewell, Hudson Taylor wrote to Emmeline Turner, on August 20. Telling her his plans, he took the trouble to explain at length how her school accounts had gone wrong through a misplaced decimal point. 'Decimals are fractions with the denominator unwritten for brevity and convenience. . . . So that .1 equals one tenth, .12 equals twelve hundredths. . . . You had payments of "$14. 6" and balance "$30.8" = total "$45.4." It should have been payments $14.06, balance $30.98 = total $45.04. . . . I feel so thankful to the Lord for bringing you out, and for making you such a help and comfort. . . . You have been able to fill an important place, and have not caused either discouragement or anxiety; I am persuaded that each year will only deepen the Christian love and confidence we feel towards you.' – the kind of letter which won him loyal colleagues.

The Rudlands and their three children arrived in Shanghai, Hudson Taylor returned from Zhenjiang with the four McCarthy children, to escort them to England, and on August 30 they and a merchant friend and his wife from Zhenjiang all sailed as third-class passengers on the French mail-boat, the men and women separated into dormitory cabins. Hudson Taylor made no reference to his back, but he was still dependent on crutches. Either his foot injury had been no mere sprain or he was taking the weight off his spine. Events soon showed which it was.

The unexpected   *September–November 1874*

The fast voyage of six weeks to Marseilles ended in a way they had not foreseen. Mary Rudland's illness had gone from bad to worse; and Hudson Taylor had developed increasingly severe spinal symptoms. When they reached Marseilles, letters were waiting to say that Emily had died after midnight early on July 25, and Catherine Duncan, worn out after ten months of continuous nursing, had been persuaded to go home to Scotland to recover. By the time they all reached Paris, Mary Rudland could go no further and Jennie had to break the journey with her. They came on a day later.

The term 'delayed concussion of the spine' sounded well as an explanation of Hudson Taylor's trouble, but was inadequate. By the time he, William Rudland and the seven children reached London on October 14, he was getting about with difficulty even on crutches and after too much activity, by the 28th was forced by pain to keep as much as possible to his room.

The longed-for happy family reunion proved impossible. His son Herbert was with his grandmother getting over scarlet fever, after being nursed by Louise Desgraz. Little Maria and Charles Edward were in quarantine at Pyrland Road, apparently sickening with the same disease. Everyone had 'deserted' Louise to cope as best as she could, except for Douthwaite's fiancée, Lily (Elizabeth) Doig, who called occasionally from outside in the street to know if they needed anything. William Faulding took Jennie and two McCarthy children to his home in Barnet, where Howard Taylor was already staying, and their merchant friends from Zhenjiang took two more. The Rudlands moved into lodgings found by Louise near by.

Using letter paper with heavy black margins for mourning, Hudson Taylor wrote to his mother on October 22, 'I am almost overwhelmed or you could have heard from me sooner.' No relative had died. The mourning almost certainly was for Emily. But no letters or diaries remain to throw more light on those harrowing days. They had reached home too late, not only to see Emily. On October 23, eight days after arriving, Mary Rudland died.

By normal timing, the news from China would have reached them at the end of October that their faithful friend, Miles Knowlton, had died at only forty-nine in an acute attack of dysentery. His wife and daughter had barely escaped with their lives, and were recovering slowly.[12] It was a sad home-coming. Even his sister Amelia and her husband Benjamin could not come to him. They were going through crises of their own.

On November 12 he wrote again to his mother. 'My spine has suffered from the vibration of railways, cabs and omnibuses, etc, since reaching land, now I am forbidden travelling at all and need to spend much time on my back.' Catherine Duncan was in London again and preparing to sail in a week's time, escorting Lily Doig and Nellie Faulding at long last to their fiancés, Arthur Douthwaite and Charles Fishe, in China. Thomas Weir of Shanghai had secured passages for them on a Castle Line ship for only £50 each. On the 28th, one of Jennie's characteristic letters (still with black margins of mourning) exhorted her mother to stop fretting about Nellie.

'The more you give way the more difficult you will find it not to go on doing so. . . . Cheer up, Ma dear, I will do all I can to be a comfort to you.' Jennie by then was six weeks from her second confinement. Scarcely a mention of the council or secretaries is to be found. With Hudson Taylor home from China, he was naturally expected to take up the reins of Mission affairs. But it had to be from his bed.

Burma trade route[13]   August 1874

As long ago as the days of the Roman empire, Chinese silks had been carried by camel caravans through Chinese Turkestan to the Caspian Sea and Bosphorus. In the seventh century, Arab dhows traded between the Red Sea and Canton. While Columbus looked for a route to the East Indies by sailing westwards – to find the Americans blocking his route – Vasco da Gama rounded the Cape of Good Hope and made his way across the Indian Ocean to Malaya (Book 1, pp 64–8). Sichuan province was one of the great sources of finely woven silk, but the three south-western provinces of Sichuan, Guizhou and Yunnan held more untapped riches which Western nations wished to exploit.

The natural outlet of the huge Sichuan basin was the Yangzi river (map, p 379) navigable by steamers from Yibin (Suifu) to Shanghai, an immense distance of 1,600 miles, through the fearsome Qutang, Wushan and Xiling gorges and rapids (only blasted clear and made safe since 1950). The plateau of Yunnan at an altitude of 5,000 feet, walled and moated to its north and west by high mountain ranges and the deep gorges of the Salween and Mekong rivers, also opened naturally to the east through Guizhou and Guangxi provinces to the Yangzi and Red Rivers. Southwards and south-eastwards the fall of land was towards Vietnam, Laos and Burma. But the Irrawaddy river was navigable as far north as Bhamo beyond Mandalay. Exploration of the south-eastern route convinced Archibald R Colquhoun (1882) that it had strong advantages over the Bhamo route, and the notorious 'Burma Road' of the Second World War followed a route through Lashio. But in 1874 Bhamo was most widely believed to hold the key, for Chinese merchants' pack-trains plied regularly between Bhamo, Tengyue (called Momein), Teng-chong, and Dali, leading to the provincial capital at Kunming. Half the inhabitants of Burmese Bhamo were Chinese.

Bhamo was the place and this the route Hudson Taylor had

wanted to exploit for Mission purposes since 1865, when he made his first proposition to John Stevenson (and consulted William Burns); only to be disappointed by an exacerbation of the Panthay Muslim rebellion in Yunnan. Either before Stevenson left China on June 7, 1874, or soon after Hudson Taylor also reached Britain, they consulted again about making an attempt to enter the western provinces of China through Burma. The passes did not lie above 8,700 feet, nor were the bridges over the roaring rapids of melted Tibetan snows below 2,500 feet. Tengchong lay at 5,500 feet, Dali at 7,000 feet, and Kunming at 6,000 feet, but in the 400 miles, eight ascents and descents had to be made, an arduous journey but not 'practically insurmountable' as Colquhoun was to describe it, and certainly not to lightly-laden pioneers of the CIM. Excitement and

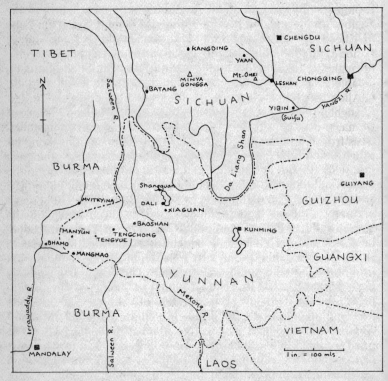

THE BURMA-YUNNAN 'TRADE ROUTE'

emotional debate over the Burma route were to flourish for a decade.

The British government had dispatched an exploratory expedition under a Colonel E B Sladen in 1868, which had been attacked by a Chinese 'Colonel' Li Zhenguo (Li Chen-kuo) close to the border. Li was therefore called 'a brigand and other hard names', although this was a foreign intrusion. So in preparing a second expedition in the year after the massacre of Muslims at Dali, greater precautions were taken. The minister in Peking, T F Wade, obtained passports from the Zongli Yamen, and two British consuls with experience in China, Clement F R Allen, formerly of Zhenjiang, and Augustus Raymond Margary of Yantai, were appointed in 1874 as interpreters to join the big new expedition under Colonel Horace A Browne. Margary had joined the consular service at 22 in 1867. An explorer named Ney Elias who had studied the new course of the Yellow River, and a surgeon-naturalist, Dr John Anderson, who had been with Sladen in 1866, with collectors, servants and an armed escort of 17 Sikhs and 150 Burmese troops (to see them safely through the tribal territory on the Burmese side of the border), completed the tally of 193 men.

Allen was sent by sea to Rangoon, but Margary, now 28, left Shanghai on August 22, 1874, one week before Hudson Taylor left China, travelling with six Chinese up the Yangzi. With introductions from the acting-viceroy of Hunan to all mandarins along his route, Margary sailed from Yueyang above Wuhan across the great Dongting complex of lakes which serves as a flood-reservoir to the Yangzi valley, and up the Yüan river into Guizhou (map, p 379). His journey was straightforward even in Yunnan, so recently the scene of rebellion and massacre. In a letter 'he dwelt much on the attention shown him by the acting-Governor' of Yunnan. Passing through Dali and Tengchong he came to Manyün (Manwyne to contemporary writers), only fifty miles from Bhamo and half that distance from the China-Burma border. There he was hospitably entertained for several days by Colonel Li Zhenguo, 'an exceedingly courteous, intelligent and straightforward man; he has done everything to facilitate the advance of the expedition', Margary reported to Wade. But in order to pass through the territory of the warlike Shan and Kachin border tribes he had to wait for an escort of forty Burmese to join him. With them he reached Bhamo on January 17, 1875.

In 1873 while Augustus Margary was on leave in Britain, he had

begun 'to think deeply about his soul's salvation' and before returning to China promised to write and tell his mother when he 'found
peace'. In Yantai he had taken part in seminars and study of the
Bible with his consular colleague Challoner Alabaster (later consul
at Wuhan) and with John Nevius and Timothy Richard. During a
bout of illness on his journey through Yunnan in November 1874 he
read his Bible and gave more thought to his own position. As a
result he wrote home from Bhamo to tell his mother of 'his own trust
in God and in Christ as his Saviour, and of his desire that prayer
should be offered by his Christian friends in England that his
journey on government matters to Burmah should end in some way
to the opening up of those wide provinces, through which he was
passing, to the preaching of the gospel.' His mother told this to John
McCarthy, who followed in Margary's footsteps in 1877.

The prospects were good. Colonel Browne completed his preparations and the expedition was to start on February 6. To officials
and tribesmen on the Chinese side of the border, ignorant of
Peking's approval of this expedition, its size must have looked
menacing.

The Huzhou, Suzhou and Ruichang riots   August–November 1874

Early in August two Chinese evangelists from Hangzhou quietly
moved into Huzhou and, after a few days at an inn, to test their
reception by the people they rented simple premises in which to
preach the gospel, plainly stating their purpose and still without
exciting opposition. For two months they were undisturbed and had
'some degree of encouragement', until they began to note the
presence of literati among their small audiences. Then on October
12 the neighbourhood *dibao* or constable came in with their landlord and ordered them to leave at once, on pain of having the place
pulled down about their ears. The Christians reported this to James
Meadows, who on his way through Hangzhou consulted the *daotai*
about the incident and obtained approval of his going to Huzhou.
Together with Arthur Douthwaite, only six months in China, he
reached Huzhou on October 31.[14]

After gathering all the facts and making sure that the rental
agreement for the Huzhou premises (a little shop with rooms above
and behind it) were satisfactory, they called on the city prefect and
offered to relinquish them if he would arrange for suitable premises
to be provided elsewhere. They told him what he would have known

already, that the anti-foreign secret society in Huzhou had threatened to destroy the house and lynch the landlord if the evangelists did not leave. The prefect was very civil, and they returned to the 'chapel' in the evening not suspecting until they arrived how serious the situation had become. In their absence a crowd had broken into the shop-front chapel, overturned the furniture and damaged the living quarters behind, where one of the evangelists was lying ill with typhus.

Leaving Douthwaite to guard the property and the sick man and his wife, if he could, Meadows returned to the prefect's *yamen* to seek official protection. In his absence the chapel and its furniture were destroyed, and after Meadows returned, deceived by the mandarins, he, Douthwaite and the sick evangelist were robbed of almost all they possessed. Promises of restitution were not kept, being only a polite way of quietening the foreigner and gaining time.

Little differed in the pattern of events from the previous riot at Huzhou, and the local literati had again proved their point, that even so near to Shanghai they would not tolerate the intrusion of foreigners. Nor had the inability of the high mandarins to control them altered at all.

Two weeks later, the American Presbyterian Mission at Suzhou, only fifty miles from Shanghai, was attacked during a teaching session for church members. The usual story of a rabble smashing and plundering was repeated, until the late intervention of a magistrate restored a semblance of order. Again one of the minor culprits was sentenced to flogging with 250 blows, considered a light sentence, but the literati were left untouched.[15]

From Jiujiang J E Cardwell reported on November 7, 'Two of the American missionaries have just had a severe beating at a city seventy-five *li* (twenty-five miles) from here. The magistrates refused to look at their passports or help them in any way. So they were left to the mercy of the mob, and barely escaped with their lives by swimming a river in darkness.' The city was Ruichang, west of Jiujiang – called Shuichang in the contemporary reports. Early in 1873 H H Hall of the American Methodist Episcopal Mission had attempted to open an outstation at Ruichang, only to be driven out by a mob employed by three of the local literati, while the chapel was attacked and its furniture and books destroyed.[16]

On October 29, 1874, V C Hart, the good friend of the Meadows and Cardwell families, and two other American missionaries made a courtesy call on the magistrate after renting another building.[17]

They then returned to Jiujiang. The next day, the two Chinese evangelists were driven out by the 'gentry' and threatened with death if they dared to return. Two missionaries and another Chinese Christian therefore took their place and went at once to the *yamen* to see the magistrate, only to be mobbed and insulted in the *yamen* itself. The *yamen* gates were thrown open to let the rabble in, and the Chinese evangelist was twice given 'a most brutal beating'. Driven out of the city, they were stoned as they fled. Both missionaries were hit often on the head, one bleeding profusely. They ran into the canal and struggled to the opposite side, illuminated by lanterns held by the literati to help the mob pelt them as they swam. Wandering about in the dark, wet and cold, it was midnight before they found their boat and could return to Jiujiang.

This was another of the 'forty quiet years' between 1860 and 1900.

CHAPTER THIRTEEN

'THE EIGHTEEN'
1875

When weak – strong!   *December 1874–January 1875*

The reports reaching Hudson Taylor as he lay partially paralysed in London, preparing *Occasional Paper* No 39, were daunting. Of Taylor himself, James Williamson, visiting London shortly after his marriage, wrote, 'Almost completely paralysed in his back and lower limbs. A rope fastened above his head enabled him to lift himself with his hands sufficiently to turn from side to side.' William Rudland had taken his motherless children to his own mother at Reading and was there, seriously ill himself, when Jennie (of all people) wrote to him, 'It seems very unlikely that either we or you will ever see China again.' The CIM was at its lowest ebb since its inception less than ten years before – but its *raison d'être* and its will to win through were unchanged.

Then on Sunday, December 13, a sudden onset of severe 'enteritis' struck Hudson Taylor. Jennie was expecting her baby at any time and avoided infection by keeping away from him. Once again the devoted Louise nursed him until his mother arrived to share the work. But during that week they thought he might die, and together witnessed his signature to a new will in which he left everything to Jennie, making her his sole executrix, 'believing that by so doing, I am consulting both her comfort and the best interests of my dear children, whom I leave with the greatest confidence to her love and care'. By then the children had been scattered to the John Eliot Howards in Tottenham, to the Grattan Guinness family and to Amelia who already had her own nine children and another well on the way.

By Christmas he was beginning to recover his strength when news came that Mr Tsiu had died. After Wang Lae-djün, Tsiu Kyuo-kwe was the one Chinese colleague who could least be spared. His loss was like a death-blow to the CIM itself. Tsiu's flogging at Xiaoshan in 1867 had steeled him to be a fearless preacher, once his natural fear of its repetition had been overcome. He was a spearhead, Wang Lae-djün the shaft, of strength and wisdom.

As Hudson Taylor lay in his 'little bed with four posts to the bottom two of which a map of China was pinned',[1] looking at it in terms of millions of people, he thought deeply about the nine provinces still denied the gospel brought by the Protestant Church, though occupied for centuries by Catholic missionaries. The task was becoming no less difficult, the casualties were mounting, the prospects were poor of his recovering to lead the way, and still no gifted leader to support or succeed him had emerged. In spirit he was uncowed. He and the Mission had been praying for two years for those eighteen men needed to launch the new offensive with the gospel. So far only Fred Baller, Henry Taylor and Arthur Douthwaite could be seen as answers to those prayers, but even from bed it was possible to rouse the Church.

The capital gift of £800 from Mrs Grace was already earmarked for pioneering, and in September 1874 Grattan Guinness told the council that she 'had engaged to place £1,000 into his hands for missionary purposes, £500 of which he had agreed with her to hand over' to the CIM.[2] But the financial shortage from which the Mission had been suffering for two long years was a shortage of funds for day-to-day continuance of established work, the unglamorous 'general purposes'. He had no sense of limitation by God, only to pray for personnel without making a public appeal for them, as he had in regard to money. The two issues were distinct. On the contrary, he knew that a challenge to unreserved commitment would be of spiritual benefit to the Church at large. 'Pray ye therefore the Lord of the harvest that he will send forth labourers into his harvest' and 'Go ye therefore' were two sides of the same coin. So, as the year ended he began to publicise an appeal for eighteen men, of a type not sought by other societies lest he undermine them, in response to prayer. *The Christian* and Spurgeon's *Sword and Trowel* and a number of other Christian periodicals carried the article in which he struck at the heart of the matter. Prayer for China in her need would bring the answer in a way no mere appeal or persuasion could.

APPEAL FOR PRAYER
ON BEHALF OF MORE THAN 150 MILLIONS OF CHINESE

There are nine provinces of China, each as large as a European kingdom, averaging a population of seventeen or eighteen millions, but all destitute of the pure Gospel. About a hundred Roman

Catholic priests from Europe live in them, but not one Protestant missionary.

Much prayer has been offered on behalf of these nine provinces by some friends of the China Inland Mission; and during the past year nearly £4,000 has been contributed on condition that it be used in these provinces alone. We have some native Christians from these regions, who have been converted in our older stations, and who are most earnestly desiring the evangelization of their native district. Our present pressing need is of missionaries to lead the way. Will each of your Christian readers at once raise his heart to God, and wait one minute in earnest prayer that God will raise up this year eighteen suitable men, to devote themselves to this work. Warm-hearted young men, who have a good knowledge of business, clerks, or assistants in shops who have come in contact with the public and learned to cover the wants and suit the wishes of purchasers, are well fitted for this work. They should possess strong faith, devoted piety, and burning zeal; be men who will gladly live, labour, suffer, and if need be, die for Christ's sake.[3]

It was a brave and defiant act, made from a paraplegic's bed, with little sign as yet of ever being ambulant again.

On the morning of January 7 his fortitude was to be taxed in quite another way. Jennie was sharing a room with a young candidate, Annie Knight. That morning, as soon as Annie had gone down to breakfast, Jennie quickly prepared for her baby to be born. She had told no one that she was in labour, thinking there was plenty of time. After breakfast all the family, but for Jennie, met for family prayers at Hudson Taylor's bedside and dispersed again. One of the children came in to see Jennie and was sent back with the message, Would Louise please come at once? 'When I reached the bedside the baby was already born,' Louise recalled, 'I ran across (to Mr T's room). He could not possibly walk so I wheeled a small sofa by the side of his bed and . . . he rolled himself slowly on to (it), then I wheeled him . . . to Mrs T's bedside. Sitting up with great difficulty he did what was absolutely necessary, then threw himself back utterly incapable of doing any more. . . . Then I wheeled him back to his bed.' To his mother he wrote, 'Jennie gave birth to a son, Ernest, about nine a m. . . . She was surprised, we more so.' He was 'a wee little mite', very slow to recover from his precipitate birth, and while not 'retarded' in the modern sense, was handicapped by frailty throughout his subsequent years as a missionary in China.

Three weeks later Louise reported to Hudson Taylor's mother

that his back was 'paining him a good deal . . . from overworking himself and twisting about in bed'. His bedroom had become the Mission's central office, with John Stevenson and other volunteers spending hours at his bedside writing to his dictation, and the council meeting in the same conditions. The response to the appeal had begun already.

Margary murdered[4]   *January–May 1875*

The council, meeting at No 6 Pyrland Road on December 14, had been startled to hear from the invalid in bed that for ten years he had contemplated sending missionaries into western and southern China via Burma, and now expected his plans to materialise very shortly. Two gentlemen from Burma, one a member of Colonel Slanden's abortive expedition, had been to see him in October, encouraging him to send missionaries soon. Colonel Browne's expedition was about to start, with approval from Peking.

John Stevenson was present at the next meeting of the council on January 25, also held at Hudson Taylor's bedside, when he announced that Stevenson 'would shortly start for Bhamo as his headquarters, and special meetings were to be arranged to bring the matter before the churches'. His wife and children would stay at home. March was set as the time for him to go, and it was hoped that by then he would have a companion.

Augustus Margary had arrived at Bhamo on January 17 with only experience of friendly co-operation by the Chinese to report. On January 26 a Chinese merchant warned the political agent at Bhamo that Colonel Browne would be opposed. Ney Elias and a small party set off by one route on February 6, through Mangmao (Maingmaw), while on February 18 Colonel Browne and the main party crossed the frontier on the Manyün road with Margary. At Mangmao 'on the insistent advice' of Colonel Li Zhenguo, Elias changed his route and, on hearing of how Browne fared, returned to Bhamo.

When Colonel Browne's party entered China he was warned by a Burmese that an ambush lay ahead of him, and between the 18th and 22nd more warnings were given. Margary and his six Chinese companions then went ahead 'to consult with Colonel Li on whose friendliness he relied', and reported that the way was safe. On the 22nd, however, Colonel Browne was hemmed in on three sides by armed men and ordered his Sikhs to fire, covering his retreat to Bhamo where he arrived on February 26. On the way, he was shown letters to Burmese in his force telling them not to be with Browne on February 23, as that night they were to be attacked. On the 25th he learned that Margary and five of the six Chinese had been 'killed on the 21st, by a body of armed Chinese'. Significantly, the only survivor was a Yunnan provincial.

If the resistance had been premeditated, who had been responsible? King Mindon at Mandalay, 'strongly opposed to the further opening of trade routes'? Or the provincial government of Yunnan, no less antagonistic to the British aims, and suspicious of British motives since Colonel Sladen's expedition had unavoidably made terms with the Panthay rebels? In any case, what trade but opium did the British Indian government want to establish through Burma? The Shans or Kachins? Or was it the border Chinese, always as independent of the central government as they could contrive to be? Colonel Li's mother was Burmese, and only six months previously a rich Burmese caravan bearing tribute to Peking had passed unmolested along this same route. Local Chinese, not Colonel Li who had been at Mangmao, were probably to blame, but ultimately the responsibility had to rest on the provincial government for an armed assault on a British mission bearing documents issued by the Zongli Yamen, and for the murder of a British consul. The acting-viceroy of Yunnan was Zeng Yüying, slaughterer of the Panthay Muslim rebels reputedly in their tens of thousands.

Thomas Wade, minister in Peking, heard of Margary's death and the repulse of Colonel Browne by a cable from the India Office, London, received on March 11. A week later, Wade presented Prince Kong with his demands: a commission of investigation to be conducted in the presence of British officers; a second expedition to be allowed; 150,000 taels to be placed in Wade's hands; and a satisfactory audience of the emperor to be given. A firm riposte could be predicted. The stage was set for another confrontation holding all the ingredients of yet another *casus belli*.

Back in London Hudson Taylor was slowly making progress. 'More power to move about' was followed on January 29 by 'Hudson walked two or three times into the next room . . . with Miss Desgraz' help'. By the end of February he was up briefly every day and in March had his bed moved into his study so that he could sit or lie at will as his back recovered. In February he wrote almost daily to Jennie, away at her parents'. 'Mrs Grace has given £300 for new provinces and £30 for Bibles – promises £50 for passage, £20 for outfit for the first of the eighteen men – and DV £100 in October (bringing the total to £500) . . . thank God.' James Williamson and his bride, 'quiet, gentle, little and tidy', so admirably suited to him, were on the verge of sailing. 'The bustle and packing are now over, and the luggage has gone to the docks.' 'Very little money has come in, the last fourteen days, for general . . . purposes. We must not cease to pray.' Why did many people prefer supporting special projects rather than faithful persistence in hard work? It was understandable, but how could Christians be educated in wise giving without the appearance of asking for funds?

At Pyrland Road again, Jennie told her mother on February 23, 'Many are taking a deep interest in the opening up of work (in west China) via Burmah. . . . Today a new friend has sent in £200. Candidates continue to offer themselves' for the nine provinces. Writing to Emmeline Turner, she said, 'He (Hudson) feels that God has done far more by him while he has been laid low than would have been done, could he have been going round the country as he hoped.' And Hudson Taylor told her, 'This mission to west China . . . is giving a wonderful impetus to interest, in the whole Mission.'

John Stevenson's farewell meetings were in progress. Both he and his wife were enthusiastic about his venture. But there was no mention of anyone going with him, until March 15, when, surprise upon surprise, the council minutes recorded that Stevenson and Henry Soltau were to sail at the end of the month. Leaving his profession, Soltau was responding to Hudson Taylor's personal challenge. The impact of such dedication upon the Christian public could not but be dramatic. The same minutes recorded that twenty young men had presented themselves in response to the call for eighteen, several of whom were promising.

No one was being naïve, out of touch with reality. Lower Burma was annexed territory, resentful of imperial aggression. Upper Burma remained free, but while a commercial treaty had been reached with King Mindon, he was under suspicion for complicity in Margary's murder. China had demonstrated her objection to any opening of her western borders to foreign trade or anything else foreign. 'The difficulties are to human strength insuperable. . . . Is not all Burmah in turmoil? Has not Margary been murdered at Manwyne? Do not the latest tidings tell of Chinese troops massing in Yunnan?' – in anticipation of a punitive strike from Burma.

They sailed from Glasgow on April 6 and reached Rangoon on May 17, to find that the British authorities were still uncertain whether King Mindon or the Chinese were to blame for Margary's death, and would not allow Stevenson and Soltau to proceed. They found a Muslim refugee to teach them the mandarin dialect of Yunnan, and started on Burmese as well. If December had seen the nadir of the China Inland Mission's early history, with 1875 and Hudson Taylor's rallying call from his bed, a new spirit became discernible among supporters, missionaries and observers alike. Compliments like Miles Knowlton's had been few and far between. Those from men of the type of Consul Medhurst (pp 220–1) were necessarily veiled. The *Chinese Recorder* tended to overlook the existence of the CIM or to treat it as an afterthought. In 1875 the tide turned, and approval began to colour the comments, as in an editorial in the *Recorder*, 'We cannot but think the Directors of the China Inland Mission have acted wisely in sending Mr Stevenson and Mr Soltau to watch their opportunity of obtaining an entrance into Western China, by way of Burmah.'[5]

'The First of the Nine'   *January–April 1875*

On January 19 Catherine Duncan and her daughter (named Mary Jane Bowyer Duncan, with good reason) reached Shanghai with Nellie Faulding and Elizabeth Doig, and on February 6 Nellie was married to Charles Fishe and Elizabeth to Arthur Douthwaite. The next issue of the *Chinese Recorder* reported the death of E C Lord's wife, his third to fall victim to infections in Ningbo. Only a few months previously Hudson Taylor in a note to Jennie during one of their travelling interludes apart, had written 'You will like the new Mrs Lord'.

April saw Henry Taylor try his wings on a fledgling penetration from Wuchang through Hubei province into southern Henan, 'the first of the nine', with an evangelist named Zhang, so becoming 'the first of the eighteen' committed to the nine provinces. For fifty-six days they toured the towns and cities of the prefectures of Nanyang and Runing (now Runan). One of Grattan Guinness's students at Harley House, named Joseph Adams, went independently to Burma after reading Hudson Taylor's January appeal, joining Stevenson, Henry Soltau and the CIM out here. Already 'the eighteen' were coming to grips with the task.

Charles Judd was at Wuchang, and in June, with one of the Hunanese Christians named Yao, and another Chinese, entered Hunan, the second of the nine provinces to be tackled. Nine years had passed since the Wesleyan Josiah Cox had visited Changsha, the provincial capital. Griffith John and Alexander Wylie had also travelled in the province. At last, however, premises were found among friendly neighbours and the Chinese Christians began work. Without difficulty they rented a house in Yueyang (Yochow) at the outlet of the Dongting lakes into the Yangzi river. But the magistrate 'demanded threateningly', Did they not know of the murder of Margary? Then how did Judd dare to come alone? When he refused them protection, 'a number of ruffians set up the cry, "The mandarin is unwilling to protect him – beat the foreign devil!"' and attacked them. Friendly Chinese defended them until the magistrate sent men in an armed boat to see them off to the next town. The Chinese evangelists returned to Yueyang later in the year.

The Garibaldi spirit   *January–April 1875*

Hudson Taylor's condition continued to improve, with setbacks he found hard to tolerate, and the response to his appeal for 'the eighteen', in the form of frank applications to serve in China, was a tonic to him. When the Mission's referees at Lord Radstock's suggestion wished to meet with him, showing strong interest in all that was happening, Hudson Taylor was unfit to oblige them, but dictated a long review of conditions in China and the prospects of the CIM. 'We hope to do *more* and *not* less than the former work, *as well as* (for the) new regions,' he said, to reassure any who might share William Berger's preference for consolidating the existing gains.

> There is nothing more evident than that the evangelization of China must be mainly effected by Christian (Chinese); and that (they) can only *effectively* work in or near their own native districts.

Elsewhere they were handicapped. They could learn a different dialect, but the tendency was for them to be treated as strangers, whereas a native of the same province was more likely to be welcomed without question.

As the number of enquiries from young men and women increased, a general form of letter became necessary, to be incorporated in each personal reply. In a Garibaldian statement he covered the essentials of the Mission's principles and practice, stressing that faith might be tested, and courage too.

If you want hard work, and little appreciation of it; value God's approbation more than you fear man's disapprobation; are prepared, if need be, to seal your testimony with your blood, and perhaps oftentimes to take joyfully the spoiling of your goods . . . you may count on a harvest of souls here, and a crown of glory that fadeth not away, and the Master's 'well done'. You would find in connection with the China Inland Mission that it is no question of 'making the best of both worlds' – the men, the only men who will be happy with us are those who have this world under their feet; and I do venture to say that such men will find such a happiness that they never dreamed of nor thought possible down here. To those who count all things but dross . . . for the 'excellence of the knowledge of Christ Jesus our Lord', He does manifest Himself in such sort that they are not inclined to rue their bargain. If after prayerfully considering the matter, you still feel drawn to engage in such work, I shall be only too glad to hear from you again.[6]

No one half-hearted need apply. For the people of the remoter provinces, unaccustomed to having foreigners among them, resolute men were needed, men who would get on with breaking new ground and *working* even when they were alone; men who would not keep looking over their shoulders to see what other foreigners thought of them. He had learned through bitter experience. From sixty applications within the year he sent fifteen whom he considered fit and ready to go. One of the first, strange as it seems, was only 18 years old, but so mature and well grounded in Scripture that Hudson Taylor chose to give him the advantage of an early start in learning the language. He himself had been only three years older when he began in China.

For two months George King served as Hudson Taylor's amanuensis, writing to his dictation from his bed, while they got to know and appreciate each other. Then King sailed unaccompanied on May 15, was shipwrecked by his vessel running on to a reef near Singapore, and arrived at Shanghai in another. Soon the report came back that the Chinese liked him, a compliment which reflected his own attitude to them. On Hudson Taylor's list of members of the CIM George King was the fifty-fifth to join. He became one of the Mission's famous pioneers, a byword for intrepid travel.

Henrietta Soltau also served as Hudson Taylor's secretary and, like King, absorbed his beliefs and statements so that she too became a lifelong asset to the Mission. Though she sat one day for an hour pleading to be allowed to go to China, he was sure that physically she could never stand the life, and would not send her. Her place was on the home staff. In time she became the trainer of the women candidates.

When George Nicoll of Dundee [to be distinguished from the disappointing Lewis Nicol of Arbroath] read the appeal, he wrote and was invited to London. The Pyrland Road ménage struck him as 'humble' and the prayers of the invalid leader 'child-like'. But family devotions round his bed with only Louise Desgraz, George King and the Taylor family present besides himself, stayed in his memory, with young Freddie, a 12-year-old, asking questions one after the other, each answered quietly and patiently by his father. Nicoll then spent two weeks at Harley House, being taught by Grattan Guinness and put through his paces as an evangelist among the rough East Enders by Tom Barnardo. Approved and approving, he returned to Scotland to settle his affairs, and was back again to work and train until he sailed in July, another illustrious pioneer.

March and April were difficult months with Louise Desgraz away at first, nursing Hudson Taylor's mother through pneumonia, and then Hudson Taylor, suffering a relapse. But by April 22 he could tell Mrs Gough (Mary Jones) that he was getting up and down stairs and into the garden. She had written on behalf of the Gough children's governess, Miss Bear, who wanted to join the CIM. He said, 'We shall probably see in a few months whether I am likely to be able to return to China again or not.' With or without him, no flicker of doubt, no mention of apprehension appears in the collected papers that the Margary affair might halt this missionary incursion in its tracks, as two government expeditions had been halted. T F Wade, minister, was being trifled with at Peking, and becoming impatient. Anything might happen. Much was indeed happening, but not only at the level of international relations. On the eve of the ambitious advance of the CIM into the farthest corners of the empire, great upheavals at dynastic levels boded ill for Christianity in China.

Ci Xi shows her hand[7]   *January–April 1875*

It was common knowledge in Peking in the winter of 1874 that the young emperor Tong Zhi and his chosen friends among the young Manchu noblemen were in the habit of frequenting incognito the brothels and opium dens of the city. The smallpox from which he died could well have been contracted accidentally, but the belief came to be widely held that because he had assumed power and dismissed his regents – the two dowager expresses – he had been eliminated. The custom of refreshing diners by the provision of steaming hot face-cloths at the end of a feast provided the opportunity. It was believed that an infected face-cloth had deliberately been used on him, or some such measure. Before he died on January 13, 1875, he was prevailed upon to issue an edict authorising the dowager empresses, Ci An and Ci Xi, to conduct the affairs of state.

The question of the succession became at once the central issue of the empire. The death of a British consul and the repulse of an expedition from Burma were matters of little moment. Tong Zhi's wife, the empress Alude, was pregnant, and her child, if a son, would automatically be the next emperor. Apart from him, one person was directly qualified to be Tong Zhi's heir, Pulun (son of the adopted son of the Dao Guang emperor's eldest son!). Next in line was the son of Prince Kong, himself Dao Guang's sixth son. But Ci Xi had contrived the marriage of her own younger sister to Prince Chun, Dao Guang's seventh son, who had a 4-year-old son named Zaitian (Tsai T'ien)! He was ineligible to occupy the Dragon Throne while Pulun and Prince Kong's son were living.

Ci Xi had thought it all through. As soon as her son Tong Zhi died, she summoned court and government in a council of state to determine the succession. The duty of the widowed empress Alude was to be beside her lord's body, so she was excluded. From the start, by sheer strength of personality Ci Xi asserted her own will upon the council. When Prince Kong proposed that the throne remain vacant and a decision be deferred until Tong Zhi's own child was born – the correct procedure – Ci Xi declared an interregnum to be too dangerous at a time of unrest and rebellion. A choice between justice and self-preservation was at once seen to be the prime concern of all present. While her relatives the imperial clansmen remained silent, desperately looking for a way to thwart her, the appointed career ministers cravenly took her side. Pulun she brushed aside as being the son of an adopted, not a natural, member of the imperial line, although an adopted son or grandson was constitutionally qualified. Prince Kong's son she dismissed from consideration without offering a reason, naming instead her nephew Zaitian. Everyone present knew this to be a breach of dynastic precedent. When the issue was put to the vote, ten princes and clansmen were for one or other of the rightful heirs, but fifteen councillors and ministers voted for Ci Xi's nomination. At her instigation the *Peking Gazette* at once published an edict declaring Zaitian as emperor with the reign title of Guang Xü, 'Continuation of Splendour'.

An appalling miscarriage of justice, precedent and protocol had been perpetrated through stark fear of an unprincipled woman. 'Thousands of memorials poured in from the censorate [*See* Appendix 2: Qing hierarchy] and the provinces, strongly protesting against . . . a violation of all ancestral custom and the time-honoured laws of succession.' Four years later one of the official censors presented a strongly-worded protest at the graveside of Tong Zhi and there and then committed suicide. Disaster for the empire was assured.

Ci Xi was taking no chances. She had sent urgently to Li Hongzhang, the new viceroy of Zhili, for troops to support her. And Yong Lu, tutor (and father, it was thought) of Tong Zhi, posted his imperial bannermen, the guards regiment, at strategic points in the Forbidden City. With his personal bodyguard of 4,000 reliable men from his own province of Anhui, Li marched the eighty miles from Tianjin in thirty-six hours, timing his arrival for midnight. With all accoutrements muffled and every man holding a chopstick in his mouth to remind him not to speak, the troops marched silently into the Forbidden City, its gates opened to them by Yong Lu's men.

The palace in which the 4-year-old Zaitian was sleeping was surrounded to protect him from conspirators, and he was taken from his bed to the imperial palace to be proclaimed emperor in the morning. As his imperial palanquin made its silent journey a dust-storm raged – another ill omen – and a phrase of profound meaning soon circulated through the empire as, for fear of reprisal, the people simply said to one another, 'And the child wept.' When day dawned on the fait accompli, such opponents and political conspirators as had not been arrested in the night knew it was too late.

The little emperor under the domination of Ci Xi was to shed many more tears and to die as Tong Zhi died, almost certainly the victim of her intrigue. And not only he: on March 27, 1875, three months after Tong Zhi's death, Alude with her child unborn died too. When Ci An, the co-regent, also died in 1881 suspicious circumstances were again to point to Ci Xi. 'There is, however, no doubt at all,' Alicia Bewicke Little wrote, 'that she did get (Alude)

. . . to commit suicide or die in some way – Chinese people generally say she was made to drink from a poisoned cup.'

Ci Xi never forgot Li Hongzhang's loyalty to her or ceased to admire the éclat of his midnight march. As soon as the situation was stable, he withdrew his men as inconspicuously as they had come. She had exposed for all to see her ruthless determination to have her own way, her unscrupulous character and her steely readiness to bide her time. No wonder, then, that neither Prince Kong nor Wen Xiang, the Grand Secretary, nor the Zongli Yamen had time or inclination to placate outraged foreigners or to find the murderer of a young man, Augustus Margary. If they knew or had an inkling of an answer, it suited them well to keep Wade dangling on prevarications of one kind after another until, enraged, he packed his bags and withdrew his embassy. That meant war – at a time when Hudson Taylor's 'eighteen' were poised to defy both mandarins and minister.

With deepening dislike of foreigners and foreign ways, Yehonala, Ci Xi, would one day turn her malice upon them and all Christians in her empire, taking thousands of lives, in an attempt to set history back 250 years, to the time of Yong Zheng and Qian Long (Book 1, pp 79–83). Through that fire would come again the triumph of the persecuted Church.

POSTSCRIPT

The last book of this series surveys the fulfilment of Robert Morrison's and Charles Gutzlaff's vision – the gospel taken to the whole of China. In it the final chapter of Hudson Taylor's life is told. In a rapidly expanding Mission his role became increasingly that of administrator, not the stuff of biographical narrative. So this chronicle will sweep through the remaining decades, a counterpoise to the first volume, describing the full flower of his dreams come true.

If the burden of his duties became administrative, it also expanded to include intercontinental travel and the growth of an international membership, losing nothing of the panache, shared at last by colleagues of the right calibre. The drama by which the Empress Dowager Ci Xi sealed the fate of dynastic China, extended barely eight years into the twentieth century; and she herself barely outlived the man whose ultimate influence on China was perhaps as great as her own. Dying at the same age as he, (Ci Xi 1835–1908; Hudson Taylor 1832–1905), she carried the ancient mores of dynastic China to the grave with her, unmourned. But the Church she had tried to exterminate went on from strength to strength, as it is still doing.

A KEY TO CHINESE PLACE NAMES
(omitting those spelt alike)

Pinyin	Wade-Giles	Postal, Press
Anqing	An-ch'ing	Anking
Beijing	Pei-ching	Peking
Changzhou	Ch'ang-chou	Changchow
Chaozhou	Ch'ao-chou	Chaochow
Chengdu	Ch'eng-tu	Chengtu
Chongqing	Ch'ung-ch'ing	Chungking
Dali	Ta-li	Tali
Danshui	Tan-shui	Tanshui
Danyang	Tan-yang	Tanyang
Dengzhou	Teng-chou	Tengchow
Fujian	Fu-chien	Fukien
Fuzhou	Fu-chou	Fuchow
Gan Jiang	Kan-chiang	Kankiang
Gansu	Kan-su	Kansu
Gaoxiong	Kao-hsiung	Kaohsiung
Guangdong	Kuang-tung	Kwangtung
Guangxi	Kuang-hsi	Kwangsi
Guazhou	Kua-chou	Kuachow
Guizhou	Kui-chou	Kweichow
Haizhou	Hai-chou	Haichow
Hangzhou	Hang-chou	Hangchow
Hankou	Han-k'ou	Hankow
Hanzhong	Han-chung	Hanchung
Hebei	Ho-peh (-pei)	Hopeh
Henan	Ho-nan	Honan
Hongkou	Hung-k'ou	Hongkew
Hubei	Hu-peh (-pei)	Hupeh
Huizhou	Hui-chou	Huichow
Huzhou (Wuxing)	Hu-chou	Huchow (Wuhsing)
Jiangxi	Chiang-hsi	Kiangsi
Jiangsu	Chiang-su	Kiangsu

Jiaxing	Chia-hsing	
Jinan	Chi-nan	Tsinan
Jinhua	Chin-hua	Chinhua
Jiujiang	Chiu-chiang	Kiukiang
Kangding	K'ang-ting	Kangting (Tatsienlu)
Kunming	K'un-ming	Kunming (Yunnanfu)
Lanxi	Lan-hsi	
Mangmao	Mang-mao	Mangmaw
Manyün	Man-yün	Manwyne
Nanjing	Nan-ching	Nanking (Nankin)
Ningbo	Ning-po	Ningpo
Pitao	P'i-t'ao	Pitaw (Pithau)
Putuo	P'u-t'u	Pootoo
Pudong	P'u-tung	Pootung
Qiantang	Ch'ien-t'ang	Tsientang
Qinghai	Ch'ing-hai	Chinghai (Tsinghai)
Qingjiangpu	Ch'ing-chiang-p'u	Tsingkiangpu
Qingpu	Ch'ing-p'u	Tsingpu
Qu Xian	Ch'ü-hsien	Chühsien
Quzhou (Lishui)	Ch'ü-chou	Chüchow
Ruichang	Jui-ch'ang	Shuichang
Runan	Ju-nan	Runing
Shaanxi	Shan-hsi	Shensi
Shandong	Shan-tung	Shantung
Shantou	Shan-t'ou	Swatow
Shanxi	Shan-hsi	Shansi
Shaoxing	Shao-hsing	Shaohsing
Sheng Xian	Sheng-hsien	Shenghsien
Sichuan	Szu-ch'uan	Szechwan
Songjiang	Sung-chiang	Sungkiang
Suzhou	Su-chou	Soochow (Suchow)
Taibei	T'ai-peh (pei)	Taipeh
Taizhou	T'ai-chou	Taichow (Taichau)
Tengyue	T'eng-yueh	Momein
Tianjin	T'ien-chin	Tientsin
Tiantai	T'ien-t'ai	Tientai
Wenzhou	Wen-chou	Wenchow
Wujiang	Wu-chiang	Wukiang
Wuxi	Wu-hsi	Wuhsi
Wuxing (Huzhou)	Wu-hsing	Huchow
Xiamen	Hsia-men	Amoy

Xinchang	Hsin-ch'ang	Sinchang
Xinjiang	Hsin-chiang	Sinkiang
Xizang	Hsi-tsang	Tibet
Xuzhou	Hsü-chou	Hsüchou
Yangzhou	Yang-chou	Yangchow
Yangzi	Yang-tse	Yangtse
Yantai	Yen-t'ai	Chefoo
Yanchou	Yenchou	Yenchow
Yueyang	Yueh-yang	Yochow
Zhejiang	Che-chiang	Chekiang
Zhenjiang	Chen-chiang	Chinkiang
Zhili	Chih-li	Chili

THE QING HIERARCHY
(The essential structure)

The empire was governed from its capital, Peking, with remarkable cohesion. Such a vast territory and population necessitated viceroys with immense powers. An autocracy totally different from the democratic system by which elected representatives decide and act *for* the people, aided by civil servants whose responsibility is to serve, the dynastic government of China was much as it had been for millennia.

Limited in power by immemorial precedents and by the unavoidable delegation of authority to his eight viceroys, the emperor was nevertheless venerated and obeyed, more for his office than for his personality or ability. By the teaching of Confucius he was the Son of Heaven, Father and Mother of the Empire, by divine right paternalistic and authoritarian in the nature of his rule. He towered above his greatest subjects and nominated his own successor. The highest mandarins attendant upon him, promoted from governing many millions in viceregal office, approached him in the throne-room of his Tartar city, with nine prostrations, the *ketou* (*see* Book 1, pp 91–2). He held the power of life and death over them, as over all. The regents of a minor received the same respect.

The emperor ruled through six principal boards or ministries, superintended by two councils comparable to the British Privy Council and Cabinet. The first advised on constitutional and international matters, and the second on administrative government. When the emperor was a minor the real power lay in the first council, as when Ci Xi, Prince Kong and Yong Lu dominated it. Each board had two presidents, a Manchu and a Chinese, and two vice-presidents like secretaries and under-secretaries of state for each department. In addition to the Zongli Yamen another, like a Colonial and Commonwealth Office, regulated the affairs of all tributary states, of Tibet and of the Mongol princes. An Office of Censorship was the watchdog of the nation with rights conceded by emperors of the past, not only to criticise the morals and behaviour of the eight viceroys and eighteen provincial governors, but the emperor and imperial family themselves. A Chief Censor on occasion did not fail to speak out, on pain of being accused of dereliction of duty, but his head never sat comfortably on his shoulders. One more body must be mentioned, the Hanlin Academy, literally the Forest of Pens. Composed of the most exalted literary graduates, it was the supreme literary establishment, the authority on correct interpretation of the classics and the arbiter of all literati.

Massive like the gates of Peking itself, and congregated in tens of thousands in strategic positions throughout the empire were the Manchu garrisons under Tartar-generals, the not-always-silent bastions of the civil power. Under them and separately in the Chinese armed forces, the military mandarins, army officers of ascending rank, served under the highest commanders, who were always literary mandarins, as seen in the case of Zeng Guofan and Li Hongzhang. In 1863 before the end of the Taiping rebellion there were 14,000 civil mandarins, graduates in the Confucian classics, and 18,000 military mandarins, successful in martial exercises. Every provincial capital had its Manchu quarter for the garrison and their families. Differing markedly from the Chinese around them (the women's unbound feet in strong contrast to the tightly-bound deformities, considered beautiful, of almost all Chinese women and girls), the Manchus, like the Romans in their empire, were accepted as part of society. Only secret revolutionaries harboured thoughts of changing the status quo.

Over every two or three provinces a viceroy presided, with a governor of each province under him. He was therefore sometimes called the governor-general. Inferior in rank to the viceroys, but accountable directly to the second board of the central government, were two directors-general of the Yellow River Conservancy and of grain transport.

The highest ranks and honours carried titles corresponding in some degree to duke, marquis, earl, baron and knight. As an ambassador in Europe, Zeng Guofan's son was known as 'Marquis Tseng' in his own right. Rank was never hereditary. On the contrary, the honour was carried back to a man's ancestors, an incentive to secure for his children the best classical education in his power to bestow.

In the provinces a roughly six-tier structure of government functioned well (Book 4, Appendix 5). Any matter was referred up or down the ladder to the level appropriate to deal with it. Second to the provincial governor or *futai* came the provincial Chief Justice or *fantai* for crimes against the state, and the Treasurer, also a *fantai*, responsible not only for provincial revenue but as the chief magistrate for civil suits. The administrative provincial prefects or *daotai* responsible to the governors for law and order in their city or cities shared approximately the same status as a *fantai*. They had a number of subordinate prefects, named according to the size and status of the city, namely *zhifu* or *zhizhou*. Smaller towns and districts and sections of cities, called *xian*, were governed by their individual magistrates or *xian zhang*, accountable to the prefects.

All prefects and magistrates were appointed by Manchu decree, a measure to forestall plots and corruption. For the same reason the tenure of office was seldom for more than three years, and with rare exceptions no governor was appointed to his native province. The unfortunate effect of this precaution tended to be an impersonal, uncaring attitude to the people governed, and the need to act swiftly to make an appointment personally profitable. Finally, each *xian* magistrate had his staff of treasurer, secretaries and lictors at his official residence, the *yamen*, and so-called 'constables' with the status of police sergeant, the *dibao*, for on-the-spot law and order in small rural areas or a few city streets.

The *yamen* or official residence of the mandarin varied in size and grandeur according to the status of its incumbent. The largest covered acres of ground with sweeping approach roads. A huge ornamental gateway always facing south, with three entrances guarded against evil influences by a high wall ornamented with a rampant dragon, led into a palisaded enclosure of successive courtyards, halls and pavilions. Lacquered, latticed woodwork, shining pillars, gilded tablets, silent, attentive underlings – an awe-inspiring sight greeted the guest or suppliant. Only through the co-operation of secretaries and underlings could the magistrate himself be reached. Surmounting the gates and doorways, carved inscriptions dressed with gold leaf on lacquer proclaimed the nature of the mandarin's office. Over the Shanghai *daotai*'s gates they read: 'Father and Mother of the people', 'Protector and Administrator of Twenty Cities' – always grandiloquent.

When he issued from his *yamen* his palanquin or sedan chair was escorted by ranks of retainers. Two or four lictors with tall hats cleared the way with whips. Boys bearing red boards inscribed with gilt characters naming the rank and titles of the mandarin led the

way, followed by a thousand-name umbrella, the symbol of popularity. His sedan chair, carried by four, eight or sixteen bearers,
according to the great man's importance, was flanked and preceded
by lesser officials. Behind followed mounted military mandarins.
(*See* illustration, p 116.)

Emperor / Regents
'Son of Heaven, Father and Mother of the Empire'
and Court

Grand Council on Constitutional and International Affairs	Council on Internal Administration

Six Boards, each with two presidents, one Manchu, one Chinese, and two vice-presidents

Office of Censors under Chief Censor, 'conscience' of emperor, imperial family, viceroys and governors	Hanlin Academy supreme literary and examining body, arbiter of interpretation of classics	Civil and Military Administrative Boards	Zongli Yamen = Foreign Office	Office of Tributary States: Tibet, Mongolia &c

Manchu garrisons under Tartar-generals in provincial capitals and main cities	Viceroys (governors-general) over 2–3 provinces	Director-General of Yellow River Conservancy	Director-General of Grain Transport (inferior to viceroys but directly accountable to Civil Board)

Provincial governors and mandarins
(see Book 4, Appendix 5)

APPENDIX 3

ROMAN CATHOLIC AND PROTESTANT PROGRESS IN CHINA
A comparative table of 1866 statistics prepared by Emily Blatchley

Comparative Table of Statistics of Roman Catholic & Protestant Missions in China 1866

PROVINCE	Roman Catholic	Protestant	No. of Foreign Rom. Cath.	No. of Foreign Protestant	No. of Native R.C.	No. of Native Protestant	No. of Christians Rom. Cath.	No. of Christians Protestant	No. of Bishops R.C.	Students	Expenses Than $
Chih-li	Lazarists & Jesuits	1,6,7,14,17,19,22,23	14	16	2	40	15	52,000	92	1	5,00	12,000
Shan-tung	Franciscans	7,9,18	1	7	7	7	6	10,750	58	1	unknown	3,800
Kiang-su	Jesuits	(4,6,7,9,11,22,28)	1	35	9	17	7	73,000	242	1	5/6	6,500
Chih-kiang	Lazarists	2,3,7,11,12,14,20,25	1	10	12	5	16,42	3,000	346	1	unknown	3,600
Fuh-kien	Dominicans	1,5,8,14,17,22	1	18	20	1	10,86	40,000	1116	1	20	7,000
Kwang-tung	Missions Étrangères	1,2,7,9,10,13,14,15,18,19,21,24,26	1	19	30	3	3,63	19,000	938	1	2,5	8,800
Hu-peh	Franciscans	21,22	1	20	31	14	5	20,000	40	1	35	5,600
Hunan-ti	Lazarists	21	1	10	1	10		12,000	none	1	unknown	3,000
Kiang-si	Franciscans	none	1	7	none	7	none	17,820	none	1	unknown	2,800
Kan-suh	Franciscans	none	1	7	none	14	none	23,000	none	1	unknown	2,800
Ho-nan	Lazarists	none	1	4	none	1	none	5,000	none	1	unknown	2,400
Hu-nan	Franciscans	none	1	6	none	11	none	3,000	none	1	35	4,000
Sze-chuen	Missions Étrangères	none	3	34	none	60	none	18,000	none	1	110	18,000
Kwei-chau	Missions Étrangères	none	1	15	none	1	none	35,000	none	1	unknown	6,400
Yun-nan	Missions Étrangères	none	1	19	none	8	none	8,000	none	1	unknown	65,300
Mongolia	Belgian	none	1	20	none	6	none	11,000	none	1	unknown	9,400
Manchuria	Missions Étrangères	none	1	10	none	1	none	7,000	none	1	unknown	5,200
Thibet	Missions Étrangères	none	1	10	none	1	none	2,000	none	1	unknown	5,100
Total			23	263	92	14	243,206		585,580	3,132	18		121,800

* Gan-huwy & Kwang-si have no Protestant Missionaries.

† A Superior, not a Bishop.

‡ It should be remembered that of these not more than a dozen are ordained helpers, while the list of Roman Catholic priests is exclusive of all lay assistants, the number of whom we have no means of ascertaining.

§ So far as derived from European sources.

THE ENROLMENT OF AN 'ADORER',
CATHOLIC CANDIDATE FOR BAPTISM

Mgr. Faurie, Vicar Apostolic of Guizhou, in 1864 described the current practice in his province. A pagan declaring his belief in one God and his desire to become a Christian was taught the sign of the cross, placed on his knees before two candles on the altar and directed to prostrate himself five times with a declaration before each prostration – first, 'I believe in God, I abjure all my past errors'; second, 'I hope that God in His infinite goodness will forgive all my sins'; third, 'I love and adore God, all beautiful, almighty, more than anything else in the world'; fourth, 'I detest with all my heart the sins of my past life and I firmly resolve never to commit them again'; fifth, 'I pray the Blessed Virgin Mary, my mother, to obtain for me from God, by her powerful intercession, the grace of final perseverance.' Again, 'After this the Apostles' Creed is recited, also Our Father, Hail Mary, and the Ten Commandments. Then is added this declaration: "The commandments of God that I have just recited are contained in these two: To love God above all things and one's neighbour as oneself. These ten commandments have been dictated by God that all nations might observe them. Those who keep them faithfully will be recompensed with eternal glory in heaven. Those who disobey them will be condemned by Him to the eternal torments of hell."'

Such information was available to the Protestant missionaries.

(Condensed from Latourette, K S: *A History of Christian Missions in China*, p 332)

HUDSON TAYLOR'S CHILDREN

JAMES HUDSON TAYLOR, b. 21 May, 1832, d. 3 June, 1905 at Changsha, Hunan
married 20 Jan, 1858, *Maria Jane Dyer*, b. 16 Jan, 1837, d. 23 July, 1870, Zhenjiang, 5 sons, 3 daughters:

Grace Dyer	b. Ningbo, 31 July, 1859, d. 23 Aug, 1867
Herbert Hudson	b. London, 3 April, 1861, d. 6 June, 1950, m. 1 Nov, 1886, nine children
Frederick Howard	b. London, 25 Nov, 1862, d. 15 Aug, 1946 m. M. Geraldine Guinness, b. 25 Dec. 1862, d. 6 June, 1949
Samuel Dyer	b. Barnsley, 24 June, 1864, d. 4 Feb, 1870
Jane Dyer	b/d London, 7 Dec, 1865
Maria Hudson	b. Hangzhou, 3 Feb, 1867, d. 1897 m. J J Coulthard, 1892
Charles Edward	b. Yangzhou, 29 Nov, 1868, d. 13 July, 1938
Noel	b. Zhenjiang, 7 July, 1870, d. 20 July, 1870

married 28 Nov, 1871, *Jane E Faulding*, b. 6 Oct, 1843, d. 30 Oct, 1904, 1 son, 1 daughter: Ernest Hamilton, b. 7 Jan, 1875; Amy, b. 1876, d. 3 July 1953

APPENDIX 5

STATIONS OF THE CHINA INLAND MISSION IN APRIL 1875
(reduced facsimile from *China's Millions*)

TABLE OF STATIONS—*continued.*

STATIONS.	DESCRIPTION.	OPENED	NATIVE ASSISTANTS.	MISSIONARIES.
VI.—Cheh-kiang Province, S.				
Wun-chau Prefecture.				
30. WUN-CHAU	Prefectural City, 240 miles S.W. of Ning-po.	Dec. 1877	Mr. Chil, E. Kying Tsing sen, C. Mr. Ing, S.	Mr. and Mrs. Stott Mr. and Mrs. Jackson.
31. Dong-ling	Village, with several converts and about 20 persons interested.		Services conducted by resident members.	
32. P'ING-YANG	District City, S. of Wun-chau.	1874	Tsiu Din-kying, C. Seng Shü-nyün, C.	
Chu-chau Prefecture.				
33. CH'U-CHAU*	Prefectural City, four days journey W. of Wun-chau.	1875	Mr. Yiang, E.	
VII.—Kiang-su Province.				
34. *NAN-KIN*	Capital of Province, former capital of the Empire. Population about 500,000.	Sept. 1867	Mr. Teng, E.	Mr. and Mrs. Cordon (absent). Mr. Harvey (absent). *Superintended by Mr. McCarthy*
35. CHIN-KIANG	Prefectural City, about 215 miles up the Yang-tse-kiang. Population about 150,000.	Jan. 1869	Mr. Chang, E. King-shu, C.	Mr. and Mrs. Hudson Taylor (absent). Mr. and Mrs. McCarthy (city). M ss Desgraz (suburbs), absent. Mrs. Duncan.
36. YANG-CHAU	Prefectural City, about 12 miles N. from Chin-kiang. Population about 360,000.	June 1868	Tsiang Soh-liang, P Lo Si-fu, C.	
37. NORTH TAI-CHAU	District City, 30 or 40 miles E. from Yang-chau.	Feb. 1873	Ch'eng Si-fu, C.	
38. TSING-KIANG-P'U	District City, 100 miles N. from Yang-chau. Population, 30,000.	Dec. 1869	Mr. Ch'un, E.	
39. SHANG-HAI	Station for Press and business purposes.	Nov. 1873	Printers.	Mr. and Mrs. E. Fishe. Mr. and Mrs. C. T. Fishe.
VIII.—Gan-hwuy Province				
40. *GAN-KING*	Capital of the Province, about 400 miles up the Yang-tse-kiang.	Jan. 1869	Chu Sien-seng, E.	Mr. and Mrs. Baller. Mr. Geo. King (expected to arrive in July).
41. CH'I-CHAU	Prefectural City, N.E. from Gan-king.	Oct. 1874	Mr. Hsü, E.	
42. Ta-t'ung	Large business Town, on the Yang-tse-kiang.	June 1873	Wu Si-fu, C. Dzing Lao-yiao, C.	
43. T'AI-P'ING FU	Prefectural City, N.W. from Nan-kin.	Sept. 1874	Mr. P'un, C.	
44. WU-HU	District City and large emporium, on the Yang-tse-kiang.	Mar. 1873	Mr. Ts, E.	
45. KWANG-TEH-CHAU	District City, near Gan-kih in Cheh-kiang Province.	April 1872	Tsiu Fûng-kying, E. (absent)	
46. NING-KWOH	Prefectural City, S. of T'ai-p'ing fu.	Dec. 1874	Wu Cheng-tsan, E.	
47. HWUY-CHAU*	Prefectural City in S.E. of Gan-hwuy.	1875	Mr. Tông, C. Lung-chung, C.	
48. LU-CHAU*	Prefectural City, near the Tsao Lake, and N. from Gan-king.	1875	Mr. Han, E. Tông Si-fu, C.	
49. FONG YANG*	Prefectural City in N.E. of Gan-hwuy.	1875	Ch'en Wen-loh, E. Tsüen-ling, C.	
IX.—Kiang-si Province.				
50. KIU-KIANG	Prefectural City, about 500 miles up the Yang-tse-kiang (the itinerant work has extended to upwards of 100 cities and towns in the province.	Dec. 1869	Mr. Yiao, E. Mr. Pen, C.	Mr. Cardwell. Mrs. Cardwell (absent). Mr. and Mrs. Williamson.
51. Ta-ku-t'ang	Large Town, on the Po-yang Lake	July 1873	Lo Gan-fuh, E.	
X.—Hu-peh Province				
52. WU-CH'ANG	Capital of Province, 650 miles up the Yang-tse-kiang.	June 1874	Yao Si-fu, C. Chang Sien-seng, E.	Mr. and Mrs. Judd. Mr. M. Henry Taylor (itinerating in Ho-nan).

Ho-nan Province.—Mr. M. Henry Taylor and the native evangelist Chang are itinerating in this province.

Yun-nan Province.—Mr. J. W. Stevenson and Mr. Henry Soltau are in Burmah, hoping in due time to make their way into Yun-nan.

TOTALS—Mission Districts, 10; Stations and Out-stations (including Shanghai), 52; Native Helpers, 56; Missionaries and their Wives, 38.
ABBREVIATIONS:—P., Pastor; E., Evangelist; C., Colporteur; S., School-teacher; B., Bible-woman; N., North; S., South; E., East; W., West.
* Work in these Stations has been recently commenced, and it is hoped that it may become permanent.

A CHRONOLOGY
1868–75

1868	
January	T T Cooper attempts China–India via Tibet
Jan 6–16	J Williamson evicted from Jinhua
Jan 28–Feb 24	JHT tours southern Zhejiang
February	Anson Burlingame to USA
March	Charles and Elizabeth Judd arrive Shanghai
April 4	Wm C Burns dies at Yingkou (Niuchuang)
April 10	Maria and party depart Hangzhou for Yangzi advance
April 11	Taiwan riots begin
April 24	Tainan RC and Presbyterian premises destroyed
April–May	Bishop C R Alford reports to R Baxter
April–Sept	A Wylie and G John travel through Sichuan
May	Nianfei rebels enter Zhili
May 23	Taylor party arrive Zhenjiang
June 1	Taylor party arrive Yangzhou
June–Dec	CIM under attack in UK
June 28	Burlingame's 'Shining Cross' speech
July 20	Yangzhou premises occupied
Aug 1–8	Threats begin at Yangzhou
Aug 16	'First disturbance': Yangzhou premises besieged
Aug 22–23	Yangzhou riot
Sept and Dec	Anson Burlingame in Britain
Sept 1–3	Zhenjiang riot
Sept 11–30	W H Medhurst rebuffed at Nanjing
Sept 13	Lewis Nicol dismissed
Sept–Oct	British merchants mobbed in Taiwan
Oct 26–Nov 6	J H T and J Williamson up Grand Canal to Qingjiangpu
Nov 9	W H Medhurst and naval squadron at Nanjing

Nov 18	JHT reinstated at Yangzhou
Nov 29	Charles Edward Taylor born at Yangzhou
Dec 28	Lord Clarendon declares new policy on China

1869

	Cutty Sark built
Jan 8	J Meadows and J Williamson arrive Anqing
Jan 20	Sharp Peak Island incident
Jan 29	'Aotingpow' incident
Jan–June	JHT's southern tour
Feb 11	Anson Burlingame dies in St Petersburg
Mar 9	House of Lords debate on China
Mar 10	*The Times* attack on Missions
May 22	M J Knowlton's defence of CIM
May 20–June 5	Putuo holiday and press attack
July 14	'Missionary Memorandum' to Sir R Alcock
July 20	G Duncan occupies Qingjiangpu
Aug 24	J Williamson of LMS murdered near Tianjin
September	'The exchanged life' revives JHT and CIM
Oct 23	Sir R Alcock's Anglo-Chinese Convention signed
Nov 2	Anqing riot
Nov 26	W A P Martin made Dean of Tong Wen Guan, Peking
December	J E Cardwell arrives Jiujiang to pioneer Jiangxi

1870

	Muslim rebellion in Gansu crushed
	Mollman of BFBS visits Shanxi (1870–72)
Feb 4	Samuel Taylor dies, aged 5
Feb 12	Timothy Richard, BMS, arrives Shanghai
Feb 23	J Meadows and J Williamson reinstated at Anqing
Mar 22	Emily Blatchley and Taylor children depart Shanghai to UK
May	Anti-RC agitation at Nanjing
June	Anti-foreign agitation widespread
June 21	Tianjin massacre
July 7	Noel Taylor born
July 19	France declares war on Prussia
July 20	Noel Taylor dies
July 23	Maria dies

July 25	News of Tianjin massacre reaches UK
Aug 22	Viceroy Ma Xinyi assassinated at Nanjing
Aug 29	J L Nevius in danger at Dengzhou, Shandong
Sept 2	Napoleon III surrenders; Republic declared
Oct 6–31	JHT to Hong Kong

1871

	Trade Unions legalised in UK
Jan–Mar	JHT ill
Jan 28	Paris capitulates
March	J E Cardwell begins Poyang Lake travels
April–June	Second Yangzhou plot
June 3	San Francisco–Shanghai telegraphic cable open
June 26	T F Wade says 'rebellion afoot'
June–Aug	'Chinese Circular' and 'Zongli Memorandum'
Aug 5	JHT, Meadows family and Jennie Faulding depart to UK
Sept 25	JHT party arrives London
Sept–Oct	G Duncan makes South Anhui journey
Oct 13	Foreign Office tells Wm Berger to curb JHT
November	J McCarthy's indigenous principles outlined
Nov 28	JHT marries Jennie Faulding
Dec 5	G Duncan makes North Anhui journey

1872

	Secret ballot introduced in UK
Jan 3	JHT acquires 6 Pyrland Rd; occupied Jan 15
Mar 18	Wm Berger retires from CIM
June	JHT tours West Country
July	R Hill proposes London Council; agreed Aug 6
Oct 4	First meeting of London Council
Oct 9	Taylors depart UK to China; arrive Nov 28
Nov 15	Tong Zhi emperor assumes power by edict

1873

	Muslim rebellion in Yunnan crushed
Feb–June	JHT's indigenous church principles stated
Feb 12	G Duncan dies
Feb 23	Tong Zhi takes control
April 12–15	Jennie's twins stillborn at Nanjing
May 3	David Livingstone dies
July 18–25	Taylors up Yangzi to Anqing, Jiujiang

| Sept–Oct | Taylor's southern tour and forced marches |
| December | Large donations for advance to 'interior' |

1874

	Northern Mandarin Bible published (NT in 1872)
Jan–July	Financial stringency in established work
Jan 2, 11	Taylor's forced marches to Crombies, Rudlands
April	Japanese expedition to Taiwan; Oct 31 treaty
April 14	Decision to advance westwards
May 3	Shanghai riot
May 30	JHT and C H Judd to Wuchang; arrive June 3
June 2	JHT's accident
June 7	J W Stevenson departs Shanghai to UK for Burma
July 25	Emily Blatchley dies
August	Second attempt to occupy Huzhou begins
Aug 22	Augustus Margary departs Shanghai to Burma
Aug 30	Taylors and Rudlands depart Shanghai to UK
Sept 10	Miles J Knowlton dies
Oct 14–15	Taylor party arrives London
Oct 23	Mary Rudland dies
October	JHT progressively paralysed
Oct 31	Second Huzhou riot
Oct–Nov	Ruichang riot
November	Suzhou riot
Dec 14	JHT's severe dysentery; renews will
Dec–Jan	JHT appeals for 18 pioneers for the nine unoccupied provinces

1875

Jan–April	Empress Dowager Ci Xi stages coup d'état
Jan 7	Ernest Hamilton Taylor born
Jan 13	Tong Zhi emperor dies of smallpox
Feb 6	Colonel Browne's expedition departs Bhamo
Feb 21	A Margary murdered at Manyün
Feb–April	JHT recovering
April 6	J W Stevenson and H Soltau depart UK; arrive Burma May 17
April	M Henry Taylor enters Henan, 'First of the Nine'

THE LONDON 'COUNCIL OF MANAGEMENT'
1873

John Challice	Hon Treasurer; company director
William Hall	deacon, Bryanston Hall
Richard Harris Hill	architect and civil engineer; married Agnes Soltau; Hon Secretary
Theodore Howard	son of Robert Howard
George Soltau	trained candidates
Henry Soltau	Hon Secretary
Joseph Weatherley	

REFEREES

Dr Thomas J Barnardo	
Henry Bewley	Dublin printer, evangelist
Robert C Chapman	solicitor; Barnstaple
The Marquis of Cholmondeley	
William Collingwood	water-colour artist; Liverpool
Revd C Graham	
H Grattan Guinness, DD	Harley House, training institute
John Eliot Howard, FRS(1874)	quinologist
William Landels, DD	Regent's Park Chapel
William G Lewis	Westbourne (Grove) Chapel
John Morley	company director
George Müller	director, orphan homes; Bristol
William Pennefather	Convenor, Mildmay Conference
Lord Radstock	evangelist
Revd W L Rosenthal	
J Denham Smith	Dublin evangelist
T B Smithies	editor
Henry Varley	evangelist
Colonel Woodfall	Bath and Brighton

(Sources: OMFA; McKay, Moira: *Faith and Facts in the History of the China Inland Mission:* MLitt. thesis)

'THE MISSIONARY MEMORANDUM'
by John Shaw Burdon, William Collins, John Dudgeon,
MD, and Joseph Edkins (abridged)

Peking, July 14th, 1869

To H.E. Sir Rutherford Alcock, K.C.B., H.M. Envoy Extraordinary and Minister Plenipotentiary, Peking.

Sir:

In recent despatches . . . you have entered somewhat at length into the subject of Protestant missions in China; and we . . . desire to address you . . . on some of the points. . . . These despatches . . . strongly advocate a restrictive policy with reference to Protestant missionary operations in the interior of China, principally on the ground of the 'implacable hostility entertained by the Chinese authorities and the official class in China towards all missionaries,' and also because of the injury that will accrue to our commercial relations with China, if missionaries are permitted to domicile themselves in the interior. (Lord Clarendon) states it as your opinion that 'it is absolutely necessary that the missionaries should not establish themselves in the interior,' and again that, 'It is expedient that the missionaries should confine themselves to the treaty ports, exercising even there great judgement.' . . .

In giving the hostility of the Chinese to missionaries as a reason why Protestant missionaries should be restrained in their operations, the nature of that hostility, and the principal causes of it, should be distinctly mentioned. . . . (It) is not directed against them as a class, but as foreigners. And the causes of the hostility are the hatred of other races which the Chinese have always had, the repeated defeats inflicted on the Chinese government by England, and the evils connected with the opium trade. The Chinese look on missionaries as representatives of all foreigners; and all foreigners they believe to be encroachers on the rights of others, seekers after money and territory, or opium sellers. Almost every abusive placard that has been issued against Protestant missionaries has charged them either with secret designs of conquest or with being engaged in the coolie or opium trades, and making the teaching of virtue a cloak for these abominations. A missionary was not long ago driven out of a large city in the province of Honan by a mob . . . these words (being) shouted after him . . . 'You burned our palace, you killed our Emperor, you sell poison to the people, and now you come professing to teach us virtue.' These charges sufficiently indicate other and deeper . . . causes of hostility than the pretensions of some Roman Catholic Bishops, or even the well known and much to be deplored protectorate of Chinese Christians by France . . . (showing) beyond a doubt that the Protestant missionary suffers not as a missionary, but as a foreigner . . . from a hostility which he has had no share in provoking. Mr Taylor's expulsion from Yang-chow is a proof of this. . . .

You have directed Lord Clarendon's special attention to a placard which was posted . . . on the gates of Shanghai. . . . It was directed principally against the Roman Catholics, and accused them of eating babies' flesh, and of gouging out the eyes of the dying . . . by no means a new charge. . . . They have arisen from the misunderstanding of the rites of baptism, the sacrament of the Host, and extreme unction . . . The ruling classes know that these charges are false but they invent them for the purpose of deluding the common people and stirring up their hatred to foreigners. . . .

The injury that will accrue to our 'material interests' in China, if missionaries are permitted to domicile themselves in the interior, you give as another reason for restraining them from doing so . . . you entertain strong opinions against 'the wisdom of present efforts for the establishment of Protestant missions beyond the circle of the ports'. You 'have no doubt whatever as to the risk incurred, and the evil consequences to be anticipated . . . in our relations with the rulers and people of China.' . . . Commerce is thus put in the foreground as the one and only object of Great Britain in China. . . . The main branch of the British commerce in China is opium . . . Let the following statistics speak for themselves: in 1867, the total amount of India opium imported into China was 88,148 piculs, 25,582 of which were *smuggled* into China from Hongkong. In silver the total value of this opium was Taels 45,071,357. In the same year (1867) the total amount of tea exported . . . Taels 33,754,009. The total amount of silk . . . Taels 15,724,380. Total value of tea and silk exported in 1867, Taels 49,478,389.

Opium then may be considered as the main branch of British commerce in China . . . It has given impetus to the growth of native opium, which (as in Szechuan) is gradually superseding the foreign article. . . . Since the opening of the Yangtze . . . the number of smokers has been trebled, 'the cultivation of the poppy' said one of the Censors in a memorial recently addressed to the Emperor . . . 'has substituted for cereal productions over vast tracts of the western and northern provinces. . . .' British commerce is responsible, and yet it is in the interests of British commerce that Protestant missionaries are to be restrained from penetrating into the interior . . .

In opposition to this, we maintain that honourable commerce has nothing to fear from Protestant missionaries, but everything to gain.

Merchants, as a rule, cannot make themselves understood among the people, as they but rarely learn their language; British officials, even if they do know the language, mix but little among the native population. Protestant missionaries learn the language, mix with the people, and throw their influence all on the side of morality, peace and good will. . . . They live among the Chinese on a friendly footing, diffuse information, receive the Chinese cheerfully in their houses. . . . The more there is of this sort of influence the better . . . especially in inland towns . . . Our merchants are urging freer access to the interior, and even permission to reside in inland towns for purposes of trade . . . When complications arise . . . will the British Minister of that day . . . advise that the merchants be confined again to the open ports? . . .

Protestant missionaries ask neither for 'gunboats' nor soldiers to protect them. The use of force in connection with missionary operations is most abhorrent to their feelings. All they ask for is that their authorities – Minister in Peking and Consuls in the ports – will exert a friendly influence . . . to insist on protection being given to all British subjects travelling or residing in the interior. . . . It is unjust to speak of missionaries as anxious to fall back on H.M. naval and military forces to help them in their work . . . Missionaries, as a rule, never travel without a passport, and this has always to be applied for at the Consulates. The Consuls therefore have every opportunity of enquiring into the movements of missionaries. . . . This system gives to H.M. government all the 'direct control' that is necessary over their proceedings. . . .

You have thought good, in enforcing your opinion 'of the necessary connection of missionary labour with commercial interests, as an obstacle to progress and improved political relations', to allude to . . . Protestant missionaries – their faulty mode of procedure, their imperfections, their disputes with each other and with the Roman Catholic missionaries, their sympathy with the Taiping rebels, and the revolutionary nature of the doctrines which they teach – as proofs that 'no good can come out of such instrumentality'. . . . You have conveyed the impression to H.M. government that Protestant missionaries make no attempt to reach the ruling class in China. . . . We assert . . . on the other hand that it is *not* a fact . . . Nearly a hundred works on science, medicine, history, geography, law, and miscellaneous subjects, have been published in China by Protestant missionaries . . . in a style so acceptable to the learned class, that men belonging to this class, when acting as Governors and Viceroys, have reprinted at their own expense not a few of them. . . . The object has been to inform the minds of the Chinese, so as to remove their prejudices, to induce them to think with candour, and thus pave the way for presenting Christianity to their attention.

We have often heard of late that missionaries are only half-educated men. . . . 'It is vain to hope,' you continue, 'for the conversion of a shrewd, rationalistic and sceptical nation like the Chinese by instrumentality so imperfect'. . . . From this and similar statements the whole Protestant missionary body has been so represented in *The Times*, the *Pall Mall Gazette*, and other newspapers. Will the following facts bear out the charge? All the Chinese dictionaries yet made for English students of Chinese are the work of Protestant missionaries; the conductors of and principal writers in the *Chinese Repository*, an invariable mine of information on almost every Chinese subject, highly prized by all who wish to become acquainted with this country, were Protestant missionaries; the author of one of the best works on China, *The Middle Kingdom*, taken as a text-book among student interpreters of the British legation, was a Protestant missionary; the translator of the Chinese Classics is a Protestant missionary; the translator into Chinese of Wheaton's *International Law*, whose work was printed at the expense of the Chinese government, is a Protestant missionary . . . Is this class of men worthy to be branded in the House of Lords as 'rascals' or 'enthusiasts', and in the leading English newspapers as ignorant, or at best half-educated men? . . .

We know of no ('unseemly') disputes between Protestant and Roman Catholic missionaries . . . Of nearly 700 publications in China . . . there is none directed specially against Roman Catholic missionaries. . . . An objection was made by M. Simon, French Vice-Consul at Ningpo to the *Pilgrim's Progress* translated some years ago into Chinese by the Rev W C Burns, now deceased. This work of Bunyan . . . has been translated into a large number of languages, and it has never been thought necessary to expunge those passages, few and brief, which referred to the Roman Catholics. . . .

You have further alluded, in strong terms of condemnation, to the sympathy which many of the Protestant missionaries manifested towards the Taiping rebels. But British naval officers, and British Consuls, and even the then Governor of Hong Kong, are involved in the same condemnation. . . . It was principally through missionaries that information respecting the self-styled Christian views of the Taipings was . . . obtained, and it will be in your recollection that Lord Clarendon sent his thanks to Dr Medhurst for his translation of certain tracts and papers issued by the insurgents. . . . It is utterly unfair to speak of the whole body of Protestant missionaries as 'hailing the Taipings as heralds of Christianity', or as men who will render 'sympathy to the first band of pirates and robbers who can gather elements of disturbance about them'. . . .

In your despatch of December fourth, you dwell much on the political and revolutionary tendencies of Christianity, and argue that as the missionary, from the very nature of the doctrines he teaches, must of necessity teach revolution, he ought to be restrained from going into the interior. . . . It is an old accusation against Christianity . . . meaning only one aspect of revolution, namely *sedition*. Christ himself was accused of 'stirring up sedition'. . . . When the Chinese accuse Christianity of being revolutionary, they also mean that it teaches sedition. Now we know this is untrue. Christianity may be revolutionary of customs and opinions, but it is not seditious. . . . But the very presence of Anglo-Saxons in the East is revolutionary . . . If Christianity is to be banished because of its tendency to produce changes, the British and American governments ought to recall every Anglo-Saxon in China. . . . The East India Company zealously excluded missionaries from India at first, and yet were the means of subverting every native government. In Japan, missionaries have not been allowed to propagate Christianity since its recent opening to foreign intercourse; and yet it is a significant fact that within ten years of this event a great revolution has taken place in the government of that country. . . . The settlement in Peking of a British Minister, at the point of a bayonet, and the demand that he shall be treated as ambassadors in the west are treated, are far more subversive of all the Chinese ideas of government than the teaching of missionaries. . . . Are the British government likely to repent of all the injury they have done to Chinese exclusiveness and pride, and to withdraw all their officials and their subjects from China, on the ground that our presence here is revolutionary? . . . China, it is admitted on all hands, needs a revolution. Its ignorance, its superstitions, its pride, its exclusiveness – all require to be changed. Until this is done, foreign intercourse of any kind will be a perpetual source of danger to individuals, and of complications between governments. The Christian religion is the only means by which such a change can be brought about, and in due time it will effect this change in China, as it has done in the nations of the west.

(*Parliamentary Papers*, 1870, Vol 69,
China, No 9, pp 4–12)

GRIFFITH JOHN'S ANSWER
TO SIR RUTHERFORD ALCOCK
(extracted)

We are informed by Lord Clarendon that there are 'grave differences between the Protestant and the Roman Catholic missionaries, of which Sir R Alcock gives us very unseemly instances'. That there is a vital difference between Roman Catholicism and Protestantism we all know and admit. For this, however, the missionary is not responsible. This he cannot and must not conceal. In preaching and teaching, both parties are bound to declare what they believe to be God's truth.

But whatever hostile feelings the two classes of missionaries may cherish towards each other, they both seem to make it a point to keep them from public view as much as possible (of the Protestant missionaries this may be said emphatically); so that wranglings and bickerings between them are things almost unknown. . . .

(Sir R Alcock) has alluded in strong terms of condemnation to the sympathy which many of the Protestant missionaries manifested towards the Taiping rebels. . . . It is a well-known fact that they (with perhaps *one* exception) *did* nothing of which the Chinese government could reasonably complain. They did not give the rebels a particle of assistance or a word of encouragement in their rebellion. . . .

Lord Clarendon informs us that Sir R Alcock has stated 'that if ever Christianity were to become general in China it would be through the upper classes, not in spite of them'. . . . As a matter of fact we do not ignore the upper classes, and it is not our desire to convert the Chinese in spite of them. . . . Among our hearers, scholars and respectable people are often to be seen. We are always glad to welcome them, and sometimes we have most interesting discussions with them. . . . Our literature, too, has been prepared with the view of meeting the wants of all classes. . . . I fear, nevertheless, that for a long period to come we shall be compelled to prosecute our labours in spite of the wise, the noble, and the mighty of the land. Pride, prejudice, worldly interests, education, prospects, and position, all combine to steel their hearts against the truth . . . Here, as elsewhere, the weak things of the world seem destined to confound the things that are mighty . . . Our Saviour commenced at the bottom of the scale, and we have to do the same. Sir R Alcock would have us reverse the order, and commence at the top. But he does not tell us how this is to be done. . . .

There is a general impression abroad that missionaries as a class are uneducated and incapable men. . . . Compared with the other classes of foreigners in China, they are not inferior either in capacity or attainments. Neither the diplomatic service, nor the Consular service, nor the mercantile enterprise can boast men of greater ability, of higher culture, and in every way better adapted to secure the ends proposed. Of the majority of the missionaries Sir R Alcock can know but little . . . and what seems unaccountable is that he should have formed such an opinion of the whole from . . . such men as Medhurst, Lockhart, Edkins, Martin, and Burns . . . But it must be confessed that some of the best missionaries are men of whom the noisy world hears least . . . the man who is to be found in season and out of season superintending his churches, schools, and Bible classes, preaching and teaching in the chapels, the streets, the tea-gardens, and other places of public resort, travelling among the surrounding towns and villages, everywhere dispensing the bread of life to perishing men . . . This is the true Apostolic succession, the mission-ary *par excellence*, the kind of man that China most needs at the present time . . . They are the real powers, though they may go to the grave unthought-of by the wise and the learned. Xavier wrote no books . . . but look at his love to God, his philanthropy, his glowing faith, his enthusiasm, his Apostolic energy, his daring, his unutter-able longings, his restless activity. 'But this I dare to say' said he, 'that whatever form of torture or death awaits me, I am ready to suffer it ten thousand times for the salvation of a single soul'. . . . Ricci, Schall, and Verbiest were men of great erudition, and did much towards paving the way for the introduction of Roman Catholicism to every province of China. But it is not from these that their successors draw their inspiration. It is the spirit of Xavier that burns within them. . . . The one class of missionaries have left behind them books of more or less value; the other class have left behind them churches of living men and women.

(Thompson, R Wardlaw: *Griffith John*, pp 252, 259–60, 263–4, 267–8)

THE PROCLAMATION BY VICEROY MA XINYI
(*see* p 219)

MA, Imperial Envoy, Minister of State, Superintendent of International Trade, Viceroy of the Two Jiang, and Member of the Imperial Boards, and YING, Junior Guardian of the Heir-apparent, Governor of Anqing, Member of the Imperial Boards, General of the Forces, and Distinguished Officer of the Emperor's bodyguard, etc, make proclamation:

Be it known unto all, that, whereas in the provincial city of Anqing disturbances were got up, and a riot took place at the chapel of the religious teachers; the Viceroy and (Governor) with their subordinate officers, have already examined into, duly considered, decided on, and settled these affairs, having apprehended and punished (the three ringleaders, one by public disgrace in a cangue, the others by prohibition from all literary examinations). We, having clear evidence of these disturbances, and the parties concerned in them, have examined the Eighth Article of the English Treaty, and find it is clearly stated that 'all preachers of religion, and those entering their religion, must certainly be protected'. Therefore, those who preach, and those who enter the religion, are guilty of no offence against the laws, and must not, in the least, be treated with disrespect, nor hindered, nor molested in any way. We also clearly understand that all Chinese subjects who enter this religion, notwithstanding that they embrace the religion of the foreigners, are still Chinese subjects, and all must still respect and treat them as such, exercising towards them the same benevolence and equity that we do. . . . From this time henceforth, people and missionaries must live at the same place in eternal peace and concord. Should you meet with missionaries in any place preaching their religion, you certainly must treat them with respect, and do not again presume to cause disturbance and riot. . . .

These religious teachers have come from a foreign country across the western ocean. In their hearts they cherish benevolent purposes, and exhort men to practise virtue; so you must receive and treat them with respect and according to propriety. From the time of the issuing of this proclamation, henceforward, you must respect, and act in accordance with the treaties; nor must you outwardly profess respect to our orders, and secretly disobey.

TUNG-CHE (Emperor) 9th Year, 2nd moon, 18th day.

NOTES

Page   Note

Preface
8   1   Fairbank, J K: *China Notes*, Div. of Overseas Ministries, NCC/USA,
              Vol X1 No 4, 1973

Prologue
27   1   Cooper, T T: *Travels of a Pioneer of Commerce*
27   2   Johnson: *The Chinese Recorder and Missionary Journal*, March 1869,
              p 240; CIM *Occasional Paper*, No 19 p 301; Foster, A: *Christian
              Progress in China*, p 126
27   3   Laughton: Morse, Hosea Ballou: *The International Relations of the
              Chinese Empire*, Vol 2 p 226
29   4   Lees: *Chinese Recorder*, Sept 1868, pp 77–82; Oct 1868
29   5   Leboucq: Morse, H B: *International Relations*, 2.224, 233f
30   6   RC: Latourette, K S: *A History of Christian Missions in China*, pp
              331, 337; Younghusband, F E: *The Heart of a Continent*, p 41;
              Medhurst, W H, Jr: *The Foreigner in Far Cathay*, pp 33–4
30   7   Hosie, A: *Three Years in Western China*; Latourette, K S: *Christian
              Missions*, pp 310, 344, 361f
31   8   Morse, H B: *International Relations*, 2.115
31   9   Hart: Morse, H B: *International Relations*, 2.140, 158–61; Vol 3,
              Preface; Little, Alicia Bewicke: *Li Hung-chang*, p 64
32   10–12 Martin: *Chinese Recorder*, 1917 p 118; 1880 p 227; Martin, W A P: *A
              Cycle of Cathay*, pp 162, 181, 222, 233–4, 238
33   13   Martin, W A P: *Cycle*, pp 294, 297–8, 301, 316–7; Morse, H B:
              International Relations, 2.474
33   14   Covell, R: *W A P Martin, Pioneer of Progress in China*, p 192
35   15   Burlingame: Little, A B: *Li Hung-chang*, pp 61–4; Morse, H B:
              International Relations, 2.186, 188, 193, 195, 203, 228; Martin,
              W A P: *Cycle*, p 377
35   16   Pott, F L Hawks: *A Short History of Shanghai*, p 106

Chapter 1
39   1   Qiantang: strictly the Fuchun river in this stretch.
41–3   2,3   OMFA 3421a; Anne and the baby, closer to the floor where carbon
              dioxide would be less concentrated, had not yet been seriously
              affected. Newspapers: Woodcock, George: *The British in the Far
              East*, pp 215–6; 1830s, the Canton community published Morrison's
              Chinese Repository, Jardine's *Canton Press*, Dent & Co's *Canton*

Gazette; 1845, Hong Kong, *China Mail* launched, then 1903, *South China Post*; 1850, Shanghai, *North China Herald*; 1864, *North China Daily News*; (? date) *Shanghai Evening Courier*, *Shanghai Recorder*. Existing chiefly to provide shipping and commercial information, they also voiced opinion which differed from the government's, put pressure on consuls, minister and British Foreign Office to be more aggressive towards China, and criticised the Imperial Maritime Customs (Robert Hart) for unwelcome impositions.

45	4	Taylor, J Hudson: *After Thirty Years*, p 32; a change of magistrate could account for this.
50	5	OMFA F423, *A Report of the Hangzhou Branch of the CIM*, pp 5, 8
53	6	OMFA 4115.31
54	7	OMFA 3412h
57	8	OMFA G126.1–6, 10
59	9	Morse, H B: *International Relations*, 2.224–5; Latourette, K S: *Christian Missions*, pp 568–9; Parl. Papers (blue books) China No 3 p 24; *Chinese Recorder*, August 1868, pp 65–8
60	10	Morse, H B: *International Relations*, 2.225; Parl. Papers, China No 3, Sir R Alcock to Admiral Sir H Keppel, Aug 14, 1868
61	11	Broomhall, M: *The Jubilee Story of the China Inland Mission*, p 56; Latourette, K S: *Christian Missions*, p 869
62	12	Broomhall, M: *The Chinese Empire*, p 88
64	13	OMFA 3 Book 5, Taylor, J H: *A Brief Account of the Progress of the China Inland Mission*, p 4
68	14	Burns, Islay: *Memoir of the Reverend William Chalmers Burns*; *Chinese Recorder*, 8.208; Broomhall, M: *Chinese Empire*, p 311; Latourette, K S: *Christian Missions*, p 396; HTCOC Book 1, p 10
68	15	Stillbirths: perhaps due to the common medicinal use of laudanum, tincture of opium.
68	16	Broomhall, M: *Jubilee Story*, p 55; Guinness, M G: *The Story of the China Inland Mission*, Vol 1, p 357; Taylor, J H: *Brief Account*, p 30; *Occasional Paper*, No 15 pp 191–2; Morse, H B: *International Relations*, 2.226
70	17	OMFA 441.11, Taylor, J H: *Summary of the Operations of the CIM*, p 12
75	18	Affidavit: OMFA G213; *China Mail*, Oct 19, 1868; Parl. Papers, China No 1, Sept 3, 1868, Medhurst to Alcock

Chapter 2

77	1	Shining cross: Morse, H B: *International Relations*, 2.223, 226
78	2	Parl. Papers, July 2, 1870
79	3	*Occasional Paper*, No 15, pp 190–1
79	4	OMFA 4126.39; 12 Book 11.178; G333
80	5	OMFA 4115.37,40
82	6	*Chinese Recorder*, Jan 1870, pp 228–9
82	7	*Occ. Paper*, No 15, pp 190–1, 210–12; No 16 p 234
85	8	Parl. Papers, 1868–69, Vol 64, China No 2 pp 3, 19, 247 (OMFA G213); *Occ. Paper*, No 15 pp 191–3
87	9	Parl. Papers, Vol 64, China No 2 p 3 (OMFA G213)
87	10	op. cit. Chinese enclosure No 2
88	11	Affidavit: OMFA 4131; G213; *Occ. Paper*, No 15 pp 191–210

91   12   Parl. Papers, Vol 64, Chinese enclosure No 3 (OMFA G213)

92   13   Extracts translated from *Le Kiangnan en 1869 (Rélation historique et descriptive par les missionaires de la Compagnie de Jésus en Chine)* (OMFA G212)

92   14   cf. Guinness, M G: *Story of the CIM*, 1.363

93   15   OMFA 12 Book 11.180; G211b; G213, 'The members of the Mission present on the occasion of the outrage (were) Mr Taylor, Mr Duncan, Mr Reid and Mr Rudland, Mrs Taylor and Mrs Rudland, Miss Desgraz, Miss Blatchley and Mrs Annie Bohannan. Children four: Herbert Taylor aged 8, Frederick Taylor aged 6, Samuel Taylor aged 4, Maria Taylor aged 2.'

96   16   *Occ. Paper*, No 12, pp 200–5; No 15 pp 198–200; OMFA 4123b, 4131, 4133d; 12 Book 11.177–95

100   17   Partial separation of the placenta.

101   18   Parl. Papers. 1868–69 (OMFA G213); *Occ. Paper*, No 15, p 205

102   19   Parl. Papers, Vol 64, enclosures 3, 5, 6

104   20   OMFA 4131, Aug 24; *Occ. Paper*, No 16, p 209

105   21   Rudland: On hearing of what her son had gone through, William Rudland's mother, 'a woman of remarkable Christian character and faith', sent him a copy of *Foxe's Book of Martyrs*, as if to keep his thoughts in perspective.

106   22   *Chinese Recorder*, 1869, p 88

107   23   Parl. Papers, China No 1, Aug 27, 1868

108   24   *China's Millions*, June 1888, p 63; circulated in Shanghai, not denied by consuls or ministers.

109   25   Parl. Papers, Vol 64, pp 19, 247

110   26   *North China Herald*, Sept 11, 1868

111   27   Parl. Papers, Vol 64, Medhurst to Alcock, Sept 3; *Occ. Paper*, No 16, pp 221–2

112   28   Parl. Papers, Vol 64, pp 17–18

113   29   Brawl: *cao-nao* (*ts'ao-nao*) instead of *chiang-an* (*ch'iang-an*)

113– 30, 31 Parl. Papers, Vol 64, No 3, enclosures 5, 4
14

114   32   *North China Herald*, Sept 5, 19, 1868

Chapter 3

115   1   Parl. Papers, Vol 64, China No 2; *North China Herald*, Sept 19; *Occ. Paper*, No 16, pp 222–4; OMFA G214

119   2   Parl. Paper, Vol 64, China No 2, enclosure 2, one among other misprints, names Mr for Mrs Taylor. Maria's bruises were still visible a full month later. As Medhurst reported to Sir Rutherford – the one-time military surgeon of the Peninsula wars, and lecturer in traumatic surgery at King's College Hospital – Mrs Taylor's injuries were 'of such a nature as to preclude personal inspection'. Her bruising was around her knee and hip. Miss Blatchley 'sustained a fracture of the outer prominence of the elbow joint', and 'Mr Reid assured me that he was unable to see clearly with the affected eye.' But Rudland's hernia was unquestionable.

119   3   *The Times*, December 1, 1868, dispatch of Oct 13.

119   4   Parl. Papers, Vol 64, China No 2; *North China Herald*, Sept 5, 11, 19,
             29, 1868; *Occ. Paper*, No 16, pp 224–6; *The Times*, Dec 1, 1868,
             dispatch of Oct 13
127   5   OMFA 13 Book 8 (MS); H11.2–4 (typed)
129   6   *Chinese Recorder*, Aug 1869, p 58. In 1874 Jane McLean was still work-
             ing in Shanghai, and JHT frequently spoke at meetings in her home.
134   7   OMFA 3322A14; HTCOC Book 4, pp 247–8
139   8   OMFA 342.11a, b; 4118.57–8, 66, 68; Wagner, Lady G: *Barnardo*,
             1979; *Children of the Empire*, 1982; Marchant, J, and Mrs Barnardo:
             Memoirs of Dr Barnardo, 1907. This section, here greatly abridged,
             is in full in HTCOC Book 5, unabridged typescript.

Chapter 4
143   1   OMFA 4115.37; 4118.58–9, 61
143   2   Stock, Eugene: *The History of the Church Missionary Society*, Vol II,
             p 650
143   3   op. cit. II.397–8
144   4   op. cit. II.584
147   5   Among Hudson Taylor's many Anglican friends, perhaps most
             notable were Burdon, Cobbold, Gough, Hobson and Pennefather.
             The CIM was later to provide three bishops in China: W W Cassels,
             F Houghton and K G Bevan.
151   6   Morse, H B: *International Relations*, 2.225; Latourette, K S:
             Christian Missions, p 469
151   7   Parl. Papers, Vol 64, Adm. Keppel to Alcock, Feb 23, 1869
152   8   Parl. Papers, Vol 64, China No 6, 1869; Morse, H B: *International
             Relations*, 2.230f
153   9   *North China Herald*, Oct 13, 17, 31; Nov 14, 1868; *The Times*, Dec 1,
             1868; Parl. Papers, China No 2, pp 43, 68–9; Alcock to Lord Stanley,
             Oct 29, 1868, and Medhurst to Alcock, Nov 13, 1868, p 54; *Chinese
             Recorder*, Sept 1869, pp 104–6; *China Mail*, Nov 18, 1868, quoting
             Shanghai Evening Courier
154   10, 11 Michie, Alexander: *The Englishman in China*, Vol 2, p 168f; *North
             China Herald*, Oct 13, 31, 1868
155   12   *The Times*, Dec 1, 1868
156   13   Little, A B: *Li Hung-chang*, p 53; cf *The Times*, Dec 29, dispatch of
             Nov 10
158   14   *North China Herald*, Nov 22, Dec 2, Oct 27
158   15   Parl. Papers, China No 2, pp 59, 69; *North China Daily News*, cited in
             China Mail, Dec 5, 1868; *North China Herald*, Sept 29, 1868
159   16   Parl. Papers, Vol 64, enclosure No 2; OMFA 12 Book 11.174
160   17   *China's Millions*, June 1888, p 63f
161   18   Little, A B: *Li Hung-chang*, p 70
161   19   On the day of reinstatement at Yangzhou, Nov 18, the Judds and
             Mary Bowyer left Hangzhou for Zhenjiang; J Meadows and family
             started from Ningbo a week later.
162   20   OMFA G128; no reference to this in JHT papers.

Chapter 5

163   1   Parliamentary Papers, Vol 64, China Nos 2, 7, 8, 1869; Morse, H B: *International Relations*, 2.228–33

164   2   Sharp Peak: Parl. Papers, China No 2, 1869, Consul Sinclair to Adm. Keppel, Jan 19, 1869

165   3   Cockchafer: Parl. Papers, China No 7, 1869, Lieut. Kerr to Commodore O J Jones, Jan 21, Apr 19, 1869, pp 1–34

166   4   Parl. Papers, China No 8, 1869, *Affairs in China*, p 5; Morse, H B: *International Relations*, 2.233; *Occ. Paper*, No 19, pp 300–1

166   5   OMFA 4133C

167   6   Parl. Papers, China No 2, 1869, p 63

168   7   Lords: *Chinese Recorder*, June 1869, pp 24–5; *The Times*, March 10, 1869

169   8   Magee: Dean of Cork and Dublin; Bishop of Peterborough; Archbishop of York; died May 5, 1891; *Chinese Recorder*, June 1869, p 25; Stock, E: *History of CMS*, 2.592

170   9   *The Times*, March 10, 1869; *Chinese Recorder*, April, June 1869, p 258; Stock, E: *History of CMS*, 2.591–2; *China's Millions*, June 1888, p 63; Spurgeon, C H: *Sword and Trowel* (magazine), Jan 1869

172   10   *Chinese Recorder*, April 1869, p 20; 1875, p 372; Challoner Alabaster, HBM Consul, Hankou

174   11   Thompson, R Wardlaw: *Griffith John*, pp 250, 231, 245

174   12   Latourette, K S: *Christian Missions*, p 388

175   13   OMFA 4221a

177   14   OMFA 4224a, b, Feb 11, May 2, 1869

178   15   *Chinese Recorder*, March 1869, p 77

178   16   *Chinese Recorder*, Nov 1874, p 360

180   17   *Chinese Recorder*, Jan 1870, pp 228–9

181   18   OMFA 4241.74, Sept 5, 1869

181   19   *Chinese Recorder*, Nov 1869, pp 172–3

182   20   OMFA 441.11, *Summary of Operations*, p 12

182   21   *The Scotsman*, April 12, 1869

183   22   Pott, F L Hawks: *Short History of Shanghai*, p 94

185   23   Burdon: *Chinese Recorder*, Sept 1869, pp 97–8

185   24   Thompson, R Wardlaw: *Griffith John*, pp 252, 259–60, 263–4, 267–8

185   25   Parl. Papers, Vol 69, 1870, China No 9, pp 4–12

186   26   *Chinese Recorder*, Sept 1869, pp 100–10

187   27   Woodcock, G: *The British in the Far East*, p 102; Neill, S C: *Colonialism and Christian Missions*, pp 147–9, citing Cohen, Paul A: *China and Christianity: The Missionary Movement and the Growth of Chinese Anti-foreignism, 1860–70*, passim.

Chapter 6

188   1   Stock, E: *The History of the CMS*, Vol II, pp 588–91

191   2   Stott: *Occasional Paper*, No 18, p 284

198   3   OMFA 4215; G331

201   4   *Chinese Recorder*, July 1869, p 56; Aug 1869, p 80

201   5   Anqing: *Occ. Paper*, No 19, p 307; Morse, H B: *International Relations*, 2.234; *Chinese Recorder*, Oct 1869, p 142; Dec 1869, p 200; OMFA 4122e; 4221h; 4216; 4241.72; 4222h, i, j

204	6	Morse, H B: *International Relations*, 2.234, citing Cordier: *Rélations de la Chine*, Vol 1, pp 335, 341
205	7	*Chinese Recorder*, Oct 1869, p 142; Dec 1869, p 200
205	8	*Chinese Recorder*, May 1870, pp 32–4
211	9	*The Exchanged Life*, a letter from JHT to his sister Amelia, published as a booklet under this title; reproduced in Taylor, F H: *Hudson Taylor's Spiritual Secret*, pp 110–16; also *Hudson Taylor and the China Inland Mission* (Vol 2) pp 168–83.
213	10	OMFA 4226a
213	11	OMFA 4241.74; 4227a
214	12	OMFA 4211b
215	13	Anqing: *Occ. Paper*, No 20, p 337; No 21, pp 360–1; OMFA 4216; 4212
216	14	Morse, H B: *International Relations*, 2.234; *Chinese Recorder*, Dec 1869, p 207, citing *Shanghai Recorder* of Nov 13
218	15	OMFA 13 Book 8 (JHT's MS manifold) p 33; typed, H12; 4241.79
218	16	Latourette, K S: *Christian Missions*, p 349; Morse H B: *International Relations*, 2.234–5; Cordier, H: *The Life of Alexander Wylie*, Vol 1, p 329
219	17	OMFA 4241.83
220	18	OMFA 441.11, *Summary of Operations*, p 14
220	19	Parl. Papers, 1869, China No 1, Lord Clarendon to R Alcock, Jan 14, 1869
221	20	OMFA 13 Book 8 (manifold), H12 (typed) pp 57, 60–1
222	21	OMFA 13 Book 8, H12, p 60; 4326a
223	22	OMFA 5423
223	23	Little, A B: *Li Hung-chang*, p 5

Chapter 7

238	1	Urakami: devastated by World War II atom bomb, RC victims.
239	2	Nevius, S C H: *Life of John Livingston Nevius*, p 287
240	3	Tianjin: HTCOC Book 3, pp 140–2; Morse, H B: *International Relations*, 2.239–40, 242, 244–5, 251–2; Latourette, K S: *A History of the Expansion of Christianity*, p 290; Stock, E: *History of CMS*, 2.592–3; *Chinese Recorder*, Nov 1870, pp 150–3; Jan 1871, pp 208–11; Parl. Papers, 1871, China No 1, *Tientsin Massacre*, 1870
243	4	As for Note 3; Latourette, K S: *Christian Missions*, p 388
246	5	OMFA 441.11, *Summary of Operations*, p 17
246	6	M G Hollingworth, A K Cunningham, F M Youd; *Chinese Recorder*, June 1870, p 15
247	7	OMFA 4228.EB7; 4324f
247	8	OMFA 4331a
248	9	OMFA 4331b
249	10	OMFA 13 Book 8 (manifold), H12, p 116
249	11	OMFA 4241.92
250	12	OMFA 13 Book 8, H12, p 119
251	13	OMFA 4241.93
252	14	OMFA 4228.75
252	15	OMFA 13 Book 8, H12, p 126
252	16	Morse, E B: *International Relations*, 2.246–8; *Chinese Recorder*, Nov

1870, p 150; Parl. Papers, 1870, July 3, p 45; 1871, China No 1, p 366; Stock, E: *History of CMS*, 2.593; Moule, A E: *Story of the Cheh-Kiang Mission*, p 137; Guinness, M G: *Story of the CIM*, 2.79, 419; OMFA 4241.94; *Days of Blessing*, pp 49–50

Chapter 8

258	1	OMFA 4228.EB8, 9; 4241.97; 4324g, h; 4228.75; 4241.96; 13 Book 8, H12, pp 129, 131, 136–7, 141, 179; 4325c; G414, G428, G429e
264	2	OMFA 13 Book 8, H12, p 179; 4325cii; 4228.97; 4324h; 4241.89
267	3	Kidner, D: Tyndale Commentary, *Genesis*, p 33, said of Abraham.
267	4	Morse, H B: *International Relations*, 2.249, 255–7; *North China Herald*, July 29, Aug 11; *Shanghai Evening Courier*, July 22
267	5	Latourette, K S: *Christian Missions*, p 351
267	6	US Foreign Relations, 1870, p 371
267	7	R Hart to Commissioner E B Drew, Sept 9, 1870: 'The spirit of all their policy is to hedge – to say "No" to the foreigner in such a way as not to provoke him, and to say "Yes" in such a way as to advance the aims of anti-foreign China.' – Morse, H B: *International Relations*, 2.256 n 85.
268	8	Heads: Parl. Papers, 1870, *Tientsin Massacre*, Wade to Lord Granville, pp 171–2. Sixteen years later, W A P Martin wrote of a succession of such events (*A Cycle of Cathay*, 1896, p 445), 'Most of these massacres have conformed to the original type [that of the Tianjin massacre] in every particular – beginning with tracts and placards as their exciting cause, followed by studied negligence on the part of mandarins (who always contrived to come too late when their aid was invoked), and finishing with an enquiry how many heads and how much money would satisfy the resulting claims.'
268	9	Assassination: Parl. Papers, op. cit., Medhurst to Wade, p 120; *Occ. Paper*, No 24, p 26
269	10	Haldane, C: *The Last Great Empress of China*, pp 67–9; Little, A B: *Li Hung-chang*, p 68
269	11	OMFA 4228.101
270	12	Hart: Morse, H B: *International Relations*, 2.255 footnote
270	13	Wade: Parl. Papers, 1870, China No 1, July 3, Wade to Lay; Morse, H B: *International Relations*, 2.243, 257–8
271	14	*North China Herald*, Feb 22, 1871
271	15	Executions: *Chinese Recorder*, Jan 1871, p 212; Morse, H B: *International Relations*, 2.257–8, 261
271	16	Cathedral: Morse, H B: *International Relations*, p 261; Latourette, K S: *Christian Missions*, p 351
272	17	Michie, A: *The Englishman in China*, 2.244
272	18	Parl. Papers, 1870, China No 1
273	19	Parl. Papers, 1870, China No 1; OMFA 13 Book 8, H12, pp 170–2, 266; OMFA 4228.99
275	20	Jennie: OMFA 432.10s, t, u
278	21	Difficulties: OMFA 4332a; G426 typed; Latourette, K̄ S: *Christian Missions*, p 388
280	22	Croup: strident respiration from laryngeal obstruction; perhaps CET

had whooping cough: UK death-rate in 1860, 42 per 1,000 cases in
infants.

Chapter 9

290	1	OMFA 13 Book 8 (manifold), H13 (typed) p 188; N8.255
292	2	No textual justification has been found (by AJB) in any source material, for the supposition that JHT ever thought of taking his own life.
297	3	Plot: OMFA N8.267–90; *Monthly Gleaner* No 6, June 1871
301	4	Wade: OMFA 13 Book 8, pp 209, 315, 320–1, 373; H13, pp 207, 210–1, 319; H14, p 252
307	5	Broomhall, M: *Jubilee Story of the CIM*, pp 73–4; Cambridge Modern History, Vol XI, p 814
307	6	OMFA 4415a, c, d
308	7	OMFA 441.11, *Summary of Operations*, p 30; H13.216; Parl. Papers, 1870–72
309	8	Change: Morse, H B: *International Relations*, 2.262–3, 267, 270; Little, A B: *Li Hung-chang*, pp 65–8; Stock, E: *History of the CMS*, 2.595–600
314	9	Opium: HTCOC Book 3, p 384 and note; *Chinese Recorder*, Sept 1874, p 258
314	10	Stock, E: *History of CMS*, 2.594
315	11	T Richard: Latourette, K S: *Christian Missions*, p 378; *Chinese Recorder*, Sept–Oct 1877, p 380
315	12,13	Nevius: Martin, W A P: *Cycle of Cathay*, p 213; Nevius, S C H: *J L Nevius*, pp 276, 287, 447
315	14	Muirhead: Broomhall, M: *The Chinese Empire*, pp 87–8

Chapter 10

324	1	*Occasional Paper*, No 28, pp 151–2; Minutes of London Council, March 24, 1873. Add Crombies and Emily Blatchley in UK, Taylors and Rudlands travelling, 32 in all, 6 years after founding of CIM in 1865 – apart from losses.
329	2	Parl. Papers, 1872; OMFA 4413a, b; 4414b, c; Stock, E: *History of CMS*, 2.593
332	3	CIM: *Occasional Paper*, Nos 20, 28, 32; *Monthly Gleaner*, 1871; OMFA H14–16; Nevius: *Chinese Recorder*, 1886–87 'Methods', March 1900, (Vol 31, No 3) p 109 (*nota bene*)
341	4	H14.224
344	5	Guinness, Joy: *Her Web of Time*, p 23
346	6	OMFA H538; N8.54: not an anachronism; Henrietta Soltau's clear recollection is of 1872, not 1873 or '74 when JHT was in China, until Nov 1874, and then immobilised on his back. June 1872, a trough in the waves, saw the venture of faith, culminating in the appeal for the Eighteen, published in Jan 1875.
346	7	Council: OMFA 4417d, e; *China's Millions*, 1909, pp 126–7; Minutes of London Council, Oct 1872
347	8	Cholmondeley: Wm Henry Hugh, 3rd marquis, hereditary Grand Chamberlain of England, member of CMS Committee.

Chapter 11

357 1 *Chinese Recorder*, Sept–Oct, 1876, pp 344–7; July–Aug, 1874, p 233
357 2 Haldane, C: *The Last Great Empress*, p 79–84; Little, A B: *Li Hung-chang*, pp 85–94; Morse, H B: *International Relations*, 2.266; *Chambers Encyclopaedia*, Vol 3, p 475
359 3 Yule, H: *Marco Polo*, 2.39
360 4 Broomhall, M: *Islam in China*, pp 123–4
366 5 Mildmay: OMFA 4533.28
367 6 Barnardo: OMFA 4523.3
370 7 Legacy: OMFA 4514p, r (£1000 may be thought of as £20,000 today)
373 8 JHT's indigenous principles: OMFA 4531.2, 5–6; 4512.8, 11; 4513f, g, h; cf C Gutzlaff, HTCOC Book 1, pp 328–30; Roland Allen, Nevius, etc.
374 9 Indigenous principle: OMFA 4531.6
375 10 Cardwell: *Occ. Paper*, No 34 pp 96–101
376 11 Ruichang: *Chinese Recorder*, Nov–Dec 1874, pp 372–3
376 12 Missions: *Chinese Recorder*, Jan 1874, p 206
378 13 Knowlton: *Chinese Recorder*, Jan 1874, p 206
380 14 OMFA Judd 2; London Council, July 27, 1873
380 15 Wylie & John: *Chinese Recorder*, Nov 1876, pp 418–26; Thompson, R Wardlaw: *Griffith John*, pp 226–8
382 16 T Howard: Chairman, Oct 5, 1875; appointed Home Director, Feb 1879
382 17 Probably Dr E P Hardy, WMMS (1870–75) who replaced Dr F Porter Smith (1864–70); *Chinese Recorder*, Nov–Dec, 1876, p 418
383 18 Yellow R: 1853 changed course from S of Shandong peninsula, Yellow Sea, to N, Gulf of Zhili (now Bo Hai).
385 19 Jennie: some entries give, born Oct 6, but on her gravestone, October 7, 1843
389 20 Baller: OMFA 4526
392 21 Minutes of London Council, Oct 8, 1872

Chapter 12

396 1 Japan: Morse, H B: *International Relations*, 2.271–7; Michie, A: *The Englishman in China*, 2.255
397 2 Douthwaite: unpublished MS by Mrs W P K Findlay.
406 3 Funds: *Occ. Paper*, No 39, pp 245–52, an edited version. Printed in *Occ. Paper*, No 37, pp 174, 193: 'If God graciously provide the men and the means (from £1500 to £1800 annually, in addition to our present outlay), we may very soon place a gospel light in each of these dark districts.' – the kind of 'appeal' about which JHT was protesting?
408 4 Funds: OMFA 4513k, 1; 4532 Challice; 4531.23; 4512
410 5 Cities: *Occ. Paper*, No 37, pp 197–8, tabulated in Broomhall, M: *Jubilee Story*, p 90
412 6 Occ. Paper, No 37, pp 194–5
413 7 OMFA 4513l
414 8 Knowlton: 441.11 *Summary of Operations*, pp 14–15
414 9 Taylor, Dr and Mrs Howard: *Hudson Taylor*, Vol 2, p 267; OMFA 4511Q, R, T; 4531.24

415	10	Weir: OMFA H517Q
417	11	Hongkew: the first CIM business centre, forerunner of the major organisation supplying up to 1300 CIM missionaries and others from Wusong Road and then Sinza Road, Shanghai.
420	12	Knowlton: *Chinese Recorder*, Nov–Dec 1874, p 360; Jan–Feb 1875, p 78
421	13	Burma: Morse, H B; *International Relations*, 2.283–7; Broomhall, M: *J W Stevenson*, pp 36–7; *Chinese Empire*, p 247; *Journal of the Royal Geographical Society*, Vol XL, 1870; Parl. Papers, 1876: *correspondence respecting the Indian Expedition to Western China and the Murder of Mr Margary; Chinese Recorder*, May 1875, p 234
424	14	Huzhou: *Occ. Paper*, No 39, pp 238–45; H511
425	15	Suzhou: *Chinese Recorder*, Nov 1874, p 371
425	16	Ruichang: *Chinese Recorder*, Nov 1874, p 372; *Occ. Paper*, No 39, p 232
425	17	A Strittmatter and J R Hykes

Chapter 13

428	1	Map: Henrietta Soltau, H538; later on wall, H537
428	2	The shares realised £400
429	3	Appeal for 18: £4000 largely from Jennie's legacy; *The Christian*, Jan 21, 1875; Broomhall, M: *Jubilee Story*, p 100; OMFA H532a; *Occ. Paper*, No 39 p 230
430	4	Margary: Morse, H B: *International Relations*, 2.287–91; Parl. Papers, *corr. resp. attack on Expedition*, 1876; memorandum by Wade, July 1875; CIM London Council Minutes, Dec 14, 1874 (Sladen's colleagues not named).
433	5	*Chinese Recorder*, Jan 1876, p 79
435	6	OMFA 511.10c
436	7	Ci Xi: Morse, H B: *International Relations*, 2.279–81; Haldane, C: *The Last Great Empress*, pp 82–94; Little, A B: *Li Hung-chang*, p 91

PERSONALIA

AITCHISON, William; Am. Board; 1854 Shanghai, Pinghu; travelled widely; d. 1861.

AITKEN, Canon W M Hay; curate to Wm Pennefather (qv) St Jude's, Mildmay; leading missioner of 1870s influenced by D L Moody 1875; an initiator of Keswick Movement, patterned on Mildmay Conferences.

ALABASTER, Challoner; HBM consul, Yantai, Shantou, Hankou.

ALCOCK, Sir John Rutherford, (1809–97); MRCS at 21; 1832–7, surgeon Marine Brigade and Spanish Legion, Peninsular Wars, Dep.-Director of Hospitals; 1835 partially paralysed; 1843 Diplomatic Service; 1846 HBM consul Fuzhou; Xiamen (Amoy), Shanghai; 1858 Consul-gen. Japan; 20 June 1862 knighted, KCB; 1859–65 HBM minister, Japan; 1865–71 HBM minister, Peking; 1876 Pres. RGS.

ALFORD, C R; principal, CMS Highbury Training College; CMS Committee; vicar, Holy Trinity, Islington; 1867 second Bishop of Victoria, Hong Kong; resigned 1872.

ALLEN, Clement F R; HBM consul, Zhenjiang; member, Col. Browne's 1875 expedition, Burma-Yunnan.

ALLEN, Young J; Am. Meth. Episc. (South); 1860 Shanghai; edited reform publications read by Chinese from peasants to emperor; 1868–74 *Church News*, *Globe News, Review of the Times*; 1882 founded Anglo-Chinese College, Shanghai; 1887 Member, Socy. for the Diffusion of Christian and General Knowledge among the Chinese; consulted by reformers.

AVELINE, Mr; one-time missionary to Demarara (Br. Guyana); personal secy. to Wm T Berger (qv).

BALFOUR, Major-Gen. Sir George, CB; Capt 1840 opium war; 1843–46 first consul Shanghai; 1865 nominated JHT for FRGS; knighted after 1865.

BALLER, Fredk. W; 1873 China, Yangzi advance; linguist; 1875 m. Mary Bowyer; 1876 with G King to Shaanxi; 1878 with Mrs Hudson Taylor, Misses Horne, Crickmay to Shanxi; 1880 took party through Hunan to Guiyang; 1885, member first China Council; 1887 began literary work, *Mandarin Primer* (used by consular service), 1900 *Analytical Chinese-English Dictionary*; translator, member Union Mandarin Bible Revision Committee.

BARCHET, Stephan Paul; German-born; 1865 Ningbo, sent by JHT; m. Mary Bausum (qv); CIM, then Am. Baptist with E C Lord (qv); later doctor of medicine, American.

BARNARDO, Thomas John (4 July 1845–19 Sept. 1905); 1862 converted; 1866 met JHT in Dublin; April 1866 to London; 1866–9 CIM candidate; 1872 CIM Referee, while developing orphan work.

BARNES, Susan; 1866 met JHT, Limerick; CIM *Lammermuir* party, Hangzhou, Shaoxing; 1868 resigned.

BATES, Rev J; CMS Islington College; 1867 Ningbo; 1884–89 B & FBS NT revision committee; 1895 still active in China.

BAUSUM, J G; independent, Penang; 1845–6 m. Maria Tarn Dyer, mother of Maria Jane Taylor née Dyer.

BAUSUM, Mrs; 2nd wife of J G Bausum; mother of Mary; 1856 Ningbo; 1861 m. E C Lord (qv); d. Jan. 15, 1869.

BAUSUM, Mary; daughter; on *Lammermuir*; 1868 at 18 m. Dr S P Barchet (qv).

BAXTER, Robert Dudley (1827–75); parliamentary lawyer in father's firm Baxter, Rose & Norton, chief Conservative election agents; cousin of C R Alford, Bishop of Victoria, Hong Kong; CES Board; chairman FES; declined nomination to stand for parliament.

BEAUCHAMP, (Rev Sir) Montagu Harry Proctor-, Bart, MA (Cantab) (1860–1939); son of Sir Thomas (qv); Cambridge Univ. oar; 1885 member of CIM 'Cambridge Seven' to China; pioneer, Shanxi, Sichuan; travelled '1000 miles' with JHT; World War I Hon. Chaplain to Forces, Egypt, Greece, Murmansk; 1915 inherited baronetcy; Oct. 1939 d. Langzhung, Sichuan.

BEAUCHAMP, Sir Thomas Proctor-, Bart; Langley Park, Norwich, 4th baronet; m. Hon Caroline Waldegrave, daughter of 2nd Baron Radstock and Dowager Lady Radstock (qv); friend, supporter of JHT, CIM, d. 1874.

BELL, Mary: Malvern, Worcs.; 1866 CIM, *Lammermuir*, Hangzhou, 1867 m. W D Rudland (qv); 1868 Yangzhou riot, Zhenjiang; 1871 Taizhou; d. Oct. 23, 1874.

BERGER, William Thomas (c 1812–99); director Samuel Berger & Co, Patent Starch manufacturer, St Leonard St, Bromley-by-Bow; CES supporter; early donor to JHT; 1865 co-founder and UK director, CIM; generous life-time donor; home at Hackney village, then Saint Hill, East Grinstead, devoted to Mission.

BERGER, Mary; wife of WTB; (c 1812–Feb 16, 1877)

BERGNE, Samuel Brodribb; Independent minister, 1854–79 co-Sec. B&FBS.

BEVAN, Francis Augustus (1840–1919); son of Robert Bevan (qv); donor to CIM; 1896 first chairman of Barclays Bank.

BEVAN, Robert Cooper Lee (1809–90); a founder of LCM; friend of CMS; first chairman of YMCA; CES Gen. Committee.

BEWLEY, Henry (1814–76); Dublin printer, built Merrion Hall, Brethren; supporter and Referee of CIM.

BISMARCK, Prince Otto Eduard Leopold von (1915–98); leading German statesman; 1862–90 Foreign Affairs; 'Iron Chancellor'; PM of Prussia; 1865 Count, 1867 Prince; defeated Austria, France; united Germany; first chancellor of Reich; 1890 'old pilot dropped'.

BLAKISTON, Capt; adventurer; 1860 attempted Shanghai to India via Tibet, forced back.

BLATCHLEY, Emily (1845–74); 1865 Home and Colonial Training Coll. grad.; 'rt.hand' secy., governess to JHT, family; 1866 CIM, *Lammermuir*, Hangzhou, 1868 Yangzhou, riot; March 1870 UK with three JHT children; 1870–74 London, guardian secretary; d. July 25, 1874.

BLODGET, Henry, DD (1825–1903); Am. Board; 'massive build and commanding presence', 'the soul of country and good breeding'; 1850–53 tutor, Yale; 1854 Shanghai with Aitchison (qv); 1860 to Tianjin with Br. forces, first Prot. to preach in streets; 1864 Peking 30 years; translator, Mandarin NT with Burdon (qv) Edkins (qv) W Martin (qv) Schereschewsky (qv), revised W H Medhurst's Southern Mandarin NT; 1870 Shanghai Vernacular NT with W J Boone, T McClatchie *et al*; 1889 'easy *wenli*' NT with Burdon (qv), Groves, J C Gibson, I Genähr, 1890 Union

Mandarin NT committee; 1890 with others submitted memorial to emperor 'setting forth the true nature of Christianity'; 1894 retired ill.

BOHANNAN, Annie; widowed sister of Mary Bell (qv); nurse to JHT children; 1868 m. Edward Fishe (qv).

BOOTH, Catherine (née Mumford) 1829–30; m. Wm Booth (qv) June 16, 1855; Salv. Army.

BOOTH, Evangeline; b. 1865 C'mas Day, to Wm and Catherine (qv); famed SA evangelist; US Natl. Commander SA; 1934–39 General, SA.

BOOTH, William (1829–1912); Methodist evangelist; June 16, 1855 m. Catherine Mumford (qv); Methodist New Connexion; 1865 'found his destiny' in London's East End and with Catherine formed The Christian Mission; 7 Aug 1878 changed name and form to Salvation Army; son Bramwell, daughter Evangeline (qv) among successors as 'General'.

BRIDGMAN, Elijah Coleman, DD (1801–61); Am. Board (ABCFM); 1830 Canton; 1832 first editor *Chinese Repository* with R Morrison; 1843–44 US treaty interpreter-negotiator; 1845–52 translator, Chinese Bible, Delegates' Committee, 1847 Shanghai.

BRIDGMAN, Mrs; 1845 Canton; 1847 Shanghai; 1864 Peking.

BROOMHALL, Benjamin (1829–1911); m. Amelia Hudson Taylor (1835–1918); 1878–95 Gen. Sec. CIM London; editor, *National Righteousness*, organ of anti-opium trade campaign, to 1911 (*see* Maxwell).

BROWNE, Colonel; Indian Army; 1875 led Burma-Yunnan expedition, repulsed, A R Margary (qv) killed.

BRUCE, Sir Fredk.; brother of Lord Elgin (qv); 1858 envoy to Peking, rebuffed; 1859 repulsed at Dagu, Tianjin; 1860 first Br. minister, Peking.

BURDON, John Shaw (1829–1907); CMS, 1853 Shanghai; pioneer evangelist; 1857 m. Burella Dyer, sister of Maria Taylor (qv); 1862 Peking; 1874 3rd bishop of Victoria, Hong Kong; Bible translator (*see* Blodget).

BURLINGAME, Anson (1820–70); barrister, Congressman, Methodist; 1861–67 US minister, Peking, appointed by Abraham Lincoln; 1867–70 ambassador-at-large for China; d. St Petersburg (Leningrad).

BURNS, Prof Islay, DD (Glas.); biographer of brother, Wm C Burns (qv).

BURNS, William Chalmers (1815–68); first English Presby. to China; 1847 Hong Kong; Amoy; 1855 Shanghai; 1856 Swatow; 1863 Peking; 1867 Niuchuang (now Yingkou), d. Niuchuang; translated *Pilgrim's Progress*; close friend of JHT.

BUXTON, Sir Edward North, Bart, MP (1812–58); son of Sir Thomas Fowell Buxton, 1st baronet; CES Gen. Committee.

CALDWELL, John R; Glasgow silk merchant, influenced by JHT, faithful CIM supporter.

CANNY, J M; merchant; French chargé d'affaires, consul Zhenjiang; friend of CIM.

CARDWELL, J E; CIM, 1867 Hangzhou; 1868 Taizhou, Zhejiang; Dec 30, 1869 Jinjiang, pioneered Jiangxi.

CAREY, William (1761–1834); Baptist Miss. Soc. founder; 1793 India, Serampore; 1800–30 Prof. of Oriental Languages, Calcutta.

CASSELS, William Wharton (1859–1925); St John's College, Cam.; 1882 ordained; one of the 'Cambridge Seven'; 1885 Shanghai, Shanxi; Sichuan; 1895 consecrated Bishop of West China, as a member of both CIM, CMS.

CAVAN, Fredk John Wm Lambart, 8th earl of, (1815–87); Lt Col 7th Dragoon

Guards; CES Gen. Committee; supporter of CIM, Mildmay Conf., D L Moody; Welbeck St Brethren.

CHALLICE, John; director of six companies, deacon, Bryanston Hall, Portman Square; 1872 member, first CIM council; hon. treasurer UK; d. 1887.

CHAPMAN, Robert Cleaver (1802–1902); High Court attorney; C of E; 1832 Strict Baptist minister; Brethren; 2nd Evang. Awakening evangelist; 1872 CIM Referee; JHT's friend.

CHEN GUORUI; brigadier, garrison commander, 1868 Yangzhou at time of riot; 1870 Tianjin, took part in riot; 1871 Yangzhou, leading part in 2nd plot.

CHOLMONDELEY, Wm. Henry Hugh, 3rd marquis (1800–84); hereditary Grand Chamberlain of England; CMS Committee; 1872 CIM Referee.

CHONGHOU; 1870 imperial commissioner for foreign affairs, Tianjin; envoy to Paris after Tianjin massacre.

CIGGIE, Grace; Glasgow, 1865 influenced by JHT, 'China's Need', recruit for Ningbo; 1866 CIM *Lammermuir* party, deferred by ill health; 1866–9 Glasgow slums; 1870 m. Geo Stott, Wenzhou.

CI XI (Ts'u Hsi) (1835–1908); Empress Dowager; Yehonala, the Concubine Yi; 1860 empress regent to Tong Zhi; 1860–1908 supreme power in China.

CLARENDON, Earl of, (1800–70); Foreign Sec. to Lord Aberdeen 1853, Lord Palmerston 1855, Lord Russell 1865, Gladstone 1868.

COBBOLD, Robert Henry; CMS, 1848–62, Ningbo; translator, Ningbo romanised vernacular NT; 1863 Rector of Broseley, Staffs; 1871–1909 Rector, Ross on Wye.

COLLINGWOOD, R G; Oxford philosopher, expert on Roman Britain; grandson of Wm Collingwood (qv).

COLLINGWOOD, W G; biographer of Ruskin; son of Wm Collingwood (qv).

COLLINGWOOD, William (1819–1903) Fellow of Royal Watercolour Society; Oxford; 1839 Liverpool; C of E until Brethren; 1850 responded to C Gutzlaff, supported CES; met JHT Sept. 1853 and supported JHT/CIM; 1872 CIM Referee.

COLLINS, W H, MRCS; 1858 CMS Shanghai; 1863 Peking.

COLQUHOUN, Archibald R; engineer, Indian govt.: 1881 travelled E–W, Canton to Burma, advised by J W Stevenson (qv) and J McCarthy (qv).

CONGLETON, John Vesey Parnell, 2nd Baron, (1805–83); 1830–37 with A N Groves, Baghdad, m. Iranian Christian widow of Shiraz; Brethren leader, Teignmouth, London, Orchard St, Welbeck St; travelled widely; donor to JHT/CIM.

COOPER, T T; adventurer, Sichuan, Tibet; agent, Calcutta Chamber of Commerce; 1862 Rangoon; 1867 Shanghai; 1868 Hankou–Tibet in Chinese clothes, forced back; 1871, author, *Travels of a Pioneer of Commerce*; proposed Yangzi–Bhamo (Irrawaddy) railway.

CORDON, Henry; 1867 CIM, sent by Berger (qv); Hangzhou; 1868 Suzhou.

COX, Josiah; 1852 Wesleyan MMS, Canton, joined G Piercy (qv); 1860 invited by Taipings (by Hong Ren) to Suzhou, Nanjing, visited, disillusioned; 1862 invited by G John (qv) Hankou, began Hubei, Hunan Miss. of WMMS; 1863 first Prot. miss. to enter antagonistic Hunan; 1865 Jiujiang; 1875 invalided to UK, d. 1906.

CRANAGE, Dr J Edward; Anglican, Old Hall, Wellington, Shrops; 1859–62 Evangelical Awakening leader (*see* Bk 3).

CRANSTON, David; Shanghai merchant, Shanghai & Putong Foundry & Engineering Co.; Feb 1874 victim in Shanghai riot; friend of CIM.

CROMBIE, George; Aberdeen farmer; 1865 JHT's second recruit, to Ningbo; 1866 CIM Fenghua.

CULBERTSON, M S, DD; Am. Presbyterian; 1850 Shanghai; co-translator of Delegates' Version, Chinese Bible (NT); with Elijah Coleman Bridgman of OT, completed 1862; d. 1862, cholera.

DAVIES, Evan, LMS Malaya; author, 1845, *China and her Spiritual Claims*; 1846 *Memoir of the Reverend Samuel Dyer*.

DAVIES, Major H R; prospected proposed Burma–Yunnan railway; travelled widely, Dali, Batang etc.

DELAMARRE, Abbé; Paris Mission; 1858–60 chief interpreter, French treaty; falsified Chinese version; 1860 dep. Peking carrying tricolor and 27 passports for SW provinces.

DENNISTON, J M; Presby. minister, London, Torquay; associated with W C Burns revivals and JHT founding CIM; co-founder Foreign Evangelist Soc.

DENNY, William; Glasgow ship-owner/builder, Wm Denny and Brothers, Dumbarton; 1865 gave free passages to China to Barchet and Crombie (qv); 1869 completed *Cutty Sark*.

DESGRAZ, Louise; Swiss governess to Wm Collingwood (qv) family, as a daughter; 1866 CIM, *Lammermuir*, Hangzhou; 1865 Yangzhou, riot; 1878 m. E Tomalin.

DISRAELI, Benj (1804–81); 1st Earl of Beaconsfield; son of Isaac d'Israeli; statesman, social novelist; 1837 MP; 1868, 1874–80 Prime Minister, bought Suez Canal shares, friend of Queen Victoria, made her 'Empress of India'.

DODD, Samuel; Canadian in Am. Presbyterian Mission; 1861 Ningbo; 1867 Hangzhou; 1875 translated *Hebrews* into *wenli*.

DOOLITTLE, Justus; Am. Board; 1850 Fuzhou; 1862 Tianjin, editor *Chinese Recorder*.

DOUGLAS, Carstairs, LL D (Glas.) (1830–77); English Presby. Mission; 1855 Amoy with W C Burns; Amoy vernacular dictionary; advocated occupying Taiwan; 1865 enlisted J L Maxwell (qv), with Maxwell began at Tainan; 1877 chairman General Miss. Conference, Shanghai; 1877 d. cholera.

DOUTHWAITE, Arthur William; 1874 Harley House; CIM, China; travelled with JHT; became surgeon; 1882 Yantai; 1884 Korea; 1886 Yantai; awarded Order of the Double Dragon for services in Sino-Japanese war; d. Oct 5, 1899.

DUDGEON, J, MD; 1863 LMS Peking.

DU HALDE, P J B; author *The General History of China* (Ldn. 1736, 1741); *A Description of the Empire of China and Chinese Tartary . . . Korea, Tibet, etc*, 2 vols (Ldn. 1741).

DUNCAN, George; Banff, Scotland, stone-mason; 1865 CIM; 1866, *Lammermuir*, Hangzhou; 1867 Lanxi, Nanjing; 1868 Yanzhou riot, m. Catherine Brown; 1872 UK; 1873 d. TB.

DYER, Burella Hunter; b. 31 May 1835; elder daughter of Samuel Dyer Sr (qv); 1857 m. J S Burdon; d. 1858.

DYER, Samuel Sr (1804–43); Cambridge law student; 1827 LMS, m. Maria Tarn, daughter of LMS director; 1827 Penang; 1829–35 Malacca, 1835–43 Singapore; d. Macao.

DYER, Samuel Jr; b. 18 Jan. 1833, son of Samuel Sr.; brother of Maria Taylor (qv); 1877 agent of B&FBS, Shanghai, after Alex Wylie (qv); expanded staff, distribution.

EDKINS, Joseph (1832–1905); LMS evangelist, linguist, translator, philologist, expert in Chinese religions, 1860 visited Suzhou Taiping rulers; 1862 Nanjing; 1848–60 Shanghai; 1860–61 first to Shandong, Yantai; 1862 Tianjin (wife died *aet*.

22) Peking; 57 years in China, 30 in Peking; 1880 retired from LMS, attached to Imperial Maritime Customs; author 1853 *Grammar Shanghai dialect*; 1857 *Mandarin Grammar*; 1859 *The Religious Condition of the Chinese*; 1878 *Religion in China*; 1880 *Chinese Buddhism*; 1875 DD (Edin.); 1877 second wife died; *aet.* 80 survived typhoid; *aet.* 81 still writing, d. Easter Sunday.

ELGIN, Earl of; son of Thomas Bruce, 7th earl (Elgin marbles); 1857 Indian mutiny; 1858 envoy, Treaty of Tientsin; treaty with Japan; 1860 second opium war, captured Peking, burned Summer Palace, negotiated Peking Convention.

FAN QISENG (Vaen Kyi-seng); evangelist, Fenghua.

FARNHAM, J M W; Presby.; 1860 Shanghai with Wm Gamble (qv); friend of CIM.

FAULDING, Jane (Jennie) Elizabeth (Oct 7, 1843–July 30, 1904); Home and Colonial Training College (with E Blatchley (qv)); 1865 assist. to JHT, London; 1866 CIM, *Lammermuir*; Hangzhou; m. JHT 28 Nov. 1871; 1877–78 led CIM team, Shanxi famine relief.

FAULDING, William F and Harriet; parents of Jane E Faulding (qv) and Ellen (Nellie); piano frame and fret manufacturer, 340 Euston Road; Regent's Park Chapel.

FENG NENGGUI; Ningbo basket-maker, member of non-idolatrous Buddhist sect; became evangelist, pastor, Fenghua, Wenzhou.

FISHBOURNE, Capt. R N; rescued Amoy victims; strong supporter of missions and anti-opium soc.; later, evangelist; CES Gen. Committee.

FISHE, Colonel; Dublin; HEIC Madras Horse Artillery (retd.); father of Edward and Charles (qv).

FISHE, Charles Thomas; son of Col Fishe, Dublin (qv); influenced by H G Guinness (qv), JHT; 1867 asst. to W T Berger (qv); 1868 CIM, Yangzhou; 1871 CIM China Secy.; 1875 m. Nellie Faulding.

FISHE, Edward; elder son of Col Fishe, Dublin (qv); 1866 influenced by H G Guinness (qv), JHT; 1867 to China independently; attached to CIM; m. Annie Bohannan (qv); 1868 Zhenjiang.

FITTACK, W H; HBM consul, 1867 Ningbo.

FLEMING, T S; 1860 CMS recruit taught by JHT; Ningbo, Hangzhou; 1863 invalided home.

FORREST, R J; 1860 HBM consular interpreter, later consul, Ningbo.

FRANCKE, August Hermann; pietist, 1696 founded Orphan Houses, extensive by C 19; prof. divinity, Halle Univ. Germany; d. 1727.

GAINFORT, Mrs; Dublin; influenced students to join CIM.

GAMBLE, William; Am. Presby. Mission Press; 1858 Ningbo; 1860 Shanghai; friend of JHT; 1866 received *Lammermuir* party, served as CIM business agent.

GARDNER, Christopher T; 1867 HBM consular interpreter, Ningbo; 1870 consul, Zhenjiang.

GARIBALDI, Giuseppe (1807–82); with Mazzini and Cavour created united Italy; 1860 freed Sicily, took Naples; Victor Immanuel proclaimed King.

GAULD, Dr Wm; Engl. Presby. Mission, *c* 1863 began med. work at Shantou (Swatow), largest in China for years; 1867 new hospital.

GILMOUR, James (1843–91); LMS; 1870 Mongolia for 20 years.

GLADSTONE, Wm Ewart (1809–98); 1832 MP; Liberal PM 1868–74, 1880–85, 1892–94.

GORDON, Lt Col Charles George (1833–85); 1860 Tianjin, Peking campaign; 1862 Shanghai, commanding Ever-Victorious Army; 1864 Taiping Rebellion ended; emperor awarded Order of the Imperial Dragon, and Queen Victoria the CB;

1865–71 London; donor to JHT; 1880 adviser to Chinese govt.; 1883–85 Major-Gen., Sudan.

GOSSE, Philip Henry (1810–88); naturalist, author: 1855–66 *Manual of Marine Zoology*; 1860–62 *Romance of Natural History*; through W T Berger joined Hackney Brethren; early donor to CIM.

GOSSE, Sir Edmund Wm (1845–1928); (aged 15–20 while JHT at Mile End); 1867–75 asst. librarian British Museum; poet and critic, 1904–10 librarian, House of Lords; author, histories of literature, and *Father and Son*, biographical.

GOUGH, Frederick Foster, DD; CMS 1849–61 Ningbo; Mary, first wife, d. 1861; 1862–69 London, Ningbo vernacular romanised NT revision with JHT; 1866 m. Mary Jones (qv); 1869 Ningbo.

GRANVILLE, Lord (1815–91); 2nd earl; 1851, 1870–74 Foreign Secretary (after Lord Clarendon), and 1880–85.

GREEN, D D; Am. Presby.; 1859 Ningbo; 1865 Hangzhou.

GRETTON, Henry; CMS 1867 Hangzhou, alone without Chinese companion after G E Moule dep.; 1870 Shaoxing.

GUANG XÜ (Kuang Hsü) emperor; 1875, 4-year-old puppet of Ci Xi (qv); son of Prince Chun, 7th son of Dao Guang emperor; 1889 assumed power; 1898 imprisoned after *coup d'état* by Ci Xi; d. 14 Nov 1908, day before Ci Xi.

GUINNESS, H Grattan, DD, FRAS (1835–1910); 1855 left New Coll. Lond. to become great evangelist of Evangelical Awakening; 1859 Ulster revival, drew thousands; 1865 offered to CIM, JHT advised continue UK; became JHT's friend; 1872 CIM Referee; 1873 founded East London Miss. Training Institute (Harley College); trained 1,330 for 40 societies of 30 denominations; 1877 Livingstone Inland Mission, 1888 Congo-Balolo Mission, 1898 initiated RBMU; NAM founded on his advice; greatly influenced Barnardo, John R Mott; author, astronomy, eschatology; 7 children, grandchildren in Christian ministry.

GUINNESS, M Geraldine (1862–1949); daughter of H Grattan Guinness (qv); 1888 CIM; 1894 m. F Howard Taylor (qv); author, biography of JHT and others.

GULICK, J T; Am. Board 1864 Peking; 1865 Kalgan (now Zhangjiakou) outside Gt. Wall.

GUTZLAFF, Charles (Karl Friedrich Augustus) (1803–51); D D Groningen 1850; 1826–28 Netherlands Miss. Soc., Batavia (Jakarta), Java; 1828 independent, Bangkok; 1829 m. Miss Newell, Malacca, first single Prot. woman missionary to E. Asia d. 1831; 1831–35 voyages up China coast; 1834 m. Miss Warnstall d. 1849; 1839 interpreter to British; 1840, 1842 governor of Chusan Is.; 1842 interpreter-negotiator, Nanking Treaty; 1843–51 Chinese Sec. to British govt. Hong Kong; initiated Chinese Union, Chinese Associations and missions; 1850 m. Miss Gabriel.

HALL, Charles J; 1857 CES missionary Ningbo; 1860 Shandong; d. 1861.

HALL, H H; Am. Meth. Episc. Mission; 1870 Jiujiang; 1873 Ruichang riot.

HALL, William; manufacturer of footwear; deacon, Bryanston Hall, Portman Square; 1872 member of first CIM London council.

HALL, William Nelthorpe; Methodist New Connexion; 1860 Shanghai; 1861 April Tianjin with J Innocent (qv); d. 1878.

HANSPACH, August; Chinese Evangelization Soc. of Berlin (Berlin Missionary Soc. for China); 1855 Hong Kong; 11 years' extensive inland travel.

HARPER, Andrew P, DD; Am. Presby. 1844–46 Macao (debarred from Canton); 1847 Canton; 1887 first president, Canton Christian Coll.

HART, Sir Robert; b. 20 Feb 1835; 1854 Ningbo, consular interpreter; 1857 Canton;

Nov. 1862 Inspector-General, Chinese Imperial Maritime Customs; 1865 Peking.

HART, V C; Am. Meth. Episc. Mission; 1866 Jiujiang, friend of CIM.

HARVEY, Thomas P; master-butcher; 1866 med. student with T J Barnardo, London Hosp., Mile End; 1869 China; 1872 Lond. Hosp. graduated; 1876 Bhamo, Burma.

HILL, David (1840–96); 1865 WMMS, Hankou (independent means); 1878–80 with J J Turner, CIM, to Shanxi famine relief; 1879 means of conversion of 'Pastor Hsi'.

HILL, Richard Harris, FRIBA; civil engineer, evangelist; helped build Mildmay Miss. Hosp., CIM Newington Green; M. Agnes, daughter of Henry W Soltau (qv); 1872 Hon. Sec. London CIM.

HODGE; Wm. Bramwell; Meth. New Connexion; 1866 Tianjin; 1869 companion of Jas. Williamson, LMS; murdered.

HOLLINGWORTH, M G; Brit. merchant, Jiujiang; friend of CIM; 1870 Jiujiang to Fuzhou, Fujian, overland.

HOLMES, J L; Am. Southern Baptist; 1860 pioneer of Shandong, Yantai (Chefoo); Oct. 1861 killed with H M Parker (qv).

HOUGHTON, John; son of Richard (qv) Liverpool; Feb. 1866 host to JHT; introduced JHT to H Grattan Guinness.

HOUGHTON, Richard; father of John (qv); 1866 as 'perfect stranger' read JHT's *China*, donated £650 (modern equiv. ?£13,000).

HOWARD, John Eliot (1807–83); quinologist, 1874 FRS, Fellow of Linnaean Soc.; manufacturing chemist; early leader of Brethren, Tottenham; member of B&FBS committee and CES Board; JHT's close friend and supporter; 1872 CIM Referee.

HOWARD, Theodore; son of Robt., nephew of John Eliot (qv), 1872 CIM Lond. Council; 1875 chairman; 1879 Home Director.

HOWELL, Alfred; Dent & Co, Japan; 1866 donor to CIM in approval of Chinese dress.

HUDSON, Benjamin Brook (c 1785–1865); Wesleyan Methodist minister; portrait-ist; grandfather of JHT.

HUDSON, T H (1800–76); General Baptist Mission; 1845 Ningbo, remained till death; 1850–66 translated NT into *wenli* (literary Chinese).

HUTCHINSON, Sir Jonathan (1828–1913); 1859 general and ophthalmic surgeon, London Hospital; 1882 FRS; 1889 President RCS; Nov. 1908 Knight Bachelor; benefactor of JHT.

INNOCENT, John (1829–1904); Methodist New Connexion evangelist; 1860 Shang-hai; 1861 Tianjin with W N Hall (qv) till 1897; 1864 visited Mongolia.

JACKSON, Josiah Alexander; carpenter, draper, Kingsland, Stoke Newington; 1865 CIM cand., 1866 *Lammermuir*, Hangzhou; 1867 Taizhou, Zhejiang; d. Shanghai 1909.

JENKINS, Horace; ABMU; 1860 Ningbo, joined Knowlton (qv), Kreyer (qv).

JOHN, Griffith (1831–1912); LMS; 1855 Shanghai; pioneer evangelist; 1861 Hankou; 1863 Wuchang; 1867 Hanyang; 1888 declined chairmanship, Congre-gational Union of Eng. and Wales; 1889 Hon. DD (Edin.); Sept. 24, 1905 jubilee in China; April 1906 retired ill.

JONES, John; CES; 1856–57 Ningbo; independent, 1857–63; early exponent of 'faith principle', influenced JHT; d. 1863.

JONES, Mary; wife of John; 1863–66 with Hudson Taylors, London; 1866 m. F F Gough; 1869 Ningbo; 1869–71 fostered Chas Edw Taylor; d. Nov. 1877.

JUDD, Charles H Sr (1842–1919); 1867 CIM through influence of T J Barnardo;

1868 Yangzhou; 1869 Zhenjiang; 1872–3 UK; 1874 Wuchang, with JHT; 1875 with two Chinese rented house at Yueyang (Yochow), Hunan, forced out; 1877 with J F Broumton via Hunan to Guiyang, Guizhou; Broumton settled, Judd via Chongqing to Wuchang; 1879 built at Yantai before school and sanatorium.

JUKES, Andrew; East India Co. officer; deacon Anglican Church; c 1842 independent minister, Brethren congregation; 1866 built Church of St John the Evangelist, Hull.

KENNAWAY, Sir John Henry, Bart, MP, PC; 1887 President of CMS; 1897 PC; 1893 coined phrase, 'Ask the Lord and tell His People' (Stock III.677).

KEPPEL, Admiral Sir Harry; Com. in Chief, Br. Far Eastern Fleet.

KERR, John G, M D, LL D; Am. Presby. North, 1854 Canton, took over Dr Peter Parker's hosp. for nearly 50 years, treated over 1 million, 480,000 surgical operations, 1300 urinary calculus, incl. US Minister, Peking; 1870 trained 260 Chinese medicals; pioneered care of insane, 1898 opened Canton Refuge for the Insane; 1887 first Pres. Med. Miss. Assn. of China; author-translator *Chinese Materia Medica*, other med. books.

KING, George; 1875 CIM, China, aged 18; pioneer of Shaanxi.

KINNAIRD, Hon Arthur Fitzgerald, 10th Baron (1814–87); supported CMS, LCM, Barnardo. Son, of same name, 11th baron m. niece of Hon and Rev Baptist W Noel; she helped found Foreign Evangelization Socy, 1871, and Zenana Bible and Medical Mission (now BMMF).

KNOWLTON, Miles Justice (Feb. 8, 1825–Sept. 10, 1874); ABMU; 1854 Ningbo; stalwart friend of JHT, rebutted slander.

KONG, Prince (Prince Kung) (1833–98); brother of Xian Feng (Hsien Feng) emperor; 1860 *et seq*, leading statesman; initiated Zongli Yamen.

KREYER, Carl T; ABMU; 1866 Hangzhou; lent his home to *Lammermuir* party; assisted CIM in Hangzhou, Huzhou crises.

LANDELS, William, DD (1823–99); minister Regent's Park Chapel (Baptist); 1872 CIM Referee.

LATOURETTE, Kenneth Scott; late Willis James and Sterling Prof. of Missions and Oriental History, Yale Univ.; author, *see* bibliography.

LAUGHTON, Richard Fredk; BMS; 1863 Shandong, Yantai; d. 1870.

LAY, Horatio N; son of George Tradescent Lay, B&FBS (1836–9) and HBM consul; HBM consul, Fuzhou, Canton; 1860 first Inspector-General, Imperial Maritime Customs; negotiated 'Lay-Osborne fleet'; 1862 dismissed; succeeded by Robt Hart (qv).

LAY, W H; HBM consul, hero of 1870 Tianjin massacre.

LECHLER, Rudolf (1824–1908); Basel Mission pioneer; 1847 Hong Kong, Guangdong (Kwangtung) Hakkas, under Gutzlaff, with Hamberg; 52 years in China, to 1899.

LEES, Jonathan; LMS; 1862 Tianjin, many years; d. 1902.

LEGGE, James, DD, LLD (1815–97); LMS; 1835 MA (Aberdeen), Congregational; 1839–43 Anglo-Chinese College, Malacca; 1843–70 Anglo-Chinese College, Hong Kong; 1861–86 translator, Chinese classics; 1875 Fellow, Corpus Christi, Oxford; 1877–97, first Prof. of Chinese, Oxford Univ.

LEWIS, William Garrett; Baptist minister, Westbourne Grove Ch., Bayswater, London; a founder of London Baptist Assn.; urged JHT to publish *China: Its Spiritual Need and Claims*; 1872 CIM Referee.

LIANG AFA (1789–1855); Canton engraver-printer; 1815 to Malacca with W Milne; 1819 Canton, colporteur; arrested, flogged; 1821 Malacca; 1828 Canton;

1834 arrested, escaped, betrayed, escaped; 1839 returned, tolerated by Lin Zexu; first Prot. pastor; 1845 mobbed; d. 1855.

LI HONGZHANG (Li Hung-chang) (1823–1901); holder of the highest academic degrees, highest honours after defeat of Taiping rebels; enlightened liberal but failed in modernisation of China; 1895 forced to cede Taiwan to Japan; the Grand Old Man of China, leading statesman until death.

LI LANFENG; 1867 printer employed by CIM, Hangzhou; converted per W D Rudland (qv); to UK with JHT 1871; pioneer evangelist, pastor.

LINDSEY, Gen Sir Alexander; 1865 host to JHT, Perth.

LING ZHUMOU; Ningbo Christian; 1868 cook-evangelist at Nanjing with G Duncan (qv) and H Reid (qv).

LI TIANFU; 1867 Ningbo Christian; 1868 Nanjing evangelist with G Duncan (qv).

LIU JINCHEN; Hangzhou evangelist; victim of 1867 Huzhou mob violence; 1868 ejected from Jinhua.

LI ZHUGUI; 1871 evangelist at Xiaoshan.

LOCKHART, William (1811–96); surgeon, FRCS; LMS; 1839 Macao; 1840 and 1843 Shanghai; 1840–41 Chusan with Gutzlaff, first British missionary Hong Kong; 1848 mobbed in 'Qingpu (Tsingpu) Outrage', Shanghai; 1861 first Prot. missionary in Peking; 1864 to UK; 1867 retired from LMS; surgeon, Blackheath.

LORD, Edward Clifford, DD (1817–87); ABMU; 1847 first Am. Baptist to Ningbo; 1853 NT Baptist version, with Dean and Goddard; 1863 independent Am. Bapt. Mission, Ningbo; 1887 still there; appointed US consul by Abraham Lincoln; JHT's friend; d. with wife, of cholera.

LORD, Mrs; (1) d. Jan. 1860; (2) Jemima (Bausum) m. 1861, d. 1869; (3) d. Feb 1875.

MACKINTOSH, William; with J Fraser initiator of FES; missionary to Cairo.

MACPHERSON, Miss Annie; mid-19th-century schoolteacher, social reformer, evangelist; 'ragged schools'; organised emigration to Canada; firm friend of CIM; introduced W D Rudland (qv).

MAGEE; Dean of Cork, Dublin; Bishop of Peterborough; Archbishop of York; d. 5 May 1891.

MARA, John; United Meth. Free Ch.; trained by JHT; 1865 Ningbo; Aug. 1869 invalided to UK.

MARGARY, Augustus Raymond; b.1845; HBM consul Yantai; 1874 as interpreter to Col. Browne's Burma–Yunnan expedition, dep. Shanghai 22 Aug 1874, via Hunan, arr. Bhamo 17 Jan 1875; murdered Feb 21 at Manyün.

MARKHAM, Sir Clements R (1830–1916); explorer, Arctic, S.Am., Ethiopia, India; Secy. and Pres. Royal Geog. Soc. (1893–1905).

MARSHALL, Thomas D; minister, Bryanston Hall, Portman Square.

MARTIN, Samuel N D; older brother of W A P Martin (qv); Am. Presby. Mission; 1850 Ningbo, i/c boys' school founded by R Q Way (qv).

MARTIN, William Alexander Parsons, DD, LL D (1827–1916); Am. Presby. Mission; educationalist; 1850–60 Ningbo; 1858 with S Wells Williams (qv) interpreter, Am. treaty; 1862 Peking; 1869 president, Tongwen Imperial College; 57 years in China; book on Christian evidences had huge circulation, China, Japan.

MATHESON, Donald; merchant partner, Jardine, Matheson, 1837 converted at Hong Kong; 1849 resigned over opium traffic; active in Presby. Missions; 1892 chairman, Soc. for the Suppression of the Opium Trade.

MAXWELL, James Laidlow, MD (b. 1836); English Presby. Mission; 1863 Amoy; 1865 Taiwan pioneer, Tainan, Dagao; 1871 invalided to UK, 8 years on his back;

publ. vernacular NT; 1883 Taiwan again; 1885 founded Medical Missionary Association (London), Secy; 1888 co-founder with B Broomhall (qv), 'Christian Union for the Severance of the Connection of the British Empire with the Opium Traffic'.

MA XINYI; Muslim; 1865–68 Gov. of Zhejiang; 1869 Viceroy of the Two Jiangs, Jiangsu, Anhui, Jiangxi; 1869–70 Nanjing; 22 August 1870 assassinated.

McAULAY, Alexander (1818–90); Wesleyan minister, missionary; 1876 Pres. Wesleyan Conf., Gen. Sec. Wes. Home Miss.; CIM Referee.

McCARTEE, Divie Bethune, MD (1820–1900); Am. Presby.; 1844 Ningbo 28 years; 1845 organised first Prot. church on Chinese soil; 1851 extended work beyond treaty ports; 1853 m. Juana Knight, first single Presby. woman to China; adopted Yu Meiying, orphaned daughter of pastor as own daughter, first Chinese woman doctor educated abroad, returned as missionary to China; 1861 met Taiping leaders, Nanjing, negotiated protection Am. citizens, Chinese Christians; Dec 1861–April 1862 earliest Prot. miss. in Japan; McC's tract translated into Japanese was first Prot. lit. in Japan; 1862–5 Shandong, Yantai; 1864 Ningbo again; 1872 Japan with Chinese envoy negotiated release of coolie prisoners on *Maria Luz* (Macao-Peru), received gold medal; 1872–77 Prof. of law and natural science, Tokyo Univ; 1877 secy. foreign affairs to Chinese legation, Japan; 1880 USA; 1889 Presby. Miss. again, Tokyo; good scholar in Greek, Chinese, Japanese; 1899 invalided USA; d. July 17, 1900. (*Chinese Recorder* 1902 Vol 33 p 497f).

McCARTHY, John; Dublin, member H G Guinness (qv) training class; Feb. 1866 influenced by JHT; 1866 CIM; 1867 Hangzhou; 1877 Jan–Aug Hankou to Bhamo, Burma on foot.

McGILVARY, Dr Daniel; 1858 arr. Thailand, Am. Presby. Mission; 1860 Chiang Mai, began medical work, schools.

McLEAN, Jane; Inverness 'Bible-woman'; 1866 Wm Pennefather's training school; CIM, *Lammermuir*; Hangzhou; 1867 engaged to John Sell (qv); 1868 resigned, worked for LMS Shanghai, later independently.

McLEAN, Margaret, twin of Jane; 1867 CIM, Hangzhou, 1868 resigned, worked for LMS Shanghai.

MEADOWS, James J (1835–1914); JHT's first recruit to Ningbo Mission, 1862, and CIM; wife Martha d. Ningbo 1863; 1866 m. Eliz. Rose (qv); 1868 began pioneering; 1869 Anqing; Shaoxing 40 years.

MEADOWS, Elizabeth; née Rose; friend of Martha Meadows; d.; 1866 CIM, *Lammermuir*, Ningbo, m. Jas Meadows (qv); 1869 Nanjing, Anqing, riot.

MEDHURST, Sir Walter Henry; son of W H Medhurst DD (qv); HBM consul-general Shanghai; minister, Peking.

MEDHURST, Walter Henry (Sr) DD (1796–1857); LMS printer; 1817–20 Malacca; 1820–21 Penang; 1822–43 Batavia, Java; 1826 toured Chinese settlements on Java coast; 1835 voyage of *Huron* up China Coast; 1843 Shanghai; 1845 inland journey in disguise; 1848 victim of 'Qingpu Outrage'; translator, Delegates' Committee, 1852 Chinese Bible; doyen of Brit. community.

MOODY, Dwight Lyman (1837–99); 19th century's greatest evangelist; 1873–75 first Br. mission; 1882 Cambridge Univ. mission stimulated 'Cambridge Seven'; 1886 first Northfield student conference led to Student Volunteer Movement.

MOULE, Arthur Evans; CMS; 1861 Ningbo; 1876 Hangzhou (Hangchow); archdeacon.

MOULE, George Evans (b. 1828); CMS; 1858 Ningbo; 1864 Hangzhou (Hang-chow); 1880 Bishop of Mid-China; over 50 years in China.

MOULE, Henry; Anglican minister; father of Handley, Bishop of Durham; George (qv) Bishop in Mid-China; and Arthur (qv) archdeacon, Ningbo.

MUIRHEAD, William, DD (1822–1900); LMS; evangelist, renowned preacher, translator, like a son to W H Medhurst; 'a gigantic worker'; 1846–90 (43 years) at Shanghai; 1848 victim of 'Qingpu (Tsingpu) Outrage', Shanghai; 1877–79 organised famine relief funds; warm friend of JHT, CIM; 'passionately fond of children'. (*Chinese Recorder* 1900 Vol 31 pp 384, 625; 1902 Vol 32 pp 1, 42).

MÜLLER, George (1805–98); German-born; married sister of A N Groves; 1832 read biography of A H Francke; 1835 founded Orphan Homes, Bristol, 2,000 children, financed 'by faith in God'; 1872 CIM Referee.

NAPOLEON III (1808–73); son of Louis Napoleon; 1848 Pres. of French Republic; 1851 *coup d'état*; 1852 emperor, second empire; 1863 occupation of Mexico; 1870 Franco-Prussian war; refugee in UK, d. at Chislehurst.

NEVIUS, John Livingston (1832–93); Am. Presby. Mission; 1854 Ningbo; 1859 Hangzhou; 1860 Japan; 1861 Shandong (Shantung); 1864 UK, USA; 1867 DD; 1869 Shandong, Denglai; Bible translator, author; 1890 Moderator, Shanghai Miss. Conf.; 1886–87 exponent of 'indigenous church' policy, Korea 1890.

NICOL, Lewis; blacksmith, Abroath, Aberdeen; 1865 CIM candidate; 1866 m. Eliza Calder, *Lammermuir*, Hangzhou; 1867 Xiaoshan, outrage; 1868 dismissed.

PARKER, H M; Am. Prot. Episc; 1861 Shandong, Yantai; Oct. killed with J L Holmes (qv).

PARKER, Dr John; brother of Dr Wm Parker; 1863 Ningbo, independent; 1865 United Presby. Ch. of Scotland, Ningbo.

PARKER, Dr Peter, MD (1804–88); Am. Board (ABCFM); 1834 Canton; first medical missionary in China (not first Western physican); 1835 Ophthalmic Hospital after T R Colledge; 1838 formed 'Medical Missionary Soc. in China'; 1838, 1843–44, semi-skilled interpreter-negotiator for US treaty; 1850 General Hosp., Canton; several times US chargé d'affaires and minister.

PARKER, Dr William; CES 1854–61; Shanghai, Ningbo; wife (1) d. 26 Aug. 1859 of cholera; m. wife (2) UK 1861; 1862 to Ningbo; d. injuries 1 Feb. 1863.

PARKES, Sir Harry Smith (1828–85); cousin m. C Gutzlaff (qv); 1841 sister m. Wm. Lockhart (qv); 1841 Macao; 1842 asst. to J R Morrison; 1842 July 21 with Sir H Pottinger at assault on Zhenjiang, *aet.* 14; present at signing of Treaty of Nanking; 1842–43 Zhoushan (Chusan) Is. with Gutzlaff; 1843 Canton consulate asst.; 1845 Fuzhou, interpreter with R Alcock (qv); August 1846 Shanghai with Alcock; 1852–54 Canton; 1853 author Parl. Paper No. 263 on *Emigration* (Coolie trade); concluded first Br. treaty with Siam for Sir John Bowring; 1856 vice-consul Canton; Oct., *Arrow* incident; 1858–60 Br. Commissioner, Canton; 1861 Hankou Feb.–Apr. with Adm. Sir Jas Hope; May 20, 1862 KCB knighthood *aet.* 34; intimate friend of Col Gordon; strongly opposed by Li Hongzhang (qv); 1865 Br. minister, Japan, 'won the most signal victory Br. diplomacy ever gained in the Far East' (Dickens, F V: *Life of Parkes*, II.44); 1871 UK; 1872–9 Japan; 1879–82 UK received KCMG, to Japan; 1883 Br. minister Peking, after Sir Thos Wade; treaty with Korea opened ports; d. March 22, 1885 'Peking fever'. (*Dicty. of Nat. Biog.* Vol XV; H B Morse).

PEARSE, George; London stockbroker; CES foreign sec.; co-founder Foreign

Evangelist Soc.; friend and adviser of JHT's; later missionary to Kabyles, N. Africa, initiated N. Africa Mission.

PENNEFATHER, William (1816–73); vicar, Christ Church, Barnet; convener, Barnet and Mildmay conferences; hymn-writer, friend of JHT; 1864 St Jude's, Mildmay, N. London; director, Mildmay Mission Conf. centre and hospital; deaconess and missionary training school; 1872 CIM Referee.

PETRIE, David; 1866 Shanghai, Jardine, Matheson agent; friendly to CIM.

PIERCY, George; 1850 to China at own expense; 1851 Canton; 1853 adopted by Wesleyan Meth. Miss. Soc.; joined by Josiah Cox (qv).

POLO, Marco (1245–1324); son of Nicolo; 1275 Peking, served Kublai Khan; *aet* 30 gov. of Yangzhou; official journeys to SW China, Burma, Indo-China, India; 1292 with Nicolo and Matteo escorted royal princess to Persia; to Venice; 1298 in war with Genoa, imprisoned, dictated travels.

PUGET, Colonel John Henry; brother of Dowager Lady Radstock (qv); generous donor to CIM.

QIAN LONG (Ch'ien Lung); sixty years (1736–96) 4th emperor, Qing (Ch'ing) dynasty; after Yong Zheng, before Jia Qing; d. 1799.

QUARTERMAN, J W; Am. Presby.; 1847–57 Ningbo; smallpox, nursed by JHT; d. 1857.

RADSTOCK, Dowager Lady; mother of Lord Radstock (qv), Lady Beauchamp (qv), Hon Miss Waldegrave (qv); sister of Col J H Puget (qv); Welbeck St Brethren; friend and supporter of JHT.

RADSTOCK, Lord; Hon Granville Augustus Wm. Waldegrave (1833–1913); 3rd Baron; converted at Crimean War; raised, commanded W. Middlesex Rifles for 6 years; evangelical Anglican evangelist in aristocratic Russian, E. European society; closely associated with Brethren; friend of JHT and CIM; 1872 CIM Referee.

RANYARD, Mrs; née Ellen White; means of conversion of M S Alexander, Prof. of Hebrew, Arabic, Bishop of Jerusalem; founded London Bible Women's Assn. and Ranyard Mission.

REID, Henry; 1867 CIM, Hangzhou; 1868 Yangzhou riot, eye injury; 1873 retired.

RICHARD, Timothy (1845–1919); converted in Evang. Awakening 1859–60, Wales; offered services to JHT, referred to BMS; 1870 Shandong; 1875 sole survivor of twelve; 1876–79 Shandong, Shanxi famine relief; educationalist, views changed, left BMS, founded Univ. of Shanxi, Taiyuan (8 years), 1891 Soc. for Diffusion of Chr. & Gen. Knowledge; 1906 Christian Literature Soc.; his policies to Christianize China akin to the techniques of Ricci; adviser to emperor, Chinese govt. and Kong Yuwei; translated *History of the Nineteenth Century* (1 mill. copies); 1885 proposed a Christian college in every prov. capital; 1901 with Boxer indemnity funds founded Taiyuan Univ. College; received two of the highest honours of the empire.

RIDGEWAY, Joseph; CMS Assoc. Sec.; editor CMS *Intelligencer*, *Record*, *Gleaner*; 1869 opposed C R Alford's proposed CMS Mission for China; d. 1871.

ROSE, Elizabeth; 1866 CIM, *Lammermuir*; m. J Meadows (qv).

RUDLAND, William D; Eversden, Cambridgeshire blacksmith/farm mechanic; 1856 CIM; 1866 *Lammermuir*, Hangzhou; 1867 m. Mary Bell (qv); 1868 printer, Yangzhou riot; 1869 Taizhou, Zhejiang many years; 1874 UK, wife died; translated (adapted) Taizhou vernacular romanised NT; 1878 m. Miss Brealey, d.; later m. Miss Knight; d. 1913.

RUSSELL, William Armstrong; CMS; 1847 Ningbo; 1872–79 first bishop in N. China; d. 1879.

RYLE, John Charles, DD; 1880–1900 Bp. of Liverpool; uncompromising Evangelical leader, writer, C H Spurgeon's 'best man in the Ch. of England'; author *Knots United*, *Holiness*, *Practical Religion*.

SCARBOROUGH, W; WMMS, 1865 Hankou with David Hill.

SCHERESCHEWSKY, Samuel Isaac Joseph (1831–1906) (pron. *Sher-e-sheff-skie*; called 'Sherry'); Russian Lithuanian rabbi, converted; 1854 USA Gen. Theol. Seminary, NY; 1859 ordained Am. Prot. Episc. Church by Bp Wm Boone Sr (Book 1, p 393); 1860 Shanghai; 1862–75 Peking, began Dicty. of Mongolian; alone translated OT into Mandarin while committee trans. NT; 1865 with J S Burdon (qv) trans. Anglican Book of Com. Prayer; 1875 nominated bishop, declined; 1876 consecrated; 1878 founded St John's College, Shanghai, and St Mary's Hall for girls; 1879 *wenli* Prayer Book, Wuchang; 1881 paralysed limbs, speech, to Europe; 1883 resigned episc. office; 1886 USA, began OT revision – impaired speech excluded Chinese help, typed with one finger, 8 hours daily – 1888–95 easy *wenli* OT, NT romanised; 1895–7 Shanghai, romanised into Ch. character; 1897 Japan, to supervise printing; 1902 OT revision publ.; sole object 'to make plain the Word of God to the Chinese'; d. Tokyo, Sept 15, 1906, *aet*. 75 in working chair. (*Chinese Recorder* 1906 Vol 37 p 615f).

SCHMIDT, Charles; 1864 officer in Ever-Victorious Army; converted through Jas. Meadows (qv); missionary in Suzhou 1867; friend of JHT, CIM.

SCOTT, William; Dunedin, Edinburgh, manufacturer; staunch friend of CIM.

SELL, John Robert; Romford, Essex; 1866 CIM, *Lammermuir*, Hangzhou; 1867 engaged to Jane McLean (qv), Ningbo, d. smallpox.

SHAFTESBURY, Lord Anthony Ashley-Cooper (1801–85); 7th earl; evangelical philanthropist; legislated to relieve ill effects of industrial revolution.

SIA SEK-ONG; minister in Meth. Episc. Church, Fuzhou; 1870 exponent of self-support of Chinese churches.

SMITH, Elizabeth; first CMS single woman to China; 1863 Fuzhou; 1864 Peking; 1869 not listed.

SOLTAU, George; son of Henry W (qv); Lamb and Flag Mission and schools, London; 1872 on first CIM London Council.

SOLTAU, Henrietta E; daughter of H W Soltau (qv); 1873 London, asst. to Emily Blatchley; Tottenham home for children of missionaries; later, CIM Women's Training Home.

SOLTAU, Henry, Jr; son of H W Soltau (qv); Aug. 1872 Hon. Sec. CIM, London with R H Hill (qv); 1875 to Bhamo, Burma with J W Stevenson (qv); 1880 with Stevenson first Westerners to cross China W. to E., Burma, Chongqing, Wuchang, Shanghai.

SOLTAU, Henry W; Chancery barrister, Plymouth and Exeter Brethren; sons George, Henry, daughters Henrietta, Agnes (m. Richard Hill qv), all in CIM.

SOLTAU, Lucy; daughter of H W Soltau (qv), d. young, 1873.

SOLTAU, William; son of H W Soltau (qv); 1875 Asst. Secy. CIM, London, with R H Hill, B Broomhall.

SPURGEON, Charles Haddon (1834–92); renowned Baptist preacher, Metropolitan Tabernacle; lifelong friend of JHT.

STACEY, Miss; one-time Quaker, member of Brook Street chapel, Tottenham; CES Ladies' Assn.; long a friend of JHT, CIM and T J Barnardo; d. 1876.

STEVENSON, John Whiteford (1844–1918); son of laird of Thriepwood, Renfrewshire; m. Anne Jolly; with G Stott (qv) first of CIM after Crombie (qv); Oct. 1865 dep. UK; 1866–74 Ningbo, Shaoxing; 1875–80 Burma; 1880 with H Soltau, Jr. (qv) crossed China W. to E., Bhamo–Chongqing–Wuchang then Shanghai; 1,900 miles, 86 days; 1885–1916 deputy director, CIM.

STOCK, Eugene (1836–1928); CMS UK staff; editor Dec. 21, 1875–Dec. 11, 1906; historian, author *The History of the Church Miss. Soc.*, Vols I–III; warm friend of CIM.

STOTT, George; Aberdeenshire schoolmaster, one leg; Oct. 1865 dep. UK; 1866 Ningbo; 1869–89 Wenzhou (Wenchow); 1870 m. G Ciggie (qv); d. 1889.

STRONACH, Alexander; LMS; 1838–39 Singapore; 1839–44 Penang; 1844–46 Singapore; 1846 Amoy.

STRONACH, John; LMS, 1838–76, 30 years without furlough; 1838–44 Singapore; 1846 Amoy; Bible translator, Delegates' Committee, 1852; S Dyer Sr's friend.

STRONACH, W G; HBM consul; son of John Stronach (qv).

SUN YAT-SEN (1866–1925); Chinese statesman; 1891 first medical graduate, Hong Kong; 1905 founded China Revolutionary League, in Europe, Japan; 1911–12 founder and first president Republic of China; m. descendant of Paul Xu (SOONG QINGLING, dep. chairman Nat. People's Congress till d. 1981).

TARN, William Jr; son of William Sr (qv); cousin of Maria Taylor; Secy. RTS.

TARN, William Sr; brother of Samuel Dyer Sr's wife; director, LMS; guardian of Burella (Mrs J S Burdon qv) and Maria Dyer (Mrs JHT qv).

TAYLOR, Frederick Howard (1862–1946); b. Beaumont St, London, Nov. 25, 1862; second son of JHT and Maria Jane (qv); 1888 MD (Lond.); 1889 MRCP; FRCS(Edin.); Jan. 1890 to China; 1894 m. M Geraldine Guinness; CIM missionary, biographer of JHT; d. Aug. 15, 1946.

TAYLOR, Grace Dyer; daughter of JHT and Maria (qv), b. Ningbo July 31, 1859; *Jubilee*, *Lammermuir* voyages; d. nr. Hangzhou, Aug. 23, 1867.

TAYLOR, Herbert Hudson; son of JHT and Maria, b. Bayswater, London, April 3, 1861; Jan. 1881 CIM, to China; c 1886 m. Jean Gray, CIM 1884; father of James Hudson Taylor II.

TAYLOR, James Hudson (21 May 1832–3 June 1905); 1853 dep. UK; 1 Mar. 1854 arr. Shanghai; 20 Jan. 1858 m. Maria Jane Dyer; 1857 with J Jones (qv) began Ningbo Mission; June 1865 founded China Inland Mission; 28 Nov. 1871 m. Jane E Faulding; 3 June 1905 d. Changsha, Hunan.

TAYLOR, Maria Jane, née Dyer (1837–70); daughter of Samuel Dyer (qv); wife of JHT; mother of Grace, Herbert Hudson, Frederick Howard, Samuel, Jane, Maria, Charles, Noel; d. Zhenjiang, July 23, 1870.

TAYLOR, Maria Hudson, daughter of JHT and Maria; b. Hangzhou, Feb. 3, 1867; 1884 CIM to China *aet*. 17; m. J J Coulthard; d. Sept. 28, 1897.

TAYLOR, Samuel Dyer, son of JHT and Maria; b. Barnsley, June 24, 1864; d. Zhenjiang, Feb. 4, 1870.

TIDMAN, Dr Arthur; Foreign Sec., LMS; member CES General Committee.

TONG TIANXI; destitute Shanghai boy, 1857 adopted, educated by JHT; worked with CIM.

TONG ZHI (T'ung Chih) (1856–75); 1862 succeeded Xian Feng emperor; d. smallpox Jan 13, 1875.

TSIANG ALIANG (*see* ZIANG).

TSIU KYUO-KWE; 1858 Ningbo Christian; evangelist; 1866 Hangzhou; Xiaoshan outrage victim; 1868–71 Zhenjiang, Nanjing; 1872 Taizhou, Hangzhou; d. Nov 1874.

UNDERHILL, C B; Sec. BMS; friend of JHT, nominated him for FRGS.

VALENTINE, Jarvis Downman; CMS recruit taught by JHT; 1864 Ningbo; 1870 Shaoxing; d. 1889.

von SOMMER, James; member, Hackney Brethren circle with W T Berger (qv) (brother-in-law) and Philip H Gosse (qv); editor, *The Missionary Reporter*.

von SOMMER, John; brother of James.

VENN, Henry 'the elder'; vicar of Huddersfield, leading promoter of first evangelical revival; grandfather of Henry Venn 'Senior'.

VENN, Henry 'the younger', known as 'Senior' (1796–1873); son of John Venn, grandson of Henry 'the elder'; St John's, Holloway; 1841–73, Hon. Sec. CMS; sent 498 clergy overseas.

VENN, Henry 'Junior'; second son of Henry 'Senior'; *c* 1869–72 Assoc. Sec. CMS.

VENN, John; rector of Clapham, member of 18th century 'Eclectic Socy.'; a founder, first chairman of CMS; father of Henry 'the younger' or 'Senior'; d. 1813.

VIGEON, James, accountant, and Mrs; 1865 recruits for Ningbo, prevented from sailing with J W Stevenson (qv) and then *Lammermuir* party.

WADE, Sir Thomas Francis; 1841 as Lieut., relief of Ningbo; Vice-Consul, Shanghai, under Alcock (qv), Battle of Muddy Flat; became Sinologue; 1870 HBM minister Peking after Alcock; pro-trade, anti-missionary.

WALDEGRAVE, Hon Miss; daughter of Dowager Lady Radstock (qv); friend, supporter of CIM.

WANG GUOYAO; 1864 peasant convert, irrepressible evangelist, village pastor, 1867 Fenghua outstations many years.

WANG LAE-DJÜN (Ch. characters not found); Ningbo Mission convert; 1860–64 with JHT London; 1867 pastor, Hangzhou, remainder of life.

WARD, Hon John E; 1859 US plenipotentiary; 1860 at capture and Convention of Peking.

WAY, R Q; Am. Presby.; 1844–59 Ningbo; established schools; brother-in-law of J W Quarterman (qv); friend of JHT; d. 1896 (*Chinese Recorder* 1896, Vol 27 p 35).

WEATHERLEY, Joseph; early CIM supporter; trustee of Maria Taylor's (qv) settlement for children's education; 1872 first chairman, CIM Lond. Council.

WEIR, Thomas; Shanghai merchant, 1865 influenced by JHT Glasgow; long a friend; negotiated reduced fares by Castle Line, UK–China, effective many years.

WILLIAMS, Samuel Wells DD (1812–84); Am. Board, printer, scholar; 1833 Canton; 1847 author *The Middle Kingdom*; 1851 succeeded E C Bridgman (qv) as editor, *Chinese Repository*; 1856 interpreter and Secy. to US minister, Peking; 9 times chargé d'affaires to 1876; 1884 *Syllabic Dicty. of Chinese Language*, 12,527 characters; prof. of Chinese, Yale Univ. 8 years.

WILLIAMSON, Alexander, LL D (1829–90); Falkirk, Scotland, b. Dec. 5, 1829, eldest of seven sons; Glasgow Univ.; 1858–63 invalided UK; 1863 National Bible Soc. of Scotland, Shandong, Yantai; 1864–69 travelled extensively distributing Scripture, Peking, Mongolia, Manchuria; Aug. 1869 brother, James Williamson, LMS, murdered near Tianjin; 1869 UK; 1871 LL D Glasgow, 1871–80, 1881–83 Yantai, NBSS and United Presby. Soc. of Scotland; 1883–85 Scotland ill, founded Book & Tract Socy. for China, later (1887) Socy. for Diffusion of Christian and General Knowledge among the Chinese (Christian Lit. Soc.); 1886 Shanghai, wife d.; 1890 d. Yantai. Author, *Natural Theology*, and others. 'Very tall, striking in appearance; intellectually also among the giants.'

WILLIAMSON, James; younger brother of Alexander W (qv); 1863 LMS Tianjin; 1869 murdered.

WILLIAMSON, James; Arbroath, Aberdeen, carpenter; 1866 CIM, *Lammermuir*, Hangzhou, JHT's assistant pioneer; 1869 Anqing riot.

WYLIE, Alexander (1815–87); LMS; 1847 Shanghai, printer, Delegates' version of Bible; 1863 Bible Soc. (B&FBS); one of the greatest Sinologues; completed distribution of the million NTs provided 1855 by Bible Soc. special fund; 1877 retired with failing eyesight; succeeded by Maria Taylor's brother Samuel Dyer, Jr (qv).

XIAN FENG (Hsien Feng) (1851–61); 7th Qing (Ch'ing) dynasty emperor.

YAKUB BEG; Muslim conqueror, 1864 captured Kashgar, Yarkand; appointed ruler by Emir of Bokhara; added Urumqi, Turfan to his kingdom; 1872 independence recognised by Russia, GB, Turkey; honoured with title only used by caliphs of Baghdad; great Muslim revival predicted, with conquest of China; but 1876 Urumqi fell to Zuo Zongtang (Tso Tsung-t'ang) (qv); May 1877 Yakub Beg died suddenly; Dec. 1877 Kashgar taken, kingdom ended.

YATES, Matthew T (1819–88); Am. S. Baptist; 1847 Shanghai; Sinologue, learned contributor to *Chinese Recorder*; Am. vice-consul; translator, Shanghai vernacular NT.

YI ZEWO; teacher, evangelist; 1867 victim, first Huzhou riot.

YÜ XIANSENG (Mr); 1867–68 Hangzhou schoolmaster; 1869–71 Yangzhou, Suzhou, Qingjiangpu, Zhenjiang; 'doctor', Chinese materia medica.

ZENG GUOFAN (Tseng Kuo-fan) (1811–72); scholar, provincial governor; 1854 defeated Taipings; viceroy of the 'Two Jiangs' (Jiangxi, Jiangsu and Anhui), then of Zhili (Chihli); 1870 after Ma Xinyi (qv) assassination returned Nanjing; d. March 11, 1872.

ZHU XINGJUN; Ningbo evangelist, pioneered Wenzhou with Stott (qv).

ZIANG ALIANG; Hangzhou laundryman; with his brother LIANGYONG became evangelist; Taizhou, Yangzhou.

ZUO ZONGTANG (Tso Tsung-t'ang); native of Hunan; successful imperial general vs. Taipings in S. China; 1860s built naval dockyard at Fuzhou; 1870 appointed to suppress Muslim rebellion in NW, completed Dec. 17, 1877, at fall of Kashgar (*see* Yakub Beg).

BIBLIOGRAPHY

British
Library ref.

BIBLE SOCIETY, *History of the B&FBS*, vols 1, 2   3129.e.76
BREDON, Juliet, *Sir Robert Hart*, Hutchinson & Co 1909   010817.de.10
BRIDGMAN, Mrs E J G, *The Life and Labors of Elijah
   Coleman Bridgman*, 1864
BRIDGMAN, Elijah C and Eliza J G, *The Pioneer of American
   Missions in China*, 1864   4985.aaa.27
BROOMHALL, Benjamin, *The Evangelization of the World*,
   CIM 1889
BROOMHALL, Marshall, *John W Stevenson: One of Christ's
   Stalwarts*, Morgan & Scott/CIM 1919   4956.aa.33
      The Jubilee Story of the China Inland Mission,
   Morgan & Scott/CIM 1915   4763.g.4
      Hudson Taylor's Legacy, Hodder & Stoughton 1931   10823.a.16
      The Chinese Empire: A General & Missionary Survey,
   Morgan & Scott/CIM 1907   4767.eeee.4
BURNS, Islay, *Memoir of the Rev William Chalmers Burns*,
   London 1885
CHINA MAIL (Hong Kong)   British Library
                                                           Colindale
CHINA'S MILLIONS, Magazine of the China Inland Mission
   1875–1951
CHINESE RECORDER AND MISSIONARY JOURNAL: Vols 1–3, 5–12
   May 1868–May 71, editor Justus Doolittle; Vol 5
   bi-monthly Jan–Dec 1874 (after 2-year interlude) – Vol 12, 1881
CLARKE, A, *The Boy from Shoreditch*, OMF Books, Clipper Series
CMS, *CM Gleaner, Intelligencer, Register, Reports,* Church
   Missionary Society
COAD, F Roy, *A History of the Brethren Movement*, The
   Paternoster Press 1968
COLLIER, Richard, *William Booth: The General Next to God*,
   Collins 1965   X.100.1629
COLLIS, Maurice Stewart, *Foreign Mud*, 1946   9059.df.15
CORDIER, Henri, *The Life of Alexander Wylie*, 1887   10803.cc.4/6
COVELL, Ralph, *W A P Martin, Pioneer of Progress in
   China*, Wm B Eerdmans Publishing Company 1978

DAVIES, Evan, *China and her Spiritual Claims*, John
　Snow 1845　　1369.b.24
　　Memoir of the Reverend Samuel Dyer, John Snow
　1846　　1372.c.20
FAIRBANK, John King, *Trade and Diplomacy on the China
　Coast*, 2 vols 1953 Edn. Cambridge, Massachusetts　　Ac.2692.10
FORBES, Archibald, *Chinese Gordon*, George Routledge &
　Sons 1884
FOREIGN OFFICE LIBRARY, Public Records Office, *A Century
　of Diplomatic Blue Books*, China FO/17
FULLERTON, W Y and WILSON, C E, *Report of the China Missions
　of the Baptist Missionary Society*, BM House, London 1908
GROVES, Mrs, *Memoir of the late Anthony Norris Groves*,
　2nd Edn, 1857
GUINNESS, M Geraldine, *The Story of the China Inland Mission*,
　2 vols, Morgan & Scott, London 1893
HALDANE, Charlotte, *The Last Great Empress of China*,
　Constable 1965
HART, Sir Robert, *These from the Land of Sinim*　　8022.cc.48/01
　　　and 0817.d.10
HOLT, Edgar C, *The Opium Wars in China*, , 1964 edn.　　X.709–581
HOOK, Brian, *China's Three Thousand Years*: Part 4
　The Modern History of China, *The Times* Newspaper
　(publishers)
HUMBLE, Richard, *Marco Polo*, Weidenfeld and Nicolson 1975
KNOLLYS, Sir Henry, *Incidents in the China War, 1860*　　9056.bb.19
　　English Life in China, 1885　　10058.e.31
LATOURETTE, Kenneth Stott, *A History of Christian
　Missions in China*, SPCK 1929　　4763.g.4
　　*A History of the Expansion of Christianity
　1800–1914*, Eyre and Spottiswoode　　4533.ff.22
　　　These Sought a Country: Tipple Lectures,
　1950 edn, Harper & Brothers　　4807.e.25
LEGGE, Helen E, *James Legge (1815–97)*, Religious Tract
　Society 1905　　04429.1.37
LITTLE, Mrs Archibald, *Li Hung-chung, His Life and Times*,
　Cassell & Co Ltd 1903
LOCKHART, William, *The Medical Missionary in China*,
　1861 edn　　10058.d.16
LYALL, L T, *A Passion for the Impossible*, Hodder
　& Stoughton 1965; OMF Books 1976
MacGILLIVRAY, Donald, *A Century of Protestant Missions
　in China* (Centennial Conference Historical Volume)
　Shanghai 1907　　4764.ff.11
McGILVARY, Daniel, *A Half Century among the Siamese and
　the Lao*, Fleming H Revell Co, 1912
MARTIN, W A P, *A Cycle of Cathay*, 1896　　010056.g.7
MEDHURST, W H, Sr, *China: Its State and Prospects*,
　John Snow 1838　　571.g.10
　　A Glance at the Interior of China in 1845,

Shanghai Mission Press 1949   10055.c.25

MEDHURST, Sir Walter H, *Curiosities of Street Literature
in China,* 1871   10057.aaa.16
    The Foreigner in Far Cathay, Edward Stanton 1872   010058.ee.35

MICHIE, Alexander, *Missionaries in China,* Edward Stanford
Ldn. 1891; 2nd edn Tientsin Press 1893   4767.ccc.10
    *The Englishman in China: as illustrated in the
Career of Sir Rutherford Alcock,* Wm Blackwood & Sons,
Edin. 1900 2 vols   09057.d.3

MORSE, Hosea Ballou, *The International Relations of the
Chinese Empire* (9 vols) vols 1–3, 1910   2386.c.17

MOULE, Arthur E, *The Story of the Cheh-Kiang Mission,*
CMS 1879

MÜLLER, George, (ed. G F Bergin), *Autobiography:
Narrative,* J Nisbet & Co, Ltd 1905

NEILL, Stephen C, *A History of Christian Missions*
(Pelican History of the Church) Penguin Books 1964;
    Colonialism and Christian Missions, Lutterworth Press:
Foundations of Christian Mission 1966

NEILL, S C *et al, Chinese Dictionary of Christian World
Mission,* United Society for Christian Literature,
London 1971

NEVIUS, Helen S C, *The Life of John Livingston Nevius,*
Revell 1895   4985.eee.5

NORTH CHINA DAILY NEWS (newspaper)   British Library, Colindale
NORTH CHINA HERALD (newspaper)   British Library, Colindale

ORR, J Edwin, *The Second Evangelical Awakening in
Britain,* Marshall Morgan & Scott 1949

PARLIAMENTARY PAPERS: Foreign Office Blue Books,
Official Publications Office

PIERSON, A T, *George Müller of Bristol,* Jas Nisbet
& Co, Ltd 1905

POLO, Marco, *The Book of Ser Marco Polo, The Venetian,
1298* First printed edition 1477 (*see* YULE)

POTT, F L Hawks, *A Short History of Shanghai,*
Kelly & Walsh 1928   010056.aaa.46

ROWDON, H H, *The Origins of the Brethren,* Pickering
& Inglis 1967

SELLMAN, R R, *An Outline Atlas of Eastern History,*
Edward Arnold Ltd

SMITH, Arthur H, *The Uplift of China,* The Young
People's Missionary Movement of America 1909

SOOTHILL, Wm E, *Timothy Richard of China,* Seeley,
Service & Co, Ltd, London 1924

STOCK, Eugene, *A History of the Church Missionary
Society,* Vols I–III 1899–1916   4765.cc.28

STOTT, Grace, *Twenty-Six Years of Missionary Work in
China,* Hodder & Stoughton 1897

TAYLOR, Dr & Mrs Howard, *Hudson Taylor in Early Years:
The Growth of a Soul,* CIM and RTS, 1911

    Hudson Taylor and the China Inland Mission:
    The Growth of a Work of God, CIM and RTS, 1918
    Hudson Taylor's Spiritual Secret, CIM, 1932
TAYLOR, Mrs Howard (M Geraldine Guinness), *The Story of*
    the China Inland Mission, 2 vols, 1892, Morgan & Scott
    Behind the Ranges: A Biography of J O Fraser, CIM
    Pastor Hsi: One of China's Scholars (2 vols), CIM
TAYLOR, J Hudson, *China: Its Spiritual Need and Claims*,
    1st–6th edns 1865 et seq, CIM
    China's Spiritual Need and Claims, 7th edn.
    1887, CIM 8th edn. 1890, CIM
    Brief Account of the Progress of the China Inland
    Mission, May 1866 to May 1868, J Nisbet & Co 1868
    A Retrospect, 1875, CIM
    After Thirty Years, 1895, Morgan & Scott and CIM
    Occasional Paper Vols 1–6, Jas Nisbet & Co
    Summary of the Operations of the China Inland
    Mission, 1865–1872, J Nisbet & Co 1872
THOMAS, W H Griffith, *The Principles of Theology*, Church
    Book Room Press, London 1945
THOMPSON, R Wardlaw, *Griffith John: The Story of Fifty*
    Years in China, The Religious Tract Society 1907
WALEY, Arthur David, *The Opium War through Chinese Eyes*,
    London 1958   09059.pp.30
WILLIAMS, Fredk Wells, *The Life and Letters of Samuel*
    Wells Williams, LL D, Missionary, Diplomatist,
    Sinologue, G P Putman & Sons,
    New York and London 1889
WILLIAMS, Samuel Wells, *The Middle Kingdom*, 1847
WOODCOCK, George, *The British in the Far East*,
    Weidenfeld & Nicolson 1969 (A Social History
    of the British Overseas)
YULE, Sir Henry, *The Book of Ser Marco Polo*
    the Venetian, 1878, 2 vols.

INDEX